Instant Messaging Systems

Cracking the Code™

Dreamtech Software Team

WILEY

Wiley Publishing, Inc.

Best-Selling Books • Digital Downloads • e-Books • Answer Networks •
e-Newsletters • Branded Web Sites • e-Learning

Instant Messaging Systems: Cracking the Code™

Published by
Wiley Publishing, Inc.
605 Third Avenue
New York, NY 10158
www.wiley.com

This book is printed on acid-free paper. ∞

Library of Congress Control Number: 2002106774

ISBN: 0-7645-4953-7

Printed in the United States of America.

10 9 8 7 6 5 4 3 2 1

1B/QW/QU/QS/IN

Dreamtech Software India Inc., Team
dreamtech@mantraonline.com
www.dreamtechsoftware.com

Dreamtech Software India Inc. is a leading provider of corporate software solutions. Based in New Delhi, India, the company is a successful pioneer of innovative solutions in e-learning technologies. Dreamtech's developers have more than 50 years of combined software-engineering experience in areas such as Java; Wireless Applications, XML, Voice-based solutions, .NET, COM/COM++ technologies, Distributed Computing, DirectX, Windows Media technologies, and security solutions.

About the Authors

Vikas Gupta is co-founder and president of Dreamtech Software. He is engaged in developing and designing new technologies in wireless applications, e-learning, and other cutting-edge areas. He is also the Managing Director of Wiley Dreamtech India (P) Ltd.

Avnish Dass, co-founder and CEO of Dreamtech Software, is a talented and seasoned programmer who has 15 years of experience in systems and application/database programming. He has developed security systems, antivirus programs, wireless and communication technologies, and ERP systems.

Gaurav Malhotra is a software developer at Dreamtech and has advanced-level programming experience in C, C++, and Java.

Pratul Katyal is a senior software developer at Dreamtech. He has two years of experience in developing software in C, C++, C#, Visual Basic, and .NET technologies.

Credits

Executive Editor
Chris Webb

Project Editors
Neil Romanosky
Kevin Kent

Technical Editor
N. R. Parsa

Copy Editors
C. M. Jones
Bill Barton

Editorial Manager
Mary Beth Wakefield

Vice President and Executive Group Publisher
Richard Swadley

Vice President and Executive Publisher
Bob Ipsen

Vice President and Publisher
Joseph B. Wikert

Executive Editorial Director
Mary Bednarek

Project Coordinator
Dale White

Proofreading
Anne Owen

Indexing
Johnna VanHoose Dinse

To our parents and family and our beloved country, India,
for providing an excellent environment
for creating and nurturing world-class IT talent.

Preface

Ever since its emergence in the early 1990s, the Internet has radically changed the way of accessing and exchanging information among desktops around the globe. Today, almost every information-hungry business banks heavily upon the Internet. The success of business in the 21st century depends not only on procuring up-to-date information but also on procuring it fast. It is in consideration of such a scenario that we have developed the Instant Messaging application described in this book. Throughout the book, the application is developed in both C# and Java, the two most popular programming languages at this time. Because the Instant Messaging application is extensible to both of these languages, it is able to meet the exacting demands of today's e-business environment.

What this Book Covers

This book details the technology for integrating an Instant Messaging application with the Jabber server. It is quite evident that there is jetlag among the Instant Messaging applications available on the market, especially when it comes to communicating with one other. This book is the first attempt in developing an application that can be integrated with the Jabber server to tide-over the barriers of cross-platform communication. The source code provided in the CD that accompanies this book has been developed with the prime emphasis on the requirements of the business world. The book has been written with focus on code, and every effort has been made to keep theory to a minimum. The source code provided in the accompanying CD is fully tested at the Dreamtech Software Research Lab, India, and is fully operational.

This book gives you complete insight into the design and implementation aspects of the application. The book begins with an introductory note on Instant Messaging and goes on to explain how Jabber clients can be built with scope for extension to meet the challenges that are likely to come up because of the rapid change in technology and increasing customer demands.

Who Should Read this Book

The book addresses programmers and developers of the intermediate to advanced level. It is meant for IT professionals who are keen to learn this specific technology. The book primarily targets innovative software designers and programmers and inspires them to impart new dimensions to the Instant Messaging application presented. IT personnel interested in exploring the open-source based Instant Messaging model, Jabber, will find this book informative. Since the application is built using the Java and C# programming languages, programmers using these two languages are offered an opportunity to sharpen their skills. An additional advantage offered by the add-on feature of this Instant Messaging application is that, because the application is built using J2ME, readers across the globe stand to reap the benefits.

Readers are expected to have a firm grip over technologies such as C# and Java. While developing the application, the fast emerging concept of Web services has also been considered. Thus, to understand the book fully, it is mandatory for the reader to have substantial knowledge of ADO.NET and RDBMS such as SQL or Sybase. Since the application closely works with the Jabber server and the communication standard of the application is XML, which has been employed to neutralize the differences arising from the variety of platforms, thorough knowledge of the XML structure as supported by Jabber is essential.

The code for the application is supplemented with exhaustive explanations.

How this Book Is Organized

Chapter 1 provides a description of the concept and scope of the Instant Messaging application and outlines its evolution to the most modern form. While discussing the concept of an Instant Messaging application, the latest form of the open-source, Instant Messaging Model (Jabber) is taken up. Since the communication standard of the Jabber server is XML based, the structure of XML as supported by the Jabber server for communication is provided in this chapter.

Chapter 2 details the designing process of the application and provides a comprehensive picture of the Instant Messaging application we intend to develop across the book. This chapter begins with a briefing regarding the prerequisites for developing the application. After this, the database design of the application is provided. When database is discussed, it must be noted that this application uses SQL Server 2000 for maintaining the database. The reader is therefore required to possess some skill in writing SQL queries and to establish the connection between the front and back ends of the application. The two modules of the application, the server and client, are detailed in this chapter, along with design considerations.

The communication that takes place between the server and the client is also discussed in this chapter. Since our application is integrating with the jabber server, various issues involved in creating and closing the session with the Jabber server are outlined in this chapter. Since this chapter involves the core designing of the application, readers such as application designers can benefit from this chapter by developing their own application based on the approach assumed in developing this application.

Chapter 3 introduces the basic principles of the Java version of the server module of this Instant Messaging application. The chapter begins with an introductory note on the Web service and the methodology involved in building and accessing the Web service. The development phase of the server module is also discussed in this chapter. Since our application works closely with the Jabber Instant Messaging model, the communication norms between the server module and the Jabber server have been clarified. Further, the role of the server in parsing and processing various client requests and the way the server interprets the messages flowing from the Jabber side have been detailed in this chapter. As mentioned earlier, since Web services are brought up in this chapter, the various Web methods deployed in our application are also discussed in this chapter. Apart from detailing the entire server module of the application, the use of IBM Xerces XML parser and the principle of server programming-socket and multithreading have been explained in this chapter.

Chapter 4 covers the C# version of the server module of the application. The chapter begins by laying down the requirements for developing the server. Various Web services used by the server module are discussed in this chapter, along with the techniques involved in creating and accessing the Web service. Since the Web service involved in our application handles the task of retrieving data from the database, the reader must have sufficient knowledge of ADO.NET and SQL Server 2000. Some familiarity with socket and thread programming is also needed. Those who possess network-programming skills stand to gain an edge over those who do not.

Since the server module communicates with the Jabber server on one hand and with the client module on the other, the communication of the server module with the Jabber server and the client module is presented in this chapter. Also, responses of various Web methods handled by the server module have been addressed this chapter. Toward the end of this chapter, the working of the various Web methods involved in our application have been discussed briefly.

The Java version of the client module for the Instant Messaging application is discussed in **Chapter 5**. The chapter begins with an introduction to client programming, which presents guidelines for developing the client module for the application. It is appropriate to mention here that the reader must have sufficient knowledge of Swing class, as it is used extensively while creating the GUI for the client module. Later, how the client module establishes the connection with the server and delivers various kinds of requests is explained in this chapter. The responses generated by the server module against the request made by the client module have also been separately presented in this chapter. The reader must be familiar with the concept of the socket and thread classes and the working and usage of the IBM Xerces parser for establishing the connection with the server.

Chapter 6 of this book covers the C# version of the client module for the Instant Messaging application. To appreciate this chapter fully, the reader must be equipped with a sound knowledge of socket and thread classes. This chapter begins with an introduction to client programming, which apprises the reader about the scope of client programming. Following this, the server module is explained. To realize the technique involved behind establishing the connection with the local server, the reader must be familiar with thread and socket classes. Since the client module is the origin of all requests, the various types of requests delivered by the client module and the processes involved in delivering the requests are presented in this chapter. The parsing of various server responses is carried out by the in-built parsing facility provided by the XML Document class present in the C# environment.

In **Chapter 7**, the add-on feature of the application is detailed. The Instant Messaging application is enhanced to bring handheld devices within its range. The client module of the Instant Messaging application is adapted to suit handheld devices. To program and understand the working involved in the background, the reader must be thorough with programming methodology that uses J2ME. Since J2ME programming is specially meant for handheld devices, programming for J2ME is outlined in this chapter, along with details of the relevant basics. The limitations of J2ME as a highly stripped-down version of J2SE are also discussed in this chapter. For programming in J2ME, the reader must be familiar with the stream connection class, an optimized version of the socket class. Since handheld devices based on J2ME have the limitation of sparse memory, the parser required for parsing the XML-based responses must be of such a kind as would work optimally under low-memory conditions. One such parser, well suited to accomplish the task under these circumstances, is kXML.

> **NOTE:** All of the source code and line-by-line code explanations for Chapter 7 can be found on this book's companion CD-ROM.

Companion CD-ROM

The CD-ROM serves to supplement the book. The entire source code to create an Instant Messaging System using both Java and C# is provided on the CD-ROM, as well as the development tools that are required to build the application. Apart from this, a complete e-book version of the book is incorporated in the CD-ROM.

Acknowledgments

We acknowledge the contributions of the following people for their support in making this book possible: V.K. Rajan, Asim Chowdhury and Priti, for their immense help in coordinating various activities throughout this project; Hema Sharma, Manish N. Srivastav, technical writers, who contributed to developing the content of this book; and Deepak Kumar Sharma, Pankaj Kumar, Yashraj Chauhan, and Pramod Sharma: a team of programmers of Dreamtech Software India, Inc. who contributed to the development of software for this book.

Contents

Chapter 1

Introduction to Instant Messaging

Instant messaging (IM) is an Internet-based protocol application that allows one-to-one communication between users employing a variety of devices. The most popular form of IM is chatting, where short, text-based messages are exchanged among computers. With the advent of technologies such as Wireless Application Protocol (WAP) and the popularity of handheld devices such as mobile phones, Short Message Service (SMS) added a new dimension to instant messaging integration.

SMS refers to sending and receiving text messages to and from mobile telephones. The text may be composed of words or numbers or may be an alphanumeric combination. SMS was created as part of the GSM Phase 1 standard. We think the first short message was sent in December 1992 from a PC to a mobile phone on the Vodafone GSM network in the U.K. Each short message ranges between 70□160 characters.SMS has a store-forward capability; this means sending messages is possible even when the recipient is not available. The user is notified when a message is waiting, as with voicemail.

Integration of SMS and instant messaging allows you to deliver short messages by using the instant messaging facility over handheld devices. Today, instant messaging can be availed free of cost. Software giants such as Yahoo!, Microsoft, and AOL are already offering free instant messaging facilities.

A Brief History of Instant Messaging

Instant Messaging has been around for more than two decades. The first major player to enter the arena of Instant Messaging was AOL, which launched its own version of instant messenger with a component used for managing all the incoming and outgoing messages and the list of friends. This component is popularly known as *buddy list*. Soon, Microsoft and Yahoo! followed AOL's trail. As a result, MSN and Yahoo! messenger appeared on the market with a variety of impressive new services. In its early days, instant messaging uses were restricted to splashing messages on bulletin boards. Gradually, instant messaging became a major area of interest for youngsters. Society acknowledges instant messaging as the most common means by which people of varying age groups, especially youngsters, communicate with one another.

Until 1990, there was no significant change in the status of instant messaging from what it had been when initially conceived, mainly because instant messaging was not taken seriously till then. Subsequently, the corporate world changed its attitude toward instant messaging, thanks to the Internet revolution. With a sudden rise in the popularity of the Internet and the arrival of new techniques like voicemail, online transactions, and so on, the corporate world started taking instant messaging seriously. The Internet led not only to a substantial increase in the number of instant messaging users but to the realization of the potential of instant messaging and to earnest attempts to eliminate the limitations of instant messaging and exploit its possibilities fully.

The business community was first to explore the potential of instant messaging and expand its capabilities, making it the useful tool it is today. Instant Messaging is now in the mainstream of WAP technology and is being used with mobile devices such as cellular phones, laptops, and pagers.

The Advantages of Instant Messaging

Instant messaging, unlike e-mail, allows spontaneous interaction among users over the network. This feature of instant messaging is extremely helpful in accessing remotely located users. Entrepreneurs often avail this attribute of instant messaging for accessing and interacting with remotely located workers. Instant messaging meets their purpose quite well and helps save time by obviating the need for writing e-mail and waiting for delivery-confirmation messages.

With the introduction of new ideas such as notification in instant messaging, the user can now be kept on the alert round the clock. Such notification features range from informing the user about in-coming mails or mobile beeps to delivering the latest information such as stock quotes.

The role of instant messaging is crucial in the business world, as it allows for quick and cheap transmissions of information. Using instant messaging to convey information that contains strings of text is much cheaper and more flexible than conveying such information over the phone or arranging to meet face to face.

Another promising feature of instant messaging is the reliable security it offers, which ensures privacy and confidentiality. In addition, you can block an unwanted incoming message and prevent yourself from being distracted. Also, you can block instant messages while using handheld devices.

The Need for Instant Messaging

Over the years, instant messaging has proven itself to be a feasible technology not only to fun-loving people but to the world of commerce and trade, where quick responses to messages are crucial. With the wide acceptance it commands, instant messaging is looked upon by the business world as an ideal tool for promoting its interests. Instant messaging has revolutionized business communication, as it is well suited for accessing remotely located workers. Also, crucial information can be delivered very quickly. Although some of you might consider e-mail the better option in this regard, e-mail lacks the spontaneous and direct person-to-person interaction instant messaging offers.

The Future of Instant Messaging

Soon, people will stop considering instant messaging merely a convenient way of chatting over the Internet. Attempts are being made to convert instant messaging into a tool that will break all the barriers encountered in device-based networking such as managing mobile-phone calls. Today, you are likely to face problems such as you will miss all your important calls if you forget to carry your mobile phone. But in the near future, you will be able to monitor your mobile-phone calls from a distance, in other words, when you are not near to your mobile phone. We hope that in a short time from now the provision to handle phone calls with instant messaging will be realized, enabling you to sit at a distance from your mobile phone and handle in-coming calls.

With instant messaging, you will be able to send a message to your mobile phone, instructing it to make a call and to deliver the message to the recipient of the call, informing him or her of your availability. You will be able to receive a message in the same manner. The possibilities of instant messaging are unlimited, but innovations are needed for the implementation of these possibilities. Instant messaging has potential far beyond chatting; in fact, it has begun to find use in other areas. Given a little time and the efforts of big software buddies, instant messaging will bloom into its full splendor.

Jabber Instant Messaging Model

Jabber Instant Messaging system is different from other instant messaging systems, as it is based on XML. The most promising feature of Jabber Instant Messaging System is the open-source XML protocol, which makes Jabber more distributed and easily accessible to all who were formerly separated by cross platforms. The architecture of Jabber is almost like that of distributed servers, wherein a client connects to its host server and delivers a message. The host server, in turn, approaches the destination server and hands the message to its intended recipient.

The Java server opts for the open-source protocol because the instant messengers currently available cannot speak with one another. Consider the following analogy. Assume that you have four friends with whom you need to communicate at the same time; you have two choices: you can meet them under some common roof, which is quite cumbersome and expensive, or, if you're friends and you're Internet surfers, you can avail the instant messaging facility to communicate with them. However, to use the latter option, you must have all the instant messengers your friends use for communication. Also, in such a case, you have to open four windows on your computer and handle incoming messages individually, which requires a lot of time.

Introduction to Jabber server

The Jabber server enables its clients to communicate with a non-Jabber client such as MSN. The Jabber server uses a component named *transport* for communicating with the foreign client. Since the Jabber server protocol is completely XML oriented and since other instant messengers maintain their own standardized protocol, the difference in communication is evitable. To bridge this communication variation, the Jabber server uses the Transport. The Transport bridges the gap between these incompatible protocols.

The Jabber server is far more complex than those of the conventional Client/Server architecture, whose simplicity may be attributed to the fact that they often overlook the client priorities. With the Jabber server, making Jabber clients for different platforms is far simpler and involves fewer headaches than with the conventional servers.

Jabber client

Initially, you will probably think of a Jabber client as a common user availing the services of Jabber instant messaging just like the MSN or the Yahoo! instant messaging client. To a certain extent, this is right. But the Jabber client is something more than an ordinary client. In simple words, a Jabber client is something that uses Jabber's ideas and protocols to get a job done. You can write your own clients that utilize the Jabber protocols. For instance, you may develop Jabber-client software that uses the Jabber protocol for instant messaging communication, allowing users of different instant messaging communities to share their views and ideas.

The Jabber server involves two major components: Base and Transports.

Jabber server Base components

Base components handle the job of delivering messages between Jabber clients in their open XML protocol. For instance, Client A and Client B have their accounts on the Jabber server. Whenever Client A sends a message to Client B, the Jabber server manages the delivery of the message to the receiving Client B in its own XML protocol. Thus, the medium of communication between the clients is a protocol, which is known to the Jabber server.

Transports

Transports are the components that bridge the gap between the Jabber and non-Jabber protocol. When you access a non-Jabber system using the Jabber server, the transports hide the system variation from you, and you do not feel that you are visiting some foreign system. When you access a non-Jabber system for the first time, you need to register yourself with Jabber transports by providing information such as the user name and the foreign system you propose to use. Once this is done, messages will be sent and received on the foreign system. We have the transports available for the well-known instant messengers AOL, ICQ, MSN, Yahoo!, and so on. Serious work is underway in developing transports to support other services such as SMS, very popular in Europe.

Structure of Jabber XML protocol

As mentioned earlier, XML is the basis of the Jabber system. Communication between the client and the Jabber server takes place on port 5222. Two XML streams are involved in the exchange of data. One stream delivers the data packet from the client to the server, and the other stream delivers the data from the server to the client. The following code snippet is an example of XML exchange between the Jabber server and the client.

```
SEND:    <stream:stream
SEND:        to='jabber.org'
SEND:        xmlns='jabber:client'
SEND:        xmlns:stream='http://etherx.jabber.org/streams'>
RECV:    <stream:stream
RECV:        xmlns:stream='http://etherx.jabber.org/streams'
RECV:        id='39ABA7D2'
RECV:        xmlns='jabber:client'
RECV:        from='jabber.org'>
      (XML for user session goes here)
SEND:    </stream:stream>
RECV:    </stream:stream>
```

Jabber's Open XML protocol contains three top-level XML elements (also called tags).

- `<presence/>` — This element determines the status of the user. The structure of the presence element is as follows:

```
<presence
from='ericmurphy@jabber.org/notebook'
to='stpeter@jabber.com/Gabber'>
<status>Online</status>
</presence>
```

Based on the status of the user to be communicated, the `<presence>` element can be evaluated on the basis of the following values:

- `probe` — This value of the `presence` element is used to send a special request to the recipient of the message without waiting for the user's presence information. Notice that the sever, not the client, processes such a request.

- `subscribe` — This sends a request that the recipient automatically send the presence information to the sender whenever the user changes its status.

- `subscribed` — This sends a notice that the sender accepts the recipient's request for presence subscription. The server now sends the recipient the sender's presence information whenever it changes.

- `unsubscribe` — If the value of the `presence` element is `unsubscribed`, the user sends the request to the recipient of the message to stop sending the messages of his/her presence.

- unsubscribed — In case the presence element holds this value, then it indicates that the user will not be able to communicate in any way with the sender of this message. In such a situation, the server no longer sends the sender's presence to the recipient of the message.

- from — This mentions the name or id of the sender of the message.

- to — This mentions the name of the recipient of the message.

- show — This displays the status of the user.

- status — This displays the description of the status.

- <message/> — This element is used for sending the messages between two Jabber users. JSM (Jabber Session Manager) is responsible for catering all messages regardless of the status of the target user. If the user is online, the JSM will instantly deliver the message; otherwise, the JSM will store the message and deliver it to the user no sooner than he or she comes online. The <message> element contains the following information:

  - to — This identifies the receiver of the message.

  - from — This mentions the name or id of the message's sender.

  - text — This element contains the message about to be delivered to the target user.

```
<message to='ericmurphy@jabber.org/notebook'
   type='chat'>
<body>hey, how's the weather today?</body>
</message>
```

- <iq/> element — This element manages the conversation between any two users on the Jabber server and allows them to pass XML-formatted queries and respond accordingly.

  The main attribute of the <iq/> element is type. The type attribute of the <iq/> element can carry the following values:

  - get — This attribute of the <iq/> element is used to retrieve the values of the fields present.

  - set — This attribute is responsible for setting or replacing the values of the fileds queried by the get attribute.

  - result — This attribute indictates the successful response to an earlier set/get type query.

```
<stream:stream from='jabber.org' id='1440203636' xmlns='jabber:client'
xmlns:stream='http://etherx.jabber.org/streams'><iq
from='gaurav@jabber.org/www.jabber.org' id='1440203636' type='result'>

<query xmlns='jabber:iq:roster'><item jid='msn.jabber.org/registered'
subscription='from'/><item jid='JohnSmith%hotmail.com@msn.jabber.org'
name='JohnSmith%hotmail.com'
```

```
subscription='both'><group>Friends</group></item><item
jid='Billy%hotmail.com@msn.jabber.org' name='Billy%hotmail.com'
subscription='both'><group>Friends</group></item></query></iq></stream
:stream>
```

Why integrate with the Jabber server?

The greatest achievements of the Jabber server are its open-source protocol and its ability to speak with other instant messaging applications. Therefore, merger with the Jabber server provides us with the opportunity to bring users around the world under the net of our application, gaining a larger distribution.

Apart from open-source protocol, the services of the Jabber server are cost-free. Availing such benefits, anyone can build his or her own Jabber client to fulfill unique requirements. Any innovative IT personnel can develop his or her own version of the Jabber client. The only point that needs to be emphasized is that the Jabber services must be used rationally. In the near future, the Jabber camp might develop a protocol that handheld devices can use to access the Jabber server. If such a protocol emerges, we will be blessed with the ability to transfer our services from personal computers to embedded systems.

Introduction to the Instant Messaging Application

Over the years, instant messaging has undergone many changes, several new innovations in the field of information technology having been incorporated in instant messaging. One such innovation is Jabber instant messaging, based upon the open-source principle. Our instant messaging application avails the benefit of this novel concept and works hand in hand with the Jabber server.

We envision an application that works on behalf of clients to interact with the Jabber server. The primary aim of our application is to develop an instant messaging solution that is compatible with clients of different platforms. In other words, an additional feature of working for Jabber server is incorporated in our application. This feature of our application not only maintains communication between the client and Jabber but also enables the client to use the application whenever desired. Our application is complete in itself; apart from handling clients for the Jabber server, it has all the characteristics of an ideal instant messaging application. No compromise has been made of the normal functions required of any instant messaging application. This application works quite efficiently in spite of the incorporation of additional features. This instant messaging application is based upon the following three components:

- Client — The client is the origin of all requests. This component manages creating XML-formatted queries and sending them to the local server.
- Local server — This component satsifies queries the client sends. The local server can act as a complete service provider to the local client; on the other hand, it can act as an intermediate layer between the local client and Jabber server. For instance, when a client

query is meant for some external source (the Jabber server), the Local server acts as the middle layer between the client and the external source and manages a synchronized flow of messages between the client and the external source. On the contrary, if the client query can be resolved locally (the query is not meant for the Jabber server but for the local server), the local server does not act as a middle layer but resolves the client query without bothering about the Jabber server.

- Jabber server — This module acts as an external source in our application. The local server approaches the Jabber server only when client queries are meant for the Jabber server. All client queries forwarded by the local server are resolved by this component. Once a query is resolved, the Jabber server returns the results to the local server, which further returns the result of the query to the intended client.

Figure 1-1 shows the functions of the various components in our application.

Work flow of the IM application for external client request

External client requests are generated by the client module for the Jabber server. Evident in Figure 1-1, our application, depicted as a local server, is handling communication from and to Jabber server for both the client and the Jabber server. The medium of communication among the client, local server, and Jabber server is XML driven. To cater to the client requests, the local server is listening on port 5555. Also, to handle multiple clients and to keep the session alive for the client and Jabber server, the local server maintains threads.

Throughout the life cycle of our application, the client and Jabber server never come face to face. The boundary of client requests is restricted to the local server, even when requests are meant for the Jabber server. To understand the workflow of our application, consider an example.

Assume a situation where Client A wishes to connect with the Jabber server. The client initiates the process by sending a query, created using a prewritten module named XML Creator. This prewritten module writes client queries in a format that the local server can understand.

Once the client successfully establishes connection with the local server, a thread is assigned by the local server for the client, which will synchronize the flow of messages to the client originating from the local server. The same thread is used up by the local server for a harmonious exchange of messages between itself and the Jabber server.

Client requests for the Jabber server are routed to the local server. Once a request is delivered to the local server, it parses the request, identifies its type, and forwards it to the Jabber server on behalf of Client A. Since the Jabber server maintains its own version of XML for communication, the local server, using its own XML Creator, creates a request that the Jabber server can recognize and hands it over to the Jabber server.

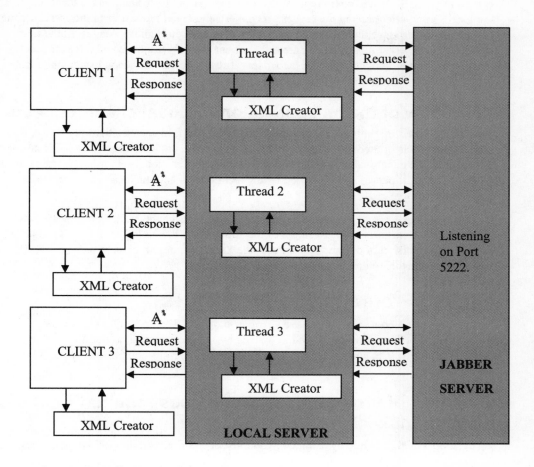

A* -- Socket Connection on Port 5555.
      Medium of Communication XML.

Figure 1-1: Instant messaging application architecture

The Jabber Server listens for all incoming requests on port 5222. Once the request is delivered to it, the Jabber Server generates some response. The local server, on behalf of client A, handles this response. Since the response generated by the Jabber server will be in its own XML format, the local server first of all parses this response for its own understanding and makes use of the XML Creator to transform the Jabber server's response to an XML format that the client can understand.

You may notice that the request for Jabber server goes through two distinct stages of XML communication. First, the client request is converted into XML format for the local server, and the local server, after parsing the request, reconverts the client request in Jabber-server format. Similarly, the response the Jabber server returns also goes through two stages. In the first stage, the local server resolves and parses the Jabber server's response and once the local server understands and analyses the Jabber server response s in the second stage, the local server converts the response for the client.

Work flow of the IM application for local client requests

The client request might be meant for the local server itself. In such a situation, communication is limited to the client and the local server, and the Jabber server has no role. All requests the client makes are handled and managed by the local server itself. The request Client A makes is parsed and identified by the local server, and the local server returns the appropriate response.

To parse the requests and responses respective components generate, the appropriate XML parser is used. Thus, in the Java version of the application, the XERCES 1_2_2 XML parser is used. The C# version of our application uses the XML Document class to parse the XML that various components return.

Required Programming Techniques

To appreciate this book, you must have a firm grip on a .NET application framework, preferably C# or Java. Besides, sound knowledge of XML is needed, as our application uses XML extensively. The communication messages among various components are in XML-based format.

Overview of programming techniques required for the C# client module

To develop a client module by using C#, you must be familiar with the following classes:

- Network stream — This class is used to manage the transportation of data between the client and local server. Whenever some data needs to be transferred, corresponding modules write the data on their network streams, which is picked up by the receiving component and is forwarded for reading.

- XML Document — This class reads the documents in XML format. The XML documents sent by the various modules to one another are nothing but requests and responses in XML format.

- Thread — The main objective of this class is to implement multitasking. The role of this class in the client module is to keep the session with the local server alive. The Thread class also sends and receives messages between the client and the local server.

Apart from the preceding classes, a separate lightweight module is required for transforming the client requests in XML format. In a nutshell, an XML Creator handles the job of creating XML-based requests.

An overview of programming techniques required for the C# server module

To develop the server module by using C#, you must have sound knowledge of the following classes:

- TCP Client — This class is used to connect the client to the host.

- TCP Listener — This class is used to create a host process that listens for connections from TCP clients. Application protocols such as FTP and HTTP are built on the TCP Listener class.

- Sockets — This class provides the core functionality of two-way communication between modules. The Sockets class in the server module of our application is used by the local server to maintain the two-way communication between clients.

- Thread — This class is used to accomplish multitasking. With regard to our application, the Thread class is used by the local server to handle the multiple incoming client requests.

- Web services — Web services can be considered a transport mechanism to access a service. The service you access is the database of the application residing on the local server. A separate module acting as a Web service is built in our application. This module enables the client to access the database the application maintains on the local server to seek out the queries.

- ADO.NET — The services in the Web service module are built by using this class. The ADO.NET class provides various methods to access the database in order to view, modify, or add data.

- MS-SQL Server 2000 — To build the database required for the application, you must be familiar with some basic operations in MS-SQL, such as creating tables and defining primary and foreign keys in the database structure. Instead of using MS-SQL, you can use some other RDBMS, such as SQL7.0 or MS Access 2000.

Apart from the previously mentioned prerequisites for the client and server modules, MS XML parser 3.0 is required for parsing the XML requests and responses of the server and the client, respectively. Client and server modules can share this XML parser accordingly.

Why C#?

Instead of selecting C#, we could have selected some other language such as Visual C++ or C++, but we've decided to choose one of the latest and fastest-developing languages in the programming world. Besides, C# is an ideal tool for developing distributed applications, especially Web-based applications. Some advantages of C# are:

- Interoperability — C# can easily be used with any programming language and development tool. It can easily be incorporated with programming languages such as Visual Basic and Visual C++. Versioning support makes C# compatible with programming languages that were on the market prior to the launching of C#.

- Simplicity — C# is simple yet powerful. To understand C#, you do not require an elaborate background of the programming techniques involved, as it is a strongly typed language. Syntax-wise, C# provides the simplicity of Visual Basic along with excellent debugger and compilation tools. Various commands in C# are easy to manipulate, as they are hybrids of the ancestral languages, C++ and C, already known to most programmers and enterprises. In simple words, we can say that C# offers the functionality of C++ and C and the simplicity of Visual Basic. Programs written in C# are easier to understand and use than those in any other language. Chances of errors are reduced to a great extent, as C# has built-in functionality for detecting errors before the execution of an application.

- Web-service enabled — Applications built using C# can easily be converted into components and can act as Web services for other applications. It is not mandatory for the application to reside on the same network over which the host application is lying or to have features specifically meant for accessing the service-providing application. Accessing a C#-enabled application is almost like accessing an Internet site for which you must know just the name of the host site. The .NET framework provides an excellent environment for creating and developing reusable components for the Internet and other applications using C#.

- Supported by XML — C# has built-in classes that support XML-based documents. There is no need for incorporating any new component to effect support for XML. Another advantage of XML support is that any C# application that uses XML as a communication medium need not bother about how the consuming application handles data; XML supports a wide range of data types and is not bound to any restriction such as COM data types. Thus, when an application receives data, it can convert it into data types it supports. The only demand on the consuming application is the ability to read the XML.

An overview of programming techniques required for the Java client module

To build the client module in Java, you must be familiar with Java's following classes:

- `Socket` — This class works like the `Socket` class of C#. The `Socket` class provides the functionality to establish two-way communication between the client and the local server.

- `Thread` — the `Thread` class in client module is responsible for handling continuous and uniform responses coming from the local server.

An overview of programming techniques required for the Java server module

To build the server module in Java, you must be familiar with Java's following classes:

- `ServerSocket` — This class is responsible for establishing the connection process between the server and the client. The connection requests that clients reach the server via some port number; in other words, the server listens for in-coming client requests on some specified port number. In our application, the local server module uses this class for catering to client requests for connection on port 5555. The `ServerSocket` class maintains the input/output stream for clients to receive requests and to send appropriate responses to the client.

- `Socket` — The local server module uses this class for maintaining connection with the Jabber server, which listens for all incoming requests on the specified port number (5222). Like the `ServerSocket` class, this class maintains an input/output stream. This occurs so that the local server can establish a connection with the Jabber server, enabling any client request meant for the Jabber server to be transferred over this socket connection; all responses that the Jabber server returns are collected by the local server.

- `Thread` — The `Thread` class that Java provides handles the job of multitasking and synchronizing the message flow occurring between respective components. With regard to our application, the local server module uses this class to handle multiple in-coming client requests for connection. Also, this class synchronizes the messages (requests and responses) exchanged between sessions that the local server for the client and the Jabber server run.

- `Vector` — This class works like a dynamic array for message queuing.

Why Java?

By itself, Java offers solutions to many problems you encounter while developing applications in the dynamically changing information-technology environment of today. Although almost all programming languages possess some unique advantages, Java, with its consistent performance, proves itself the ideal choice for developers. Java is highly efficient in managing time and cost factors, which makes it popular among entrepreneurs. Several other features of Java contribute to the fact that developers favor it. Some of these features are as follows:

- Platform-independent — Java is built to run on various platforms and easily mingles with networking distinctions. This feature of Java eliminates the complexity encountered by applications while running on different platforms. An application built in Java seldom requires platform configurations and networking topologies, making its reach wider and more distributive for the users.

- Simplicity — Among the popular object-oriented languages, Java is far simpler and easier to use than C and C++. Complex features of the C++ language, such as pointers, are eliminated in Java. Multiple inheritance is replaced by the simple structure known as *interface*. Memory allocation and garbage collection in Java occur automatically, whereas in C++ you need to allocate memory and collect garbage on your own.

- Distributed and platform independent — Java eliminates the need to write lengthy coding, as modules can be built separately and integrated later to carve out the final application. Besides, once the code is written, there is no need for compiling it over and over again; applications built in Java are compiled into byte-code.

- Security — So far, no programming language has succeeded in providing absolute security. Java is no exception. But Java maintains an upper edge over its rival programming languages as it is equipped with a series of security measures deployed at various stages in consideration of the requirements of the enterprise world and also those of the end user.

- Robust — Java is robust, which means it provides reliability. Java, in the true sense, is a reliable language; it can easily detect possible coding errors well in advance of execution.We know Java does not support pointers and thereby avoids complexities. The reason behind not incorporating pointers is to restrict memory from being overwritten, providing more reliability in data management.

Summary

In this chapter, we explore the history of instant messaging and discuss its potential trends. In the overview, we discuss the requirements for using instant messaging and the advantages of instant messaging. The overview of instant messaging is followed by the most discussed form of instant messaging — Jabber. We briefly outline the working of the Jabber instant messaging server, along with details of some of the major technical aspects of the Jabber server: the main elements involved in XML-based, open-source protocol of the Jabber server and the purpose of integrating an application with the Jabber server. A glimpse of the working of our application and the programming techniques required for developing it is also presented in this chapter.

Toward the end of the chapter, the reasons for choosing some of the programming languages for developing this application are explained, and the merits of these languages are discussed.

Chapter 2

Designing the Instant Messaging Application

This chapter focuses on the design of the Instant Messaging application and integrating it with the Jabber instant messaging server.

Application Design Considerations

The nature and purpose of this application is innovative in itself, and in the near future this application might gain wider acceptance. While designing this application, we have used the approach presented in this chapter.

As mentioned earlier, the mode of this application is meant for a global scale, which makes it mandatory that the application is well equipped to encounter and overpower networking differences. Often, excess traffic on the network challenges the boundaries of the application's memory-management. Thus, while you are deploying the application over the network, you must twice consider the limits set for the excess networking traffic to avoid network congestion.

The most crucial aspect of application design is customer needs. History has proven that designing applications without considering customer needs ultimately leads to failure. And it is clear that users sometimes resist interacting with an application based on our approach, preferring to use the application according to their specific needs. Some corporate tycoons might deploy a similar application for their trade and commerce purposes, while other users such as students might be interested in availing the benefits of an application by sharing their ideas of the community, using this application on the University level. Hence, the application must possess enough versatility to hide the differences between local area networks (LANs) and wide area networks (WANs) and should provide the same enjoyment and task force for the user.

Another important consideration of the application designer is the simplicity of the application. The design of the application must provide a carefree environment, and should not make the user feel confused or isolated. You can use GUI forms and the well-framed Help feature to let the user handle the application with ease.

Last, consider some provisions for the future existence of the application. There is hardly any need to mention to IT personnel that technology in today's world changes with the blink of an eye. While designing the application, keep some free space to incorporate new extensions to encounter any change in technology and customer demand. When the add-ons are about to be integrated in the application, the basic purpose and functionality of the application must not be axed.

Database Design Considerations

The database of the application maintains the name and required information of all registered users. Like the application-design phase, database design involves lots of considerations. After form normalizations are complete, the final picture of the database emerges. The approach you have decided upon to build the application can be different from ours. As a result, the database design can also vary. But there are some common points that you must consider while designing the database:

- Maintain at least two tables, and assign the primary key in each table along with a foreign key, if required.

- Keep one table for general purposes (storing user information such as the login name, password, residential address, contact number, and so on).

- In the table you are using for general purposes, make sure the login name and password are not left blank.

- The other table in the database can be used for a list of names of friends of the corresponding user. You can achieve this by assigning the primary key of a later table as a foreign key in the present table and vice-versa.

Based on the design considerations of the database, the preferred table structure is like the one shown in Figure 2-1.

Server Module Design Considerations

Whether you are interested in designing the local server module in C# or in Java, keep the following design considerations in mind.

Connectivity

The first consideration that needs to be emphasized is how the local server allows clients to connect with it. In more precise terms, we need to know on what port number the local server waits for the client's connection request. Further, the mechanisms involved in establishing connections with the client cannot be ignored. On the Jabber side, the local server must know the port number on which Jabber listens to all incoming requests and how the connection with the Jabber server can be established.

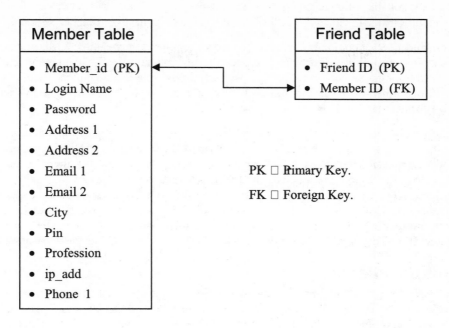

Figure 2-1: Structure of the application database

The listed prerequisites for the connection process can be achieved via a socket connection. Server modules built using C# and Java can use respective classes and methods to accomplish the connection procedure. The port number can be resolved by selecting the port number for the local server as in our application. In our application, the local server is listening to all in-coming client requests for connection on port 5555. In a parallel manner, the Jabber server is listening to all in-coming requests on port 5222. In case the local server receives a client request for establishing connection with the Jabber server, the local server must be able to establish a session and socket connection with the Jabber server.

Communication

The communication mechanism of the local server must be flexible; on one hand, it must be able to understand the contents of the client request and to respond in such layout that the client can read. On the other hand, while interacting with the Jabber server, the local server must have suitable arrangements for communicating with Jabber server. You can divide two submodules inside the local server for listening to client requests and Jabber responses.

Since Jabber server communicates only in its own supported open-source XML protocol, the local server must be able to formulate requests for the Jabber server. While receiving a response from the Jabber server, the local server must be able to recognize the Jabber server's response. Further, the local server must deliver the response to its final destination client in such a format that the client can recognize.

Creating requests for the Jabber server and reformatting them in a client-supported format can be achieved by writing a component that can write requests according to Jabber-server standards and can retranslate the Jabber response for the client. However, the local server can only deliver the response returned by the Jabber server to the client when the local server understands the response. In technical terms, there should be some specification to parsing the Jabber response. To handle such cross-platform dissimilarities, you can use methods and classes present in programming language you have selected for designing the local-server module. If the language you select does not have such support, XML parsers can assist you.

Multiple clients

The local server must bear the potential to cater to multiple-client requests and process them simultaneously. To meet this requirement, you can use the `Thread` class in C# and in the Java version of server module. The class present in C# and in the Java environment serve the common purpose of multitasking.

Message synchronization

As mentioned earlier, the local server needs to be handy while handling clients. Similarly, it becomes mandatory that the local server have the provisions to manage the messages flowing from the Jabber server and from itself for the client. To encounter such a problem, you can incorporate some functionality that queued up the messages for clients so that respective the client can flush them. When messages are queued up, make sure they contain the ID of the recipient client.

Web services

Web services are among the most widely discussed concepts of today's Internet era. Web services are particularly helpful in downsizing the working of the server by accomplishing certain tasks on its behalf. For example, in the conventional client/server architecture client requests such as authentication, logout, view some information, and so on were processed by the server itself which increases the server's work load. With introduction of Web services the servers could be designed to handle core tasks such as implementation of logic, and so on.

Usually, the server is responsible for calling the appropriate Web service after determining the nature of the request received from the client. The Web service, on being called by the server, processes the request and delivers the computed result to the server. In an ideal scenario, the

Web service and server communicate with each other in XML standards, as in our application. In our application, the Web services and the local server communicate with each other in XML protocol. Whenever the Web service needs to deliver a result to the server, it creates appropriate XML and vice-versa. Thus, the role of the server shrinks from processing the request to merely delivering the result in response to the client. Figure 2-2 shows the workflow of Web services. Figure 2-3 shows the workflow of the entire server module.

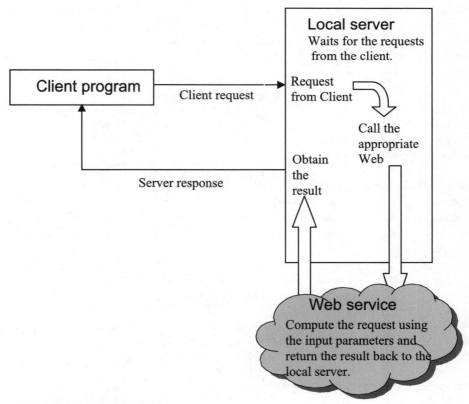

Figure 2-2: Working of Web services

Figure 2-3a: Work flow of the local server module

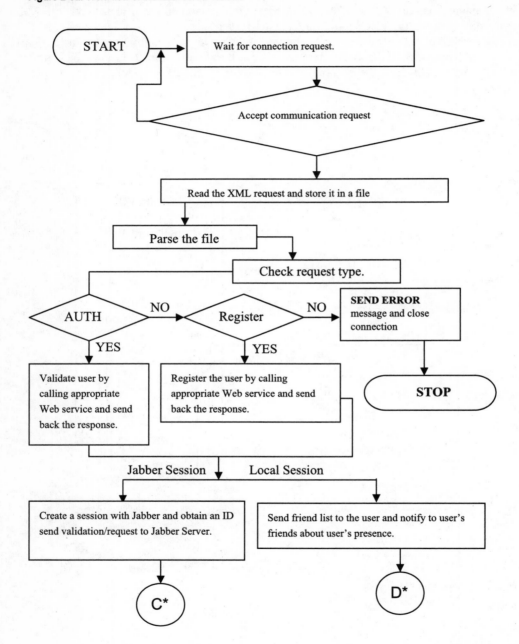

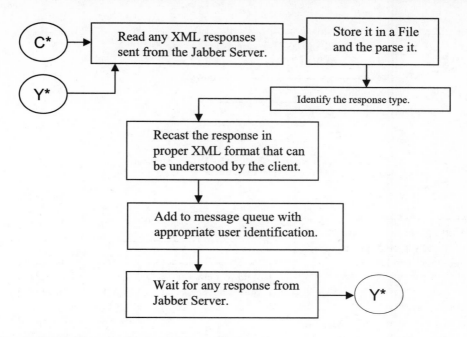

Figure 2-3b: Work flow of the local server module (continued)

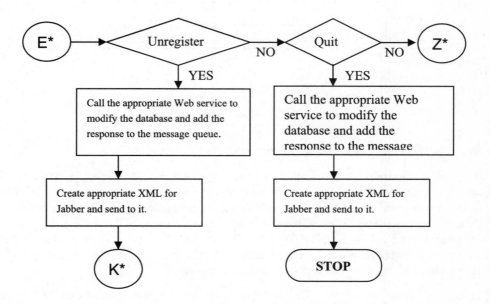

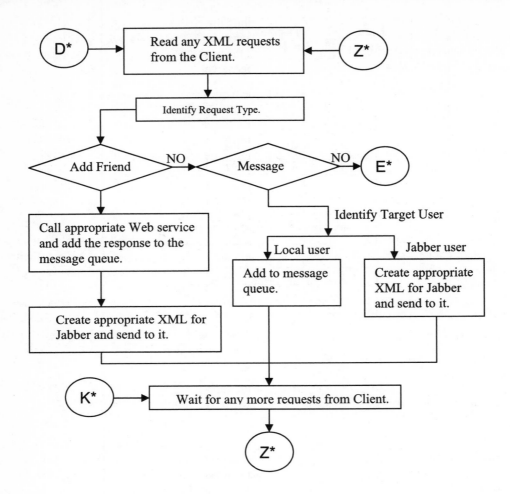

Figure 2-3c: Work flow of the local server module

The local server is designed to handle all in-coming client requests on port 5555. At the start up of the process, the local server waits for clients to make a connection request. No sooner than the client makes the request, the local server reads the request and stores it in a file. The local server then parses the client request to determine the mode of the request. The nature of the client request at this stage is either for authentication or logging on (if user is registered) or for registration (if user is new). You can assume this stage is equal to the signing or registration process that uses your desired instant messenger.

If the local server receives an authentication request, the appropriate validations are performed for the client request, such as verifying the login name, the password, and the choice made for the local server or Jabber server to log on by calling the Web service responsible for performing this task. Once the authentication process is over, the local server returns the appropriate response to the client; consequently, the session is created for the client, either locally (on the local server itself) or for the Jabber server.

On the other hand, if the local server receives the request for registration, calls to the appropriate Web services are made, and appropriate responses are returned to the client. The response generated during the registration process can either be for successful completion of the registration process or for some validations mismatch such as leaving some mandatory "fields empty" or a "user already exists" exception. After completion of the registration process, an appropriate session is created for the client. The creation of sessions entirely depends upon the selection made by the user for servers. Exceptionally, if the client request neither carries the request for authentication nor registration, an error message is raised by the local server, and immediately the connection is closed.

In case the client request is demanding an interaction with the Jabber server, the local server, on behalf of client request, creates the session with the Jabber server and forwards the client request and obtains an ID for the session. The Jabber server also generates and returns a response. The response from the Jabber server is first attended to by the local server. After reading the response, the local server stores the response in the file and parses it to determine its nature. Once the process of reading and parsing is over, the local server reformats the Jabber response in an XML format the client can comprehend. In the next step, the local server adds the response in the message queue with the client ID, so that corresponding clients can flush their messages.

The local server waits for more responses from the Jabber server. In such a case, the entire cycle of reading, parsing, and adding responses to the message queue recurs until the last response of the Jabber server is not delivered to the receiving client.

On the other hand, if the client request wants to deal with the local server, the Local Server at start up returns the list of friends to the client and sends notification to all friends of the client about his or her presence and waits for the client to make any requests. At this stage, the possible client requests received by the local server can be for:

- Adding a friend
- Delivering a message to another user
- Unregistering (removing account)
- Quiting the application and coming out of the network

The local server determines the previously mentioned client requests by reading them and determining their type. Once the local server determines the request type, it initiates the rest of the process. Table 2-1 contains a description of various client requests the local server makes.

Table 2-1: Local Server Client Requests

Request	Explanation
Add Friend	If the client requests to add a new friend, the local server calls the appropriate Web service to accomplish the task and to send responses to the client. The local server informs the Jabber server about the new friend the client has added by creating an appropriate response and delivering it to the Jabber server. After finishing the task, the local server waits for more client requests.
Message	Apart from adding a friend, a client can also send a message to the user. In such a scenario, the local server determines the location of the recipient of the message (whether the message is to be delivered for the local user or the user who belongs to the Jabber server). If the message is meant for some local user, the local server adds the message in the message queue from where the message is flushed by the recipient users. Conversely, if the message is destined for some user of the Jabber server, the local server creates the appropriate request for the Jabber server on behalf of client and delivers it.
Unregister	Rarely, but quite possibly, the client can opt to unregister itself from the service. The local server manages this request by calling the appropriate Web service, which handles the process of deleting the user account from the application database. Once the user account is removed and the database is updated, a response is generated by the local server and added in the message queue for the client. After completing the task, the local server creates an appropriate request for the Jabber server to inform it about the changes that have taken place. The local server then waits to fulfill more client requests.
Quit	The local server finalizes such a client request by making a call to the appropriate Web service, which accesses the application database and performs necessary updates. Once the database is updated, the message is once again added to the message queue, which is retrieved by the client. Next, the local server informs the Jabber server about the logged out status of the client by making an appropriate request and sending it to the Jabber server. Finally, the application stops.

Apart from the aforementioned requests, the local server might receive such a client request that is not supported or cannot be fulfilled. In such a case, an error is raised by the server and is communicated to the client.

Required Web services for the application

Web services handle the login procedure of the client. Web services must handle the task of validating the user and making appropriate updates each time the user logs in. Similarly, when the user is moving out from the application, there must be appropriate Web services to provide smooth access to the client. Apart from handling the tasks of logging in and logging out the user, there can be other Web services to cater to user requirements such as sending notification to friends whenever a user logs in and logs out. Similarly, a Web service must remain present, which allows the client to include and delete other users in and from his or her friend's list.

Based on our approach to developing the application, the following Web service can square up the tasks on behalf of the server.

While designing such an application, the required Web services for meeting the requirements of the application can be:

- Login Web service: This Web service is responsible for providing access on the application network to the client whenever the client logs in. Apart from providing access to the client, this Web service is also responsible for authenticating the client input during login time with the help of the login name and login password.

- Register Web service: The Primary task of this Web service is to organize and accomplish the registration procedure for the new client, with due regard for database validations.

- FriendList Web service: Whenever the user successfully logs on to the application network, this Web service produces the list of friends (all friends who are online and offline) for the user, along with their statuses.

- Add Friend Web service: This Web service allows the user to add a new friend to his or her list of friends. While performing the task, this Web service keeps in notice the prior presence of a friend from the Friend list. If the Web service finds that a friend is already present in the Friend list, the user is immediately informed.

- DeleteContact Web Service: This Web service permits the user to remove a friend from the Friend list. Whenever the user initiates this task, the Web service informs the opposite user that he or she has been deleted from the Friend list of the user.

- UnRegister Web Service: This Web service removes the user's account permanately from the database of the application. When this Web service completes its task, the user no longer remains an eligible client to use the services of the application.

- Logout Web service: Whenever the user wishes to leave the application, this Web service comes into action. Apart from providing easy departure to the user, this Web service handles the task of updating the status of the user in the database (from online to offline).

Login Web service

The main task of the Login Web service (Figure 2-4) is to authenticate the client attempting to set up the connection with the server. For authentication, this Web service uses two parameters □ login name and password □ entered by the user while logging in. At the beginning of the validation process, the Login Web service picks the login name entered by the user and consults the appropriate table (member) maintained by the application database. While scrolling the table's records, if the Web service finds that the user name does not exist, an error is raised by the Web service, and delivered to the server. The server, on receiving such an error, generates the appropriate XML for the client, and the process of authorizing the client stops.

The login name entered by the user might be correct, but the password might not match the password stored in the database. In such a scenario, the Web service once again raises an error and hands it to the Web service. The server, on receiving such response from the Web service, generates the appropriate XML and delivers it to the client.

Customarily, when the connection with the server is established without facing any errors, the Login Web service determines the IP Address of the client. In the next step, this Web service updates the status of the client in the database from offline to online. Consequently, after successful log on, the Web service generates the appropriate code, which is followed by a formulation of the appropriate XML. Finally, this XML is delivered to the respective client, mentioning that the user has successfully logged on. Thus the role of this Web service ends.

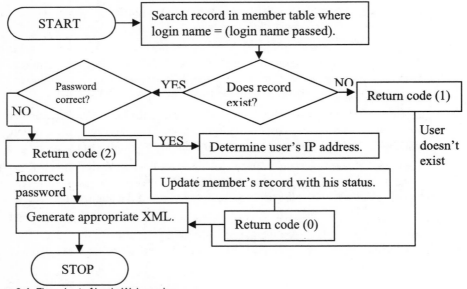

Figure 2-4: Flow chart of Login Web service

Register Web service

The Register Web service (Figure 2-5) is responsible for adding new clients in the application net. Whenever the server receives the client request for registration, Register Web service is called. This Web service considers the login name, the password, and some optional fields as parameters that were filled by the client during the registration process. Once the information is filled by the client, the server hands over the client information to the Web service for appropriate validation. The Register Web service initiates the process of validating the user information by looking for the login name opted by the user; this prevents the occurrence of two users with the same login name.

If, while consulting the database records, the Web service finds that the login name chosen by the user is already taken by some other client, the Web service raises an error, mentioning that the user already exists. Consequently, an appropriate XML is generated and handed over to the server, which informs the client.

Generally, when no error is encountered by the Web service, user information such as login name, password, and optional field entered by the user are added in the application database, and 0 is returned by the Web service to the server to notify that the user has been successfully included in the application database and is now a registered client.

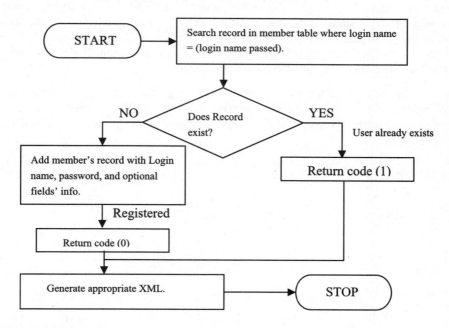

Figure 2-5: Flow chart of Register Web service

FriendList Web service

The FriendList Web Service (Figure 2-6) comes into action after the client has successfully logged on to the application network. The primary task of this Web service is to return the friend list to the user, along with his or her present login status of friends (who are online or offline). To start the process of returning the friendlist to the user, this Web service looks for the member ID corresponding to the login name passed by the user. In the next step, this Web service searches the ID of friends in another table by considering the login ID of the client as a parameter. In other words, you can say that the FriendList Web service manages the task of obtaining the IDs of all users who are friends of the present client from the Friends table of the database, which is related to the previously discussed Member table by means of the primary and foreign key algorithm.

While searching for the friend's ID, if the Web dervice finds that no friend is present in the Friends table, an empty freindlist is returned by the Web service. Positively, when the Friends table holds some IDs of users who are friends of the client, the Web service starts searching the name and IP address in the Members table corresponding to the friend's ID. When the Web service is through with resolving the names and IP addresses on the basis of ID, it generates a list comprising the names of friends.

In the next step, the Web service checks the status of the friends by considering their IP addresses. Since the status of the friends can either be 0 (offline) or 1 (online), the Web service, after determining the value of the field in the Member table responsible for storing and managing the IP Address, appends the status of the friend appropriately in the list, so that the user can know well in advance who is available for conversing.

Finally, after putting together all required blocks of information in sequential order, the Web service returns the list to the server and generates appropriate XML for the server. The server, on receiving this XML response from the Web service, determines its type and delivers it to the target user.

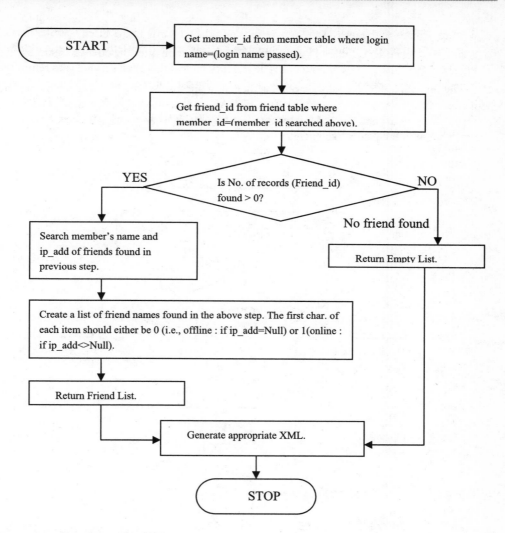

Figure 2-6: Flow chart of FriendList Web service

NotifyFriends Web service

The NotifyFriends Web service (Figure 2-7) handles the job of generating the list of friends to whom a notification has to be delivered whenever the client logs on to the application network. The local server manages the task of sending notification. This Web service is merely forming the list to let the server know who the target users are for delivering the notification. Initially, when Web service is called, it consults the Friends table and obtains the ID of all those clients who are friends to the user. The Web service might find no ID in the Friends table. In such a case, the Web service returns no list. Suitable XML is created for letting the server know about the situation.

Normally, when the Web service obtains the list, it approaches the Member table to resolve the names of the users corresponding to their IDs. After resolving the names, the Web service formulates the list and generates appropriate XML for the server, so that it can deliver notification to the respective clients.

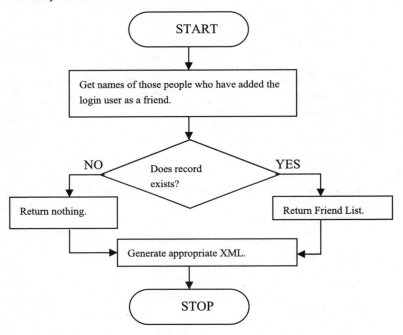

Figure 2-7: Flow chart for NotifyFriends Web service

AddFriend Web service

The AddFriend Web Service (Figure 2-8) enables the user to add a new friend to his or her Friend list. For accomplishing the task, this Web Service takes login names as parameter of the client who is adding the user in the Friend list and the login name of the user who is to be added to the Friend list. On being called from the server, this Web service searches the member ID of the client by its login name who (the client) is interested in adding the new user in the Friend list. In the next step, Web service seeks the Member ID of the user who is about to be included in the Friend list of the later user.

The Web service carries out this check to determine whether the friend in whom the user is interested really exists on the application database. If the Web service finds that the desired member does not exist in the application database, it returns error code 1 and generates an appropriate XML for the server to notify the user that the member selected by the user as friend does not exist on the application database.

Commonly, when the Web service does not face nonexistence issues of the member, it carries out another validation to make sure that the member opted by the user for his or her Friend list might not already exist in the Friend list. For ensuring such coexistence in the Friend list, the Web service looks for the member ID and the friend ID in the Friend table to ensure that no other friend for the corresponding member ID exists. Unfortunately, when the Web service finds that the member already exists in the Friend list of the user, error code 2 is returned by the Web service, followed by an XML response for the server. The server then forwards this information to the user to let him/her know that the member is already in his/her Friend list.

When the Web service finds neither nonexistence nor duplicity of members, it adds the member in the Friend list of the user. For doing so, a field is inserted in the Friend table containing the member ID of the user and his or her friend. After successful inclusion of the member in the Friend list of the user, the Web service returns code 0 and generates appropriate XML for the server. The server then forwards this information to the client to let him know about the completion of the task

DeleteContact Web service

The DeleteContact Web service (Figure 2-9) allows the client to delete a friend from his or her Friend list. To facilitate the user, the Web service must know who is deleting whom? The Web service starts its working by looking for the member ID of the client, and the ID of the friend who is about to be deleted by the client in the Member Table, on the basis of login names.

Once the Web service obtains the ID of the member and his or her friend, it removes the member ID of the client and the IDs of his or her friends from the Friends Table. To verify that the record has been deleted successfully, the Web service performs a check. If the record is deleted successfully, the Web service returns 0 code, which signifies successful deletion of the record. It is possible that, due to technical reasons, records sometimes cannot be deleted. In such a case, the Web service raises an error code 2 to notify that an error has occurred. Depending upon the situation faced by the Web service, appropriate errors are generated by the Web services, followed by the suitable XML for explaining the situation to the server.

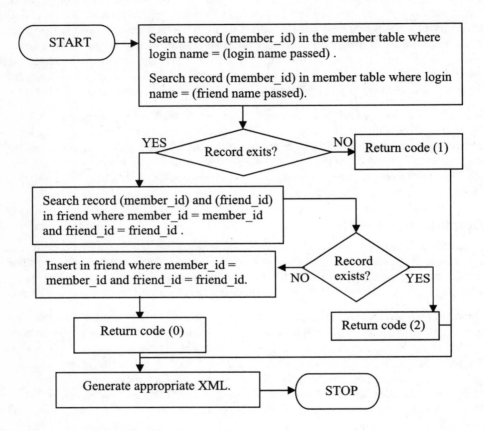

Figure 2-8: Flow chart of the AddFriend Web service

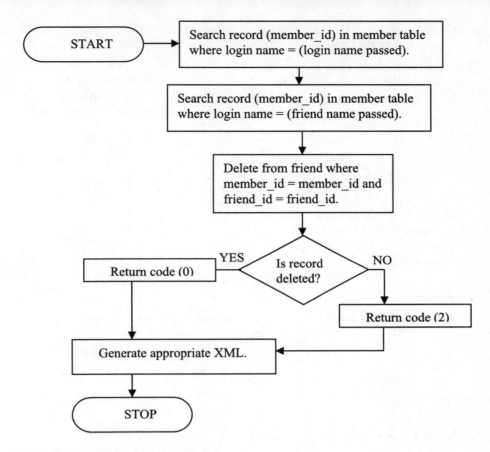

Figure 2-9: Flow chart of DeleteContact Web service

UnRegister Web service

The UnRegister Web service (Figure 2-10) is used to remove the account of the user from the application database. Whenever this Web service is called, it starts looking for the records of the login name about to be deleted. It is rare but possible that the user is attempting to delete the account of such a user who has never existed in the records of the application. On encountering such a situation, the Web service raises the appropriate error code (1) to signify that user does not exist.

By and large, when the Web service finds the record for the Login name in the Member table, it removes the login name, password, and other related information from the table. After deleting the record of the client, the Web service returns an appropriate code (0) to confirm that the record is deleted. It must be remembered that when the client account is removed from the application database, he or she is no longer entitled to avail the services of the application. So try to avoid using the UnRegister Web service.

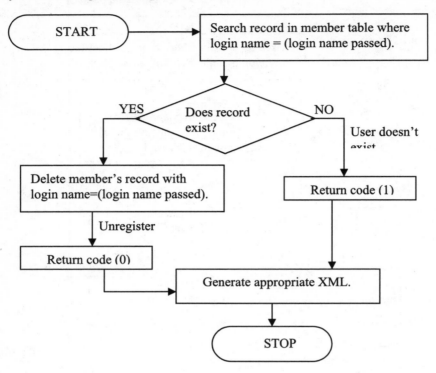

Figure 2-10: Flow chart of UnRegister Web service

Logout Web service

The primary task of the Logout Web service (Figure 2-11) is to provide a smooth exit to the user whenever he or she wishes to quit the application. Simultaneously, the Logout Web service updates the database. On receiving such a request, the local server makes a call to this Web service. To begin logging out the user from the application, this Web service takes the login name of the user as a parameter. At start up, this Web service searches the login name in the application database to change its status from online to offline. It is rare but possible that while calling the Web service, the wrong parameters, such as the name of the user, which never existed in the database of the application, are passed. In such exceptional cases, the Web service raises an error code 2, which symbolizes that the user does not exist. This error code is handed over to the server, which, after determining the nature of the error, forms the appropriate XML and returns it to the client. After exchanging errors and XML, the process is stopped until further action takes place on the client side.

The possibility exists that the Web service receives a request for logging out a client who has already logged out. On encountering such a request, the Web service raises the error code 1 to notify the server that the user to whom the exit door is about to be shown has already gone through it. The server, on receiving such a response from the Web Service, generates the appropriate XML for client notification.

Under normal circumstances, the Web service process the logout request by setting the IP address field in the database as NULL, signifying the offline status of the client. After performing the task, the computed result is handed over to the server. The server, on receiving such a response, formulates the appropriate XML and posts it to the concerned client.

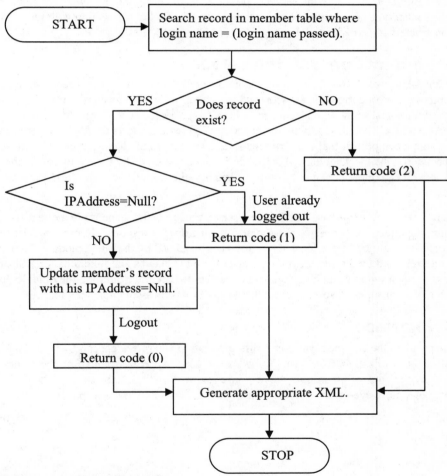

Figure 2-11: Flow chart of Logout Web service

Client Module Design Considerations

The client module is the source of all client requests, and it handles the task of delivering the requests to the server and receiving the responses returned by the server. While designing the client module, either of the following design considerations must be taken into account: connectivity with the server or communication with the server.

Connectivity with the server

To initiate any communication with the server, the client module, ahead of all tasks, needs to establish a connection with the server. Once the connection with the server is established, further communication with the server is possible. While designing the client module, you can use the socket type connections to reach the server. The socket connection with the server can be constructed at the dedicated port number (5555) assigned to the server.

Communication with the server

Like the Jabber server, the local server maintains certain communication specifications. The client module must communicate with the local server in its deployed standards. Generally, client communication with the local server is request oriented. The format of the request must be recognized and supported by the local server. To create requests for the local server, you can design a component that can write requests according to the local server's specifications. Consequently, the local server will respond to the request made by the client. Inside the client module, you can implement a submodule to listen to the response coming from the local server.

Although we have mentioned that the local server typecasts the response in a client-friendly manner, the client needs to fetch the actual content from the response. In more precise terms, the response returned by the local server needs to be parsed by the client module. To parse the response returned by the server, you can manipulate the classes and functions for XML parsing present in the programming language you have decided upon for building the module. In the absence of such support, you can use suitable XML parsers available on the market.

GUI interface

To encapsulate the complex working of the application and provide a carefree environment for handling the application, GUI-based forms can be used. Apart from initiating the request process by the click of the mouse, the response returned by the local server can be presented to the user in a more eye-catching form by using the form related to the response.

Work flow of the client module

Figure 2-12 illustrates the work flow of the Instant Messaging application's client module.

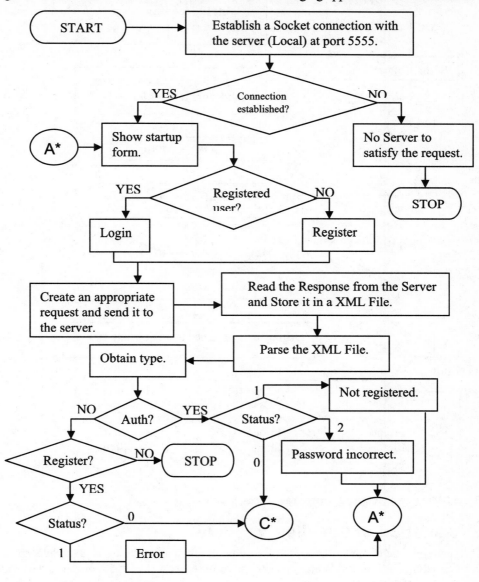

Figure 2-12a: Flow chart of the client module

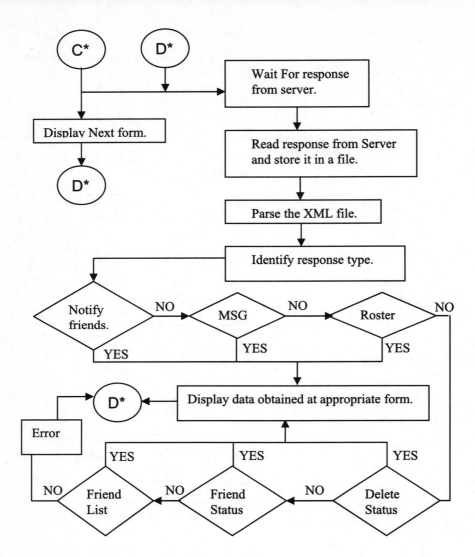

Figure 2-12b: Flow chart of the client module (continued)

Explanation of the client module

The client module of our application is the origin of all client requests. This module, apart from initiating the connection process with the local server at port 5555, manages the creation and delivery of requests to the local server and displays the response returned by the local server in appropriate GUI-based forms. At the beginning of the process, the client module attempts to make the connection with the local server. In case the server (local or Jabber) is unavailable to fulfill the request of the user, the application stops immediately.

Customarily, when the connection is established with the local server, some sort of login form is displayed to the user containing two options: one for logging onto the network and another for registration (if the user is new). Based upon the option selected by the user, the client module makes the appropriate response, delivers it to the local server, and waits for a response. When the server responds, the client module reads the response and stores it in an XML file for parsing the response. Since the process is still in its initial stages, the response returned by the server is either for authentication or for registration. When client module parses the server response, it obtains the type of the response.

If the client module obtains the authentication response, it parses the response to determine its nature. The response generated by the server against authentication most likely encompasses login failure, successful login, or a response for any such attempt where the unregistered user tries to log on. Except in the case of successful login, a start-up form is redisplayed to the user. After the user gains access, the client module displays the start-up form of the application to the user, which comprises of various options such as message delivery, provision of sending notification to other users, adding friends, and so on.

In contrast, the response type obtained by the client module is of registration type; it determines the mode of the response. If the response returned by the server is for successful registration, the start-up form is displayed to the user. Unfortunately, if the server returns some errors during the registration process, the client module displays the login form to the user. When the client module receives a response for an unrecognized request, it leads to an error, and the application stops in the next step.

Once the user successfully (either through the logging or registration process) enters the network, the start-up form is displayed for the user to carry on his or her activities. From this point onward, all requests are generated from this form. The response returned by the server is parsed to obtain the response's nature, and it is displayed in respective GUI forms. For example, if the server is returning the list of friends, the appropriate form is displayed containing the Friend list. The user at one moment of time can possibly perform one out of six activities from the start-up form; consequently, the server responds appropriately to the corresponding user action.

After delivering the request to the server, the client module waits for the response. Once the response is obtained, the client module reads the server response, saves it in the file, and identifies the type of the response. The server response holds the ID of the recipient. Based upon the response type and the user ID, the client module invokes the corresponding GUI form and displays the response as a result to the user.

Remember that whenever the client module encounters the response for the 'Notify Friends' request, it becomes the responsibility of the client module to display not only the list of users or client localities to the local server but also the global list of users' friends, which includes users from Jabber and other instant messaging services so that the user can perform activities such as adding or deleting friends and can see the refreshed list of friends.

Similarly, if the response is of the roster type, the list of friends to the user comes up. However, this list carries names of global users only. In other words, we can say that the list of friends apart from the local server is displayed to the user in appropriate form.

Another important point to note is that the response types 'Delete Status' and 'Friend Status' encompass only clients of the local server. If the client receives such types of responses, data is displayed in appropriate forms and is shown to the user.

Application Communication Standards

Before we start discussing the communication models of our application, it is better to bring to your notice that the mode of communication in our application is XML oriented. Various modules involved in our application converse with each other in XML queries and responses. In the next section, you observe that the format of XML in the request/response mechanism varies between the modules involved, as in the case of the Jabber and local servers. In our application, this communication gap has been overpowered using a prewritten module-XML Creator. Modules for generating XML queries in such a format, which is recognized and supported by the receiving module, use this component. Similarly, the response generated by the modules can vary, as in case of Jabber server. To seek this problem, the built-in functions and methods provided by the programming language are consumed. If support is not available, parsers are used.

Communication models

This section pertains to the communication involved between various modules of the Instant messaging application. As mentioned earlier in the chapter, the standard of communication for our application is XML oriented; in this section we will discuss how various modules communicate with each other in XML based queries. On one hand, the communication between the client and the local server is discussed, and XMLs involved in the communications are quoted. On the other hand, the server-to-server communication (that is, between the local server to the Jabber server) is discussed, and the XMLs involved in the communications are illustrated.

Server to client communication model

The communication between the client and the local server starts with displaying a login window. In the login window, you are required to enter information required for authentication. Once the Client / user gets authenticated, the client and the local server are ready to communicate with each other. It must be remembered that communication between the client and the local server is taking place on the socket connection.

In client/server architecture, the client is responsible for initiating the communication process; a request is created by the client for the local server by using the XML Creator, so that the local server can recognize and understand it. On receiving the request, the local server assigns a thread for the client request. This thread interacts with the client and delivers the response generated by the local server. The local server, on the opposite end, generates the responses for client requests by using its own XML Creator for the sake of convenience to the user and places the response in the assigned thread, which delivers it to the user. Once obtained by the client, the response is parsed, and the final output of the request is displayed to the user.

As mentioned earlier, the communication mode of our application is XML. The modules involved in our application use common XMLs regardless of the C# version and Java version. In the following section, a glimpse of requests/responses involved between modules is presented to you. For your better understanding, a simple process of client authentication is depicted in this section.

The process of communicating and exchanging information is initiated by the client module. At start up, the client module makes the authentication request and submits it to the local server. The structure of the client-authentication request appears as displayed in Listing 2-1.

Listing 2-1: Authentication XML

```
<?xml version="1.0" encoding="utf-8" ?>
-<InstantMessenger>
-<Auth>
 <UserName>johnsmith</UserName>
  <Password>smithy</Password>
  </Auth>
</InstantMessenger>
```

Consequently, the Local Server responds against the client-authentication request. The structure of the server response appears like the one shown in Listing 2-2.

Listing 2-2: Result of Authentication XML

```
<?xml version="1.0" ?>
-<InstantMessenger>
-<auth>
  <int>0</int>
</auth>
</InstantMessenger>
```

The 0 between the int tags represents the successful login of the client. In the case of a failed login, the value is 1.

When the client logs onto the network, the local server returns the Friend list to the client with information about its login status — online of offline. The structure of the Friend list returned by the local server is as shown in Listing 2-3.

Listing 2-3: Friend list XML

```
<?xml version="1.0" ?>
-<InstantMessenger>
-<FriendList>
    <UserName>johnsmith</UserName>
        <FriendName>Billy</FriendName>
        <Status>1</Status>
        <FriendName>Joe</FriendName>
        <Status>1</Status>
</FriendList>
</InstantMessenger>
```

Besides returning the Friend list to the client, the local server sends the notification to all friends of the client. If the friend of the client is offline, the local server stores the notification for such a friend and displays it when he or she has logged in. The structure of the notification XML generated by the local server appears as displayed in Listing 2-4.

Listing 2-4: Friends' status XML

```
<?xml version="1.0" ?>
-<InstantMessenger>
-<NotifyFriends>
    <UserName>johnsmith</UserName>
        <Status>On-Line</Status>
        <FriendName>Billy</FriendName>
        <FriendName>Joe</FriendName>
</NotifyFriends>
</InstantMessenger>
```

Server to Jabber server communication model

The communication between the Jabber server and the server of our application initiates only when the client requests to interact with some user, which is foreign to our local server i.e. a client who does not exist in the records of applications' database, for example a client belonging to MSN or Jabber networks. Whenever the local server receives such a request, it creates a session with the Jabber server and obtains a reference of such a session to maintain distinction between requests flowing for the Jabber client. In the next phase, after establishing a session, the local server sends a user-authentication request to the Jabber server. The local server traps the response returned by the Jabber server and stores it in the file. Since the response returned by the Jabber server is in its own XML format, the local server parses the request by using XML Creator to re-create the response in a user-friendly format and deliver it to the client.

The Jabber server dominates the communication between itself and the local server. Since Jabber has to listen to clients from all corners of the world, it maintains its open-source XML protocol. To get the job done, it is our responsibility to communicate with Jabber in its own spoken and recognized language. Once again, to understand the standards of communication between the Jabber server and the local server, let's consider the process of client authentication.

The communication between the local server and the Jabber server comes into play only when the client submits the request to the local server for communicating with foreign clients such as the Jabber client. The process is initiated by the local server; at the beginning of the procedure, the local server formats the request for the Jabber server to start the session for further communication. The structure of the request for creating the session with the Jabber server is in the format that follows.

```
<stream:stream to="jabber.org" xmlns="jabber:client"
xmlns:stream="http://etherx.jabber.org/streams" />
```

In the preceding code, the request for creating the session by the local server is dominated by the stream element. This element is responsible for opening the stream for the socket connection between the local and Jabber servers. It must be remembered that the local server only attempts to open the stream with the Jabber server, which can be refused by Jabber if the server is unavailable, which is quite rare.

Once the stream is open, the Jabber server returns a unique session ID to the local server. The structure of the response returned by the Jabber server to the local server for creating the session is as follows:

```
<stream:stream from="jabber.org" id="1919892175" xmlns="jabber:client"
xmlns:stream="http://etherx.jabber.org/streams" />
```

After opening the stream and obtaining the session ID, the local server sends the client-authentication request to the Jabber server. The structure of the client-authentication request for the Jabber server is depicted in Listing 2-5.

Listing 2-5: Authorization XML for the Jabber server

```
-<iq type="set" id="unique id">
-<query xmlns="jabber:iq:auth">
  <username>johnsmith</username>
  <password>smithy</password>
  <resource>work</resource>
  </query>
  </iq>
```

The Jabber server returns the response of the client-authentication request. This request, when received by the local server, appears as follows:

```
< iq id ='Unique id' type="result"/>
```

Upon successful authentication of the client information, the type attribute of the iq element is assigned value. In contrast, the authentication fails for the client; instead, the value of the type attribute becomes an error, and error code is shown in the response.

Once the Jabber server approves the client, he or she is free to interact with other clients. From this point onward, the Local server manages the task of translating the client requests in Jabber doctrine; on receiving the response, it again typecasts the Jabber response in client standards. The following listings help you to figure out the transformation of requests and responses being exchanged between the local and the Jabber servers.

Assume that the client asks the local server to provide him or her the roster from Jabber. On receiving such a request, the local server reformats the client request in Jabber norms. The local server, as depicted in the following code, reframes the structure of client request for the roster:

```
-<iq type="get" id="1020054725">
  <query xmlns="jabber:iq:roster" />
  </iq>
```

In reply to the roster request, the Jabber server hands over the list to the local server. The roster faced by the local server appears as shown in Listing 2-6.

Listing 2-6: Roster/Friend list XML from the Jabber server

```
-<stream:stream from="jabber.org" id="1020054725" xmlns="jabber:client"
xmlns:stream="http://etherx.jabber.org/streams">
-<iq from="johnsmith@jabber.org/www.jabber.org" id="1020054725"
type="result">
-<query xmlns="jabber:iq:roster">
  <item jid="msn.jabber.org/registered" subscription="from" />
 -<item jid="sonia%hotmail.com@msn.jabber.org" name="sonia%hotmail.com"
     subscription="both">
  <group>Friends</group>
 </item>
 -<item jid="victor%hotmail.com@msn.jabber.org"
name="victor%hotmail.com"subscription="both">
  <group>Friends</group>
 </item>
 -<item jid="derek%hotmail.com@msn.jabber.org" name="derek%hotmail.com"
     subscription="both">
  <group>Friends</group>
 </item>
 -<item jid="julia%hotmail.com@msn.jabber.org" name="julia%hotmail.com"
     subscription="both">
  <group>Friends</group>
 </item>
</query>
</iq>
</stream:stream>
```

The roster received by the local server is not recognized by the recipient client. The local server reforms the roster so that it can be readable by the client. The restructured roster for the client appears as shown in Listing 2-7.

Listing 2-7: Roster/Friend list XML received be the local client

```
<?xml version="1.0" encoding="utf-8" ?>
-<InstantMessanger>
-<Roster>
  <FriendID>sonia%hotmail.com@msn.jabber.org</FriendID>
  <Subscription>both</Subscription>
  <FriendID>victor%hotmail.com@msn.jabber.org</FriendID>
  <Subscription>both</Subscription>
  <FriendID>derek%hotmail.com@msn.jabber.org</FriendID>
  <Subscription>both</Subscription>
  <FriendID>julia%hotmail.com@msn.jabber.org</FriendID>
  <Subscription>both</Subscription>
</Roster>
</InstantMessanger>
```

Similarly, when the client delivers the message to the Jabber client, the local server recycles the client message in Jabber protocol and delivers it to the Jabber server, which in turn delivers it to the target client. The structure of the message sent to the Jabber client is shown in Listing 2-8.

Listing 2-8: Message XML for the Jabber server for MSN/Jabber clients

```
-<message to="derek%hotmail.com@msn.jabber.org" type="chat"
  from="johnsmith">
  <body>Good Morning Derek</body>
</message>
```

When the Jabber client replies, the local server receives this message. The structure of the message received by the local server in Jabber norms appears as displayed in Listing 2-9.

Listing 2-9: Message XML received by the local server

```
-<stream:stream from="jabber.org" id="1781647817" xmlns="jabber:client"
  xmlns:stream="http://etherx.jabber.org/streams">
-<message from="derek %hotmail.com@msn.jabber.org"
to="johnsmith@jabber.org"         type="chat">
  <thread>271a6e85b5c68292fe7664492ff1cf09516ed9d0</thread>
  <body>Hello! Derek..</body>
</message>
</stream:stream>
```

Issues Involved in Creating the Session

In our application, the connection between the modules can easily be made via sockets. But merely establishing the connection is not enough. To facilitate any further communication between the modules, sessions must be created and maintained by the time the last communication occurs between the modules. To accomplish such a task, two-sided sessions are created one between the local server and the client, with another session between the local and the Jabber server. In both cases, streams are used to create and run the sessions; to keep rotating the communication process, threads are maintained.

The local server is responsible for maintaining and running the session. In our application, whenever the client interacts with the local server, a thread is assigned to the client, which rotated the conversation process occurring with the client. Since the mode of the connection is socket-based, respective modules maintain input/output streams for a to and fro flow of communication. Using the output stream, respective modules deliver the response, request, or message to the target module. The target module receives it's the request, response or message by using its input stream.

As mentioned earlier, it is likely that the local server can receive the client request for foreign clients such as Jabber users. On receiving such a request, the local server starts a two-sided session. For dealing with the Jabber server, the local server keeps another socket in reserve. Using this reserved socket, the local server sets up the socket connection with the Jabber server.

The Jabber server, on receiving request from the local server, opens the stream. Consequently, input/output streams work for exchanging the requests and responses between the local and the Jabber Server. The Jabber server writes its responses over the stream, which is obtained by the local server. Further, the local server, after parsing the response in client mode, delivers the response to the intended client.

Issues Involved in Closing the Stream

The sessions running between various modules usually come to an end when the client requests to log out of the application. On receiving such a request, the local server sends a notification to all local friends of the client, mentioning that the client/user is logging out. After sending the notification to the local clients, the local server sends another notification to the jabber server to inform him/her that the client is logging out. The jabber server separately handles the task of sending notification to its clients.

Once the notification is delivered to concerned recipients, the local server shuts down the stream running between itself and the client. Similarly, the stream running between the local and the Jabber Server comes to close. To close the stream running on this end, the local server sends the request to the Jabber server, mentioning that the stream running on the opposite end (between itself and client) has closed down and asks Jabber to close its stream also. The Jabber server, on receiving such a request, closes the stream running with the local server.

The request delivered to the Jabber server contains the `</stream:stream>` tag. This tag is responsible for establishing the stream between the local and the Jabber server. Similarly, when the session is about to be closed, this tag comes into action. But this time it contains the contents for closing the stream.

If the local server is maintaining some log file or view while closing the stream, the entry of the client who has logged out must be removed from the log. Very likely, the local server can be keeping a temporary file of client requests by its login name. This file must be deleted or removed when the session comes to end.

Summary

In this chapter, the process of designing applications and an overall view of the Instant Messaging application and required technical knowledge are provided to you. Apart from design considerations, boundaries of the server and client are detailed here, followed by various flow charts to enhance your understanding of this application. Apart from bringing the client and the server modules under consideration, the required Web services for the application are discussed comprehensively. In the chapters that follow, you will find more in-depth discussions over working and designing of the Web services. Side by side, the communication process between the server and the client is elaborated and backed-up with techniques required for instantiating communication between the server and the client.

Toward the end of this chapter, the subjects involved in creating the session between various modules are brought into consideration. Similarly, the issues involved in closing the stream between various modules are discussed.

Chapter 3

Instant Messaging Server (Java)

In Chapter 2, we introduced you to the general design aspects of the Instant Messaging application. We discussed the underlying database structure and the model(s) on which the client-server and server-Jabber Server communication are based. In this chapter, we examine how the design concepts introduced in Chapter 2 are implemented practically in the Java version of our Instant Messaging application. (The Instant Messaging Application is a client-server application, and the design of the client and the server is being discussed separately. Thus, the terms "Server/Server Application" and "Client/Client Application" throughout this book refer to the server and client part of the Instant Messaging application, respectively.) This chapter begins with an introduction to Java Web Services □ howthey are built, deployed, and accessed. This discussion is followed by a brief introduction to the predefined Java classes that play a pivotal role in the development of the Server application. We then discuss the user-defined classes that perform various server-side tasks such as handling and processing requests, generating responses, transferring messages, and so on. Finally comes the technical documentation of the code, with line-by-line explanations and corresponding flow charts.

Java Web Services

A *Web service* is any service that can receive, process (if required), and respond to requests from Web clients. Any self-contained software component/application or piece of code that can be deployed on a Web server and, subsequently, be invoked over the Web by Web clients, qualifies as a Web service. The realm of Web services varies from simple acknowledgement of a client's request to complex business processes. Web services are instrumental in providing what's known as "dynamic content" in Web parlance. Contemporary Web services are usually based on the ubiquitous HTTP (Hyper Text Transfer Protocol) and the dynamic XML (eXtensible Markup Language) that helps generate dynamic content on the fly and makes the data portable.

Java Web services are powerful tools for developing high-performance, scalable solutions for two-tier, three-tier, or multitier architecture. The Java platform provides enough APIs (Application Programming Interfaces) to build a variety of Web services and also simplify the development process. On the client side, you have Java's Swing component to create interactive GUIs, while on the server side, you have servlets and JSPs. Java's J2EE (Java 2

Enterprise Edition), on the application-server side, is a complete platform in itself and provides integrated support to develop, sustain, and run Web services.

In this section, we see how you can develop and implement the Java Web services.

J2EE — Java's Web services development platform

J2EE APIs provide developers with tools to develop business and presentation logic. Apart from providing support for XML operations, servlets, JSPs, and Enterprise Java Beans (EJBs), J2EE APIs provide a plethora of utilities to communicate with Web service technologies such as SOAP, UDDI, and WSDL (which we discuss in the section on Java APIs for XML, later in this chapter). They also provide functionality to communicate with databases. Figure 3-1 gives a diagrammatic presentation of a J2EE-based Web-service environment.

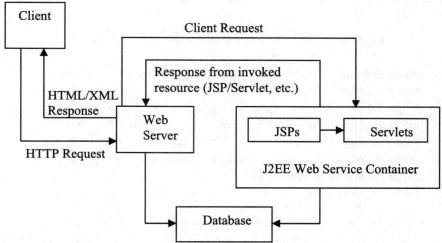

Figure 3-1: The J2EE environment

As shown in Figure 3-1, Java Web services run within the J2EE Web container. The J2EE container interfaces with the Web server to receive client requests from it and invokes the J2EE resource — say, a servlet —that the client requests. After the resource processes the request, it passes an appropriate response to the container, which forwards the response to the Web server. The Web server then sends the response to the client. If the J2EE container is unable to invoke a resource for any reason — or if a requested resource is unavailable — the container generates an error message and forwards it to the Web server to send to the client.

As is evident from the discussions in Chapter 2, XML is very important in the sphere of Web services. XML technologies play a vital part in the development of applications for deployment over the Web. Java provides a separate package for XML support — namely, the JAX (Java APIs for XML) pack. The JAX package provides XML functionality through the following APIs:

- Java API for XML Parsing (JAXP), to parse XML.

- Java API for XML Binding (JAXB), which maps XML to Java classes.

- Java API for XML Messaging (JAXM), which sends messages over the Web by using SOAP (Simple Object Access protocol).

- Java API for XML Registries (JAXR), which provides an interface for UDDI (Universal description, discovery, and integration) and other registries say ebXML registries.

- Java API for XML-based Remote Process Communication (JAXRPC), which provides support for sending requests to operations on remote servers.

Utilities such as the XSLT compiler (XSL TC), which compiles XSLT transformations into Java byte code, and Java-based DOM (JDOM), which enables reading and writing by using XML, are supplements to the APIs and are very useful to developers. The JAX pack supports the following:

- **XML (eXtensible Markup Language):** The favorite language of Web-service developers that's fast becoming the de-facto language for Web applications.

- **SOAP (Simple Object Access Protocol) and XMLP (XML protocol):** XML-based protocols that enable interaction with objects on remote systems.

- **WSDL (Web Services Definition Language):** An XML-based language that you use to utilize services you're providing on remote servers and various platforms in the form of communication objects, much like CORBA IDL specifications.

- **UDDI (Universal Description, Discovery, and Integration):** An open specification that implements a universal registry containing businesses and services available from various vendors along with their specifications. The idea is that prospective users/customers should be able to get this information over the Web so that they can build applications taking advantage of these services. The users can achieve this by creating their own communication objects, based on the specifications that they download by using the UDDI global catalogue.

The advantages that Java APIs for XML offer are as follows:

- These APIs support industry standards and hence enable interoperability.

- Because these APIs define strict compatibility requirements, the final implementations offer standard functionality.

- They offer developers great flexibility — for example, you may use various messaging protocols over SOAP as you're using JAXM code.

Thus, you can safely conclude that J2EE and Java APIs for XML provide a strong infrastructure to build and implement optimized and flexible Web services that are compatible with contemporary standards and technologies. The following sections describe how you can deploy and access Java Web services.

How to access Web services

To deploy Java's Web services, you need a container that includes the necessary Java packages and Java APIs that the Java Web services/components use. Additionally, you also need this container to provide an environment in which you can design, develop, test, and finally run these services. Currently, Apache's Tomcat is the only implementation available that supports both servlets and JSPs, although you can develop servlets alone by using Java Web Server or Java Servlet Development Kit (JSDK). *Tomcat* is a Java runtime environment that implements the Java Servlet API and provides support for processing JSP. At certain places, you find people referring Tomcat to as Jakarta Tomcat; hence, you should know that Jakarta is the name of the umbrella project under which Apache's is developing Tomcat. *Watchdog* (the one that checks whether the Servlets/JSP page is consistent with the Servlet/JSP specifications) and *Taglibs* (a repository of tag libraries) are the other two projects under the Jakarta umbrella.

Tomcat

Tomcat is the code name for Apache's Software Foundation's reference implementation of a Servlet/JSP container. This container is called the *reference implementation* because you use it as a reference for any software that's supposed to implement the servlet or JSP technologies. Tomcat is a free, open-source implementation of a Servlet/JSP container that Apache and Sun Microsystems are developing, with a host of other developers contributing to it. Although Tomcat is Apache's endeavor, Tomcat doesn't need an Apache Web server to run on; it also runs on iPlanet Web Server, BEA WebLogic, IBM WebSphere, and so on.

Tomcat offers the following three types of versions for downloading:

- Nightly builds: These downloads include the latest pieces of code added to the Tomcat implementation. Because these versions are not tried or tested and are still under development, however, they're only of use to those who are helping in the development of the technology. These versions are not for users seeking implementation technologies, because they're highly unstable.

- Milestone builds: These downloads are more stable than nightly builds, but are still not tested and debugged. Hence they are likely to prove buggy and untrustworthy for implementation purposes. Advanced users can used them to explore future improvements and report bugs.

- Release builds: These versions are ready for use. They are reviewed by the QA team at Sun Microsystems before release.

We developed the Instant Messaging application that we describe in this book by using Tomcat 3.0, although we've also tested it with Tomcat 4.0.1, and it works as well with the later version(CHECK). You can download and install Tomcat from the download section of Apache's Web site at `http://jakarta.apache.org/tomcat`.

Before you use Tomcat to develop and run servlets or JSPs, knowing its directory structure is essential. The following list describes this structure, assuming that you've installed Tomcat at `c:\tomcat\`, and applies to Tomcat 3.0, the version that we used to develop this application):

- **Where JSPs are stored:** `C:\tomcat\` serves as the default or root directory for all JSP pages — that is, the Tomcat implementation processes any JSP file at this location or in any subfolders under this directory. A JSP file named `TestJSP.jsp`, for example, may exist at `c:\tomcat\TestJSP.jsp`, at `c:\tomcat\JSP\TestJSP.jsp`, or at `c:\tomcat\ApplFiles\JSPFiles\TestJSP.jsp` (and so on).

- **Where servlets are compiled:** After writing a servlet, you save its JAVA file at `c:\tomcat\src` and compile it from this path to create the respective CLASS file. For example, you should save the code of a servlet named `TestServlet.java` at `c:\tomcat\src\TestServlet.java` and compile the same file at `c:\tomcat\src>javac TestServlet.java`.

- **Where servlets run:** The CLASS file created after you compile a servlet should go in `c:\tomcat\examples\WEB-INF\classes\`, which serves as the default context for all Servlets. For you to invoke the `TestServlet` in the preceding paragraph, for example, its CLASS file must exist at `c:\tomcat\ examples\WEB-INF\classes\TestServlet.class`. (You can configure the servlet's default context by using deployment descriptors; that discussion, however, is beyond the scope of this book.)

- **How to invoke a servlet:** To invoke a servlet — say, the `TestServlet` — give the path as `http:/localhost:8080/servlets/TestServlet`. Replace "*localhost*" with the name of the computer or IP address of the computer that hosts Tomcat. In the case of a Web site, replace *localhost* with the domain name of the site — for example, `mysite.com`. Notice that the path `/servlets/` maps to the `/examples/WEB-INF/classes` folder.

- **How to call a JSP page:** You can call a JSP page as `http:/localhost:8080/TestJSP.jsp` if it is in the root directory. If it is within, say, the JSP folder under the root directory, the path is `http:/localhost:8080/JSP/TestJSP.jsp`. Replace *localhost* with the respective computer or domain name, as we explaine in the preceding paragraph.

NOTE: Since JSPs are not explicitly compiled (as any one-time compilation of code such as a JSP declaration occurs at the time of the first call to the JSP page), we mention no such directory for them.

How to build Web services

Servlets and JSPs are two Java components that are widely used for implementing Java Web services by communicating with the Web clients through HTTP. A client request may invoke either a servlet or a JSP page. Although both servlets and JSPs are capable of retrieving parameters from client requests, obtaining additional information from request headers, and sending out a response page to the client, they differ in their syntax, utility, and code behavior. Following are the points of difference:

- A servlet is a piece of pure Java code and strictly adheres to the Java rules. a servlet is defined within a class, for example, and the filename must be the same as the class name. It is saved as a JAVA file and is compiled to create the CLASS file., This CLASS file is used against client requests. A JSP page, which you save with a JSP extension, however, is actually an HTML page containing Java statements. A JSP page contains HTML or XML interspersed with fragments of Java code. Furthermore, a JSP page may be interspersed with HTML or XML.

- A Servlet is compiled once, and the same CLASS file is run to handle client requests. Only if the servlet file is reloaded or the server on which the servlet is running is restarted does the code get recompiled. ( ) On the other hand, different JSP elements behave differently as follows:

  - **Declarations:** These are compiled only once — when the JSP page is called for the first time. Variables initiallized within declarations retain the same value while methods defined within declarationsremain the same until the JSP page is reloaded.

  - **Scriptlets:** These are executed/compiled every time the JSP page is called and may contain a complete Java code or fragments of code — say, an `if-else` statement.

  - **Expressions:** These are executed/compiled every time the JSP page is called and are very useful in writing values from a Java variable within an HTML code.

- Servlets are pure Java and thus enjoy complete support from the vast class libraries of Java. JSP, on the other hand, is more an improvement on server-side scripting languages because it incorporates Java functionality and carries Java's platform-independence.

- Servlets deliver programmatic content generation (that is, HTML or XML, if any, must be generated through the `ServletResponse` object within the servlet), while JSPs implement template-based content generation, because JSP pages are nothing but HTML, XML, or XHTML templates with special processing information contained in the form of JSP tags.

In essence, JSP is just an extension of servlets, and you use the two in tandem to create optimal Web applications.

Example

We now give a very simple example of a servlet (named FirstServlet.java) and a JSP page (named FirstJSP.jsp), both of which perform the following functions:

- Retrieve a user's login name, given by `sLoginName`.
- Retrieve the IP address of the client sending the request.
- Write the retrieved login name and IP address to an XML document.

Assumptions

- Tomcat, the small JSP container developed by Apache for testing purposes, is used to run servlets and JSP pages.

- Both the client and the Tomcat server are on the same machine — that is, client and server programs are run on the same machine for testing.

- All servlet CLASS files, JSPs, and HTML files are located in their respective folders under the Tomcat default or root directory — that is, c:\tomcat \examples\WEB-INF\classes\, c:\tomcat \JSP\ and c:\tomcat \HTMLFiles\, respectively.

First, create an HTML form with a single text box named sLoginName and that uses the HTTP POST method to invoke the servlet. Name the HTML page ServletOne.htm. Following is the appropriate code:

```
<HTML>
<HEAD>
<TITLE>My First Servlet</TITLE>
</HEAD>
<BODY>
<P> Please enter your Login Name to proceed: <BR><BR>
<FORM action="http://localhost:8080/examples/servlets/FirstServlet"
method="post">
<INPUT type="text" name="sLoginName"><BR><BR>
<INPUT type=submit value="submit Form">
</FORM>
</BODY>
</HTML>
```

Save this code as ServletOne.htm (at c:\tomcat\HTMLFiles\ServletOne.htm, as we mention earlier).

Following is the code for FirstServlet:

```
import java.io.*;
import javax.servlet.*;
import javax.servlet.http.*;
public class FirstServlet extends HttpServlet
{
 public void service( HttpServletRequest req, HttpServletResponse
res)throws IOException
 {
  String m_LoginName;
  String m_RemoteAddress;

  PrintStream m_OutputStream = new PrintStream( res.getOutputStream());

  m_LoginName             = req.getParameter("sLoginName");
  m_RemoteAddress   = req.getRemoteAddr();
```

```
    res.setStatus( HttpServletResponse.SC_OK);
    res.setContentType(" text/html ");

    m_OutputStream.println("<FirstServlet>");
    m_OutputStream.println("<LoginName>"+m_LoginName+"</LoginName>");

    m_OutputStream.println("<RemoteAddress>"+m_RemoteAddress+"</RemoteAddre
ss>");
    m_OutputStream.println("</FirstServlet>");
    }
}
```

Save the preceding code as `FirstServlet.java` at `c:\tomcat\src` and compile it from this location to create the CLASS file. Put the CLASS file at `c:\tomcat \examples\WEB-INF\classes\FirstServlet.class`.

Notice that `FirstServlet` extends `HTTPServlet` because it handles an HTTP request from the client. After the servlet receives the request, it carries out the following actions:

- It creates an `OutputStream` to generate the output, `m_OutputStream`.
- It uses the `getParameter()` method of the `HTTPRequest` object to request the login name supplied by the user and stores it in the variable m_LoginName.
- It uses the `getRemoteAddr()` method of the `HTTPRequest` object to request the IP address of the client and stores it in the variable m_RemoteAddress.
- It sets the status of the response as `SC_OK` (code 200) to confirm that the request was normally processed.
- It sets the content type of the response as "`text/html`" by using the `HTTPResponse` object's `setContentType()` method to inform the client that the response sent contains markup text that the browser needs to decode.
- It uses the output stream to generate the desired XML code.

Output of `FirstServlet` is as follows:

```
<FirstServlet>
<LoginName>UserLoginName</LoginName>
<RemoteAddress>UserIPAddress</RemoteAddress>
</FirstServlet>
```

Now use JSP to achieve the same result. Replace the action attribute in the `<FORM>` tag of `ServletOne.htm` as follows, and the rest of the HTML code remains the same:

```
<FORM action="http://localhost:8080/JSP/FirstJSP.jsp" method="post">
```

The code for `FirstJSP.jsp` is as follows:

```
<?xml version="1.0" ?>
<InstantMessenger>
<% String m_LoginName = request.getParameter("sLoginName"); %>
<% String m_RemoteIp = request.getRemoteAddr(); %>
<%response.setContentType("text/html ");%>
<FirstJSP>
<LoginName> <%=m_LoginName%> </LoginName>
<RemoteAddress> <%=m_RemoteIp%> </RemoteAddress>
</FirstJSP>
</InstantMessenger>
```

Save the code as `FirstJSP.jsp` (at `c:\tomcat\JSP\FirstJSP.jsp`).

After the HTML form is submitted using the Submit Form button, the JSP code executes as follows:

- The JSP `request` object is used within JSP scriptlets to obtain the user's login name and client's IP address and to store them in their respective variables.

- The `response` object is used to set the content type of the response.

- JSP expressions are used to place the values of the two variables within the respective XML tags.

The output from `FirstJSP.jsp` is as follows:

```
<InstantMessenger>
<FirstJSP>
<LoginName>UserLoginName</LoginName>
<RemoteAddress>UserIPAddress</RemoteAddress>
</FirstJSP>
</InstantMessenger>
```

As we mention earlier in this section, whether you use a servlet or JSP depends on what optimizes the performance, and the Web-application developer can best decide that. In most practical-life applications, both servlets and JSPs are used in conjunction to achieve the desired functionality to boost performance.

Server Development

Because a basic working knowledge of Java, JSP, Servlets, SQL and XML is a prerequisite for reading this book, we presume that the readers are familiar with various Java classes that are used by the classes of this Instant Messaging application. In this section, however, we discuss some of the Java classes that play a pivotal role in developing this Instant Messaging Server.

Server application

Five predefined classes in the Java Standard Library facilitate development of the core server classes of our application. These classes are as follows:

- Socket class
- ServerSocket class
- Thread class
- URLConnection class
- Vector class

Socket class

The Socket class in the java.net package is used for communication between the client and the server. The communication is through the input and output streams associated with the socket. In our application, for example, the StartUpScreen class creates the socket sc on the server in response to the first client request. This socket is then used to create the input stream from the client, as follows:

```
sc = server_soc.accept()
StreamFromClient = new BufferedInputStream(sc.getInputStream())
```

Similarly, a socket is created by the Server class on the server to communicate with the Jabber server through the respective Input and Output streams created for the purpose, as follows:

```
m_socketToJabber = new Socket(address,5222)
StreamFromJabber = new
BufferedInputStream(m_socketToJabber.getInputStream())
StreamToJabber = new
BufferedOutputStream(m_socketToJabber.getOutputStream())
```

Here, address gives the IP address of the Jabber server — that is, www.jabber.org.

The socket sc thus carries messages/requests and responses to and from the client, and m_socketToJabber carries messages/requests and responses to and from the Jabber server.

ServerSocket class

Another class from the java.net package, the ServerSocket class, is used by our application to implement the *listener service* on our server. The ServerSocket class provides the capability to listen at a specified port for client requests and accept them. Because a client always initiates a request, the server needs to be a listening program and, hence, the need for a ServerSocket.

In our server application, the StartUpScreen class creates the server socket that listens at the port 5555. Please notice that you need to make sure that the port at which the listener listens isn't used by any other application on the server machine. The port, 5555 in our case, becomes dedicated to the listener. Following line of code creates an object of the class ServerSocket.

```
ServerSocket server_soc = new ServerSocket (5555)
```

As we mention in the discussion on the `Socket` class in the preceding section, this `server_soc` accepts a client connection and opens another socket `sc` on the server machine, thereby paving the way for an input and output stream to open with the client.

A similar `ServerSocket` on the Jabber server that listens for client requests accepts the request that the `Server` class sends it and creates a corresponding socket on the Jabber server.

Thread class

A *thread* is a piece of code that you can execute independently. An application such as our Instant Messaging application is a typical example of a multithreaded environment. In response to the first request from the client, a new server thread begins to control communication with the client. Simultaneously, another client thread begins for Jabber server, wherein the server of our application acts as a client to the Jabber server. This action starts a second corresponding thread that controls communication with the Jabber server. Figure 3-2 illustrates this concept.

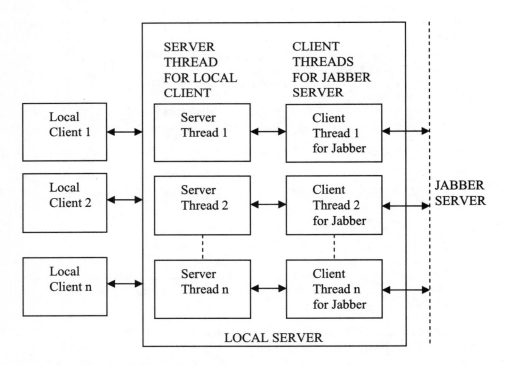

Figure 3-2: The multithreaded environment of the local server

Every new thread is invoked by the `StartUpScreen` class through the following code:

```
new Server(this, sc);
```

In this code, `this` is an object of the `StartUpScreen` class, and `sc` is the socket on the server machine created to communicate with this particular client.

The thread for Jabber server is created through the following code:

```
ListenerFor Jabber listener = new ListenerForJabber(this,
StreamToJabber, StreamFromJabber)
```

This time, `this` is an object of the `Server` class, `StreamToJabber` is the output stream, and `StreamFrom Jabber` is the input stream.

These two threads together manage the various requests from the client and also handle the to-and-from communication between a client and his/her contacts.

URLConnection class

The `URLConnection` class provides a higher-level alternative to sockets for communicating with resources over the Web. Although Sockets are more suitable for lower-level client-server communication, however, `URLConnection` is more suitable for communicating with HTTP URLs because it centers on HTTP. Hence, in our application, the methods of the `Server` class that call the various Web services use the `URLConnection` class to send requests to the JSPs and servlets and receive responses from them. Again, the actual reading/writing process is carried out through input/output streams.

The `localAuthorization()` method in the `Server` class, for example, calls `Login.jsp` by using the `URLConnection` class. First, the URL is built, as follows:

```
URL url = new URL(urlName)
```

Here, `urlName` provides the address of the resource with which communication is sought. The following line of code sets the value for the variable `urlName`:

```
urlName = "http://localhost:8080/examples/Login.jsp?sLoginName=" +
values[0] + "&sPassword=" + values[1]
```

The `URLConnection` class explicitly opens a connection and uses the `URLConnection` object to create the input and output streams, as in the following code:

```
URLConnection connection = url.openConnection();
BufferedInputStream ResponseStream = new BufferedInputStream(
connection.getInputStream())
```

Vector class

The `Vector` class from the `java.util` package is used to implement a dynamic array of objects, the capacity of which increases or decreases depending on the elements in the dynamic array. In our Instant Messaging application, the `Server` class needs to maintain a list of online users, a list of messages in queue, a list containing objects for each of the clients, and so on. Because the number of users using the Instant Messaging application at any given time varies constantly as users log in and log out, the message queue also varies as messages are added to and deleted from it. Optimum utilization of memory space demands that you use an array of variable dimensions. Thus you use the `Vector` class to store all such lists of elements for which you cannot predict a maximum or minimum number.

The following statements in the `Server` class create the `Vectors` required:

```
static Vector       UserList        = new Vector();
static Vector       MessageQueue    = new Vector();
static Vector       JabberId        = new Vector();
static Vector       ListenerList    = new Vector();
```

The initial capacity of all the `Vectors` so created is 32 bytes, and the incremental capacity also is 32 bytes — that is, whenever the number of elements exceeds the last allocated capacity, another 32 bytes are added. Similarly, if the number of elements falls and 32 bytes are free, the `Vector`'s capacity decrements by 32 bytes.

Java Web services

In this section we discuss Java classes that have been used in our Instant Messaging application to develop various Web services. One of those is the JSP `request` object.

You use the JSP `request` object to retrieve parameters from an HTTP request. The JSP `request` object provides various methods that you can use to retrieve not only parameter values, but also additional client information such as his/her IP address, method of the HTTP request, and so on.

The methods that we use in this Instant Messaging application's JSPs are as follows:

- `GetParameter(String ParameterName)`: This method returns the value of the parameter whose name `ParameterName` specifies. In the following sections, for example, you see the JSP statement `String l_name = request.getParameter("sLoginName")` repeatedly. Here, the login name of a user that is passing in the query string variable `sLoginName` is retrieved in the string variable `l_name`. If the user's name is, say, Jack, on execution of this statement, `l_name` contains the value `Jack`.

- `GetRemoteAddress()`: This method provides the IP address of the client from whom the request is received. On execution of the statement, `String l_ip = request.getRemoteAddr()`, for example, the variable `l_ip` has a value such as `206.214.0.99`.

HTTPServlet

The only servlet within Web services, Notify Friends, extends the `HTTPServlet` class because our Instant Messaging application is Web-based, and communication across the Web is carried out through the HTTP protocol. `HTTPServlet` provides methods specific to the HTTP protocol, and its `service()` method automatically separates requests by type and sends the request to the respective handler defined in `HTTPServlet` class. The `service()` method, for example, automatically sends an HTTP `GET` request to the `doGet()` method and a `POST` request to the `doPost()` method.

The `service()` method of an `HTTPServlet` receives two parameters, one is an `HTTPServletRequest` object and the second is an `HTTPServletResponse` object. In the following code, `req` is the `HttpServletRequest` object and `res` is the `HttpServletResponse` object:

```
public void service( HttpServletRequest req, HttpServletResponse res )
```

The `HTTPServletRequest` object provides a mechanism to receive a client request while the `HTTPServletResponse` object provides a mechanism to write back a response to the client. Methods in these two interfaces also enable additional information to be read from the client or written to the client.

Methods of HTTPServletRequest interface

The HTTPServletRequest Interface provides the `getParameter()` method that is used to obtain values of parameters passed with the request. The name of the variable whose value is to be retrieved is passed as an argument to the method and the return value is a String. For example, when we say `String m_status= req.getParameter("sStatus")` the `req` object uses the `getParameter()` method to get the value of a user's status that is being sent in the variable `sStatus`. The output is assigned to the String variable `m_status`.

Methods of HTTPServletResponse interface

The following methods of the HTTPServletResponse interface have been used in our Instant Messaging application:

- `setContentType(String type)`: This method is used to specify the MIME type of the response written to the client. The statement `res.setContentType(" text/plain ")`, for example, specifies that you read the response as plain text.

- `setStatus(int statusCode)`: This method is used to set the status of the response. The method is used to inform the client whether or not the request succeeds. The statement `res.setStatus( HttpServletResponse.SC_OK)`, for example, denotes that the request was successfully serviced. Notice that `public static final int SC_OK` is equivalent to the status code `200` and hence the parameter (`statusCode`) is of type `int`.

- `getOutputStream()`: This method is used to return a `ServletOutputStream` suitable for writing binary data in the client response. The response is committed by calling the method `flush()` on the `ServletOutputStream`. Notice the following piece of code, where the output is contained in the `response` variable, which is a `byte` array:

```
m_BresponseStream = new BufferedOutputStream (res.getOutputStream());
m_BresponseStream.write(response, 0, response.length);
m_BresponseStream.flush();
```

The JDBC API

The Java Web services make extensive use of the JDBC API that's used for communication with the Database Management System (DBMS). We discuss in the following list the three basic objects that you use to retrieve, add, or modify data in the database:

- The `Connection` object: You use this object to open a connection with a database by using an appropriate driver. In our application, we use the JDBC-ODBC Bridge driver, as follows:

```
java.sql.Connection db =
java.sql.DriverManager.getConnection("jdbc:odbc:messenger","sa","")
```

  The `getConnection()` method accepts three parameters: the fully qualified jdbc:odbc bridge name, `messenger`, the login name for the database, `sa,` while the third parameter, the password is blank (since the database we used had no password).

- The `Statement` object: This object sends the SQL statements to the DBMS. A `Statement` object is created and then executed, supplying the appropriate execute method (depending on the SQL statement). For a `SELECT` statement, the method used is `executeQuery`. For statements that create or modify tables, the method used is `executeUpdate`. The following codes shows how SQL queries are executed using JDBC API methods[what?]:

```
st1.executeQuery("select count(login_name) from member where
login_name = " + "'" + l_name + "'" + ";")
st3.executeUpdate("INSERT INTO member ( member_id, login_name, ..........)
VALUES ( " + m_Id + " , '" + LoginName + "............. "' )
```

  In the preceding code, `st1` and `st3` are the `Statement` objects.

- The `ResultSet` object: You use this object to store the result from an executed query. you can retrieve the results of the first `SELECT` query given in the discussion on `Statement` object, for example, in a `ResultSet` object, as follows:

```
ResultSet rs1 = st1.executeQuery("select count(login_name) from member
where login_name = " + "'" + l_name + "'" + ";")
```

  The `rs1` now contains all the rows obtained from the `SELECT` query, and you can access each record row sequentially by using the `rs1.next()` method. You can obtain the values in a variable by using the appropriate `getXXX` method of the `ResultSet` object. Here you can retrieve, for example, the count, which is an integer, by using the `getInt()` method, as follows:

```
int b_Id = rs1.getInt("count(login_name)")
```

If you were retrieving, say, a string, you'd use the `getString()` method.

Now we're going to move on to the concepts of the server application.

Inside the Server Application

This section discusses the five user-defined Java classes that together form the server application. These classes are as follows:

- `Server`: This class is at the core of the server application; it coordinates various activities, ranging from receiving the client request to communicating with the class that handles responses from the Jabber server by calling appropriate classes, JSPs, and servlets.

- `ListenerForJabber`: This class controls and coordinates all communication with clients ouside the local server, such as Yahoo! clients, MSN clients, and so on.

- `XMLParser`: This class parses the XML requests and returns the following:

  - An integer representing the request type, authorization, login, and so on.

  - A vector containing the attribute names enclosed in the given XML.

  - A vector containing the attribute values in the given XML.

The following additional return values may be present, depending on the type of request:

- `CreateXML`: You use this class after a communication is received from the Jabber server for a client who is logged onto the local server (local client). This class converts the Jabber response to an XML format that the local client can recognize and returns this XML as a string value.

- `StartUpScreen`: This is the class that provides a Graphical User Interface (GUI) to the user to start the Instant Messaging application. This class serves as the starting point for a new client thread to begin.

> **NOTE:** In this section, the terms *client* and *user* are used interchangeably, depending on the suitability. If we talk abouit "friends" or "contacts", for example, the term *user's friends* sounds more appropriate than *client's friends*. If we discuss client-to-server communication in which user's actions are implicit, however, the phrase *client request* sounds appropriate.

Before we start the main discussion of the server application, consider Figure 3-3, which sums up the working of the server application. It also provides a fair idea about the basic workflow of the server appliation and the roles that various classes play.

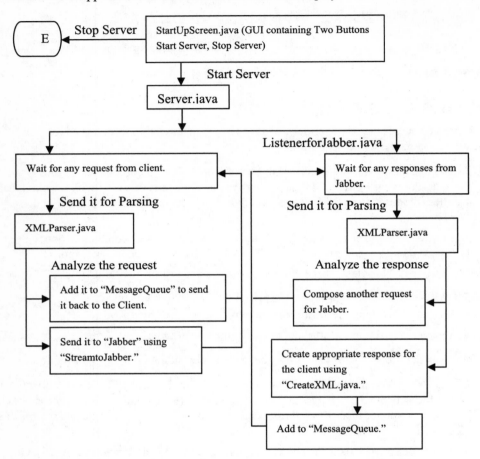

Figure 3-3: Work flow of the server application

How to handle requests from the client

The Graphical User Interface (GUI), defined in the StartUpScreen class, provides the option of starting or stopping the server, as shown in Figure 3-4.

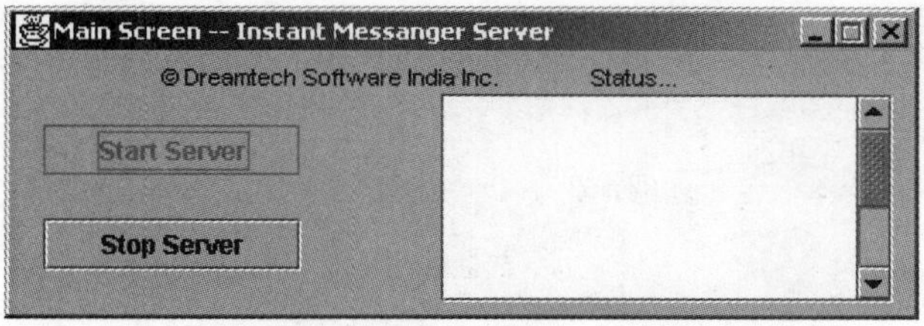

Figure 3-4: The Startup screen window

After a user clicks the Start Server button, the `StartUpScreen` class creates an instance of the main `Server` class and begins a new client thread, as follows:

```
ServerSocket server_soc = new ServerSocket (5555);
  Socket sc;

  while (true)
  {
  System.out.println("Here 1");
  sc = server_soc.accept();
  new Server(this, sc);
  }
```

This instance of the `Server` class [what?] invokes the constructor of `Server` class and serves as the entry point to the server application. Hereafter, the `Server` class starts servicing this new user thread by opening a channel of communication (a stream) between the client and the server.

While the user thread is running, the `Server` class performs a series of operations to carry out operations that the client requests and to carry message/data to and from the client. These operations are summarized as follows:

1. The constructor of `Server` class takes two parameters: an object of the `StartUpServer` class and a `Socket` object. It uses this `Socket` to create an input stream to receive requests from the client and an output stream to write responses to the client, as follows:

```
StreamFromClient = new BufferedInputStream(sc.getInputStream());
StreamToClient = new BufferedOutputStream(sc.getOutputStream());
```

2. The `Server` class tries to connect to the Jabber server to enable to-and-from communication with the user's contacts outside the local server's scope — for example, Jabber clients. If it succeeds in making the contact, the flag `m_FlagJabberPresent` is set to 1, and an input and an output stream open for communication. If any exception occurs during the connecting process, the flag `m_FlagJabberPresent` is set to 0. In all future communication with the Jabber server, this flag is checked to see whether the Jabber Server can be contacted, as illustrated by the following code:.

```
try
            {
                    InetAddress address =
InetAddress.getByName("www.jabber.org");
                    m_socketToJabber = new Socket(address,5222);

                    StreamFromJabber       = new
BufferedInputStream(m_socketToJabber.getInputStream());
                    StreamToJabber         = new
BufferedOutputStream(m_socketToJabber.getOutputStream());

                    m_FlagJabberPresent = 1;
            }
            catch(Exception SException)
            {
                    System.out.println(SException);
                    m_FlagJabberPresent = 0;
            }
```

3. The constructor then calls the `run()` method that runs in an infinite loop, waiting for client communication. If a client request is available, it is read by using an object of the class `BufferedInputStream` called `StreamFromClient`. This request is written to `request.xml` if the request signifies that a thread is commencing — for example, an authorization or registration request. Otherwise, it's written to a file with a name that's generated by appending the user's login name to the filename. If a user's name is, say, James, the request is written to `requestJames.xml` as illustrated by the following code:

> **NOTE:** The server application works in a multithreaded environment, where multiple requests are processed simultaneously. If a single file is used for writing the request data, a subsequent request may overwrite a previous, yet-to-be processed request, resulting in random and erratic request-processing. To ensure that each request from the client is satisfactorily processed, therefore, more than one file is used.

```
while (loop != 0)
            {
                    temp = StreamFromClient.read(request, 0, 32);
                    String str    =       new String (request, 0,
temp);

                    FinalString   =       FinalString + str;

                    loop = StreamFromClient.available();
            }

                    byte [] tempbytes = FinalString.getBytes();
                    if (getName().indexOf("Thread") != -1)
                        TempOutFile= new
FileOutputStream("request.xml");
```

```
                        else
                            TempOutFile= new
FileOutputStream("request"+getName()+".xml");
                        TempOutFile.write(tempbytes, 0,
tempbytes.length);

                        TempOutFile.close();
```

4. The name of the XML file thus generated is forwarded to the `perform()` method of `XMLParser` class for parsing the XML before the request can be processed by the `Server` class.

```
if (getName().indexOf("Thread") != -1)
        Parser.perform("request.xml");
else
        Parser.perform("request"+getName()+".xml");
```

5. Any cycle that contains no client request is utilized by the server to write messages from the message queue to the respective clients.

```
        if (loop == 0)
            SendMessageToClient();
        else
        {
.................................................. .
.................................................. .
```

How to process requests

The request sent by a client is in XML format. On receiving a request from the client, the first step performed by the `Server` class is to parse it, for which `XMLParser` class is called. This class calls the `parse()` function to parse the XML and takes the following actions in using the parsed values:

1. It assigns a value to the variable `requestType` to indicate the type of request, as follows:

```
if (localName.equalsIgnoreCase("AUTH"))
        {
            requestType = 1;
        }
        else if (localName.equalsIgnoreCase("REGISTER"))
        {
            requestType = 2;
        }
        else if (localName.equalsIgnoreCase("MSG"))
        {
.................................................. .
.................................................. .
```

2. It retrieves parameters specific to the request type — for example, for a `requestType` 8 that denotes a message, the `m_attributeName` vector is used to store the attribute names, `m_attributes` is used to store the attribute values (such that the index of a value is the same as the index of the corresponding name in `m_attributeName`), and the String array `Val` is used to store the message, as follows:

```
if (requestType == 8)
            {
                    if
((atts.getLocalName(i).equalsIgnoreCase("from"))||(atts.getLocalName(i
).equalsIgnoreCase("to"))||(atts.getLocalName(i).equalsIgnoreCase("typ
e")))

m_attributeName.add(atts.getLocalName(i)) ;
                }
            else
             m_attributeName.add(atts.getLocalName(i)) ;

            if (styleFlag)
            {
                m_attributeName.add(atts.getLocalName(i)) ;
                m_attributes.add(atts.getValue(i)) ;

            }
..................................................................... .
..................................................................... .

String temp;
        temp            = new String(ch,start,end).trim();
        if (temp.length() != 0)
        {
                Val[j] = temp;
                j++;
        }
```

These return values are then sent to back to the `Server` class, which interprets the return values and sends them to the appropriate handlers (JSPs/servlets) for further processing. The return values from the XML class are checked to see whether they pertain to the local server, and appropriate handlers are invoked for each type of request, as we describe in the following sections.

Authorization/login request

This request is recognized by the value 1 for its request-type. After this value is recognized, the `Server` class calls the `MaintainClientList()` method to respond to the request, as follows:

```
if (Parser.getType() == 1)
  {
    int returnVal       = 0;

    MaintainClientList(values[0]);
    screen.m_Logger.append(values[0]+" "+ sc.getInetAddress()+"\n");

    returnVal           = LocalAuthorization(values);
    localNotifyFriends(values, 1);
    GetFriendList(values);
```

1. The method `MaintainClientList()` adds the user's name to the `UserList` vector, as follows:

```
void MaintainClientList(String userName)
{
..................................................... .
..................................................... .
  {
    if ((String)UserList.elementAt(i) == userName)
    {
        setName(userName);
        checkFlag = 1;
    }
  }
  if (checkFlag == 0)
  {
    UserList.add((Object)userName);
    setName(userName);
  }
}
..................................................... .
..................................................... .
```

2. The user's name and IP address get appended onto the designated area on the start up screen.

3. The method `LocalAuthorization()` is called that, in turn, calls `Login.jsp`, the handler for handling login requests. The XML output from `Login.jsp` is written to the client using the output stream meant for the purpose, as follows:

```
int LocalAuthorization(String values[])
{
..................................................... .
..................................................... .
urlName = "http://localhost:8080/examples/Login.jsp?sLoginName=" +
values[0] + "&sPassword=" + values[1] ;

try
{
```

```
  URL url = new URL(urlName);
  URLConnection connection = url.openConnection();

  BufferedInputStream ResponseStream = new BufferedInputStream(
connection.getInputStream());
......................................................... .
......................................................... .

}
```

4. **LocalNotifyFriends** is called to send a notification to all contacts in the user's friends list, informing them that the user is now online. (See the section "Request to notify friends of user's status," later in this chapter, for more information.)

5. The user's Friend List is retrieved for display on the client machine, along with the status of each friend. (See the section "Request to notify friends of user's status, later in this chapter.)

Registration request

This request is recognized by a request-type value of 2, which the getVal() method of the XMLParser class returns, as follows:

```
else if (Parser.getType() == 2)
    {
    int returnVal       = 0;

    MaintainClientList(values[0]);

    returnVal           = LocalRegistration(values);
```

When a registration request is received, the code execution follows the following sequence:

1. The method MaintainClientList() is called and adds the user's name to the UserList vector.

2. The method LocalRegistration() is called and, in turn, calls Register.jsp and sends its output XML to the client by using the client's output stream.

Request to send a message

The request to send a message is recognized by the value 3, which the getType() method of XMLParser class return, as follows:

```
else if (Parser.getType() == 3)
    {
......................................................... .
......................................................... .

    if (dummy == 1)
    {
```

```
        responseFromServer(values[0]+"^"+FinalString);
    }
```

When a request to send a message is received, the code execution follows the following sequence:

1. The `dummy` variable specifies whether the message is meant for a local or a Jabber user. The value `1` for `dummy` denotes a local user.

2. The `responseFromServer()` method is called, which appends the message to the message queue, as follows:

```
void responseFromServer(String str)
{
MessageQueue.add((Object)str);
}
```

Request to add a friend

The request-type `9` denotes a request to add a friend to the user's friend list, as follows:

```
else if (Parser.getType() == 9) // AddFriend...
    {
    int returnVal = -1;
    returnVal    = addFriendLocally(values);
    }
```

The `addFriendLocally()` method is called and, in turn, calls `AddFriend.jsp`. The output from `AddFriend.jsp` is appended to the `ServerResponse.xml` file. Again, the `XMLParser` class is used to parse this XML, and depending on the return type specified by the `getType()` method of the `XMLParser` class., an appropriate response is appended to the message queue, as follows:

```
int addFriendLocally(String tempStr[])
{
..........................................
 urlName = "http://localhost:8080/examples/AddFriend.jsp?sLoginName=" +
tempStr[0]+"&sFriendName="+tempStr[1];

 try
 {
   URL url = new URL(urlName);
   URLConnection connection = url.openConnection();

   BufferedInputStream ResponseStream = new BufferedInputStream(
connection.getInputStream());
..............................................  .
..............................................  .
```

Request to delete a friend

A request to delete a friend is recognized by a request-type value of 11, as follows:

```
else if (Parser.getType() == 11) // DeleteFriend...
    {
      removeFriendLocally(values);
    }
```

The removeFriendLocally() method is called and, in turn, calls DeleteContact.jsp and outputs the resultant XML to the client through the output stream, as follows:

```
void removeFriendLocally(String tempStr[])
{
................................................. .
................................................. .

 urlName =
"http://localhost:8080/examples/DeleteContact.jsp?sLoginName=" +
tempStr[0]+"&sFriendName="+tempString;

 try
 {
   URL url = new URL(urlName);
   URLConnection connection = url.openConnection();

   BufferedInputStream ResponseStream = new BufferedInputStream(
connection.getInputStream());
................................................. .
................................................. .
```

Logout request

If the XMLParser class returns the value 4 in its getType() method, it denotes a logout request from a user, as follows:

```
else if (Parser.getType() == 4)
    {
      int index = -1;
      for (int i =0;i<UserList.size() ;i++ )
      {
        if
(((String)UserList.elementAt(i)).equalsIgnoreCase(getName()))
        {
        UserList.removeElementAt(i);
        index = i;
        }
      }
      if (index > -1)
      {
        ListenerList.removeElementAt(index);
```

```
        JabberId.removeElementAt(index);
        }

        int result = localLogout(values);
        File userFile        = new File("request"+getName()+".xml");
        userFile.delete();
------------------
localNotifyFriends(values, 0);
        StreamToClient.close();
        StreamFromClient.close();
```

When a logout request is received, the code execution follows the following sequence:

1. The user name is removed from the vector `UserList`.

2. The object corresponding to the user is removed from the `ListenerList` vector that contains the objects for all users currently logged into the Instant Messaging application.

3. The user's ID is removed from the `JabberID` vector that stores the Jabber session IDs for each user.

4. The method `localLogout()` is called, which invokes `Logout.jsp` and outputs the contents by using client output stream as shown in the following code:

```
int localLogout(String values[])
  {
..............................................................
..............................................................

urlName = "http://localhost:8080/examples/Logout.jsp?sLoginName=" +
values[0];

try
{
  URL url = new URL(urlName);
  URLConnection connection = url.openConnection();

  BufferedInputStream ResponseStream = new BufferedInputStream(
connection.getInputStream());

..............................................................
..............................................................
```

5. The XML file created for storing user requests is deleted.

6. `localNotifyFriends()` is called to inform all contacts that user is now offline.

7. The client output and input streams are closed.

Unregister request

If the getType() method of XMLParser returns the value 16 on parsing, a user has made an unregister request, as follows:

```
else if (Parser.getType() == 16)
    {
............................................................ .
............................................................ .


    unregisterUser (values);
    }
```

When an unregister request is received, the code execution follows the following sequence:

1. The unregisterUser() method is called and, in turn, calls Unregister.jsp to unregister a user, as follows:

```
void unregisterUser(String values[])
{
............................................................ .
............................................................ .

urlName = "http://localhost:8080/examples/Unregister.jsp?sLoginName="
+ values[0];
}
```

2. The method then writes the XML generated by Unregister.jsp to the client.

Request to notify friends of user's status

This request is called automatically whenever a user logs in or logs out. This request notifies a user's friends whether the user's gone offline or come online. The following operation is carried out to notify the user's friends:

The output of NotifyFriends is written to the ServerResponse.xml file, which is parsed, and messages notifying each friend individually of the user's status are appended to the message queue, as follows:

```
int localNotifyFriends(String name[], int status)
{
............................ .
 urlName =
"http://localhost:8080/examples/servlet/NotifyFriends?sLoginName=" +
name[0]+"&sStatus="+status;

 try
 {
   URL url = new URL(urlName);
   URLConnection connection = url.openConnection();
```

```
    BufferedInputStream ResponseStream = new BufferedInputStream(
connection.getInputStream());

    ................................................... .
    ................................................... .
```

Request to generate user's friend list

This request is generated automatically whenever a user logs in. This request ensures that a user is presented with his/her friends list as soon as the login operation succeeds. A call to FriendList.jsp is made, and its output is written to the message queue, as follows:

```
void GetFriendList(String values[])
{
.....................

 urlName = "http://localhost:8080/examples/FriendList.jsp?sLoginName=" +
values[0];

 try
 {
   URL url = new URL(urlName);
   URLConnection connection = url.openConnection();

   BufferedInputStream ResponseStream = new BufferedInputStream(
connection.getInputStream());
   ................................................... .
   ................................................... .
```

Request to add a gateway

This request is sent by a client to communicate with his/her friends on the Hotmail® Instant Messenger Service. The gateway that's added interfaces with the Hotmail server via the Jabber server to facilitate two-way communication between a user and his/her friends. To make an AddGateway request, a user needs to have a valid account on the Hotmail/MSN server.

The AddGateway request is recognized by the return value 15 in the getType() method of XMLParser. The program's execution follows these steps after receiving this request:

1. The Server class calls the method addMSNGateway(), as follows:

```
else if (Parser.getType() == 15) // AddGateway...
            {
            try
            {
                    addMSNGateway(values);
            }
            catch (Exception e)
```

```
                    {
                System.out.println("Exception occured in Add
MSNGateway:"+e);
                    }
```

2. The method `addMSNGateway()` forms an XML request to add a gateway and sends it to the Jabber server. This request contains the username and password provided by the user for the purpose of authentication before the gateway is added, as follows:

```
void addMSNGateway(String tempStr[]) throws Exception
 {
................................................................
................................................................
String addGatewayRequest      = "<iq to='msn.jabber.org'
type='set'><query
xmlns='jabber:iq:register'><username>"+msnUserName+"</username>
<password>"+rawPassword+"</password></query></iq>";

        byte [] bytesAuthString      = addGatewayRequest.getBytes();
    StreamToJabber.write(bytesAuthString, 0,bytesAuthString.length);
        StreamToJabber.flush();
................................................................
................................................................
 }
```

Generate requests for the Jabber Server

The requests just discussed may involve communication with the Jabber server — for example, if a user sends a message to a friend who's a Jabber client, the message is forwarded to the Jabber server in a format that it can understand. The Jabber server then sends the message to the user for whom its meant. Similarly, if a user logs in, the list of his/her friends who are clients of another Instant Messaging application is retrieved from the Jabber server.

The `ListenerForJabber` class receives requests from Jabber server to communicate to the local server and vice versa. We discuss in the following sections cases where the parsed XML return values are checked to determine whether communication with the Jabber Server is required. Notice that the `Server` class checks the value of the flag, `m_FlagJabberPresent`. The value 1 for this flag 1 indicates that connection with the Jabber server exists.

Obtain the global friends list from the Jabber server

If the `Server` class receives an authorization request, it forms an XML request for the `ListenerForJabber` to request the user's friends list outside the local server's scope, as follows:

```
if (Parser.getType() == 1)
```

```
    {
...............
        if (m_FlagJabberPresent != 0)
        {
        listener =   new ListenerForJabber(this, StreamToJabber,
StreamFromJabber);
        addToListenerList(listener);
        }


        if ((returnVal == 1)&&(m_FlagJabberPresent == 1))
        {
         /* Send it to Jabber to get the Global Userlist */
         String authString1 = "<stream:stream
\nto=\"jabber.org\"\nxmlns=\"jabber:client\"
\nxmlns:stream=\"http://etherx.jabber.org/streams\">";
         m_userName = values[0];
         m_passWord = values[1];
         String authString = authString1;
         byte [] bytesAuthString  = authString.getBytes();
         StreamToJabber.write(bytesAuthString, 0,bytesAuthString.length);
         StreamToJabber.flush();
        }
        else
        {
...............
```

Send a message to a client outside the local server

The Server class checks the dummy variable, and if its value isn't 1 — meaning that the client for whom the message is meant isn't within the local server's database — a request is generated for the ListenerForJabber containing the required attribute values, such as the name of sender, the target user, the message, and so on. The output stream, StreamToJabber, is used to write the request to ListenerForJabber, as follows:

```
if (dummy == 1)
    {
       // message for Local User....
    }
    else if (m_FlagJabberPresent == 1)
    {

    String m_targetUser = values[0]+"@msn.jabber.org";
    String m_sender    = values[1]+"@jabber.org";
    String m_Message   = values[2];
    String m_JabberID;

    int   index  =      UserList.indexOf((Object)values[1]);
    if (index != -1)
```

```
        {
            m_JabberID        = (String)JabberId.elementAt(index);
        }

    String m_MessageXML = "<message to=\""+m_targetUser+"\"
type=\"chat\" from=\""+values[1]+"\">";
    m_MessageXML += "<body>"+values[2]+"</body>";
    m_MessageXML += "</message>";

    byte [] bytesAuthString   = m_MessageXML.getBytes();
    StreamToJabber.write(bytesAuthString, 0,bytesAuthString.length);
    StreamToJabber.flush();
    }
  }
```

Inform the Jabber server when a user logs out

If a logout request is received, the `Server` class sends a request to the
`ListenerForJabber`, informing it of the name of the user who's made the logout request.
The `ListenerForJabber` then closes the session that it started with the local server for that
user and informs Jabber clients who are in the user's friends list of his/her offline status, as
follows:

```
if ((result == 1)&&(m_FlagJabberPresent == 1))
    {
        byte [] logoutRequest = "</stream:stream>".getBytes();

 StreamToJabber.write(logoutRequest, 0,logoutRequest.length);
        StreamToJabber.flush();
    }
```

How to handle responses

As we show you in the preceding sections, the last step in processing a request is forwarding it
to the respective handler, which is either a JSP page or a servlet. These handlers generate
XML responses in a format that can be sent directly to the client and also sent back to the
calling function as a string. The calling function then reads the response through an input
stream. This response is then either sent directly to the client or added to the message queue in
byte form.

We discuss in the following sections how the responses for each type of request are handled by
the calling function in the `Server` class.

How to handle responses from Web services

In this section, we discuss, how the `Server` class calls various JSPs and/or servlets and how it
handles the XMLs that they generate.

Response to an authorization request

This is the same as a login request. The Server class responds to this request by calling the method LocalAuthorization(), which in turn calls Login.jsp and reads the XML output from Login.jsp in the string variable FinalString. It then converts this string to bytes and uses the client's output stream to write the response directly to the client, as follows:

```
int LocalAuthorization(String values[])
{
............................................................ .
............................................................ .


  while (loop != 0)
  {
   temp            = ResponseStream.read(buffer, 0, 32);
   String str      = new String (buffer, 0, temp);
   FinalString     = FinalString + str;
   loop            = ResponseStream.available();
  }

  ResponseStream.close();

  byte [] response = FinalString.getBytes();
    StreamToClient.write(response, 0, response.length);
............................................................ .
............................................................ .

}
```

Response to a registration request

To respond to a registration request, the Server class calls its method LocalRegistration(). The method LocalRegistration() calls Register.jsp and reads the XML generated by it in the byte array buffer. The value in the byte array is converted to a string and stored in the variable FinalString. FinalString is then converted into bytes again and sent to the client, as follows:

```
int LocalRegistration(String values[])
{
............................................................ .
............................................................ .


  while (loop != 0)
  {
   temp            = ResponseStream.read(buffer, 0, 32);
   String str      = new String (buffer, 0, temp);
   FinalString     = FinalString + str;
   loop            = ResponseStream.available();
  }
```

```
ResponseStream.close();

byte [] response = FinalString.getBytes();
  StreamToClient.write(response, 0, response.length);
StreamToClient.flush();
```

Response to request for sending a message

If a request seeks to send a message, the parsed XML response is appended to the message queue to send to the target user during a free request cycle, as in the following steps:

1. The `Server` class calls the method `responseFromServer()`, as follows:

```
else if (Parser.getType() == 3)
                    {
                        int dummy = 0;
                            for (int i = 0;i<UserList.size();i++)
                            {
                                    String str =
(String)UserList.elementAt(i);

                                    if
(str.equalsIgnoreCase(values[0]))
                                    {
                                            dummy = 1;
                                    }
                            }
                            if (dummy == 1)
                            {
responseFromServer(values[0]+"^"+FinalString);
                            }
```

2. The `responseFromServer()` method appends the message to the message queue. Notice that, after a user logs on, the message goes into the message queue instead of being sent directly to the user. This is because, on login, a new thread pertaining to that user begins. This thread can then be used to determine whether a message for the user is in the message queue, as follows:

```
void responseFromServer(String str)
{
MessageQueue.add((Object)str);
}
```

Response to an AddFriend request

The `addFriendLocally()` method in `Server` class calls `AddFriend.jsp`. The output from `AddFriend.jsp` is written to the `ServerResponse.xml` file. Again, the

XMLParser class is used to parse this XML, and depending on the request type specified by
the method, getType(), the FinalString variable is generated. This variable contains the
output XML as a string. This string is converted to bytes and added to the message queue, as
follows

```java
int addFriendLocally(String tempStr[])
{
........................................................ .
........................................................ .

   while (loop != 0)
   {
    temp           = ResponseStream.read(buffer, 0, 32);
    String str     = new String (buffer, 0, temp);
    FinalString    = FinalString + str;
    loop           = ResponseStream.available();
   }
   ResponseStream.close();

 byte [] tempbytes = FinalString.getBytes();
 FileOutputStream TempOutFile    = new
FileOutputStream("ServerResponse.xml");
 TempOutFile.write(tempbytes, 0, tempbytes.length);
 TempOutFile.close();

 Parser.perform("ServerResponse.xml");
 String values[] = Parser.getVal();
 String userName = new String();

 if (Parser.getType() == 10)
 {
  if (values[2].equalsIgnoreCase("0"))
  {
    userName = values[0];
     FinalString = userName+"^"+FinalString;
    responseFromServer(FinalString);
    return 0;
  }
  else if (values[2].equalsIgnoreCase("2"))
  {
    userName = values[0];
     FinalString = userName+"^"+FinalString;
    responseFromServer(FinalString);
    return 0;
  }

........................................................ .
........................................................ .
```

Response to a DeleteFriend request

The `removeFriendLocally()` method in `Server` class calls `DeleteContact.jsp`. The output from `DeleteContact.jsp` is written to the `ServerResponse.xml` file. Again, the `XMLParser` class is used to parse this XML, and depending on the request type specified by the method, `getType()`, the `FinalString` variable is generated. This variable contains the output XML as a string. Finally, this string is converted to bytes and added to the message queue, as follows:

```
void removeFriendLocally(String tempStr[])
{
.......................................................... .
.......................................................... .

 urlName =
"http://localhost:8080/examples/DeleteContact.jsp?sLoginName=" +
tempStr[0]+"&sFriendName="+tempString;

 try
 {
   URL url = new URL(urlName);
   URLConnection connection = url.openConnection();

   BufferedInputStream ResponseStream = new BufferedInputStream(
connection.getInputStream());

   while (loop != 0)
   {
    temp            = ResponseStream.read(buffer, 0, 32);
    String str      = new String (buffer, 0, temp);
    FinalString     = FinalString + str;
    loop            = ResponseStream.available();
   }
   ResponseStream.close();

 byte [] tempbytes = FinalString.getBytes();
 FileOutputStream TempOutFile    = new
FileOutputStream("ServerResponse.xml");
 TempOutFile.write(tempbytes, 0, tempbytes.length);
 TempOutFile.close();

 Parser.perform("ServerResponse.xml");
 String values[] = Parser.getVal();
 String userName = new String();
 if (Parser.getType() == 12)
 {
  if (values[2].equalsIgnoreCase("0"))
  {
    userName = values[0];
```

```
      FinalString = userName+"^"+FinalString;
      responseFromServer(FinalString);
   }
   else if (values[2].equalsIgnoreCase("1"))
...............................................  .
...............................................  .
```

Response to a logout request

The method `localLogout()` in `Server` class invokes `Logout.jsp` and obtains the output by using an input stream. Notice that, because this is a logout request, no message is sent to the client, either directly or through the message queue, as the following code shows:

```
int localLogout(String values[])
 {
...............................................  .
...............................................  .

   BufferedInputStream ResponseStream = new BufferedInputStream(
connection.getInputStream());

   while (loop != 0)
   {
    temp           = ResponseStream.read(buffer, 0, 32);
    String str     = new String (buffer, 0, temp);
    FinalString    = FinalString + str;
    loop           = ResponseStream.available();
   }

   ResponseStream.close();
...............................................  .
...............................................  .
```

Response to an UnRegister request

The `unregisterUser()` method in `Server` class calls `Unregister.jsp` to unregister a user, as follows:

```
void unregisterUser(String values[])
{
...............................................  .
...............................................  .

urlName = "http://localhost:8080/examples/Unregister.jsp?sLoginName=" +
values[0];
}
```

Response to NotifyFriends request

The output from the servlet `NotifyFriends` is written to the `ServerResponse.xml` file, which is parsed, and messages notifying each friend individually are appended to the message queue, as follows:

```
int localNotifyFriends(String name[], int status)
{
............................................................ .
............................................................ .


    BufferedInputStream ResponseStream = new BufferedInputStream(
connection.getInputStream());

    while (loop != 0)
    {
     temp             = ResponseStream.read(buffer, 0, 32);
     String str       = new String (buffer, 0, temp);
     FinalString      = FinalString + str;
     loop             = ResponseStream.available();
    }

    ResponseStream.close();
 byte [] tempbytes = FinalString.getBytes();
 FileOutputStream TempOutFile    = new
FileOutputStream("ServerResponse.xml");
 TempOutFile.write(tempbytes, 0, tempbytes.length);
 TempOutFile.close();

 Parser.perform("ServerResponse.xml");
 String values[] = Parser.getVal();

 if (Parser.getType() == 6)
 {
............................................................ .
............................................................ .

     responseFromServer(FinalString);
    }
  }
 }
```

Response to a generate FriendList request

The `GetFriendList()` method in the `Server` class calls `FriendList.jsp`, reads its output through an input stream, generates the `FinalString` variable containing the name of the target user and the output XML and writes it to the message queue, as follows:

```
void GetFriendList(String values[])
{
............................................................ .
```

```
   BufferedInputStream ResponseStream = new BufferedInputStream(
connection.getInputStream());

  while (loop != 0)
  {
   temp             = ResponseStream.read(buffer, 0, 32);
   String str       = new String (buffer, 0, temp);
   FinalString      = FinalString + str;
   loop             = ResponseStream.available();
  }

   ResponseStream.close();
 addToMessageQueue(FinalString);
 }
```

Process responses from Jabber Server

The ListenerForJabber class waits in an infinite loop, listening to communication from
the Jabber server. If it receives a request/response from the Jabber server, the
ListenerForJabber class performs a series of steps to analyze the request that it receives
and to modify it in a manner that makes it suitable for communicating to local clients. These
steps are as follows:

1. The ListenerForJabber class uses the input stream StreamFromJabber to read
   any requests from the Jabber server, one byte at a time. It reads the request this way
   because the size of the XML data that it's receiving from the JabberServer isn't
   known, as the following code shows:

   ```
   temp             = StreamFromJabber.read(m_request, 0, 1);
   ```

2. The value of the variable loop determines whether the complete XML was received.
   This is done by setting the value of the loop variable through the method
   checkForCompleteXML(), which is repeatedly called to check for completeness of
   the received XML, as the following code shows:

   ```
   while (loop != 0)
               {
                   temp             = StreamFromJabber.read(m_request,
   0, 1);
                   if (temp < 0)
                     break;
                   String str      = new String (m_request, 0, temp);
                   FinalString     = FinalString + str;

                   for (int i =0;i<str.length();i++ )
                   {
   ```

```
                               if (str.charAt(i) == '<')
                               {
                                       m_loopCtrl++;
                               }
                               else if (str.charAt(i) == '>')
                               {
                                       m_loopCtrl--;
                               }


                       }
                       if (m_loopCtrl  == 0)
                       {
                         loop = checkForCompleteXML(FinalString);
                       }
```

3. The method `checkForCompleteXML()` uses `if-else` clauses to check for the
    presence or absence of XML starting tags and their corresponding ending tags. It returns
    an integer value that sets the value of the variable `loop` to 0 or 1, depending on whether
    or not it detects the XML as complete, as follows:

```
int checkForCompleteXML(String m_XMLString)
{
boolean        query  = false;
boolean        status = false;


if (m_XMLString.indexOf("<stream:stream") == 0)
{
       return 0;
}
else if (m_XMLString.indexOf("<iq") != -1)
{
   if ((m_XMLString.indexOf("query") != -
1)||(m_XMLString.indexOf("<error") != -1))
     {
               query = true;
     }
   if (!query)
   {
     if (m_XMLString.lastIndexOf("/>") == (m_XMLString.length() - 2))
        {
          return 0;
        }
        else
          return 1;
   }
   else if(query)
     {
```

```
          if (m_XMLString.lastIndexOf("</iq>") == (m_XMLString.length()
- 5))
          {
            return 0;
          }
          else
            return 1;
     }
}
else if (m_XMLString.indexOf("<presence") != -1)
{
  if ((m_XMLString.indexOf("<status") != -
1)||(m_XMLString.indexOf("<error") != -1))
    {
              status = true;
    }
  if(!status)
    {
      if (m_XMLString.lastIndexOf("/>") == (m_XMLString.length() - 2))
        {
          return 0;
        }
        else
          return 1;
    }
    else
    {
        if (m_XMLString.lastIndexOf("</presence>") ==
(m_XMLString.length() - 11))
        {
          return 0;
        }
        else
         return 1;
    }
}
else if (m_XMLString.indexOf("<message") != -1)
{
    if (m_XMLString.lastIndexOf("</message>") ==
(m_XMLString.length() - 10))
        {
          return 0;
        }
        else
          return 1;
}
  return 1;
}
```

4. After the XML is complete, a 0 value is returned to the `loop` variable, causing an exit from the `while` loop. The `ListenerForJabber` class then checks for the root XML tag, `<stream:stream>`, and its corresponding closing tag. If either or both the starting or closing tags are missing, they're prefixed or suffixed to the request, as the case may be, as follows:

```
if (FinalString.indexOf("<stream:stream from=\'jabber.org\'")!= -1)
            {
                    FinalString += "</stream:stream>";
                    m_requestType  = "ID";
            }
            else if (FinalString.indexOf("</stream:stream>")!= -1)
            {
                    FinalString = "<stream:stream from='jabber.org'
id='"+m_id+"' xmlns='jabber:client'

xmlns:stream='http://etherx.jabber.org/streams'>"+FinalString;

                    StreamToJabber.close();
                    StreamFromJabber.close();
                    thread = false;
                    //destroy();
            }
            else
            {
                    FinalString = "<stream:stream from='jabber.org'
id='"+m_id+"'

xmlns='jabber:client'
xmlns:stream='http://etherx.jabber.org/streams'>"+FinalString;
                    FinalString += "</stream:stream>";
            }
```

5. The request is then written to the `requestJabber.xml` file that you parse by calling the `perform()` method of class `XMLParser`, as follows:

```
byte [] tempbytes = FinalString.getBytes();
            FileOutputStream TempOutFile= new
FileOutputStream("requestJabber.xml");
            TempOutFile.write(tempbytes, 0, tempbytes.length);
            TempOutFile.close();
            Parser.perform("requestJabber.xml");

            String values[]                         = Parser.getVal();
            m_attributes                   = Parser.getAttributes();
            m_attributeNames               =
Parser.getAttributeNames();
```

```
                            m_namespaceType                          =
Parser.getNameSpaceType();
                            m_tagType                        = Parser.getType();
```

6. Depending on the type of request, the `ListenerForJabber` class sends a request to Jabber server — for example, for an Authorization request, the user's friends list is requested — as follows:

```
else if (m_requestType.equalsIgnoreCase("AUTH"))
                {
                        int index =
m_attributeNames.indexOf((Object)"type");

                        if
(((String)m_attributes.elementAt(index)).equalsIgnoreCase("result"))
                        {
                                        // if Logged On then Get
UserList...
                                m_requestType = "JABBER";
                                String authString3 = "<iq type='get'
id='"+m_id+"'>\n<query
xmlns='jabber:iq:roster'/>\n</iq>";

                                String authString = authString3;
                                byte [] bytesAuthString      =
authString.getBytes();
                                StreamToJabber.write(bytesAuthString,
0,bytesAuthString.length);
                                StreamToJabber.flush();
................................................................ .
................................................................ .
```

7. After the request-type is determined, a call to the `CreateXML` class is made by passing a parameter value that denotes the type of response that needs to be generated, as follows:

```
                        CreateXML m_XMLResponse = new
CreateXML("ROSTER", m_attributes);
                String  response          =
m_XMLResponse.returnResult();
```

8. The `CreateXML` class generates response for three types of requests: `ROSTER` (denoting a `FriendList` request), `PRESENCE` (denoting a `NotifyFriends` request) and `MESSAGE` (if a message request is received). These methods are `CreateRosterXML()`, `CreatePresenceXML()`, and `CreateMessageXML()`, respectively, and they generate XML responses that the local client's can understand, as follows:

```
CreateXML(String type, Vector param)
{
```

```
        XMLString                    = "<?xml version=\'1.0\'
encoding=\'utf-8\'?><InstantMessenger>";
    if (type.equalsIgnoreCase("ROSTER"))
    {
        CreateRosterXML(param);
    }
    else if (type.equalsIgnoreCase("PRESENCE"))
    {
        CreatePresenceXML(param);
    }
    else if (type.equalsIgnoreCase("MESSAGE"))
    {
        CreateMessageXML(param);
    }
}
.............................................
.............................................
void CreateMessageXML(Vector param)
{
        XMLString += "<MSG>";
        XMLString += "<Target>"     + (String)param.elementAt(1) +
"</Target>";
        XMLString += "<Source>"     + (String)param.elementAt(0) +
"</Source>";
        XMLString += "<Message>"+ (String)param.elementAt(2) +
"</Message>";
        XMLString += "</MSG>";
}
```

9. Finally, the `ListenerForJabber` class uses the `Server` class's
   `responseFromServer()` method to add the `CreateXML` class's response to the
   message queue. The `parentClass` is an object of the `Server` class, and
   `m_XMLResponse` is an object of the class `CreateXML`, which contains the output XML
   from the `CreateXML` class, as follows:

```
String    response                = m_XMLResponse.returnResult();

        String m_TempUserName = parentClass.getName();

        m_TempUserName += "^";

        response =  m_TempUserName + response;

        parentClass.responseFromServer(response);
```

Response to an AddGateway request

If the gateway is successfully added, the names of the user's friends on the Hotmail/MSN network appear on the main screen window. If, however, the gateway can't be added, an error message is sent to the client by the `ListenerForJabber` class, as follows:

```
else if (parentClass.Parser.getType() == 15)
{
.................................................... .

.................................................... .


  if (idString.indexOf("type-error") != -1)
  {
    CreateXML m_XMLResponse = new CreateXML("AddGateway", data);
    String  response        = m_XMLResponse.returnResult();
    byte [] responseBytes = response.getBytes();
    parentClass.StreamToClient.write(responseBytes, 0,
responseBytes.length);
    parentClass.StreamToClient.flush();
  }
}
```

The discussions in this chapter, up to this point, sum up the description of the server application. Notice how the five classes `Server`, `ListenerForJabber`, `XMLParser`, createXML, and `StartUpScreen` form modules with independent functions but work in conjunction to serve the purpose of the complete server application.

We discuss in the following sections the various Web Services that act as handlers for the final response generation for local clients.

Inside Java Web Services

- This section introduces the various JSP files and servlets that work at the server to provide the client utilities, such as logging in, logging out, registering, adding a friend, and so on, and briefly describes their basic operations.

Log into the Instant Messaging application

If a user wants to log in to the Instant Messaging application, an authorization type request is generated, which the `<auth>` tag identifies. After the request XML is parsed, the two parameters required for verification — namely, login name and password — are sent as query string variables named `sLoginName` and `sPassword`, respectively, to `Login.jsp`. The `Login.jsp` file performs the following steps to generate an appropriate response:

1. It requests the two parameters, login name and password, for verification as well as the IP address of the user, as follows:

```
<% String l_name = request.getParameter("sLoginName"); %>
<% String l_password = request.getParameter("sPassword"); %>
```

```
<% String l_ip = request.getRemoteAddr(); %>
```

2. It opens a connection to the database containing the user information, as follows:

```
<% java.sql.Connection db =
java.sql.DriverManager.getConnection("jdbc:odbc:messenger","sa","" );
%>
```

3. It executes a query to check whether the login name exists in the member table, as follows:

```
<% rs1 = st1.executeQuery("select member_id from member where
login_name = " + "'" + l_name + "'" + ";"); %>
```

4. If the login name exists, it executes a second query to check whether the password is correct, as follows:

```
<% rs2 = st2.executeQuery("select member_id from member where
login_name = " + "'" + l_name + "' and password = " + "'" + l_password
+ "'" + ";"); %>
```

5. If the query returns a record that corresponds to the given login name and password, the file executes a third query to update the member table with the IP address of the user, as follows:

```
<% ip = st3.executeUpdate(" UPDATE member SET ip_add =" + "'" + l_ip +
"'" +  " WHERE member.login_name = " + "'" + l_name + "'" + ";"); %>
```

6. It creates the output XML with the return value, which it stores in variable r_value, as follows:

```
<?xml version="1.0" ?>
<InstantMessenger>
<auth>
<int> <%= r_value %> </int>
</auth>
</InstantMessenger>
```

The *return value* is an integer that is set as follows:

- r_value = 1, if login name doesn't exist.
- r_value = 2, if password is incorrect.
- r_value = 0, if login name and password are both correct.
- r_value = -1, if the login name and password are correct but the update query fails for any reasons (note that ☐1is the initialization value of the variable).

Log out of the Instant Messaging application

A logout request is sent to end a user session and is identified by the `<Quit>` tag in the request XML. After it's parsed, the logout request is sent to `Logout.jsp`, with the login name sent as the query string variable `sLoginName`. `Logout.jsp` performs the following steps:

1. It retrieves the user's login name, as follows:

```
<% String l_name = request.getParameter("sLoginName"); %>
```

2. It opens the database connection (as in `Login.jsp`).

3. It sets the IP address field to `null` against the login name that's requesting to log out, as follows:

```
<% ip = st.executeUpdate(" UPDATE member SET ip_add =" + "'" + "'" + "
WHERE member.login_name =" + "'" + l_name + "'" + ";"); %>
```

4. It creates the output XML with the return value, which it stores in the variable `r_value`, as follows:

```
<?xml version="1.0" ?>
<InstantMessenger>
<int> <%= r_value %> </int>
</InstantMessenger>
```

The return value is an integer that is set as follows:

- `r_value = 0`, if the update query succeeds.
- `r_value = -1`, if the update query fails (note that ☐1 is the initialization value of the variable).

Register a new user

A new user needs to register with the Instant Messaging application before he can send messages through it. The registration request is identified by the `<Register>` tag in the request XML, and after it's parsed, the user information stored in XML value tags is passed as query string variables to `Register.jsp`. `Register.jsp` handles the registration request from the user by following these steps:

1. It retrieves the parameters that contain the user's information — such as the login name, password, e-mail address, telephone number, address, city, pin code, and profession — as follows:.

```
<% String LoginName = request.getParameter("sLoginName"); %>
<% String Password = request.getParameter("sPassword"); %>
<% String Add1 = request.getParameter("sAdd1"); %>
<% String Add2 = request.getParameter("sAdd2"); %>
<% String Phone1 = request.getParameter("sPhone1"); %>
```

```
<% String Phone2 = request.getParameter("sPhone2"); %>
<% String Email1 = request.getParameter("sEmail1"); %>
<% String Email2 = request.getParameter("sEmail2"); %>
<% String Pin = request.getParameter("sPin"); %>
<% String City = request.getParameter("sCity"); %>
<% String Profession = request.getParameter("sProfession"); %>
```

2. It opens the database connection (as in Login.jsp).

3. It executes a query to check whether the given login name already exists in the member table. (The login name must be unique for each of the users, as per the member table design; hence, a login name that already exists in the member table can't be assigned to any other new user.) It does so as follows:

```
<% rs1 = st1.executeQuery("select member_id from member where
login_name = " + "'" + LoginName + "'" + ";"); %>
```

4. If the given login name doesn't exist, the member ID is incremented, and a query is executed to add a new record to the member table, containing information for the user who's sent the registration request, as follows:

```
<% row_count = st3.executeUpdate("INSERT INTO member ( member_id,
login_name, password, address_1, address_2, email_1, email_2, city,
pin, profession ) VALUES ( " + m_Id + " , '" + LoginName + "', '" +
Password + "', '" + Add1 + "', '" + Add2 + "', '" + Email1 + "', '" +
Email2 + "', '" + City + "', '" + Pin + "', '" + Profession + "' );
"); %>
```

5. It creates the output XML with the return value, which it stores in the variable r_value, as follows:

```
<?xml version="1.0" ?>
<InstantMessenger>
<Register>
<int> <%= r_value %> </int>
</Register>
</InstantMessenger>
```

The return value is an integer that's set as follows:

- r_value = 1, if the given login name already exists.
- r_value = 0, if the user's registration succeeds.
- r_value = -1, if the update query fails (note that □1 is the initialization value of the variable).

Unregister an existing user

If a user doesn't want to remain registered with the Instant Messaging application, he can send an unregistration request. An unregistration request is identified by the `<Unregister >` tag in the request XML and login name and password are passed to `Unregister.jsp` in the form of query string variables. After a user is successfully unregistered, he/she can't use the Instant Messaging application until after reregistering. `Unregister.jsp` performs the following steps:

1. It retrieves the two parameters, login name and password, for authenticating the request, as follows:

```
<% String LoginName = request.getParameter("sLoginName"); %>
<% String Password = request.getParameter("sPassword"); %>
```

2. It opens the database connection (as in `Login.jsp`).

3. It executes a query to check whether a record corresponding to the given login name exists, as follows:

```
<% rs1 = st1.executeQuery(""select member_id from member where
login_name = " + "'" + LoginName + "'" + ";"); %>
```

4. If the record exists, it executes a second query to delete that particular record, as follows:

```
<% row_count = st2.executeUpdate("delete from member where login_name
= " + "'" + LoginName + "'" + ";"); %>
```

5. It creates the output XML with the return value, which it stores in the variable `r_value`, as follows:

```
<?xml version="1.0" ?>
<InstantMessenger>
<UnRegister> <%= r_value %> </UnRegister>
</InstantMessenger>
```

The return value is an integer that's set as follows:

- `r_value = 0`, if deletion of user record succeeds.
- `r_value = -1`, if unregistration fails.

Add a friend to the friends list

If a user wants to add a friend to his friend list, he does so by providing the login name of the friend. (The user's name is implicitly sent by the Instant Messaging application running at the user's end.) `AddFriend.jsp` performs the following steps to add the friend:

1. It retrieves the two parameters, the user's login name and the friend's loginname, as follows:

```
<% String LoginName = request.getParameter("sLoginName"); %>
<% String FriendName = request.getParameter("sFriendName"); %>
```

2. It opens the database connection (as in `Login.jsp`).

3. It executes a query to retrieve the member IDs corresponding to the user's and the friend's login names, respectively, as follows:

```
<% rs1 = st1.executeQuery("select member_id from member where
login_name = " + "'" + LoginName + "'" + ";"); %>
<% rs2 = st2.executeQuery("select member_id from member where
login_name = " + "'" + FriendName + "'" + ";"); %>
```

4. If the member IDs are retrieved, it checks the `friend` table to determine whether the user's already added this friend to his friends list on any previous occasion, as follows:

```
<% rs3 = st3.executeQuery("select member_id from friend where
member_id = " +  m_Id + " and friend_id = " + f_Id + ";"); %>
```

5. If the friend doesn't exist in the user's friends list, it adds the friend to the `friend` table against the user's member ID, as follows:

```
<% row_count = st4.executeUpdate("INSERT INTO friend ( member_id,
friend_id, status ) VALUES ( " + m_Id + " , " + f_Id + " , " +
statusVar + ");"); %>
```

6. It creates the output XML with the return value, which it stores in the variable `r_value`, as follows:

```
<?xml version="1.0" ?>
<InstantMessenger>
<FriendStatus>
<UserName><%=LoginName%></UserName>
<FriendName><%=FriendName%></FriendName>
<Status><%= r_value %></Status>
</FriendStatus>
</InstantMessenger>
```

The return value is an integer that's set as follows:

- `r_value` = 0, if a friend is successfully added to the `friend` table.
- `r_value` = 1, if the friend's name doesn't exist in the `member` table.
- `r_value` = 2, if the friend already exists in the `friend` table of the user.
- `r_value` = 3, if the friend's member ID is same as the user's member ID — that is, the user is trying to add himself as his friend!
- `r_value` = -1, if the friend cannot be added.

Retrieve the friends list from the server

After a user logs in, his/her friends list automatically appears on-screen, along with the respective status of each friend— that is, whether the friend's online or offline. `FriendList.jsp` performs the following steps to retrieve and generate a user's friends list and the status of each friend:

1. It retrieves one parameter, the user's login-name, as follows:

```
<% String l_name = request.getParameter("sLoginName"); %>
```

2. It opens the database connection (as in `Login.jsp`).

3. It executes a query to select the login name and status of the logged-in user's friends from the `friend_list` view, as follows:

```
<% rs = st.executeQuery(" SELECT login_name_a, ip_add  FROM
friend_list WHERE friend_list.login_name =" + "'" + l_name + "'" +
";"); %>
```

4. It executes a `while` loop to generate the friends list and the respective status of each friend, as follows:

```
<% while (rs.next()) { %>
..................................................................... .
..................................................................... .
<FriendName><%= name %></FriendName>
<Status><%= ip %></Status>

<% } %>
```

5. It creates the output XML containing the friends list, as follows:

```
<?xml version="1.0" ?>
<InstantMessenger>
<FriendList>
<FriendName>FriendName1</FriendName>
<Status>IPAddress1</Status>
<FriendName>FriendName2</FriendName>
<Status>IPAddress2</Status>
..................................................................... .
..................................................................... .
<FriendList>
</InstantMessenger>
```

Send a user's status to his/her friends

After a user logs in or logs out, a message is sent to all the contacts in his/her friends list, informing them of his/her status. The HTTP servlet `NotifyFriends` handles the notification process through the following steps:

1. It retrieves the user's login name and status, as follows:

```
m_SuserName= req.getParameter("sLoginName");
m_status= req.getParameter("sStatus");
```

2. It generates the notification XML string (partial), as follows:

```
m_SxmlString    = "<?xml version=\"1.0\"?>";
m_SxmlString         += "<InstantMessenger>";
m_SxmlString         += "<NotifyFriends>";
m_SxmlString         += "<UserName>";
m_SxmlString         += m_SuserName;
m_SxmlString         += "</UserName>";
m_SxmlString         += "<Status>";
 if (m_status.equalsIgnoreCase("1"))
m_SxmlString    += "On-Line";
else
m_SxmlString    += "Off-Line";
m_SxmlString    += "</Status>";
```

3. It opens a connection to the database, as follows:

```
m_Cconnection = DriverManager.getConnection(
"jdbc:odbc:messenger","sa","");
```

4. It executes a query to retrieve the login names of friends from the `friend_list` view, as follows:

```
m_CresultSet = m_Cstatement.executeQuery(" SELECT
friend_list.login_name FROM friend_list  WHERE
friend_list.login_name_a = " + "'" + m_SuserName + "'" +";");
```

5. It uses a `while` loop to create the XML for each of the friends that it retrieves through the `SELECT` query and completes the XML, as follows:

```
while(m_CresultSet.next())
{
String str1    = m_CresultSet.getString(1);
m_SxmlString    += "<FriendName>";
m_SxmlString    += str1;
m_SxmlString    += "</FriendName>";
}

m_SxmlString    += "</NotifyFriends>";
m_SxmlString    += "</InstantMessenger>";
```

6. It creates an output stream and uses it to output the XML string (with `res` as the `HTTPServletResponse` object), as follows:

```
m_BresponseStream = new BufferedOutputStream (res.getOutputStream());
byte [] response = m_SxmlString.getBytes();
```

```
m_BresponseStream.write(response, 0, response.length);
```

7. It closes the connection, as follows:

```
m_Cconnection.close();
```

Delete a friend from the friend list

If a user wants to delete a contact from his/her friends list, the request is handled by
DeleteContact.jsp, which performs the following steps:

1. It retrieves the two parameters, the user's and the friend's login names, as follows:

```
<% String LoginName = request.getParameter("sLoginName"); %>
<% String FriendName = request.getParameter("sFriendName"); %>
```

2. It opens the database connection (as in Login.jsp).

3. It executes a query to retrieve the member IDs corresponding to the user's and the
   friend's login names, respectively, as follows:

```
<% rs1 = st1.executeQuery("select member_id from member where
login_name = " + "'" + LoginName + "'" + ";"); %>
<% rs2 = st2.executeQuery("select member_id from member where
login_name = " + "'" + FriendName + "'" + ";"); %>
```

4. If it retrieves the IDs, it deletes the friend's entry from the friend table against the
   user's member ID, as follows:

```
<% row_count = st4.executeUpdate("Delete friend where
member_id="+m_Id+"and friend_id="+f_Id+";"); %>
```

5. It creates the output XML with the return value, which it stores in the variable r_value:

```
<?xml version="1.0" ?>
<InstantMessenger>
<DeleteStatus>
<UserName><%=LoginName%></UserName>
<FriendName><%=FriendName%></FriendName>
<Status><%= r_value %></Status>
</DeleteStatus>
</InstantMessenger>
```

The return value is an integer that's set as follows:

- r_value = 0, if the friend is successfully deleted from the friend table.
- r_value = 1, if the delete query fails.
- r_value = 2, if friend's login-name does not exist in member table.
- r_value = -1, if the friend cannot be deleted.

Technical Documentation

We now list all the codes (servlets/ JSPs) that we use in the Instant Messaging application with a line-by-line explanation of the code.

Server application classes

The server-application classes include the following:

- `StartUpScreen` class
- `Server` class
- `XMLParser` class
- `ListenerForJabber` class
- `CreateXML` class

StartUpScreen class

Figure 3-5 gives the technical-flow diagram that summarizes the working of the `StartUpScreen` class. Listing 3-1 contains the code for this class, followed by a detailed description of the code.

Listing 3-1: StartUpScreen.java

```
1.    import javax.swing.*;
2.    import javax.swing.event.*;
3.    import java.awt.*;
4.    import java.awt.event.*;
5.    import java.net.*;
6.    import java.io.*;
7.    import java.util.Vector;
8.
9.    /********************* StartUpScreen ***************************/
10.
11.   public class StartUpScreen extends JFrame implements
ActionListener, Runnable
12.   {
13.
14.   JLabel                      m_CompanyLogo;
15.   JLabel                      m_Information;
16.   JTextArea                   m_Logger;
17.   JButton                     m_StopServer;
18.   JButton                     m_StartServer;
19.   Container                   m_ContentPane;
20.   JScrollPane                 m_ScrollPane1;
21.   boolean                     startServer         = false;
```

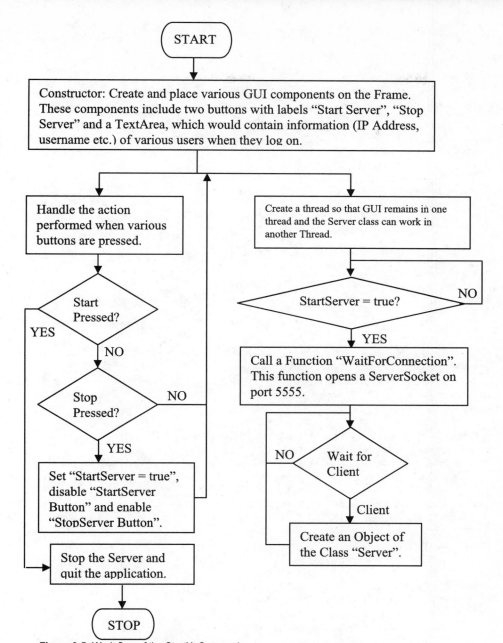

Figure 3-5: Work flow of the StartUpScreen class

```
22.
23.    /**************** StartUpScreen  Constructor ***************/
24.
25.    StartUpScreen()
26.    {
27.
28.     setTitle("Main Screen -- Instant Messenger Server");
29.     setResizable(false);
30.
31.     m_ContentPane = getContentPane();
32.
33.     m_ContentPane.setLayout(null);
34.
35.     setSize(425,150);
36.     setLocation(250,150);
37.
38.     addWindowListener (new java.awt.event.WindowAdapter () {
39.      public void windowClosing (java.awt.event.WindowEvent evt) {
40.      System.exit(0);
41.     }
42.     }
43.     );
44.
45.     m_CompanyLogo = new JLabel("© Dreamtech Software India Inc.");
46.     m_CompanyLogo.setFont(new Font("sansSerif", Font.PLAIN, 11));
47.     m_CompanyLogo.setBounds(70, 7, 200, 10);
48.     m_CompanyLogo.setForeground(Color.blue);
49.     m_ContentPane.add(m_CompanyLogo);
50.
51.     m_StartServer = new JButton("Start Server");
52.     m_StartServer.setBounds(15, 35, 120, 25);
53.     m_StartServer.addActionListener(this);
54.     m_ContentPane.add(m_StartServer);
55.
56.     m_StopServer = new JButton("Stop Server");
57.     m_StopServer.setBounds(15,80, 120, 25);
58.     m_StopServer.addActionListener(this);
59.     m_StopServer.setEnabled(false);
60.     m_ContentPane.add(m_StopServer);
61.
62.     m_Information = new JLabel("Status...");
63.     m_Information.setFont(new Font("sansSerif", Font.PLAIN, 11));
64.     m_Information.setBounds(270, 7, 200, 10);
65.     m_Information.setForeground(Color.blue);
66.     m_ContentPane.add(m_Information);
67.
68.     m_Logger       = new JTextArea(10, 15);
69.     m_Logger.setEnabled(false);
```

```
70.    m_ScrollPanel = new JScrollPane(m_Logger);
71.    m_ScrollPanel.setBounds(200, 20, 210, 100);
72.    m_ContentPane.add(m_ScrollPanel);
73.
74.    Thread       t = new Thread(this);
75.    t.start();
76.  }
77.
78.  /********************** actionPerformed ************************/
79.
80.  public void actionPerformed(ActionEvent ae)
81.  {
82.   if (ae.getSource() == m_StartServer)
83.   {
84.    startServer = true;
85.    m_StartServer.setEnabled(false);
86.    m_StopServer.setEnabled(true);
87.   }
88.   else if (ae.getSource() == m_StopServer)
89.   {
90.    System.exit(0);
91.   }
92.  }
93.
94.  /********************** run() ****************************/
95.
96.  public void run()
97.  {
98.   try
99.   {
100.    while (true)
101.    {
102.   if (startServer)
103.   {
104.      WaitForConnection();
105.      startServer = false;
106.      this.toBack();
107.   }
108.    }
109.   }
110.   catch(Exception e)
111.   {
112.   System.out.println("ThreadException   :"+e);
113.   }
114.  }
115.
116.  /********************** WaitForConnection
**********************/
117.
```

```
118.   public void WaitForConnection() throws Exception
119.   {
120.
121.     ServerSocket server_soc = new ServerSocket (5555);
122.     Socket sc;
123.
124.     while (true)
125.     {
126.         System.out.println("Server is Ready\nListening for
Requests...");
127.         sc = server_soc.accept();
128.         new Server(this, sc);
129.     }
130.   }
131.
132.   /********************** main  ***************************/
133.
134.   public static void main(String[] args)
135.   {
136.     StartUpScreen  mainScreen = new StartUpScreen();
137.     mainScreen.show();
138.   }
139.   }// End StartUpScreen....
```

- Lines 1□7: Java import statements that import the Java packages necessary for creating the GUI — for example the javax.swing package is the base package, the classes of which you use to create the GUI elements such as buttons (JButton class), text areas (JTextArea class), and so on.

- Line 11: The class declaration.

- Lines 14□21:Variable declarations for various elements that you use to create the GUI.

- Line 25: Declares the class constructor.

- Line 28: Sets the title of the GUI window to Main Screen -- Instant Messenger Server.

- Line 29: Sets the Resizable property of the GUI wondow to false, which means that a user can't resize it.

- Line 31: Calls the getContentPane() method to obtain a Container object that contains the components of the GUI.

- Line 33: A null is passed to the setLayout() method to set an absolute positioning for the content pane.

- Line 35: Sets the size of the GUI window, in pixels, to 425 x 150 (width x height).

- Line 36: Sets the position of the GUI window on-screen. (x-coordinate from top left and y-coordinate from topleft).

- Line 38: Adds a window listener to the container/GUI window.

- Lines 39□41:The `windowClosing()` method implements the window listener by specifying (in Line 40) that the program is to exit after the window closes.

- Line 45: Creates a label named `m_CompanyLogo`.

- Line 46: Sets the font for `m_CompanyLogo`.

- Line 47: Sets the bounds (where the label should appear — that is, the x-coordinate, y-coordinate, width, and height) for `m_CompanyLogo`.

- Line 48: Sets the foreground (text) color for the label `m_CompanyLogo`.

- Line 49: Adds `m_CompanyLogo` to the content pane.

- Lines 51□52:Create a new button, `m_StartServer`, and set its boundaries.

- Line 53: Adds an action listener to the button `m_StartServer`.

- Line 54: Adds the button `m_StartServer` to the content pane.

- Lines 56□60:Create a new button, `m_StopServer` (Line 56), set its bounds (Line 57), add an action listener (Line 58), set the `setEnable` to false (Line 59) to disable the button, and add it to the content pane (Line 60).

- Lines 62□66: Create a new label,`m_information` (Line 62), set its font (Line 63), set its boundaries (Line 64), set its foreground color (Line 65), and add it to the content pane (Line 66).

- Lines 68: Creates a new text area, `m_Logger`, with 10 rows and 15 columns.

- Line 69: Sets the `Enabled` property of `m_Logger` to `false` so that a user can't write in it.

- Lines 70□72: Createa scroll pane within the text area `m_Logger`, set its bounds and add it to the content pane.

- Lines 74□76: Create a new thread and start it.`t.start()` calls the `run()` method of the class.

- Line 80: Declares the `actionPerformed()` method.

- Lines 82□87: Check whether the source of theAction event is `m_StartServer` — that is, whether the user's clicked the `m_StartServer` button — and list the steps to take in such an event:

  - Line 84: Sets the Boolean variable `startServer` to true.

  - Line 85: Disables the `m_StartServer` button.

  - Line 86: Enables the `m_StopServer` button.

- Lines 88□91: Check whether the source of theAction event is `m_StopServer` — that is, whether the user's clicked the `m_StopServer` button — and specify that the program (the Instant Messaging application in this case) should exit (Line 90).

- Lines 96□114:Declare and define the `run()` method of the `StartUpScreen` class within a `try-catch` block:

  - Line 102: Checks whether the variable `startServer` is true.

  - Line 104: Calls the `WaitForConnection()` method that creates an object of the `Server` class.

  - Line 105: Sets the variable `startServer` to false to ensure that another new instance of `Server` class isn't created after control returns to the `while` condition of Line 100.

  - Line 106: Sends the GUI window to the back of the screen.

  - Line 110: Catches any `Exception` thrown by the `try` block of Line 88.

  - Line 112: Prints the `Exception` description.

- Lines 118□130: Declare and definethe `WaitForConnection()` method:

  - Line 121: Creates a new `ServerSocket`.

  - Line 122: Declares a socket.

  - Line 126: Prints the line `Server is Ready\Listening for Requests . . .` to the server console, thereby confirming that the server is ready to service requests.

  - Line 127: Creates aa `ServerSocket` on the client side, represented by the socket `sc`.

  - Line 128: Instantiates the `Server` class by creating its object.

- Lines 134□138: Definethe `main()` function that serves as the starting point for the program by creating an object of the `StartUpScreen` class and making it visible (Line 137).

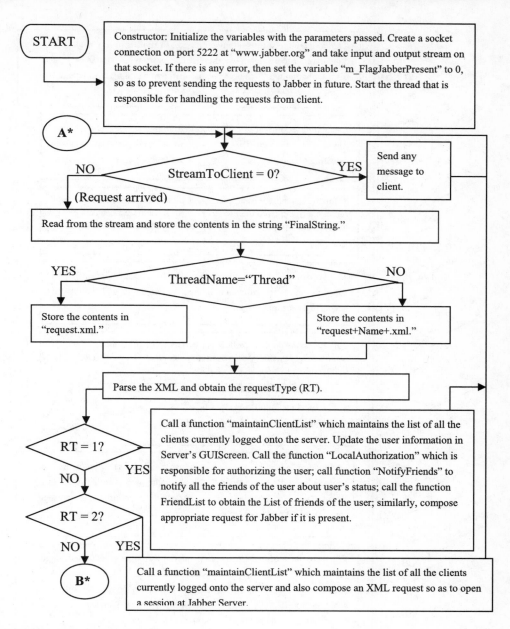

Figure 3-6a: Flow chart of the Server class

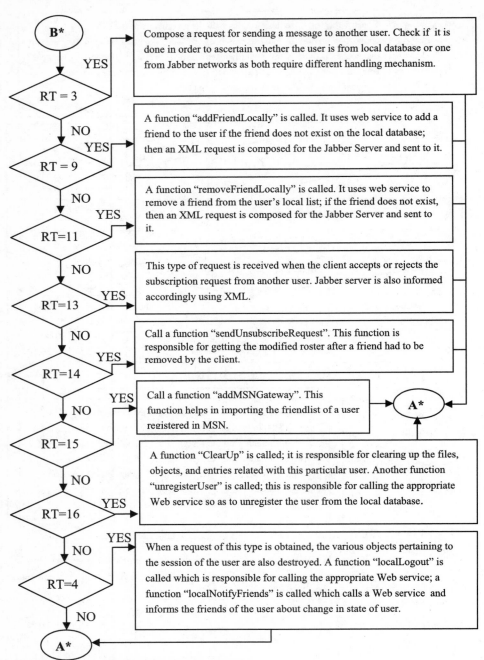

Figure 3-6b: Flow chart of the Server class (continued)

Server class

Figure 3-6 gives the technical flow diagram that summarizes the working of the Server class. Listing 3-2 contains the code for this class, followed by a detailed description of that code.

Listing 3-2: Server.java

```
1.   import java.io.*;
2.   import java.net.*;
3.   import java.util.*;
4.
5.   /*********** Class Declaration ************/
6.
7.   public class Server extends Thread
8.   {
9.     BufferedInputStream          StreamFromClient;
10.    BufferedOutputStream         StreamToClient;
11.
12.    BufferedInputStream          StreamFromJabber;
13.    BufferedOutputStream         StreamToJabber;
14.
15.    Socket                       ClientSocketOnServer;
16.    Socket                       sc;
17.    Socket                       m_socketToJabber;
18.
19.    int                          m_FlagJabberPresent;
20.
21.    XMLParser                    Parser = new XMLParser();
22.
23.    static    Vector             UserList       = new
Vector();
24.    static    Vector             MessageQueue  = new Vector();
25.    static    Vector             JabberId       = new
Vector();
26.    static    Vector             ListenerList  = new Vector();
27.
28.
29.    String                       m_requestType = new String();
30.    String                       m_userName     = new
String();
31.    String                       m_passWord     = new
String();
32.
33.    int                          m_CriticalSection      = 0;
34.    FileOutputStream             TempOutFile;
35.    ListenerForJabber            listener;
36.    StartUpScreen                screen;
37.    boolean          unregister         = false;
38.    boolean          addGatewayFlag     = false;
```

```
39.
40.   /************ Constructor *************/
41.
42.   Server(StartUpScreen screen, Socket sc) throws IOException
43.   {
44.    this.sc             =      sc;
45.    m_FlagJabberPresent       =      1;
46.    this.screen =      screen;
47.    StreamFromClient = new BufferedInputStream(sc.getInputStream());
48.     StreamToClient = new BufferedOutputStream(sc.getOutputStream());

49.    try
50.    {
51.     InetAddress address = InetAddress.getByName("www.jabber.org");
52.     m_socketToJabber = new Socket(address,5222);
53.
54.     StreamFromJabber   = new
BufferedInputStream(m_socketToJabber.getInputStream());
55.     StreamToJabber          = new
BufferedOutputStream(m_socketToJabber.getOutputStream());
56.
57.     m_FlagJabberPresent = 1;
58.    }
59.    catch(Exception SException)
60.    {
61.     System.out.println(SException);
62.     m_FlagJabberPresent = 0;
63.    }
64.    start();
65.   }
66.
67.   /************ run *************/
68.
69.   public void run()
70.   {
71.    try
72.    {
73.    while (true)
74.    {
75.   // Read the Request from Client....
76.   // Debug it....
77.   // Send it to the Jabber Server...
78.   // Wait for the response...
79.   // if resonse comes send it on StreamTo Client...
80.
81.    byte []              request       =      new byte[32];
82.    int                 temp          =      0;
83.    int                 loop          =      100;
84.    String              FinalString   = new String();
```

```
85.
86.    // Request Taken from The Client....
87.
88.    loop = StreamFromClient.available();
89.
90.    if (loop == 0)
91.      SendMessageToClient();
92.    else
93.    {
94.    while (loop != 0)
95.    {
96.     temp = StreamFromClient.read(request, 0, 32);
97.     String str =      new String (request, 0, temp);
98.     FinalString =       FinalString + str;
99.     loop = StreamFromClient.available();
100.    }
101.
102.        byte [] tempbytes = FinalString.getBytes();
103.        if (getName().indexOf("Thread") != -1)
104.           TempOutFile= new FileOutputStream("request.xml");
105.        else
106.           TempOutFile= new
FileOutputStream("request"+getName()+".xml");
107.        TempOutFile.write(tempbytes, 0, tempbytes.length);
108.        TempOutFile.close();
109.
110.        if (getName().indexOf("Thread") != -1)
111.            Parser.perform("request.xml");
112.        else
113.            Parser.perform("request"+getName()+".xml");
114.
115.        String values[] = Parser.getVal();
116.
117.        if (Parser.getType() == 1)
118.        {
119.            //         Compose the Request For The Authorization..
120.        int returnVal = 0;
121.
122.        MaintainClientList(values[0]);
123.        screen.m_Logger.append(values[0]+"
"+sc.getInetAddress()+"\n");
124.        returnVal          = LocalAuthorization(values);
125.        localNotifyFriends(values, 1);
126.        GetFriendList(values);
127.
128.        if (m_FlagJabberPresent != 0)
129.        {
130.        listener =    new ListenerForJabber(this, StreamToJabber,
StreamFromJabber);
```

```
131.        addToListenerList(listener);
132.        }
133.
134.
135.        if ((returnVal == 1)&&(m_FlagJabberPresent == 1))
136.        {
137.             /* Send it to Jabber to get the Global Userlist */
138.             String authString1 = "<stream:stream
\nto=\"jabber.org\"\nxmlns=\"jabber:client\"
\nxmlns:stream=\"http://etherx.jabber.org/streams\">";
139.             m_userName = values[0];
140.             m_passWord = values[1];
141.             String authString = authString1;
142.             byte [] bytesAuthString    = authString.getBytes();
143.             StreamToJabber.write(bytesAuthString,
0,bytesAuthString.length);
144.             StreamToJabber.flush();
145.             }
146.        }
147.        else if (Parser.getType() == 2)
148.        {
149.             //        Compose the Request For Registering the
user..
150.
151.             int returnVal = 0;
152.
153.             MaintainClientList(values[0]);
154.
155.             returnVal = 1;
156.             if ((returnVal == 1)&&(m_FlagJabberPresent == 1))
157.             {
158.                  /* Send it to Jabber to Register the User */
159.        if (m_FlagJabberPresent != 0)
160.        {
161.        listener =    new ListenerForJabber(this, StreamToJabber,
StreamFromJabber);
162.        addToListenerList(listener);
163.        }
164.
165.             m_userName = values[0];
166.             m_passWord = values[1];
167.
168.             setRequestType("REGISTER");
169.             String authString1 = "<stream:stream \n
to=\"jabber.org\"\nxmlns=\"jabber:client\"
\nxmlns:stream=\"http://etherx.jabber.org/streams\">";
170.             String authString = authString1;
171.             byte [] bytesAuthString    = authString.getBytes();
```

```
172.                StreamToJabber.write(bytesAuthString,
0,bytesAuthString.length);
173.                StreamToJabber.flush();
174.                }
175.        }
176.        else if (Parser.getType() == 3)
177.        {
178.            //          Compose the Request For The Sending Message
To another user..
179.
180.            int dummy = 0;
181.            for (int i = 0;i<UserList.size();i++)
182.            {
183.                String str = (String)UserList.elementAt(i);
184.                if (str.equalsIgnoreCase(values[0]))
185.                {
186.                    dummy = 1;
187.                }
188.            }
189.            if (dummy == 1)
190.            {
191.                // message for Local User....
192.                // Add To Message Queue... (Intended
User+"^"+FinalString)
193.                responseFromServer(values[0]+"^"+FinalString);
194.            }
195.            else if (m_FlagJabberPresent == 1)
196.        {
197.            //   Message For the Jabber Client.. Compose the
request Accordingly .
198.            String m_targetUser  =new String();
199.
200.            if (values[0].indexOf("%")!= -1)
201.                m_targetUser = values[0]+"@msn.jabber.org";
202.            else
203.                m_targetUser = values[0]+"@jabber.org";
204.
205.            String m_sender      = values[1]+"@jabber.org";
206.            String m_Message     = values[2];
207.            String m_JabberID;
208.
209.            String m_MessageXML = "<message
to=\""+m_targetUser+"\" type=\"chat\" from=\""+values[1]+"\">";
210.            m_MessageXML += "<body>"+values[2]+"</body>";
211.            m_MessageXML += "</message>";
212.
213.            byte [] bytesAuthString      =
m_MessageXML.getBytes();
```

```
214.             StreamToJabber.write(bytesAuthString,
0,bytesAuthString.length);
215.             StreamToJabber.flush();
216.       }
217.       }
218.       else if (Parser.getType() == 9) // AddFriend...
219.       {
220.             int returnVal = -1;
221.             returnVal     = addFriendLocally(values);
222.       }
223.       else if (Parser.getType() == 11) // DeleteFriend...
224.       {
225.             removeFriendLocally(values);
226.       }
227.       else if (Parser.getType() == 13) // AcceptFriend...
228.       {
229.
230.             values[0] = values[0] + "@jabber.org";
231.             int i = values[1].indexOf("%");
232.             int j = values[1].indexOf("@msn.jabber.org");
233.             if ((i != -1)&&(j == -1))
234.             {
235.                   values[1] = values[1] + "@msn.jabber.org";
236.             }
237.             else if ((i != -1)&&(j != -1))
238.             {
239.                   values[1] = values[1];
240.             }
241.             else
242.             {
243.                   values[1] = values[1] + "@jabber.org";
244.             }
245.
246.       if (values[2].equalsIgnoreCase("0"))
247.       {
248.             String m_AddFriendXML = "<presence
from=\""+values[0]+"\" to=\""+values[1]+"\" type=\"subscribed\"/>";
249.
250.
251.             byte [] bytesAuthString     =
m_AddFriendXML.getBytes();
252.             StreamToJabber.write(bytesAuthString,
0,bytesAuthString.length);
253.             StreamToJabber.flush();

254.
255.             m_AddFriendXML = "<presence from=\""+values[0]+"\"
to=\""+values[1]+"\" type=\"subscribe\"/>";
256.
```

```
257.              bytesAuthString      = m_AddFriendXML.getBytes();
258.              StreamToJabber.write(bytesAuthString,
0,bytesAuthString.length);
259.              StreamToJabber.flush();

260.
261.              String authString3 = "<iq type='get'>\n<query
xmlns='jabber:iq:roster'/>\n</iq>";
262.              String authString = authString3;
263.              bytesAuthString      = authString.getBytes();
264.              StreamToJabber.write(bytesAuthString,
0,bytesAuthString.length);
265.              StreamToJabber.flush();
266.
267.              }
268.              else if (values[2].equalsIgnoreCase("1"))
269.              {
270.
271.              String m_AddFriendXML = "<presence
from=\""+values[0]+"\" to=\""+values[1]+"\" type=\"unsubscribe\"/>";
272.
273.              byte [] bytesAuthString      =
m_AddFriendXML.getBytes();
274.              StreamToJabber.write(bytesAuthString,
0,bytesAuthString.length);
275.              StreamToJabber.flush();

276.
277.              String authString3 = "<iq type='get'>\n<query
xmlns='jabber:iq:roster'/>\n</iq>";
278.              String authString = authString3;
279.              bytesAuthString      = authString.getBytes();
280.              StreamToJabber.write(bytesAuthString,
0,bytesAuthString.length);
281.              StreamToJabber.flush();
282.
283.              }
284.
285.         }
286.      else if (Parser.getType() == 14) // UnSubscribeRequest...
287.      {
288.              sendUnSubscribedRequest(values);
289.      }
290.      else if (Parser.getType() == 15) // AddGateway...
291.      {
292.      try
293.      {
294.              addMSNGateway(values);
295.      }
```

```
296.        catch (Exception e)
297.        {
298.          System.out.println("Exception occured in Add
MSNGateway:"+e);
299.        }
300.
301.        }
302.        else if (Parser.getType() == 16) // Unregister...
303.        {
304.             clearUp(values);
305.             unregisterUser(values);
306.        }
307.        else if (Parser.getType() == 4)
308.        {
309.        int index = -1;
310.
311.        String strTemp  = screen.m_Logger.getText();
312.        char [] tempArray = strTemp.toCharArray();
313.        for (int i =0;i<tempArray.length;i++ )
314.        {
315.             if (tempArray[i]=='\n')
316.                tempArray[i] = '|';
317.        }
318.        strTemp = new String(tempArray);
319.        String targetString  = values[0]+" "+sc.getInetAddress();
320.        StringTokenizer      st = new StringTokenizer(strTemp, "|");
321.        String strTemp1        = new String();
322.        while (st.hasMoreElements())
323.        {
324.           String str = new String();
325.           str = st.nextToken();
326.           if (!(str.equalsIgnoreCase(targetString)))
327.           {
328.                strTemp1 += str+"|";
329.           }
330.           else
331.           {
332.                strTemp1 += "~";
333.           }
334.        }
335.
336.
337.             tempArray = strTemp1.toCharArray();
338.             for (int i=1;i<tempArray.length;i++ )
339.             {
340.                  if (tempArray[i]=='|')
341.                   tempArray[i] = '\n';
342.                  else if (tempArray[i]=='~')
343.                   tempArray[i] = ' ';
```

```
344.                    }
345.                    if ((tempArray[0] == '|')||(tempArray[0] == '~'))
346.                       strTemp1 = new String();
347.                    else
348.                     {
349.                       strTemp1 = new String(tempArray);
350.                       strTemp1.trim();
351.                     }
352.                    screen.m_Logger.setText(strTemp1);
353.
354.
355.          for (int i =0;i<UserList.size() ;i++ )
356.          {
357.            if
(((String)UserList.elementAt(i)).equalsIgnoreCase(getName()))
358.             {
359.                    UserList.removeElementAt(i);
360.                    index = i;
361.             }
362.          }
363.          if ((index > -1)&&(m_FlagJabberPresent == 1))
364.          {
365.                    ListenerList.removeElementAt(index);
366.          }
367.
368.          int result = localLogout(values);
369.          File userFile = new File("request"+getName()+".xml");
370.          userFile.delete();
371.
372.          if ((result == 1)&&(m_FlagJabberPresent == 1))
373.          {
374.                    // Send To Jabber As Well
375.                    byte [] logoutRequest =
"</stream:stream>".getBytes();
 StreamToJabber.write(logoutRequest, 0,logoutRequest.length);
376.                    StreamToJabber.flush();
377.          }
378.          localNotifyFriends(values, 0);
379.          StreamToClient.close();
380.          StreamFromClient.close();
381.       }
382.       }          // End While..
383.    }
384.
385.    }          // End Try Block..
386.    catch(Exception ae)
387.    {
388.
389.    int index = -1;
```

```
390.
391.    for (int i =0;i<UserList.size() ;i++ )
392.    {
393.       if
(((String)UserList.elementAt(i)).equalsIgnoreCase(getName()))
394.       {
395.           UserList.removeElementAt(i);
396.           index = i;
397.       }
398.    }
399.
400.    if (index > -1)
401.    {
402.           ListenerList.removeElementAt(index);
403.    }
404.    String [] values = new String[1];
405.    values[0] = getName();
406.
407.    File userFile      = new File("request"+getName()+".xml");
408.    userFile.delete();
409.
410.    int temp = localLogout(values);
411.    if ((temp == 1)&&(m_FlagJabberPresent == 1))
412.    {
413.        // Send To Jabber As Well
414.        byte [] logoutRequest = "</stream:stream>".getBytes();

415.        try
416.        {
417.        StreamToJabber.write(logoutRequest, 0,logoutRequest.length);
418.        StreamToJabber.flush();
419.        }
420.        catch (Exception e)
421.        {
422.          System.out.println("Exception occured: in Closing Stream
of Jabber"+e);
423.           e.printStackTrace(System.out);
424.        }
425.    }
426.
427.    try
428.    {
429.    StreamFromClient.close();
430.    StreamToClient.close();
431.    }
432.    catch(Exception e)
433.    {
434.        System.out.println("Exception in Stream Closing..." +e);
435.    }
```

```
436.    }
437.  }
438.
439.
440.  /*********** LocalAuthorization ************/
441.
442.  int LocalAuthorization(String values[])
443.  {
444.
445.  String        urlName       = new String();
446.  int           loop          = 100;
447.  byte[]        buffer        = new byte[32];
448.  int           temp          = 0;
449.  String        FinalString   = new String();
450.
451.  urlName = "http://localhost:8080/examples/Login.jsp?sLoginName=" +
values[0] + "&sPassword=" + values[1] ;
452.
453.  try
454.  {
455.    URL url = new URL(urlName);
456.    URLConnection connection = url.openConnection();
457.
458.    BufferedInputStream ResponseStream = new BufferedInputStream(
connection.getInputStream());
459.
460.    while (loop != 0)
461.    {
462.        temp          = ResponseStream.read(buffer, 0, 32);
463.        String str    = new String (buffer, 0, temp);
464.        FinalString   = FinalString + str;
465.        loop          = ResponseStream.available();
466.    }
467.
468.    ResponseStream.close();
469.
470.  /*** Using the Stream of the Client (StreamToClient) Send it to
the Client to parse. ***/
471.
472.    byte [] response = FinalString.getBytes();
473.    StreamToClient.write(response, 0, response.length);
474.    StreamToClient.flush();
475.  return 1;
476.  }
477.  catch(Exception e)
478.  {
479.   System.out.println("Exception Occurred In LocalAuthorization :
"+e);
480.   return 0;
```

```
481.   }
482.   }
483.
484.   /*********** LocalRegistration *************/
485.
486.   int LocalRegistration(String values[])
487.   {
488.   String        urlName         = new String();
489.   int           loop            = 100;
490.   byte[]        buffer          = new byte[32];
491.   int           temp            = 0;
492.   String        FinalString     = new String();
493.
494.   urlName =
"http://localhost:8080/examples/Register.jsp?sLoginName=" + values[0] +
"&sPassword=" + values[1] + "&sAdd1=" + values[3] + "&sAdd2=" +
values[4] + "&sPhone1=" + values[5] + "&sPhone2=" + values[6] +
"&sEmail1=" + values[7] + "&sEmail2=" + values[8] + "&sPin=" + values[9]
+ "&sCity=" + values[10] + "&sProfession=" + values[11];
495.
496.   try
497.   {
498.     URL url = new URL(urlName);
499.     URLConnection connection = url.openConnection();
500.
501.     BufferedInputStream ResponseStream = new BufferedInputStream(
connection.getInputStream());
502.
503.     while (loop != 0)
504.     {
505.         temp            = ResponseStream.read(buffer, 0, 32);
506.         String str      = new String (buffer, 0, temp);
507.         FinalString     = FinalString + str;
508.         loop            = ResponseStream.available();
509.     }
510.
511.     ResponseStream.close();
512.
513.
514.
515.   /*** Using the Stream of the Client (StreamToClient) Send it to
the Client to parse. ***/
516.
517.     byte [] response = FinalString.getBytes();
518.     StreamToClient.write(response, 0, response.length);
519.     StreamToClient.flush();
520.   return 1;
521.   }
522.   catch(Exception e)
```

```
523.   {
524.     System.out.println("Exception Occurred In LocalRegistration :
"+e);
525.     return 0;
526.   }
527.  }
528.
529.  /*********** GetFriendList *****************/
530.
531.  void GetFriendList(String values[])
532.  {
533.  String        urlName      = new String();
534.  int           loop         = 100;
535.  byte[]        buffer       = new byte[32];
536.  int           temp         = 0;
537.  String        FinalString  = new String();
538.
539.  urlName =
"http://localhost:8080/examples/FriendList.jsp?sLoginName=" + values[0];
540.
541.  try
542.  {
543.    URL url = new URL(urlName);
544.    URLConnection connection = url.openConnection();
545.
546.    BufferedInputStream ResponseStream = new BufferedInputStream(
connection.getInputStream());
547.
548.    while (loop != 0)
549.    {
550.        temp          = ResponseStream.read(buffer, 0, 32);
551.        String str    = new String (buffer, 0, temp);
552.        FinalString   = FinalString + str;
553.        loop          = ResponseStream.available();
554.    }
555.
556.    ResponseStream.close();
557.
558.  addToMessageQueue(FinalString);
559.  }
560.  catch(Exception e)
561.  {
562.    System.out.println("Exception Occurred In GetFriendList : "+e);
563.  }
564.  }
565.
566.  /****** addFriendLocally ***************/
567.
568.  int addFriendLocally(String tempStr[])
```

```
569.  {
570.  String       urlName      = new String();
571.  int          loop         = 100;
572.  byte[]       buffer       = new byte[32];
573.  int          temp         = 0;
574.  String       FinalString  = new String();
575.
576.  urlName =
"http://localhost:8080/examples/AddFriend.jsp?sLoginName=" +
tempStr[0]+"&sFriendName="+tempStr[1];
577.
578.  try
579.  {
580.    URL url = new URL(urlName);
581.    URLConnection connection = url.openConnection();
582.
583.    BufferedInputStream ResponseStream = new BufferedInputStream(
connection.getInputStream());
584.
585.    while (loop != 0)
586.    {
587.        temp            = ResponseStream.read(buffer, 0, 32);
588.        String str      = new String (buffer, 0, temp);
589.        FinalString     = FinalString + str;
590.        loop            = ResponseStream.available();
591.    }
592.    ResponseStream.close();
593.
594.  byte [] tempbytes = FinalString.getBytes();
595.  FileOutputStream TempOutFile       = new
FileOutputStream("ServerResponse.xml");
596.  TempOutFile.write(tempbytes, 0, tempbytes.length);
597.  TempOutFile.close();
598.
599.  Parser.perform("ServerResponse.xml");
600.  String values[] = Parser.getVal();
601.  String userName = new String();
602.
603.  if (Parser.getType() == 10)
604.  {
605.   if (values[2].equalsIgnoreCase("0"))
606.   {
607.     userName = values[0];
608.     FinalString = userName+"^"+FinalString;
609.     responseFromServer(FinalString);
610.     return 0;
611.   }
612.   else if (values[2].equalsIgnoreCase("2"))
613.   {
```

```
614.     userName = values[0];
615.     FinalString = userName+"^"+FinalString;
616.     responseFromServer(FinalString);
617.     return 0;
618.    }
619.   else if (values[2].equalsIgnoreCase("1"))
620.    {
621. int    index   =     UserList.indexOf((Object)values[0]);
622.
623. values[0] = values[0] + "@jabber.org";
624. int i =  values[1].indexOf("@");
625. if (i != -1)
626. {
627. int j =  values[1].indexOf("hotmail.com");
628. if (j != -1)
629. {
630. String str11 = values[1].substring(0, i);
631. str11 = str11+"%";
632. str11 = str11+values[1].substring(i+1);
633.
634. values[1] = str11;
635. values[1] = values[1] + "@msn.jabber.org";
636. }
637. }
638. else
639. {
640. values[1] = values[1] + "@jabber.org";
641. }
642.
643.   String m_AddFriendXML = "<presence to=\""+values[1]+"\"
type=\"subscribe\"/>";
644.   byte [] bytesAuthString   = m_AddFriendXML.getBytes();
645.   StreamToJabber.write(bytesAuthString, 0,bytesAuthString.length);
646.   StreamToJabber.flush();
647.
648.
649.   String authString3 = "<iq type='get'>\n<query
xmlns='jabber:iq:roster'/>\n</iq>";
650.   String authString = authString3;
651.   byte [] bytesAuthString1   = authString.getBytes();
652.   StreamToJabber.write(bytesAuthString1, 0,bytesAuthString1.length);
653.   StreamToJabber.flush();
654.    }
655.    }     // End If...
656. }// End Try..
657. catch(Exception e)
658. {
659.   System.out.println("Exception Occurred In GetFriendList : "+e);
660.   }
```

```
661.    return 1;
662.    }
663.
664.    /************* removeFriendLocally ****************/
665.
666.    void removeFriendLocally(String tempStr[])
667.    {
668.    String       urlName      = new String();
669.    int          loop         = 100;
670.    byte[]       buffer       = new byte[32];
671.    int          temp         = 0;
672.    String       FinalString  = new String();
673.
674.    String       tempString   = new String();
675.
676.    int          indexPercent= tempStr[1].indexOf("%");
677.    if (indexPercent != -1)
678.    {
679.      tempString        = tempStr[1].substring(0, indexPercent);
680.      tempString        = tempString +"@";
681.      tempString        = tempString +
tempStr[1].substring(indexPercent+1);
682.    }
683.    else
684.    {
685.      tempString        = tempStr[1];
686.    }
687.    urlName =
"http://localhost:8080/examples/DeleteContact.jsp?sLoginName=" +
tempStr[0]+"&sFriendName="+tempString;
688.
689.    try
690.    {
691.      URL url = new URL(urlName);
692.      URLConnection connection = url.openConnection();
693.
694.      BufferedInputStream ResponseStream = new BufferedInputStream(
connection.getInputStream());
695.
696.      while (loop != 0)
697.      {
698.          temp          = ResponseStream.read(buffer, 0, 32);
699.          String str    = new String (buffer, 0, temp);
700.          FinalString   = FinalString + str;
701.          loop          = ResponseStream.available();
702.      }
703.      ResponseStream.close();
704.
705.    byte [] tempbytes = FinalString.getBytes();
```

```
706.   FileOutputStream TempOutFile        = new
FileOutputStream("ServerResponse.xml");
707.   TempOutFile.write(tempbytes, 0, tempbytes.length);
708.   TempOutFile.close();
709.
710.   Parser.perform("ServerResponse.xml");
711.   String values[] = Parser.getVal();
712.   String userName = new String();
713.   if (Parser.getType() == 12)
714.   {
715.    if (values[2].equalsIgnoreCase("0"))
716.    {
717.      userName = values[0];
718.      FinalString = userName+"^"+FinalString;
719.      responseFromServer(FinalString);
720.    }
721.    else if
(values[2].equalsIgnoreCase("2")||(values[2].equalsIgnoreCase("1")))
722.    {
723.        indexPercent  = 0;
724.        tempString            = new String();
725.
726.        values[0] = values[0] + "@jabber.org";
727.
728.        indexPercent= values[1].indexOf("@");
729.        if (indexPercent != -1)
730.        {
731.          tempString          = values[1].substring(0, indexPercent);
732.          tempString          = tempString +"%";
733.          tempString          = tempString +
values[1].substring(indexPercent+1);
734.          values[1]                   = tempString;
735.          values[1]                   = values[1] + "@msn.jabber.org";
736.
737.        }
738.        else
739.        {
740.          tempString          = values[1]+"@jabber.org";
741.          values[1]                   = tempString;
742.        }
743.
744.    String m_RemoveFriendXML = "<presence to=\""+values[1]+"\"
type=\"unsubscribe\"/>";
745.    byte [] bytesAuthString   = m_RemoveFriendXML.getBytes();
746.    StreamToJabber.write(bytesAuthString, 0,bytesAuthString.length);
747.    StreamToJabber.flush();
748.
749.    String authString3 = "<iq type='get'>\n<query
xmlns='jabber:iq:roster'/>\n</iq>";
```

```
750.
751.    String authString = authString3;
752.    bytesAuthString   = authString.getBytes();
753.    StreamToJabber.write(bytesAuthString, 0,bytesAuthString.length);
754.    StreamToJabber.flush();
755.    }
756.    }     // End If...
757.  }// End Try..
758.  catch(Exception e)
759.  {
760.    System.out.println("Exception Occurred In removeFriendLocally:
"+e);
761.  }
762.  }
763.
764.  /*********** addMSNGateway *************/
765.
766.  void addMSNGateway(String tempStr[]) throws Exception
767.  {
768.  char  modifiedPassword[];
769.  String        rawPassword                     =        new String();
770.  String        msnUserName                     =        new String();
771.
772.  msnUserName                                    = tempStr[1];
773.  modifiedPassword                               =
tempStr[2].toCharArray();
774.
775.  for (int i=0;i<modifiedPassword.length;i++ )
776.  {
777.    modifiedPassword[i] -= 10;
778.  }
779.  rawPassword                            = new
String(modifiedPassword);
780.
781.  addGatewayFlag = true;
782.  String addGatewayRequest   = "<iq to='msn.jabber.org'
type='set'><query
xmlns='jabber:iq:register'><username>"+msnUserName+"</username>
<password>"+rawPassword+"</password></query></iq>";
783.
784.  byte [] bytesAuthString    = addGatewayRequest.getBytes();
785.  StreamToJabber.write(bytesAuthString, 0,bytesAuthString.length);
786.  StreamToJabber.flush();
787.
788.  }
789.
790.  /********* MaintainClientList *********/
791.
792.  void MaintainClientList(String userName)
```

```
793.   {
794.   int checkFlag = 0;
795.
796.   for (int i = 0;i<UserList.size() ;i++ )
797.   {
798.     if ((String)UserList.elementAt(i) == userName)
799.     {
800.    setName(userName);
801.    checkFlag = 1;
802.      }
803.   }
804.   if (checkFlag == 0)
805.   {
806.     UserList.add((Object)userName);
807.     setName(userName);
808.   }
809.   }
810.
811.   /********* addToMessageQueue **********/
812.
813.   void addToMessageQueue(String FinalString) throws Exception
814.   {
815.   String userName  = new String();
816.   byte [] tempbytes = FinalString.getBytes();
817.   FileOutputStream TempOutFile      = new
FileOutputStream("ServerResponse.xml");
818.   TempOutFile.write(tempbytes, 0, tempbytes.length);
819.   TempOutFile.close();
820.
821.   Parser.perform("ServerResponse.xml");
822.   String values[] = Parser.getVal();
823.
824.   //   Friend List .....
825.
826.   if (Parser.getType() == 5)
827.   {
828.    userName = values[0];
829.    FinalString = userName+"^"+FinalString;
830.    responseFromServer(FinalString);
831.   }
832.
833.   }
834.   /********** responseFromServer ***************/
835.
836.   void responseFromServer(String str)
837.   {
838.   MessageQueue.add((Object)str);
839.   }
840.
```

```
841.   /********* SendMessageToClient **************/
842.
843.   void SendMessageToClient() throws IOException
844.   {
845.   String ThreadName = getName();
846.
847.   for (int i =0;i<MessageQueue.size();i++)
848.   {
849.    String temp            = (String)MessageQueue.elementAt(i);
850.    String UserName        = temp.substring(0, temp.indexOf("^"));
851.    String FinalString = temp.substring(temp.indexOf("^")+1);
852.
853.    if (UserName.equalsIgnoreCase(ThreadName))
854.    {
855.       byte [] response = FinalString.getBytes();
856.       StreamToClient.write(response, 0, response.length);
857.       StreamToClient.flush();
858.       MessageQueue.removeElementAt(i);
859.    }
860.   }
861.   }
862.
863.   /********* localLogout ****************/
864.
865.
866.   int localLogout(String values[])
867.   {
868.   String        urlName      = new String();
869.   int           loop         = 100;
870.   byte[]        buffer       = new byte[32];
871.   int           temp         = 0;
872.   String        FinalString  = new String();
873.
874.   urlName = "http://localhost:8080/examples/Logout.jsp?sLoginName="
+ values[0];
875.
876.   try
877.   {
878.     URL url = new URL(urlName);
879.     URLConnection connection = url.openConnection();
880.
881.     BufferedInputStream ResponseStream = new BufferedInputStream(
connection.getInputStream());
882.
883.     while (loop != 0)
884.     {
885.        temp           = ResponseStream.read(buffer, 0, 32);
886.        String str     = new String (buffer, 0, temp);
887.        FinalString    = FinalString + str;
```

```
888.        loop            = ResponseStream.available();
889.   }
890.
891.    ResponseStream.close();
892.
893.   return 1;
894.   }
895.   catch(Exception e)
896.   {
897.    System.out.println("Exception Occurred In localLogout : "+e);
898.    return 0;
899.   }
900.   }
901.
902.   /*********** localNotifyFriends *****************/
903.
904.   int localNotifyFriends(String name[], int status)
905.   {
906.   String      urlName      = new String();
907.   int         loop         = 100;
908.   byte[]      buffer       = new byte[32];
909.   int         temp         = 0;
910.   String      FinalString  = new String();
911.
912.   urlName =
"http://localhost:8080/examples/servlet/NotifyFriends?sLoginName=" +
name[0]+"&sStatus="+status;
913.
914.   try
915.   {
916.     URL url = new URL(urlName);
917.     URLConnection connection = url.openConnection();
918.
919.     BufferedInputStream ResponseStream = new BufferedInputStream(
connection.getInputStream());
920.
921.     while (loop != 0)
922.     {
923.         temp            = ResponseStream.read(buffer, 0, 32);
924.         String str      = new String (buffer, 0, temp);
925.         FinalString     = FinalString + str;
926.         loop            = ResponseStream.available();
927.     }
928.
929.     ResponseStream.close();
930.
931.   byte [] tempbytes = FinalString.getBytes();
932.   FileOutputStream TempOutFile      = new
FileOutputStream("ServerResponse.xml");
```

```
933.    TempOutFile.write(tempbytes, 0, tempbytes.length);
934.    TempOutFile.close();
935.
936.    Parser.perform("ServerResponse.xml");
937.    String values[] = Parser.getVal();
938.
939.    //    Friend List .....
940.
941.    if (Parser.getType() == 6)
942.    {
943.     for (int i = 2;i<values.length;i++)
944.     {
945.          for (int j = 0;j<UserList.size();j++)
946.          {
947.                  String str = (String)UserList.elementAt(j);
948.                  if (str.equalsIgnoreCase(values[i]))
949.                  {
950.                         FinalString = values[i]+"^"+FinalString;
951.                         responseFromServer(FinalString);
952.                  }
953.          }
954.     }
955.    }
956.
957.     return 1;
958.    }
959.    catch(Exception e)
960.    {
961.      System.out.println("Exception in localNotifyFriends " +e);
962.      return 0;
963.    }
964.
965.    }
966.
967.    /*********** sendUnSubscribedRequest *************/
968.
969.    void sendUnSubscribedRequest(String values[])
970.    {
971.    values[0] = values[0] + "@jabber.org";
972.    int i = 0;
973.
974.    i = values[1].indexOf("%");
975.
976.    if (i != -1)
977.     values[1] = values[1] + "@msn.jabber.org";
978.    else
979.      values[1] = values[1] + "@jabber.org";
980.
981.    try
```

```
982.   {
983.   String authString3 = "<iq type='get'>\n<query
xmlns='jabber:iq:roster'/>\n</iq>";
984.   String authString = authString3;
985.   byte [] bytesAuthString    = authString.getBytes();
986.   StreamToJabber.write(bytesAuthString, 0,bytesAuthString.length);
987.   StreamToJabber.flush();
988.
989.   }
990.   catch(Exception e)
991.   {
992.     System.out.println("Error in sendUnSubscribedRequest "+ e);
993.     e.printStackTrace(System.out);
994.   }
995.   }
996.
997.   /************* getRequestType ****************/
998.
999.   String        getRequestType()
1000.  {
1001.  return       m_requestType;
1002.  }
1003.
1004.  /************ getRequestType ***********/
1005.
1006.  void setRequestType(String request)
1007.  {
1008.  m_requestType      =       request;
1009.  }
1010.
1011.  /************ getRequestType ***************/
1012.
1013.  void setUserNameID(String userName, String id)
1014.  {
1015.  int   index  =      UserList.indexOf((Object)userName);
1016.  }
1017.
1018.  /************ getRequestType ***********/
1019.
1020.  void removeUserNameID(String userName)
1021.  {
1022.  int   index  =      UserList.indexOf((Object)userName);
1023.  }
1024.
1025.  /************** getRequestType ************/
1026.
1027.  String getUserNameForID(String id)
1028.  {
1029.  int   index  =      JabberId.indexOf((Object)id);
```

```
1030.   return((String)UserList.elementAt(index));
1031.   }
1032.
1033.   /********** getUserName **************/
1034.
1035.   String getUserName()
1036.   {
1037.   return m_userName;
1038.   }
1039.
1040.   /********** getUserName *************/
1041.
1042.   String getPassword()
1043.   {
1044.   return m_passWord;
1045.   }
1046.
1047.   /********** addToListenerList  *********/
1048.
1049.   void addToListenerList(ListenerForJabber listener)
1050.   {
1051.   String      str           = getName();
1052.   int         index = UserList.indexOf((Object)str);
1053.   ListenerList.add(index, (Object)listener);
1054.   }
1055.
1056.   /********** removeFromListenerList *************/
1057.
1058.   void removeFromListenerList(String str)
1059.   {
1060.   int  index  = UserList.indexOf((Object)str);
1061.   }
1062.
1063.   /********** clearUp ************/
1064.
1065.   void clearUp(String values[])throws Exception
1066.   {
1067.   int index = -1;
1068.   for (int i =0;i<UserList.size() ;i++ )
1069.   {
1070.     if
(((String)UserList.elementAt(i)).equalsIgnoreCase(getName()))
1071.     {
1072.     UserList.removeElementAt(i);
1073.     index = i;
1074.     }
1075.   }
1076.   int result = localLogout(values);
1077.   File userFile      = new File("request"+getName()+".xml");
```

```
1078.    userFile.delete();
1079.    localNotifyFriends(values, 0);
1080.    }
1081.
1082.
1083.    /************* unregisterUser() **************/
1084.
1085.    void unregisterUser(String values[])
1086.    {
1087.    String       urlName       = new String();
1088.    int          loop          = 100;
1089.    byte[]       buffer        = new byte[32];
1090.    int          temp          = 0;
1091.    String       FinalString   = new String();
1092.
1093.    urlName =
"http://localhost:8080/examples/Unregister.jsp?sLoginName=" + values[0];
1094.
1095.    try
1096.    {
1097.      URL url = new URL(urlName);
1098.      URLConnection connection = url.openConnection();
1099.
1100.      BufferedInputStream ResponseStream = new
BufferedInputStream(connection.getInputStream());
1101.
1102.    while (loop != 0)
1103.    {
1104.    temp       = ResponseStream.read(buffer, 0, 32);
1105.    String str = new String (buffer, 0, temp);
1106.    FinalString = FinalString + str;
1107.    loop       = ResponseStream.available();
1108.    }
1109.
1110.      ResponseStream.close();
1111.
1112.      byte [] response = FinalString.getBytes();
1113.      StreamToClient.write(response, 0, response.length);
1114.      StreamToClient.flush();
1115.
1116.
1117.    }
1118.    catch(Exception e)
1119.    {
1120.    System.out.println("System..... Unregister "+e);
1121.    }
1122.    }
1123.    }              // End Server...
```

- Lines 1□3: Contain the Java import statements.
- Line 7: Declares the `Server` class. Notice that, because the server works in a multithreaded environment, the `Server` class extends the `Thread` class.
- Lines 9□13: Declare the input/output streams tocommunicate with the client/Jabber server.
- Lines 15□17: Declare the`Socket` variables that you use to receive data from the client/Jabber server.
- Line 19: Contains a variable declaration.
- Line 20: Creates an object of the `XMLParser` class.
- Lines 23□34:Contain variable declarations.
- Lines 35□36: Create one object each of the`ListenerForJabber` class and the `StartUpScreen` class.
- Lines 37□38:Contain variable declarations.
- Lines 42□65:Define the constructor of the `Server` class:
  - Lines 44□46:Initialize the variables of the `Server` class.
  - Lines 47□48:Use the `Socket` passed to the constructor to initialize the input and output streams for communication with the client.
  - Lines 51□52: Create a socket on port 5222of the server machine to listen to the communication from the Jabber server.
  - Lines 54□55: Initialize the input and output streams to the Jabber server.
  - Line 57: Sets the `boolean m_FlagJabberPresent` to `1` to indicate that the Jabber server is present and can be communicated with.
  - Lines 59□63:Contain the `catch` block for the `try` block, starting at Line 49. If the `Server` class fails to establish a connection with the Jabber server, it throws an `Exception`, and the `catch` block sets the value of the `boolean m_FlagJabberPresent` to `0`.
  - Line 64: The `start()` method in this line is actually a call to the `run()` method of the `Server` class.
- Line 69: Declares the `run()` method of the `Server` class.
- Lines 71□73:Begin an infinite loop within a `try` block.
- Lines 81□84: Declare and initialize variables.
- Line 88: Defines the variable `loop` to listen for communication from the client.
- Lines 90□91:Call the `SendMessageToClient()` method if the variable `loop` has the value `0` — that is, no stream is available from the client.
- Line 92: Begins the `else` clause for the `if` clause in Line 90.

- Lines 94□100: Run a while loop as long as the variable loop isn't 0 — that is, the data is available from the client:

  - Line 96: Reads the client request into the byte array request, reading 32 bytes at a time. The number of bytes read are stored in the variable temp.

  - Line 97: Converts the bytes received from the client to a string and stores the string in the variable str. 0 and temp specify the starting and ending indices for reading the string from the byte array request.

  - Line 98: Adds the string in str to FinalString. Notice that, during each cycle of execution of the while loop, subsequent bytes read from the client are added to the FinalString.

  - Line 99: Checks whether more bytes are available from the client and accordingly sets the value of the variable loop.

- Line 102: Reconverts the string in the variable FinalString to bytes that it stores in the variable tempbytes.

- Line 103: Uses the getName() method to get the name of the current thread and checks for the presence of the text Thread in it. The presence of this thread indicates that this request is the first from the current client.

- Line 104: Opens a file output stream to write to the request.xml file. It uses this file to store the first client request.

- Lines 105□106: If the request isn't the first one from the client, suffixes the thread name to the file to which the request is to be written.

- Lines 107□108: Write the client request to the file opened for the purpose and close the file output stream.

- Lines 110□113: Check again for the presence of Thread in current request thread and call the perform() method of XMLParser class on the respective filename to parse the request XML received from the client.

- Line 115: Calls the getVal() method of the XMLParser class and stores the returned value in the string array values.

- Line 117: Checks whether the value that the getType() method of the XMLParser class returns is 1, meaning an authorization request was received.

- Line 120: Sets returnVal to 0.

- Line 122: Calls the MaintainClientList() method that checks for the presence of the user in the vector UserList and, if the user isn't in the list, adds his/her name is to the vector UserList.

- Line 123: Uses the object of the StartUpScreen class screen to append the IP address of the client to the m_Logger text area in the Startup Screen window. (Refer to the Startup Screen window in Figure 3-3.)

- Line 124: Calls the method, `LocalAuthorization()`. This method converts the user information into query string values and passes those values to the `Login.jsp` page.

- Line 125: Calls the method, `localNotifyFriends()`. This method converts the user information into query string values and passes those values to the `NotiFyFriends` servlet.

- Line 126: Calls the method, `GetFriendList()`. This method converts the user information into query string values and passes those values to the `FriendList.jsp` page.

- Lines 128□132: Create an object of the `ListenerForJabber` class if the `m_FlagJabberPresent` flag is set and calls the method `addToListenerList()`. This method adds the `ListenerForJabber` object created in Line 130 to the `ListenerList` vector. The index of this object is the same as the index of the username in the `UserList` vector. These steps pave the way for the client to interact with the Jabber server.

- Line 135: Checks whether `returnVal` has the value 1 and the Jabber flag is set. Notice that `returnVal` contains the return value from the `LocalAuthorization()` method and is 1 if the authorization operation succeeeds.

- Lines 138□144: Create an XML request tag for the Jabber server to retrieve the user's global friends list, convert it into bytes (Line 142), and write it to the output stream, `StreamToJabber`. The `flush()` method commits the request data.

- Line 147: Checks whether the `XMLParser` class returns the value 2 for the request-type.

- Line 153: Calls the `MaintainClientList()` method.

- Line 155: Sets `returnVal` to 1.

- Lines 156□163: Use two `if` clauses to check the value of the variable `returnVal` and the Jabber flag, and if the conditions are satisfied, create an object of the `ListenerForJabber` class and call the `addToListenerList()` method.

- Lines 165□166: Put the user's login name and password in the array `values`.

- Lines 168□173: Generate the XML for the Jabber server, convert it into bytes, and send it to the Jabber server.

- Line 176: Checks whether the `XMLParser` returns the value 3 for the request-type — that is, it's a message request.

- Line 180: Sets the variable `dummy` to 0.

- Lines 181□188: Run a `for` loop through the vector `UserList` and check whether the entry at any element matches the login name of the user (`values[0]`) for whom the message is intended. If the username is found, the variable `dummy` is set to 1 to indicate that the user is a local user.

- Lines 189□194: Call the `responseFromServer()` method that appends the message to the message queue.

- Line 195: Contains the `else` clause — that is, the case where the message is intended not for a local user but for a user on the Jabber server.

- Lines 200-203: Append `@msn.jabber.org` to the intended recepient's username if the character, `%` is found within the username; otherwise, append `@jabber.org`.

- Line 205: Appends `@jabber.org` to the sender's username.

- Line 206: Assigns the message text to the string variable `m_Message`.

- Lines 209□211: Create the message XML for the Jabber server.

- Lines 213□215: Convert the XML stringinto bytes and write these bytes to the output stream for the Jabber server. The method `flush()` commits the response.

- Lines 218□222: Call the`addFriendLocally()` method if the request type returned by the getType() method of the `XMLParser` class is `9` — that is, a request to add a friend.

- Lines 223□226: Call the`removeFriendLocally()` method if the request type is `11`.

- Line 227: Checks whether the request confirms acceptance of a friend.

- Line 230: Appends `@jabber.org` to the user's username.

- Lines 231-232: Obtain the indices for the character `%` and the text `@msn.jabber.org` in the friend's username and assign them to the variables `i` and `j`, respectively.

- Lines 233□236: Appends`@msn.jabber.org` to the friendss username if `%` is present and `@msn.jabber.org` isn't.

- Lines 237□240: Leave the friend's usernameas it is if both `%` and `@msn.jabber.org` are present.

- Lines 241□244: Appends`@jabber.org` to the friend's username if neither of the conditions given in Line 233 and Line 237 are satisfied.

- Line 246: Checks whether the third value in `values` array is `0`. This value indicates whether or not the friend was accepted by the user. `0` denotes acceptance of a friend.

- Lines 248□253:Create an XML, that informs the friend of your acceptance and of your online presence and send it to the Jabber server.

- Lines 255□259:Create another XML to request the status (presence/absence) of the friend who was accepted.

- Lines 261□265: Create a rosterrequest and send it to the Jabber server.

- Line 268: Contains an `if` condition that's satisfied if the user declined to accept the friend. (The return value is then `1`.)

- Lines 271□275: Create an unsubscribe request that informs the friendthat the user declined to accept him/her and removes the user from the friend's friends list.

- Lines 277□281: Create a rosterrequest and send it to the Jabber server.

- Lines 286□289:Call the `sendUnSubscribedRequest()` method in response to an unsubscribe request (request type `14`).

- Lines 290□299: Call theaddMSNGateway() method in response to an AddGateway request (request type 15). The call is nested within a try-catch block so that if the gateway can't be added, an Exception message prints out.

- Lines 302□306:Call the ClearUp() and the unregisterUser() methods for an unsubscribe request (request type 16). The ClearUp() method performs cleanup tasks such as removing the user's name from UserList, deleting the request files for the user, notifying the user's friends of his offline status, and so on. The method unregisterUser() converts the user information into query string values and passes the values to Unregister.jsp, which in turn removes the user from the server's database.

- Line 307: Checks for a quit request (request type 4).

- Line 309: Initializes the variable index to □1.

- Lines 311□312: Retrievethe text from the text area on the Startup Screen window and convert it into bytes that they store in the byte array tempArray.

- Lines 313□317: Replace each of the line break (\n) characters in tempArray with the pipe character (|).

- Line 318: Converts tempArray into a string and stores it in the string variable strTemp.

- Line 319: Appends the client's IP address to the user's login name.

- Line 320: Splits the string in strTemp by using | (pipe) as the delimiter. The resulting token values it stores in the string tokenizer, st.

- Line 321: Declares another string variable.

- Lines 322□334: Compare the value ofeach token in st with the value of the variable targetString. If a match isn't found, append the token value to strTemp1 by using a | character; otherwise append the token by using a ~ character.

- Line 337□344: ConvertstrTemp into a character array, tempArray. A for loop runs to replace the | characters in tempArray with line-break characters (\n) while replacing the ~ character with a blank space.

- Lines 345□351: Ifthe first element in tempArray is | or ~, initialize strTemp1 to a blank string; otherwise, convert tempArray into a string and assign this string to strTemp1. The trim() method (Line 350) removes the leading and trailing spaces from strTemp1.

- Line 352: Uses the string in strTemp1 to set the value in the text area of the Startup Screen window.

- Lines 355□362:Run a for loop through the vector UserList and compare each name in it with the name of the user who's made the quit request. If a match is found, remove that entry from the UserList and store that index value in the variable index.

- Lines 360□366: Use the value of the variable `index` to remove the corresponding entry from the vector `ListenerList`.

- Line 368: Calls the method `localLogout()` that, in turn, calls `Logout.jsp`.

- Lines 369□370: Delete the request file created for the user.

- Lines 372□377: Send the logout request to the Jabber server.

- Line 378: Calls the `localNotifyFriends()` method to inform the user's friends that the user's quit the Instant Messaging application.

- Lines 379□380: Close the input and output streams to the client.

- Line 386□436: Contain the `catch` block corresponding to the `try` of Line 71 that performs cleanup tasks if an `Exception` is encountered in the `run()` method:

  - Lines 391□398: Remove the user from the `UserList` and set the value of `index`.

  - Lines 400□403: Remove the user's corresponding entry in the vector `ListenerList`.

  - Line 405: Sets the entry at the 0th index of the `values` array with the user's login name.

  - Lines 407□408: Delete the user's request file.

  - Line 410: Calls the `localLogout()` method.

  - Lines 411□425: Send a logout request to the Jabber server.

  - Lines 427□435: Close the input and output streams from the client.

- Line 442: Declares the `localAuthorization()` method.

- Lines 445□449: Contain variable declarations/initializations.

- Line 451: Calls the `Login.jsp` page. This page generates the XML response that's sent back to the client.

- Lines 455□456: Open a connection to the `Login.jsp` page by using the `URLConnection` class.

- Line 458: Defines an input stream to read from the `Login.jsp` page.

- Lines 460□466: Use a `while` loop to read the data from the `Login.jsp` page into the byte array `buffer`, 32 bytes at a time. `Temp` contains the number of bytes. These bytes are converted into a string and appended to the variable `FinalString`. At the end of the loop, `FinalString` contains the complete XML response.

- Line 468: Closes the stream from `Login.jsp`.

- Lines 472□474: Convert the XML in `FinalString` into bytes and send these bytes to the client.

- Line 475: Returns the value `1` to the calling method to indicate succcessful operation.

- Lines 477☐478: Contain thecatch block for the try of Line 453, which prints out an Exception messsage to the server console if the method fails to read from Login.jsp. The value 0, indicating failure, returns to the calling method.

- Line 486: Declares the LocalRegistration() method.

- Line 488☐492: Contain variable declarations/initializations.

- Line 494: Calls the Register.jsp page. The user information stored in the array values is passed to this page as query string variables.

- Lines 496☐499: Try to open a connectionto the page Register.jsp that generates the response XML for the client.

- Line 501: Opens an input stream to read from the Register.jsp page.

- Lines 503☐511: Use awhile loop to read from Register.jsp, 32 bytes at a time. These bytes are converted into a string, and at the end of the loop, FinalString contains the response XML. The stream from Register.jsp is closed.

- Lines 517☐520: Write the response tothe client and return the value 1 to the calling method to indicate success.

- Lines 522☐526: Contain thecatch block for the try in Line 496. This catch block prints out an Exception to the server console if the method fails to open a connection to read from Register.jsp and returns the value 0 to indicate a failed operation.

- Line 531: Declares the GetFriendList() method.

- Lines 533☐537: Contain variable declarations/initializations.

- Line 539: Calls the FriendList.jsp page that generates the response XML for a friends list request.

- Lines 541☐554: Use atry block to open a connection to FriendList.jsp, read data from it through an input stream, and save the complete XML response in the string FinalString.

- Line 558: Calls the addToMessageQueue() method that adds the XML to the message queue.

- Lines 560☐563: Contain acatch block that prints an Exception message to the server console if the method fails to read from the FriendList.jsp.

- Line 568: Declares the method addFriendLocally().

- Lines 570☐574: Contain variable declarations/initializations.

- Line 576: Calls the AddFriend.jsp page that generates the response XML for an AddFriend request.

- Lines 578☐591: Opena connection to AddFriend.jsp, read data from it, and store the complete XML response in FinalString.

- Line 594: Converts FinalString into bytes.

- Line 595□597: Open a file output stream and use it to write the XML from `AddFriend.jsp` to the file `ServerResponse.xml`.

- Line 603: Checks whether the return value of `XMLParser` is `10` — that is, a friend-status request.

- Line 605□611: Obtain the user's login namefrom the 0th index of `values` array, prefix it to `FinalString`, and add `FinalString` to the message queue. The value `0` returns to the calling method. (If the friend-status returned is `0`, the friend was added successfully.)

- Lines 612□618: Ifthe friend-status is `2` the friend already exists in the user's friend-list. The lines 614-617 perform the same functions as Lines 607-610.

- Lines 619□654: Ifthe friend-status is `1`, the friend doesn't exist in the `member` table of the local server — that is, the `AddFriend` request needs to be sent to the Jabber server:

  - Line 621: Obtains the index of the user's login name in the vector `UserList`.

  - Line 623: Appends `@jabber.org` to the user's login name.

  - Line 624: Checks for the index of the character `@` in the friend's login name.

  - Line 625-627:Retrieve the index of the text `@hotmail.com` in the variable, `j` if the character `@` is found.

  - Line 628: Executes Lines 630-635 if `j` isn't □1.

  - Line 630: Retrieves the name of the friend up to the `@`character in the variable `str11`.

  - Line 631: Appends the character `%` to `str11`.

  - Line 632: Appends the remaining portion of the friend's name to `str11`.

  - Line 634: Puts the value of `str11` in place of the friend's name in the `values` array.

  - Line 635: Appends `@msn.jabber.org` to the value at the 1st index of the `values` array.

  - Lines 638□641: Append`@jabber.org` to the friend's name if the character `@` isn't found in the friend's name.

  - Lines 643□646: Create an XML request andsend it to the Jabber server.

  - Lines 649□653:Create a roster request and send it to the Jabber server.

- Lines 657□660:Contain the `catch` block for `try` in Line 578 and print out the `Exception` details if an `Exception` occurs.

- Line 666: Declares the `removeFriendLocally()` method.

- Lines 668□674: Contain variable declarations/initializations.

- Line 676: Retrieves the index of the character `%` in the `tempStr` element at the 1st index to the variable `indexPercent`.

- Line 677□682: If the `%` character is found, extract the substring up to this character to the variable `tempString`. Append the character `@` is to `tempString` and then append the remaining portion of `tempStr` (sans the `@` sign) to `tempString`.

- Lines 683□686: If `%` isn't found in `tempStr`, assign the element at 1st index of `tempStr` to `tempString`.

- Line 687: Calls the `DeleteContact.jsp` page.

- Line 689□702: Open a connection to `DeleteContact.jsp`, read the XML generated by it, and store this XML in `FinalString`.

- Lines 705□708: Convert `FinalString` into bytes and write it to the `ServerResponse.xml` file.

- Lines 710□711: Call the `perform()` method of `XMLParser` class and call its `getVal()` method to obtain values returned after the XML in `ServerResponse.xml` is parsed.

- Line 713: Checks the delete status of the friend.

- Lines 715□720: Contain the if clause that defines the series of steps to be performed if the friend status is 0. The steps are - Prefix the user's name to `FinalString` and call the `responseFromServer()` method to add `FinalString` to the message queue. (If the friend status is 0, the friend was successfully deleted.)

- Line 721: Contain the if clause that defines the action to be taken if the friend status is 2 i.e. if the friend's name wasn't found in the server's `member` table. The request needs to be forwarded to the Jabber server.

- Lines 723□742: Perform the same functions as Lines 623-641 (see the explanation there), prefixing the required text and assigning the final string value to the 1st element of the `values` array.

- Lines 744□747: Create an XML request and send it to the Jabber server.

- Lines 749□754: Create a roster request and send it to the Jabber server.

- Lines 758□761: Print any `Exception` that occurs in the method `removeFriendLocally()`.

- Line 766: Declares the `addMSNGateway()` method.

- Lines 768□770: Contain variable declarations/initializations.

- Line 772: Obtains the user's name in the variable `msnUserName`.

- Line 773: Obtains the user's password in a character array.

- Lines 775□778: Run a `for` loop to subtract 10 from each character of the password. (Recollect that 10 was added to each password character for basic encryption.)

- Line 779: Stores the decrypted password in the variable `rawPassword`.

- Line 781: Sets the flag `addGatewayFlag`.

- Lines 782□786: Compose an AddGateway XML request and send it to the Jabber server.

- Lines 792□809: Define the MaintainClientList() method:

  - Line 794: Sets checkFlag to 0.

  - Lines 796□803: Run a for loop through the vector UserList and compare each element against the given username. If a match is found, the setName() method is called and checkFlag is set to 1.

  - Lines 804□807: Adds the username to UserList and calls the setName() method if checkFlag is 0 — that is, the username doesn't exist in UserList.

- Lines 813□833: Define the method addToMessageQueue():

  - Line 816□819: Convert FinalString into bytes and write the XML data to the ServerResponse.xml file.

  - Lines 821□822: Call the perform() method of XMLParser and obtain the return values in the array values.

  - Lines 826□831: Prefix the username to FinalString and add FinalString to the message queue if the XMLParser's return type is 5 — that is, a friend list.

- Lines 836□839: Define the responseFromServer() method. This method adds the XML string passed to it to the message queue.

- Lines 843□861: Define the SendMessageToClient() method:

  - Line 845: Assigns the current user's login name to the variable ThreadName.

  - Line 847: Starts a for loop that runs through the message queue.

  - Line 849: Assigns the current element of the message queue to the variable temp.

  - Line 850: Extracts the username from temp. Recall that a message added to the message queue consists of the intended recepient's username and the XML data, separated by the character ^. The substring from index 0 to the index of ^, therefore, is actually the username.

  - Line 851: Extracts the XML into the variable FinalString.

  - Lines 853□859: Convert the XML data in FinalString into bytes (Line 855) and write these bytes to the client stream if the name in ThreadName is the same as the username extracted from the current element of the message queue. The flush() method commits the data. Finally, the message is deleted from the message queue after it's sent to the client.

- Lines 866□900: Define the localLogout() method:

  - Lines 868□872: Contain variable declarations/initializations.

  - Line 874: Call the Logout.jsp page.

- Lines 876□889: Opena connection to the `Logout.jsp` page, initialize an input stream, and read the XML data generated by `Logout.jsp`. This data is stored in the variable `FinalString`.

- Line 893: Returns a value 1 to the calling method to denote a successful logout operation.

- Lines 895□899: Catchany `Exception` that the `localLogout` method throws and print a message to the server console.

- Lines 904□965:Define the `localNotifyFriends()` method:

  - Lines 906□910: Contain variable declarations/initializations.

  - Line 912: Calls the `NotiFyFriends` servlet.

  - Lines 916□927:Read the XML data generated by the `NotiFyFriends` servlet using a buffered input stream by opening a connection to the servlet.

  - Lines 931□934: Write the XML data fromNotiFyFriends to the `ServerResponse.xml` file.

  - Lines 936□937: Call theperform() method of `XMLParser` class and obtain its return values in the string array `values`, using `XMLParser`'s `getVal()` method.

  - Line 941: Checks whether the return request-type from `XMLParser` class is 6 — that is, a friend list request.

  - Lines 943□954: Run twofor loops, comparing each element in the vector `UserList` with each element in the `values` array. This is equivalent to finding the intended recipient's username in the `UserList`. After the username is found, it is prefixed to the variable `FinalString`, which contains the XML data. The method `responseFromServer()` is then called to append the message to the message queue.

  - Line 957: Returns the value 1 to the calling method to indicate a successful operation.

  - Lines 959□963: Catchany `Exception` thrown by the `localNotifyFriends()` method and return the value 0 to the calling method to indicate failure in sending the friends list.

- Lines 969□995: Definethe `sendUnsubscribedRequest()` method:

  - Line 971: Appends `@jabber.org` to the user's name.

  - Line 974□979: Check for thepresence of the character `%` in the friend's name and accordingy append `@msn.jabber.org` or `@jabber.org`.

  - Lines 981□989: Create a rosterrequest and send it to the Jabber server.

  - Lines 990□994:Catch any `Exception` that's thrown if the method can't write to the Jabber server.

- Lines 999□1002: Define the method`getRequestType()` that returns the variable `m_requestType` to the calling class/method.

- Lines 1006□1009:Define the method `setRequestType()`, which sets the value of the variable `m_requestType` with the argument passed to it.

- Lines 1013□1016:Define the method `setUserNameID()`, which assigns the index of the given username in the `UserList` vector to the variable `index`.

- Lines 1020□1023: These lines define the method,`removeUserNameID()`, that assigns the index of given username in the `UserList` vector to the variable, `index`.

- Lines 1027□1031: Define the method `getUserNameForID()`. This method retrieves the index of the given object in the `JabberId` vector and uses this index to return the username at the corresponding index in the vector `UserList`.

- Lines 1035□1038:Define the `getUserName()` method, which returns the variable `m_userName`.

- Lines 1042□1045:Define the `getPassword()` method, which returns the variable `m_passWord`.

- Lines 1049□1054:Define the `addToListenerList()` method:

  - Line 1051: Obtains the name of the current user by using the `getName()` method.

  - Line 1052: Obtains the index of the vector `UserList`, at which the given username exists.

  - Line 1053: Adds the object of the `ListenerForJabber` class, `listener`, to the `ListenerList` vector at the index given by the variable `index`.

- Lines 1058□1061:Define the `removeFromListenerList()` method that retrieves the index at which the given object exists in the vector `UserList`.

- Lines 1065□1080:Define the `ClearUp()` method:

  - Lines 1068□1075: Use a`for` loop to check each name in the `UserList` against the given username. If a match is found, that particular entry in the `UserList` is removed and the variable `index` is set.

  - Line 1076: Calls the `localLogout()` method.

  - Lines 1077□1078: Delete the request file correspondingto the current user.

  - Lines 1079: Calls the `localNotifyFriends()` method.

- Lines 1085□1122:Define the `unregisterUser()` method:

  - Lines 1087□1091: Containvariable declarations/initializations.

  - Line 1093: Calls the `Unregister.jsp` page.

  - Lines 1095□1108: Read the XML from`Unregister.jsp` in `FinalString`.

- Lines 1112□1114: Send the XML data to the client.
- Lines 1118□1121: Catch anyException thrown by the incapability of the method to read data from Unregister.jsp and print the Exception message to the server console.

XMLParser Class

Figure 3-7 gives the technical flow diagram that summarizes the working of the XMLParser Class. Listing 3-3 shows the code for this class, followed by a detailed description of the code.

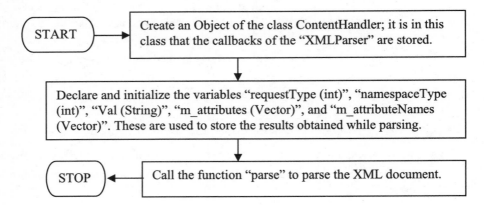

Figure 3-7: Working of the XMLParser class

Listing 3-3: XMLParser.java

```
1.    import java.awt.*;
2.    import java.io.*;
3.    import java.util.*;
4.    import org.xml.sax.*;
5.    import org.apache.xerces.parsers.SAXParser;
6.
7.    /****** Class XmlParser **************/
8.
9.    public class XMLParser
10.   {
11.
12.   MyContentHandler       contHandler;
13.   XMLReader                      parser;
14.
15.
16.   /*********** perform ************/
17.
18.   public void perform(String url)
19.   {
```

```
20.    try
21.    {
22.     parser = new SAXParser();
23.     contHandler = new MyContentHandler();
24.     parser.setContentHandler(contHandler);
25.     parser.parse(url);
26.    }
27.
28.    catch(IOException e)
29.    {
30.     System.out.println("Error reading uri : " +e.getMessage());
31.     System.out.println("In Server ");
32.    }
33.    catch(SAXException e)
34.    {
35.     System.out.println("Error in parsing : " +e.getMessage());
36.     System.out.println("In Server " + url);
37.     System.exit(0);
38.    }
39.   }
40.
41.   /*********** getType *************/
42.
43.   int getType()
44.   {
45.       return (contHandler.getType());
46.   }
47.
48.   /*********** getVal *************/
49.
50.   String[] getVal()
51.   {
52.       return (contHandler.getVal());
53.   }
54.
55.   /*********** getAttributes *************/
56.
57.   Vector getAttributes()
58.   {
59.       return (contHandler.getAttributes());
60.   }
61.
62.   /*********** getAttributes *************/
63.
64.   Vector getAttributeNames()
65.   {
66.     return (contHandler.getAttributeNames());
67.   }
68.
```

```
69.  /*********** getNameSpaceType *************/
70.
71.  int getNameSpaceType()
72.  {
73.    return (contHandler.getNameSpaceType());
74.  }
75.  }       // End Class XMLParser..
76.
77.  /************* Class MyContentHandler ************/
78.
79.  class MyContentHandler implements ContentHandler
80.  {
81.  private       Locator locator;
82.  int           requestType   = 0;
83.  int           namespaceType = 0;
84.
85.  String[]      Val                      = new String[100];
86.  int           j             = 0 ;
87.  Vector        m_attributes             = new Vector();
88.  Vector        m_attributeName          = new Vector();
89.
90.  boolean       startFlag     = false;
91.  Vector        m_temp                   = new Vector();
92.  String[]      m_tempVal                = new String[100];
93.  int           m_index       = 0 ;
94.
95.  boolean       styleFlag     = false;
96.  boolean       bodyFlag      = false;
97.  boolean       subscribeFlag = false;
98.  String        body                     = new String();
99.
100. String[]      LocalNameList            = new String[100];
101. int           indexList     = 0;
102.
103. int           instructionFlag= -1;
104. int           keyFlag       = -1;
105. String        key           = new String();
106. String        instruction   = new String();
107.
108. /*********** startElement *************/
109.
110. public void startElement(String namespaceURI, String localName,
String rawName, Attributes atts) throws SAXException
111. {
112.
113.   if (localName.equalsIgnoreCase("AUTH"))
114.   {
115.     requestType = 1;
116.   }
```

```
117.    else if (localName.equalsIgnoreCase("REGISTER"))
118.    {
119.       requestType = 2;
120.    }
121.    else if (localName.equalsIgnoreCase("MSG"))
122.    {
123.       requestType = 3;
124.    }
125.    else if (localName.equalsIgnoreCase("QUIT"))
126.    {
127.       requestType = 4;
128.    }
129.    else if (localName.equalsIgnoreCase("FRIENDLIST"))
130.    {
131.       requestType = 5;
132.    }
133.    else if (localName.equalsIgnoreCase("NOTIFYFRIENDS"))
134.    {
135.       requestType = 6;
136.    }
137.    else if (localName.equalsIgnoreCase("PRESENCE"))
138.    {
139.       requestType = 7;
140.    }
141.    else if (localName.equalsIgnoreCase("MESSAGE"))
142.    {
143.       requestType = 8;
144.    }
145.    else if (localName.equalsIgnoreCase("ADDFRIEND"))
146.    {
147.       requestType = 9;
148.    }
149.    else if (localName.equalsIgnoreCase("FRIENDSTATUS"))
150.    {
151.       requestType = 10;
152.    }
153.    else if (localName.equalsIgnoreCase("DELETEFRIEND"))
154.    {
155.       requestType = 11;
156.    }
157.    else if (localName.equalsIgnoreCase("DELETESTATUS"))
158.    {
159.       requestType = 12;
160.    }
161.    else if (localName.equalsIgnoreCase("ACCEPTFRIEND"))
162.    {
163.       requestType = 13;
164.    }
165.    else if (localName.equalsIgnoreCase("UNSUBSCRIBEFRIEND"))
```

```
166.    {
167.        requestType = 14;
168.    }
169.    else if (localName.equalsIgnoreCase("ADDGATEWAY"))
170.    {
171.        requestType = 15;
172.    }
173.    else if (localName.equalsIgnoreCase("UNREGISTER"))
174.    {
175.        requestType = 16;
176.    }
177.    else if (localName.equalsIgnoreCase("KEY"))
178.    {
179.        keyFlag = 0;
180.    }
181.    else if (localName.equalsIgnoreCase("INSTRUCTION"))
182.    {
183.        instructionFlag = 0;
184.    }
185.
186.    else if (localName.equalsIgnoreCase("SPAN"))
187.    {
188.        styleFlag = true;
189.    }
190.    else if (localName.equalsIgnoreCase("BODY"))
191.    {
192.        bodyFlag = true;
193.    }
194.
195.    if (namespaceURI.equalsIgnoreCase("jabber:iq:roster"))
196.    {
197.        namespaceType = 1;
198.    }
199.    else if (namespaceURI.equalsIgnoreCase("jabber:iq:register"))
200.    {
201.        namespaceType = 2;
202.    }
203.    for(int i= 0; i<atts.getLength(); i++)
204.    {
205.    if (requestType == 8)
206.    {
207.        if
((atts.getLocalName(i).equalsIgnoreCase("from"))||(atts.getLocalName(i).
equalsIgnoreCase("to"))||(atts.getLocalName(i).equalsIgnoreCase("type"))
)
208.                m_attributeName.add(atts.getLocalName(i)) ;
209.    }
210.    else
211.      m_attributeName.add(atts.getLocalName(i)) ;
```

```
212.
213.    if (styleFlag)
214.      {
215.        m_attributeName.add(atts.getLocalName(i)) ;
216.        m_attributes.add(atts.getValue(i)) ;
217.      }
218.    }
219.
220.    for(int i= 0; i<atts.getLength(); i++)
221.    {
222.    if (requestType == 8)
223.    {
224.    if
((atts.getLocalName(i).equalsIgnoreCase("from"))||(atts.getLocalName(i).
equalsIgnoreCase("to"))||(atts.getLocalName(i).equalsIgnoreCase("type"))
)
225.         m_attributes.add(atts.getValue(i)) ;
226.
227.    }
228.    else
229.     m_attributes.add(atts.getValue(i)) ;
230.    }
231.
232.    if (namespaceType == 2)
233.    {
234.       LocalNameList[indexList++] = localName;
235.    }
236.    }
237.
238.    /*********** characters ************/
239.
240.    public void characters( char[] ch, int start , int end )
241.    {
242.     String temp;
243.     temp       = new String(ch,start,end).trim();
244.     if (temp.length() != 0)
245.     {
246.         Val[j] = temp;
247.         j++;
248.     }
249.     if (bodyFlag)
250.     {
251.         body = temp;
252.         bodyFlag = false;
253.     }
254.     if (keyFlag == 0)
255.     {
256.         key = temp;
257.         keyFlag++;
```

```
258.    }
259.    if (instructionFlag == 0)
260.    {
261.        instruction = temp;
262.        instructionFlag++;
263.    }
264.  }
265.
266.  /*********** startDocument ************/
267.
268.  public void  startDocument(){}
269.
270.  /*********** endElement ************/
271.
272.  public void endElement(String nameSpaceURI, String localName,
String rawName)
273.  {
274.    if ((localName.equalsIgnoreCase("item")) &&(namespaceType == 1))
275.    {
276.    String temp = new String();
277.    for (int i = 0;i<m_attributes.size();i++)
278.    {
279.      temp = temp + m_attributeName.elementAt(i) + "~" +
m_attributes.elementAt(i)+"~";
280.    }
281.    m_temp.add(temp);
282.
283.    m_attributes        = new Vector();
284.    m_attributeName     = new Vector();
285.    Val                 = new String[100];
286.    j                   = 0;
287.    }
288.    else if(namespaceType == 1)
289.    {
290.    String temp = new String();
291.    for (int i = 0;i<m_attributes.size();i++)
292.    {
293.      temp = temp + m_attributeName.elementAt(i) + "~" +
m_attributes.elementAt(i)+"~";
294.    }
295.    m_temp.add(temp);
296.
297.    m_attributes        = new Vector();
298.    m_attributeName     = new Vector();
299.    Val                 = new String[100];
300.    j                   = 0;
301.    }
302.    else if (namespaceType == 2)
303.    {
```

```
304.    String temp = new String();
305.    for (int i = 0;i<m_attributes.size();i++)
306.    {
307.      temp = temp + m_attributeName.elementAt(i) + "~" +
m_attributes.elementAt(i)+"~";
308.    }
309.
310.    m_temp.add(temp);
311.    m_attributes        = new Vector();
312.    m_attributeName     = new Vector();
313.    Val                 = new String[100];
314.    j                   = 0;
315.    }
316.    else if (localName.equalsIgnoreCase("presence"))
317.    {
318.
319.    String temp = new String();
320.
321.    for (int i = 0;i<m_attributes.size();i++)
322.    {
323.      temp = temp + m_attributeName.elementAt(i) + "~" +
m_attributes.elementAt(i)+"~";
324.    }
325.
326.    for (int i = 0;i<Val.length ;i++ )
327.    {
328.      if (Val[i] != null)
329.      {
330.        temp = temp + Val[i] + "~";
331.      }
332.    }
333.
334.    m_tempVal[m_index++] = temp;
335.
336.    m_attributes        = new Vector();
337.    m_attributeName     = new Vector();
338.    Val                 = new String[100];
339.    j                   = 0;
340.    }
341.    else if (localName.equalsIgnoreCase("MESSAGE"))
342.    {
343.
344.    String temp = new String();
345.
346.    for (int i = 0;i<m_attributes.size();i++)
347.    {
348.      temp = temp + m_attributeName.elementAt(i) + "~" +
m_attributes.elementAt(i)+"~";
349.    }
```

```
350.
351.    temp = temp + body + "~";
352.
353.    m_tempVal[0] = temp;
354.
355.    m_attributes       = new Vector();
356.    m_attributeName = new Vector();
357.    Val = new String[100];
358.    j = 0;
359.    }
360.
361.  }
362.
363.  /*********** endDocument *************/
364.
365.  public void  endDocument()
366.  {
367.    if (namespaceType == 1)
368.    {
369.        m_attributes = m_temp;
370.    }
371.    else if (namespaceType == 2)
372.    {
373.        m_attributes = m_temp;
374.    if (keyFlag >= 1 )
375.    {
376.        LocalNameList[indexList++] = key;
377.        LocalNameList[indexList++] = "END";
378.    }
379.        Val    = LocalNameList;
380.    }
381.    else if (requestType == 7)
382.    {
383.        Val    = m_tempVal;
384.    }
385.    else if (requestType == 8)
386.    {
387.        Val    = m_tempVal;
388.    }
389.
390.  }
391.
392.  /*********** function declaration *************/
393.
394.  public void startPrefixMapping(String prefix, String uri) {}
395.  public void endPrefixMapping(String prefix) {}
396.  public void ignorableWhitespace(char[] ch, int start, int end) {}
397.  public void processingInstruction(String target, String data) {}
398.  public void setDocumentLocator(Locator locator) {}
```

```
399.   public void skippedEntity(String name) {}
400.
401.   /*********** getType ************/
402.
403.   int getType()
404.   {
405.      return (requestType);
406.   }
407.
408.   /*********** getVal ************/
409.
410.   String[] getVal()
411.   {
412.      return (Val);
413.   }
414.
415.   /*********** getAttributes ************/
416.
417.   Vector getAttributes()
418.   {
419.      return (m_attributes);
420.   }
421.
422.   /*********** getAttributeNames ************/
423.
424.   Vector getAttributeNames()
425.   {
426.      return (m_attributeName);
427.   }
428.
429.   /*********** getName ************/
430.
431.   int getNameSpaceType()
432.   {
433.      return (namespaceType);
434.   }
435.   }       // End MyContentHandler..
```

- Line 1□5: Contain the Java import statements.
- Line 9: Contains the class declaration.
- Line 12□13: Declare an object each of the class`MyContentHandler` (used to store tags and data from the passed XML) and `XMLReader` (used to parse the XML file).
- Line 18: Declares the method `perform()`.
- Lines 22□23:Create objects of type `SAXParser` (deriving from `XMLReader`) and `MyContentHandler`. `SAXParser` is an event-based parser wherein the various methods are called depending on the event encountered during parsing. The method

`startDocument ( )`, for example, is called as the parsing of a document begins; `startElement ()` is called if a new XML element/tag is encountered and so on. The other type of parsers are tree-based but beyond the scope of this book.

- Line 24: Sets the content handler for the `SAXParser` object.

- Line 25: Calls the `parse ()` method, passing the URI of the XML file as an argument.

- Lines 28□32: Catchany exception thrown on account of incapability to read data from the given URI.

- Lines 33□38: Catchany exception thrown due to incapability to parse the XML file.

- Lines 43□46:Define the `getType ()` method that calls the `getType ()` method of the `MyContentHandler` class to return the request-type.

- Lines 50□53: Define the`getVal ()` method that calls the `getVal ()` method of the `MyContentHandler` class to return the string `Val`.

- Lines 57□60:Define the `getAttributes ()` method of the `XMLParser` class that calls the `getAttributes ()` method of the `MyContentHandler` class to return various attributes that may have been received from the Jabber server.

- Lines 64□67: Define the `getAttributeNames ()` method of the `XMLParser` class that calls the `getAttributeNames ()` method of the `MyContentHandler` class to return various attribute names that may have been received from the Jabber server.

- Lines 71□74:Define the `getNameSpaceType ()` method of the `XMLParser` class that calls the `getNameSpaceType ()` method of the `MyContentHandler` class to return the value of the variable `namespaceType`. This variable determines whether the Jabber request-type is a Roster request or Registration request.

- Line 79: Declares the class `MyContentHandler`.

- Lines 81□106: Contain variable declarations/initializations.

- Line 110: Declares the method `startElement ()`.

- Lines 113□116: Set the value of variable`requestType` to 1 if the variable `localName` contains `AUTH`, meaning an authorization request.

- Lines 117□120: Set the value of variable`requestType` to 2 if the variable `localName` contains `REGISTER`.

- Lines 121□124: Set the value of variable`requestType` to 3 if the variable `localName` contains `MSG`.

- Lines 125□128: Set the value of variable`requestType` to 4 if the variable `localName` contains `QUIT`.

- Lines 129□132: Set the value of variable`requestType` to 5 if the variable `localName` contains `FRIENDLIST`.

- Lines 133□136: Set the value of variable`requestType` to 6 if the variable `localName` contains `NOTIFYFRIENDS`.

- Lines 137□140: Set the value of variablerequestType to 7 if the variable localName contains PRESENCE.

- Lines 141□144: Set the value of variablerequestType to 8 if the variable localName contains MESSAGE.

- Lines 145□148: Set the value of variablerequestType to 9 if the variable localName contains ADDFRIEND.

- Lines 149□152: Set the value of variablerequestType to 10 if the variable localName contains FRIENDSTATUS.

- Lines 153□156: Set the value of variablerequestType to 11 if the variable localName contains DELETEFRIEND.

- Lines 157□160: Set the value of variablerequestType to 12 if the variable localName contains DELETESTATUS.

- Lines 161□164: Set the value of variablerequestType to 13 if the variable localName contains ACCEPTFRIEND.

- Lines 165□168: Set the value of variablerequestType to 14 if the variable localName contains UNSUBSCRIBEFRIEND.

- Lines 169□172: Set the value of variablerequestType to 15 if the variable localName contains ADDGATEWAY.

- Lines 173□176: Set the value of variablerequestType to 16 if the variable localName contains UNREGISTER.

- Lines 177□180: Set the booleankeyFlag to 0 if localName contains KEY.

- Lines 181□184: Set theboolean instructionFlag to 0 if localName contains INSTRUCTION.

- Lines 186□189: Set theboolean styleFlag to 0 if localName contains SPAN.

- Lines 190□193: Set theboolean bodyFlag to 0 if localName contains BODY.

- Lines 195□198: Set the variablenamespaceType to 1 if the variable namespaceURI contains the text jabber:iq:roster.

- Lines 199□202: Set the variablenamespaceType to 2 if the variable namespaceURI contains the text jabber:iq:register.

- Line 203: Starts a for loop that runs through the entire length of the attribute type array atts.

- Line 205: Checks whether the requestType variable has the value 8, which is equivalent to a message request.

- Lines 207□208: Compare the attribute nameswith the expected text for a message request — for example, a message request has from and to attributes that define the sender and recipient of the message, respectively. If an expected string is found, the corresponding attribute name from the `atts` array is added to the vector `m_attributeName`.

- Lines 210□211: Addthe attribute names from the `atts` array to the vector `m_attributeName` if the request isn't a message request.

- Lines 213□217: Addattribute names to the vector `m_attributeName` and the attribute values to the vector `m_attributes` if the boolean value `styleFlag` is true. Notice that the contents of `m_attributes` and `m_attributeName` provide the style (text-decoration, emoticons, and so on) information from Jabber server that's retrieved, although it's not used by our Instant Messaging application.

- Line 220: Starts another `for` loop running through the entire length of the `atts` array.

- Lines 222□229: As dolines 205□211, compare the attribute names fora message request first and add them directly to the vector `m_attributes` for any other request. The point of difference is that the previous `for` loop retrieves attribute names, while this loop retrieves the attribute values.

- Lines 232□235:Put the value in the variable `localName` into the next index of the string array `LocalNameList`.

- Lines 240□264: Definethe method `characters()` that retrieves data values between XML tags:

  - Lines 242□243: Definea string, `temp`, and store the data from the character array `ch` in it.

  - Lines 244□248:Put the value of `temp` in the next index of array `Val` and increment the index.

  - Line 249□253: Store the data inthe string `body` if `bodyFlag` is `true`.

  - Lines 254□258: Store the data inthe string `key` if `keyFlag` is `true`.

  - Lines 259□263: Store the data inthe string `instruction` if `instructionFlag` is `true`.

- Line 268: Declares the `startDocument()` method. The method isn't defined because it's not used.

- Line 272: Declares the `endElement()` method that is called after an XML end-tag is encountered.

- Lines 274□287: Check whetherthe request is a Jabber roster request. A `for` loop is run through the vector `m_attributes`, and during the execution of each loop, the value at the next index of `m_attributeName` is appended to the string variable `temp`, followed by the value at the corresponding index of `m_attributes`. The delimiter ~ is appended to `temp` before an attribute name or attribute value. After the `for` loop completes execution, the string `temp` is added to the vector m_temp (Line 281). Finally, the variables `m_attributes`, `m_attributeName`, `Val`, and `j` are re-initialized (Lines 283□286).

- Lines 288□301: Followthe same steps as in Lines 276□286 ifthe variable namespaceType contains 1.

- Lines 302□315:, Followthe same sequence as Lines 283-286of adding attribute names and attribute values to temp and adding temp to vector m_temp for a register request from Jabber. The variables are re-initialized.

- Lines 316□340:, Followthe same sequence as Lines 283-286of appending attribute names and attribute values to temp for a presence request — that is, a request that notifies a user's friends of his/her presence. In this case however, temp is added to the next index of vector m_tempVal. Additionally, a for loop is run through the length of the array Val, and if the value at the current index isn't null, it's appended to the string temp. The character ~ is again appended between subsequent values.

- Lines 341□359: Appendthe body to the string temp for a message request, after the attribute names and attribute values are appended to temp, the string in variable. temp is then added to the vector m_tempVal at the 0th index, and the variables are re-initialized.

- Line 365: Declares the endDocument() method that is called after the end of a document is reached.

- Lines 367□370: Assignthe value of temp to m_attributes for a roster request.

- Lines 371□380: Assignthe value of temp to m_attributes for a registration request. Simultaneously, if the keyFlag is true, the string in the variable key is added to the next index of array, LocalNameList. The text END" is added at the index next to the key value The value of LocalNameList is assigned to Val.

- Lines 381□388: Assignthe value of temp to Val for a presence or message request: requestTypes 7 and 8, respectively.

- Lines 394□399: Declare methods that aren't used bythe XMLParser class but need to be declared to satisfy the Java implementation specification.

- Lines 403□406:Define the method getType(), which returns the value of variable requestType to the calling method/class.

- Lines 410□413: Definethe method getVal(), which returns the value of string array, Val to the calling method/class.

- Lines 417□420: Definethe method getAttributes(), which returns the value of the vector m_attributes to the calling method/class.

- Lines 424□427: Definethe method getAttributeNames(), which returns the value of the vector m_attributeName to the calling method/class.

- Lines 431□434: Definethe method getNameSpaceType(), which returns the value of variable namespaceType to the calling method/class.

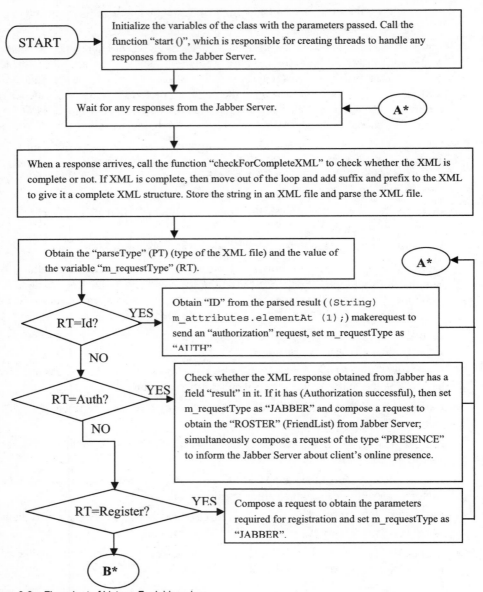

Figure 3-8a: Flow chart of ListenerForJabber class

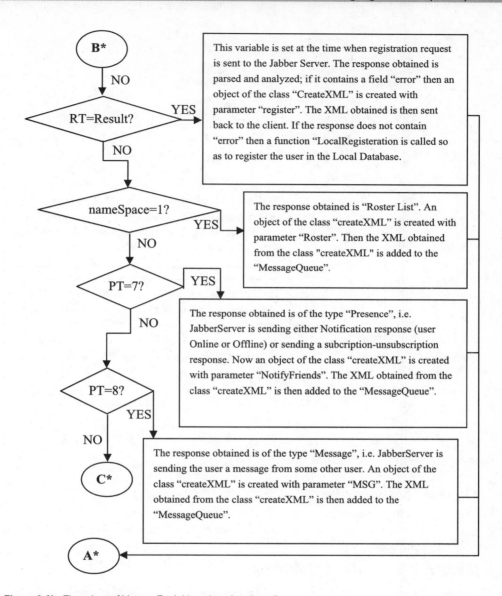

Figure 3-8b: Flow chart of ListenerForJabber class (continued)

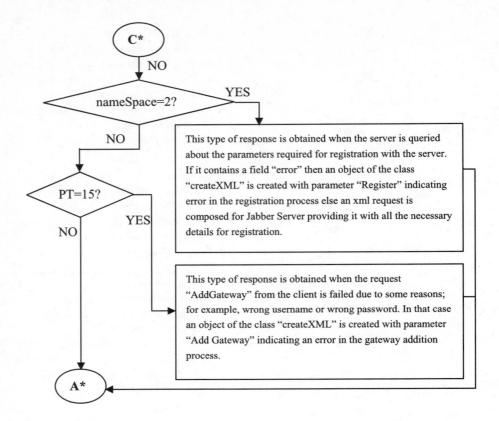

Figure 3-8c: Working of ListenerForJabber dlass (continued)

ListenerForJabber class

Figure 3-8 gives the technical flow diagram that summarizes the working of the ListenerForJabber class. Listing 3-4 shows the code for this class, followed by a detailed description of the code.

Listing 3-4: ListenerForJabber.java

```
1.   import java.io.*;
2.   import java.net.*;
3.   import java.util.*;
4.
5.   /****** Class Declaration ********/
6.
7.   public class ListenerForJabber extends Thread
8.   {
```

```
9.    BufferedInputStream         StreamFromJabber;
10.   BufferedOutputStream        StreamToJabber;
11.   Server                      parentClass;
12.   int                         FirstRequest   =      -1;
13.   XMLParser                   Parser         = new XMLParser();
14.
15.   String                      m_id           = new String();

16.   String                      m_userName     = new String();

17.   String                      m_passWord     = new String();

18.   int                         m_case         = 1;
19.   int                         m_type         = 1;
20.
21.   String                      m_requestType  = new String();
22.   boolean                     thread         = true;
23.   int                         fileIndex      = 0;
24.   int                         FirstRegistration = 1;
25.
26.   /*********  Constructor *********/
27.
28.   ListenerForJabber(Server parentClass, BufferedOutputStream
OutStream, BufferedInputStream InStream) throws IOException
29.   {
30.    StreamToJabber     = OutStream;
31.    StreamFromJabber   = InStream;
32.    this.parentClass   = parentClass;
33.
34.    start();
35.   }
36.
37.   /********** run() ************/
38.
39.   public void run()
40.   {
41.    try
42.    {
43.     while (thread)
44.     {
45.     int                         temp           =      0;
46.     int                         loop           =      100;
47.     int                         m_loopCtrl     =      0;
48.     String                      FinalString    =      new
String();
49.     StringBuffer m_readBuffer  =      new StringBuffer();
50.     byte[]                      m_request      =      new
byte[1];
51.
```

```
52.
53.    int       m_namespaceType                    = 0;
54.    int       m_tagType                          = 0;
55.    Vector m_attributes                          = new Vector();
56.    Vector m_attributeNames                      = new Vector();
57.
58.    // Response From the Jabber Server...
59.
60.    while (loop != 0)
61.    {
62.     temp           = StreamFromJabber.read(m_request, 0, 1);
63.     if (temp < 0)
64.       break;
65.     String str  = new String (m_request, 0, temp);
66.     FinalString = FinalString + str;
67.     for (int i =0;i<str.length();i++ )
68.     {
69.        if (str.charAt(i) == '<')
70.        {
71.            m_loopCtrl++;
72.        }
73.        else if (str.charAt(i) == '>')
74.        {
75.            m_loopCtrl--;
76.        }
77.     }
78.     if (m_loopCtrl  == 0)
79.     {
80.       loop = checkForCompleteXML(FinalString);
81.     }
82.    }
83.
84.    if (FinalString.indexOf("<stream:stream from=\'jabber.org\'")!= -
1)
85.    {
86.     FinalString += "</stream:stream>";
87.     if (!parentClass.getRequestType().equalsIgnoreCase("Register"))
88.     {
89.        m_requestType  = "ID";
90.     }
91.     else
92.     {
93.        m_requestType  = "REGISTER";
94.     }
95.    }
96.    else if (FinalString.indexOf("</stream:stream>")!= -1)
97.    {
98.      FinalString = "<stream:stream from='jabber.org' id='"+m_id+"'
xmlns='jabber:client'
```

```
xmlns:stream='http://etherx.jabber.org/streams'>"+FinalString;

99.       StreamToJabber.close();
100.       StreamFromJabber.close();
101.       thread = false;
102.     }
103.     else
104.     {
105.         FinalString = "<stream:stream from='jabber.org'
id='"+m_id+"' xmlns='jabber:client'
xmlns:stream='http://etherx.jabber.org/streams'>"+FinalString;
106.         FinalString += "</stream:stream>";
107.     }
108.
109.     byte [] tempbytes = FinalString.getBytes();
110.     FileOutputStream TempOutFile      = new
FileOutputStream("requestJabber.xml");
111.     TempOutFile.write(tempbytes, 0, tempbytes.length);
112.     TempOutFile.close();
113.     Parser.perform("requestJabber.xml");
114.
115.     String values[]                 = Parser.getVal();
116.     m_attributes                    = Parser.getAttributes();
117.     m_attributeNames                = Parser.getAttributeNames();
118.     m_namespaceType                 = Parser.getNameSpaceType();
119.     m_tagType                       = Parser.getType();
120.
121.     if (m_requestType.equalsIgnoreCase("ID"))
122.     {
123.         m_userName    =        parentClass.getUserName();
124.         m_passWord    =        parentClass.getPassword();
125.         m_id          =        (String)m_attributes.elementAt(1);
126.
127.         String authString2 = "<iq type='set' id='"+m_id+"'>\n<query
xmlns='jabber:iq:auth'>\n<username>" + m_userName+
"</username>\n<password>" + m_passWord +
"</password>\n<resource>jabber.org</resource>\n</query>\n</iq>";
128.
129.         String authString = authString2;
130.         byte [] bytesAuthString     = authString.getBytes();
131.         StreamToJabber.write(bytesAuthString,
0,bytesAuthString.length);
132.         StreamToJabber.flush();
133.         m_requestType = "AUTH";
134.     }
135.     else if (m_requestType.equalsIgnoreCase("AUTH"))
136.     {
137.         int index = m_attributeNames.indexOf((Object)"type");
138.
```

```
139.        if
(((String)m_attributes.elementAt(index)).equalsIgnoreCase("result"))
140.        {
141.                    // if Logged On then Get UserList...
142.            m_requestType = "JABBER";
143.
144.            String authString3 = "<iq type='get'
id='"+m_id+"'>\n<query xmlns='jabber:iq:roster'/>\n</iq>";
145.
146.            String authString = authString3;
147.            byte [] bytesAuthString    = authString.getBytes();
148.            StreamToJabber.write(bytesAuthString,
0,bytesAuthString.length);
149.            StreamToJabber.flush();
150.
151. //                    Notify The Friends...
152.
153.            authString3  = "<presence from =
'"+m_userName+"@jabber.org/jabber.org' id ='"+m_id+"'/>";
154.
155.            authString = authString3;
156.            bytesAuthString      = authString.getBytes();
157.            StreamToJabber.write(bytesAuthString,
0,bytesAuthString.length);
158.            StreamToJabber.flush();
159.        }
160.    }
161.    else if (m_requestType.equalsIgnoreCase("REGISTER"))
162.    {
163.    m_id            =       (String)m_attributes.elementAt(1);
164.
165.    String authString1 = "<iq type=\"get\" id=\""+m_id+"\"
to=\"jabber.org\"><query xmlns=\"jabber:iq:register\"/></iq>";
166.    String authString = authString1;
167.
168.    m_requestType = "JABBER";
169.
170.    byte [] bytesAuthString = authString.getBytes();
171.    StreamToJabber.write(bytesAuthString,
0,bytesAuthString.length);
172.    StreamToJabber.flush();
173.    }
174.    else if (m_requestType.equalsIgnoreCase("RESULT"))
175.    {
176.      m_requestType = "JABBER";
177.
178.     String  idString     = (String)m_attributes.elementAt(0);
179.     String  type         = new String();
```

```
180.        boolean setFlag          = false;
181.        StringTokenizer st = new StringTokenizer(idString, "~");
182.
183.        while (st.hasMoreTokens())
184.          {
185.            if (st.nextToken().equalsIgnoreCase("type"))
186.            {
187.               type = st.nextToken();
188.               break;
189.            }
190.          }
191.        m_attributes.removeElementAt(0);
192.        if (type.equalsIgnoreCase("error"))
193.        {
194.                    // Compose Cannnot register Error.... in Registration
XML....
195.                    Vector data =new Vector();
196.                    data.add((Object)"1");
197.                    CreateXML m_XMLResponse = new CreateXML("Register",
data);
198.                    String  response           =
m_XMLResponse.returnResult();
199.
200.                    byte [] responseBytes = response.getBytes();
201.                    parentClass.StreamToClient.write(responseBytes, 0,
responseBytes.length);
202.                    parentClass.StreamToClient.flush();
203.        }
204.        else
205.        {
206.                    String [] val = new String [12];
207.                    val[0] = parentClass.getUserName();;
208.                    val[1] = parentClass.getPassword();
209.                    parentClass.LocalRegistration(val);
210.          }
211.        }
212.      else
213.      {
214.    //   Handle The  Parsed Response Appropriately....
215.    if (m_namespaceType == 1)
216.    {
217.
218.       String   idString       = (String)m_attributes.elementAt(0);
219.       String   id                     = new String();
220.       boolean setFlag        = false;
221.       StringTokenizer st = new StringTokenizer(idString, "~");
222.
223.       while (st.hasMoreTokens())
```

```
224.          {
225.            if (st.nextToken().equalsIgnoreCase("id"))
226.            {
227.              id = st.nextToken();
228.              break;
229.            }
230.          }
231.
232.    if (idString.indexOf("type~set")!= -1)
233.    {
234.      setFlag            = true;
235.    }
236.
237.      if (idString.indexOf("type~result~jid~msn.jabber.org") != -1)
238.      {
239.        m_attributes.removeElementAt(0);
240.      }
241.
242.    if (!setFlag)
243.    {
244.      CreateXML m_XMLResponse = new CreateXML("ROSTER",
m_attributes);
245.      String response        = m_XMLResponse.returnResult();
246.      String m_TempUserName = parentClass.getName();

247.      m_TempUserName += "^";
248.      response =  m_TempUserName + response;
249.      parentClass.responseFromServer(response);
250.    }
251.    }
252.    if (m_tagType == 7)
253.    {
254.    int type = 0;
255.
256.    for (int i=0;i < values.length && values[i] != null;i++ )
257.    {
258.    if (values[i].indexOf("registered") != -1)
259.    {
260.        type++;
261.    }
262.    if (values[i].indexOf("from~msn.jabber.org") != -1)
263.    {
264.        type++;
265.    }
266.    if (values[i].indexOf("error~code") != -1)
267.    {
268.        type++;
269.    }
```

```
270.    if (((values[i].indexOf("from~msn.jabber.org") != -
1)&&(values[i].indexOf("type~subscribe") != -
1))&&(parentClass.addGatewayFlag))
271.     {
272.         String automaticResponse = "<presence to='msn.jabber.org'
type='subscribed'/>";
273.         byte [] bytesAuthString    = automaticResponse.getBytes();
274.         StreamToJabber.write(bytesAuthString,
0,bytesAuthString.length);
275.         StreamToJabber.flush();
276.         parentClass.addGatewayFlag = false;
277.     }
278.
279.
280.    if (type == 0)
281.     {
282.         String                id = new String();
283.         StringTokenizer       st = new StringTokenizer(values[i],
"~");
284.
285.         if(values[i].lastIndexOf(")") == -1)
286.         {
287.             Vector  m_TempVal           = new Vector();
288.             m_TempVal.add(values[i]);
289.             CreateXML m_XMLResponse     = new
CreateXML("PRESENCE", m_TempVal);
290.             String  response           =
m_XMLResponse.returnResult();
291.             String m_TempUserName = parentClass.getName();
292.             m_TempUserName += "^";
293.             response = m_TempUserName + response;
294.             parentClass.responseFromServer(response);
295.         }
296.     }
297.    }
298.    }
299.    if (m_tagType == 8)
300.    {
301.    String               id     = new String();
302.    StringTokenizer      st             = new StringTokenizer(values[0],
"~");
303.
304.    Vector               data   = new Vector();
305.    int                  tokens = st.countTokens();
306.    String               m_TempValues[]= new String[tokens];
307.    int                  index  = 0;
308.    String               m_user = new String();
309.
310.    while (st.hasMoreTokens())
```

```
311.        m_TempValues[index++] = st.nextToken();
312.
313.
314.    for (int i = 0;i<index;i++)
315.    {
316.      String    tempVal = m_TempValues[i];
317.
318.      if (tempVal.equalsIgnoreCase("from"))
319.      {
320.        String check = m_TempValues[i+1];
321.        if (!(check.equalsIgnoreCase("jabber.org")))
322.        {
323.            check = check.substring(0, check.indexOf("@"));
324.            data.add((Object)check);
325.        }
326.      }
327.      else if (tempVal.equalsIgnoreCase("TO"))
328.      {
329.        tempVal               = m_TempValues[i+1];
330.        tempVal               = tempVal.substring(0,
tempVal.indexOf("@"));
331.        data.add((Object)tempVal);
332.        m_user                = tempVal;
333.      }
334.    }
335.    data.add(m_TempValues[m_TempValues.length-1]);
336.    CreateXML m_XMLResponse = new CreateXML("MESSAGE", data);
337.    String  response        = m_XMLResponse.returnResult();
338.
339.    String m_TempUserName = parentClass.getName();
340.
341.    m_TempUserName += "^";
342.
343.    response =  m_TempUserName + response;
344.
345.    parentClass.responseFromServer(response);
346.    }
347.     else if (m_namespaceType == 2)
348.     {
349.    if ((FirstRegistration == 1)&&(parentClass.Parser.getType() !=
15))
350.    {
351.      String        idString      =
(String)m_attributes.elementAt(0);
352.      String        type          = new String();
353.      boolean       setFlag       = false;
354.      StringTokenizer st          = new StringTokenizer(idString,
"~");
```

```
355.
356.        FirstRegistration++;
357.
358.        while (st.hasMoreTokens())
359.          {
360.           if (st.nextToken().equalsIgnoreCase("type"))
361.            {
362.             type = st.nextToken();
363.             break;
364.            }
365.          }
366.        m_attributes.removeElementAt(0);
367.
368.        if (type.equalsIgnoreCase("error"))
369.          {
370.                // Compose Cannnot register Errrorr.... in
Registration XML....
371.                Vector data =new Vector();
372.                data.add((Object)"0");
373.                CreateXML m_XMLResponse = new CreateXML("Register",
data);
374.                String   response              =
m_XMLResponse.returnResult();
375.
376.                byte [] responseBytes = response.getBytes();
377.                parentClass.StreamToClient.write(responseBytes, 0,
responseBytes.length);
378.                parentClass.StreamToClient.flush();
379.          }
380.        else if (type.equalsIgnoreCase("result"))
381.          {
382.           boolean    keyFound       = false;
383.           int        indexEnd       = -1;
384.           String     keyValue       = new String();
385.           for (int i = 0;i<values.length && values[i] != null;i++)
386.            {
387.                if (values[i].equalsIgnoreCase("key"))
388.                 {
389.                    keyFound        = true;
390.                 }
391.                if ((keyFound ==
true)&&(values[i].equalsIgnoreCase("End")))
392.                  {
393.                     indexEnd    = i;
394.                  }
395.                }
396.
397.                m_userName    =       parentClass.getUserName();
398.                m_passWord    =       parentClass.getPassword();
```

```
399.
400.              String authString3 = "<iq type=\"set\"
to=\"jabber.org\" id=\""+m_id+"\"><query
xmlns=\"jabber:iq:register\"><username>"+m_userName+"</username><passwor
d>"+m_passWord+"</password>";
401.              if (keyFound)
402.              {
403.                  authString3 += "<key>"+values[indexEnd-1]+"</key>";

404.              }
405.              authString3    += "</query></iq>";
406.              String authString = authString3;
407.              byte [] bytesAuthString    = authString.getBytes();
408.              StreamToJabber.write(bytesAuthString,
0,bytesAuthString.length);
409.              StreamToJabber.flush();
410.
411.               m_requestType = "RESULT";
412.      }
413.      }
414.    else if (parentClass.Parser.getType() == 15)
415.    {
416.     String   idString   = (String)m_attributes.elementAt(0);

417.     String   type         = new String();
418.
419.     if (idString.indexOf("type~error")!= -1)
420.     {
421.              Vector data =new Vector();
422.              data.add((Object)"0");
423.              CreateXML m_XMLResponse = new CreateXML("AddGateway",
data);
424.              String  response         =
m_XMLResponse.returnResult();
425.
426.              byte [] responseBytes = response.getBytes();
427.              parentClass.StreamToClient.write(responseBytes, 0,
responseBytes.length);
428.              parentClass.StreamToClient.flush();
429.      }
430.
431.      }
432.      }
433.  }
434.    }    // End while
435.    }    // End Try..
436.  catch(Exception e)
437.    {
```

```
438.      System.out.println("Exception in ListenerForJabber.. run
Method" + e);
439.      e.printStackTrace(System.out);
440.  }
441.  }      // End Run.
442.
443.  /******* checkForCompleteXML ************/
444.
445.  int checkForCompleteXML(String m_XMLString)
446.  {
447.  boolean            query  = false;
448.  boolean            status = false;
449.
450.
451.  if (m_XMLString.indexOf("<stream:stream") == 0)
452.  {
453.   return 0;
454.  }
455.  else if (m_XMLString.indexOf("<iq") != -1)
456.  {
457.      if ((m_XMLString.indexOf("query") != -
1)||(m_XMLString.indexOf("<error") != -
1)||(m_XMLString.indexOf("<service") != -1))
458.      {
459.         query = true;
460.      }
461.      if (!query)
462.      {
463.      if (m_XMLString.lastIndexOf("/>") == (m_XMLString.length() - 2))
464.      {
465.        return 0;
466.      }
467.      else
468.        return 1;
469.      }
470.      else if(query)
471.      {
472.      if (m_XMLString.lastIndexOf("</iq>") == (m_XMLString.length() -
5))
473.      {
474.        return 0;
475.      }
476.      else
477.        return 1;
478.      }
479.  }
480.   else if (m_XMLString.indexOf("<presence") != -1)
481.   {
```

```
482.    if ((m_XMLString.indexOf("<status") != -
1)||(m_XMLString.indexOf("<error") != -1)||(m_XMLString.indexOf("<x") !=
-1))
483.     {
484.        status = true;
485.     }
486.     if(!status)
487.     {
488.     if (m_XMLString.lastIndexOf("/>") == (m_XMLString.length() - 2))
489.     {
490.       return 0;
491.     }
492.     else
493.       return 1;
494.     }
495.      else
496.      {
497.      if (m_XMLString.lastIndexOf("</presence>") ==
(m_XMLString.length() - 11))
498.      {
499.        return 0;
500.      }
501.      else
502.       return 1;
503.       }
504.     }
505.  else if (m_XMLString.indexOf("<message") != -1)
506.   {
507.      if (m_XMLString.lastIndexOf("</message>") ==
(m_XMLString.length() - 10))
508.      {
509.        return 0;
510.      }
511.      else
512.        return 1;
513.   }
514.   return 1;
515.   }
516.   }// End of Class ListenerForJabber...
```

- Lines 1□3: Contain the Java import statements.
- Line 7: Contains the class declaration.
- Lines 9□10: Declare user-definedvariables.
- Line 11: Declares an object of class `Server`.
- Line 12: Contains a variable declaration.
- Line 13: Declares an object of the class `XMLParser`.

- Lines 15☐24:Contain variable declarations/initialization.

- Lines 28☐35:Define the constructor of class `ListenerForJabber`.

- Lines 30☐32: Initiallize the input/outputstreams and the object of the `Server` class by using the argument values supplied to the constructor's parameters.

- Line 34: Calls the `run()` method.

- Line 39: Declares the `run()` method.

- Lines 41☐43:The `run()` method starts an infinite `while` loop within a `try` block to listen to communication from the Jabber server.

- Lines 45☐56:Declare/initialize variables.

- Line 60: Starts a code loop that reads from the Jabber server as long as it doesn't receive a complete XML request.

- Line 62: Reads the request data sent by the Jabber server into the byte array `m_request` one byte at a time and saves the number of bytes read in the variable `temp`. Notice that, because the length of the request data from the Jabber server isn't known, one byte is read at a time and analyzed (see code explanation for Lines 443-516) to check whether the last XML element/tag was read.

- Lines 63☐64:Exit the `while` loop of Line 60 if no bytes are read/available.

- Line 65: Converts the byte array `m_request` into a string. All the values within the starting index (`0`) and last index (`temp`) are read and converted to a string. This string value is then stored in the variable, `str`.

- Line 66: Appends `str` to the variable `FinalString`.

- Lines 67☐77:Contain a `for` loop that loops through the length of the string `str`. If it encounters the character < (the beginning of an XML tag), the variable `m_loopCtrl` is incremented; if it encounters the character > (the ending of an XML tag), the variable `m_loopCtrl` is decremented. After the `for` loop completes execution, if `m_loopCtrl` is `0` — that is, a complete XML element was received (only then does it contain both the characters < and >) — the method `checkForCompleteXML()` is called, and its return value is assigned to the loop control variable `loop`. Notice that `checkForCompleteXML()` returns `0` if it recognizes an ending XML tag and the execution of the `while` loop of Line 60 is terminated; otherwise, `checkForCompleteXML()` returns a value other than `0`, and program control goes back to the `while` loop of Line 60 to read further bytes from the Jabber server.

- Lines 78☐81:, Call the method`checkForCompleteXML()`to check whether the end of XML stream was reached if `m_loopCtrl` is `0` (which means that a complete XML tag was received). The value returned by `checkForCompleteXML()` is assigned to the control condition of the `while` loop (Line 60). If the returned value is `0`, the program execution exits the `while` loop; otherwise, the `while` loop executes again.

- Line 84: Checks for the presence of the start-of-the-XML-stream tag fragment `<stream:stream from=\'jabber.org\'`.

- Line 86:, Append the end-of-the-XML-stream tag `</stream:stream>` to `FinalString` if the tag in Line 84 is present to complete the XML received from the Jabber server.

- Lines 87□94:Use the object of class `Server`, `parentClass`, to check whether the request is a registration request. If so, the variable `m_requestType` is assigned the string `ID`; otherwise, it's assigned the string `"REGISTER"`.

- Lines 96□102: Check whether the end-of-the-stream tag`</stream:stream>` is present in the XML received from the Jabber server:

  - Line 98: Appends the start-of-the-stream tag at the beginning of the variable `FinalString` to complete the XML.

  - Lines 99□100: Close the input and output streams from/to the Jabber server.

  - Line 101: Sets the boolean `thread` to `false`.

- Lines 103□107: Contain the`else` clause corresponding to the `if` clause of Line 84 and `else-if` clause of Line 96. If neither the start-of-the-stream nor the end-of-the-stream tags are present in the XML received from the Jabber server, they're appended at the beginning and end of `FinalString`, respectively.

- Line 109: Converts `FinalString` into a byte array, `tempbytes`.

- Line 110: Creates a file output stream, `TempOutFile`, to write to the file `requestJabber.xml`.

- Lines 111□112: Write the bytes received from the Jabberserver to the file designated for the purpose and close the file output stream.

- Line 113: Calls the `perform()` method of `XMLParser` to parse the XML in the file `requestJabber.xml`.

- Lines 115□119: Call the methods of class `XMLParser` that return the required values to the calling class (in this case, `ListenerForJabber` class).

- Line 121: Checks whether the request is a Jabber ID request.

- Line 123□125: Retrieve the user's login name, password and Jabber ID into respective variables.

- Line 127: Creates the authorization XML and stores it in the string variable `authString2`.

- Line 129: Converts `authString2` into bytes.

- Lines 131□132: Write the request bytes in the byte array `bytesAuthString` to the Jabber server. The method `flush()` commits the data written to the output stream.

- Line 133: Assigns the string `AUTH` to the variable `m_requestType`.

- Line 135: Checks whether an authorization request was received.

- Line 137: Retrieves the index of the object type from the vector m_attributeNames.

- Line 139: Checks whether the value contained at the preceding index (see Line 137) in the vector m_attributes is result.

- Line 142: Assigns the string JABBER to the variable m_requestType.

- Lines 144☐149: Create the XML roster request and write it tothe Jabber server.

- Lines 153☐159: Create an XML presence request and write it tothe Jabber server to notify a user's friends of his/her presence.

- Lines 161☐173: Check whetherthe request is a registration request. The user's ID is then retrieved in the variable m_id and the request XML is created (Line 165), converted into bytes (Line 170), and written to the Jabber server (Lines 171-172). The variable m_requestType is assigned the string value JABBER.

- Line 174: Checks whether the variable m_requestType contains the string RESULT.

- Line 176: Sets m_requestType to JABBER.

- Line 178: Obtains the value at 0th index of vector m_attributes into the variable idstring.

- Lines 179☐180: Contain variable declarations/initializations.

- Line 181: Splits the string idstring, using ~ as the delimiter, and stores the token values in the string tokenizer st.

- Line 183☐190: Execute awhile loop that runs through all the token values and compares the token value with the string type (Line 185). If this token value is found, the next token value is assigned to the variable type, and the execution of the loop is terminated.

- Line 191: Removes the 0th element from the vector m_attributes.

- Line 192: Checks whether the variable type contains the string error.

- Lines 195☐196: Create a new vector,data, and add 1 to the vector. Notice that 1 is stored as an object within the vector and that it signifies an error in the request.

- Lines 197☐198: Call theCreateXML class to form a registration request, and the XML returned is stored in the string variable response.

- Lines 200☐202: Convert the XML received from the classCreateXML into bytes and write them to the client. Notice that the XML received from the CreateXML class informs the user of a failed registration request.

- Line 204: Contains the else clause corresponding to the if of Line 192.

- Lines 206☐208: Create the stringarray val and store in it the user's login name and password.

- Line 209: Calls the localRegistration() method of the Server class.

- Line 212: Declares the `else` clause if the XML received contains none of the request types given previously (in Lines 121, 135, 161, and 174).

- Line 215: Checks whether the namespace variable contains 1 — that is, a roster request.

- Line 218: Retrieves the 0th element from the vector `m_attributes`.

- Line 219☐220:Contain variable declarations.

- Line 221: Splits `idstring` into token values.

- Lines 223☐230: Run a `T` loop to check each token value against the string "id". If this token value is found, the next token value is assigned to the variable `id`, and the execution of the `while` loop is terminated.

- Lines 232☐235: Set the boolean`setFlag` to `true` if `idstring` contains "type~set".

- Lines 237☐240: Remove`the` 0th element from the vector `m_attributes` if `idString` contains "type~result~jid~msn.jabber.org".

- Line 242: Checks whether the boolean `setFlag` is `false`.

- Lines 244☐245: Call the`CreateXML` class to form a roster request and assign the returned values to the string `response`.

- Lines 246☐247: Use the object of`the` `Server` class to obtain the user's login name and append the character ^ to it.

- Line 248: Appends the user's login name at the beginning of the XML response so that, after this XML is added to the message queue (see Line 249), the program can identify the user that it's meant for.

- Line 249: Calls the `responsefromServer()` method of the `Server` class. Notice that this method adds the XML to the message queue.

- Line 252: Checks whether the value of the variable `m_tagType` is 7. (This value denotes a presence request.)

- Line 254: Sets the value of the variable `type`.

- Line 256: Starts a `for` loop till that runs through the array `values`. `values` contains parsed values returned by `XMLParser` class.

- Lines 258☐269: Increment the value of`the` variable `type` if the current value of the array `values` contains any of the strings `registered`, `from~msn.jabber.org`, or `error~code`.

- Lines 270☐277: Create a presence XML tag (Line 272), convert`it` into bytes (Line 273), and write it to the Jabber server if the current value of the array `values` contains the strings `from~msn.jabber.org` and `type~subscribe`, and the `addGatewayFlag` of the `Server` class is `true`. The flag `addGatewayFlag` is set to `false`.

- Line 280: Checks whether the integer variable `type` contains the value 0.

- Line 283: Splits the current value of the array `values` and stores the token values in the string tokenizer `st`.

- Line 285: Checks for the absence of a closing curved bracket —) — in the current value of the `values` array.

- Lines 287□288: Create a vector,`m_TempVal`, and add to it the current element of the array `values`.

- Lines 289□290: Call the class`CreateXML` to form a presence XML and assign the returned XML to the variable `response`.

- Lines 291□293: Obtain the login name of the user and append it at the beginning of the XML, with the character ^ serving as the delimiter.

- Ine 294: Calls the `responseFromServer()` method of the `Server` class that adds the XML to the message queue.

- Line 299: Checks whether `m_tagType` has the value 8. (This value signifies a message request.)

- Line 302: Splits the 0th value of the `values` array and stores the token values in the string tokenizer `st`.

- Lines 304□308: Contain variable declarations/initializations.

- Line 310□311: Contain a`while` loop that adds each of the token values to the subsequent index of the array `m_TempValues`.

- Lines 314□334: Run a`for` loop through the array, `m_TempValues`:

  - Line 316: Puts the value at current index of`m_TempValues` into the string variable `tempVal`.

  - Lines 318□326: Check the next`value` in the `m_TempValues` array if `tempVal` contains the string `from`. If the next value isn't equal to the string `jabber.org`, the substring from the index 0 to the index of the character @ is extracted from the next value of `m_TempValues` and added to the vector `data`. Notice that this substring is the login name of the sender of the message.

  - Lines 327□333: Extract the name of`the` recipient of the message from the i+1th value of `m_TempValues` and add it to the vector `data` if `tempVal` contains the string `TO`.The value of `tempVal` is assigned to `m_user`.

- Line 335: Adds the value at the last index of `m_TempValues` to the vector `data`.

- Lines 336□337: Call the`CreateXML` class to form a message request and assign the return XML to the variable `response`.

- Lines 339□343: Obtain the user's`login name and append it to the beginning of the XML.

- Line 345: Calls the `responseFromServer()` method of `Server` class that adds the XML to the message queue.

- Line 347: Checks whether the namespace variable has the value 2, which indicates a registration request.
- Line 349: Checks whether the variable `FirstRegistration` is 1 and the value returned by the `getType()` method of `XMLParser` class isn't 15.
- Line 351: Assigns the 0th element of `values` array to `idString`.
- Lines 352□353: Contain variable declarations/initializations.
- Line 354: Splits `idString` and stores the token values in the string tokenizer `st`.
- Line 356: Increments the variable `FirstRegistration`.
- Line 358: Starts a `while` loop up to the last token value in `st`.
- Lines 360□364: Assignthe next token value to the variable `type` if a token value of `type` is reached and the execution of the loop is terminated.
- Line 366: Removes the 0th element of vector `m_attributes`.
- Line 368: Checks whether the variable `type` contains the value `error`.
- Lines 371□372: Create a new vector,`data`, and add to it the value 0.
- Lines 373□374: Call the class`CreateXML` to form a registration request and assign the returned XML to the variable `response`.
- Lines 376□378: Write the XML tothe client.
- Line 380: Checks whether the variable `type` contains the string `result`.
- Lines 382□385: Declare andinitialize variables.
- Line 385: Starts a `for` loop that runs through all values in the array `values`.
- Lines 387□390: Set the flag`keyFound` to `true` if the current value of the array `values` is the string `key`.
- Lines 391□394: assigned the value of`i` to the variable `indexEnd` if the `keyFlag` is set to `true` and the current value of `values` array is the string `End`.
- Lines 397□398: Obtain the user'slogin name and password.
- Line 400: Creates a registration XML.
- Lines 401□404: Assignthe element before the element containing `End` to the value tag `<key>` and append it to authString3 if the `keyFlag` is set to `true`.
- Lines 405□406: Appendthe closing XML tags to `authString3` and assign its value to `authString`.
- Lines 407□409: Convert`authString` to bytes and write it to the Jabber server.
- Line 411: Sets the value of variable `m_requestType` to "RESULT".
- Line 414: Contains an `else-if` clause that checks whether the request-type is 15, meaning an `AddGateway` request.

- Line 416: Assigns to idString the 0th element of the array m_attributes.

- Line 419□421:, Add the value 0to the vector data, call the CreateXML class to form an AddGateway request, and write this request is to the client after converting it into bytes if the text type~error exists in idString.

- Line 436□440: Contain thecatch block corresponding to the try of Line 41.

- Line 445: Define the method checkForCompleteXML().

- Lines 447□448: Declare andinitialize variables.

- Lines 451□454:The method returns the value 0 if the tag fragment <stream:stream doesn't exist in m_XMLString.

- Line 455: Checks for the presence of the tag fragment <iq in m_XMLString.

- Line 457□460: Set the variablequery to true if any of the tag fragments query, <error and <service exist in m_XMLString,.

- Line 461: Checks whether the boolean query is false.

- Line 463□468: Return the value0 if the character /> is the last-but-one character at the given index in the string m_XMLString; otherwise, return the value 1.

- Line 470: Checks whether the boolean query is true.

- Lines 472□477: Set the return value to0 if the fragment </iq> is at the fourth index from the last character; otherwise, set the return value to 1.

- Line 480: Checks for the presence of the tag fragment <presence in m_XMLString.

- Lines 482□485: Set theboolean status to true if any of the tag fragments <status, <error, andin m_XMLString is as per the index in Line 488. If the condition of line 488 isn't satisfied, 1 is returned.

- Lines 495□503:Return the value 0 if status is true and the last occurrence of the tag fragment <presence is as per the index in Line 497; otherwse, 1 is returned.

- Lines 505□513: Returnthe value 0 if the tag fragment <message is present in m_XMLString and the last occurrence of the tag <message> is as per the condition in Line 507; otherwise, 1 is returned.

- Line 514: Returns the value 1 if none of the closing tags match.

CreateXML class

Figure 3-9 gives the technical flow diagram that summarizes the working of the CreateXML class. Listing 3-5 contains the code for this class, followed by a detailed description of the code.

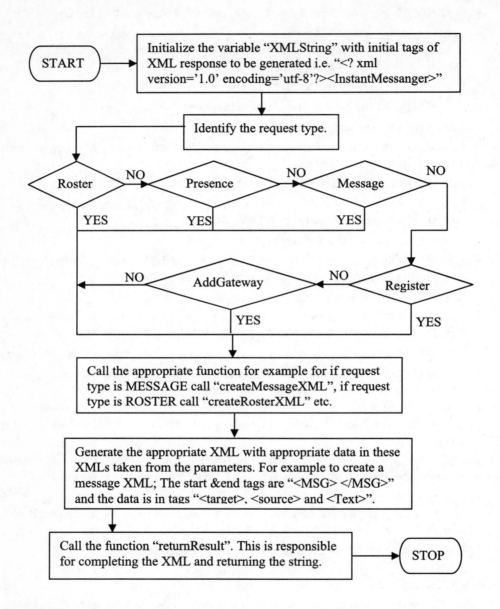

Figure 3-9: Working of CreateXML class

Listing 3-5: CreateXML.java

```
1.   import java.util.*;
2.
3.   public class CreateXML
4.   {
5.
6.   String          XMLString    =       new String();
7.   boolean         tempFlag     =       false;
8.
9.   /************** Constructor ***************/
10.
11.   CreateXML(String type, Vector param)
12.   {
13.
14.    XMLString                   = "<?xml version=\'1.0\'
 encoding=\'utf-8\'?><InstantMessenger>";
15.
16.     if (type.equalsIgnoreCase("ROSTER"))
17.     {
18.    CreateRosterXML(param);
19.     }
20.     else if (type.equalsIgnoreCase("PRESENCE"))
21.     {
22.    CreatePresenceXML(param);
23.     }
24.     else if (type.equalsIgnoreCase("MESSAGE"))
25.     {
26.    CreateMessageXML(param);
27.     }
28.     else if (type.equalsIgnoreCase("REGISTER"))
29.     {
30.    CreateRegistrationXML(param);
31.     }
32.     else if (type.equalsIgnoreCase("ADDGATEWAY"))
33.     {
34.    CreateAddGatewayXML(param);
35.     }
36.   }
37.
38.   /*********** CreateRosterXML ***********/
39.
40.   void CreateRosterXML(Vector param)
41.   {
42.   XMLString += "<Roster>";
43.
44.   for (int i = 0;i<param.size();i++)
45.   {
46.    String              temp                = (String)param.elementAt(i);
```

```java
47.   StringTokenizer    st              = new StringTokenizer(temp,
"~");
48.   if (st.countTokens() < 4)
49.     tempFlag = false;
50.   else
51.     tempFlag = true;
52.   while ((st.hasMoreTokens()) &&(tempFlag))
53.   {
54.      String    str              = st.nextToken();
55.      String    tempName         = new String();
56.      String    tempSubscription = new String();
57.      boolean   skipFlag         = false;
58.
59.    if (str.equalsIgnoreCase("jid"))
60.    {
61.        tempName = st.nextToken();
62.        XMLString += "<FriendID>" + tempName + "</FriendID>";
63.    }
64.    else if (str.equalsIgnoreCase("subscription"))
65.    {
66.        tempSubscription = st.nextToken();
67.        XMLString += "<Subscription>" + tempSubscription +
"</Subscription>";
68.    }
69.   }
70.  }
71.
72.  XMLString += "</Roster>";
73.  }
74.
75.  /**************    CreatePresenceXML *****************/
76.
77.  void CreatePresenceXML(Vector param)
78.  {
79.   XMLString                += "<NotifyFriends>";
80.   String                   m_TempStr           =
(String)param.elementAt(0);
81.   StringTokenizer    st                          = new
StringTokenizer(m_TempStr, "~");
82.   int                    m_numberOfTokens = st.countTokens();
83.   boolean                m_typeFlag       = false;
84.   boolean                m_done           = false;
85.
86.
87.   while(st.hasMoreTokens())
88.   {
89.    String str  = st.nextToken();
90.
91.     if ((str.equalsIgnoreCase("from"))&&(!m_done))
```

```
92.      {
93.      String temp  = st.nextToken();
94.      if (!(temp.equalsIgnoreCase("jabber.org")))
95.      {
96.        int index = temp.indexOf("@");
97.        if (index != -1)
98.            temp = temp.substring(0, index);
99.      XMLString += "<UserName>" + temp + "</UserName>";
100.          m_done = true;
101.        }
102.      }
103.      else if (str.equalsIgnoreCase("type"))
104.      {
105.         String temp  = st.nextToken();
106.         if (temp.equalsIgnoreCase("unavailable"))
107.            XMLString += "<Status>Off-Line</Status>";
108.         if (temp.equalsIgnoreCase("subscribe"))
109.            XMLString += "<Status>Subscribe</Status>";
110.         if (temp.equalsIgnoreCase("unsubscribe"))
111.            XMLString += "<Status>UnSubscribe</Status>";
112.         if (temp.equalsIgnoreCase("unsubscribed"))
113.            XMLString += "<Status>UnSubscribed</Status>";
114.         if (temp.equalsIgnoreCase("Subscribed"))
115.            XMLString += "<Status>Subscribed</Status>";
116.
117.
118.         m_typeFlag = true;
119.      }
120.    }
121.   if (!m_typeFlag)
122.     XMLString += "<Status>On-Line</Status>";
123.   XMLString += "</NotifyFriends>";
124.  }
125.
126. /*************** CreateMessageXML *********************/
127.
128. void CreateMessageXML(Vector param)
129. {
130.   XMLString += "<MSG>";
131.   XMLString += "<Target>"   + (String)param.elementAt(1) +
"</Target>";
132.   XMLString += "<Source>"   + (String)param.elementAt(0) +
"</Source>";
133.   XMLString += "<Text>"+ (String)param.elementAt(2) + "</Text>";
134.   XMLString += "</MSG>";
135. }
136.
137. /************          CreateRegistrationXML **************/
138.
```

```
139.  void CreateRegistrationXML(Vector param)
140.  {
141.   XMLString += "<Register>";
142.   String      str = (String)param.elementAt(0);
143.   if (str.equalsIgnoreCase("0"))
144.   {
145.     XMLString += "<int>-1</int>";
146.   }
147.   else if (str.equalsIgnoreCase("1"))
148.   {
149.     XMLString += "<int>1</int>";
150.   }
151.   XMLString += "</Register>";
152.  }
153.
154.  /*********** AddGateway ************/
155.
156.  void CreateAddGatewayXML(Vector param)
157.  {
158.   XMLString += "<AddGateway>";
159.   String      str = (String)param.elementAt(0);
160.   if (str.equalsIgnoreCase("0"))
161.   {
162.     XMLString += "<code>-1</code>";
163.   }
164.   XMLString += "</AddGateway>";
165.  }
166.
167.  /***************** returnResult ***************/
168.
169.  String returnResult()
170.  {
171.   XMLString += "</InstantMessenger>";
172.   return XMLString;
173.  }
174.  }      //  End CreateXML..
```

- Line 1: Contains the Java import statement for the `java.util` package that contains the class `StringTokenizer` used by the `CreateXML` class.

- Line 3: Contains a class declaration.

- Lines 6□7: Contain variabledeclarations.

- Line 11: Contains the constructor declaration.

- Line 14: Initializes the string `XMLString` with two XML tags that form the beginning of every XML request.

- Lines 16□19:Call the method `CreateRosterXML()` if the argument passed to the parameter `type` is ROSTER. The vector parameter `param`, received from the calling class/method, is passed to the `CreateRosterXML()` method. Notice that this vector contains data for the value XML tags for a particular type of request.

- Lines 20□23: Call the method`CreatePresenceXML()` if the argument passed against the parameter `type` is "`PRESENCE`".

- Lines 24□27: Call the method`CreateMessageXML()` if the argument passed against the parameter `type` is "`MESSAGE`".

- Lines 28□31: Call the method`CreateRegistrationXML()` if the argument passed against the parameter `type` is "`REGISTER`".

- Lines 32□35: Call the method`CreateAddGatewayXML()` if the argument passed against the parameter `type` is "`ADDGATEWAY`".

- Lines 40□73: Define the method `CreateRosterXML()`.

  - Line 42: Adds the tag `<Roster>` to the string `XMLString`.

  - Line 44: Begins a `for` loop that runs through the entire vector `param`.

  - Line 46: Retrieves the ith element of the Vector, `param` into the String `temp`.

  - Line 47: Splits the string `temp` by using the delimiter ~ and uses the variable `st`, of the type `StringTokenizer`, to store the token values.

  - Lines 48□51:Set the `boolean` `tempFlag` to `false` if the count of the tokens in `st` is less than 4; otherwise, set it to `true`.

  - Line 52: Starts a `while` loop that executes if more tokens exist in the `StringTokenizer` and `tempFlag` is true.

  - Line 54: Retrieves the next token value in the variable `str`. Notice that this value indicates the XML tag whose value is contained in the subsequent token.

  - Lines 55□57: Declare two string variables and set the`boolean` `skipFlag` to `false`.

  - Lines 59□63: Obtain the next token value in the variable`tempName` if the variable `str` contains the text `jid`. Notice that `tempName` now contains the Jabber ID of a friend in the friends list. This ID is appended to the `XMLString` within its respective tags.

  - Lines 64□68: Obtain the next token value in the variable`tempName` if the variable `str` contains the text `subscription`. Notice that `tempName` now contains the subscription status of a friend in the friends list. This status is added to the `XMLString` within its respective tags. (The subscription status determines whether the subscription is two-way or one-way — that is, you've requested to add a friend, but the friend hasn't yet accepted/declined your invitation.)

  - Line 72: Adds the closing XML tag for the type of request.

- Lines 77□124: Define the method`CreatePresenceXML()`:

  - Line 79: Adds the request-type starting tag `<NotifyFreinds>` to `XMLString`.

- Line 80: Retrieves the 0th element of the vector `param` into the variable `m_TempStr`.
- Line 81: Splits the string `m_TempStr` by using ~ as delimiter and retrieves the token values in the string tokenizer, `st`.
- Line 82: Counts the number of tokens.
- Line 83□84: Contain variable declarations.
- Line 87: Starts a `while` loop that checks whether more tokens exist in the `StringTokenizer`.
- Line 89: Retrieves the next token into the variable `str`.
- Line 91: Contains an `if` statement that checks whether the string contained in `str` is `from` and `boolean m_done` is `false`.
- Line 93: Retrieves the next token value in variable `temp`.
- Lines 94□101: Extract the name of the user by using the substring value from index0 to the index at which the character @ exists if the token value in the variable `temp` isn't `jabber.org` and the character @ exists in `temp`. The username is appended to `XMLString` within its respective tags (Line 99), and `m_done` is set to `true`.
- Line 103: Specifies the `else-if` clause for the `if` in Line 91. The clause checks whether the variable `str` contains the string `type`.
- Lines 105□115: Retrievethe value of the next token in the variable `temp` and check its value to ascertain what the presence status of the user is — that is, whether the user is offline or has unsubscribed and so on. The status is then enclosed within the respective XML tags and appended to `XMLString`.
- Lines121□122: Set the status to online if`m_typeFlag` is `false`.

- Lines 128□135: Definethe `CreateMessageXML()` method:

  - Line 130: Appends to `XMLString` the starting XML tag denoting the type of request.
  - Lines 131□133:Append the value tags denoting receipient of message, sender of message, and the message text, with their respective data, to `XMLString`.
  - Line 134: Closes the XML tag for request type.

- Lines 139□152: Definethe `CreateRegistrationXML()` method:

  - Line 141: Appends the request-type XMLtag to `XMLString`.
  - Line 142: Obtains the value of the 0th element of the vector `param` into the string variable `str`.
  - Lines 143□146: Set the value within the`<int>` tag to –1 if `str` contains 0.
  - Lines 147□150: Set the value within the`<int>` tag to 1 if `str` contains 1.
  - Line 151: Closes the request-type tag.

- Lines 156☐165: Definethe method `CreateAddGatewayXML()`:
  - Line 158: Appends the XML starting tag for request-type to `XMLString`.
  - Line 159: Obtains the value of the 0th element of the vector `param` into the string variable `str`.
  - Line 160☐163: Set the value-1 within the tag `<int>` if `str` contains 0.
  - Line 164: Sets the closing XML tag.
- Lines 169☐173: Definethe method `returnResult()` that appends the closing XML tag to `XMLString` and returns it to the calling method/ class.

Web services

These services include the following Java Server Pages (JSPs) and servlet:

- `Login.jsp`
- `Logout.jsp`
- `Register.jsp`
- `Unregister.jsp`
- `AddFriend.jsp`
- `FriendList.jsp`
- `NotifyFriends.java`
- `DeleteContact.jsp`

Login.jsp

Listing 3-6 contains the code for the `Login.jsp` Web service and is followed by a detailed description of the code.

Listing 3-6: Login.jsp

```
1.   <?xml version="1.0" ?>
2.   <InstantMessenger>
3.   <% Class.forName("sun.jdbc.odbc.JdbcOdbcDriver");%>
4.   <% int r_value = -1 ; %>
5.
6.   <% try { java.sql.Connection db =
java.sql.DriverManager.getConnection("jdbc:odbc:messenger","sa","" );
%>
7.
8.   <% java.sql.Statement st1 = db.createStatement(); %>
9.   <% java.sql.Statement st2 = db.createStatement(); %>
10.  <% java.sql.Statement st3 = db.createStatement(); %>
11.
```

```
12.  <% java.net.InetAddress addr ; %>
13.
14.  <% java.sql.ResultSet rs1  ;  %>
15.  <% java.sql.ResultSet rs2  ;  %>
16.
17.  <% String l_name = request.getParameter("sLoginName"); %>
18.  <% String l_password = request.getParameter("sPassword"); %>
19.  <% String l_ip = request.getRemoteAddr(); %>
20.
21.  <% int ip = 0 ; %>
22.  <% int l_count = 0 ; %>
23.  <% int p_count = 0 ; %>
24.
25.  <% rs1 = st1.executeQuery("select member_id from member where
login_name = " + "'" + l_name + "'" + ";"); %>
26.
27.  <% if (rs1.next()) { %>
28.  <% l_count = rs1.getInt("member_id");  %>
29.  <% } %>
30.
31.  <% if (l_count <= 0) { %>
32.  <% r_value = 1 ; %>
33.  <%  } else if (l_count > 0) { %>
34.
35.  <% rs2 = st2.executeQuery("select member_id from member where
login_name = " + "'" + l_name + "' and password = " + "'" + l_password +
"'" + ";"); %>
36.
37.  <% if (rs2.next()) { %>
38.   <% p_count = rs2.getInt("member_id");  %>
39.  <% } %>
40.
41.  <% if (p_count <= 0) { %>
42.   <% r_value = 2; %>
43.  <%  } else if (p_count > 0) { %>
44.
45.  <% ip = st3.executeUpdate(" UPDATE member SET ip_add =" + "'" +
l_ip + "'" +  " WHERE member.login_name = " + "'" + l_name + "'" + ";");
%>
46.
47.   <% if (ip == 1 ) { r_value = 0 ;  %>
48.   <% } else { r_value = -1;  %>
49.   <% } %>
50.  <% } %>
51.  <% } %>
52.  <auth>
53.  <int> <%= r_value %> </int>
54.  </auth>
55.  <% } catch (java.sql.SQLException ex) { %>
```

```
56.
57.   <int> <%= r_value %> </int>
58.
59.   <% } %>
60.
61.   </InstantMessenger>
```

- Line 1: Contains the tag that declares that XML 1.0 version is being used.

- Line 2: Contains the starting XML tag.

- Line 3: Contains a standard Java statement that loads the JDBC-ODBC bridge driver for use in establishing a connection with a database.

- Line 4: Declares the user-defined variable r_value, containing the return value, and initializes it.

- Line 6: Tries to establish a connection with the database within a try block, with messenger the Data Source Name, sa the login name, and the password blank. db is the Connection object.

- Lines 8□10: Use theConnection object's createStatement() method to create three Statement objects, st1, st2, and st3; Statement objects send the SQL queries to the Database Management System.

- Line 12: Declares the variable addr of the type InetAddress.

- Lines 14□15: Declare twoResultSet objects used to store results from the execution of a query.

- Lines 17□18:Use the JSP's request object's getParameter() method to retrieve the values of the user's login name and password by supplying the query string variable names as arguments.

- Line 19: Uses the request object's getRemoteAddr() method to get the IP address of the user making the request.

- Lines 21□23:Declare and initialize the user-defined variables.

- Line 25: Executes a SELECT query to get the member_id where the login_name field matches the login name that the user provides.

- Lines 27□29:Use an if statement to retrieve the member_id into the variable l_count as a result of executing the preceding query(Line 25).

- Lines 31□35: Check the value of the variablel_count. If its value is less than 0, r_value is set to 1; otherwise, if l_count is greater than 0 (meaning a record exists for the particular login-name), a second query executes that verifies the password by selecting the member_id where login_name and password fields match the user's login name and password, respectively.

- Lines 37□39:Retrieve the member_id in the variable p_count.

- Lines 41☐45:Use an if-else loop to take appropriate actions based on the value of p_count, as follows:

  - If the value of p_count is 0 or less, indicating that no record was found corresponding to both the given login name and password, the return value is set to 2.

  - If p_count is greater than 0, indicating that a match was found, a third query executes to update the member table by setting the value of ip_add field to the IP address of the user in the corresponding record.

- Lines 47☐48: Check the value of the result setip, containing the result of the update query, to set the return value accordingly, as follows.

  - If ip contains 1, indicating successful updating of the table, the return value is set to 0, meaning successful login.

  - If ip contains 0, indicating that the update query was unsuccessful, the default return value of −1 is set.

- Line 52: Starts the identification tag that indicates the type of request. The <auth> tag represents an authorization request.

- Line 53: Contains the value tag <int>, containing the return value.

- Line 54: Contains the XML closing tag for the authorization type.

- Lines 55☐59:Close the try block of Line 6 and start the catch block that catches any Exception of the type SQLException that may occur if the connection can't be made —if, for example, the database server is down — and outputs the initialized return value of −1 through the value tag <int>.

- Line 61: Contains the XML closing tag.

Logout.jsp

Listing 3-7 contains the code for the Logout.jsp Web service and is followed by a detailed description of the code.

Listing 3-7: Logout.jsp

```
1.   <?xml version="1.0" ?>
2.   <InstantMessenger>
3.   <% Class.forName("sun.jdbc.odbc.JdbcOdbcDriver");%>
4.
5.
6.   <% int r_value = -1 ; %>
7.
8.   <% try { java.sql.Connection db =
java.sql.DriverManager.getConnection("jdbc:odbc:messenger","sa","" );
%>
9.
```

```
10.    <% java.sql.Statement st = db.createStatement(); %>
11.    <% java.net.InetAddress addr ; %>
12.    <% java.sql.ResultSet rs ;   %>
13.
14.    <% String l_name = request.getParameter("sLoginName"); %>
15.
16.    <% int ip = 0 ; %>
17.
18.    <% ip = st.executeUpdate(" UPDATE member SET ip_add =" + "'" + "'"
+ " WHERE member.login_name =" + "'" +

l_name + "'" + ";"); %>
19.
20.    <% if (ip == 1) { %>
21.    <% r_value = 0 ; %>
22.    <% } %>
23.
24.    <int> <%= r_value %> </int>
25.
26.    <% } catch (java.sql.SQLException ex) { %>
27.
28.    <int> <%= r_value %> </int>
29.
30.    <% } %>
31.    </InstantMessenger>
```

- Line 1: Contains the tag that declares that XML 1.0 version is being used.

- Line 2: Contains the starting XML tag.

- Line 3: Contains a standard Java statement that loads the JDBC-ODBC bridge driver for use in establishing a connection with a database.

- Line 6: Declares the user-defined variable r_value, containing the return value, and initializes it.

- Line 8: Tries to establish a connection with the database within a try block, with messenger the Data Source Name, sa the login name, and the password blank. db is the Connection object.

- Line 10: Creates the Statement object

- Line 11: Declares a variable of type InetAddress.

- Line 12: Declares a ResultSet object to store the results from execution of a query.

- Line 14: Uses the request object's getParameter() method to retrieve the login name by supplying the query string variable name as an argument.

- Line 16: Contains a variable declaration.

- Line 18: Executes an update query to set the `ip_addr` field for the corresponding user's record in the `member` table to blank (indicating an offline status); the query result is stored in the variable `ip`.

- Lines 20□22:Use an `if` condition to set the value of the return variable to `0` if the result set `ip` contains 1, indicating that the update query of Line 18 was successful. The return value `0` denotes that user was successully logged out.

- Line 24: Puts the return value in the value tag `<int>` within the `try` block that starts at Line 8.

- Line 26□30: Closes the`try` block of Line 8, starts the `catch` block, and sets within it the value tag `<int>` with the default value of the return variable, which is `-1`. □1 is returned if the `try` statement fails.

- Line 31: Contains the XML closing tag.

Register.jsp

Listing 3-8 contains the code for the `Register.jsp` Web service and is followed by a detailed description of the code.

Listing 3-8: Register.jsp

```
1.   <?xml version="1.0" ?>
2.   <InstantMessenger>
3.   <Register>
4.   <% Class.forName("sun.jdbc.odbc.JdbcOdbcDriver");%>
5.
6.   <% String LoginName = request.getParameter("sLoginName"); %>
7.   <% String Password = request.getParameter("sPassword"); %>
8.   <% String Add1 = request.getParameter("sAdd1"); %>
9.   <% String Add2 = request.getParameter("sAdd2"); %>
10.  <% String Phone1 = request.getParameter("sPhone1"); %>
11.  <% String Phone2 = request.getParameter("sPhone2"); %>
12.  <% String Email1 = request.getParameter("sEmail1"); %>
13.  <% String Email2 = request.getParameter("sEmail2"); %>
14.  <% String Pin = request.getParameter("sPin"); %>
15.  <% String City = request.getParameter("sCity"); %>
16.  <% String Profession = request.getParameter("sProfession"); %>
17.
18.  <% int r_value = -1 ; %>
19.
20.  <% try { java.sql.Connection db =
java.sql.DriverManager.getConnection("jdbc:odbc:messenger","sa","" );
%>
21.
22.  <% java.sql.Statement st1 = db.createStatement(); %>
23.  <% java.sql.Statement st2 = db.createStatement(); %>
24.  <% java.sql.Statement st3 = db.createStatement(); %>
```

```
25.
26.    <% java.sql.ResultSet rs1 ;   %>
27.    <% java.sql.ResultSet rs2 ;   %>
28.    <% int b_Id = 0; %>
29.    <% int m_Id = 0; %>
30.
31.    <% int row_count = 1; %>
32.    <% rs1 = st1.executeQuery("select member_id from member where
login_name = " + "'" + LoginName + "'" + ";"); %>
33.
34.    <% if(rs1.next()) { %>
35.    <% b_Id = rs1.getInt("member_id");  %>
36.    <% } %>
37.
38.    <% if (b_Id == 0) { %>
39.
40.    <% row_count = st3.executeUpdate("INSERT INTO member ( login_name,
password, address_1, address_2, email_1, email_2, city, pin, profession
) VALUES ( '" + LoginName + "', '" + Password + "', '" + Add1 + "', '" +
Add2 + "', '" + Email1 + "', '" + Email2 + "', '" + City + "', '" + Pin
+ "', '" + Profession + "' ); "); %>
41.
42.    <% if (row_count == 1) { %>
43.     <% r_value = 0 ; %>
44.    <% } else { %>
45.     <% r_value = -1 ; }  } %>
46.
47.    <% } else if (b_Id > 0) { %>
48.
49.    <%  r_value = 1 ;  %>
50.
51.    <% } else { %>
52.
53.    <%  r_value = -1 ; } %>
54.
55.    <% rs1.close(); %>
56.
57.    <int> <%= r_value %> </int>
58.
59.    <% } catch (java.sql.SQLException ex) { %>
60.
61.    <int> <%= r_value %> </int>
62.
63.    <%  } %>
64.    </Register>
65.    </InstantMessenger>
```

- Line 1: Contains the tag that declares that XML 1.0 version is being used.
- Line 2: Contains the starting XML tag.

- Line 3: Contains the starting identification tag that specifies a registration request.
- Line 4: Contains a standard Java statement that loads the JDBC-ODBC bridge driver for use in establishing a connection with a database.
- Lines 6□16: Request user information, login name, password, address, and so on by passing the respective query string variable name as argument to the getParameter() method.
- Line 18: Declares the return variable and initializes it.
- Line 20: Tries to establish a connection with the database within a try block, with messenger the Data Source Name, sa the login name, and the password blank. db is the Connection object.
- Lines 22□24:Create three Statement objects.
- Lines 26□27:Create two ResultSet objects.
- Lines 28□31:Contain variable declarations and initializations.
- Line 32: Executes a query to select the member_id, where the login_name field corresponds to the user's login name, and stores the result in the ResultSet object rs1.
- Lines 34□36:Use an if statement to get the result stored in the result set object into the variable b_Id.
- Lines 38□40:Use an if condition to check the value of the variable b_Id and, if it's 0, indicating that a given login name doesn't previously exist in the member table, executes a second query to add a new record to the member table. This record contains the user information of the user from whom the registration request is received.
- Lines 42□45:Set the return value, depending on the value stored in row_count, as follows:
  - If row_count is 1, meaning that the update query was successful, r_value is set to 0 to denote successful registration.
  - If row count is not 1, r_value is set to its default –1 to denote that the requested operation didn't succeed.
- Line 47: Contains else-if clause from Line 38; checks whether b_id is greater than 0, indicating that a record with the given login name already exists in the member table, and if so, sets r_value to 1.
- Line 51□53: Contains anelse clause following the else if of Line 47, which sets the r_value to its default –1, indicating that the result of the first SELECT query (Line 32) can't be interpreted correctly.
- Line 55: Closes the ResultSet object rs1.
- Line 57: Puts the return value in the value tag <int>.

- Line 59: Closes the `try` block of Line 20 and starts the `catch` block.

- Line 61: Puts the return value in the value tag `<int>` within the `catch` block. This value is the default value –1.

- Line 64☐65: Contain XML closing tags.

Unregister.jsp

Listing 3-9 contains the code for the `Unregister.jsp` Web service and is followed by a detailed description of the code.

Listing 3-9: Unregister.jsp

```
1.    <?xml version="1.0" ?>
2.    <InstantMessenger>
3.    <% String LoginName = request.getParameter("sLoginName"); %>
4.
5.    <% Class.forName("sun.jdbc.odbc.JdbcOdbcDriver");%>
6.
7.    <% int r_value = -1 ; %>
8.
9.    <% try { java.sql.Connection db =
java.sql.DriverManager.getConnection("jdbc:odbc:messenger","sa","" );
%>
10.
11.   <% java.sql.Statement st1 = db.createStatement(); %>
12.   <% java.sql.Statement st2 = db.createStatement(); %>
13.   <% java.sql.Statement st3 = db.createStatement(); %>
14.
15.   <% java.sql.ResultSet rs1 ;   %>
16.   <% java.sql.ResultSet rs2 ;   %>
17.   <% int b_Id = 0; %>
18.   <% int m_Id = 0; %>
19.   <% int row_count = 0; %>
20.
21.   <% rs1 = st1.executeQuery("select member_id from member where
login_name = " + "'" + LoginName + "'" + ";"); %>
22.
23.   <% if (rs1.next()) { %>
24.    <% b_Id = rs1.getInt("member_id");  %>
25.   <% } %>
26.
27.   <% if (b_Id > 0) { %>
28.    <% row_count = st2.executeUpdate("delete from member where
login_name = " + "'" + LoginName + "'" + ";"); %>
29.   <% }  %>
30.
31.   <% if (row_count == 1) { %>
32.    <% r_value = 0 ; %>
```

```
33.    <%  }  %>
34.
35.    <% rs1.close();  %>
36.
37.    <UnRegister> <%= r_value %> </UnRegister>
38.
39.    <% } catch (java.sql.SQLException ex) { %>
40.
41.    <UnRegister> <%= r_value %> </UnRegister>
42.
43.    <%  }  %>
44.    </InstantMessenger>
```

- Line 1: Contains the tag that declares that XML 1.0 version is being used.
- Line 2: Contains the starting XML tag.
- Line 3: Requests login name by passing the query string variable name as an argument to the getParameter() method.
- Line 5: Contains a standard Java statement that loads the JDBC-ODBC bridge driver for use in establishing a connection with a database.
- Line 7: Declares the return variable and initializes it.
- Line 9: Tries to establish a connection with the database within a try block, with messenger the Data Source Name, sa the login name, and the password blank. db is the Connection object.
- Line 11□13: Create threeStatement objects.
- Line 15□16: Create twoResultSet objects.
- Line 17□19:Contain variable declarations and initializations.
- Line 21: Executes a query to select the member_id, where the login_name field corresponds to user's login name, and stores the result in the ResultSet object rs1.
- Line 23□25:Use an if statement to store the result in the ResultSet object rs1 into the variable b_Id.
- Line 27□29: Use an if condition to check the value of b_Id. If b_Id is greater than 0, meaning that a record exists, a second query executes to delete the record corresponding to the given login name, and its result is stored in row_count.
- Line 31□33: Set the return variable to 0if the value of the variable row_count is 1, indicating that the delete operation succeeded.
- Line 35: Closes the ResultSet object rs1.
- Line 37: Puts the return value within the value tag <UnRegister> within the try block.
- Line 39: Closes the try block of Line 10 and starts the catch block.

- Line 41: Puts the default return value, -1, within the value tag <UnRegister> within the catch block. —
- Line 44: Contains the XML closing tag.

AddFriend.jsp

Listing 3-10 contains the code for the AddFriend.jsp Web service and is followed by a detailed description of the code.

Listing 3-10: AddFriend.jsp

```
1.   <?xml version="1.0" ?>
2.   <InstantMessenger>
3.   <FriendStatus>
4.
5.
6.   <% String LoginName = request.getParameter("sLoginName"); %>
7.   <% String FriendName = request.getParameter("sFriendName"); %>
8.
9.   <UserName><%=LoginName%></UserName>
10.  <FriendName><%=FriendName%></FriendName>
11.
12.  <% int r_value = -3 ; %>
13.  <% int ip = 0 ;        %>
14.  <% Class.forName("sun.jdbc.odbc.JdbcOdbcDriver");%>
15.
16.  <% try { java.sql.Connection db =
java.sql.DriverManager.getConnection("jdbc:odbc:messenger","sa","" );
%>
17.
18.  <% java.sql.Statement st1 = db.createStatement(); %>
19.  <% java.sql.Statement st2 = db.createStatement(); %>
20.  <% java.sql.Statement st3 = db.createStatement(); %>
21.  <% java.sql.Statement st4 = db.createStatement(); %>
22.
23.  <% java.sql.ResultSet rs1 ;   %>
24.  <% java.sql.ResultSet rs2 ;   %>
25.  <% java.sql.ResultSet rs3 ;   %>
26.
27.  <% int m_Id = 0; %>
28.  <% int f_Id = 0; %>
29.  <% int statusVar = 1; %>
30.
31.  <% int row_count = 0; %>
32.  <% int rcount = 0; %>
33.
34.  <% rs1 = st1.executeQuery("select member_id from member where
login_name = " + "'" + LoginName + "'" + ";"); %>
```

```
35.    <% if (rs1.next()) { %>
36.      <% m_Id = rs1.getInt("member_id");  %>
37.    <% } %>
38.
39.    <% rs2 = st2.executeQuery("select member_id from member where
login_name = " + "'" + FriendName + "'" + ";"); %>
40.    <% if (rs2.next()) { %>
41.      <% f_Id = rs2.getInt("member_id");  %>
42.    <% } %>
43.
44.    <% if (f_Id > 0) { %>
45.      <% rs3 = st3.executeQuery("select member_id from friend where
member_id = " +  m_Id + " and friend_id = " + f_Id + ";"); %>
46.      <% if (rs3.next()) { %>
47.        <% rcount = rs3.getInt("member_id");  %>
48.      <% } %>
49.    <% } %>
50.
51.    <% if ( f_Id >= 0 & rcount <= 0 & f_Id != m_Id ) { %>
52.      <% row_count = st4.executeUpdate("INSERT INTO friend ( member_id,
friend_id ) VALUES ( " + m_Id + " , " + f_Id + "  );"); %>
53.      <% r_value = 0; %>
54.    <% } %>
55.
56.    <% if (f_Id <= 0) {  %>
57.    <% r_value = 1; %>
58.    <% }  %>
59.
60.    <% if (rcount > 0) { %>
61.      <% r_value = 2; %>
62.    <% }  %>
63.
64.    <% if (f_Id == m_Id) { %>
65.    <% r_value = 3; %>
66.    <% }  %>
67.
68.    <Status><%= r_value %></Status>
69.
70.    <% String ip_add = new String(" ");
71.      rs3 = st3.executeQuery(" SELECT ip_add FROM member WHERE
login_name =" + "'" + FriendName + "'" + ";");
72.      if (rs3.next())
73.      {
74.       ip_add = rs3.getString("ip_add");
75.       if ( ip_add.trim().equals("")||(ip_add.equals(" ")))
76.       {
77.        ip = 0 ; ip_add = "null";
78.       }
79.      else
```

```
80.          {
81.            ip = 1 ;
82.          }
83.        }
84.    %>
85.
86.    <% rs2.close(); %>
87.    <% rs1.close(); %>
88.
89.    <% } catch (java.sql.SQLException ex) { %>
90.    <Exception><%=ex%></Exception>
91.    <Status><%= r_value %></Status>
92.
93.    <%  } %>
94.    <Online><%= ip %></Online>
95.    </FriendStatus>
96.    </InstantMessenger>
```

- Line 1: Contains the tag that declares that XML 1.0 version is being used.
- Line 2: Contains the starting XML tag.
- Line 3: Containst the identification tag that specifies an AddFriend request.
- Lines 6□7: Request the user's login name and the friend's login name by passing the respective query string variable name as an argument to the getParameter() method.
- Lines 9□10: Contain XML value tags containing the user's and friend's login names.
- Line 12: Declares the return variable and initializes it.
- Line 13: Initializes the variable ip to 0.
- Line 14: Contain a standard Java statement that loads the JDBC-ODBC bridge driver for use in establishing a connection with a database.
- Line 16: Tries to establish a connection with the database within a try block, with messenger the Data Source Name, sa the login name, and the password blank. db is the Connection object.
- Lines 18□21:Create four Statement objects.
- Lines 23□25:Create three ResultSet objects.
- Lines 27□32:Contain. variable declarations and initializations.
- Lines 34: Executes a query that selects the member ID of the user and stores it in rs1.
- Lines 35□37: Retrieve the member ID from theResultSet object rs1 to the variable m_id.
- Line 39: Executes a query to select the friend's member ID and stores it in rs2.
- Lines 40□42:Retrieve the friend's member ID from the ResultSet object rs2 to the variable f_id.

- Lines 44□45:Use an `if` condition to check value of `f_id`. If `f_id` is greater than 0, meaning that the friend's ID was found, execute a query to check whether the `friend` table contains an entry where `member_id` field has the same value as the user's member ID and `friend_id` has the same value as the friend's member ID. The result of this query is stored in `rs3`.

- Lines 46□48:Use the variable `rcount` to obtain value of `rs3`.

- Lines 51□52:Check the following three conditions before executing a query that adds the friend to the user's friends list by entering a record into the `friend` table:

  - That `f_id` isn't 0, which means that the friend's ID doesn't exist in the `member` table.

  - That `rcount` isn't greater than 0, which means that the user's already added the given friend to his/her friends list.

  - That `f_id` isn't the same as `m_id`, which means that the user is trying to add herself as a friend!

- Line 53: Sets the value of the return variable to 0.

- Lines 56□58: Use an `if` clause to set `r_value` to 1 in the event that `f_id` is 0 or less than 0 — that is, the friend's ID doesn't exist in the `member` table.

- Lines 60□62:Use an `if` clause to set `r_value` to 2 in the event that `rcount` is greater than 0 — that is, the friend already exists in the user's friends list.

- Lines 64□66:Use an `if` clause to set `r_value` to 2 in the event that `f_id` is the same as `m_id` — that is, the user is trying to add himself/herself to his/her friends list.

- Line 68: Puts the return value within the XML value tags.

- Line 70: Creates a new empty string, `ip_add`.

- Line 71: Executes a third query that selects the value of the `ip_add` field corresponding to the given friend's name. This value indicates the online or offline status of a friend.

- Lines 72□74:Retrieve `ip_add` from the `ResultSet` object to the variable `ip_add`.

- Lines 75□78:Set the variable `ip` to 0 and the variable `ip_add` to `null` if `ip_add` is a blank string.

- Lines 79□82:Set `ip` to 1 if `ip_add` isn't a blank string.

- Lines 86□87:Close the two `ResultSet` objects.

- Line 89: Closes the `try` block of Line 15 and starts the `catch` block.

- Lines 90□91:Put the `Exception` description and the return value within the respective XML tags in the event that the `catch` block executes. `r_value` then contains the default value of -1.

- Line 94: Puts the status of the friend within the respective value tag. If `ip` is 1, it indicates an online friend; otherwise, it denotes an offline friend.

- Lines 95□96: Contain the closing XML tags.

FriendList.jsp

Listing 3-11 contains the code for the `FriendList.jsp` Web service and is followed by a detailed description of the code.

Listing 3-11: FriendList.jsp

```
1.   <?xml version="1.0" ?>
2.   <InstantMessenger>
3.   <FriendList>
4.   <% Class.forName("sun.jdbc.odbc.JdbcOdbcDriver");%>
5.   <% java.sql.Connection db =
java.sql.DriverManager.getConnection("jdbc:odbc:messenger","sa","");  %>
6.   <% java.sql.Statement st = db.createStatement(); %>
7.
8.   <% java.sql.ResultSet rs ;  %>
9.
10.  <% String l_name = request.getParameter("sLoginName"); %>
11.  <% int ip = 0 ; %>
12.  <% String ip_add = "" ; %>
13.  <% rs = st.executeQuery(" SELECT login_name_a, ip_add  FROM
friend_list WHERE friend_list.login_name =" + "'" + l_name + "'" + ";");
%>
14.  <UserName><%= l_name %></UserName>
15.
16.  <% while (rs.next()) { %>
17.  <% String name = rs.getString("login_name_a"); %>
18.  <% ip_add = rs.getString("ip_add"); %>
19.  <% if ( ip_add.trim().equals("")||(ip_add.equals(" "))){ ip = 0 ;
ip_add = "null"; %>
20.  <% } else { ip = 1 ;  } %>
21.
22.  <FriendName><%= name %></FriendName>
23.  <Status><%= ip %></Status>
24.
25.  <% } %>
26.  <% rs.close(); %>
27.  </FriendList>
28.  </InstantMessenger>
```

- Line 1: Contains the tag that declares that XML 1.0 version is being used.

- Line 2: Contains the starting XML tag.

- Line 3: Contains the starting identification tag.

- Line 4: Contains a standard Java statement that loads the JDBC-ODBC bridge driver for use in establishing a connection with a database.

- Line 5: Tries to establish a connection with the database, with `messenger` the Data Source Name, `sa` the login name, and the password blank. `db` is the `Connection` object.

- Line 6: Creates a `Statement` object.

- Line 8: Creates a `ResultSet` objects.

- Line 10: Requests the user's login name

- Lines 11☐12:Contain variable declarations and initializations.

- Line 13: Executes a query that selects all the friends' names and their respective status from the `friend_list` view.

- Line 14: Puts the user's login name within the respective XML value tags.

- Lines 16☐25:Contain a `while` loop that performs the following steps:

  - Line 16: Checks whether result set has more records.

  - Lines 17-18: Retrieve the friend's name and his IP address into the variables `name` and `ip_add`, respectively.

  - Lines 19☐20:Execute an `if-else` loop. If the friend's IP address field is `null` or blank, variable `ip` is set to `0` to denote offline status; otherwise, `ip` is set to `1` to denote online status.

  - Lines 22☐23: Set the friend's nameand status values within the respective XML tags. These tags and their values are generated repeatedly as long as the `while` condition is satisfied — that is, the result set has more records.

- Line 26: Closes the `ResultSet` object.

- Lines 27☐28: Contain XML closing tags.

NotifyFriends

Listing 3-12 contains the code for the `NotifyFriends.java` Web service and is followed by a detailed description of the code.

Listing 3-12: NotifyFriend.java

```
1.   import java.io.*;
2.   import javax.servlet.*;
3.   import javax.servlet.http.*;
4.   import java.sql.*;
5.   import java.util.*;
6.   import java.io.*;
7.
8.
9.   public class NotifyFriends extends HttpServlet
10.  {
11.  BufferedOutputStream m_BresponseStream;
```

```
12.   String                            m_SuserName;
13.   String                            m_status;
14.   String                            m_SxmlString;
15.   Connection                        m_Cconnection;
16.   Statement                         m_Cstatement;
17.   ResultSet                         m_CresultSet;
18.
19.
20.   public void service( HttpServletRequest req, HttpServletResponse
res )
21.   {
22.   m_SuserName          = new String();
23.   m_SxmlString = new String();
24.   m_status             = new String();
25.
26.   try
27.   {
28.
29.    ServletContext sc = getServletContext();
30.    res.setStatus( HttpServletResponse.SC_OK);
31.    res.setContentType(" text/plain ");
32.
33.    m_SuserName= req.getParameter("sLoginName");
34.    m_status= req.getParameter("sStatus");
35.
36.
37.    m_SxmlString = "<?xml version=\"1.0\"?>";
38.    m_SxmlString    += "<InstantMessenger>";
39.    m_SxmlString    += "<NotifyFriends>";
40.    m_SxmlString    += "<UserName>";
41.    m_SxmlString    += m_SuserName;
42.    m_SxmlString    += "</UserName>";
43.    m_SxmlString    += "<Status>";
44.    if (m_status.equalsIgnoreCase("1"))
45.      m_SxmlString    += "On-Line";
46.    else
47.      m_SxmlString    += "Off-Line";
48.    m_SxmlString    += "</Status>";
49.
50.
51.    m_BresponseStream = new BufferedOutputStream
(res.getOutputStream());
52.
53.    try
54.    {
55.     Class.forName("sun.jdbc.odbc.JdbcOdbcDriver");
56.    }
57.    catch (ClassNotFoundException ef)
58.    {
```

```
59.     System.out.println("Class not Found Exception "+ef);

60.   }
61.
62.   try
63.   {
64.     m_Cconnection = DriverManager.getConnection(
"jdbc:odbc:messenger","sa","");
65.     m_Cstatement = m_Cconnection.createStatement();
66.     m_CresultSet = m_Cstatement.executeQuery(" SELECT
friend_list.login_name FROM friend_list  WHERE friend_list.login_name_a
= " + "'" + m_SuserName + "'" +";");
67.   }
68.   catch(Exception g)
69.   {
70.     System.out.println("Exception in Connection Statement");
71.
72.   }
73.
74.   while(m_CresultSet.next())
75.   {
76.     String str1      = m_CresultSet.getString(1);
77.     m_SxmlString    += "<FriendName>";
78.     m_SxmlString    += str1;
79.     m_SxmlString    += "</FriendName>";
80.   }
81.
82.   m_SxmlString    += "</NotifyFriends>";
83.   m_SxmlString    += "</InstantMessenger>";
84.
85.   byte [] response = m_SxmlString.getBytes();
86.   m_BresponseStream.write(response, 0, response.length);
87.   m_BresponseStream.flush();
88.   m_BresponseStream.close();
89.   m_Cconnection.close();
90.   }
91.   catch (Exception e)
92.   {
93.     System.out.println("Exception occured:"+e);
94.   }
95.
96.   }
}
```

- Lines 1☐6: Contain import statements that import various Java packages used by the NotifyFriends class.

- Line 9: Declares NotifyFriends as a subclass of the HTTPServlet class.

- Lines 11☐17:Contain object/variable declarations:

- Line 11: Declares the `BufferedOutputStream` object that is used to write the response.

- Lines 12□14: Declare the string variables to contain string elements such as the user's login name, status, and the output XML string.

- Line 15: Declares the `Connection` object used to connect to the database.

- Line 16: Declares the `Statement` object used to send queries to the Database Management System for execution.

- Line 17: Declares the `ResultSet` object to store the result of a query-execution.

- Line 20: Declares the `service()` method of the `NotifyFriends` servlet that takes an `HTTPServletRequest` and `HTTPServletResponse` object as parameters.

- Lines 22□24:Initializes the string variables.

- Line 26: Starts a `try` block to enclose the operations that the servlet is required to perform and that may throw an `Exception`.

- Line 29: Gets the context in which the servlet is running.

- Line 30: Sets the status of the response to `SC_OK`, which denotes that the resource requested by the client — in this case, the `NotifyServlet` — is available to service client request.

- Line 31: Sets the content type of the response object so that the client may know how to interpret the response. `text/plain` signifies that response contains only data and no markup.

- Lines 33□34:Pass the query string variable `names` as arguments to the `getParameter()` method of the request object `req` to obtain the user's login name and status.

- Lines 37□48: Build the output XML string containing the servlet's response.

  - Lines 44□47:Contain an `if-else` loop that checks the value of variable `m_status` against the value 1 and sets the value of the XML `<status>` tag accordingly: If `m_status` is 1, the status is set to indicate that the user is online; otherwise, the status is set to offline.

- Line 51: Initializes the buffered output stream.

- Lines 53□60: Nest the standard Java statement (Line 55) that loads the JDBC-ODBC driver to establish a database connection within a `try-catch` block. If the specified driver can't load/isn't found, the `catch` block prints out the message `Class not Found Exception` along with the `Exception` definition.

- Lines 62□72:Contain another `try-catch` block that contains statements to establish a connection with the database (Line 64) and execute a query to retrieve names of the friends from the `friend_list` view (Line 66). The results of the query are stored in the variable `m_CresultSet`. If the connection with the database can't be made, a general `Exception` is thrown that's caught by the `catch` statement, and the message `Exception in Connection Statement` prints out to the server console.

- Lines 74□80:Contain a `while` loop that sequentially loops through the result set and generates a `<FriendName>` value tag corresponding to the name of each friend contained in the result set.

- Lines 82□83: Contain XML closing tags that complete the XML response stored in the the string variable `m_SxmlString`.

- Line 85: Converts the response string into bytes and stores them in the response variable.

- Lines 86□88: Write the XML response bytes to the client, flush out the contents of the output stream, and close it.

- Line 89: Closes the connection to the database.

- Lines 91□94:Contain the `catch` statement following the first `try` block of Line 26. It catches a general `Exception` if the `try` block fails and prints out the message `Exception occured` along with the description of the `Exception` on the server console.

DeleteContact.jsp

Listing 3-13 contains the code for the `DeleteContact.jsp` Web service and is followed by a detailed description of the code.

Listing 3-13: DeleteContact.jsp

```
1.   <?xml version="1.0" ?>
2.   <InstantMessenger>
3.   <DeleteStatus>
4.
5.   <% String LoginName   = request.getParameter("sLoginName"); %>
6.   <% String FriendName  = request.getParameter("sFriendName"); %>
7.
8.   <UserName><%=LoginName%></UserName>
9.   <FriendName><%=FriendName%></FriendName>
10.
11.  <% int r_value = -1 ; %>
12.
13.  <% Class.forName("sun.jdbc.odbc.JdbcOdbcDriver");%>
14.
15.  <% try { java.sql.Connection db =
java.sql.DriverManager.getConnection("jdbc:odbc:messenger","sa","" );
%>
16.
17.  <% java.sql.Statement st1 = db.createStatement(); %>
18.  <% java.sql.Statement st2 = db.createStatement(); %>
19.  <% java.sql.Statement st3 = db.createStatement(); %>
20.  <% java.sql.Statement st4 = db.createStatement(); %>
```

```
21.
22.    <% java.sql.ResultSet rs1 ;   %>
23.    <% java.sql.ResultSet rs2 ;   %>
24.    <% java.sql.ResultSet rs3 ;   %>
25.
26.    <% int m_Id = 0; %>
27.    <% int f_Id = 0; %>
28.    <% int statusVar = 1; %>
29.
30.    <% int row_count = 0; %>
31.
32.    <% int count = 0; %>
33.
34.    <% rs1 = st1.executeQuery("select member_id from member where
login_name = " + "'" + LoginName + "'" + ";"); %>
35.
36.    <% while (rs1.next()) { %>
37.     <% m_Id = rs1.getInt("member_id");  %>
38.    <% } %>
39.
40.    <% rs2 = st2.executeQuery("select member_id from member where
login_name = " + "'" + FriendName + "'" + ";"); %>
41.
42.    <% while (rs2.next()) { %>
43.     <% f_Id = rs2.getInt("member_id");  %>
44.    <% } %>
45.
46.    <% if (f_Id > 0)
47.    {
48.     row_count = st4.executeUpdate("Delete friend where
member_id="+m_Id+"and friend_id="+f_Id+";");
49.     if (row_count > 0)
50.       r_value = 0;
51.     else
52.       r_value = 1;
53.    }
54.    else if (f_Id == 0)
55.        r_value = 2;
56.    %>
57.
58.    <Status><%= r_value %></Status>
59.
60.    <% rs2.close(); %>
61.    <% rs1.close(); %>
62.    <% } catch (java.sql.SQLException ex) { %>
63.    <Status><%= r_value %></Status>
64.    <% } %>
65.    </DeleteStatus>
66.    </InstantMessenger>
```

- Line 1: Contains the tag that declares that XML 1.0 version is being used.

- Line 2: Contains the starting XML tag.

- Line 3: Contains the identification tag that specifies a delete contact/friend request.

- Line 5☐6: Request the user's login name and friend's login name by passing the respective query string variable name as an argument to the getParameter() method.

- Line 8☐9: Contain XML value tags containing the user's and friend's login names.

- Line 11: Declares the return variable and initializes it.

- Line 13: Contains a standard Java statement that loads the JDBC-ODBC bridge driver for use in establishing a connection with a database.

- Line 15: Tries to establish a connection with the database within a try block, with messenger the Data Source Name, sa the login name, and the password blank. Db is the Connection object.

- Line 17☐20: Create fourStatement objects.

- Line 22☐24:Create three ResultSet objects.

- Line 26☐32:Contain variable declarations and initializations.

- Line 34: Executes a query that selects the member ID of the user and stores it in rs1.

- Line 36☐38: Retrieve the member ID fromResultSet object rs1 to variable m_id.

- Line 40: Executes a query to select a friend's member ID and stores it in rs2.

- Lines 42☐44:Retrieve the friend's member ID from ResultSet object rs2 into the variable f_id.

- Lines 46☐48:Use an if condition to check the value of f_id. If f_id is greater than 0, meaning friend ID was found, execute a query to delete the entry from the friend table where the value of the member_id field is the same as m_id and friend_id field has a value the same as f_id. The outcome of this query is stored in the variable row_count.

- Lines 49☐53:Set r_value depending on the value of row_count,as follows:

  - If row_count is greater than 0, r_value is set to 0 to indicate that the given contact/friend was successfully deleted.

  - If row_count is less than or equal to 0, r_value is set to 1 to indicate that the delete operation failed.

- Lines 54☐56:Contain the else-if clause following the if statement of Line 46. If f_id is 0, meaning that the contact/friend's ID wasn't found in the member table, r_value is set to 2.

- Line 58: Sets the return value within the XML value tag <Status>.

- Lines 60☐61: Close the two result sets,rs1 and rs2.

- Lines 62□64:Contain the `catch` statement that catches an `Exception` of type `SQLException` thrown by the `try` statement of Line 15 and puts the default value of `r_value` within XML value tags.

- Line 65□66: Contain the closing XML tags.

Summary

In this chapter, we discuss the server (Java) architecture for the Instant Messaging application. As the discussions in this chapter indicate, the server application clearly lies at the root of the Instant Messaging application. Here, you've seen that you can classify the Java Server Application classes into two categories: the core Java classes □ for example,`Server.java`, `XMLParser.java`, and so on — and Web-service classes/JSP □ for example, `NotifyFriends.java`, `AddFriend.jsp`, and so on. Although the Web services generate the final XML to send to the client, the core classes support the basic functionality of the server. The chapter also clearly demonstrates that the `Server` class is at the heart of the Instant Messaging application. Various `Server` classes in this chapter are described through the use of flow diagrams to clarify the concepts behind them. In the next chapter, we discuss the C# server.

Chapter 4

Instant Messaging Server (C#)

In Chapter 3, we discuss the Java version of the server module. This chapter discusses the design and implementation processes of the Server module for the Instant Messaging application. As an introduction to the topic of Web services, the chapter describes how the Server module processes various types of client requests and Jabber responses. The chapter also includes a brief discussion on ADO.NET and an inclusive discussion about how various Web methods work. Toward the end of the chapter, we provide the technical documentation for the server module. To facilitate a better understanding of the text, we also supply flow charts throughout this chapter.

Web Services

The concept of Web services gained momentum with the launch of the much-awaited Microsoft product .NET, which is dedicated to development of Web-centric applications. Web services are specifications to build an application that can be deployed over any system, irrespective of the platform that it supports. Such an application also supports the Internet. A consuming application can use the Web services that you deploy on the Web to build a higher level of the application, thereby saving precious time and effort. The standard platform for Web services is HTTP with XML. A very useful example of a Web service is the Passport service that Microsoft provides.

How to build a Web service

In the .NET environment, you can create Web services with ease. In this section, you are guided through a small tutorial showing you how to build a Web service in the .NET environment by using the C# programming language. As you start building a Web service, make sure that the system you selected for deploying the Web service has IIS server installed on it.

As you start coding for a Web service, include the header tag at the beginning of the coding. The header tag that follows this paragraph mentions the name of the programming language chosen for building the Web service and the name of the Web-service class:

```
<%@ WebService Language="C#" class="HelloWorld" %>
```

Now just follow these steps:

1. After creating the header tag, add the namespaces necessary for building the Web service. The following code snippet lists some important namespaces that you must include while coding the Web service:

```
using System;
using System.Collections;
using System.Configuration;
using System.ComponentModel;
using System.Diagnostics;
using System.Web; //provides the functionality required to
                        communicate over web.
using System.Web.Services; // provides the functionality required by
                                web services.
```

2. Add another tag listing the protocol to use to access the Web service and the name of the machine that is acting as a server for hosting the Web service. In the following code, the protocol is http and the name of the server is pratul:

```
[WebService(Namespace="http://ankur/")]
```

3. Declare a publicly accessible class HelloWorld (same as what you declared in the header tag), which is inherited from System.Web.Services.WebService class. Inside the default constructor of HelloWorld class, the InitializeComponent() function is implemented. This function initializes the controls that the Web service uses. The following code depicts the implementation of the default constructor of the class and its required functions:

```
public class HelloWorld : System.Web.Services.WebService
{
public HelloWorld()
{
    InitializeComponent();
}
private void InitializeComponent()
{

}
public void Dispose()
{
        // this will release the memory occupied by the control
initialized
        // by the constructor.
}
}
```

4. After implementation of the default constructor, you deploy a Web method with public accessibility, as shown in the following code snippet. This code implements the Web method DisplayMessage(), which returns the string "Hello World!" on

execution. Make sure that, whenever you implement any Web method, you put the [WebMethod] tag at the start of the method.

```
[WebMethod]
public String DisplayMessage()
{
        return "Hello World!";
}

}
```

5. After you finish implementation of the DisplayMessage() Web method, save the file with an asmx extension in the root folder or any subfolder of the IIS server.

How to access the Web service

To access the Web service, the user must know the name of the server that's hosting the Web service and have certain rights to use the Web services, such as those obtained by registering with the server that's hosting the Web service. Usually, on accessing the Web service, the user must authenticate himself/herself by providing information such as a login name and password, but some Web services are free and open for everyone — for example, the Web service we deploy in our application. Also remember that, to access the Web services, the user must have access to the World Wide Web. Suppose, for example, that you want to access the Web service SampleWS that the server ankur hosts. Just follow these steps:

1. First of all create a new project using the Microsoft® Visual Studio .NET Development Environment. Let the project name be WindowsApplication1.

2. To access a Web service, you need to add the reference of this Web service to the project. To add the reference of the Web service to the project, right-click the mouse anywhere in the Solution Explorer window. If the Solution Explorer window is not visible then go to the View menu on the tool bar of the Microsoft® Visual Studio .NET Development Environment and select Solution Explorer option to make the Solution explorer window visible.

3. From the pop-up menu that appears, choose Add Web Reference, as shown in Figure 4-1.

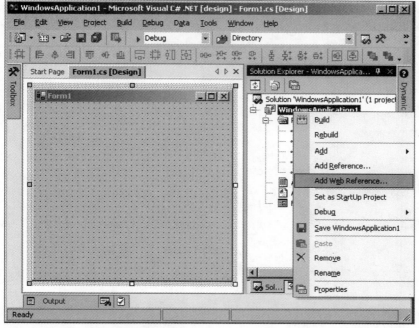

Figure 4-1: Adding a Web service reference

4. In the Address bar of the window that opens, you must enter the nameof the Web service and the server that's hosting it. In our example, the name of the server that's hosting the SampleWS Web service is `ankur`. Thus the address for accessing the required Web service is `http://ankur/SampleWS.asmx`, as shown in Figure 4-2.(You can access any other Web service similarly.) After typing the required address in the Address bar, press the Enter key or click the Go button.

5. If you successfully call the Web service, a new window appears, as shown in Figure 4-3. On the left-hand side of the window is the list of all Web methods present in the Web service. The right-hand side of the window contains the reference for the Web service and its description. The Web server automatically creates the description and associated Help for the Web service.

6. After you press the Add Reference button as shown in Figure 4-3, all Web methods of this service are also included in the project and become part of the project See the changes to the Solution Explorer window to the right side of the screen (Figure 4-4).

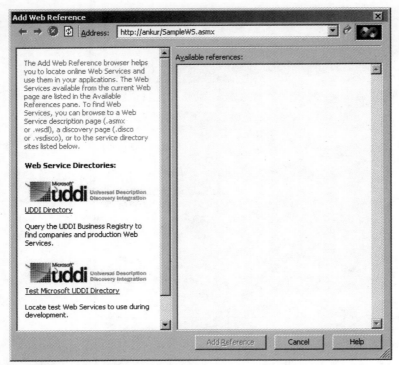

Figure 4-2: Calling a Web service

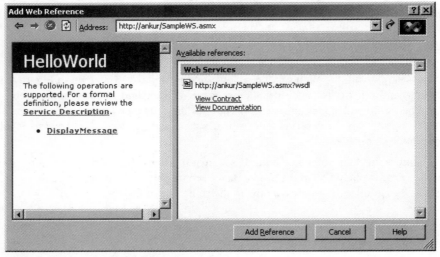

Figure 4-3: Successful calling of the Web service

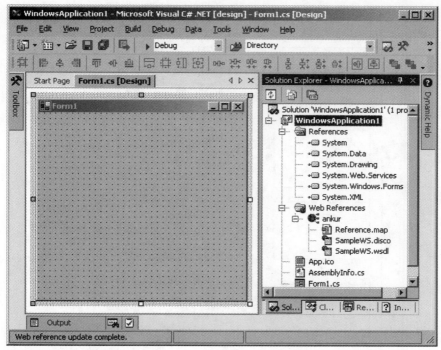

Figure 4-4: Web methods

Developing the Server

Based on the approach of the Instant Messaging application that we're developing, the Server module maintains a two-way communication — one with the Client module and the other with the Jabber server. Thus, while developing the Server module, you must make sure that the module maintains an equilibrium with the Jabber server as well as with the Client module. The Server module must be complete in itself. In the absence of the Jabber server, the Server module must keep functioning smoothly without disappointing its local client.

We show you the preferred design of the Server module in Figure 4-5. As you can see from Figure.4-5, various threads are deployed in the Server module to bridge the parallel communication. The Server module maintains the parallel communication between itself and local clients on one hand and on the other hand Server module maintains the communication with Jabber Server. At the beginning of the session with a client, the local server allots a separate thread to the client. Along with the client threads, the Server module maintains threads for reading the messages flowing from the Jabber server side. These messages are iterated by their means of threads, and the process continues by the until session between the Server module and Jabber Server does not come to an end.

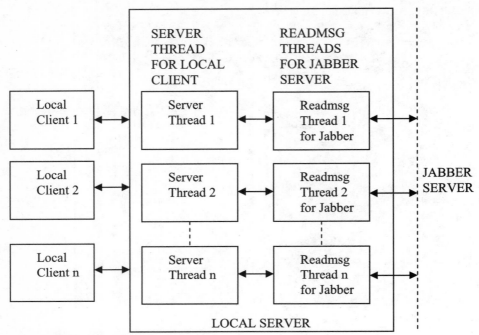

Figure 4-5: Work flow of the C# server

An Introduction to ADO.NET

ADO.NET is the latest Universal Data Access (UDA) technology, unveiled along with the launch of the .NET platform. Although ADO.NET functions like its ancestor, ADO, some enhanced features incorporated into the ADO.NET architecture make it superior to ADO alone. One such feature is its nondependence on databases that results from the use of XML for data traversing. Despite certain differences between ADO.NET and ADO, those well-versed with the working of ADO don't find understanding the workings and behavior of ADO.NET difficult. The following list discusses some prominent features of ADO.NET:

- **Interoperability:** In ADO.NET architecture, the medium of data transmission is XML-oriented, which relieves both parent and consuming application from the headache of data formatting. When the consuming application, equipped with ADO.NET, recieves the data from the parent application, the consuming application is not bothered about in which format does the parent application transmits the data because at the recieving end the consuming application is equipped with ADO.NET, which has XML support. Due to XML support available in ADO.NET, the consuming application is not concerned about the data types and data formats supported by the parent application as XML is not restricts till upto limited data types like COM.

- **Scalability:** Any application using ADO.NET, if deployed over the Web, can handle large number of simultaneous connections, because ADO.NET works on the principle of a disconnected access database, where it has no need to maintain a constant connection with the server. Thus an application using ADO.NET doesn't maintain a database lock for long this reduces the load on server as there will be no bottlenecks and there will fast query processing.

- **Introduction of `DataSet`:** `DataSet` is one of the key modules on which the working of the entire ADO.NET architecture depends. The other key module is the *.NET Provider*. In ADO.NET, `DataSet` is a replacement for the `RecordSet` class present in ADO. `DataSet` can be considered as a small database that holds the records of more than one table without applying any `JOIN`. It also represents the relationship between the tables. The data that `DataSet` represents is the copy of the original data, and whatever modification is necessary is made to the copy of the data. After the required changes are made, `DataSet` submits the copy of modified data back to the data source for the final update. Thus throughout the entire process of modification, the data remains secure and away from the data source. This arrangement prevents any direct intervention in the data source.

Architecture of ADO.NET

The architecture of ADO.NET has two main components: the .NET Provider and `DataSet`.

The .NET Provider handles tasks such as establishing connection between the application and the database, processing various queries pertaining to data retrieval, and obtaining the results from the database. The following four submodules are present under the .NET Provider:

- **Connection:** Establishes the connection with the data source.
- **Command:** Executes certain commands on the data source.
- **Data Reader:** Reads the data from the data source in read-only and forward-only streams.
- **Data Adapter:** Populates the `DataSet` with the data that the database returns.

The `DataSet` component of ADO.NET also comprises the following submodules:

- **Data Table:** Represents all the tables held by the `DataSet`.
- **Data Relation:** Represents the relation between various tables present in the `Dataset`.

Comparison between ADO and ADO.NET

The `RecordSet` class present in the ADO environment was capable of retrieving records from multiple tables, but it needed the help of a `JOIN` clause. In the case of `DataSet`, you have no need of the JOIN clause in retrieving data from multiple tables.

Another significant difference between ADO and ADO.NET is in cursor types. In ADO.NET, the `DataSet` is represented as the static cursor of ADO, while the `DataReader` replaces the read-only cursor of ADO.

In ADO.NET, you use XML for transmitting the data across different applications, whereas in ADO, you use COM, so the data types must be COM-centric. ADO.NET places no such restriction on data types, however, and through it, you can send more rich-formatted data than you can with ADO.

Server application

Primarily, the Server module of our Instant Messaging application undertakes two tasks — first, it listens to client requests, and second, it handles the responses coming from the Jabber server. Remember that, sometimes, the Server module may need to contact the Jabber server while listening to the client requests, and sometimes it may not. After the Server module starts, it waits for a client request for connection. On receiving the client request, the Server module performs the required authentication of the client, and on successful authorization, the client is permitted to log on. After the logon, a client is most likely to make some request, which is handed over to the Server module. The server, on receiving the client request, analyzes it. If, after analyzing the client request, the server finds that it can fulfill the request without bothering the Jabber server, it responds in appropriate XML structure, which the Client module can read and understand. To form the responses, the Server module uses the services of `XmlFormat` class. To deliver the server's responses to the client, the `SendMsg()` function is implemented in the `SocketThread` class.

In some situations, however, the local server isn't in a position to execute the client request. In that case, the server simply hands over the request to the Jabber server. In handing over the client request to the Jabber server, the local server transforms the client request into Jabber standards. In other words, the local server reformats the client request in the XML structure that the Jabber server supports. After delivering the request to the Jabber server, the Server module waits for the reply of the Jabber server. After the response from the Jabber server arrives, the Server module reads it and parses it. To analyze the Jabber server's responses, the `SocketThread` class implements a separate function, `parseJabberXml()` in. The `parseJabberXml()` function determines the type and contents of the Jabber response. While parsing the Jabber response, the Server module may need to make another request to the Jabber server. In such a situation, the Server module sends the request to the Jabber server and again waits for the response.

As we just mentioned, the Jabber server has its own standard of XML, so whenever a request is delivered to the Jabber server, it must be in the XML format that the Jabber server understands. To create various types of requests in Jabber norms, the Server module implements the `JabberXml()` function.

After the process of sending the requests to and receiving the responses from the Jabber server is complete, the local server re-creates the Jabber response in the XML format that the Client module understands. To form the Jabber response in client standards, the XmlFormat class is called on. After formatting the Jabber response in client standards, the local server hands it over to the SendMsg() function, which delivers it to the client.

Web Services

The Web services that we deploy in the Instant Messaging application primarily handle tasks such as data retrieval and resolving updates with the application database. A Web service is implemented in the application so that workload on the local server is reduced and the Server can devote maximum attention to dealing with the clients. To deal with all possible types of client requests, the Web service deploys various Web methods in. Each Web method fulfills a certain client request that the local server forwards.

Whenever the local server requires the services of the Web service, it makes the HTTP request to the nearest Web server. The Web server searches the Web service that can fulfill the request of the client. After locating the required Web service, the server hands the client request over to that service. In return, the Web method capable of fulfilling the client demand is executed, and the response of the Web method is returned to the Web server. The Web server, in turn, returns the response to the client in XML format. Figure 4-6 displays the workings of the Web service.

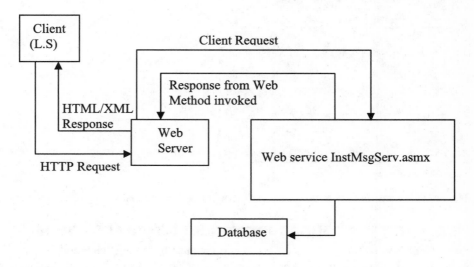

Figure 4-6: Work flow of a Web service

Inside the Server Application

The Server module of the Instant Messaging application works between the Client module and the Jabber server. On the one hand, it listens and caters to the requests coming from the Client module, and on the other, it acts as the Jabber client, delivering the requests to the Jabber server on behalf of the Client module. Hence, the Server module primarily performs the following tasks:

- Receiving a connection request from the client and starting the session for the client.

- Processing client requests by means of various Web methods that the Web service deployed in the application implements. For processing the client requests, the server may need to approach the Jabber server. In that case, the local server must deliver the client request in the XML format that the Jabber server supports and recognizes.

- Processing the responses that the Jabber server returns.

Whenever the Server module is run, a small window appears, as shown in Figure 4-7. In the window, you see two buttons, one for starting the server and the other for stopping the server, as well as a label showing the number of active connections on the server.

Figure 4-7: Startup window of server

The next sections discuss how the Server module handles the tasks that we just discussed.

Receiving the connection request from the client

First, the Server module receives the connection request from the Client module. The `StartConn()` function of `frmLocalServer` class is responsible for accepting connection requests. The local server receives all connection requests on its socket. After the connection request arrives, a new thread is assigned to it, and the thread starts. The following code illustrates this process:

```
public class frmLocalServer : System.Windows.Forms.Form
{
```

```
private void StartConn()
{
    
Socket sock;
sock=sck.AcceptSocket(); //accept connection req.
SocketThread sckThrd=new SocketThread(sock);//assign it to a new thread
Thread thrd=new Thread(new ThreadStart(sckThrd.StartSession));
thrd.Start();
    
  }
}
```

After accepting the client's connection request and assigning a new thread to it, the next task of the Server module is to start the session for the client. The StartSession() function of the SocketThread class handles the task of starting the new session for the incoming connection request.

After the StartSession() function assigns the thread, it searches for the data available on the socket. If data is available on the socket, the StartSession() function sets the size of byte type array equal to the length of the message available on the socket and the entire data is received in the byte array. After creating the byte type array and putting the message into it, the data is further converted into a string-type format. Converting the data into a string type is mandatory, as the data is later written in a temporary XML file, which supports only string-formatted data. The following code depicts the working of StartSession() function:

```
public class SocketThread
{
    
  public void StartSession()
  {
    if (sck.Available>0)
    {
      iDataAvailable=sck.Available;
      
      bData=new byte[iDataAvailable];
      sck.Receive(bData);
      for (int i=0;i<iDataAvailable;i++)
      {
        strMsg+=((char)bData[i]).ToString();
      }
      
```

To write the data in a temporary file, a new instance of StreamWriter class (streamXml) is created. Before creating the file, the Exists() method of StreamWriter class[what?] makes sure that such a file doesn't already exist. The file if any that was created earlier is deleted and new version of file is created and the data is written into it. After the data is written to the file, the parseXml() function is called for parsing the file to determine its type and contents. The `Integer` value that the `parseXml()` function returns to notify the type of request present in the file is trapped in an integer-type variable (`iCode`). Later, the `processXml()` function is called with the value returned by the `parseXml()` as a parameter to perform suitable actions and deliver the results. The following code illustrates the creation of a temporary XML file and also shows the role of `parseXml()` and `processXml()` functions:

```
    System.IO.StreamWriter streamXml;
    if (System.IO.File.Exists("temp" + iFileNo.ToString()+".xml"))
    {
      System.IO.File.Delete("temp" + iFileNo.ToString()+".xml");
    }
    streamXml=System.IO.File.CreateText("temp" +
iFileNo.ToString()+".xml");
    iCode=parseXml("temp" + iFileNo.ToString()+".xml");
    iPCode=processXml(iCode);
    ...............................
  }
}
```

Processing various client requests

The Server module of the Instant Messaging application is entitled to process various client requests. The requests that the Server module receives can vary from authentication to unregistration requests. To handle the processing of different kinds of client requests, the `SocketThread` class deploys a separate function, `prcessXml()`. The `processXml()` function considers the integer value that the `parseXml()` function returns, while parsing the requests to determine their type. Based on the return value of `parseXml()` function, the `processXml()` function decides the suitable course of action. Usually, the steps that the `processXml()` chooses to accomplish the given task consist of calls to various other methods implemented in the application.

Authorization request

An *authorization request* comes if the user logs on to the application. If such a request arises, the `processXml()` function calls the `Login()` Web method. The result that the `Login()` Web method returns is assigned to an integer-type variable (`iResult`). If the result is 0, the user is a registered client of the application, and the `AddUser()` function is called to add the login name of the user and the reference for his/her message queue to the array list of the users. The following code illustrates the process:

```
public class SocketThread
{
private int processXml(int iXmlType)
{
case 0: //Auth.
```

```
iResult=frmLocalServer.webServiceJIM.Login(strXmlElements[0],
strXmlElements[1]);
if (iResult==0)
{
    ........................
AddUser();
}
```

Furthermore, the constructor of the XmlFormat class is called with AUTH as a parameter to formulate the message about the successful login in suitable XML structure. The server uses the XmlFormat class to structure its responses in the XML format that the Client module can read, understand, and analyze. After the message is structured, the SendMsg() function is assigned the responsibility of delivering the message to the target user. The SendMsg() function is responsible for sending local-server responses to the local users. Later, the Web method FriendList() is called to obtain the friends list of the user who's just logged in. This friends list is handed over to the XmlFormat class's constructor with a FRIENDLIST parameter to structure it in the suitable XML format. After the friend list is formatted, the SendMsg() function is called to deliver the friends list to the user.

Apart from delivering the authentication message and friends list to the user, the SendMessage() function also sends a notification to those users to whom the logged in user is a friend, to notify the friends that the user is online now. To send the notification, the Server module calls the Web method FriendsToNotify(), which searches the total number of friends, along with their login names and IP addresses. The result that the FriendsToNotify() method returns is stored in string-type variable strNotify. After accessing the login names and IP addresses of the friends, the Server module calls the NotifyFriends() function to deliver the notification to all those friends who're present in the result that FriendsToNotify() returns, along with the online status of each user.

Finally, the authorization request is also delivered to the Jabber user. To deliver the request to the Jabber server, the Server module uses the xmlAuth() function of the JabberXml class. This function structures the authorization request for the Jabber server in the XML format that it supports. After the request is formatted, the WriteMsg() function is called to write the request on the stream. The following code illustrates the processing of the user's authorization request:

```
xmlLocalResult=new XmlFormat("AUTH",strParam);
SendMsg(xmlLocalResult.GetXml());

strParam=frmLocalServer.webServiceJIM.FriendsList(strLogin);
xmlLocalResult=new XmlFormat("FRIENDLIST",strParam);
SendMsg(xmlLocalResult.GetXml());

strNotify=frmLocalServer.webServiceJIM.FriendsToNotify(strLogin);
NotifyFriends(strNotify,"1");
........................
strJabberXml+=xmlJabber.xmlAuth(strXmlElements[0],strXmlElements[1]);
```

```
    WriteMsg(strJabberXml);
}
}
```

Registration request

To registering a user, the Jabber server must be available. Hence, the Server module opens the stream for the Jabber server. After opening the required stream, the Server module calls the xmlRegister() function of the JabberXml class to form the registration request in the Jabber standard. After the request is formed, the WriteMsg() function is assigned the task to deliver the request to the Jabber server. The following code shows how the registration request is delivered to the Jabber server:

```
case 1: //Register
........................
strJabberXml=xmlJabber.xmlOpenStream();
strJabberXml+=xmlJabber.xmlRegister(strXmlElements[0],strXmlElements[1])
;
WriteMsg(strJabberXml);
return 1;
```

If the host isn't available to register the user, the constructor of the XmlFormat class is called, with REGISTER as a parameter, to form the error response for the failed registration request. Finally, the SendMsg() function is assigned the task of delivering the message (error response) to the client. The following code shows how the server delivers the registration failure notice to the client:

```
else
{
........................
strParam[0]="-1";
XmlFormat xmlRegs=new XmlFormat("REGISTER",strParam);
SendMsg(xmlRegs.GetXml());
........................
}
```

Message request

The local server can also receive the client request for delivering the message to the other user. The target user of the message can be either a local user or some foreign/remote user, such as the Jabber user. To determine the type of target user, the local server refers to the message queue. If the target user is found in the message queue, the receiver of the message is local. In this case, the constructor of XmlFormat class is called with the MSG parameter to formulate the message in the XML format that the recipient can understand. To deliver the message, the AddMessage() function is called, which puts the message in the message queue of the target user, from which the user retrieves it. The following code illustrates the process of adding the message in the message queue of the user:

```
case 2: //Msg
........................
if
(queUser.strUserName.Trim().ToUpper()==strXmlElements[0].Trim().ToUpper(
));
xmlMsg=new XmlFormat("MSG",strXmlElements);
AddMessage(xmlMsg.GetXml(),strXmlElements[0]);
```

If the recipient of the message isn't a local user but belongs to the Jabber server, the ID of the recipient is formatted according to the standards of the Jabber server. The conversion of ID of the recipient of the message facilitates the Jabber server in identifying the recipient of the message. Finally, the local server calls the `WriteMsg()` function to post the request to the Jabber server. The following code depicts the working of `WriteMsg()` function in delivering the message to the Jabber server:

```
if (bJLogin)
{
  strXmlElements[0]=FormatUserId(strXmlElements[0]);
  strXmlElements[1]=FormatUserId(strXmlElements[1]);
  WriteMsg(strJabberXml);
}
```

AddFriend request

The local server receives an `AddFriend` request if some user wants to include another user in his/her friends list. Whenever a friend is about to be added to the friends list of the user, the local server first tries to add the name in the friends list as a Hotmail user. To determine the type of the user, the Server module calculates and stores the index position of `@HOTMAIL.COM` in an `Integer` type variable `iIdx`. In the next step, the Web method `AddFriend()` is called to add the friend to the friends list. If the user belongs to Hotmail, `%hotmail.com` is appended to the login name of the user. Unfortunately, if the user can't be included in the friends list of the user who's currently logged in, the Server module uses `XmlFormat` class to formulate the response, mentioning the incapability to add the user to the friends list. The following code depicts this process:

```
case 3: //add local
........................
iIdx=strXmlElements[1].ToUpper().IndexOf("@HOTMAIL.COM");
if (iIdx==-1)
{
  ........................
  strResult=frmLocalServer.webServiceJIM.Addfriend(strXmlElements[0],
  strXmlElements[1]);
  ........................
  else
  {
  strResult="01";
  ........................
```

```
strXmlElements[1]+="%hotmail.com";
if (strResult!="01")
{
  xmlLocalResult=new XmlFormat("FRIENDSTATUS",strParam);
  iResult=SendMsg(xmlLocalResult.GetXml());
}
  ...........................
```

Sometimes, a friend can't be added to the friends list of the user. In that case, another attempt is made to add the friend as a Jabber user. To accomplish this task, the Server module manufactures a notification through the `xmlNotify()` function of the `JabberXml` class. After the required notification is built, it's handed over to the `WriteMsg()` function. The `WriteMsg()` function then delivers the notification to the Jabber server, as shown in the following code:

```
if (bJLogin)
strJabberXml=xmlJabber.xmlNotify(FormatUserId(strXmlElements[0]),
          FormatUserId(strXmlElements[1]),0);
MessageBox.Show(strJabberXml,"xml send");
WriteMsg(strJabberXml);
```

Delete friend request

The local server encounters the delete-friend request if a user wants to delete his/her friend from the friends list. On receiving such a request, the local server calls the Web method `DeleteFriend()` to process the request. The `DeleteFriend()` method returns an `Integer` value, which is assigned to the integer-type variable. The `Integer` value that the Web method returns is checked to ensure that the friend that the user wants to delete really exists. If the friend really exists (`iResult!=2`), the constructor of `XmlFormat` class is called, with a `DELETESTATUS` parameter, to form the server response to tell the user that the friend was deleted successfully. Finally, the `SendMsg()` function delivers the message to the initiator of the request. The following code shows the processing of the user's delete-friend request:

```
case 4: //del local
iResult=frmLocalServer.webServiceJIM.DeleteFriend(strXmlElements[0],
        strXmlElements[1]);
if (iResult!=2)
{
  ...........................
  xmlLocalResult=new XmlFormat("DELETESTATUS",strParam);
  iResult=SendMsg(xmlLocalResult.GetXml());
}
```

Occasionally, the friend that the user wants to delete is a foreign/remote user and belongs to the Jabber server. In such a situation, the local server has a `xmlNotify()` function of the `JabberXml` class formulate the notification to the Jabber user concerning the deletion request of the local user. After the notification is formed, the `WriteMsg()` function is called to deliver the notification to the Jabber server, as the following code illustrates:

```
strJabberXml=xmlJabber.xmlNotify(FormatUserId(strXmlElements[0]),
          FormatUserId(strXmlElements[1]),2);
WriteMsg(strJabberXml);
```

Accept friendship request from the Jabber User

Another request that the local server may face is a friendship request to a local user from a Jabber user. If the local user accepts the friendship offer from the Jabber user, the local server sends notification to the Jabber server that the local user accepted the friendship offer from the Jabber user. To structure the notification for the Jabber user, the Server module calls the `xmlNotify()` function of the `JabberXml` class; in the `xmlNotify()` function, the formatted IDs of the users who made and accepted the friendship request are sent as parameters. After the IDs are formatted and the notification built, the Server module calls the `WriteMsg()` function to deliver the message to the Jabber server. Because acceptance of the friendship offer adds one more friend to the friends list of the local user, a refreshed roster list is requested from the Jabber server by the Server module. The `xmlRosterReq()` function of the `JabberXml` class is called to form the request for the roster list in the appropriate XML structure for the Jabber server to understand. Finally, the request is handed over to the `WriteMsg()` function for delivery to the Jabber server. The following code depicts the process involved in accepting the friendship request from the Jabber user:

```
case 5: //accept
if (strXmlElements[2]=="0") //Accept
{
 strJabberXml=xmlJabber.xmlNotify(FormatUserId(strXmlElements[0]),
  FormatUserId(strXmlElements[1]),1);
 WriteMsg(strJabberXml);

 strJabberXml=xmlJabber.xmlRosterReq(strJSessionID);
 WriteMsg(strJabberXml);

 strJabberXml=xmlJabber.xmlNotify(FormatUserId(strXmlElements[0]),
 FormatUserId(strXmlElements[1]),3);
 WriteMsg(strJabberXml);
```

Client request to unsubscribe the Jabber User

Whenever the user wants that a particular Jabber friend could not receive his/her ON-LINE/OFF-LINE status the user sends the Server module a request of the type unsubscribe. If such a situation arises, the Server module calls the `xmlNotify()` function of the `JabberXml` class to formulate the notification in the XML structure that the Jabber server supports and understands. After the notification is formed, the task of delivering it to the Jabber server is handed over to the `WriteMsg()` function. After the Jabber user is deleted, the friends list of the user changes, so a request for the refreshed roster list is made to the Jabber server by the Server module. The local server uses the `xmlRosterReq()` function of the `JabberXml` class for get a fresh roster list. The `xmlRosterReq()` forms the roster for the Jabber server in appropriate XML structure, and the `WriteMsg()` function is called to deliver the message to the Jabber server. The following code illustrates the process:

```
case 6: //unsubscribe
if (bJLogin)
{
 strJabberXml=xmlJabber.xmlNotify(FormatUserId(strXmlElements[0]),
 FormatUserId(strXmlElements[1]),3);
 WriteMsg(strJabberXml);

 strJabberXml=xmlJabber.xmlRosterReq(strJSessionID);
 WriteMsg(strJabberXml);
............................
}
```

Unregistration request of the user

Sometimes a user may want to remove his/her account from the Instant messaging service. In that case, the local server calls the `Unregister()` Web method to remove the record of the user from the application. After the `Unregister()` Web method finishes its work, the local server looks to the constructor of `XmlFormat` to formulate a response to inform the user whether or not he/she was deleted successfully from the application. If the user's deleted from the application, another Web method, `FreindsToNotify()`, is called to calculate the number of friends the users have and their login names and IP addresses. Furthermore, the `NotifyFriend()` function is called to deliver the notification to all the friends, telling them that the user was removed from the application. The following code illustrates the steps involved in unregistration:

```
case 7: //unregister
............................
iResult=frmLocalServer.webServiceJIM.Unregister(strXmlElements[0]);
xmlLocalResult=new XmlFormat("UNREGISTER",strParam);
iResult=SendMsg(xmlLocalResult.GetXml());

strNotify=frmLocalServer.webServiceJIM.FriendsToNotify(strLogin);
NotifyFriends(strNotify,"0");
............................
```

Request to quit the application

Any user who logs on to the application sooner or later leaves it. On getting the clients request to quit the application, the local server calls the `Logout()` Web method, which provides a smooth exit for the user. After the user leaves the application, the `Logout()` Web method sets the status of the user to offline for the sake of his/her friends. Then the `FriendsToNotify()` Web method is called to calculate the total number of friends to

whom to deliver the notification that the user is logged out. Furthermore, the
NotifyFriends() function is called to deliver the notification to the user's friends,
suggesting that he/she's logged out and is no longer available. The user may also have some
friends on the Jabber side. To deliver the same notifcation to them, the Server module calls
the xmlOnline() function of JabberXml class to form the notification in Jabber server
standards. While the function is forming the notification for the Jabber server, the online status
of the user is set to FALSE to note that the user's logged out. As usual, the WriteMsg()
function is called to deliver the notification to the Jabber server. After delivering notification
to the Jabber server, the Server module forms the request to close down the stream for the
logged-out user, with the help of the xmlClose() function of the JabberXml class, and the
request is posted to the Jabber server. The following code depicts the process involved
whenever the user quits the application:

```
case 8: //quit
iResult=frmLocalServer.webServiceJIM.Logout(strXmlElements[0]);
strNotify=frmLocalServer.webServiceJIM.FriendsToNotify(strLogin);
NotifyFriends(strNotify,"0");
..............
strJabberXml=xmlJabber.xmlOnLine(false);
WriteMsg(strJabberXml);
strJabberXml=xmlJabber.xmlClose();
WriteMsg(strJabberXml);
```

Request to add gateway

The server encounters the request to include the gateway for the MSN Instant Messaging
service if a user wants to communicate with friends on MSN. To fulfill this request, the local
server calls the xmlAddGateWay() function of the JabberXml class to form the request in
the XML structure that the Jabber Server supports. While forming the request for a gateway,
the Server module passes as a parameter the login name and password of the user to log on to
MSN. To deliver the request to the Jabber server, the WriteMsg() function is called. If the
request of the user can't be processed (strParam[0]="-1"), the constructor of the
XmlFormat class is called, and ADDGATEWAY and the failed processing status of the request
are passed as parameters. To deliver the response back to the user, SendMsg() function is
called. The following code depicts how the add-gateway request is processed by the server:

```
case 9: //add gateway
..............
strJabberXml=xmlJabber.xmlAddGateWay(strXmlElements[1],strXmlElements[2]
);
WriteMsg(strJabberXml);
..............
strParam[0]="-1";
XmlFormat xmlAddGateWay=new XmlFormat("ADDGATEWAY",strParam);
SendMsg(xmlAddGateWay.GetXml());
```

Handling Jabber responses

Whenever the local server forwards some client request to the Jabber server for processing, the Jabber server, after performing the required actions on the client request, responds back to the local server. Because the Jabber Server maintains its own XML standard for communication, the Server module must translate the Jabber server response into predefined communication standards between client module and the Server module before delivering it to the end user. parseJabberXml(), a separate function for parsing the Jabber server responses, is used by the Server module; it then performs the task of analyzing the Jabber response. After the Server module understands the Jabber response, it hands the response over to processJabberXml(). The processJabberXml() function processes various types of responses that the Jabber server returns after receiving different kinds of requests from the local server.

Handling a Jabber response for an authorization request

On receiving the Jabber response to the authorization request, the local server searches the value of the iq attribute. If the value of the "iq" attribute is Result, the user request was processed without any failures, such as a technical error or an invalid stream error. After the Jabber server successfully authenticates the user, the local server sends a request for the roster list. The xmlRosterReq() function of the JabberXml class forms the request for the roster list and passes it to the WriteMsg() function as a parameter. The Server module uses the WriteMsg() function to deliver various types of requests to the Jabber server. After the request for a roster list is delivered to the Jabber server, another request to upgrade the status of the user is sent. This request sets the status of the user to online as soon as he/she logs in the application. To form the request to promote the user status, the xmlOnline() function of the JabberXml class is called on. The xmlOnline() function is called with the TRUE parameter to notify the Jabber server that the user status must be set as online. After the request is formed, it passes as a parameter to the WriteMsg() function for delivery to the Jabber server. The following code shows the process of the response for an authorization request:

```
private int processJabberXml(int iXmlType)
{
case 0: //Auth.
if (strType.ToUpper()=="RESULT")
bJLogin=true;
  ........................
WriteMsg(xmlJabber.xmlRosterReq(strJSessionID));
WriteMsg(xmlJabber.xmlOnLine(true));
```

Handling a Jabber response for a registration request

Whenever a new local user wants to register for the application, the consensus of the Jabber server is required to make sure that the user about to be registered doesn't exist on the Jabber side. To register the user, the Server module calls the Web method Register(). During the registration process, such information as login name, password, residence address, and so on that the user enters pass to the `Register()` Web method as parameters. The `Integer` type value that the `Register()` method returns to notify the Server module of the successful or unsuccessful registration of the user is assigned to an `Integer` type variable (`iResult`), which is converted into a string and kept in a string type variable (`strParam`).

If the value that returns is 1, a user with the same login name already exists on the application. The `WriteMsg()` function is then called to deliver a request to the Jabber server to close down the session. Furthermore, the Server module also informs the user about the registration failure via a message sent through the `SendMsg()` function. The following code depicts the work involved in processing the response of the Jabber server:

```
if (strType.ToUpper()=="RESULT")
{
iResult=frmLocalServer.webServiceJIM.Register(strXmlElements[0],strXmlEl
ements[1],strXmlElements[2],strXmlElements[3],strXmlElements[4],strXmlEl
ements[5],strXmlElements[6],strXmlElements[7],strXmlElements[8],strXmlEl
ements[9],strXmlElements[10]);

 strParam[0]=iResult.ToString();

 strParam[0]="1";
 WriteMsg(xmlJabber.xmlClose());

 xmlLocalResponse=new XmlFormat("REGISTER",strParam);
 iResult=SendMsg(xmlLocalResponse.GetXml());
```

Handling a Jabber response for an add gateway request

Whenever the local server delivers the client request to add a gateway, the Jabber server responds by stating whether the user's request is processed successfully or not. If the gateway request is processed successfully, the local server sends another request for the roster list to the Jabber server. While delivering the roster list request to the Jabber Server via the `WriteMsg()` function, the Server module supplies as a parameter the session ID that the Jabber server allots to the Server module at the start of session.

If the gateway request of the user can't be fulfilled due to some technical reasons, the local server sends the failure message to the user through the `SendMsg()` function. The following code depicts how the Jabber server response to an add gateway request:

```
if (strType.ToUpper()=="RESULT")
{
WriteMsg(xmlJabber.xmlRosterReq(strJSessionID));

strParam[0]="-1";
xmlLocalResponse=new XmlFormat("ADDGATEWAY",strParam);
SendMsg(xmlLocalResponse.GetXml());
```

Processing the roster list returned by the Jabber server

Another kind of request that the local server can hand over to the Jabber server is a request for the roster list. The roster list coming from the Jabber server contains the full login name of the user — for example, john_smith@yahoo.com — along with the type of subscription. The roster list obtained from the Jabber Server is assigned to a string type variable. In the following code, the roster list received from the Jabber server is already in the string type variable (strJID). While processing the roster list, the Length() method of string type variable-strJID calculates the length of the roster list and assigns it to an Integer type variable (iCount). Furthermore, in a string type array (strParam) is delcared inside the processJabberXml() function, which will be used later to store the roster list. The length of strParam array is twice the length of the roster list so that the initials of the roster list that is Login name and subscription type could be accommodated in the array. The following code snippet illustrates the process of obtaining and handling the roster list:

```
case 3: //Roster
iCount=strJID.Length;
strParam=new String[iCount*2];
```

After the string array is created, the items present in the roster list are added to it one by one. After all the items are placed in the array, the next task of the Server module is to deliver the roster list to the user. For this job, the Server module calls the constructor of XmlFormat class to form the response in a format that the receiving user can understand. In the constructor of the XmlFormat class parameters Roster and strParam are passed. After the response is formulated, the SendMsg() function is called to deliver the response to the target user. The following code helps you see how the server obtains the roster list and delivers it to the client:

```
for (i=0;i<iCount;i++)
{
  strParam[2*i]=strJID[i];
  strParam[(2*i)+1]=strSubscription[i];
}
........................................
xmlLocalResponse=new XmlFormat("ROSTER",strParam);
SendMsg(xmlLocalResponse.GetXml());
```

Handling the presence returned by the Jabber server

On receiving the presence from the Jabber server, the Server module looks for its type by considering its name. Based on the type of presence received, the local server returns a string type value. If the Server module receives the presence of a SUBSCRIBE type, string value 2 is assigned to the array strParam. On acceptance of the friendship request that the local user makes to the Jabber user, the string value 3 is assigned to the array strParam to notify the Server module Jabber server's notification is of SUBSCRIBED type. On the receiving a SUBSCRIBED type notification, the Server module delivers the request for a roster list to the

Jabber server with the help of the `WriteMsg()` function. The following code depicts how the server handles subscription type notifications:

```
switch(strType.Trim().ToUpper())
{
 case "SUBSCRIBE":
 strParam[1]="2";
 break;
 case "SUBSCRIBED":
 WriteMsg(xmlJabber.xmlRosterReq(strJSessionID));
 break;
 strParam[1]="3";
```

The Server module receives an UNSUBSCRIBE notification if a Jabber user deletes the local user from the friends list. In such a situation, the string value 4 is assigned to the array strParam. Alternatively, if a local user deletes the Jabber user, the Jabber Server sends an UNSUBSCRIBED notification on accepting the deletion by the Jabber user. The Server module, on receiving such a notification from the Jabber server, quickly delivers a request for an updated roster from the Jabber server. The string value 5 is assigned to array strParam, which returns an UNSUBSCRIBED notification. If the Jabber user with whom the local user wants to communicate isn't available, the Server module receives an UNAVAILABLE notification instead of UNSUBSCRIBED type of notification and the UNSUBSCRIBED type notation will be received by the Server module when the Jabber user comes ON-LINE and accepts the UNSUBSCRIBE request. The following code illustrates the three situations that this paragraph discusses:

```
 case "UNSUBSCRIBE":
 strParam[1]="4";
 break;
 case "UNSUBSCRIBED":
 WriteMsg(xmlJabber.xmlRosterReq(strJSessionID));
 strParam[1]="5";
 break;
 case "UNAVAILABLE":
 strParam[1]="0";
 break;
}
```

The Server module also receives messages from the Jabber server that are meant for the local user. On receiving such a message, the Server module searches the name of the target user in the array list that it maintains to hold user login names and references for their message queues. If the user ID is found in the array list, the message is delivered to the user. A requirement for delivery, however, is that the messages are formatted so that the user can read them. To format the message as required, the Server module calls the constructor of XmlFormat class. The constructor shapes the message in the XML structure that the client's application could analyze and understood supports. After the message is formatted, it's assigned to the `AddUser()` function to add to the user's message queue. The following code shows the processing of messages from the Jabber user:

```
case 5: //Message
.....................
foreach(UserQueue queUser in arrUser)
{
  if (queUser.strUserName.Trim().ToUpper()==strTo.Trim().ToUpper())
  xmlLocalResponse=new XmlFormat("MSG",strParam);
  AddMessage(xmlLocalResponse.GetXml(),strTo.Trim().ToUpper());
```

Handling messages

After the local server is assigned the responsibility of delivering a message to the user, it uses the `AddMessage()` function of the `SocketThread` class to do so. On receiving the message, the server calls the `AddMessage()` function to add the message to the message queue of the target user. The `AddMessage()` function looks for the login name of the user in the message queue. After finding the login name, it puts the message in the message queue of the target user, who can then retrieve it. The following code illustrates the work of the `AddMessage()` function:

```
private void AddMessage(string strMessage,string strMsgFor)
{
  foreach(object obj in arrUser)
  {
    if (((UserQueue)obj).strUserName.Trim().ToUpper()==
    strMsgFor.Trim().ToUpper())
    {
      ((UserQueue)obj).refQueue.Enqueue((object)strMessage);
    }
  }
}
```

To help the user retrieve the message added to his/her message queue, our application deploys the `RetrieveMessage()` function. The `RetrieveMessage()` function fetches the message from the user's message queue and hands it over to the user. The following code depicts the work of the `RetrieveMessage()` function:

```
private object RetrieveMessage()
{
  if (msgQueue.Count>0)
  return msgQueue.Dequeue();
  else
  return null;
}
```

Inside a Web Service

In this section, we focus on the various Web methods that our application uses. In our application, the Web methods retrieve data from the application's database by using the core functionality of ADO.NET. While developing the Web methods, the Web service uses various functions and properties of OleDbCommand and OleDbDataReader. The OleDbCommand class is necessary to execute the SQL query for data retrieval from the application database, whereas OleDbDataReader is necessary to take care of the result that the database returns on execution of the SQL query.

Login() Web method

Whenever the user logs on to the application, he/she must provide a login name and password for authentication so that he/she can be validated as a registered user. Each time that a user logs on to the application, his/her login name and password are checked. As soon as the user enters his/her login name and password, the Login() Web method comes into play. The information that the user enters is checked by searching the table of the application database to determine whether the user really exists in the database's records. The user can log on to the application only if a user with the supplied login name and the correct password exists in the database. Otherwise, error codes 1 and 2 return: nonexistence of the user and false password, respectively. The following code illustrates the work of Login() Web method:

```
public int Login(String strLoginName, String strPassword)
{
 OleDbCommand logCmd = Conn.CreateCommand();
 logCmd.CommandText = "Select member_id,password from member where
 Login_name='"+strLoginName+"'";
 ....................
 logReader=logCmd.ExecuteReader();
 if (logReader.Read()==false)
 {
    return(1);
 }

 ....................
if (strpass==strPassword)
{
 String[]
strArr=this.Context.Request.ServerVariables.GetValues("REMOTE_ADDR");
 logCmd.CommandText ="update member set ip_add='" + strIpAdd + "' where
 member_id=" + iMemberId;
 ....................
 int rows_affected=logCmd.ExecuteNonQuery();
 else
 {
    return(2);
 }
}
```

Logout() Web method

The Logout() Web method manages the task of updating the database table member whenever the user wants to quit the application. Whenever such a request is raised, the Logout() web method searches out the login name of the user in the member table by using an SQL query. In case the user doesn't exist or already logged out from the application, error codes 2 and 1 return, respectively. Otherwise, the IP address of the user is set to NULL. The following code illustrates the work of the Logout() Web method:

```csharp
public int Logout(String sLoginName)
{
 strSql="Select member_id,ip_add from member where login_name='" +
sLoginName + "'";
 ........................
 logReader=logCmd.ExecuteReader();
 if (logReader.Read()==false)
 {
  return(2);
 }
 if (logReader.IsDBNull(1))
 {
  return(1);
 }
 ........................
logCmd.CommandText ="update member set ip_add=null,login_time=null where
member_id=" + iMemberId;
 ........................
}
```

Register() Web method

The Register() Web method comes into play whenever some new user needs to register on the application. A SQL query is executed by the Register() Web method to ensure that the user doesn't already exist in the records of the application. If the user doesn't exist, the information that the user enters during the registration process is inserted in the member table. On a successful entry of the record, error code 0 returns. If the login name that the new user chose already exists, the error code 1 returns. The following code illustrates the work of the Register() Web method:

```csharp
public int Register(String sLoginName, String sPassword,String sAdd1,
.................)
{
regCmd.CommandText = "Select * from member where
Login_name='"+sLoginName+"'";
 if (regReader.Read()==false)
 {
  ........................
```

```
   String strSql="Insert into

 member(login_name,password,address_1,address_2,phone_1,phone_2,email_1,
email_2,pin,city,profession) "+"values('" + sLoginName +"','" +
sPassword + "'," +strAdd1 + strAdd2 + strPhone1 + strPhone2 +
strEmail1 +strEmail2 + strPin +  strCity + strProfession + ")";
 ........................


 return(0);
 }
 else
 {
  return(1);
 }
}
```

FriendList() Web method

The FriendList() Web method obtains the friends list for the user. To get the friends list, two nested SQL queries are used by the FriendList() Web method. The first nested query finds the number of friends for the user, while the second query determines the friends' names. After the friends list for the user is retrieved, the FriendList() Web method picks up the user's login name and then checks the login status of the user. If the friend of the user is offline, 0 is appended to the login name of the user; otherwise, 1 is appended. The process of retrieving the login name and determining the status of the friend continues until all the friends of the user are checked. The following code illustrates the work of the FriendList() Web method:

```
public String[] FriendsList(String sLoginName)
{
 String strSql1="Select Count(login_name) from member,friend where " +
 "friend.member_id = (Select member_id from member where login_name='" +
 sLoginName + "') and member.member_id=friend.friend_id";

  String strSql="Select login_name,ip_add,(" + strSql1 + ") from
member,friend          where " + "friend.member_id = (Select
member_id from member where          login_name='" +
 sLoginName + "') and member.member_id=friend.friend_id";

  frdReader=frdCmd.ExecuteReader();
 ........................
 frdReader=frdCmd.ExecuteReader();
 if (!frdReader.Read())
 {
  strFriendList= new String[1];
  strFriendList[0]=sLoginName;
  return(strFriendList);
}
```

```
strFriendList= new String[(2*iRows)+1];
strFriendList[0]=sLoginName;

if (frdReader.IsDBNull(1))
{
  strFriendList[i+1]="0";
}
else
{
  strFriendList[i+1]="1";
}
}
```

Unregister() Web method

The Unregister() Web method executes after a user raises the unregistration request to remove his/her account from the application. To begin processing the user's request, the Unregister() Web method executes an SQL query to search the login name of the user. If the name of the user doesn't exist in the application records, error code 1 returns; otherwise, another SQL query to delete the user is written to accomplish the task. The following code illustrates the work of the Unregister() Web method:

```
public int Unregister (string sLoginName)
{
 regCmd.CommandText = "Select member_id from member where
                            Login_name='"+sLoginName+"'";
.......................
 if (regReader.Read()==false)
 {
  regReader.Close();
  return(1);
 }

 ........................
 regCmd.CommandText="Delete from member where member_id=" +
   iMemberId.ToString();
 ........................
}
```

AddFriend() Web method

The AddFriend() Web method processes the user's request to add another user to his/her friends list. The AddFriend() method is called to process the user's request and executes an SQL query to obtain the member ID of the friend from the member table. If the result of the SQL query shows that the friend that the user selected for inclusion in the friends list doesn't exist in the member table, error code 1 returns. Similarly, if the user who's making the add-friend request doesn't exist in the member table, error code 3 returns. Another exception may arise if the friend that the user selects for addition already exists in the friends list. In such a situation, error code 2 returns. If both the user and the friend are valid users and the friend doesn't exist in the user's friends list, the SQL query for including the friend in the user's friends list executes. The following code illustrates the work of `AddFriend()` Web method:

```
public string Addfriend(String sLoginName,String sFriendName)
{
 if (sLoginName.Trim().ToUpper()==sFriendName.Trim().ToUpper())
 return "-1";

 frCmd.CommandText = "Select member_id,ip_add from member where
Login_name='" + sFriendName + "'";
........................
 if (frReader.Read()==false)
 {
  frReader.Close();
  return("01");
 }

........................
 frCmd.CommandText="Select member_id from member where Login_name='"+
                           sLoginName +"'";

........................
 if (!frReader.Read())
 {
  frReader.Close();
  return("03");
 }
 if (frReader.Read())
 {
  return("02");
  Else
 {
  frCmd.CommandText="Insert into friend values(" + iMemberId.ToString()
+ "," + iFriendId.ToString() + ")";
........................
 }
}
```

DeleteFriend() Web method

The `DeleteFriend()` Web method enables a user to delete a friend from the friends list. The `DeleteFriend()` method runs the SQL query to attain the member ID and login name of the friend that the user selects for deletion. If the ID of the friend and the user can't be located, error codes 2 and 3 return, respectively. Otherwise, the SQL query to delete the friend from the user's friends list is executes to complete the process. The following code illustrates the work of the `DeleteFriend()` Web method:

```
public int DeleteFriend(String sLoginName,String strFriend)
{
 regCmd.CommandText = "Select member_id,Login_name from member where
  Login_name='"+sLoginName+"' or Login_name='" + strFriend + "'";
```

```
.................
if (iFriendId==-1)
return 2;

if (iMemberId==-1)
return 3;

regCmd.CommandText="Delete from friend where member_id="
+iMemberId.ToString()+ " and friend_id=" + iFriendId.ToString();
int rows_affected=regCmd.ExecuteNonQuery();
.................
}
```

FriendsToNotify() Web method

The FriendsToNotify() Web method is called to deliver the user's notification i.e. the user has come ON-LINE or has gone OFF-LINE to the friends and executes an SQL query to retrieve the login name of the user whose notification it needs to deliver. After it obtains the user's login name, it recovers the login names and the IP addresses of the friends to determine where to deliver the notification. The following code illustrates the work of the FriendsToNotify() Web method:

```
public string FriendsToNotify(String sLoginName)
{
 String strSubSql="(Select member_id from member where login_name='" +
sLoginName + "')";
 String strSql="Select login_name,ip_add from member,friend where
member.member_id=friend.member_id and friend.friend_id=" + strSubSql;
 if (!frdReader.Read())
 {
  return "";
 }
 do
 {
  if (!frdReader.IsDBNull(1))
  strFriendList+=frdReader.GetString(0) + "^";
 }
 while(frdReader.Read());
}
```

Technical Documentation

In this section the coding part of the Server module is discussed. For the better understanding to the readers, flow charts of various classes are provided backed up with the line-by-line explanation of the code that is deployed to build the Server.

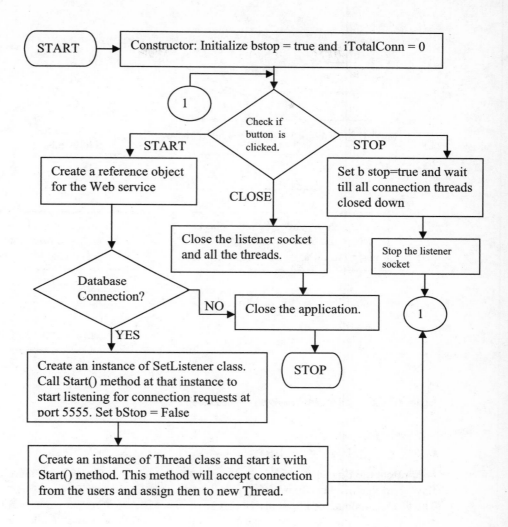

Figure 4-8: Flow Chart of Server application

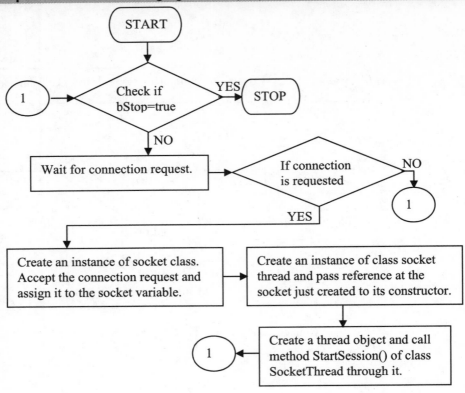

Figure 4-9: Flow chart of thread deployed in frmLocalServer class

frmLocalServer class

We present the flow chart for the `frmLocalServer` class in Figure 4-8. Figure 4-9 is another flow chart that displays the working of a thread implemented in the `frmLocalServer` class. The thread implemented in the `frmLocalServer` caters to all client requests for a connection. Listing 4-1 contains the code for this class, followed by a detailed description of the code.

Listing 4-1: frmLocalServer.cs

```
1 using System;
2 using System.Drawing;
3 using System.Collections;
4 using System.ComponentModel;
5 using System.Windows.Forms;
6 using System.Data;
```

```
 7 using System.Data.OleDb;
 8 using System.Net;
 9 using System.Net.Sockets;
10 using System.Threading;
11 using JIM;
12 using JIM.pratul;
13
14 namespace JIM
15 {
16  /// <summary>
17  /// Summary description for Form1.
18  /// </summary>
19  public class frmLocalServer : System.Windows.Forms.Form
20  {
21       private System.Windows.Forms.Button cmdStart;
22       private System.Windows.Forms.Label lblStatus;
23       private System.Windows.Forms.Button cmdStop;
24       private System.Windows.Forms.Label label1;
25       private System.Windows.Forms.Label label2;
26       private System.Windows.Forms.StatusBar statusBarIM;
27       private System.Windows.Forms.Panel panelIM;
28       private System.Windows.Forms.Label label3;
29       private System.Windows.Forms.Timer timer1;
30       private System.ComponentModel.IContainer components;
31
32       private SckListener sck;
33       public static bool bStop;
34       public static int iTotalConn;
35       public static InstMsgServ webServiceJIM=null;
36
37       public frmLocalServer()
38       {
39               //
40               // Required for Windows Form Designer support
41               //
42               InitializeComponent();
43
44 //
45 // TODO: Add any constructor code after InitializeComponent call
46               //
47               bStop=true;
48               iTotalConn=0;
49
50       }
51
52       /// <summary>
53       /// Clean up any resources being used.
54       /// </summary>
55       protected override void Dispose( bool disposing )
```

```
56        {
57         if( disposing )
58          {
59           if (components != null)
60            {
61             components.Dispose();
62            }
63          }
64        base.Dispose( disposing );
65        }
66
67        #region Windows Form Designer generated code
68        /// <summary>
69        /// Required method for Designer support - do not modify
70        /// the contents of this method with the code editor.
71        /// </summary>
72        private void InitializeComponent()
73        {
74        this.components = new System.ComponentModel.Container();
75        this.panelIM = new System.Windows.Forms.Panel();
76        this.cmdStart = new System.Windows.Forms.Button();
77        this.lblStatus = new System.Windows.Forms.Label();
78        this.cmdStop = new System.Windows.Forms.Button();
79        this.label1 = new System.Windows.Forms.Label();
80        this.label2 = new System.Windows.Forms.Label();
81        this.label3 = new System.Windows.Forms.Label();
82        this.timer1 = new
System.Windows.Forms.Timer(this.components);
83        this.statusBarIM = new System.Windows.Forms.StatusBar();
84        this.panelIM.SuspendLayout();
85        this.SuspendLayout();
86            //
87            // panelIM
88            //
89        this.panelIM.BorderStyle =
System.Windows.Forms.BorderStyle.Fixed3D;
90        this.panelIM.Controls.AddRange(new
                            System.Windows.Forms.Control[] {
91        this.cmdStart,
92        this.lblStatus,
93        this.cmdStop,
94        this.label1,
95        this.label2});
96        this.panelIM.Location = new System.Drawing.Point(8, 24);
97        this.panelIM.Name = "panelIM";
98        this.panelIM.Size = new System.Drawing.Size(224, 112);
99        this.panelIM.TabIndex = 1;
100           //
101           // cmdStart
```

```
102              //
103         this.cmdStart.Location = new System.Drawing.Point(56, 16);
104         this.cmdStart.Name = "cmdStart";
105         this.cmdStart.Size = new System.Drawing.Size(40, 24);
106         this.cmdStart.TabIndex = 0;
107         this.cmdStart.Text = ">>";
108         this.cmdStart.Click += new
System.EventHandler(this.cmdStart_Click);
109              //
110              // lblStatus
111              //
112         this.lblStatus.BorderStyle =
System.Windows.Forms.BorderStyle.FixedSingle;
113         this.lblStatus.Location = new System.Drawing.Point(32, 88);
114         this.lblStatus.Name = "lblStatus";
115         this.lblStatus.Size = new System.Drawing.Size(168, 16);
116         this.lblStatus.TabIndex = 4;
117         this.lblStatus.Text = "0 Connections";
118         this.lblStatus.TextAlign =
System.Drawing.ContentAlignment.MiddleCenter;
119              //
120              // cmdStop
121              //
122         this.cmdStop.Location = new System.Drawing.Point(56, 48);
123         this.cmdStop.Name = "cmdStop";
124         this.cmdStop.Size = new System.Drawing.Size(40, 24);
125         this.cmdStop.TabIndex = 1;
126         this.cmdStop.Text = "#";
127         this.cmdStop.Click += new
System.EventHandler(this.cmdStop_Click);
128              //
129              // label1
130              //
131         this.label1.Location = new System.Drawing.Point(104, 24);
132         this.label1.Name = "label1";
133         this.label1.Size = new System.Drawing.Size(88, 24);
134         this.label1.TabIndex = 2;
135         this.label1.Text = "Start Server";
136              //
137              // label2
138              //
139         this.label2.Location = new System.Drawing.Point(104, 56);
140         this.label2.Name = "label2";
141         this.label2.Size = new System.Drawing.Size(88, 16);
142         this.label2.TabIndex = 3;
143         this.label2.Text = "Stop Server";
144              //
145              // label3
146              //
```

```
147          this.label3.ForeColor = System.Drawing.Color.Blue;
148          this.label3.Location = new System.Drawing.Point(8, 8);
149          this.label3.Name = "label3";
150          this.label3.Size = new System.Drawing.Size(232, 16);
151          this.label3.TabIndex = 2;
152          this.label3.Text = "© Dreamtech Software India Inc.";
153          this.label3.TextAlign =
System.Drawing.ContentAlignment.MiddleCenter;
154          //
155          // timer1
156          //
157      this.timer1.Enabled = true;
158      this.timer1.Tick += new
                              System.EventHandler(this.timer1_Tick);
159          //
160          // statusBarIM
161          //
162      this.statusBarIM.Location = new System.Drawing.Point(0,
147);
163      this.statusBarIM.Name = "statusBarIM";
164          this.statusBarIM.Size = new System.Drawing.Size(246,
16);
165      this.statusBarIM.TabIndex = 0;
166      this.statusBarIM.Text = "Ready";
167          //
168          // frmLocalServer
169          //
170      this.AutoScaleBaseSize = new System.Drawing.Size(5, 13);
171      this.ClientSize = new System.Drawing.Size(246, 163);
172      this.Controls.AddRange(new System.Windows.Forms.Control[] {
173      this.label3,
174      this.panelIM,
175      this.statusBarIM});
176      this.FormBorderStyle =
System.Windows.Forms.FormBorderStyle.FixedDialog;
177      this.MaximizeBox = false;
178      this.Name = "frmLocalServer";
179      this.StartPosition =
System.Windows.Forms.FormStartPosition.CenterScreen;
180      this.Text = "JIM Local Server";
181      this.Closing += new
System.ComponentModel.CancelEventHandler(this.frmLocalServer_Closing);
182      this.panelIM.ResumeLayout(false);
183      this.ResumeLayout(false);
184
185      }
186      #endregion
187
188      /// <summary>
```

```
189         /// The main entry point for the application.
190         /// </summary>
191         [STAThread]
192         static void Main()
193         {
194           Application.Run(new frmLocalServer());
195         }
196
197         private void cmdStop_Click(object sender, System.EventArgs
e)
198         {
199             if (bStop)
200             {
201               statusBarIM.Text="Server already closed";
202               return;
203             }
204             bStop=true;
205
206             try
207             {
208                 //close Web Services.
209               webServiceJIM.Dispose();
210               webServiceJIM=null;
211
212               statusBarIM.Text="Listener  Stoped.......";
213               Thread.Sleep(1000);
214               statusBarIM.Text="Closing Socket connections &
Threads";
215               while (iTotalConn>0); //make sure that no threads
// remain active.
216               //force server to stop(i.e exit // this statement) if
some //threads
217         //fails to stop at it own.
218               Thread.Sleep(1000);
219               statusBarIM.Text="Server Stopped.......";
220               sck.Stop();
221         }
222             catch(Exception ex)
223             {
224               MessageBox.Show(ex.Message,"Error : Closing
                                      Application");
225               Application.Exit();
226               return;
227             }
228         }
229
230         private void cmdStart_Click(object sender, System.EventArgs
e)
231         {
```

```
232              if (!bStop)
233              {
234                statusBarIM.Text="Server already running";
235                return;
236              }
237
238              try
239              {
240                webServiceJIM=new InstMsgServ(); //web obj. created
// once for the server
241                if (!webServiceJIM.IsConnected())
242                    {
243                        MessageBox.Show("Database connection
                                failed.","Closing Application");
244                        //this.Close();
245                        Application.Exit();
246                        return;
247                    }
248              }
249              catch(System.Net.WebException ex)
250              {
251                MessageBox.Show(ex.Message,"Web Services not
found.");
252                //this.Close();
253                Application.Exit();
254                return;
255              }
256
257      try
258      {
259        sck=new SckListener(5555);
260        sck.Start();
261        statusBarIM.Text="Server Started........";
262        bStop=false;
263
264        Thread thrd=new Thread(new ThreadStart(StartConn));
265        thrd.Start();
266      }
267      catch(Exception ex)
268      {
269      MessageBox.Show(ex.Message,"Closing Application.");
270      //this.Close();
271      Application.Exit();
272      return;
273      }
274    }
275
276      private void StartConn()
277      {
```

```
278        while (!bStop)
279        {
280              //if (bStop) return;
281              try
282              {
283              Socket sock;
284              while (true) //wait for connection request.
285              {
286              Thread.Sleep(10);
287              Application.DoEvents();
288              if (bStop) return; //break on new conn req.
289              if (sck.Pending()) break;
290        };
291        sock=sck.AcceptSocket(); //accept connection required
292        SocketThread sckThrd=new SocketThread(sock);
           //assign it to a new thread
293        Thread thrd=new Thread(new
                 ThreadStart(sckThrd.StartSession));
294        thrd.Start();
295        Thread.Sleep(100);
296   }
297        catch(Exception ex)
298         {
299         MessageBox.Show(ex.Message,"Error : Closing
           Listener  Thread.");
300         return;
301         }
302        }
303        }
304
305        private void timer1_Tick(object sender, System.EventArgs e)
306        {
307        lblStatus.Text=iTotalConn.ToString() + " Connection(s)";
308        }
309
310        private void frmLocalServer_Closing(object sender,
System.ComponentModel.CancelEventArgs e)
311        {
312              if (!bStop) cmdStop_Click(sender,e);
313        }
314   }
315 }
```

- Lines 1□12: Includes the necessary namespacesrequired for building the application.

- Line 19: Declares the publicly accessible class frmLocalServer, which is getting inherited from the System.Windows.Forms.Form class.

- Lines 21□30:Declare various designer variables necessary for building the GUI for frmLocalServer.

- Lines 32□35: Declare some user-definedvariables, which are used up later during the development process of the application,.

- Lines 37□50: Implements the default constructor of the frmLocalServer class.

- Lines 55□65:Implements the Dispose() function, which performs the cleanup task by releasing all resources previously acquired by the application.

- Lines 72□185:Deploys the InitializeComponent() function, which is a must for designer variables. Because the coding of this function is auto-generated, users are requested not to alter the coding and, thereby, prevent a chance of error in the overall working of the application.

- Lines 192□195: Implement theMain() function, which acts as the main entry point for the application.

- Lines 197□228:Executes after the Stop button of the local server is clicked.

  - Lines 199□203: Executes afterthe Stop button of the local server is clicked, even if the local server was stopped earlier. To notify the user, the status bar is populated with a message indicating that the local server has already stopped.

  - Lines 206□220: Comeinto effect if the local server is yet to close. To begin closing down the local server, the Web method Dispose() is called to release all resources, and a message is shown on the status bar stating that the Listener has stopped. After waiting for 1,000 milliseconds, the event handler for the Stop button displays another message on the status bar notifying the user that all socket connections and threads involved in the communication process are closed down. In closing the Server mdule, make sure that no more threads remain active. If some thread is unable to stop itself, the local server must stop it. Finally, after closing all the threads, the event handler the Stop button displays the message Server Stopped on the status bar.

  - Lines 222□228: Comeinto action if some exception occurrs while closing the server. On execution of this code, an error message appears and the application closes.

- Lines 230□274- Executesafter the Start button of the Server module is clicked by the user to start the Server module.

  - Lines 232□236: Execute is theServer module is already running. To notify the user the event handler of the Start button diplays the message on the status bar mentioning that the Server module is already running.

  - Lines 238□248: Createsa new object webServiceJIM of the web service InstMsgServ. The web method IsConnected checks whether the connection between the web service and the Server module gets established or not. Incase the connection could not be established the event handler of the Start button displays the message to the user notifying that connection with the database could not established and due to such a reason application (Server module) is closing down. After displaying the message to the user, the application is closed with the help of `Exit()` method.

- Lines 249□255: Checkswhether the Server module managed to found the web service. Incase the Server module could not found the web service, a message box is shown by the event handler of the Start button to notify the user that Server module is unable to locate the web service. Consequently, the application(Server module) is closed down with the help of `Exit()` method.

- Lines 257□274: Creates an objectsck of class `SckListener` class. The port number `5555` is passed as parameter, which signifies that Server module will going handle all incoming client requests on the specified port number. A message is displayed to the user notifying that the Server is getting started. Also, a new object thrd of `Thread` class is created and as parameter the `StartConn()` function is passed. The `StartConn()` function is discussed in lines to follow. Incase the Server module does not starts an exception occurs and as a result a message box is displayed to the user notifying him/her that the application(Server module) is closing down.

- Lines 276□303: Implement thestartConn() function, which lays down the foundation for establishing the connection between the server and the client:

  - Lines 283□290: Create a new instanceSock of `Socket` class, and the Server waits for the connection request.

  - Lines 291□295: Use theAcceptSocket() function to accept the connection request. After the server receives the request, it puts the request in the thread and immediately assigns a new thread to this connection request, which releases the main thread of the server.

  - Lines 297□301: Execute if the server can't fulfill the connection request. In sucha situation, an error message appears.

- Lines 305□308: Display the numberof connection on the server.

- Lines 310□313: Deploys the frmLocalServer Closing() function whichis responsible for closing the Server module. The coding deployed for the Stop button is used for this function.

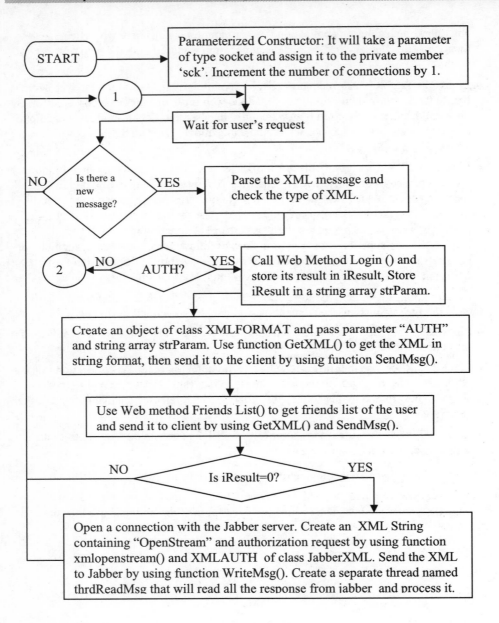

Figure 4-10 (a): Flow chart for the SocketThread class

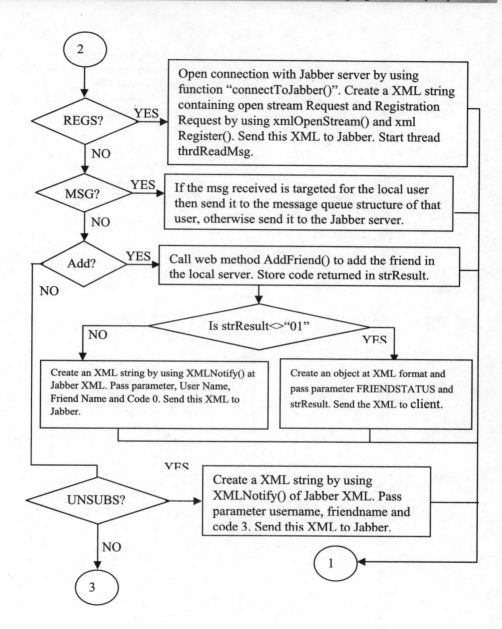

Figure 4-10 (b): Flow chart for the SocketThread class

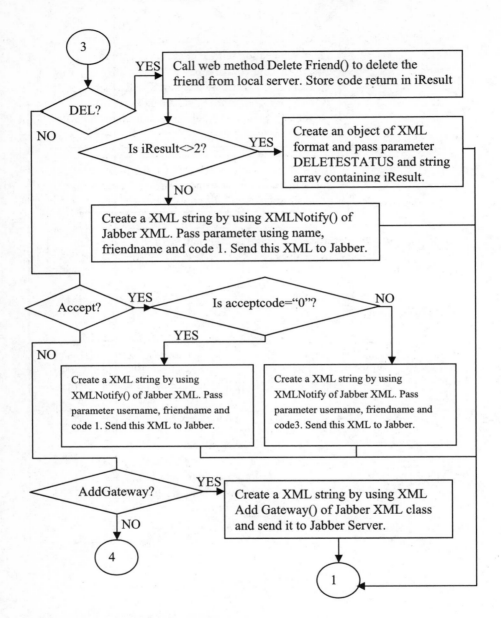

Figure 10 (c): Flow chart for the SocketThread class

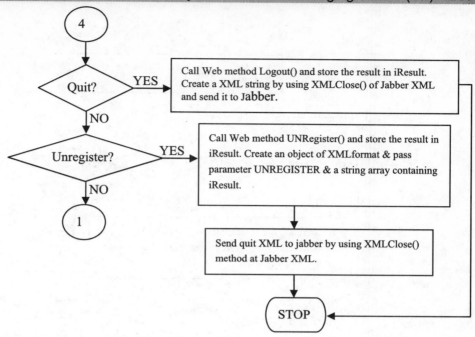

Figure 4-10 (d): Flow chart for the SocketThread class

SocketThread class

We present the flow chart for the `SocketThread` class in Figure 4-10. Figure 4-11 shows another flow chart that displays a thread deployed in the `SocketThread` class for reading messages. Listing 4-2 contains the code for this class, followed by a detailed description of that code.

Flow Chart of Thread Deployment for Reading Messages from the Jabber Server

The following flow chart depicts the process of message reading by the Server module. The message read by the Server module could be coming from the Jabber Server. To accomplish the task of reading messages in a synchronized way, a thread is deployed. The following flowchart illustrates the process of reading Jabber messages.

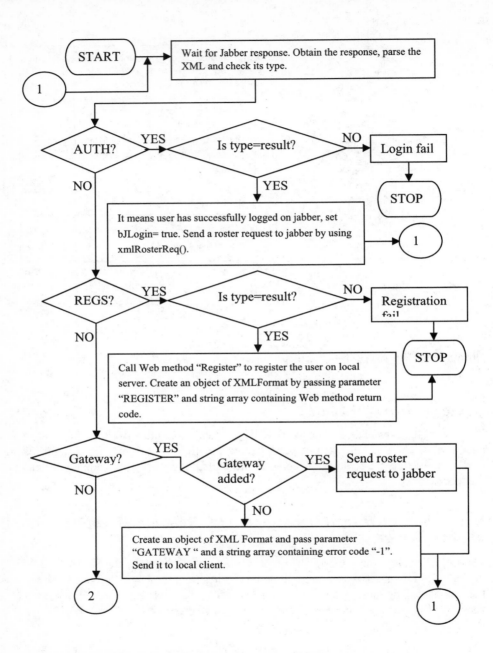

Figure 4-11 (a): Flow chart of the Thread deployed in the Socket Thread Class

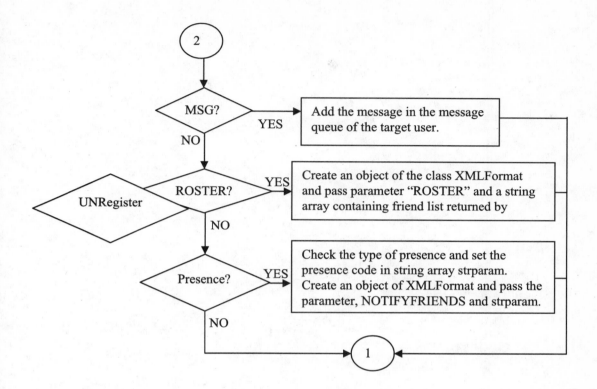

Figure 4-11 (b): Flow chart of the Thread deployed in the Socket Thread Class

Listing 4-2: SocketThread.cs

```
1 using System;
2 using System.Drawing;
3 using System.Collections;
4 using System.ComponentModel;
5 using System.Windows.Forms;
6 using System.Data;
7 using System.Net;
8 using System.Net.Sockets;
9 using System.Threading;
```

```
10 using JIM;
11 using JIM.pratul;
12
13 namespace JIM
14 {
15 /// <summary>
16 /// Summary description for SocketThread.
17 /// </summary>
18 public class SocketThread
19 {
20      private Socket sck;
21      static ArrayList arrUser=new ArrayList();
22      private string []strXmlElements=null;
23      private bool bLogin;
24      private string strLogin="";
25
26      private Queue msgQueue=new Queue();
27
28      private TcpClient sckJabber=null;
29      private Thread thrdReadMsg=null;
30      private NetworkStream netStream=null;
31      private bool bAvailable=false,bJLogin=false;
32      private static int iStFileNo=0;
33      private int iFileNo;
34      private string strJSessionID="";
35      private string strId="",strType="",strTo="",
                 strFrom="",strMessage="",strStatus="",strXmlns="";
36      private string []strJID=null;
37      private string []strSubscription=null;
38
39
40      //private bool bClose;
41
42      public SocketThread(Socket sck)
43      {
44       this.sck=sck;
45       frmLocalServer.iTotalConn++;
46       iFileNo=iStFileNo;
47       iStFileNo++;
48      }
49
50      private int ConnectToJabber()
51      {
52       try
53         {
54          sckJabber=new TcpClient();
55          sckJabber.Connect("jabber.org",5222);
56          netStream=sckJabber.GetStream();
57          bAvailable=true;
```

```
58              StartReadingMsg();
59              return 0;
60          }
61          catch(Exception ex)
62          {
63           bAvailable=false;
64           return -1;
65          }
66      }
67
68      private void StartReadingMsg()
69      {
70       thrdReadMsg=new Thread(new ThreadStart(ReadMessage));
71       thrdReadMsg.Start();
72      }
73
74      public int WriteMsg(string strMsg) //send Msg. to jabber.
75      {
76       if (netStream==null)
77        return 1;
78       if (!netStream.CanWrite)
79        return 1;
80
81       int len=strMsg.Length;
82       char []chData=new Char[len];
83       byte []bData=new byte[len];
84
85       chData=strMsg.ToCharArray();
86       for (int i=0;i<len;i++)
87        {
88         bData[i]=(byte)chData[i];
89        }
90       try
91        {
92         netStream.Write(bData,0,len);
93        }
94       catch
95        {
96         bData=null;
97         chData=null;
98         return 1;
99        }
100      bData=null;
101      chData=null;
102      return 0;
103     }
104
105     private void ReadMessage()
106     {
```

```
107        byte []bData=null;
108        string str="";
109
110      while (true)
111      {
112       if (!bAvailable)
113       {
114        //if (netStream!=null)
115        //read jbr closed on logout
116        netStream=null;
117        return;
118       }
119       if (frmLocalServer.bStop)
120        {
121        //MessageBox.Show("read jbr closed on srvr down");
122        netStream=null;
123        return;
124        }
125        Application.DoEvents();
126        //if (bClose) return; //bclose is set at Quit() or
                                          //execption
127
128       try
129       {
130
131        while (netStream.DataAvailable)
132        {
133        //if (bClose) return;
134        Application.DoEvents();
135
136        bData=new Byte[512];
137        int iRead=netStream.Read(bData,0,512);
138
139        for (int i=0;i<iRead;i++)
140
          str+=((char)bData[i]).ToString();
141        bData=null;
142
143        str=FormatXml(str);
144
145        if (str==null)
146        {
147        //null recv. ending
148        return;
149        }
150       }
151      }
152     catch(Exception ex)
153     {
```

```
154          //close session on error
155

             //MessageBox.Show(ex.ToString(),"Session closed
         //on error");
156           bClose=true;
157           //return;
158           break;
159         }
160        }
161      }
162
163      private string FormatXml(string str)
164      {
165       char []chBlank={' ','\t','\r','\n'};
166       string strLocal,strXml="";
167       char []chXml=null;
168
169
170       byte bData;
171       string strTag="",strEndTag="/>";
172       char []chEndTag=new char[strEndTag.Length];
173       chEndTag=strEndTag.ToCharArray();
174       char []chEndFullTag=null;
175       int i=0,j=0,k=0;
176       bool bCharFound;
177       bool bIn,bEnd,bComplete;
178       bCharFound=bIn=bEnd=bComplete=false;
179       int iCode=-1;
180
181       while (str.Trim()!="") //(true)
182       {
183
184       Application.DoEvents();
185
186       try
187       {
188        str=str.TrimStart(chBlank);
189        strLocal=str;
190
191      if
                         (strLocal.Substring(0,8).ToUpper()=="<STREAM:"
                 )
192        {
193        if
           (strLocal.Substring(8,6).ToUpper()=="STREAM")
194        {
195        int iIdIndex=strLocal.ToUpper().IndexOf("ID='");
196
197        strLocal=strLocal.Substring(iIdIndex+4);
```

```
198          strJSessionID=strLocal.Substring(0,
          strLocal.IndexOf("'"));
199          iIdIndex=strLocal.ToUpper().IndexOf

("'http://etherx.jabber.org/streams'>".ToUpper());
200          if (iIdIndex==-1)
201          {
202           strJSessionID="";
203          return str;
204          }
205          else
206          {
207           strLocal=strLocal.Substring(iIdIndex+
          "'http://etherx.jabber.org/streams'>".Length);
208          str=strLocal;
209          //return strLocal; //return the remaining string;
210          }
211          }
212          else //error in opening the stream
213          {
214           if (strJSessionID.Trim()=="")
          //if error rcv. before stream rcvd.
215          {
216          bAvailable=false;
217          bJLogin=false;
218          //MessageBox.Show("stop:Error in opening the stream");
219          if (netStream!=null)
220          netStream.Close();
221
222      netStream=null;
223          return null;
224            }
225          }
226          }
227          else if (strLocal.Trim().ToUpper()=="</STREAM:STREAM>")
228          {
229          bAvailable=false;
230          bJLogin=false;
231
232          if (netStream!=null)
233           netStream.Close();
234           netStream=null;
235           return null;
236          }
237          else
238          {
239           bComplete=false;
240           bIn=false;
241           bEnd=false;
```

```
242            bCharFound=false;
243            j=k=0;
244            chEndFullTag=null;
245
246            strXml="";
247            strTag="";
248
249            chXml=new char[strLocal.Length];
250            chXml=strLocal.ToCharArray();
251
252            for (i=0;i<chXml.Length;i++)
253            {
254              Application.DoEvents();
255
256              if (!bCharFound)
257              {
258              if (chXml[i]==' ' || chXml[i]=='\r' || chXml[i]=='\n' ||
                 chXml[i]=='\t')
259              {
260              continue;
261              }
262              else
263              {
264              bCharFound=true;
265              if (chXml[i]=='<')
266              {
267              bIn=true;
268              bEnd=true;
269              }
270              }
271              }
272
273              if (bEnd)
274              {
275              if (chXml[i]!='<')
276              {
277              if (chEndTag[j]==chXml[i])
278              j++;
279              else
280              j=0;
281
282              if (bIn)
283              {
284              if(((chXml[i]==' ' && strTag.Trim()!="") ||
                     (chXml[i]=='>'))))
285              {
286                 bIn=false;
287                 chEndFullTag=new char[strTag.Length+2];
288                 chEndFullTag=("/" +strTag + ">").ToCharArray();
```

```
289             }
290          else
291             strTag+=chXml[i].ToString();
292       }
293          if(chXml[i]=='>')
294          {
295          bEnd=false;
296          }
297          }
298        strTag=strTag.Trim();
299       }
300          strXml+=chXml[i].ToString();
301
302          if (j==chEndTag.Length)
303          {
304          bComplete=true;
305             break;
306             }
307             if ((!bEnd) &&
                  (chEndFullTag[k]==chXml[i]))
308          k++;
309          else
310          k=0;
311             if ((!bEnd) &&
                  (k==chEndFullTag.Length))
312       {
313          bComplete=true;
314          break;
315             }
316          }
317          }
318
319          if (bComplete)
320          {
321          bComplete=false;
322          System.IO.StreamWriter streamXml;
323          if (System.IO.File.Exists(strLogin +
                     ".xml"))
324          {
325       System.IO.File.Delete(strLogin +
                                    ".xml");
326                                 }
327 streamXml=System.IO.File.CreateText(strLogin +".xml");
328       streamXml.Write("<JIM>" + strXml + "</JIM>");
329  streamXml.Close();
330
331  iCode=parseJabberXml(strLogin + ".xml");
332  System.IO.File.Delete(strLogin + ".xml");
333
```

```
334 if (processJabberXml(iCode)==1) //close
                                //session after
                                //processing
         //Registration
  //Request
335  {
336  if (netStream!=null)
337  netStream.Close();
338  netStream=null;
339  bAvailable=false;
340

341  return null;
342  }
343
344  //clear var. for re-use..
345  strId="";
346  strType="";
347  strXmlns="";
348  strJID=null;
349  strSubscription=null;
350  strTo="";
351  strFrom="";
352  strStatus="";
353  strMessage="";
354
355 i++;
356  if (i>9)
357  i=0;
358
359  str=str.Substring(strXml.Length);
360 }
361  else
362  {
363      return strLocal;
364  }
365  }
366  catch(Exception ex)
367  {
368      //close session on error
369      //MessageBox.Show(ex.ToString(),"Session closed
                //on error");
370 //bClose=true;
371  netStream=null;
372  bAvailable=false;
373
374 return null;
375  break;
376  }
```

```
377  }
378     return "";
379  }
380
381
382  private int parseJabberXml(string strFile)
383  {
384  System.Xml.XmlDocument xmlDoc=new System.Xml.XmlDocument();
385  System.Xml.XmlNode xNode;
386
387     try
388     {
389            xmlDoc.Load(strFile); //"c:\\pk.xml");
390            //JCOM_0'
391
392            xNode=xmlDoc.FirstChild;;
393  if(xmlDoc.FirstChild.Name.ToUpper().CompareTo
("JIM")!=0)
394  {
395     return -1;
396     }
397
398  if (xNode.FirstChild.Name.Trim().ToUpper()=="IQ")
399     {
400     for (int i=0;i<xNode.FirstChild.Attributes.Count;i++)
401  {
402  if (xNode.FirstChild.Attributes[i].Name.ToUpper()=="ID")
403    strId=xNode.FirstChild.Attributes[i].Value;
404  if (xNode.FirstChild.Attributes[i].Name.ToUpper()=="TYPE")
405    strType=xNode.FirstChild.Attributes[i].Value;
406  }
407  if (strId.ToUpper()=="AUTH")
408  {
409     return 0; //return code for auth
410  }
411  else if (strId.ToUpper()=="REGISTER")
412  {
413            return 1; //regs
414  }
415  else if (strId.ToUpper()=="ADDGATEWAY")
416  {
417     return 2; //GateWay
418  }
419  else
420  {
421  if (strType.ToUpper()!="RESULT")
422  return -1;
423  for (int i=0;i<xNode.FirstChild.ChildNodes.Count;i++)
424  {
```

```
425  if (xNode.FirstChild.ChildNodes[i].Name.ToUpper()=="QUERY")
426  {
427  //MessageBox.Show("Query type");
428 for (int
j=0;j<xNode.FirstChild.ChildNodes[i].Attributes.Count;j++)
429  {
430
 if(xNode.FirstChild.ChildNodes[i].Attributes[j].Name.ToUpper()=="XMLNS"
)
431 strXmlns=xNode.FirstChild.ChildNodes[i].Attributes[j].Value;
432  }
433
434  if (strXmlns.ToUpper()=="JABBER:IQ:ROSTER")
435  {
436  int iLen=xNode.FirstChild.ChildNodes[i].ChildNodes.Count;
437  if (iLen>0)
438  {
439      strJID=new string[iLen];
440      strSubscription=new string[iLen];
441  }
442  for (int j=0;j<iLen;j++)
443  {
444  if
(xNode.FirstChild.ChildNodes[i].ChildNodes[j].Name.ToUpper()=="ITEM")
445  {
446 for (int
k=0;k<xNode.FirstChild.ChildNodes[i].ChildNodes[j].Attributes.Count;k++)
447  {
448 if
(xNode.FirstChild.ChildNodes[i].ChildNodes[j].Attributes[k].Name.ToUpper
()=="ASK")
449  {
450  strJID[j]="";
451  strSubscription[j]="";
452  break;
453
     }
454 if
(xNode.FirstChild.ChildNodes[i].ChildNodes[j].Attributes[k].Name.ToUpper
()=="JID")
455
 {
456  int iIndex=-1;
457
 strJID[j]=xNode.FirstChild.ChildNodes[i].ChildNodes[j].Attributes[k].Va
lue;
458  iIndex=strJID[j].IndexOf("@");
459  if (iIndex!=-1)
460  strJID[j]=strJID[j].Substring(0,iIndex);
```

```
461   }
462   if
(xNode.FirstChild.ChildNodes[i].ChildNodes[j].Attributes[k].Name.ToUpper
()=="SUBSCRIPTION")
463   {
464
strSubscription[j]=xNode.FirstChild.ChildNodes[i].ChildNodes[j].Attribu
tes[k].Value;
465        }
466       }
467      }
468     }
469    }
470   }
471  }
472 }
473   return 3; //roster
474   }
475   else if (xNode.FirstChild.Name.Trim().ToUpper()=="PRESENCE")
476   {
477   for (int i=0;i<xNode.FirstChild.Attributes.Count;i++)
478   {
479   if (xNode.FirstChild.Attributes[i].Name.ToUpper()=="TO")
480       strTo=xNode.FirstChild.Attributes[i].Value;
481   if (xNode.FirstChild.Attributes[i].Name.ToUpper()=="FROM")
482       strFrom=xNode.FirstChild.Attributes[i].Value;
483   if (xNode.FirstChild.Attributes[i].Name.ToUpper()=="TYPE")
484       strType=xNode.FirstChild.Attributes[i].Value;
485   }
486   for (int i=0;i<xNode.FirstChild.ChildNodes.Count;i++)
487   {
488   if (xNode.FirstChild.ChildNodes[i].Name.ToUpper()=="STATUS")
489   {
490   strStatus=xNode.FirstChild.ChildNodes[i].InnerText;
491   }
492   }
493   if (strFrom.ToUpper().IndexOf("MSN.JABBER.ORG/")!=0)
494   {
495       int iIndex=strFrom.IndexOf("@");
496       if (iIndex!=-1)
497       strFrom=strFrom.Substring(0,iIndex);
498       return 4; //presence
499   }
500   else
501   return -1; //skip in case of msn.jabber.org
502   }
503        else if (xNode.FirstChild.Name.Trim().ToUpper()=="MESSAGE")
504        {
505        for (int i=0;i<xNode.FirstChild.Attributes.Count;i++)
```

```
506          {
507          if (xNode.FirstChild.Attributes[i].Name.ToUpper()=="TO")
508           strTo=xNode.FirstChild.Attributes[i].Value;
509          if (xNode.FirstChild.Attributes[i].Name.ToUpper()=="FROM")
510           strFrom=xNode.FirstChild.Attributes[i].Value;
511          if (xNode.FirstChild.Attributes[i].Name.ToUpper()=="TYPE")
512          strType=xNode.FirstChild.Attributes[i].Value;
513          }
514          for (int i=0;i<xNode.FirstChild.ChildNodes.Count;i++)
515          {
516          if (xNode.FirstChild.ChildNodes[i].Name.ToUpper()=="BODY")
517          {
518          strMessage=xNode.FirstChild.ChildNodes[i].InnerText;
519          }
520          }
521          if (strType.ToUpper()=="CHAT" || strType=="")
522          {
523          MessageBox.Show("To -> " + strTo + " : From -> " +strFrom +
    " : Message -> " + strMessage);
524          return 5; //message
525          }
526          else
527                  return -1; //invalid msg type
528          }
529
530          }
531          catch(Exception ex)
532          {
533          //MessageBox.Show(ex.ToString(),"error in xml : server");
534          return -1;
535          }
536          return -1; //error
537          }
538
539          private int processJabberXml(int iXmlType)
540          {
541                  XmlFormat xmlLocalResponse=null;
542                  string []strParam=null;
543                  int iResult=-1;
544                  JabberXml xmlJabber=new JabberXml();
545                  int i,iCount;
546
547          try
548          {
549          switch (iXmlType) //Xml Type
550          {
551          case 0: //Auth.
552          if (strType.ToUpper()=="RESULT")
553          {
```

```
554          bJLogin=true; //bJLogin=true;
555          WriteMsg(xmlJabber.xmlRosterReq(strJSessionID));
556          WriteMsg(xmlJabber.xmlOnLine(true));
557          }
558          else
559          {
560                  bAvailable=false; //Close jabber session
561                  bJLogin=false;;
562          }
563          return 0;
564          break;
565          case 1: //Regs
566                  strParam=new String[1];
567                  if (strType.ToUpper()=="RESULT")
568                  {
569
iResult=frmLocalServer.webServiceJIM.Register(strXmlElements[0],strXmlE
lements[1],strXmlElements[2],strXmlElements[3],strXmlElements[4],strXmlE
lements[5],strXmlElements[6],strXmlElements[7],strXmlElements[8],strXmlE
lements[9],strXmlElements[10]);
570                  strParam[0]=iResult.ToString();
571                  }
572                  else
573                  {
574                          strParam[0]="1"; //-1
575                  }
576                  WriteMsg(xmlJabber.xmlClose()); //end session.
577
578                  xmlLocalResponse=new XmlFormat("REGISTER",strParam);
579                  iResult=SendMsg(xmlLocalResponse.GetXml());
580                  return 0; //check if return code 1 is req.
581                  break;
582          case 2: //Gateway
583                  if (strType.ToUpper()=="RESULT")
584                  {
585                  WriteMsg(xmlJabber.xmlRosterReq(strJSessionID));
586                  }
587                  else
588                  {
589                  strParam=new String[1];
590                  strParam[0]="-1";
591                  xmlLocalResponse=new
XmlFormat("ADDGATEWAY",strParam);
592                  SendMsg(xmlLocalResponse.GetXml());
593                  xmlLocalResponse=null;
594                  }
595                  return 0;
596                  break;
597                  case 3: //Roster
```

```
598                    if (strJID==null) return 0;
599                    iCount=strJID.Length;
600                    strParam=new String[iCount*2];
601                    for (i=0;i<iCount;i++)
602                    {
603                    strParam[2*i]=strJID[i];
604                    strParam[(2*i)+1]=strSubscription[i];
605                    }
606
607               xmlLocalResponse=new XmlFormat("ROSTER",strParam);
608               SendMsg(xmlLocalResponse.GetXml());
609               xmlLocalResponse=null;
610               return 0;
611               break;
612          case 4: //Presence
613        //don't send presence if either sender or recv. is null
614                    if (strFrom.Trim()=="" || strTo.Trim()=="")
615                    return 0;
616                    strParam=new string[2];
617                    strParam[0]=strFrom;
618                    switch(strType.Trim().ToUpper())
619                    {
620                    case "SUBSCRIBE":
621                    strParam[1]="2";
622                    //is it req. xmlNotify(0)
623
624         //check it
625 //WriteMsg(xmlJabber.xmlNotify(FormatUserId(strLogin),strFrom,0));
626               break;
627          case "SUBSCRIBED":
628 //WriteMsg(xmlJabber.xmlNotify(FormatUserId(strLogin),strFrom,1));
629
630    //Roster Req. on getting subscribed
631    WriteMsg(xmlJabber.xmlRosterReq(strJSessionID));
632
633                    strParam[1]="3";
634                    break;
635          case "UNSUBSCRIBE":
636                    strParam[1]="4";
637
638                    //check it
639 //WriteMsg(xmlJabber.xmlNotify(FormatUserId(strLogin),strFrom,2));
640                    break;
641          case "UNSUBSCRIBED":
642
//WriteMsg(xmlJabber.xmlNotify(FormatUserId(strLogin),strFrom,3));
643
644 //Roster Req. on getting unsubscribed
645               WriteMsg(xmlJabber.xmlRosterReq(strJSessionID));
```

```
646
647                 strParam[1]="5";
648
649                 break;
650         case "UNAVAILABLE":
651                 strParam[1]="0";
652                 break;
653         default:
654                 strParam[1]="1";
655                 break;
656         }
657         xmlLocalResponse=new XmlFormat("NOTIFYFRIENDS",strParam);
658         SendMsg(xmlLocalResponse.GetXml());
659         return 0;
660         break;
661         case 5: //Message
662                 strParam=new string[3];
663                 if (arrUser!=null)
664                 {
665                 int iIndex=strTo.IndexOf("@");
666                 if (iIndex!=-1) strTo=strTo.Substring(0,iIndex);
667                 iIndex=strFrom.IndexOf("@");
668                 if (iIndex!=-1) strFrom=strFrom.Substring(0,iIndex);
669
670                 foreach(UserQueue queUser in arrUser)
671                 {
672                 //if target user is found in local list then
673                 //send msg locally
674 if (queUser.strUserName.Trim().ToUpper()==strTo.Trim().ToUpper())
675 {
676     strParam[0]=strTo;
677     strParam[1]=strFrom;
678     strParam[2]=strMessage;
679     xmlLocalResponse=new XmlFormat("MSG",strParam);
680     AddMessage(xmlLocalResponse.GetXml(),strTo.Trim().ToUpper());
681     xmlLocalResponse=null;
682     return 0;
683 }
684 }
685 }
686     return 0;
687     break;
688 }
689 }
690 catch(Exception ex)
691 {
692     //MessageBox.Show(ex.ToString());
693 }
694 return -1;
```

```
695   }
696
697   private void DisConnect()
698   {
699   }
700
701   private void StopJabberThread()
702   {
703   }
704
705   private void AddUser()
706   {
707       UserQueue queUser=new UserQueue();
708       queUser.strUserName=strLogin;
709       queUser.refQueue=this.msgQueue;
710
711       arrUser.Add((object)queUser);
712   }
713
714   private void DeleteUser()
715   {
716       foreach (UserQueue queUser in arrUser)
717       {
718        if
(queUser.strUserName.Trim().ToUpper()==strLogin.Trim().ToUpper())
719        {
720               queUser.refQueue=null;
721               arrUser.Remove(queUser);
722               return;
723        }
724      }
725   }
726
727   private void AddMessage(string strMessage,string strMsgFor)
728   {
729   foreach(object obj in arrUser)
730   {
731   if
(((UserQueue)obj).strUserName.Trim().ToUpper()==strMsgFor.Trim().ToUpper
())
732   {
733   ((UserQueue)obj).refQueue.Enqueue((object)strMessage);
734   }
735   }
736   }
737
738   private object RetrieveMessage()
739   {
740   if (msgQueue.Count>0)
```

```
741         return msgQueue.Dequeue();
742  else
743  return null;
744  //convert it into string.
745  }
746
747  public void StartSession()
748  {
749      int id=0,pid=0,iCode=-1,iPCode=-1;
750      int iDataAvailable=0;
751      byte []bData=null;
752      string strMsg="",match="</InstantMessenger>",str="";
753      char []chWhiteSpace={' ','\t','\r','\n'};
754
755      //while((!frmLocalServer.bStop) && (!bQuit))
756
757      while(true)
758      {
759      Thread.Sleep(10);
760      Application.DoEvents();
761
762      if (frmLocalServer.bStop)
763      {
764      CloseClientConnection(sck);
765    //MessageBox.Show("socket close on server stopped");
766      return;
767      }
768
769      try
770      {
771      if (sck.Available>0)
772      {
773      iDataAvailable=sck.Available;
774      Thread.Sleep(10);
775      Application.DoEvents();
776      bData=null;
777      bData=new byte[iDataAvailable];
778
779      sck.Receive(bData);
780      for (int i=0;i<iDataAvailable;i++)
781      {
782        strMsg+=((char)bData[i]).ToString();
783      }
784
785      id=pid=0;
786      while (pid<strMsg.Length)
787      {
788      str="";
789
```

```
790          id=strMsg.IndexOf(match,pid);
791          if (id!=-1)
792          {
793                  str=strMsg.Substring(pid,id-pid+match.Length);
794                  pid=id+match.Length;
795
796                  System.IO.StreamWriter streamXml;
797
798  if (System.IO.File.Exists("temp" + iFileNo.ToString()+".xml"))
799  {
800  System.IO.File.Delete("temp" + iFileNo.ToString()+".xml");
801  }
802  streamXml=System.IO.File.CreateText("temp" +
      iFileNo.ToString()+".xml");
803  //System.IO.File.OpenWrite("pk.xml");
804
805
806  str=str.TrimStart(chWhiteSpace);
807  streamXml.Write(str);
808  streamXml.Close();
809
810  iCode=parseXml("temp" + iFileNo.ToString()+".xml");
811  //System.IO.File.Delete("temp" + iFileNo.ToString()+".xml");
812
813  if (iCode!=-1)
814  {
815      iPCode=processXml(iCode);
816      if (iPCode==1)  //On quit close the session.
817      {
818      while (bAvailable)
819      {
820      //wait till connection is closed by the jabber
821      Thread.Sleep(10);
822      }
823      CloseClientConnection(sck);
824      //MessageBox.Show("Socket close on Quit req....","Server");
825      return;
826      }
827      }
828  }
829  else
830      break;
831  }
832  strMsg=strMsg.Substring(pid);
833  if (id!=-1)
834  {
835      if (strMsg.Trim()=="")
836      strMsg="";
837      }
```

```
838        bData=null;
839        bData=new byte[512];
840        //strMsg="";
841  }
842  else
843  {
844  /*if (bLogin && sck.Poll(10,SelectMode.SelectRead))
845  {
846  MessageBox.Show("can't read from server on client
     stream","Stop");
847  CloseClientConnection(sck);
848      return;
849  }
850  */
851  }
852
853  object objMsg=RetrieveMessage();
854
855  if (objMsg!=null) //Retrieve message from the user's queue.
856  {
857  SendMsg((string)objMsg); //send it to the user.
858  }
859  }
860  catch (Exception ex)
861  {
862      CloseClientConnection(sck);
863  //MessageBox.Show("Socket close on exception","Server");
864  return;
865  }
866  }
867  }
868
869  private void CloseClientConnection(Socket sck)
870  {
871  if (sck!=null && sck.Connected)
872  sck.Close();
873  sck=null;
874  frmLocalServer.iTotalConn--;
875  }
876
877  private int SendMsg(string strMsg) //to local client
878  {
879   if (!sck.Poll(100,SelectMode.SelectWrite))
880   {
881  //MessageBox.Show("Can't send to client");
882  return 1;
883  }
884
885      int len=strMsg.Length;
```

```
886        char []chData=new Char[len];
887        byte []bData=new byte[len];
888
889        chData=strMsg.ToCharArray();
890        for (int i=0;i<len;i++)
891        {
892                bData[i]=(byte)chData[i];
893        }
894        try
895        {
896        sck.Send(bData);
897        }
898        catch //(Exception ex)
899        {
900        bData=null;
901        chData=null;
902        return 1;
903        }
904        bData=null;
905        chData=null;
906        return 0;
907        }
908        private int parseXml(string strFile)
909        {
910        System.Xml.XmlDocument xmlDoc=new System.Xml.XmlDocument();
911        System.Xml.XmlNode xNode;
912
913        strXmlElements=null;
914
915        try
916        {
917        xmlDoc.Load(strFile);
918        if (xmlDoc.ChildNodes.Count<2) //invalid Xml.
919        {
920        return(-1);
921        }
922        xNode=xmlDoc.ChildNodes.Item(1);
923 if (xNode.Name.Trim().ToUpper().CompareTo("INSTANTMESSENGER")!=0)
924        {
925        return(-1);
926        }
927
928        if (xNode.FirstChild.Name.ToUpper().CompareTo("AUTH")==0)
929        {
930        strXmlElements=new string[2];
931        strXmlElements[0]=strXmlElements[1]="";
932
933  for (int j=0;j<xNode.FirstChild.ChildNodes.Count;j++)
934 {
```

```
 935 if
(xNode.FirstChild.ChildNodes.Item(j).Name.ToUpper().CompareTo("USERNAME"
)==0)
 936  strXmlElements[0]=xNode.FirstChild.ChildNodes.Item(j).InnerText;
 937  if
(xNode.FirstChild.ChildNodes.Item(j).Name.ToUpper().CompareTo("PASSWORD"
)==0)
 938
strXmlElements[1]=xNode.FirstChild.ChildNodes.Item(j).InnerText.Trim();
 939  }
 940  return 0;
 941  }
 942  else if
(xNode.FirstChild.Name.ToUpper().CompareTo("REGISTER")==0)
 943  {
 944  strXmlElements=new string[11];
 945  strXmlElements[0]=strXmlElements[1]="";
 946  for (int j=0;j<xNode.FirstChild.ChildNodes.Count;j++)
 947  {
 948  if
(xNode.FirstChild.ChildNodes.Item(j).Name.ToUpper().CompareTo("USERNAME"
)==0)
 949 strXmlElements[0]=xNode.FirstChild.ChildNodes.Item(j).InnerText;
 950 if
(xNode.FirstChild.ChildNodes.Item(j).Name.ToUpper().CompareTo("PASSWORD"
)==0)
 951
 strXmlElements[1]=xNode.FirstChild.ChildNodes.Item(j).InnerText.Trim();
 952  if
(xNode.FirstChild.ChildNodes.Item(j).Name.ToUpper().CompareTo("SADD1")==
0)
 953
 strXmlElements[2]=xNode.FirstChild.ChildNodes.Item(j).InnerText.Trim();
 954  if
(xNode.FirstChild.ChildNodes.Item(j).Name.ToUpper().CompareTo("SADD2")==
0)
 955
 strXmlElements[3]=xNode.FirstChild.ChildNodes.Item(j).InnerText.Trim();
 956 if
(xNode.FirstChild.ChildNodes.Item(j).Name.ToUpper().CompareTo("SPHONE1")
==0)
 957
 strXmlElements[4]=xNode.FirstChild.ChildNodes.Item(j).InnerText.Trim();
 958                                    if
(xNode.FirstChild.ChildNodes.Item(j).Name.ToUpper().CompareTo("SPHONE2")
==0)
 959
 strXmlElements[5]=xNode.FirstChild.ChildNodes.Item(j).InnerText.Trim();
```

```
 960  if
(xNode.FirstChild.ChildNodes.Item(j).Name.ToUpper().CompareTo("SEMAIL1")
==0)
 961
 strXmlElements[6]=xNode.FirstChild.ChildNodes.Item(j).InnerText.Trim();
 962  if
(xNode.FirstChild.ChildNodes.Item(j).Name.ToUpper().CompareTo("SEMAIL2")
==0)
 963
 strXmlElements[7]=xNode.FirstChild.ChildNodes.Item(j).InnerText.Trim();
 964  if
(xNode.FirstChild.ChildNodes.Item(j).Name.ToUpper().CompareTo("SPIN")==0
)
 965
 strXmlElements[8]=xNode.FirstChild.ChildNodes.Item(j).InnerText.Trim();
 966  if
(xNode.FirstChild.ChildNodes.Item(j).Name.ToUpper().CompareTo("SCITY")==
0)
 967
 strXmlElements[9]=xNode.FirstChild.ChildNodes.Item(j).InnerText.Trim();
 968  if
(xNode.FirstChild.ChildNodes.Item(j).Name.ToUpper().CompareTo("SPROFESSI
ON")==0)
 969
 strXmlElements[10]=xNode.FirstChild.ChildNodes.Item(j).InnerText.Trim()
;
 970        }
 971  for (int j=0;j<xNode.FirstChild.ChildNodes.Count;j++)
 972  {
 973  }
 974  return 1;
 975  }
 976  else if (xNode.FirstChild.Name.ToUpper().CompareTo("MSG")==0)
 977  {
 978  strXmlElements=new string[3];
 979  strXmlElements[0]=strXmlElements[1]=strXmlElements[2]="";
 980  for (int j=0;j<xNode.FirstChild.ChildNodes.Count;j++)
 981  {
 982  if
(xNode.FirstChild.ChildNodes.Item(j).Name.ToUpper().CompareTo("TARGET")=
=0)
 983
 strXmlElements[0]=xNode.FirstChild.ChildNodes.Item(j).InnerText;
 984  if
(xNode.FirstChild.ChildNodes.Item(j).Name.ToUpper().CompareTo("SOURCE")=
=0)
 985
 strXmlElements[1]=xNode.FirstChild.ChildNodes.Item(j).InnerText.Trim();
```

```
 986                          if
(xNode.FirstChild.ChildNodes.Item(j).Name.ToUpper().CompareTo("TEXT")==0
)
 987
 strXmlElements[2]=xNode.FirstChild.ChildNodes.Item(j).InnerText.Trim();
 988        }
 989     return 2;
 990  }
 991  else if
(xNode.FirstChild.Name.ToUpper().CompareTo("ADDFRIEND")==0)
 992  {
 993  strXmlElements=new string[2];
 994  strXmlElements[0]=strXmlElements[1]="";
 995  for (int j=0;j<xNode.FirstChild.ChildNodes.Count;j++)
 996  {
 997  if
(xNode.FirstChild.ChildNodes.Item(j).Name.ToUpper().CompareTo("USERNAME"
)==0)
 998
 strXmlElements[0]=xNode.FirstChild.ChildNodes.Item(j).InnerText;
 999  if
(xNode.FirstChild.ChildNodes.Item(j).Name.ToUpper().CompareTo("FRIENDNAM
E")==0)
 1000
 strXmlElements[1]=xNode.FirstChild.ChildNodes.Item(j).InnerText.Trim();
 1001  }
 1002  return 3;
 1003  }
 1004  else if
(xNode.FirstChild.Name.ToUpper().CompareTo("DELETEFRIEND")==0)
 1005  {
 1006      strXmlElements=new string[2];
 1007      strXmlElements[0]=strXmlElements[1]="";
 1008      for (int j=0;j<xNode.FirstChild.ChildNodes.Count;j++)
 1009  {
 1010      if
(xNode.FirstChild.ChildNodes.Item(j).Name.ToUpper().CompareTo("USERNAME"
)==0)
 1011
 strXmlElements[0]=xNode.FirstChild.ChildNodes.Item(j).InnerText;
 1012  if
(xNode.FirstChild.ChildNodes.Item(j).Name.ToUpper().CompareTo("FRIENDNAM
E")==0)
 1013
 strXmlElements[1]=xNode.FirstChild.ChildNodes.Item(j).InnerText.Trim();
 1014  }
 1015  return 4;
 1016  }
```

```
1017        else if
(xNode.FirstChild.Name.ToUpper().CompareTo("ACCEPTFRIEND")==0)
1018   {
1019   strXmlElements=new string[3];
1020   strXmlElements[0]=strXmlElements[1]=strXmlElements[2]="";
1021   for (int j=0;j<xNode.FirstChild.ChildNodes.Count;j++)
1022   {
1023   if
(xNode.FirstChild.ChildNodes.Item(j).Name.ToUpper().CompareTo("USERNAME"
)==0)
1024   strXmlElements[0]=xNode.FirstChild.ChildNodes.Item(j).InnerText;
1025   if
(xNode.FirstChild.ChildNodes.Item(j).Name.ToUpper().CompareTo("FRIENDNAM
E")==0)
1026
 strXmlElements[1]=xNode.FirstChild.ChildNodes.Item(j).InnerText.Trim();
1027   if
(xNode.FirstChild.ChildNodes.Item(j).Name.ToUpper().CompareTo("STATUS")=
=0)
1028
 strXmlElements[2]=xNode.FirstChild.ChildNodes.Item(j).InnerText.Trim();
1029        }
1030   return 5;
1031   }
1032   else if
(xNode.FirstChild.Name.ToUpper().CompareTo("UNSUBSCRIBEFRIEND")==0)
1033   {
1034   strXmlElements=new string[2];
1035   strXmlElements[0]=strXmlElements[1]="";
1036   for (int j=0;j<xNode.FirstChild.ChildNodes.Count;j++)
1037   {
1038   if
(xNode.FirstChild.ChildNodes.Item(j).Name.ToUpper().CompareTo("USERNAME"
)==0)
1039   strXmlElements[0]=xNode.FirstChild.ChildNodes.Item(j).InnerText;
1040   if
(xNode.FirstChild.ChildNodes.Item(j).Name.ToUpper().CompareTo("FRIENDNAM
E")==0)
1041
 strXmlElements[1]=xNode.FirstChild.ChildNodes.Item(j).InnerText.Trim();
1042   }
1043   return 6;
1044   }
1045   else if
(xNode.FirstChild.Name.ToUpper().CompareTo("UNREGISTER")==0)
1046   {
1047   strXmlElements=new string[1];
1048   strXmlElements[0]=xNode.FirstChild.InnerText.Trim().ToUpper();
1049   return 7;
```

```
1050        }
1051    else if (xNode.FirstChild.Name.ToUpper().CompareTo("QUIT")==0)
1052    {
1053        strXmlElements=new string[1];
1054        if
(xNode.FirstChild.ChildNodes.Item(0).Name.ToUpper().CompareTo("USERNAME"
)==0)
1055    strXmlElements[0]=xNode.FirstChild.ChildNodes.Item(0).InnerText;
1056    //MessageBox.Show(strXmlElements[0],"quit server");
1057    return 8;
1058    }
1059    else if
(xNode.FirstChild.Name.ToUpper().CompareTo("ADDGATEWAY")==0)
1060    {
1061    strXmlElements=new string[3];
1062    strXmlElements[0]=strXmlElements[1]=strXmlElements[2]="";
1063    for (int j=0;j<xNode.FirstChild.ChildNodes.Count;j++)
1064    {
1065    if
(xNode.FirstChild.ChildNodes.Item(j).Name.ToUpper().CompareTo("USERNAME"
)==0)
1066    strXmlElements[0]=xNode.FirstChild.ChildNodes.Item(j).InnerText;
1067    if
(xNode.FirstChild.ChildNodes.Item(j).Name.ToUpper().CompareTo("MSNUSERNA
ME")==0)
1068
strXmlElements[1]=xNode.FirstChild.ChildNodes.Item(j).InnerText.Trim();
1069    if
(xNode.FirstChild.ChildNodes.Item(j).Name.ToUpper().CompareTo("MSNPASSWO
RD")==0)
1070
strXmlElements[2]=xNode.FirstChild.ChildNodes.Item(j).InnerText.Trim();
1071        }
1072        return 9;
1073        }
1074        }
1075        catch(Exception ex)
1076        {
1077    //MessageBox.Show(ex.ToString(),"error in xml : server");
1078        return(-1);
1079    }
1080    return -1;
1081    }
1082
1083    private int processXml(int iXmlType)
1084    {
1085        XmlFormat xmlLocalResult=null;
1086        string []strParam=null;
1087        int iResult=-1,iIdx=-1;
```

```
1088        string strResult=null,strNotify="",strJabberXml="";
1089        XmlFormat xmlMsg;
1090        JabberXml xmlJabber=new JabberXml();
1091
1092        try
1093
1094        switch (iXmlType) //Xml Type
1095        {
1096        case 0: //Auth.
1097
iResult=frmLocalServer.webServiceJIM.Login(strXmlElements[0],strXmlElem
ents[1]);
1098        if (iResult==0)
1099        {
1100        strLogin=strXmlElements[0];
1101        bLogin=true;
1102        AddUser();
1103
1104        }
1105
1106        strParam=new String[1];
1107        strParam[0]=iResult.ToString();
1108
1109        xmlLocalResult=new XmlFormat("AUTH",strParam);
1110        SendMsg(xmlLocalResult.GetXml());
1111
1112       strParam=frmLocalServer.webServiceJIM.FriendsList(strLogin);
1113        xmlLocalResult=new XmlFormat("FRIENDLIST",strParam);
1114        SendMsg(xmlLocalResult.GetXml());
1115
1116
strNotify=frmLocalServer.webServiceJIM.FriendsToNotify(strLogin);
1117        NotifyFriends(strNotify,"1");
1118
1119        if (iResult==0 && ConnectToJabber()==0)
1120        {
1121        //bAvailable=true; //make it available on Auth response.
1122        strJabberXml=xmlJabber.xmlOpenStream();
1123
strJabberXml+=xmlJabber.xmlAuth(strXmlElements[0],strXmlElements[1]);
1124        WriteMsg(strJabberXml);
1125        }
1126
1127        return 0;
1128        break;
1129        case 1: //Register
1130                if (ConnectToJabber()==0)
1131                {
1132                        bAvailable=true;
```

```
1133        strJabberXml=xmlJabber.xmlOpenStream();
1134
 strJabberXml+=xmlJabber.xmlRegister(strXmlElements[0],strXmlElements[1]
);
1135        WriteMsg(strJabberXml);
1136        return 1;
1137  //on local stream after reading reg's result from jabber stream..
1138        }
1139  else //can't register as the host is not available.
1140  {
1141        strParam=new String[1];
1142        strParam[0]="-1";
1143        XmlFormat xmlRegs=new XmlFormat("REGISTER",strParam);
1144        SendMsg(xmlRegs.GetXml());
1145        xmlRegs=null;
1146        return 1;
1147  }
1148
1149  /*    WebServiceJIM=new InstMsgServ();
1150
 iResult=webServiceJIM.Register(strXmlElements[0],strXmlElements[1],strX
mlElements[2],strXmlElements[3],strXmlElements[4],strXmlElements[5],strX
mlElements[6],strXmlElements[7],strXmlElements[8],strXmlElements[9],strX
mlElements[10]);
1151
1152
1153        strParam=new String[1];
1154        strParam[0]=iResult.ToString();
1155
1156        xmlLocalResult=new XmlFormat("REGISTER",strParam);
1157        iResult=SendMsg(xmlLocalResult.GetXml());
1158
1159        bAvailable=false;
1160
1161        return 1;*/
1162        break;
1163        case 2: //Msg
1164        if (!bLogin) return -1;
1165
1166        if (arrUser!=null)
1167        {
1168        foreach(UserQueue queUser in arrUser)
1169        {
1170        //if target user is found in local list then
1171        //send msg locally
1172        if
(queUser.strUserName.Trim().ToUpper()==strXmlElements[0].Trim().ToUpper(
))
1173        {
```

```
1174          xmlMsg=new XmlFormat("MSG",strXmlElements);
1175          AddMessage(xmlMsg.GetXml(),strXmlElements[0]);
1176          xmlMsg=null;
1177          return 0;
1178          }
1179          }
1180        }
1181     if (bJLogin) //send msg to jabber user.
1182     {
1183        // change the format of reciever id.
1184        strXmlElements[0]=FormatUserId(strXmlElements[0]);
1185        strXmlElements[1]=FormatUserId(strXmlElements[1]);
1186        strJabberXml=xmlJabber.SendMessage(strXmlElements);
1187        WriteMsg(strJabberXml);
1188     }
1189        return 0;
1190        break;
1191        case 3: //add local
1192            if (!bLogin) return -1;
1193
1194     strParam=new String[3];
1195      iIdx=strXmlElements[1].ToUpper().IndexOf("@HOTMAIL.COM");
1196
1197            if (iIdx==-1)
1198            {
1199
strResult=frmLocalServer.webServiceJIM.Addfriend(strXmlElements[0],strX
mlElements[1]);
1200            strParam[0]=strXmlElements[1];
1201            strParam[1]=strResult.Substring(1);
1202            strParam[2]=strResult.Substring(0,1);
1203     }
1204     else
1205     {
1206            strResult="01";
1207            strXmlElements[1]=strXmlElements[1].Substring(0,iIdx);
1208            strXmlElements[1]+="%hotmail.com";
1209     }
1210
1211     if (strResult!="01")
1212     {
1213     xmlLocalResult=new XmlFormat("FRIENDSTATUS",strParam);
1214     iResult=SendMsg(xmlLocalResult.GetXml());
1215     }
1216     else
1217     {
1218     //if friend is not a local user then try to add him
1219                                              //as a jabber user.
1220     if (bJLogin)
```

```
1221                                                    {
1222
strJabberXml=xmlJabber.xmlNotify(FormatUserId(strXmlElements[0]),Format
UserId(strXmlElements[1]),0);
1223   MessageBox.Show(strJabberXml,"xml send");
1224   WriteMsg(strJabberXml); //send request for addition
1225
1226   //MessageBox.Show(strJabberXml,"Add local req. sent to jabber");
1227       }
1228     }
1229   return 0;
1230   break;
1231   case 4: //del local
1232   if (!bLogin) return -1;
1233
1234   strParam=new String[3];
1235
iResult=frmLocalServer.webServiceJIM.DeleteFriend(strXmlElements[0],str
XmlElements[1]);
1236
1237   if (iResult!=2)
1238   {
1239   strParam=new String[2];
1240   strParam[0]=strXmlElements[1];
1241   strParam[1]=iResult.ToString();
1242
1243   xmlLocalResult=new XmlFormat("DELETESTATUS",strParam);
1244   iResult=SendMsg(xmlLocalResult.GetXml());
1245   }
1246   else
1247   {
1248     if (bJLogin)
1249       {
1250
strJabberXml=xmlJabber.xmlNotify(FormatUserId(strXmlElements[0]),Format
UserId(strXmlElements[1]),2);
1251     WriteMsg(strJabberXml); //send request for deletion
1252     }
1253   }
1254   return 0;
1255   break;
1256   case 5: //accept
1257       if (!bLogin) return -1;
1258       if (bJLogin)
1259       {
1260       if (strXmlElements[2]=="0") //Accept
1261       {
```

```
1262
strJabberXml=xmlJabber.xmlNotify(FormatUserId(strXmlElements[0]),Format
UserId(strXmlElements[1]),1);
1263        WriteMsg(strJabberXml);
1264
1265        //Roster Req. after accepting subscribe
1266        strJabberXml=xmlJabber.xmlRosterReq(strJSessionID);
1267        WriteMsg(strJabberXml);
1268
1269
strJabberXml=xmlJabber.xmlNotify(FormatUserId(strXmlElements[0]),Format
UserId(strXmlElements[1]),0);
1270        WriteMsg(strJabberXml);
1271        }
1272        else
1273        {
1274
strJabberXml=xmlJabber.xmlNotify(FormatUserId(strXmlElements[0]),Format
UserId(strXmlElements[1]),3); //unsubscribed.
1275        WriteMsg(strJabberXml);
1276        }
1277    }
1278    return 0;
1279    break;
1280    case 6: //unsubs
1281    if (!bLogin) return -1;
1282        if (bJLogin)
1283        {
1284
strJabberXml=xmlJabber.xmlNotify(FormatUserId(strXmlElements[0]),Format
UserId(strXmlElements[1]),3);
1285        WriteMsg(strJabberXml);
1286
1287        //Roster Req. after accepting unsubscribe.
1288        strJabberXml=xmlJabber.xmlRosterReq(strJSessionID);
1289        WriteMsg(strJabberXml);
1290
1291
strJabberXml=xmlJabber.xmlNotify(FormatUserId(strXmlElements[0]),Format
UserId(strXmlElements[1]),2);
1292        WriteMsg(strJabberXml);
1293        }
1294    return 0;
1295    break;
1296        case 7: //unregister
1297        if (!bLogin) return -1;
1298
1299
iResult=frmLocalServer.webServiceJIM.Unregister(strXmlElements[0]);
```

```
1300
1301        strParam=new String[1];
1302        strParam[0]=iResult.ToString();
1303
1304        xmlLocalResult=new XmlFormat("UNREGISTER",strParam);
1305        iResult=SendMsg(xmlLocalResult.GetXml());
1306
1307
strNotify=frmLocalServer.webServiceJIM.FriendsToNotify(strLogin);
1308        NotifyFriends(strNotify,"0");
1309
1310        DeleteUser();
1311
1312        if (bAvailable)
1313        {
1314        strJabberXml=xmlJabber.xmlOnLine(false);
1315        WriteMsg(strJabberXml);
1316
1317        strJabberXml=xmlJabber.xmlClose();
1318        WriteMsg(strJabberXml);
1319        }
1320        return 1;
1321        break;
1322        case 8: //quit
1323                if (!bLogin) return -1;
1324
1325
iResult=frmLocalServer.webServiceJIM.Logout(strXmlElements[0]);
1326
1327
strNotify=frmLocalServer.webServiceJIM.FriendsToNotify(strLogin);
1328        NotifyFriends(strNotify,"0");
1329
1330        DeleteUser();
1331        if (bJLogin)
1332        {
1333        strJabberXml=xmlJabber.xmlOnLine(false);
1334        WriteMsg(strJabberXml);
1335
1336        strJabberXml=xmlJabber.xmlClose();
1337        WriteMsg(strJabberXml);
1338        }
1339        return 1;
1340        break;
1341        case 9: //add gateway
1342                if (!bLogin) return -1;
1343                if (bJLogin &&
(strLogin.Trim().ToUpper()==strXmlElements[0].Trim().ToUpper()))
1344                {
```

```
1345
strJabberXml=xmlJabber.xmlAddGateWay(strXmlElements[1],strXmlElements[2
]);
1346       WriteMsg(strJabberXml); //send request for add GateWay
1347       }
1348       else
1349       {
1350       strParam=new String[1];
1351       strParam[0]="-1";
1352       XmlFormat xmlAddGateWay=new
XmlFormat("ADDGATEWAY",strParam);
1353       SendMsg(xmlAddGateWay.GetXml());
1354       xmlAddGateWay=null;
1355       }
1356       return 0;
1357       break;
1358       }
1359     }
1360     catch(Exception ex)
1361     {
1362       //MessageBox.Show(ex.ToString());
1363     }
1364     return -1;
1365   }
1366
1367   private string FormatUserId(string strId)
1368   {
1369     if (strId.IndexOf("%")==-1)
1370       strId+="@jabber.org";
1371     else
1372       strId+="@msn.jabber.org";
1373   return strId;
1374 }
1375
1376   private void NotifyFriends(string strNotify,string status)
1377   {
1378       if (strNotify==null) return;
1379
1380       string []strParam=new string[2];
1381       int iNotifyIndex=strNotify.IndexOf("^");
1382
1383       while (iNotifyIndex!=-1)
1384       {
1385       strParam[0]=strLogin;
1386       strParam[1]=status;
1387       XmlFormat xmlLocalResult=new
        XmlFormat("NOTIFYFRIENDS",strParam);
```

```
1388
AddMessage(xmlLocalResult.GetXml(),strNotify.Substring(0,iNotifyIndex).
ToUpper());
1389
1390        strNotify=strNotify.Substring(iNotifyIndex+1);
1391        iNotifyIndex=strNotify.IndexOf("^");
1392      }
1393    }
1394  }
1395
1396  public class UserQueue
1397  {
1398        public string strUserName;
1399        public Queue refQueue;
1400  }
1401 }
```

- Lines 1□11: Include necessary namespacesrequired for building the server.

- Line 18: Declares the publicly accessible class `SocketThread`.

- Lines 20□37:Declare various user-defined variables.

- Lines 42□48:Deploy the default constructor of the `SocketThread` class. The constructor keeps the track of incoming connection requests for the local server.

- Lines 50□66:Implement the `ConnectToJabber()` function, which establishes the connection of the local server with the Jabber server on port number 5222. For further communication with the Jabber server, a stream is obtained. If the Jabber server is available (bAvailable=true), the `StartReadingMsg()`starts reading the message flowing from the Jabber server. If the Jabber server is unavailable, an exception is raised and −1 returns.

- Lines 68□72:Implement the `StartReadingMsg()` function. This function reads the messages coming from the Jabber server. To do so, the `StartReadingMsg()`uses a thread.

- Lines 74□103: Hold the executionpath of the `WriteMsg()` function, which sends the message to the Jabber server:

  - Lines 76□79: Comeinto existence if the message to be sent is `NULL` or the `netStream` can't write the message.

  - Lines 81□83: Calculate the total length of the message and store it in the`Len` variable. After assessing the total length of the message, the `WriteMsg()` functionconverts the message into a `char` type array, and then converts the message into `byte` type. The dual conversion of the message is necessary because the string type message can't be put on the network stream.

- Lines 85□93: Convert each character of the messageinto the byte type and store it in the variable `bData`, after which the message is handed over to `netStream` for writing.

- Lines 94□102: Set the variables`bData` and `chData` to NULL whether the message is delivered successfully or unsuccessfully. The only difference comes in the return value. On successfully writing the message, the `WriteMsg()` function returns `0`; otherwise, `1` returns.

- Lines 105□160: Deploys the`ReadMessage()` function, which reads the messages coming from the Jabber server:

  - Lines 112□118: Check the availability ofthe Jabber server. If the Jabber Server is unavailable, the `netStream` is set to NULL and the process of reading the messages from Jabber server stops with immediate effect.

  - Lines 119□124:If theServer module stops the `netStream` is set to NULL.

  - Lines 131□137: Check the availability of dataon the `netStream`. If the data is available, a byte type array is created to read the message in blocks of 512 bytes. (You can say that the local server in a single instance can read 512 bytes of data.) After the data is read, the actual number of bytes that the local server reads is returned and stored in the `iRead` variable.

  - Lines 139□143: Convert the data storedin the `iRead` variable into a string type and puts it into the variable `str`. After the entire message is processed, the `FormatXml()` function is called, which assigns suitable formatting to the message read from the Jabber server.

  - Lines 144-158:Checks whether the complete XML is received from the Jabber server or not. In case the XML is complete then the `FormatXML()` function returns a NULL value which terminates the execution of the `while` loop. In case some error occurs while reading the XML, an exception is thrown.

- Lines 163□379: Implement the`FormatXml()` function. Because the messages that the Jabber server returns aren't in the correct format, the `FormatXml()` function accesses the messages that the Jabber server returns and applies suitable formatting to bring the message structure into shape:

  - Lines 165□179: Declare various user-defined variables.

  - Lines 181□189:Implements the `while` loop. At the beginning of the `while` loop all the blank characters are removed from the XML using the function `TrimStart()`.

  - Lines 191□199: Check the opening ofthe stream. If the stream is open, the Jabber session ID is retrieved.

  - Lines 200□210: Comeinto play if the XML is incomplete (`iIdIndex==-1`). If so, the original string returns; otherwise, the remaining string returns.

- Lines 212□226: Execute ifan error occurs before the stream opens with the Jabber server. As a result, the Jabber server becomes unavailable, and the user's login status is set to `false`. Consequently, the stream of the local server also closes down.

- Lines 227□235:Close down the stream and the Jabber server on receiving the tag `</STREAM:STREAM>` and the login status of the user is set to `false`.

- Lines 239□247: Assigningvalues to various user-defined variables.

- Lines 249□250: Declare achar type array, `chXml`. The length of `chXml` is equal to the length of the variable `strLocal`, which holds the string that returns if the stream with the Jabber is open. The message that `strLocal` stores is converted into `char` type and handed over to the `chXml` array.

- Lines 252-255: Implements a `for` loop which checks the validity of the XML by iterating through the XML, character by character.

- Lines 256□269: Ignore newlines, white spaces, and tab spaces while calculating the length of the message, now stored in `chXml`. After any character is found, the variables `bIn` and `bEnd` are set to `true`.

- Lines 273□280: Lookfor the opening tag (`<`).

- Lines 282□289: Searchfor the closing tag (`>`). If the tag is found, the name of the tag is searched in the XML, and as a result, variable `bIn` is set to `false`. The variable `bIn` remains `true` if ending tag isn't found. Usually the closing tag (`>`) marks the end of a single statement that's present in the XML.

- Lines 300□308: Searchfor the full closing tag (`/>`). If the full closing tag is found, variable `bComplete` is set to `true`.

- Lines 311□315: Searches the end tag ofthe XML. If the end tag is found in the XML variable `bComplete` is set to `true`.

- Lines 322□329: Makethe instance `streamXml` of `StreamWriter` create a file that uses the login name of the user as its filename. If the file already exists under that name, it's deleted, and a new version of file is created with the same filename. The instance `streamXML` of the class `StreamWriter` writes the message to the file using `Write()` function after writing the message, `streamXML` closes the stream using `Close()` method.

- Lines 331□332: Call theparseJabberXml() function to process the XML that the Jabber server returns. After the `parseJabberXml()` function completes its task, the file is deleted.

- Lines 334□342:Place control of the application into the hands of the `processJabberXml()` function after parsing the message from the Jabber server. If the `processJabberXml()` function finds that the message from the Jabber server is a registration request, the stream that's open between the local and Jabber servers closes down, and the Jabber server becomes unavailable.

- Lines 345□353: Cleanup the variables for further re-usability.

- Lines 355-357: Checks whether the loop control variable i (Line 252)exceeds the value 9, if the value of i is greater than 9 then the variable i is reinitialized to 0;

- Lines 359: Retrieves the remaining XML, appends it with the original XML.

- Lines 360-365: In case during the execution of the function FormatXML() the xml obtained from the Jabber server is not complete then the a string type variable strLocal which indicates the string passed to the function FormatXML() earlier is returned to the calling function ReadMsg().

- Lines 366□378: Execute incase of an exception. After this coding comes into action, the netStream is set to NULL, and the Jabber server becomes unavailable.

- Lines 382□537: Deploythe parseJabberXml() function, which takes the string type parameter. The parameter usually holds the Jabber message, which needs to be parsed:

  - Lines 384□385: Inthese lines Create new instances of the XmlDocument and Xmlnode classes.

  - Lines 389□396: Loadthe XML file. The name of the first child node is stored in xNode. If the name of the first child node isn't JIM, -1 is returned by the parseJabberXml () function to notify an error to the Server module.

  - Lines 398□406: Determine the nameof the first child node of the Jabber XML. If the name of the node is IQ, the name of the attributes are determined. If the names of the attributes are ID and TYPE, the values of the attributes are obtained and stored in variables strId and strType.

  - Lines 407□418: Determine the value ofthe TYPE attribute, and based on the value of the TYPE attribute, returns the suitable integer value.

  - Lines 421□422: Determine the typeof the IQ node after retrieving its value attribute. If the type of the IQ node isn't TYPE, the process of parsing the Jabber XML stops.

  - Lines 423□428: Calculate the number ofelements inside the name of the first child node if its name is QUERY to determine the total number. For this task, the for loop is used, which increases the value of variable j by 1 whenever any attribute is found.

  - Lines 430□431: Execute ifthe name of the attribute inside QUERY is XMLNS and find the value of the attribute is and put it into the variable strXmlns.

  - Lines 434□441: Execute ifthe value of strXmlns variable (QUERY attribute) is JABBER:IQ:ROSTER, which means that the request made is for Roster. All the elements are calculated to find out the total number. The possible elements present under the JABBER:IQ:ROSTER are the query ID, type of Subscription, and ASK element. In our application, we concentrate only on the query ID and type of Subscription. To retain the values of the query ID and Subscription type, the string type arrays strJID and strSubscription are declared.

- Lines 442-453: Initializes a for loop which itertrates to calculate the attributes present in the various child nodes.

- Lines 436: Determines the total length of the child node QUERY.

- Lines 454□461: Execute ifthe type of attribute is JID. Detemines the number of subitems present under QUERY and the number of attributes present in each subitem.

- Lines 462□465: Determine the value ofattribute SUBSCRIPTION in each subitem of QUERY and stores each sub item in a string type arraystrSubscription.

- Lines 475□485: Comeinto action if the name of the first child node is PRESENCE. Determine the total number of attributes present under the node and fetch the value of each attribute to store in string type variables.

- Lines 486□492: Determine the total number ofsubelements present under the PRESENCE node. Out of the total number of subelements obtained, the loop control variable i searches the STATUS subelement. On finding the STATUS, sub item the variable strStatus stores its value

- Lines 493□501: Check whether or not the messageis the address itself (MSN.JABBER.ORG/). If the message is the address, fetches string prior to @ character, which is the login name of the user.

- Lines 503□513: Count the numberof attributes present in the node if the first child node is a MESSAGE type and get the value of each attribute. The variables strTo, strFrom, and strType hold the values of TO, FROM, and TYPE attributes, respectively.

- Lines 514□520:Calculates the subelements in the node. After calculating the subelements, the loop control variable i is used to search the sub item BODY. The contents of the sub item BODY are stored in a string type variable strMessage.

- Lines 521□527: Determine the value ofattribute TYPE. If the value is CHAT, it indicates that the type of the message is normal, integer value 5 returns; otherwise −1 returns to indicate an invalid message type.

- Lines 539□695: Setup the processJabberXml() function, which processes the Jabber messages that the parseJabberXml() function parsed earlier. During the processing stage, the processJabberXml() function calls the Web service and other related functions to analyze the Jabber responses and messages:

  - Lines 541□545: Declare the user-defined variables that are the processJabberXml() function uses later.

  - Line 549: Initializes a switch statement to handle various response types from Jabber server.

  - Lines 551□563: Sendthe request for the Roster and the Online presence to the Jabber server by using the WriteMsg() function if the type of the XML that the Jabber server returns is an authorization type and is successfully processed. If the Jabber server isn't available, the connection with the Jabber server closes down, and the login of the user is set to NULL.

- Lines 565☐576: Process the Jabber response for a registrationtype request. To process the response, the `processJabberXml ()` method calls the Web method `Register()`, and the return value of the `Register()` Web method is stored in `strParam`. If the user can't be registered on the Jabber server (`strParam[0]="1"`), the session with the Jabber server closes.

- Lines 578☐581: Generates the appropriate XML if the user successfullyregisters on the Jabber server by using the constructor of `XmlFormat` class, with `REGISTER` and `strParam` as parameters.

- Lines 582☐586: Appliedafter the Jabber responds back against the successful inclusion of the MSN gateway. After the gateway is added, the request for roster list (MSN Friend's List) is sent to the Jabber server.

- Lines 587☐595: Call the constructor ofthe `XmlFormat` class and pass the parameters `ADDGATEWAY` and `strParam` to it if the add gateway request can't be fulfilled (`strParam[0]="-1"`). Finally, the `SendMsg()` function is called to deliver the message to the Jabber server.

- Lines 597☐600: Findthe length of `strJID` and put it into the `iCount` variable. After determining the length, the `parseJabberXml()` method creates an array, `strParam`, that's twice the size of the `strJID` variable.

- Lines 601☐611: Put the value of`strJID` and `strSubscription` in the indexes of the array `strParam` in continuous form. Again, the constructor of the `Xmlformat` class is called with `ROSTER` and `strParam` as parameters. This time, the local server uses the `XmlFormat` class to deliver to the end user the roster listthat the Jabber server returns.

- Lines 612☐617: These lines check Jabberserver's PRESENCE type response.If the name of the sender or receiver is empty, the process stops and 0 returns.

- Lines 620☐626: Execute ifthe PRESENCE type is `Subscribe`, and, as a result, 2 is assigned to `strParam`.

- Lines 627☐634: Implement ifthe PRESENCE type is `Subscribed`. If so, the request for a refreshed roster is sent by using the `WriteMsg()` function. Otherwise, 3 is assigned to `strParam`.

- Lines 635☐640: Execute ifthe PRESENCE type is `Unsubscribe`. The value of `strParam` becomes 4.

- Lines 641☐649: Execute ifthe PRESENCE type is `Unsubscribed`. The `WriteMsg()` function is called to deliver a message asking for a refreshed roster to the Jabber server, and the value of `strParam` becomes 5.

- Lines 650☐656: Execute ifthe user isn't available. Consequently, the value of `strParam` is set to 0. However note that the default value of `strParam` is set to 1.

- Lines 657☐660: Call the constructor of the `XmlFormat` class, which takes `NOTIFYFRIENDS` and `strParam` as parameters. The `SendMsg()` function is called to deliver the notification to the intended user.

- Lines 661☐687: Process the message from the Jabber server.

- Lines 665☐668: Retrieve the entire string, up to the index position of the special character @, from the names of the sender and receiver of the message.

- Lines 670☐685: Send the message to the locally available target user. A separate queue for each target user is maintained; each queue is accessible by its target user. Whenever a message arrives for the user, it goes directly into the message queue. Side-by-side string type arrays, each with a capacity of three indexes, are used to hold the names of the sender and the receiver of the message, as well as the content of the message. The constructor of the `XmlFormat` class is called with parameters `MSG` and `strParam`. Finally, the `AddMessage()` function is called, which adds the message to the message queue.

- Lines 690☐694: Execute if any exception occurs during the processing of the XML.

- Lines 705☐712: Implement the `AddUser()` function, which creates a new queue for the user whenever he/she logs in. This queue is necessary for each user to manage his/her incoming messages and notifications:

  - Lines 707☐711: Create a new instance of the `UserQueue` class to obtain the login name of the user and his/her message queue reference, and call the `Add()` function of the `ArrayList` class to add the information in the array list, which holds the users' names and the references for their message queues.

- Lines 714☐725: Implement the `DeleteUser()` function to remove the name and message queue reference of the user from the `ArrayList` whenever he/she logs out of the application.

- Lines 727☐736: Deploy the `AddMessage()` function, which searches the array list for the message queue reference of the target user. After locating the message queue reference, the `AddMessage()` function dumps the message in the user's queue.

- Lines 738☐745: Hold the execution path of the `RetrieveMessage()` function, which picks up the message from the message queue by using the `Dequeue()` method.

- Lines 747☐867: Hold the execution of the `StartSession()` function for the local server:

  - Lines 749☐752: Declare certain user-defined variables, which are used later in the StartSession() function.

  - Line 753: line Lines up and stores all the characters that create empty spaces in the message in the `Char` type array `WhiteSpace`.

  - Lines 757☐767: Check the availability of the local server. If the local server isn't available, the connection with the local server closes.

- Lines 771□777: Check whether or not any data is available onthe stream. If the data is available, it's assigned to the iDataAvailable variable. Once the entire data is stored in iDataAvailable, it is converted into bytes and assigned further to variable bData.

- Lines 779□783: Retrieveand convert the byte formatted data into string type by using the `Receive()` function.

- Lines 786□790: Check whetherthe message length stored in `strMsg` is less than the value of the `pid` variable.

- Lines 791□794: Extract the content fromthe XML message through the last character of the end tag of the XML (`</InstantMessenger>`).

- Lines 796□802: Create a new instance ofthe `StreamWriter` class to build a temporary XML file. If the file already exists, it's deleted and re-created.

- Lines 807□810:Use the `Write()` function to write to the file. After all the data is written down, the `parseXml()` function is called to parse the file. The parseXml() function returns an integer type value, which is assigned to the `iCode` variable.

- Lines 813□823: Check the validity ofthe XML file that the `parseXml()` function parses. If the parsed file is valid, it's handed over to the `processXml()` function. Meanwhile, if the XML file contains the `QUIT` request, the connection with the Jabber server is closes after waiting for 10 milliseconds.

- Lines 832-839: Performs the cleanup operation, assigns `NULL` value all variables.

- Lines 853□859:Obtains the message from the user's message queue of. Later, the `SendMsg()` function delivers the message to the user.

- Lines 860□865:Executed if an error occurs in establishing the session. In such a situation, the server calls the `CloseClientConnection()` function to close the socket connection with the client.

- Lines 869□875: Implement theCloseClientConnection() function, which closes down the connection between the local server and the local client.

- Lines 877□907:Implement the SendMsg() function:

  - Line 879: Determines whether or not the message can be written in the stream. To determine the availability of writing mode, this function waits for 100 milliseconds.

  - Lines 880-884: Gets executed when the `SendMsg()` function is unable to send the data to the local client. On such a failure integer value 1 is returned.

  - Lines 885□887:Store the entire length of the message in the variable `len`. Two arrays, chData and bData, of char and byte type, respectively, are declared. The size of these two arrays is equal to the length of the message.

  - Lines 889□897: Converts the messageinto char type with the help of ToCharArray() method and assigns to the array chData. After conversion into

Char type, each character of the message is converted into byte type and stored in bData; finally, the SendMsg() function is called to deliver the message.

- Lines 898☐906: Indicate the successful or unsuccessfulcompletion of the process. If any exception occurs, 1 returns; otherwise, 0 returns. In both cases, the arrays are set to NULL either to rehandle the conversion process or to take care of the new messages.

- Lines 908☐1081: Set up theparseXml() function, which is responsible for parsing the XML and determining its type:

  - Lines 910☐921:Create new instances xmlDoc and xNode, of classes XmlDocument and XmlNode, respectively, and load the file for parsing. Immediately after it loads, the Count() method of xmlDoc determines the validity of the file by checking the number of child nodes present in the file. If the number of child nodes is more than 2, integer value -1 returns to reveal that the file is carrying an invalid XML structure.

  - Lines 923☐926: Performanother check on the structure of the XML by looking for the name of the node in the file. If the name of the node is not INSTANTMESSENGER, which is a sign of invalid XML structure for our application, -1 returns to show the error.

  - Lines 928☐940:Execute if no error is found in the XML structure and the name of the first child node is AUTH. The parseXml() function uses the for looping structure to keep the count of child nodes present under the first child node (AUTH). The names of the child nodes are checked and their text is obtained and stored in the string type array strXmlElements. On a successful parsing and retrieval of the contents of the AUTH type XML, integer value 0 returns.

NOTE: Remember that while parsing the XML, the for loop's structure determines the number of child nodes present under various types of first child nodes.

- Lines 942☐974: Execute ifthe name of the first child node is REGISTER, which means that the type of the XML is for registering the user. The content of various child nodes present under the first child node is obtained and put into the array strXmlElements. The child nodes contain the information necessary for registering the user, such as login name, password, e-mail address, residence address, and so on. Once the XML for registering the user is parsed by the parseXml() function, integer value 1 is returned by the parseXml() function.

- Lines 976-989: Executes if the name of the first child node is MSG, which means that the type of XML for delivering the message to the intended client. The contents of various child nodes present under the first child nodes are obtained and assigned to the array strXmlElements. The child nodes TARGET and SOURCE conatains the information about the sender and reciever of the message respectively. The child node TEXT contains the contents of the message that is about to be delivered to the reciever of the message.

- Lines 991□1003: Execute if the nameof the first child node is ADDFRIEND and is meant to include the other user in the friends list. The name of the user and the name of the friend are retrieved from the child nodes present under the first child node and assigned to strXmlElements. On completion of the process, 3 returns.

- Lines 1004□1016: Execute if the type of the XML is meant todelete a friend from the friends list. The name of the first child node, DELETEFRIEND, represents such an XML type. The names of the user and the friend are retrieved from the child nodes and put into strXmlElements. On completion of the parsing task, 4 returns.

- Lines 1017□1030:Parse the XML that ACCEPTFRIEND represents as the name of the first child node. ACCEPTFRIENDXML usually occurs whenever the user sends the request to another user to make him/her a friend and include him/ her in the friends list. The content from the child nodes, which contains the user and friend names, is retrieved. And the child node STATUS states whether the friend accepts or rejects the friendship offer that the user makes. After the XML is parsed, 5 returns.

- Lines 1032□1044: Parse the XML meant todelete a foreign friend of the user, such an MSN friend. Names of the user and his/her friend are obtained from the child nodes of first child node UNSUBSCRIBEFRIEND and allocated to strXmlElements. Once the parsing is complete, integer value 6 is returned.

- Lines 1045□1050: Hold the execution path for parsing the XML thatUNREGISTER denotes, which usually appears if a user wants to unregister himself/herself from the application. The login name of the user for the application is obtained from the child node and assigned to strXmlElements. After the parsing is complete, 7 returns.

- Lines 1051□1058: Execute if the name of the first child node isQUIT. Such an XML arises if the user wants to quit the application. The login name of the user is acquired from the child node and put into strXmlElements. On a successful parsing of the XML, 8 returns.

- Lines 1059□1072: Execute if the name of the first child node isADDGATEWAY. Such XML emerges if the user wants to add the gateway for the MSN Instant Messaging service to communicate with his/her friends on MSN. Information such as login name of the user for the Instant Messaging application (that we intend to develop), login name of the user for MSN Instant Messaging service and password for logging the MSN Instant Messaging service are obtained from the child nodes. The information is then stored in strXmlElements.The integer value 9 returns on successful parsing.

- Lines 1075□1080:Execute if an exception occurrs whle parsing the XML, such as an invalid type of XML or missing child nodes. To notify error to the end user, -1 returns.

- Lines 1083□1365:Hold the execution path of the processXml() function, which is responsible for taking suitable actions on the parsed XML. Usually in the list of actions, the local server for the end user calls other functions to accomplish the task and deliver the final result. In processing the XML, the value that the parseXml() function returns while parsing the XML is considered a guideline in determining the type of XML:

- Lines 1096□1128:Process the AUTH type of XML. First, the Web method Login() is called and, on successful authorization of the user (iResult==0), the AddUser() function is called. Next, the constructor of the XmlFormat class is used to structure the authorization result in suitable XML format for the end user. Thereafter, through use of the SendMsg() function, the XML is delivered to the local user. After delivering the login result to the local user, web method FriendsList() is called from the processXml() function by the Server module. Then the constructor of the XmlFormat class and the SendMsg() function are used to deliver the friends list to the intended user. Simultaneously, the related notification is sent to the user's friends with the help of the FriendsToNotify() Web method. Finally, on a successful authorization, the Jabber server becomes available to the user and the stream with the Jabber server is opened by the xmlOpenStream() function. Next, the WriteMsg() function wipes out the process by writing the message on the stream. After the task is completed successfully, 0 returns.

- Lines 1129□1147:Process the REGISTER type XML. Because the Jabber server must remain available during the registration process, the accessibility of the Jabber server is checked (ConnectToJabber()==0). If the Jabber Server is available, the stream opens to the Jabber server. In next move, the xmlRegister() function of JabberXml class creates the appropriate XML for registering the userand writes it down on the stream with the help of the WriteMsg() function. If the host isn't available for registering the user, the constructor of the XmlFormat class loads, with the parameters REGISTER and strParam, and the message is delivered to the user via the SendMsg() function.

- Lines 1163□1180:Process the MSG type of XML, which is exchanged between users for delivering messages. The first part (Lines 1164□1180) checks the locationof the user. If the target user is local, a constructor of the XmlFormat class executes to deliver the message, and the message is appended to the message queue of the user with the help of the AddMessage() function. The message queue of the target user obtains the message. The second half of the coding (Lines 1181□1188)is responsible for delivering the message to the Jabber user if it isn't meant for the local user.

- Lines 1181□1188:Formats the IDs of the reciever and sender of the message in the Jabber server's XML norms. To begin with delivering the message to the Jabber user, first of all the SendMesage() function of the JabberXml class is called. The SendMessage() fucntion of the JabberXml class formats the message in the Jabber server norms. Once the message is formatted in the Jabber server norms, the WriteMsg() function is called to write down the message on the stream for delivering the message to the Jabber server. On recieving the message the Jabber server will take care of delivering the message to its intented user.

- Lines 1191□1229: Process the XML for adding another user to the friends list of the currently logged-in user. First, the member selected for inclusion in the friends list is verified — whether or not he/she belongs to Hotmail. If the member isn't a Hotmail user, an attempt is made to add him/her as a local user in the friends list of the user. To accomplish this task web method AddFriend() is called from the processXml() function by the Server module. If the member belongs to Hotmail (strResult="0"), he/she is added to the user's friends list and %hotmail.com is appended to the name of the new entry on the friends list. If the member can't be added as Hotmail user, the server delivers the required notification through the XmlFormat class. The constructor of XmlFormat class is called with FRIENDSTATUS and strParam as parameters. Later, the SendMsg() function delivers the server's response to the user. If the member that the user selects definitely can't be added to the user's friends list as a local or a Hotmail user, the Server module makes another attempt to add the selected member to the friends list as a Jabber user. To do so, the server uses the xmlNotify() function of the JabberXml class, which formulates the request in Jabber norms. Finally, the WriteMsg() function sends the request to the Jabber server.

- Lines 1231□1255:Process the XML for deleting a friend of the user from his/her friends list. The Web method DeleteFriend() is called, which returns an integer value of 2 on a successful deletion of the friend. Then, if the friend to be deleted is local, a constructor of XmlFormat forms the appropriate XML, and the SendMsg() function delivers the notification to the user. If the user is a Jabber side user, the xmlNotify() function of the JabberXml class is called to formulate the appropriate XML in Jabber standards. Finally the WriteMsg() function delivers the message to the Jabber user, notifying him/her of the deletion request by the user.

- Lines 1256□1279:Process the XML of ACCEPTFRIEND type. If the Jabber user accepts the friendship of the local user (strXmlElements[2]=="0"), the xmlNotify() function is called to form the suitable XML structure to deliver the message to the Jabber user. After xmlNotify() completes its task, the WriteMsg()writes the message. The request for roster list is then sent to the Jabber server and managed by the xmlRosterReq() function. The WriteMsg() function also delivers this request.

- Lines 1280□1293:Execute if the XML for deleting a foreign user needs to be processed (UNSUBSCRIBEFRIEND type). The xmlNotify() function is called to form the suitable XML for conveying the notification to the target user, and the WriteMsg() function writes the message for the Jabber server. After the friend is deleted, the Server module makes the request for an updated roster listby using the xmlRosterReq() function and then hands over the refreshed roster list requestto the WriteMsg() function.

- Lines 1296□1321:Execute whenever XML of the UNREGISTER type needs to be processed. The Web method Unregister() is called, and then the constructor of the

XmlFormat class is called to form the XML. The SendMsg() function is then called to deliver the message to the user. A notification is sent to the friend of the user about his/her unregistration through the Web method FriendsToNotify(), and the DeleteUser() function is called. If the Jabber server remains available even after unregistration of the user, the xmlOnline() function of the JabberXml class is called with the parameter FALSE to form the XML as to the current status of the user (offline). Thereafter, the WriteMsg() function is called to deliver the message to the Jabber server. Finally, the xmlClose() function of the JabberXml is called to form the request to the Jabber server for closing down the session, and as usual, the task of delivering the message is assigned to the WriteMsg() function.

- Lines 1322□1340:This coding processes the QUIT type of XML, which usually generates if the user wants to log out from the application. To log out the user from the application, the Web method Logout() is called. After the Logout() method completes its task of, the Web method FriendsToNotify() is called to send notification to the friends of the user. The DeleteUser() function is called to clean up the message queue of the user.Information on the status of the user is delivered to the Jabber server by the xmlOnLine() function. The request to close the session is conveyed to the Jabber server via xmlClose() function of the JabberXml class Both requests are transported to the Jabber server with the help of the WriteMsg() function.

- Lines 1341□1357:Processes XML of the ADDGATEWAY type that's generally produced after the user requests to include the gateway in the application. If the user belongs to the Jabber server (bJLogin), the xmlAddGateway() function of the JabberXml class is called to formulate the request and hand it over to the WriteMsg() function to send. If the request for adding the gateway can't be processed due to some error, the constructor of the XmlFormat class is called to formulate the failure notice in the appropriate XML format, and the responsibility of sending the message goes to the SendMsg() function

- Lines 1360□1364:Execute if an exception occurs during the processing of XMLs, and -1 is returned to notify the user of the error.

- Lines 1367□1374: Format the user's login name by appending@msn.jabber.org to the login name and converting '@' sign of the original login name to '%' sign.

- Lines 1376□1393: Implement the NotifyFriends() function to send notification to the local users. The friend names are separated by the ^ character. To send the notification to the friends, the constructor of the XmlFormat class is called with NOTIFYFRIENDS and strParam as parameters. The strParam holds the name of the friends and their status. Finally, the AddMessage() function adds the message to the message queue of the target user.

- Lines 1396□1400: Implements the publiclyaccessible class UserQueue, which has two member variables, strUserName and refQueue. strUserName holds the login name of the user, whereas `refQueue` maintains the reference of the message queue for the user.

InstMsgServ.asmx

Listing 4-3 contains the code for the Web service named as `InstMsgServ`, followed by a detailed description of the code. The Web service `InstMsgServ` has an extension `.asmx`. Inside the Web service various Web methods are deployed. The Web methods are called by the Server module to carry out tasks like authorization, registration of the user, etc. On completing the task the web methods hands over the result to the Server module. On receiving the result from the Web methods, the Server module analyzes the result and delivers it to the end user.

Listing 4-3: InstMsgServ.asmx

```
1 <%@ WebService Language="C#" class="InstMsgServ" %>
2
3 /*
4  This WebService acts as a server side of our Application.
5  This WebService provide several methods which enables a person to
6  register him on the server, to log-on to the server, get friends
   list
7  & their status, to send notification to friends and to add a new
   friend.
8 */
9
10
11 using System; // provide the basic functionality of .Net
12 using System.Collections; // provides the different type of class
                            // collections
13 using System.Configuration;
14 using System.ComponentModel; // provides the functionality of
using                                                              //
components
15 using System.Diagnostics;
16 using System.Web; // provides the functionality required to
                     // communicate over web.
17 using System.Web.Services; // provides the functionality required
                            // by web services.
18
19 // List of additional namespace used by our web service
20 using System.Data; // provides the functionality to work with
data.
21 using System.Data.OleDb;
22 using System.Net; // provides the net related functionality.
23 using System.Net.Sockets; // provides the functionality of
sockets.
```

```
24 using System.Threading; // provides the functionality of threads.
25
26 // Namespace used to access our WebService
27 [WebService(Namespace="http://pratul/")]
28 // here http: is the protocol &  //pratul is the
29 // server name on which our WebService is hosted.
30
31 public class InstMsgServ : System.Web.Services.WebService
32 {
33  public OleDbConnection Conn;
34  public bool bConnected;
35  public InstMsgServ()
36  {
37      // default Constructor used by the class
38
39   InitializeComponent();
40  // this will initialize the control used (if any) by our
    // webservice.
41
42
43   // Connection object require to connect to database.
44   Conn = new OleDbConnection("Provider=SQLOLEDB.1;Persist Security
     Info=False;User ID=charul;password=charul;Initial
     Catalog=Messanger; Data Source=DEVELOPERS");
45
46  try
47  {
48  // try to open the database("Messanger") connection.
49  Conn.Open();
50  bConnected=true;
51  }
52  catch(System.Data.OleDb.OleDbException ex)
53  {
54  // if connection failed then this execption will
55  // raise.Set bConnected=false..
56  bConnected=false;
57  }
58  }
59
60  private void InitializeComponent()
61  {
62      // nothing to initailize.
63  }
64
65     public  void Dispose()
66     {
67         // this will release the memory occupied by the control
initialized
68         // by the constructor.
```

```
69
70      Conn.Close();
71      Conn=null;
72    }
73
74  [WebMethod]
75  public bool IsConnected()
76  {
77  return bConnected;
78  }
79
80  /*********** Login() ********/
81  // This function is used to authenticate a valid user by
82  // checking his/her login name & password.
83  // If the user is a valid user then this function will return
84  // 0 otherwise the appropriate error code.
85
86  [WebMethod]
87  public int Login(String strLoginName, String strPassword)
88  {
89  int iMemberId;
90  String strIpAdd;
91
92  try
93  {
94  // OleDbCommand object require to execute a Sql Query.
95  OleDbCommand logCmd = Conn.CreateCommand();
96  logCmd.CommandText = "Select member_id,password from member
                  where Login_name='"+strLoginName+"'";
97
98  // OleDbDataReader  object which will store the records
    // return by the Sql query.
99  OleDbDataReader logReader=null;
100
101  // fill the datareader.
102  logReader=logCmd.ExecuteReader();
103
104  if (logReader.Read()==false)
105  {
106  // myReader.Read()==false means that the user doesn't exist.
107      return(1); //1: It means user doesn't exist.
108  }
109
110  // GetString(n) GetString() gets a string type
111  // field at col. no. n from the table/query.
112  string strpass=logReader.GetString(1); // col1: password
113  iMemberId=logReader.GetInt32(0);
114  logReader.Close();
115
```

```
116    // if password matches then update the status of the user
117    // by adding his/her IpAddress.
118    if (strpass==strPassword)
119    {
120         // Get Client IP Address
121    String[] strArr=
            this.Context.Request.ServerVariables.
            GetValues("REMOTE_ADDR");
122    strIpAdd=strArr[0];
123
124    // Sql: for updating ipAdd
125    logCmd.CommandText ="update member set ip_add='" +
            strIpAdd + "' where member_id=" + iMemberId;
126
127    // Update IP Add.
128    int rows_affected=logCmd.ExecuteNonQuery();
129    return(0); // succesfuly Login.
130    }
131    else
132    {
133    return(2); // In-Correct Password
134         // if password mismatch then return error code(2).
135         }
136      }
137      catch //(System.Data.OleDb.OleDbException ex)
138      {
139         // on exception return error(-1)
140         return(-1);
141      }
142    }
143    /******** End of Login *******/
144
145
146    /*********** Logout() **********/
147    // this function is use to logout the user from
148    // InstantMessanger Server.
149    [WebMethod]
150
151    public int Logout(String sLoginName)
152    {
153    String strSql;
154    strSql="Select member_id,ip_add from member where login_name='" +
                sLoginName + "'";
155
156    try
157    {
158    // OleDbCommand object require to execute a Sql Query.
159    OleDbCommand logCmd = Conn.CreateCommand();
160    logCmd.CommandText =strSql;
```

```
161
162  // OleDbDataReader object which will store the  records return by
                 // the Sql query.
163  OleDbDataReader logReader=null;
164
165  // fill the datareader.
166  logReader=logCmd.ExecuteReader();
167
168  if (logReader.Read()==false)
169  {
170  // myReader.Read()==false mean that user doesn't exist.
171      return(2);
172        //Error : User doesn't exist.
173  }
174
175  if (logReader.IsDBNull(1))
176  {
177  // if ip_address(field(1)) is null then it mean that the user
178  // is already logout.
179  return(1);
180  }
181
182  int iMemberId=logReader.GetInt32(0);
183  String strIpAdd=logReader.GetString(1);
184  logReader.Close();
185
186  // if ip_address is not null then it mean that the user
187  // is curently loged in, so log him out.
188  logCmd.CommandText ="update member set
     ip_add=null,login_time=null where member_id=" + iMemberId;
189  // update member set ip_add=null ,login_time=null;
190
191  int rows_affected=logCmd.ExecuteNonQuery();
192  return(0);//Logout
193  }
194  catch //(System.Data.OleDb.OleDbException ex)
195  {
196  // on exception return error(-1)
197  return(-1);
198  }
199
200  }
201  /*********** End of Logout **********/
202
203
204  /********* FriendList() ********/
205  // This function will return the friend list of the user.
206  // friend list is return as an array of string.
207  // each string element's first char. indicate whether the
```

```csharp
208   // friend is online("1") or offline("0").
209
210   [WebMethod]
211
212   public String[] FriendsList(String sLoginName)
213   {
214   String strSql1="Select Count(login_name) from member,friend
          where " +
215       "friend.member_id = (Select member_id from member where
                                              login_name='" +
216       sLoginName + "') and member.member_id=friend.friend_id";

217
218       String strSql="Select login_name,ip_add,(" + strSql1 + ")
                from member,friend where " +
219       "friend.member_id = (Select member_id from member where
                                       login_name='" +
220       sLoginName + "') and member.member_id=friend.friend_id";

221
222   try
223   {
224   //OleDbCommand object require to execute a Sql Query.
225   OleDbCommand frdCmd = Conn.CreateCommand();
226   String[] strFriendList;
227   frdCmd.CommandText =strSql;
228
229   // OleDbDataReader  object which will store the records
      // return by the Sql query.
230   OleDbDataReader frdReader=null;
231
232   // fill the datareader.
233   frdReader=frdCmd.ExecuteReader();
234
235   if (!frdReader.Read())
236   {
237   strFriendList= new String[1];
238   strFriendList[0]=sLoginName;
239   return(strFriendList);
240   }
241   int iRows=frdReader.GetInt32(2);
242   // String of friends
243   strFriendList= new String[(2*iRows)+1];
244   strFriendList[0]=sLoginName;
245   int i=1;
246
247   do
248   {
249   strFriendList[i]=frdReader.GetString(0);
```

```
250   if (frdReader.IsDBNull(1))
251   {
252   // if ip_add of friend is null
253   // then it mean that the friend is offline.
254   strFriendList[i+1]="0";
255   }
256   else
257   {
258   strFriendList[i+1]="1";
259   }
260   i+=2;
261   }
262   while(frdReader.Read());
263
264   return(strFriendList);
265   }
266    catch //(System.Data.OleDb.OleDbException ex)
267    {
268        String []strFriendList= new String[1];
269        strFriendList[0]=sLoginName;
270        return(strFriendList);
271    }
272   }
273   /******* End of FriendList *********/
274
275
276   /**************** Register() ******/
277   // This function helps a person in registering him
278   // on the Instant Messanger server.
279
280   [WebMethod]
281   public int Register(String sLoginName, String sPassword,String
          sAdd1,String sAdd2,String sPhone1, String sPhone2,String
          sEmail1, String sEmail2,String sPin,String sCity,String
          sProfession)
282       {
283       String  strAdd1,strAdd2,strPhone1, strPhone2, strEmail1,
              strEmail2, strPin, strCity, strProfession;
284
285       try
286       {
287       // OleDbCommand object require to execute a Sql Query.
288       OleDbCommand regCmd = Conn.CreateCommand();
289       regCmd.CommandText = "Select * from member where
          Login_name='"+sLoginName+"'";
290
291       // OleDbDataReader  object which will store the
          // records return by the Sql query.
292       OleDbDataReader regReader=null;
```

```
293
294        // fill the datareader.
295        regReader=regCmd.ExecuteReader();
296
297        if (regReader.Read()==false)
298        {
299        // myReader.Read()==false mean user doesn't exist.
300        // so add it in the user list.
301        regReader.Close();
302
303        /* regCmd.CommandText="Select member_id from member where
           member_id=(select max(member_id) from member)";
304        regReader=regCmd.ExecuteReader();
305        int iMemberId;
306        if (regReader.Read())
307        {
308            iMemberId=regReader.GetInt32(0)+1;
309        }
310        else
311        {
312            iMemberId=1;
313        }
314        regReader.Close();
315        */
316        strAdd1=(sAdd1.Trim()==""?"null,":"'" + sAdd1 + "',");
317        strAdd2=(sAdd2.Trim()==""?"null,":"'" + sAdd2 + "',");
318        strPhone1=(sPhone1.Trim()==""?"null,":"'" + sPhone1 + "',");
319        strPhone2=(sPhone2.Trim()==""?"null,":"'" + sPhone2 + "',");
320        strEmail1=(sEmail1.Trim()==""?"null,":"'" + sEmail1 + "',");
321        strEmail2=(sEmail2.Trim()==""?"null,":"'" + sEmail2 + "',");
322        strPin=(sPin.Trim()==""?"null,":"'" + sPin + "',");
323        strCity=(sCity.Trim()==""?"null,":"'" + sCity + "',");
324        strProfession=(sProfession.Trim()==""?"null":"'" +
                          sProfession + "'");
325
326        String strSql="Insert into member
(login_name,password,address_1,address_2,phone_1,phone_2,email_1,email_2
,pin,city,profession) "+
327        "values('" + sLoginName +"','" + sPassword + "',"  +
328        strAdd1 + strAdd2 + strPhone1 + strPhone2 + strEmail1 +
329        strEmail2 + strPin + strCity + strProfession + ")";
330        /*
331        String strSql="Insert into member "+
332        "values("+iMemberId.ToString() +",'" +sLoginName +"','" +
           sPassword + "',"  +
333        strAdd1 + strAdd2 + strPhone1 + strPhone2 + strEmail1 +
334        strEmail2 + strPin + strCity + strProfession +
335        "null,null,null)";
336        */
```

```
337        regCmd.CommandText =strSql;
338
339        int rows_affected=regCmd.ExecuteNonQuery();

340        return(0); //It means user doesn't exist.so add a new user.
341        }
342        else
343        {
344        return(1);
345        //it means a user with the requested login_name
346        //already exist.
347        }
348        }
349        catch //(System.Data.OleDb.OleDbException ex)
350        {
351        // on exception return error(-1)
352        return(-1);
353        }
354
355 }
356
357 /************* End of Register *************/
358
359
360 /*********** UnRegister() **********/
361 // This function is used to unregister a user.
362 // Once a user is unregister he lost his use status
363 // and he must be logged off from the server by the web service.
364
365 [WebMethod]
366 public int Unregister (string sLoginName)
367 {
368 try
369 {
370        // OleDbCommand object require to execute a Sql Query.
371        OleDbCommand regCmd = Conn.CreateCommand();
372        //sql-query : search the user.
373        regCmd.CommandText = "Select member_id from member where
                        Login_name='"+sLoginName+"'";
374
375        // OleDbDataReader  object which will store the records
           / return by the Sql query.
376        OleDbDataReader regReader=null;
377
378        // fill the datareader.
379        regReader=regCmd.ExecuteReader();
380
381        if (regReader.Read()==false)
382        {
```

```
383                // myReader.Read()==false mean that user doesn't
                   // exist.
384                // so return error code(1)
385        regReader.Close();
386        return(1);
387        }
388        else
389        {
390                int iMemberId=regReader.GetInt32(0);
391                regReader.Close();
392
393        // delete the record of the user to be unregister.
394        regCmd.CommandText="Delete from member where member_id=" +
                        iMemberId.ToString();
395
396        int rows_affected=regCmd.ExecuteNonQuery();
397
397        return(0);
398            }
399        }
400        catch //(System.Data.OleDb.OleDbException ex)
401        {
402                // on exception return error(-1)
403                return(-1);
404        }
405
406    }
407
408    /*********** End of UnRegister *********/
409
410
411    /*********** AddFriend() ********/
412    // This function lets a user add another user in his
413    // friend list
414
415    [WebMethod]
416    public string Addfriend(String sLoginName,String sFriendName)
417    {
418        int iMemberId,iFriendId;
419        string strAddStatus="";
420
421        try
422        {
423    if (sLoginName.Trim().ToUpper()==sFriendName.Trim().ToUpper())
424        return "-1";
425        // OleDbCommand object require to execute a Sql Query.
426        OleDbCommand frCmd = Conn.CreateCommand();
427        // Sql: get the member_id of the friend to be added.
```

```
428    frCmd.CommandText = "Select member_id,ip_add from member
       where Login_name='" + sFriendName + "'";
429
430    // OleDbDataReader  object which will store the records
       // return by the Sql query.
431    OleDbDataReader frReader=null;
432
433    // fill the datareader.
434    frReader=frCmd.ExecuteReader();
435
436    if (frReader.Read()==false)
437    {
438    // myReader.Read()==false mean that friend doesn't exist.
439    frReader.Close();
440    return("01");
441    // retunr error(1) : Friend is not a register user.
442    }
443    iFriendId=frReader.GetInt32(0);
444    if (frReader.IsDBNull(1))
445    strAddStatus="0";
446    else
447    strAddStatus="1";
448    frReader.Close();
449
450    frCmd.CommandText="Select member_id from member where
            Login_name='"+ sLoginName +"'";
451    frReader=frCmd.ExecuteReader();
452
453    if (!frReader.Read())
454    {
455    // myReader.Read()==false mean that user doesn't exist.
456    frReader.Close();
457    return("03");
458    // return error(-1)
459    }
460
461    iMemberId=frReader.GetInt32(0);
462    frReader.Close();
463    // Sql: Check whether friend is already in the friend list.
464    frCmd.CommandText="Select * from friend where member_id=" +
       iMemberId.ToString() + " and Friend_id=" +
       iFriendId.ToString();
465    frReader=frCmd.ExecuteReader();
466
467    if (frReader.Read())
468    {
469    // if friend's record exist then return error code(2)
470    return("02"); // Friend already exist.
471    }
```

```
472        else
473        {
474        // It means user is not found in friend list.
475        // Add it to the friend list.
476        frReader.Close();
477        frCmd.CommandText="Insert into friend values(" +
           iMemberId.ToString() + "," + iFriendId.ToString() + ")";
478
479        int rows_affected=frCmd.ExecuteNonQuery();
480        // friend added.
481        strAddStatus+="0";
482        return(strAddStatus); //status + 0(added)
483        }
484        }
485        catch //(System.Data.OleDb.OleDbException ex)
486        {
487        // on exception return error(-1)
488        return(null);
489        }
490
491    }
492
493    /********** End of AddFriend *********/
494
495
496    [WebMethod]
497        public int DeleteFriend(String sLoginName,String strFriend)
498        {
499        int iMemberId,iFriendId;
500        try
501        {
502        if (sLoginName.Trim().ToUpper()==strFriend.Trim().ToUpper())
503              return -1;
504
505        OleDbCommand regCmd = Conn.CreateCommand();
506        regCmd.CommandText = "Select member_id,Login_name from
member                                       where
Login_name='"+sLoginName+"' or Login_name='" +
    strFriend + "'";
507
508        OleDbDataReader regReader=null;
509
510        regReader=regCmd.ExecuteReader();
511
512        iMemberId=iFriendId=-1;
513        while (regReader.Read())
514        {
515 if (regReader.GetString(1).ToUpper().Trim()==sLoginName.ToUpper())
516        iMemberId=regReader.GetInt32(0);
```

```
517    if (regReader.GetString(1).ToUpper().Trim()==strFriend.ToUpper())
518                                      iFriendId=regReader.GetInt32(0);
519        }
520        regReader.Close();
521
522        if (iFriendId==-1)
523        return 2;
524        if (iMemberId==-1)
525        return 3;
526
527    regCmd.CommandText="Delete from friend where member_id="
       +iMemberId.ToString() + " and friend_id=" + iFriendId.ToString();
528
529        int rows_affected=regCmd.ExecuteNonQuery();
530
531        if (rows_affected>0)
532             return(0);
533        else
534        return(1);
535        }
536        catch //(System.Data.OleDb.OleDbException ex)
537        {
538        return(-1);
539        }
540    }
541
542
543    [WebMethod]
544        public string FriendsToNotify(String sLoginName)
545        {
546        String strSubSql="(Select member_id from member where
                login_name='" + sLoginName + "')";
547        String strSql="Select login_name,ip_add from member,friend
           where member.member_id=friend.member_id and
           friend.friend_id=" + strSubSql;
548
549        try
550        {
551        OleDbCommand frdCmd = Conn.CreateCommand();
552        frdCmd.CommandText =strSql;
553
554        OleDbDataReader frdReader=null;
555
556        frdReader=frdCmd.ExecuteReader();
557
558        if (!frdReader.Read())
559        {
560        // no friend found
```

```
561          return "";
562          }
563          // String of friends
564          String strFriendList="";
565
566          do
567          {
568          if (!frdReader.IsDBNull(1))
569          strFriendList+=frdReader.GetString(0) + "^";
570          }
571          while(frdReader.Read());
572
573          return(strFriendList);
574          }
575          catch
576          {
577          return "";
578          }
579
580          }
```

- Lines 11□24:Include necessary namespaces required for creating the Web Service.

- Line 27: `pratul` is the name of the server on which our Web service is hosted.

- Line 31: Declares the publicly accessible class `InstMsgServ`.

- Lines 35□58: Implement the default constructor of the `InstMsgServ` class. Inside the constructor, a connection with the database is made with the help of the object `Conn` of the `OleDbConnection` class. The connection class object is initialized with information necessary for authorizing the user and the location of the database:

  - Lines 46□57: Attempt toopen the connection with the database of our application, named Messenger. If the connection opens successfully, the `boolean` variable `bConnected` is set to `True`. If the connection with the database fails, an exception is raised and `bConnected` is set to `false`.

- Lines 59-64: Implements the `InitializeComponent()` function. The `InitializeComponent()` function initializes the various controls used in the web service.

- Lines 65□72:Implement the `Dispose()` function, which releases the memory occupied by the controls that the constructor initializes.

- Lines 74-78: Implements the `IsConnected()` web method. The `IsConnected()` web method checks the connectivity between Server module and database by returning a `boolean` type variable `bConnected`.

- Lines 87☐142: Hold the work of the Web method `Login()`, which is used to authenticate a valid user by checking his/her login name and password. If the user is a valid user, this function returns 0; otherwise, it returns the appropriate error code:
  - Lines 95☐108:Create object `logCmd` of `OleDbCommand` class to execute the SQL query. In the `CommandText` property of `logCmd`, the SQL query is written to obtain the login name and password of the user. Another object, `logReader` of `OleDbDataReader`, is created, which stores the records that the SQL query returns. If, after executing the SQL query, that the user is found not to exist (`logReader.Read()==false`), 1 returns.
  - Lines 112☐114: Retrievethe login name and password of the user from the string type field located at the corresponding column number in the table.
  - Lines 118☐125: Determine the passwordthat the user enters. If the password is correct, the status of the user is updated in the membertable by adding the IP address of the user.
  - Lines 128☐141: Use theExecuteNonQuery() method of `logCmd` to see how many rows are affected in the table to confirm that the SQL query for updating the table executes successfully. If the password that the user enters is incorrect, 2 returns.
- Lines 151☐200: Deploy the Web method`Logout()`. After the user quits the application, the `Logout()` method updates the member table by setting the `member_id` and `ip_addr` fields as empty:
  - Lines 153☐154: Declare a stringtype variable is, which is filled with the SQL query that obtains the member ID and the IP address of the user per the login name that the user supplies.
  - Lines 159☐166: Create an object,logCmd of the `OleDbCommand` class, to execute the SQL query.The SQL query passes in the `CommandText` property of `logCmd`, and the results that the SQL query return are received by the object `logReader` of the `OleDbDataReader` class.
  - Lines 168☐173: Execute ifthe user ID in the SQL query doesn't exist.
  - Lines 175☐180: Execute ifthe user of the user ID passed in the SQL query logged out earlier.
  - Line 188: Sets the member ID and the IP address of the user to `NULL` to notify the Server module that the user is logged out.
- Lines 212☐272: Implement the Web methodFriendsList(), which obtains the friends list for the user:
  - Lines 214☐220: Implement two nested SQL queries. The first SQL query obtains the number of friends for the logged-in user, while the second SQL query retrieves the names of all those members who are friends of the user.

- Lines 222-233: Creates an object `frdCmd` of class `OleDbCommand` to execute the SQL query. Also a `string` type array `strFriendList` is created. In the `CommandText` property of `frdCmd`, variable `strSql` is passed. Another object frdReader of class `OleDbDataReader` is created, which will store the records returned by the SQL query. With the help of `ExecuteReader()` method of `frdCmd` the SQL query is executed and records returned on execution of the SQL query are getting stored in `frdReader`.

- Lines 235□240: Store the login nameof the friend in the string type array `strFriendList`.

- Lines 241-245: Calculates the number records present in `frdReader`. Also a string type array `strFriendList` is created to store the string of friends which contains information like login name and status of the friend.

- Lines 249□262: Lookfor the IP address of the friend. If this IP address is `NULL`, the friend is offline, and `0` is appended to the login name of the friend to notify the Server module of his/her offline status; otherwise, 1 is added to the login name of the friend.

- Lines 281□355: Deploy the Web method`Register()`, which is responsible for registering the new user to the application after ensuring all validations:

  - Line 283: Declares the string type variables, which are necessary to store the information that the user fills in during registration.

  - Lines 288□289: Create the object`regCmd` of the `OleDbCommand` class, and assign the `CommandText` property to the SQL query to select all the information per the login name that the user supplies.

  - Lines 292□324:Attain through `regReader`, an object of `OleDbDataReader` class, the result that the SQL query returns. If the result that returns shows that no current user has the login name that the user chose (`regReader.Read()==false`), the information that the user entered is picked up and assigned to the corresponding variable.

  - Lines 326□329: Write the SQL query toinsert the information for the user in the member table.

  - Lines 342□347:Execute if some other user already has the login name that the user adopted. If so, an integer value of 1 returns to notify the Server moduleof the cause of the registration failure.

- Lines 366□406: Implements the Web method`Uregister()`, which comes into play if a user wants to unregister himself/herself from the application:

  - Line 373: Writes the SQL query that searches the member table for the name of the user who wants to unregister himself/herself.

  - Line 379: Populates the `regReader` object of the class `OleDbDataReader` with the result of the SQL query.

- Lines 381□387: Execute ifthe user who's about to unregister from the application doesn't exist in the application's database (`regReader.Read()=false`). As a result the `regReader` closes and returns an integer value of 1.

- Line 394: Deletes the user from the member table on the application's database if the user does exist.

- Lines 416□491:Set up the Web method `AddFriend()`, which enables the user to include other users of the application in his/her friend list:

  - Line 423: Raises an error if the login name of the user is same as the name of the friend that he/she wants to include is and returns `-1` to the Server module because you can't have two users with identical login name.

  - Lines 423-427: Checks the name of the friend that user wants to add. In case the login names of the user and the friend are same then `-1` is returned by the `AddFriend()` web method to the Server module to notify the error. On the other hand if error does not exist then an object `frCmd` of class `OleDbCommand` is created, which is required to execute a SQL query.

  - Line 428: Writes an SQL query that retrieves the `member_ID` of the friend that the user wants to add.

  - Lines 431-434: Creates an object frReader of class OleDbDataReader. Later, on execution of the SQL query, frReader is initialized with records.

  - Lines 436□442:Execute if the friend that the user selectes for inclusion in the friends list doesn't exist in the member table. (`frReader.Read()==false`). As a result, error code 01 returns.

  - Lines 443□448: Searchthe status of the friend in the record that the data reader returns. If the status field is NULL, then status of the friend is set to 0; otherwise, it's set to 1.

  - Lines 450□459: Execute todetermine whether or not the user who's added another user as a friend is a valid user. If the user isn't a valid user, error code 03 returns.

  - Lines 464□471: Write anSQL query to determine whether or not the friend that the user wants to add already exists in the friends list. If the friend does exist in the user's friend list, error code 02 returns.

  - Line 477: Writes an SQL query to add the friend to the friends list of the user if the friend is a valid user but isn't already in the user's friends list.

- Lines 497□540: Implementthe Web method `DeleteFriend()`, which processes the user request to delete his/her friend from the friends list:

  - Lines 502□506:Check whether or not the login name of the user and friend are the same. If the names are the same, `-1` returns as an error code; otherwise, the query is written to select the member ID and login name from the `member` table.

- Lines 508□510: Execute the query to delete the friend,and the result of the query is stored in `regReader`.

- Lines 513□519: retrievethe member IDs of the user and the friend that returnefrom `regReader`.

- Lines 522□534: Returnerror codes 2 and 3, respectively, if after executing the query, the friend and member ID can't retrieved because they don't exist in the table,. Otherwise, another SQL query is written to delete the friend from the table. The `ExecuteNonQuery()` method of `regCmd` executes the query and determines the number of rows affected. If no rows are affetcted, the delete friend query fails, and error code 1 returns; otherwise, 0 returns.

- Lines 544□580: Lay downthe execution path of the Web method `FriendsToNotify()`, which is used to send notification to the friends of the user:

  - Line 546: Writes an SQL query that retrieves the member ID of the user per his/her login name. This SQL query is assigned to string type variable `strSubSql`.

  - Line 547: In Writes another SQL query to determine the IP address of other users to whom the notification is to be delivered. This SQL query is assigned to string type variable `strSql`.

  - Line 551: Creates an object frdCmd of class OleDbCommand, which will be required to execute the SQL query.

  - Lines 552□556: Create objectsfrdCmd and frdReader, of classes `OleDbCommand` and `OleDbDataReader`, respectively. In the `CommandText` property of frdCmd, the string type variable `strSql` passes. The `ExecuteReader()` function of frdCmd executes, and the result that the query returns is collected by frdReader.

  - Lines 558□562: Executedif no friend is found (`!frdReader.Read()`), and as a result, nothing returns.

  - Lines 564□573:Declare a string type variable, `strFriendList`. The names of the friends are obtained from frdReader and assigned to strFriendList. The names of the friends are seperated by a `^` character.

JabberXml.cs

Listing 4-4 contains the code for `JabberXml.cs`, followed by a detailed description of the code. The JabberXml class has various functions that Server module uses to form different type of requests like request for roster, message delivery to the Jabber server.

Listing 4-4: JabberXml.cs

```
1 using System;
2
3 namespace JIM
4 {
```

```
 5   /// <summary>
 6   /// Summary description for JabberXml.
 7   /// </summary>
 8   public class JabberXml
 9   {
10       private string strXml="";
11       public JabberXml()
12       {
13               //
14               // TODO: Add constructor logic here
15               //
16       }
17
18   public string xmlOpenStream()
19   {
20       strXml="";
21       strXml="<stream:stream\r\n" +
22       "to=\"jabber.org\"\r\n" +
23       "xmlns = \"jabber:client\"\r\n" +
24       "xmlns:stream=\"http://etherx.jabber.org/streams\">";
25
26       return strXml;
27   }
28
29   public string xmlAuth(string strUsername,string strPassword)
30   {
31       strXml="";
32       strXml="<iq type='set' id='AUTH'>\r\n" +
33       "<query xmlns='jabber:iq:auth'>" +
34       "<username>" + strUsername + "</username>" +
35       "<password>" + strPassword + "</password>" +
36       "<resource>work</resource>" +
37         "</query>" +
38         "</iq>";
39
40       return strXml;
41   }
42   public string xmlOnLine(bool bStatus)
43   {
44       strXml="";
45       string strStatus=(bStatus?"OnLine":"OffLine");
46
47       strXml="<presence>" +
48       "<status>" + strStatus + "</status>" +
49       "</presence>";
50
51       return strXml;
52   }
53
```

```
54    public string xmlNotify(string strUser,string strFriend,int
                                               iNotify)
55    {
56        strXml="<presence " +
57        "from=\"" + strUser + "\" " +
58        "to=\"" + strFriend + "\" " +
59        "type=\"";
60
61        switch(iNotify)
62        {
63        case 0:
64                strXml+="subscribe";
65                break;
66        case 1:
67                strXml+="subscribed";
68                    break;
69        case 2:
70                strXml+="unsubscribe";
71                break;
72        case 3:
73                strXml+="unsubscribed";
74                break;
75        }
76
77        strXml+="\"/>";
78
79        return strXml;
80    }
81
82    public string xmlRosterReq(string strID)
83    {
84        strXml="";
85        strXml="<iq type='get' id='" + strID + "'>" +
86        "<query xmlns='jabber:iq:roster' /> " +
87        "</iq>";
88
89        return strXml;
90    }
91    public string SendMessage(string []param)
92    {
93        strXml="";
94        strXml="<message to='" + param[0]+ "' from='" + param[1] +
"'                                         >" +
95        "<body>" + param[2] + "</body></message>";
96
97        return strXml;
98    }
99    public string xmlClose()
100   {
```

```
101        strXml="";
102        strXml="</stream:stream>";
103
104        return strXml;
105    }
106
107    public string xmlRegister(string strUserName,string strPassword)
108    {
109        strXml="<iq id='REGISTER' type='set'>" +
110        "<query xmlns='jabber:iq:register'>" +
111        "<username>" + strUserName + "</username>" +
112        "<resource>work</resource>" +
113        "<password>" + strPassword + "</password>" +
114        "</query>" +
115        "</iq>";
116
117        return strXml;
118    }
119
120    public string xmlAddGateWay(string msnUserName,string
                                        msnPassword)
121    {
122        char []chPass=msnPassword.ToCharArray();
123        string msnPass="";
124
125        for (int i=0;i<chPass.Length;i++)
126        {
127        msnPass+=((char)((byte)chPass[i]-10)).ToString();
128        }
129    strXml="<iq to='msn.jabber.org' type='set' id='ADDGATEWAY'>" +
130        "<query xmlns='jabber:iq:register'><username>" +
131        msnUserName +"</username><password>" +
132        msnPass +"</password></query></iq>";
133
134        return strXml;
135    }
136    }
137 }
```

- Line 8-10: Declares the publicly accessible class `JabberXml`. This class holds various functionsthat are responsible for forming different types of requests, notifications, or messages in an XML format that the Jabber server supports.Also a string type variable `strXml` is created.

- Lines 11□16: Set up default constructor ofJabberXml class.

- Lines 18□27:Implement `xmlOpenStream()` function, which returns a string. The returned string usually holds the request in XML format to open the stream with the Jabber server as well as the protocol for the Jabber server.

- Lines 29☐41:Contain the xmlAuth() function. Whenever the user's authorization request needs to be delivered to the Jabber server, the Server module use the xmlAuth() function. In delivering the request, the xmlAuth() function mentions the type of request and information like user's login name, password and resource name are appended in the request. The authorization request is headed by <AUTH> ID for an IQ type of XML.

- Lines 42☐51:Hold the execution path of the xmlOnline() function, which is used to send the presence notification to the friends of the user whenever he/she logs in or logs out. The xmlOnline() function takes the status of the user as a parameter. A notification of this type is represented by the <presence> ID.

- Lines 54☐80:Implement the xmlNotify() function. The xmlNotify() function takes the names of the user and friend and the type of notification as parameters. Integer values in upcoming lines identify the types of the notifications:

  - Lines 56☐59:Make Creates an appropriate XML structure necessary for sending the notification.

  - Lines 61☐75: Group various types of notifications. Eachtype of notification is headed by an integer value ranging between 0—and 3.

- Lines 82☐90:Implement the xmlRoster() function, which is usually necessary for sending the roster request to the Jabber server in the appropriate XML format.

- Lines 91☐98:Applies to the working of the SendMessage() function. The SendMessage() function holds the names of the sender and the receiver of the message, along with the content of the message, which is enclosed between the <body> element.

- Lines 99☐105: Implement thexmlClose() function, which closes the stream and terminates the session running with the Jabber server.

- Lines 107☐118: Sets upthe xmlRegister() function, which formulates the registration request for the Jabber server. In sending the request, the Server module sends the login name, password, and resource name as mandatory information.

- Lines 120☐134: Implement thexmlAddGateway() function, which sends the request of the user to add a gateway. Because the user's password to log on to MSN is also required to include the gateway, the password is converted into char type. To decrypt the password, the xmlAddGateway() function subtracts 10 from the ASCII value of each character present in the password, and then this decrypted password is converted into string type and put into the string type variable msnPass.

XmlFormat.cs

The XmlFormat class handles the task of formulating the XML according to the norms of the application. The Server module uses the functions present under the XmlFormat class to deliver the response to the local user. Listing 4-5 contains the code for XmlFormat.cs, followed by a detailed description of the code.

Listing 4-5: XmlFormat.cs

```
 1 using System;
 2
 3 namespace JIM
 4 {
 5 /// <summary>
 6 /// Summary description for XmlFormat.
 7 /// </summary>
 8 public class XmlFormat
 9 {
10 private string strXml;
11 public XmlFormat()
12 {
13     //
14     // TODO: Add constructor logic here
15     //
16 }
17 //overloaded constructor
18 public XmlFormat(string strType,string []param)
19 {
20     strXml= "<?xml version=\'1.0\' encoding=\'utf-
                8\'?><InstantMessenger>";
21
22     if (strType.ToUpper().CompareTo("AUTH")==0)
23     {
24     AuthXML(param);
25     }
26     else if (strType.ToUpper().CompareTo("REGISTER")==0)
27     {
28     RegisterXML(param);
29     }
30     else if (strType.ToUpper().CompareTo("FRIENDLIST")==0)
31     {
32     FriendListXML(param);
33     }
34     else if (strType.ToUpper().CompareTo("MSG")==0)
35     {
36     MessageXML(param);
37     }
38     else if (strType.ToUpper().CompareTo("ROSTER")==0)
39     {
40     RosterXML(param);
41     }
42     else if (strType.ToUpper().CompareTo("NOTIFYFRIENDS")==0)
43     {
```

```
44          NotifyFriendsXML(param);
45          }
46          else if (strType.ToUpper().CompareTo("FRIENDSTATUS")==0)
47          {
48          FriendStatusXML(param);
49          }
50          else if (strType.ToUpper().CompareTo("DELETESTATUS")==0)
51          {
52          DeleteStatusXML(param);
53          }
54          else if (strType.ToUpper().CompareTo("UNREGISTER")==0)
55          {
56          UnRegisterXML(param);
57          }
58          else if (strType.ToUpper().CompareTo("ADDGATEWAY")==0)
59          {
60          AddGatewayXML(param);
61          }
62          strXml+= "</InstantMessenger>";
63
64  }
65  private void AuthXML(String []param)
66  {
67          strXml+= "<auth>";
68          strXml+= "<int>"+param[0]+"</int>";
69          strXml+= "</auth>";
70  }
71
72  private void RegisterXML(String []param)
73  {
74          strXml+= "<Register>";
75          strXml+= "<int>"+param[0]+"</int>";
76          strXml+= "</Register>";
77  }
78
79  private void FriendListXML(String []param)
80  {
81          strXml+= "<FriendList>";
82          strXml+= "<username>"+param[0]+"</username>";
83
84          for (int i=1;i<param.Length;i+=2)
85          {
86          strXml+= "<FriendName>"+param[i]+"</FriendName>";
87          strXml+= "<status>"+param[i+1]+"</status>";
88          }
89          strXml+= "</FriendList>";
90  }
91
92  private void MessageXML(String []param)
```

```
 93   {
 94         strXml+= "<MSG>";
 95         strXml+= "<Target>"   + param[0] + "</Target>";
 96         strXml+= "<Source>"   + param[1] + "</Source>";
 97         strXml+= "<Text>"+ param[2] + "</Text>";
 98         strXml+= "</MSG>";
 99   }
100
101   private void RosterXML(String []param)
102   {
103         strXml+= "<Roster>";
104         for (int i=0;i<param.Length;i+=2)
105         {
106         //DON'T SEND MSN ITEM IN ROSTER LIST and null values.
107         if ((param[i].ToUpper().IndexOf("MSN.JABBER.ORG/")!=0) &&
                    param[i]!="")
108         {
109         strXml+= "<FriendId>"+param[i]+"</FriendId>";
110         strXml+= "<Subscription>"+param[i+1]+"</Subscription>";
111         }
112         }
113         strXml+= "</Roster>";
114   }
115
116   private void NotifyFriendsXML(String []param)
117   {
118         strXml+= "<NotifyFriends>";
119         for (int i=0;i<param.Length;i+=2)
120         {
121         strXml+= "<UserName>"+param[i]+"</UserName>";
122         switch (param[i+1].ToCharArray()[0])
123         {
124         case '0':
125               strXml+= "<Status>OFF-LINE</Status>";
126               break;
127         case '1':
128               strXml+= "<Status>ON-LINE</Status>";
129               break;
130         case '2':
131               strXml+= "<Status>SUBSCRIBE</Status>";
132               break;
133         case '3':
134               strXml+= "<Status>SUBSCRIBED</Status>";
135               break;
136         case '4':
137               strXml+= "<Status>UNSUBSCRIBE</Status>";
138               break;
139         case '5':
140               strXml+= "<Status>UNSUBSCRIBED</Status>";
```

```
141                 break;
142         }
143     }
144         strXml+= "</NotifyFriends>";
145 }
146
147 private void FriendStatusXML(String []param)
148 {
149         strXml+= "<FriendStatus>";
150         strXml+= "<FriendName>"+param[0]+"</FriendName>";
151         strXml+= "<Status>"+param[1]+"</Status>";
152         strXml+= "<OnLine>"+param[2]+"</OnLine>";
153         strXml+= "</FriendStatus>";
154 }
155
156 private void DeleteStatusXML(String []param)
157 {
158         strXml+= "<DeleteStatus>";
159         strXml+= "<FriendName>"+param[0]+"</FriendName>";
160         strXml+= "<Status>"+param[1]+"</Status>";
161         strXml+= "</DeleteStatus>";
162 }
163 private void UnRegisterXML(String []param)
164 {
165         strXml+= "<UnRegister>";
166         strXml+= param[0];
167         strXml+= "</UnRegister>";
168 }
169 private void AddGatewayXML(String []param)
170 {
171         strXml+= "<AddGateway>";
172         strXml+= param[0];
173         strXml+= "</AddGateway>";
174 }
175
176 public string GetXml()
177 {
178         return strXml;
179     }
180 }
181 }
```

- Line 8: Declares the publicly accessible Xml Format class.

- Lines 11☐16:Set up the default constructor of the XmlFormat class.

- Lines 18☐64: Implement the overloaded constructor of theXmlFomat class. Various functions line up under the constructor. After the type of XML is determined by the constructor, a corresponding function is called to take over the responsibility of formulating the server's response XML format, which the Client module can understndd and read.

- Lines 65☐70:Executes the `AuthXML()` function. The `AuthXML()` function frames the authorization result that the server returns. The `<int>` element holds the integer value that indicates a successful or failed login.

- Lines 72☐77:Implements `RegisterXML()` function, which determines the XML format for delivering the registration result. The local server uses this function to deliver the registration result to the Client module. The `<int>` element carries the value to notify the successful or unsuccessful registration of the user.

- Lines 79☐90: Implement the `FriendListXML()` function. The local server uses this function to deliver the friend list to the Client module. The elements `<FriendName>` and `<status>` hold the name of the friend and his/her status.

- Lines 92☐99:Apply to the `MessageXML()` function. The local server uses this function to deliver the message to the Client module. The name of the sender, the receiver of the message, and the text of the message are delivered as information to the Client module. The `<Target>` element mentions the name of the target user, whereas the `<Source>` element gives the sender's name. The `<Text>` element contains the text of the message.

- Lines 101☐114: Implement the`RosterXML()` function. The local sever uses this function to deliver the names of the Jabber users who are friends to the local user. In sending the list of friends, [what?] doesn't put the names of the MSN friends and `NULL` items in the roster list. The `<FriendID>` element holds the name of the friend, whereas the `<Subscription>` element describes the type of subscription between the user and the Jabber friends.

- Lines 116☐145: Organizes the working ofthe `NotifyFriendsXML()` function. The local server uses the `NotifyFriendsXml()` function to deliver notification to the friends of the user in suitable XML format. The `NotifyFriendsXML()` function groups various types of notifications. Each type of notification is recognized by a distinct value ranging between 0 and 5:

  - Lines 124☐129: Executed whena notification about the offline or online status of the user needs to be delivered to friends. The notification for the offline status of the user is recognized by 0, whereas the online notification is headed by 1.

  - Lines 130☐132:Forms the SUBSCRIBE type of notification. Usually, this type of notification arises when the currently logged in user sends a friendship request to some other user. The SUBSCRIBE type of notification is recognized by 2.

  - Lines 133☐135: Forms the SUBSCRIBEDtype of notification. This type of notification arises when the user replies to the SUBSCRIBE type of notification.

  - Lines 136☐138:Forms the UNSUBSCRIBE type of notification in appropriate XML format. This type of notification arises when the currently logged in user removes other users from the friend list.

- Lines 139□141: Forms the UNSUBSCRIBEDtype of notification. This type of notification arises when the user replies to the UNSUBSCRIBE type of notification.

- Lines 147□154: Implements theFriendStatusXML() function. The local server uses the FriendStatusXML() function to notify the user as to whether or not the friend has been successfully included in the friend list and as to his or her status — online or offline.

- Lines 156□162: Enabledwhen the local server needs to respond to the client module to deliver the result of the Delete Friend request. The DeleteStatusXML() function implemented in this coding hands over the result to the client module. The result can be the successful or unsuccessful deletion of the friend.

- Lines 163□168: Enabled when the local server needsto reply to the client module for an unregistration type of request. To handle the task, the UnRegisterXML() function is deployed in this coding; the function sends the result of the unregistration request.

- Lines 169□174: Implements theAddGatewayXML() function. The local server uses this function to deliver the request result to the client module in the appropriate XML structure. The result can be success or failure.

- Lines 176□179: Deploys theGetXml() function, which returns the string type variable strXml. The strXml variable contains the XML format that the local server usually uses while delivering the response to the client module.

SckListener.cs

The Server module uses the SckListener.cs class to establish connection with the Client module in order to listen the client's request. Listing 4-6 contains the code for SckListener.cs, followed by a detailed description of the code.

Listing 4-6: SckListener.cs

```
1 using System;
2 using System.Net;
3 using System.Net.Sockets;
4
5 namespace JIM
6 {
7  /// <summary>
8  /// Summary description for SckListener.
9  /// </summary>
10  public class SckListener : System.Net.Sockets.TcpListener
11  {
12       public SckListener(int port) : base(port)
13       {
14              //this(port);
15       }
16       public bool IsConnected()
```

```
17        {
18                return this.Active;
19        }
20  }
21 }
```

- Lines 1□3: Include necessary namespaces.

- Line 10: Declares the publicly accessible class SckListener, which is inherited from System.Net.Sockets.TcpListener class.

- Lines 12□15: Sets up the default constructor of theSckListener class.

- Lines 16□19: This code snippet implements theIsConnected() function, which returns a boolean value.

Summary

In this chapter, the complete design and implementation phase of the server module is presented. The chapter begins with a note about Web services and proceeds to detail the working and deployment of the Web services. Later, the chapter discusses how the server module handles various types of client requests. The key code snippet responsible for executing the client request is comprehensively discussed, as is the method by which the server module analyzes and processes various types of Jabber responses. The working of the various Web methods deployed in the Web service used by the application is explained. Finally, the technical documentation of the server module, clarified by technical flow charts and the line-by-line discussion of code provided toward the end of the chapter, offers handy tools to help you create your own applications.

Chapter 5

The Instant Messaging Client
(Java)

In Chapters 3 and 4, we discuss the server architecture. We discuss how the server was developed and the classes that form its core components. From those two chapters, it is clear that regardless of the technology used — Java or C# — the implementation of the server ensures that it works as the central coordination unit among various clients. In both implementations, the server provides various Web services to clients, communicates with the database(s), and provides interoperability by sitting between the client and the Jabber server. The point to be noted here is that the server works behind the scenes, and its presence remains hidden from the end user using the Instant Messenger Service. The immediate question that comes to mind is the following: if the end user is oblivious of the server, what or whom does the end user communicate with? The answer to this question is the client application that provides the necessary user interface(s) that the user can communicate with.

It is incumbent on the client to perform tasks that happen at the center stage (that is, at the user's end). These tasks are:

- To present the user with one or more graphical user interfaces that are easy to use and easy to understand.

- To act as an interface between the end user and the server by converting the user commands into a format that can be understood and, if required, processed by the server application.

- To transmit user requests to the server and receive responses from it.

- To interpret and convert the server's responses to a format that can be displayed on the GUI in a user-friendly manner. An example is status messages that appear on a GUI, informing the user as to what actions are being taken by the client application or whether or not a user request can be fulfilled, something like, "your message has been sent," "contacting the server, please wait," and so on.

Though these tasks are generic and apply to practically all Instant Messenger clients, the client in our Instant Messenger application also provides the same functionality. Our client application is the subject of discussion in this chapter.

Basic Implementation of the Client

If you have ever used any Instant Messenger service, you know that there is a general sequence of operations followed by Instant Messenger applications:

1. At the start, the Instant Messenger service asks you to login, with a message like, "click here to login." Along with the login option is another option for new users to register themselves. For example, if you are using the Instant Messenger service MyInstantMessenger and do not have an account with them, you can choose this option. The Instant Messenger service then presents you with a form that seeks details like a such as login name, password, and so on. A successful registration means that your information has been logged in the Instant Messenger service's database.

2. Once you have registered yourself, the Instant Messenger service asks you to login. A successful login means that verification of your login name and password against the user database has established you as a bonafide user and that the Instant Messenger server is now ready to serve your requests. You are now presented with a window that contains a friend or contact list sorted on the basis of "Online" and "Offline" contacts. If you are a new user, you will probably be shown an empty friend list stating something like "You have no contacts in your friend list. Do you want to add one now?" You may then add contacts to your list and begin chatting with them if they are online.

3. While you are logged in, you can chat with your contacts and add or delete contacts. A new message window is opened for every new contact you choose to chat with or vice-versa. Alerts are received when a contact comes online or goes offline or when you receive a message.

4. When you choose the logout option or close the main Instant Messenger window, the program exits. These days, however, you have Instant Messenger services that keep running in the background when the main window is closed.

Contemporary Instant Messenger services provide a hoard of additional utilities such as using emotions (images representing various emotions or graphics like a flower, a heart, and so on); working in invisible mode; ignoring a friend; setting the font and color properties of the messages; receiving a notification with an accept and decline option when someone adds you as a friend; and so on. However, at the core, an Instant Messenger service remains one that allows you to chat privately with your friends by adding them to your friend list.

The client application of our Instant Messenger service concentrates on the basic Instant Messenger utilities, though it provides some additional functionality by way of changing message colors. This is amply clear from Figure 5-1, which summarizes the working of our client-side application. The client application follows the following execution path:

1. It presents the user with a GUI that provides a login/registration option.

2. Simultaneously, it starts a user session. This session is created by opening a connection with the server. If the client fails to create a session, it displays a label saying "There is no

Server to satisfy your request" on the user GUI and exits the program. If, however, the session is created, further processing of user request(s) continues.

3. The first request — a login or registration — is sent to the server via the session class that is responsible for creating the session.

4. Upon successful login/registration, the client application presents the user with a GUI that has menus/buttons providing him/her with various Instant Messenger utilities such as adding a friend, sending a message, logging out, accepting a friend, unregistering with the Instant Messenger Service, and so on. Also, displayed on GUI is the user's friend list that is classified as "Online " and "Offline" friends. It may be noted that no request is sent by the client as such to retrieve the client list. Rather, when a user sends a login request that is authentic, the server automatically retrieves his/her friend list and sends it with the response confirming authorization.

5. While the user is logged in, the client application sends requests to the server and recieves responses from it to fulfill the tasks requested by the user. As shown in Figure 5-1, requests subsequent to the login request are sent by the class behind the main GUI window (the `MainScreen` class) or by separate classes meant for special requests. (See Associated Classes in Figure 5-1.)

6. All responses after login are handled by the `MainScreen` class that calls the `SParser` class to parse the XML response received from the server. Appropriate messages, dialog boxes, and so on are then displayed to inform the user of the server's response. For example, if the user receives a message from a friend, the message is written to the message window that the user has opened for that particular friend; if a friend logs out, a dialog box pops up informing the user of his friend's offline status. The friend's name is shifted to the "Offline" entries in the friend list on the user's main screen.

The client application runs until the user logs out, closes the main screen window, or unregisters. Then the client application ends the user session and closes the GUI window.

Figure 5-1: Workflow of the client application

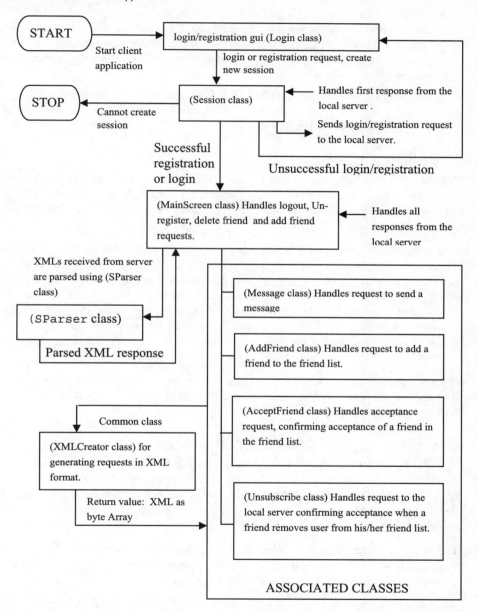

From Figure 5-1 and the preceding discussions, it is clear that two basic operations form the core of our client application. These operations are:

- Creating a user session: Creation of a session is intrinsic to the working of the client application. If a user session cannot be created, the client application cannot function. The server is the only gateway through which a user can communicate with his/her friends; if a session with the server cannot be created, the client application on its own cannot service user requests.

- Creating Graphical User Interface(s): A GUI, that is, a window, a message box, a form, and son on, is the mode through which the client can receive inputs from the user and display responses for him/her.

Creating a user session

A *session* may be defined as an entity used by the server to recognize a client. A user session makes every client unique, since it has a particular ID/server thread associated with it. A user session also serves as an indication to the server that a certain client is logged into a service and may request server resources.

In our Instant Messenger service, the Session class is responsible for starting a session by creating a socket on the client machine that has input and output streams associated with it to communicate with the server. Chapter 3 discusses how a similar socket is also created on the server. The socket on the client machine acts as the other end point of communication between the client and the server. A session is created if the client application manages to open a connection with the server. In such a case, the value of the variable sessionVal in the Session class is set to 1. However, if the client fails to establish a connection, sessionVal is set to □1.

Once a session is established, the Session class gives up control to the MainScreen class for receiving server responses, while the requests are handled by individual classes defined for each type of request.

Creating a graphical user interface

Swing components have been used to create the main GUI in the MainScreen class. The javax.swing and javax.swing.tree packages are central to the development of the GUI. The former is being used to create the menus and buttons that provide a user with the Instant Messenger Service options, while the later is being used for the tree-view structure of the friend list being displayed on the main window.

The structure of the friend list is an important feature you need to understand to be able to understand code explanations given later in this chapter. This tree structure is repeatedly used to identify source objects for mouse events.

As shown in Figure 5-2, 'Friend List for the "User 1"' is the parent node of the tree; the 'ON-LINE' and 'OFF-LINE' friends are its two subnodes, and the names of friends are the leaves.

The Parent-Child relationship dictates that 'Friend List for "User 1"' is the Parent; "ON-LINE" and "OFF-LINE" are Parent-Child nodes, and Friend 1, Friend 2, Friend 3, Friend 4, and Friend 5 are the Parent-Child-Child nodes. Each row in the tree structure is assigned a number, in ascending order. Thus, 'Friend List for the "User 1"' is row 1; "ON-LINE" is row 2; "Friend 1" is row 3 and so on. In code explanations, the path to a row is always ascertained. The path to a row returns a value that specifies whether the clicked row is the Parent row or Parent-Child row or Parent-Child-Child row and so on. Thus, the path to "Friend 1" is Parent-Child-Child. Another value ascertained is the last node within a path. For example, if a user clicks Friend 2, the last node for this path is Friend 5. Similarly, the last node for the path to "ON-LINE" row is "OFF-LINE." Notice that the last node has the same path as that of the row for which the path has been determined. The last node for 'Friend List for t "User 1"' is 'Friend List for "User 1"' itself.

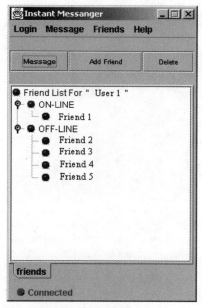

Figure 5-2: The Main window

Establishing a Connection with the Local Server

The client is connected to and communicates with his/her contacts via the server. All requests have to be processed by the server, and all messages are routed through the server. Thus, connection with the local server is central to the working of the client application. Without being connected to the server, the client application cannot fulfill user requests.

The connection with the server is retained through the session created by the `Session` class. The constructor of the `Session` class tries to create a socket on the client machine for communication with the server and creates input and output streams associated with this socket. If the `Session` class succeeds in making a connection, it sets the return value to 1; if it fails to connect to the server, it sets the return value to □1.

```
Session()
 {
 try
 {

   socket= new Socket (ServerIP, 5555);

   StreamFromLocalServer  = new
BufferedInputStream(socket.getInputStream());

   StreamToLocalServer    = new
BufferedOutputStream(socket.getOutputStream());
   sessionVal= 1;
 }
 catch(Exception e)
 {
   System.out.println("Exception in Constructor of Session.java" + e);
   sessionVal = -1;
 }
 }

 int returnResult()
 {
   return  sessionVal;
 }
```

> **NOTE:** The variable `ServerIP` in the above code indicates a place holder where you have to specify the IP address for your server machine. For example, if the server code is being run on a machine with IP address "192.168.1.105", then, you need to replace ServerIP in the above code with "192.168.1.105".

When the user starts the client application, the first GUI screen that comes up is the login controlled by the `Login` class. The constructor of the `Login` class is overloaded. One is a constructor without parameters; the other accepts parameters. In the first instance, the no-parameter version is called that creates an object of the `Session` class and checks the return value to ascertain whether a session has been initiated or not. If the session has not been created, the `Login` class displays an error message to the effect that the server could not be reached, and the program exits. However, if the session has been initiated, the `Login` class presents the login screen to the user and waits for his/her action event, against which a suitable method call can be made.

```
userSession =      new Session();
if (userSession.returnResult() == -1)
 {
```

```
JOptionPane.showMessageDialog(this,"There is No Server To Satisfy your
Request ","Instant Messenger",JOptionPane.INFORMATION_MESSAGE);
System.exit(0);
}
```

Regardless of whether the user is an existing one who chooses to login or a new one who opts for registration, the first authorization or registration request is sent through the sendRequest() method of the Session class that also waits in a loop for the server's response. If the login attempt is successful, the Session class relinquishes control to the MainScreen class by passing to it the user's name, password, and the input and output streams associated with the server connection.

```
MainScreen showScreen = new MainScreen(userName, passWord,
StreamFromLocalServer, StreamToLocalServer)
```

The object of the Session class is no longer required and doesn't play any part in further request/response transmission. However, note that it is the session created by the Session class that handles communication with the server until the user exits the session. The connection to the server is made only once and the input/output stream objects created by the Session class are passed back and forth between classes to communicate with the server. Another point to be noted is that while respective classes such as Message and AddFriend handle transmission of respective request(s) to the server, all responses from the server are written to the "response.xml" file and are handled solely by the MainScreen class.

Programming Client Requests

In this section, we discuss the various requests that a user may send to the server. The classes that handle the formation of the request and the sending of the request to the server are explained with code snippets.

Registration request from a new user

As mentioned in the previous section, when a user starts the client application, Login is the first class that comes into play. The login screen also has a Register button for new users who do not have a login name and password already. When a user wanting to register himself/herself clicks the Register button, the Login class creates an object of the Register class that handles registration and passes it two parameters: one is an instance of the Login class itself, and the other is an instance of the Session class.

```
if(source.equals(m_Register))
{
 register = new Register(this, userSession);
 register.register_list();
}
```

The method `register_list()` creates the registration GUI for the user with requisite text fields, labels, and so on to accept user information (see Figure 5-3).

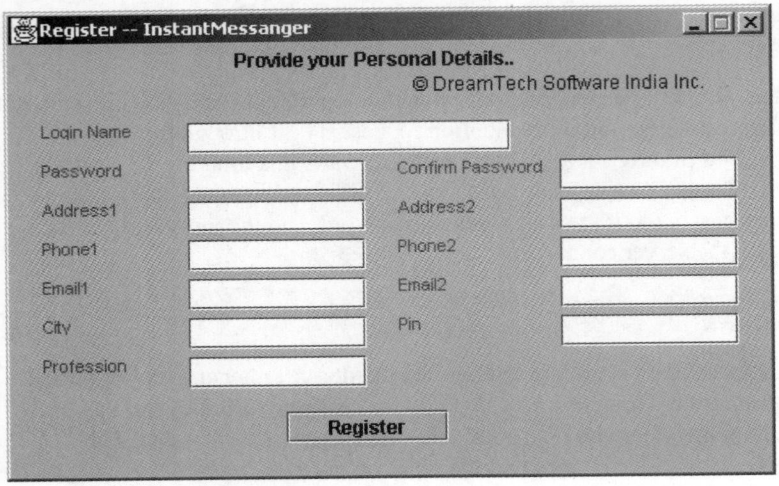

Figure 5-3: The Registration window

When the user fills in his/her information and presses the Register button, the program execution follows the following course:

1. The class `XMLCreator` is called to create an XML request in the desired format.

```
public void actionPerformed(ActionEvent e)
{
if(e.getSource() == b_register)
{

        XMLCreator              createRequest;
................................................................... .
................................................................... .


createRequest = new XMLCreator("REGISTER", requestString);
RequestGenerated      = createRequest.returnResult();
................................................................... .
................................................................... .


}
```

2. `XMLCreator` calls the appropriate method to generate a registration request in the required XML format. Notice that `XMLCreator` returns the result in the form of a byte array, whereas the `CreateXML` class of the server returns the XML as a string.

```
XMLCreator(String type, String params[])
```

```
{

        XMLString= "<?xml version=\'1.0\'  encoding=\'utf-
8\'?><InstantMessenger>";

    if (type.equalsIgnoreCase("AUTH"))
    {
        CreateAuthXML(params);
    }
    else if (type.equalsIgnoreCase("REGISTER"))
    {
        CreateRegisterXML(params);
    }
.............................................. .
.............................................. .

void CreateRegisterXML(String params[])
{
        XMLString += "<Register>";
        XMLString += "<UserName>"+params[0]+"</UserName>";
        XMLString += "<Password>"+params[1]+"</Password>";
        XMLString += "<sAdd1>"+params[3]+"</sAdd1>";
        XMLString += "<sAdd2>"+params[4]+"</sAdd2>";
        XMLString += "<sPhone1>"+params[5]+"</sPhone1>";
        XMLString += "<sPhone2>"+params[6]+"</sPhone2>";
        XMLString += "<sEmail1>"+params[7]+"</sEmail1>";
        XMLString += "<sEmail2>"+params[8]+"</sEmail2>";
        XMLString += "<sPin>"+params[9]+"</sPin>";
        XMLString += "<sCity>"+params[10]+"</sCity>";
        XMLString += "<sProfession>"+params[11]+"</sProfession>";
        XMLString += "</Register>";
}
.............................................. .
.............................................. .

}
```

3. The `Register` class then forwards the XML request received from `XMLCreator` to the `sendRequest()` method of the `Session` class.

```
userSession.sendRequest(screen, RequestGenerated, this)
```

4. The `sendRequest()` method of the `Session` class sends the request to the local server.

```
void sendRequest(Login screen, byte request[], Register regScreen)
  {
```

```
                  .
                  .

    try
     {
       StreamToLocalServer.write(request, 0, request.length);
       StreamToLocalServer.flush();

                  .
                  .
```

Login request from an existing user

The Login GUI is presented to the user when he/she starts the application (see Figure 5-4).

Figure 5-4: The Login window

When a user supplies his/her login name and password and clicks on the Login button, the following cycle of program execution is performed:

1. The `Login` class calls `XMLCreator` to form an authorization-type request.

```
public void actionPerformed(ActionEvent at)
{
        Object source = at.getSource();

                  .
                  .
        else if(source.equals(m_Login))
        {
                  .
                  .

            val[0]= m_EnterLoginName.getText();
            val[1]= new String(m_EnterPassword.getPassword());

            createRequest      = new XMLCreator("AUTH", val);
```

```
            RequestGenerated = createRequest.returnResult();
..........................................................................
..........................................................................
```

2. The XMLCreator calls tha CreateAuthXML() method to create the XML request for authorization and returns this XML as a byte array to the Login class.

```
void CreateAuthXML(String params[])
{
        XMLString += "<Auth>";
        XMLString += "<UserName>"+params[0]+"</UserName>";
        XMLString += "<Password>"+params[1]+"</Password>";
        XMLString += "</Auth>";
}
```

3. The Login class calls the sendRequest() method of the Session class that sends the request to the local server, just as it happens in the registration request.

Logout request from a user

The Logout request is handled by the MainScreen class itself. This request ends a user session and informs the server that the client need not be serviced any more.

1. When a user chooses the "Exit" option from the menu, the method logoutUser() is called. Also, if the user closes the MainScreen window, a windowClosing event is generated that calls logoutUser().

```
if (ae.getSource() == m_SignOutMenuItem)
{
        try
        {
                logoutUser();
        }
..........................................................................
..........................................................................


addWindowListener( new WindowAdapter()
        { public void windowClosing(WindowEvent e)
                {
                        try
                        {
                                logoutUser();
                        }
..........................................................................
..........................................................................
```

2. The `logoutUser()` method calls the `XMLCreator` to form a logout request, sends this request to the server, and closes the main window.

```
void logoutUser() throws IOException
{
        String [] values = new String[1];
        values [0] = userName;

        XMLCreator createRequest;
        byte[]                RequestGenerated;

        createRequest      = new XMLCreator("QUIT", values);
        RequestGenerated   = createRequest.returnResult();

        StreamToServer.write(RequestGenerated, 0,
RequestGenerated.length);
        StreamToServer.flush();
    }
```

3. The `XMLCreator` calls the `CreateQuitXML()` method to generate the quit request.

```
void CreateQuitXML(String params[])
{
        XMLString += "<Quit>";
        XMLString += "<UserName>"+params[0]+"</UserName>";
        XMLString += "</Quit>";
}
```

4. The request is sent to the server by the `MainScreen` class, and the program exits.

Request to add a friend to the friend list

The `AddFriend` class handles the request to add a friend. This request is made when the user wants to add a new person to his/her friend list using his/her username.

1. When a user chooses to add a friend, the `MainScreen` class calls the `AddFriend` class.

```
if (ae.getSource() == m_AddFriendMenuItem)
{
        m_addFriendInList = new AddFriend(this, userName);
}
```

2. The `AddFriend` class presents the user with a GUI that seeks the user's ID (login name) and friend's ID (see Figure 5-5).

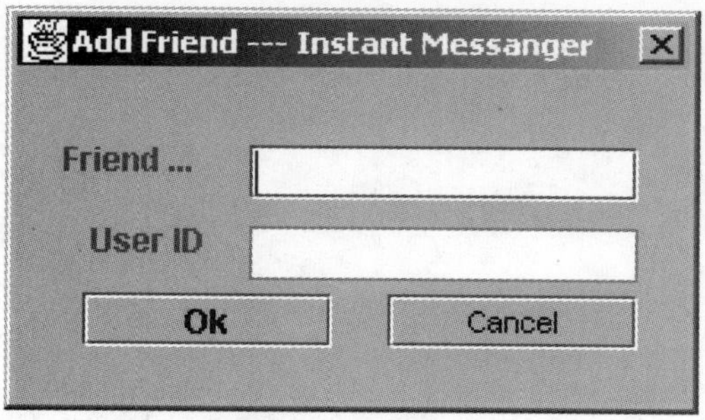

Figure 5-5: The window to add a friend

3. If the user provides the two IDs and clicks the Okbutton, the XMLCreator is called to form an add friend request.

```
else if(source.equals(b_friends_name))
        {
................................................. .
................................................. .
            createRequest = new XMLCreator("ADDFRIEND", values);
            RequestGenerated  = createRequest.returnResult();
................................................. .
................................................. .
```

4. The XMLCreator calls the CreateAddFriendXML() method to generate the request.

```
void CreateAddFriendXML(String params[])
{
        XMLString += "<AddFriend>";
        XMLString += "<UserName>"+params[0]+"</UserName>";
        XMLString += "<FriendName>"+params[1]+"</FriendName>";
        XMLString += "</AddFriend>";
}
```

5. The request is then sent to the server by the AddFriend class.

Request to delete a friend

A friend can be deleted by highlighting the friend's name and clicking the Delete Friend button or by choosing the delete option from the pop-up menu that appears upon right-clicking a friend's name.

1. The deleteFriend() method within the MainScreen is called.

```
if (ae.getSource() == m_PopMenuItem1)
{
        deleteFriend();
```

```
}
if (ae.getSource() == m_Delete)
{
        deleteFriend();
}
```

2. The friend's name is deleted from the friend list; XMLCreator is called to create the delete friend request.

```
void deleteFriend()
{
·············································· .
createRequest  = new XMLCreator("DELETEFRIEND", values);
RequestGenerated = createRequest.returnResult();
·············································· .
}
```

3. XMLCreator calls the method CreateDeleteFriendXML() to form the request.

```
void CreateDeleteFriendXML(String params[])
{
        XMLString += "<DeleteFriend>";
        XMLString += "<UserName>"+params[0]+"</UserName>";
        XMLString += "<FriendName>"+params[1]+"</FriendName>";
        XMLString += "</DeleteFriend>";
}
```

4. The MainScreen class then sends this request to the server.

Request to send a message

A user chats with his/her friends through Instant Message windows that are opened for each friend with whom the user initiates a chat. The user can send a message to a friend by highlighting a friend's name and choosing the "Send a message" menu item or by pressing the "Send" button or right-clicking a friend's name in the main window and choosing the "Send an Instant Message" option.

1. If the user chooses to send a message to one of his/her friends, the MainScreen class calls the showMessageWindow() method.

```
if (ae.getSource() == m_Message)
{
        showMessageWindow();
}
if (ae.getSource() == m_PopMenuItem)
{
        showMessageWindow();
```

```
}
```

2. The `showMessageWindow()` method checks whether or not the friend's status is online. If the friend is offline, a dialog box is displayed that alerts the user that a message cannot be sent to an offline friend.

```
void showMessageWindow()
{
        int result = -11;
int clickedRow = m_friendsOnline.getRowForLocation(m_posOnScreenX,
m_posOnScreenY);

if (clickedRow > 0)
{
 TreePath path= m_friendsOnline.getPathForRow(clickedRow);
 TreeNode node     = (TreeNode)path.getLastPathComponent();

 if (((node.getParent()).toString()).equalsIgnoreCase("OFF-LINE"))
        {
            result = -2;
        JOptionPane.showMessageDialog(this,"Cannot Send Message to an
OFF-Line User.","Instant Messenger",JOptionPane.INFORMATION_MESSAGE);
        }
.................................................................. .
.................................................................. .
```

3. If the friend is online, the `CheckBeforeOpening()` method is called to check if an object corresponding to the message window for the friend already exists in the `ListOfMessageWindowsByName` vector. If it does, its index value is returned; otherwise, □1 is returned, indicating that the message window for the friend needs to be opened.

```
result = CheckBeforeOpening(node.toString())
.................................................................. .
.................................................................. .

int CheckBeforeOpening(String toUser)
{
        for (int i = 0;i<ListOfMessageWindowsByName.size() ;i++ )
        {
            String str = new String();
            str     =
(String)ListOfMessageWindowsByName.elementAt(i);
            if (str.equalsIgnoreCase(toUser))
                {

                return i;
```

```
                }
        }
        return -1;
}
```

4. If the window does not exist, a new window is opened, and the name and message window object for that friend is added to the respective vectors. Simultaneously, the Message class is called that presents the user with a GUI to type and send messages (see Figure 5-6).

Figure 5-6: The Instant Message window

```
if (result == -1)
{
MessagemsgWindow = new Message(user, node.toString(), this,
StreamToServer);
        msgWindow.show();

ListOfMessageWindowsByName.add((Object)node.toString());
ListOfMessageWindowsByObject.add((Object)msgWindow);
}
```

5. When the user types a message and presses the send button, the sendMessage()
    method is called. This method calls the XMLCreator to generate a request to send the
    message.

```
void sendMessage()
{
....................................................... .
....................................................... .


createRequest  = new XMLCreator("MSG", values);
RequestGenerated      = createRequest.returnResult();
....................................................... .
....................................................... .
}
```

6. The XMLCreator calls the CreateMessageXML() method to generate the XML
    request.

```
void CreateMessageXML(String params[])
{
      XMLString += "<MSG>";
      XMLString += "<Target>"     + params[0] + "</Target>";
      XMLString += "<Source>"     + params[1] + "</Source>";
      XMLString += "<Text>"+ params[2] + "</Text>";
      XMLString += "</MSG>";
}
```

7. The XML created is sent to the server by the Message class.

The Instant Message window provides additional features such as setting font colors for
messages, the sender's name, and so on. If the user presses the color button, the
ColorPreferences class is called that presents a GUI for the user to choose a color (see
Figure 5-7).

```
else if (ae.getSource() == m_BKColor)
{
ColorPreference colorPreference = new ColorPreference(this, "Color
Preferences", true);
colorPreference.show();
addStyle();
}
```

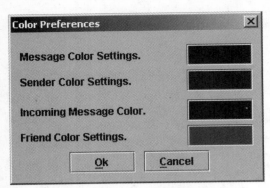

Figure 5-7: The window to set the color preferences

The addStyle() method then sets the color for incoming and outgoing messages in the message window per user preferences.

```
void addStyle()
{
m_Style = m_StyleContext.addStyle(null, null);
StyleConstants.setBold(m_Style, true);
StyleConstants.setForeground(m_Style, m_SenderColor);
m_Attributes.put("sender", m_Style);

m_Style = m_StyleContext.addStyle(null, null);
StyleConstants.setBold(m_Style, true);
StyleConstants.setForeground(m_Style, m_messageSendColor);
m_Attributes.put("senderMessage", m_Style);

m_Style = m_StyleContext.addStyle(null, null);
StyleConstants.setBold(m_Style, true);
StyleConstants.setForeground(m_Style, m_ReceiverColor);
m_Attributes.put("receiver", m_Style);

m_Style = m_StyleContext.addStyle(null, null);
StyleConstants.setBold(m_Style, true);
StyleConstants.setForeground(m_Style, m_messageReceivedColor);
m_Attributes.put("receiverMessage", m_Style);
 }
}
```

Unregistration request from an existing user

When a user chooses the "Unregister" option from the menu on the main screen, the MainScreen class calls the unregisterUser() method to remove the user from the client list of the server. This deletes the user's record from the server's database and deletes records pertaining to his/her friend list. Subsequent to unregistration, the user's name is freed, and his/her login name can now be taken by another user registering with the Instant Messenger Service. The process can be summarized as follows:

1. The `MainScreen` class calls the `unregisterUser()` method.

```
if (ae.getSource() == m_UnregisterMenuItem)
{
        try
        {
                unregisterUser();
        }
.................................................... .
.................................................... .
}
```

2. The `unregisterUser()` method calls the `XMLCreator` to form an unregister request.

```
void unregisterUser()throws Exception
{
.................................................... .
.................................................... .
  XMLCreator  createRequest;
  byte []            RequestGenerated;

  createRequest      = new XMLCreator("UNREGISTER", values);
  RequestGenerated   = createRequest.returnResult();
.................................................... .
.................................................... .
  }
```

3. The `XMLCreator` calls the `CreateUnregisterXML()` method to create the unregister request.

```
void CreateUnregisterXML(String params[])
     {
             XMLString += "<Unregister>";
             XMLString += "<UserName>"+params[0]+"</UserName>";
             XMLString += "</Unregister>";
     }
```

4. The `MainScreen` class writes this request to the server.

Sending a notification confirming acceptance of a friend

When a second person using the Instant Messenger Service adds the user as a friend, the Instant Messenger Service sends a notification to the user saying so and so has added you to his/her friend list. The dialog box that informs the user of this action provides him/her with two options: to accept the second person as a friend or to refuse to accept. The sequence of operations following the appearance of this dialog box is as follows:

1. When the user receives a notification that another user wants to add him/her as a friend, he/she has two options: to accept or to decline. The `AcceptFriend` class calls the `createReply()` method to create the confirmation accordingly.

```java
public void actionPerformed(ActionEvent e)
{

        Object source = e.getSource();

        if(source.equals(b_decline))
        {
                createReply("1");
                dispose();
        }   // end of if (source.equals(b_cancel))

        else if(source.equals(b_accept))
        {
                createReply("0");
.............................................................. .
.............................................................. .
```

2. The `createReply()` mehtod calls the `XMLCreator` to form an the Accept friend request as per the option chosen by the user.

```java
void createReply(String str)
{
        XMLCreator createRequest;
        byte [] RequestGenerated;

        String[] values = new String[3];
        values[0] = userName;
        values[1] = FriendName;
        values[2] = str;

        createRequest = new XMLCreator("ACCEPTFRIEND", values);
        RequestGenerated  = createRequest.returnResult();
.............................................................. .
.............................................................. .
```

3. The `XMLCreator` calls the `CreateAcceptFriendXML()` method to create the XML.

```java
void CreateAcceptFriendXML(String params[])
{
        XMLString += "<AcceptFriend>";
```

```
        XMLString += "<UserName>"+params[0]+"</UserName>";
        XMLString += "<FriendName>"+params[1]+"</FriendName>";
        XMLString += "<Status>"+params[2]+"</Status>";
        XMLString += "</AcceptFriend>";
}
```

4. The `createReply()` method forwards the request/notification to the server.

Sending an Add Gateway request

When a user registered with the local or the Jabber server wants to chat with his/her friends on the MSN or Hotmail Instant Messenger network, he/she needs to add a gateway. This gateway interfaces with the Jabber Instant Messenger server to facilitate communication between the user and his/her friends. It also enables importing of the user's MSN or Hotmail friend list and sending of notifications regarding user's/friends' status to either network. This is how it works: after a user has successfully added the gateway, his/her friend list and each friend's status are displayed on the main window. If the user sends a message to a Hotmail friend, this message request passes through the gateway and is converted to a form that can be accepted by the MSN server. The MSN server then forwards the request to the friend on its network for whom the message is intended. A reverse procedure is followed when a friend sends a message for the user. A prerequisite for the Add Gateway request is that the user has an account with Hotmail or MSN.

The Add Gateway request is handled by the `AddGateway` class. The request originates when the user chooses the "Add Gateway" menu item in the `MainScreen` Class. Following are the steps that define the generation of the request:

1. The `actionPerformed()` method of `MainScreen` Class calls the `AddGateway` class when this menu item is chosen.

```
if (ae.getSource() == m_AddGatewayMenuItem)
  {
  System.out.println("Add Gateway...");

      AddGateway GatewayScreen = new AddGateway(this,userName);
      GatewayScreen.show();
  }
```

2. The constructor of the class `AddGateway` presents the user with a GUI window that seeks the user's MSN/Hotmail login name and password (see Figure 5-8).

Figure 5-8: The window to add a Gateway

3. The `actionPerformed()` method recognizes when the Add button is pressed. It then checks that the login name contains the character "@" since this character is a must for an e-mail ID; if the character is found, it calls `XMLCreator` to form the `ADDGATEWAY` request; otherwise, it calls the second constructor of the `AddGateway` class with the message "Wrong User Name Please Try Again!"

```
else if(source.equals(m_AddIt))
{
 XMLCreator    createRequest;
......................................................... .
......................................................... .
char [] rawPassword  = m_EnterPassword.getPassword();

for (int i=0;i<rawPassword.length;i++ )
 {
  rawPassword[i] += 10;
 }
  val[2] = new String(rawPassword);

if (val[1].indexOf("@") == -1)
 {
  this.dispose();
  AddGateway AddGateway = new AddGateway(screen,userName,"Wrong User
Name Please Try Again!");
  AddGateway.show();
 }
else
 {
  createRequest       = new XMLCreator("ADDGATEWAY", val);
  RequestGenerated    = createRequest.returnResult();
```

4. The `XMLCreator` class calls the method `CreateAddGatewayXML()` to form the required XML.

```
void CreateAddGatewayXML(String params[])
    {
              XMLString += "<AddGateway>";
              XMLString += "<UserName>"+params[0]+"</UserName>";
              XMLString +=
"<MSNUserName>"+params[1]+"</MSNUserName>";
        XMLString += "<MSNPassword>"+params[2]+"</MSNPassword>";
        XMLString += "</AddGateway>";
        }
```

5. The `AddGateway` class then writes the request to the server.

```
try
  {
  StreamToServer.write(RequestGenerated, 0, RequestGenerated.length);
  StreamToServer.flush();
  }
```

Handling Responses

This section discusses how the client handles various responses it receives from the server and how these responses are processed and displayed in an appropriate GUI. All the responses received by the client application are handled by the `MainScreen` class, except for the first login or registration request. Thus, the `MainScreen` class is the starting point for receipt of all responses.

Response to a Registration request

A registration request entails checking the previously existing login names to see if the given login name already exists. If it does not, the server makes a new entry for the user attempting registration and sends a response confirming registration; otherwise, the server sends a response saying that the user name already exists; please retry. The server response comes as an integer return value, and it is left to the client to decode the return value and display the appropriate response. The response is processed as follows:

1. After sending the registration request, the `sendRequest()` method of the `Session` class waits in a loop to receive the response to a Registration request.

```
void sendRequest(Login screen, byte request[], Register regScreen)
    {
```

```
        while (loop != 0)
        {
                temp              = StreamFromLocalServer.read(buffer, 0,
32);
                String str        = new String (buffer, 0, temp);
                FinalString       = FinalString + str;
                loop              = StreamFromLocalServer.available();


        }
```

2. When it receives a response, it writes the response to the "`response.xml`" file and
   calls the `SParser` class to parse the XML.

```
byte [] tempbytes = FinalString.getBytes();
FileOutputStream TempOutFile = new FileOutputStream(""response.xml"");
TempOutFile.write(tempbytes, 0, tempbytes.length);
TempOutFile.close();

Parser.perform(""response.xml"");
```

3. The `SParser` class parses the XML and returns an integer denoting the request type and
   a string containing the XML data.

```
else if (localName.equalsIgnoreCase("REGISTER"))
{
 requestType = 2;
}


int getType()
{
  return (requestType);
}

public String valueReturn()
{
        return st;
}
```

4. The `Session` class then calls the `checkRegistration()` method to check the response received from the server. Whether or not the registration is successful, the control is passed back to the `Login` class with the appropriate message displayed as a label; for example, the value 0 denotes that registration is successful; 1 denotes that username already exists, and so on.

```java
if (Parser.getType() == 2)
        {
            checkRegistration();
        }
................................................................. .
................................................................. .

void checkRegistration() throws Exception
 {
String value = Parser.valueReturn();
char info = value.charAt(0);

if(info == '0')
{
................................................................. .
................................................................. .
Login loginAgain = new Login(userName, passWord,"Registration
Successful.. Press Login to Log !");
 loginAgain.show();

 }
else if(info == '1')
{
................................................................. .
................................................................. .
        Login loginAgain = new Login("", "","User Already Exits... Try
Again !");
        loginAgain.show();

 }
else
{
................................................................. .
................................................................. .
        Login loginAgain = new Login("", "","Critical Error... Please
Try Again !");
        loginAgain.show();
 }
................................................................. .
................................................................. .
```

5. On this occasion, the second constructor of the `Login` class is called that accepts three parameters: the user's name, the password, and the message label.

```
Login(String Name, String PassWord, String MessageLabel)
{
        this.LoginName = Name;
        this.PassWord = PassWord;
        this.MessageLabel = MessageLabel;
        initForm();
}
```

If the registration is successful, the user is prompted to login with the registered login name and password, and the login procedure described in the next section is followed; otherwise, the previous registration cycle repeats.

Response to a Login request

When a user sends a login request, the login name and password provided by him/her are checked against the user database; if a match is found, the login attempt is declared successful; otherwise, the server returns an error code. Once again, the client application decodes the return value to display an appropriate message for the user and to call the necessary classes/methods. The response is handled as follows:

1. The response to the Login request is handled by the `Session` class that waits in a loop to receive the server's response.

2. The server response is once again written to the "response.xml" file and the `SParser` class is called to parse the response, as in the registration request.

3. The class `SParser` parses the response received from the server and returns the request type, login in this case, and the corresponding XML data.

4. The `Session` class calls the `checkAuthorization()` method to evaluate the parsed response and to call the appropriate class depending on the return value; the value 0 means successful registration; 1 signifies unregistered user, 2 signifies invalid password; any other undefined value indicates an error somewhere along the processing chain.

```
void checkAuthorization() throws Exception
  {
String value = Parser.valueReturn();
char info = value.charAt(0);

if(info == '0')
  {
..................................................... .
..................................................... .
```

```
        MainScreen showScreen = new MainScreen(userName, passWord,
StreamFromLocalServer, StreamToLocalServer);

        screen.dispose();
}
else if(info == '1')
{
        screen.dispose();
..........................................................

..........................................................

        Login loginAgain = new Login("", "","UnRegistered User");
        loginAgain.show();
}
else if(info == '2')
{

..........................................................

..........................................................

        Login loginAgain = new Login("", "","Invalid Password");
        loginAgain.show();

}
else
{

..........................................................

..........................................................

        Login loginAgain = new Login("", "","Critical Error Try
Again.");
        loginAgain.show();

}
}
```

If the Login attempt is successful, the Session class transfers control to the MainScreen class; otherwise, it calls the parameterized version of Login class with the respective error message, and the same Login process is repeated. Upon successful login, all subsequent requests are sent directly to the Server by the respective classes meant to handle each type of request. The Session class isn't more called to forward requests anymore, though each class uses the same Input and Output Streams that were originally initiated by the Session class. Also, the responses are now received by the MainScreen class instead of the Session class.

Receiving the friend list

When a user logs in, he/she need not send a request to obtain his/her friend List. This list is automatically retrieved by the server and sent to the client application. The client application performs the following operations to receive the friend list from the server.

1. Upon successful login, the `MainScreen` class receives all the responses from the server. The `run()` method of the `MainScreen` class waits in a loop to read responses from the server.

```
public void run()
{
 try
  {
  while (true)
   {
..................................................... .
..................................................... .

   while (loop != 0)
   {
   temp = StreamFromServer.read(buffer, 0, 1);
   if (temp < 0)
   break;
   String str = new String (buffer, 0, temp);
   FinalString = FinalString + str;
   loop = StreamFromServer.available();
   if (FinalString.indexOf("</InstantMessenger>") != -1)
   break;
      }
..................................................... .
..................................................... .
```

2. When a user logs in, the server retrieves and sends his/her friend List to the client application. Just like the `Session` class, the `MainScreen` class writes the response to the "response.xml" file and calls the `SParser` class to parse the response XML.

```
FileOutputStream TempOutFile = new FileOutputStream(""response.xml"");
TempOutFile.write(tempbytes, 0, tempbytes.length);
TempOutFile.close();

String ReturnVal = new String();

Parser.perform(""response.xml"");
ReturnVal      = Parser.valueReturn();
```

3. The `SParser` class sets the `requestType` to 5, which denotes a friend list.

```
else if (localName.equalsIgnoreCase("FRIENDLIST"))
        {
            requestType = 5;
        }
```

4. The `MainScreen` puts the names of the friends and their status in vector variables and adds each name to the tree structure on the user's main screen according to the status. The friends who are logged into their respective Instant Messenger services are added to the ON-LINE listings, and those who are not logged in are added to the OFF-LINE listings.

```
if (Parser.getType() == 5)
{
 StringTokenizer tokens = null;
 tokens = new StringTokenizer(ReturnVal,"~");
 Vector FriendName            = new Vector();
 Vector FriendIP              = new Vector();
 Vector FriendStatus  = new Vector();
 String userName = new String();
 userName = tokens.nextToken();

 while (tokens.hasMoreTokens())
  {

   FriendName.add(tokens.nextToken());

   FriendStatus.add(tokens.nextToken());
  }

  this.user               = userName;
  this.FriendName         = FriendName;
  this.FriendIP           = FriendIP;
  this.FriendStatus  = FriendStatus;
  getContentPane().setCursor(new   Cursor(Cursor.WAIT_CURSOR));
  AddToTree(0);
      getContentPane().setCursor(new Cursor(Cursor.DEFAULT_CURSOR));

      m_ConnectionStatus.setIcon(new ImageIcon("pink-ball.gif"));
      m_ConnectionStatus.setText("Connected");
.................................................................. .
.................................................................. .
```

The point to be noted here is that when the user's global friend list is received from the Jabber Server, the `SParser` sets the `requestType` to 7. In this case, the Vectors used to store the friends' names and their status are different, `JabberFriendID` and `JabberFriendSubscription`, respectively, but the procedure followed to display the friends on the main screen remains the same as followed for the local friend list.

Receiving a message

When a friend sends a message to the user, the message is displayed in the Instant Message window for that particular friend; otherwise, if the friend has initiated communication, a new message window is opened on the client machine. The message from the server is processed as follows:

1. When a message is received for the user, the SParser class sets the requestType to 3.

```java
else if (localName.equalsIgnoreCase("MSG"))
      {
          requestType = 3;
      }
```

2. The MainScreen class retrieves the sender's name, the receiver's name, and the message text from the string returned by the SParser class and calls the CheckBeforeOpening() method of the MainScreen class.

```java
else if (Parser.getType() == 3)
      {
..................................................... .
..................................................... .

              tokens = new StringTokenizer(ReturnVal,"~");

              receiver      = tokens.nextToken();
              sender        = tokens.nextToken();
              userMessage = tokens.nextToken();
              int result = CheckBeforeOpening(sender);
```

3. The CheckBeforeOpening() method sifts through the ListOfMessageWindowsByName vector to check if the sender's name exists in the vector elements. If it does, the corresponding index of the ListOfMessageWindowsByName vector is returned; otherwise, -1 is returned.

```java
int CheckBeforeOpening(String toUser)
{
        for (int i = 0;i<ListOfMessageWindowsByName.size() ;i++ )
        {
                String str = new String();
                str      =
(String)ListOfMessageWindowsByName.elementAt(i);
                if (str.equalsIgnoreCase(toUser))
                {

                    return i;
                }
```

```
        }
        return -1;
}
```

4. As mentioned previously, an entry in the `ListOfMessageWindowsByName` indicates that a message window is open on the client machine for a particular user. If the `CheckBeforeOpening()` method returns -1, it means a message window does not exist for the sender. The `MainScreen` class then opens a new window for the sender by creating an object of the `Message` class and makes the sender's entry to the `ListOfMessageWindowsByName` and `ListOfMessageWindowsByObject` vectors. If, however, an index value is returned, the `MainScreen` class looks for the object in the `ListOfMessageWindowsByObject` vector at the returned index to identify the message window object. This object (message window) is then brought to the front, and the message is appended to its screen.

```
if (result == -1)
  {
 Message msgWindow = new Message(receiver, sender, this,
StreamToServer);
 msgWindow.show();
 ListOfMessageWindowsByName.add((Object)sender);
 ListOfMessageWindowsByObject.add((Object)msgWindow);

 Style m_TempStyle   = (Style)
msgWindow.m_Attributes.get("receiver");
 try
  {

msgWindow.m_Document.insertString(msgWindow.m_Document.getLength(),
sender+" :\n", m_TempStyle);

 m_TempStyle   = (Style)msgWindow.m_Attributes.get("receiverMessage");


msgWindow.m_Document.insertString(msgWindow.m_Document.getLength(),
userMessage+"\n", m_TempStyle);
 }
 catch (Exception e)
  {
   System.out.println("Exception occured:"+e);
 }

}
else
  {
   Message msg
=(Message)(ListOfMessageWindowsByObject.elementAt(result));
```

```
 msg.toFront();
 msg.show();
 Style m_TempStyle = (Style) msg.m_Attributes.get("receiver");
 try
 {
  msg.m_Document.insertString(msg.m_Document.getLength(), sender+"
:\n", m_TempStyle);

  m_TempStyle = (Style) msg.m_Attributes.get("receiverMessage");

  msg.m_Document.insertString(msg.m_Document.getLength(),
userMessage+"\n", m_TempStyle);
}
```

Friend status notification

A notification is received in the form of a pop-up dialog box that appears every time an online friend goes offline or vice versa. This response informs the client application that a friend's status has changed and nudges it into action to refresh the user's friend list to reflect the changed status of the friend. For example, if an online friend goes offline, his/her name is removed from the online list and added to the offline list. The response is handled as follows:

1. When the status of a friend is reversed, that is, when an online friend goes offline or vice versa, the MainScreen receives a notification for it. The SParser sets the requestType to 6 for notification information.

```
else if (localName.equalsIgnoreCase("NOTIFYFRIENDS"))
        {
            requestType = 6;
        }
```

2. The MainScreen class then creates a dialog box that remains visible for 5 seconds and displays the notification. For example, if a friend named Daniel has signed in, the dialog box will display the message "Daniel is ON-LINE."

```
........................................................ .
........................................................ .
{
 m_notifyDialog = new JDialog();
 m_notifyDialog.setTitle("Friend");
 m_notifyDialog.setSize(150, 100);
 m_notifyDialog.getContentPane().setLayout(null);
 m_gc   = m_notifyDialog.getGraphicsConfiguration();
 bounds = m_gc.getBounds();
 m_notifyDialog.setLocation(bounds.width -150, bounds.height-140);
```

```
String tempName      = m_FriendName;
int indexP = tempName.indexOf("%");
if (indexP!= -1)
  {
  tempName     =        tempName.substring(0, indexP);
  }
m_label = new JLabel(tempName);


m_notifyDialog.getContentPane().add(m_label);

m_label1 = new JLabel(" is ");


m_notifyDialog.getContentPane().add(m_label1);

m_label2 = new JLabel(m_status);


m_notifyDialog.getContentPane().add(m_label2);
m_notifyDialog.setVisible(true);



try
  {
  Thread.sleep(5000);
  }


 m_notifyDialog.setVisible(false);
}

```

3. Simultaneously, the friend list on the user's main screen is updated to reflect the changed status of the friend.

When a user adds you to his/her friend list

Another user is able to add you as a friend; in such an event, the server sends a notification to the client application, informing the name of the friend who wants to add the user as a friend. The response is handled as follows:

1. In this case, too, the requestType is set to 6 by the SParser class.

2. The MainScreen class identifies the notification by the "SUBSCRIBE" tag value and calls the AcceptFriend class.

```
if (m_status.equalsIgnoreCase("SUBSCRIBE"))
{
 AcceptFriend acceptRequest = new AcceptFriend(this, m_FriendName,
userName);
 acceptRequest.show();
}
```

3. The `AcceptFriend` class displays a dialog box that informs the user as to who wants to add him/her to his/her friend list and presents him/her with two options: to accept or to decline.

```
AcceptFriend(MainScreen  screen, String FriendName, String userName)
{
        setTitle("Accept Friend --- Instant Messenger");
..................................................... .
..................................................... .
        setVisible(true);
        cont = getContentPane();
        cont.setLayout(null);
..................................................... .
..................................................... .
        addWindowListener( new WindowAdapter()
        { public void windowClosing(WindowEvent e)
                {
                        dispose();
                }
        });

 l_friends_name = new JLabel(FriendName);
.......................................................  .
 cont.add(l_friends_name);

 l_friends_name = new JLabel("Wants to View Your Online Presence.. ");
.......................................................  .
 cont.add(l_friends_name);

 b_accept = new JButton("Accept");
.......................................................  .
.......................................................  .
 cont.add(b_accept);
 b_decline = new JButton("Decline");
.......................................................  .
.......................................................  .
 cont.add(b_decline);
}
```

4. Dependingupon the option that the user chooses, a notification is sent to the server.

5. The user's friend list is updated if he/she chooses to accept the friend.

When a user deletes you from his/her friend list

Another user may choose to delete you from his/her friend list. In such an event, the server sends you a notification informing that you have been deleted from the friend's friend list. The notification response from the server is handled as follows:

1. Once again, the `requestType` is set to 6 by the `SParser` class.

2. The `MainScreen` class identifies the notification by the "UNSUBSCRIBE" tag value and calls the `UnsubscribeFriend` class.

```java
else if (m_status.equalsIgnoreCase("UNSUBSCRIBE"))
  {
   UnsubscribeFriend unsubscribeRequest = new UnsubscribeFriend(this,
m_FriendName, userName);
   unsubscribeRequest.show();
  }
```

3. The `UnsubscribeFriend` class presents a dialog box with a message saying "FriendName Has removed you from his/her Friend List" and a confirmation option through an "Ok" button.

```java
UnsubscribeFriend(MainScreen  screen, String FriendName, String
userName)
 {
        setTitle("UnSubscribe --- Instant Messenger");
        .................................................

..............................................
        cont = getContentPane();
        cont.setLayout(null);

..............................................
..............................................
        addWindowListener( new WindowAdapter()
        { public void windowClosing(WindowEvent e)
                {
                        dispose();
                        createReply();
                }
        });

        m_FriendName = new JLabel(FriendName);
..............................................
..............................................
```

```
        cont.add(m_FriendName);


        m_StaticText = new JLabel("Has removed You from his/her Friend
List.. ");
..................................................................................
..................................................................................
        cont.add(m_StaticText);

        m_Ok = new JButton("Accept");
..................................................................................
..................................................................................
        cont.add(m_Ok);
}
```

4. The confirmation is then sent to the server.

Response to an Add Friend request

When you make an Add Friend request, the server sends a notification to the friend at the other end, informing him/her of your attempt. Depending on whether or not the friend accepts you, the server sends a response informing you of whether the friend has accepted you or declined to accept you as a friend. This response is handled as follows:

1. The SParser sets the requestType to 8 to denote the status of the friend who is to be added.

```
else if (localName.equalsIgnoreCase("FRIENDSTATUS"))
        {
            requestType = 8;
        }
```

2. The MainScreen class updates the user's friend list if a new friend is being added; if the friend already exists in his/her friend list, a message saying so is displayed.

```
else if (Parser.getType() == 8)
        {
// update friend list
..................................................................................
..................................................................................
            }
                else if (val[2].equalsIgnoreCase("2"))
                {
                    JOptionPane.showMessageDialog(this,"Friend \"" +
val[1] +"\" Already exists...","Instant
Messenger",JOptionPane.INFORMATION_MESSAGE);
                }
```

```
        }
```

Response to an Add Gateway request

When the user sends an Add Gateway request to add the gateway for communicating with his/her MSN friends, the server responds with a confirmation that the gateway has been added or with an error message. Like all other responses, this response is handled by the MainScreen class. The steps for handling this response are as follows.

1. When the MainScreen class receives a request type value of 11, it interprets it as a failed Add Gateway request and calls the constructor of the AddGateway class with an error message.

```
else if (Parser.getType() == 11)
  {
    AddGateway AddGateway = new AddGateway(this,userName,"Wrong User
Name or Password Please Try Again!");
    AddGateway.show();
  }
```

2. The AddGateway class again presents the user with its GUI window seeking the login name and password and displays the message "Wrong User Name or Password Please Try Again!"

3. If the gateway is successfully added, the user's friend list from MSN is imported.

Technical Documentation

In this section, we list complete, working codes for various client classes, followed by line-by-line explanation of the code.

XMLCreator class

The flow chart of the XMLCreator class is presented in Figure 5-9. Listing 5-1 contains the code for this class, followed by a detailed description of the code.

Figure 5-9: Technical flow chart for the XMLCreator class

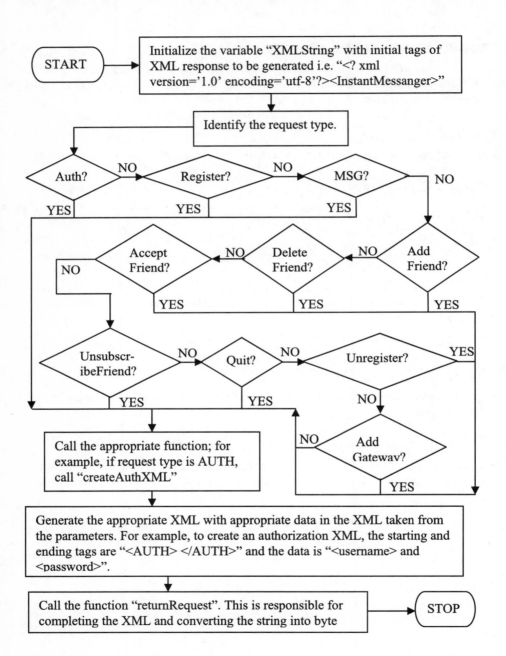

Listing 5-1: XMLCreator.java

```
1.   public class XMLCreator
2.   {
3.
4.    String XMLString      =       new String();
5.
6.
7.    XMLCreator(String type, String params[])
8.    {
9.
10.     XMLString = "<?xml version=\'1.0\'       encoding=\'utf-
8\'?><InstantMessenger>";
11.
12.        if (type.equalsIgnoreCase("AUTH"))
13.        {
14.      CreateAuthXML(params);
15.        }
16.        else if (type.equalsIgnoreCase("REGISTER"))
17.        {
18.      CreateRegisterXML(params);
19.        }
20.        else if (type.equalsIgnoreCase("MSG"))
21.        {
22.      CreateMessageXML(params);
23.        }
24.        else if (type.equalsIgnoreCase("ADDFRIEND"))
25.        {
26.      CreateAddFriendXML(params);
27.        }
28.        else if (type.equalsIgnoreCase("DELETEFRIEND"))
29.        {
30.      CreateDeleteFriendXML(params);
31.        }
32.        else if (type.equalsIgnoreCase("ACCEPTFRIEND"))
33.        {
34.            CreateAcceptFriendXML(params);
35.        }
36.        else if (type.equalsIgnoreCase("UNSUBSCRIBEFRIEND"))
37.        {
38.            CreateUnsubscribeFriendXML(params);
39.        }
40.        else if (type.equalsIgnoreCase("QUIT"))
41.        {
42.      CreateQuitXML(params);
43.        }
44.        else if (type.equalsIgnoreCase("UNREGISTER"))
45.        {
46.      CreateUnregisterXML(params);
```

```
47.        }
48.        else if (type.equalsIgnoreCase("ADDGATEWAY"))
49.        CreateAddGatewayXML(params);
50.    }
51.    void CreateAuthXML(String params[])
52.    {
53.      XMLString += "<Auth>";
54.      XMLString += "<UserName>"+params[0]+"</UserName>";
55.      XMLString += "<Password>"+params[1]+"</Password>";
56.      XMLString += "</Auth>";
57.    }
58.
59.    void CreateAddFriendXML(String params[])
60.    {
61.      XMLString += "<AddFriend>";
62.      XMLString += "<UserName>"+params[0]+"</UserName>";
63.      XMLString += "<FriendName>"+params[1]+"</FriendName>";
64.      XMLString += "</AddFriend>";
65.    }
66.    void CreateDeleteFriendXML(String params[])
67.    {
68.      XMLString += "<DeleteFriend>";
69.      XMLString += "<UserName>"+params[0]+"</UserName>";
70.      XMLString += "<FriendName>"+params[1]+"</FriendName>";
71.      XMLString += "</DeleteFriend>";
72.    }
73.    void CreateAcceptFriendXML(String params[])
74.    {
75.      XMLString += "<AcceptFriend>";
76.      XMLString += "<UserName>"+params[0]+"</UserName>";
77.      XMLString += "<FriendName>"+params[1]+"</FriendName>";
78.      XMLString += "<Status>"+params[2]+"</Status>";
79.      XMLString += "</AcceptFriend>";
80.    }
81.    void CreateUnsubscribeFriendXML(String params[])
82.    {
83.      XMLString += "<UnsubscribeFriend>";
84.      XMLString += "<UserName>"+params[0]+"</UserName>";
85.      XMLString += "<FriendName>"+params[1]+"</FriendName>";
86.      XMLString += "</UnsubscribeFriend>";
87.    }
88.    void CreateRegisterXML(String params[])
89.    {
90.      XMLString += "<Register>";
91.      XMLString += "<UserName>"+params[0]+"</UserName>";
92.      XMLString += "<Password>"+params[1]+"</Password>";
93.      XMLString += "<sAdd1>"+params[3]+"</sAdd1>";
94.      XMLString += "<sAdd2>"+params[4]+"</sAdd2>";
95.      XMLString += "<sPhone1>"+params[5]+"</sPhone1>";
```

```
96.      XMLString += "<sPhone2>"+params[6]+"</sPhone2>";
97.      XMLString += "<sEmail1>"+params[7]+"</sEmail1>";
98.      XMLString += "<sEmail2>"+params[8]+"</sEmail2>";
99.      XMLString += "<sPin>"+params[9]+"</sPin>";
100.     XMLString += "<sCity>"+params[10]+"</sCity>";
101.     XMLString += "<sProfession>"+params[11]+"</sProfession>";
102.     XMLString += "</Register>";
103.     }
104.
105.   void CreateQuitXML(String params[])
106.     {
107.     XMLString += "<Quit>";
108.     XMLString += "<UserName>"+params[0]+"</UserName>";
109.     XMLString += "</Quit>";
110.     }
111.
112.     void CreateUnregisterXML(String params[])
113.     {
114.     XMLString += "<Unregister>";
115.     XMLString += "<UserName>"+params[0]+"</UserName>";
116.     XMLString += "</Unregister>";
117.     }
118.     void CreateMessageXML(String params[])
119.     {
120.     XMLString += "<MSG>";
121.     XMLString += "<Target>"    + params[0] + "</Target>";
122.     XMLString += "<Source>"    + params[1] + "</Source>";
123.     XMLString += "<Text>"              + params[2] + "</Text>";
124.     XMLString += "</MSG>";
125.     }
126.     void CreateAddGatewayXML(String params[])
127.     {
128.     XMLString += "<AddGateway>";
129.     XMLString += "<UserName>"+params[0]+"</UserName>";
130.     XMLString += "<MSNUserName>"+params[1]+"</MSNUserName>";
131.     XMLString += "<MSNPassword>"+params[2]+"</MSNPassword>";
132.     XMLString += "</AddGateway>";
133.     }
134.     byte[] returnResult()
135.     {
136.     XMLString += "</InstantMessenger>";
137.     return XMLString.getBytes();
138.     }
139. }
```

- Line 1: Declares the class XMLCreator.
- Line 4: Declares XMLString as a blank String variable.

- Line 7: Declares the constructor for XMLCreator class.

- Line 10: Initializesthe variable XMLString with the XML tag containing the version declaration and the starting XML tag <InstantMessenger>.

- Lines 12□15: Check the value of thefirst parameter value received by the constructor (that is, the variable type) and call the CreateAuthXML() method, if type contains the string "AUTH."

- Lines 16□19:Call the CreateRegisterXML() method, if the String type contains "REGISTER."

- Lines 20□23:Call the CreateMessageXML() method, if the String type contains "MSG."

- Lines 24□27:Call the CreateAddFriendXML() method, if the String type contains "ADDFRIEND."

- Lines 28□31:Call the CreateDeleteFriendXML() method, if the String type contains "DELETEFRIEND."

- Lines 32□35:Call the method CreateAcceptFriendXML(), if the String type contains "ACCEPTFRIEND."

- Lines 36□39:Call the method CreateUnsubscribeFriendXML(), if the string type contains "UNSUBSCRIBEFRIEND."

- Lines 40□43:Call the method CreateQuitXML(), if the String type contains "QUIT."

- Lines 44□47: These linescall the method CreateUnregisterXML(), if the String type contains "UNREGISTER".

- Lines 48□49:Call the method CreateAddGatewayXML(), if the String type contains "ADDGATEWAY."

- Lines 51□57: These lines define theCreateAuthXML() method that creates an authorization tag.

  - Line 53: Appends the XML tag representing the request type to XMLString.

  - Line 54: Appends to XMLString the value tag <userName> with the username being retrieved from the 0th index of the String array params[].

  - Line 55: Appends to XMLString the value tag <password> with the password value being retrieved from the 1st index of params array.

  - Line 56: Closes the request type tag.

- Lines 59□65:Define the CreateAddFriendXML() method. The request type tag <AddFriend> and the value tags <UserName> and <FriendName> are appended to the String XMLString along with their respective data and closing tags.

- Lines 66☐72:Define the `CreateDeleteFriendXML()` method. The request type tag `<DeleteFriend>` and the value tags `<UserName>` and `<FriendName>` are appended to the String `XMLString`, along with their respective data and closing tags.

- Lines 73☐80:Define the `CreateAcceptFriendXML()` method. The request type tag `<AcceptFriend>` and value tags `<UserName>`, `<FriendName>`, and `<Status>` (denotes whether or not a friend has been accepted) are appended to the `XMLString`, along with their respective data and closing tags.

- Lines 81☐87:Define the `CreateUnsubscribeFriendXML()` method. The request type tag `<UnsubscribeFriend>` and the value tags `<Username>` and `<FriendName>` are appended to the `XMLString`, along with their respective data and closing tags.

- Lines 88☐103: Define the`CreateRegisterXML()` method. The request type tag `<Register>` and the user information within respective value tags are appended to the `XMLString`, along with the closing tags.

- Lines 105☐110: Definethe `CreateQuitXML()` method. The request type tag `<Quit>` and the value tag `<UserName>` containing the user's name are appended to `XMLString` along with the closing tags.

- Lines 112☐117: Definethe `CreateUnregisterXML()` method. The request type tag `<Unregister>` and the value tag `<UserName>` are appended to the `XMLString`, along with respective data and closing tags.

- Lines 118☐125:Define the `CreateMessageXML()` method. The request type tag `<MSG>` and the value tags `<Target>`, `<Source>`, and `<Text>` are appended to the `XMLString`, along with respective data and closing tags.

- Lines 126☐133: Definethe `CreateAddGatewayXML()` method. The request type tag `<AddGateway>` and the value tags `<UserName>`, `<MSNUserName>`, and `<MSNPassword>` are appended to the `XMLString` alongwith respective data and closing tags.

- Lines134☐138: Define the method`returnResult()` that returns the request XML generated by the `XMLCreator` class.

  - Line 136: Completes the XML requested by appending the closing tag corresponding to the opening XML tag.

  - Line 137: Returns the XML generated by the `XMLCreator` class as a byte array.

SParser class

The flow chart of the `SParser` class is presented in Figure 5-10. Listing 5-2 contains the code for this class, followed by a detailed description of the code.

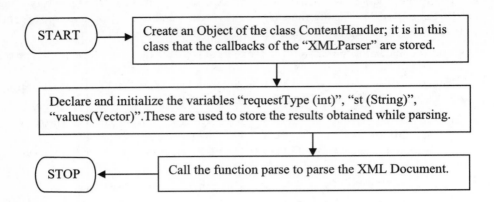

Figure 5-10: Technical flow chart for the SParser class

Listing 5-2: SParser.java

```
1.    import java.awt.*;
2.    import java.io.*;
3.    import java.util.*;
4.    import org.xml.sax.*;
5.    import org.apache.xerces.parsers.SAXParser;
6.
7.    /*********** SParser *************/
8.
9.    public class SParser
10.   {
11.
12.   XMLReader                    parser;
13.   MyContentHandler     contHandler;
14.
15.   /*********** perform *************/
16.
17.   public void perform(String uri)
18.   {
19.    try
20.    {
21.     parser = new SAXParser();
22.     contHandler = new MyContentHandler();
23.     parser.setContentHandler(contHandler);
24.     parser.parse(uri);
25.
26.    }
```

```
27.
28.    catch(IOException e)
29.    {
30.      System.out.println("Error reading uri : " +e.getMessage());
31.    }
32.    catch(SAXException e)
33.    {
34.      System.out.println("Error in parsing : " +e.getMessage());
35.    }
36.  }
37.
38.  /*********** valueReturn ************/
39.
40.  public String valueReturn()
41.  {
42.    return contHandler.valueReturn();
43.  }
44.
45.  /*********** vectorReturn ************/
46.
47.  public Vector vectorReturn()
48.  {
49.    return contHandler.vectorReturn();
50.  }
51.
52.  /*********** getType ************/
53.
54.  int getType()
55.  {
56.      return (contHandler.getType());
57.  }
58.
59.  } // End SParser
60.
61.  /*********** Class Declaration ************/
62.
63.  class MyContentHandler implements ContentHandler
64.  {
65.  private Locator locator;
66.  String st = new String();
67.  Vector values = new Vector();
68.  int requestType = 0;
69.  int j = 0 ;
70.
71.  /*********** startElement ************/
72.
73.  public void startElement(String namespaceURI, String localName,
String rawName, Attributes atts) throws SAXException
74.  {
```

```
75.
76.   if (localName.equalsIgnoreCase("AUTH"))
77.   {
78.      requestType = 1;
79.   }
80.   else if (localName.equalsIgnoreCase("REGISTER"))
81.   {
82.      requestType = 2;
83.   }
84.   else if (localName.equalsIgnoreCase("MSG"))
85.   {
86.      requestType = 3;
87.   }
88.   else if (localName.equalsIgnoreCase("QUIT"))
89.   {
90.      requestType = 4;
91.   }
92.   else if (localName.equalsIgnoreCase("FRIENDLIST"))
93.   {
94.      requestType = 5;
95.   }
96.   else if (localName.equalsIgnoreCase("NOTIFYFRIENDS"))
97.   {
98.      requestType = 6;
99.   }
100.   else if (localName.equalsIgnoreCase("ROSTER"))
101.   {
102.      requestType = 7;
103.   }
104.   else if (localName.equalsIgnoreCase("FRIENDSTATUS"))
105.   {
106.      requestType = 8;
107.   }
108.   else if (localName.equalsIgnoreCase("DELETESTATUS"))
109.   {
110.      requestType = 9;
111.   }
112.   else if (localName.equalsIgnoreCase("UNREGISTER"))
113.   {
114.      requestType = 10;
115.   }
116.   else if (localName.equalsIgnoreCase("ADDGATEWAY"))
117.   {
118.      requestType = 11;
119.   }
120.
121.   for(int i= 0; i<atts.getLength(); i++)
122.   {
123.        if (atts.getLocalName(i).equals("name"))
```

```
124.          {
125.                values.add(atts.getValue(i)) ;
126.                j++;
127.          }
128.    }
129.  }
130.
131.  /*********** characters ************/
132.
133.  public void characters( char[] ch, int start , int end )
134.  {
135.   String temp = new String(ch,start,end).trim();
136.   if (temp.length() != 0)
137.     st = st + temp + "~" ;
138.  }
139.
140.  /*********** startDocument ************/
141.
142.  public void  startDocument()
143.  {
144.   st = "";
145.  }
146.
147.  /*********** endDocument ************/
148.
149.  public void  endDocument()
150.  {}
151.  public void endElement(String nameSpaceURI, String localName,
      String rawName) {}
152.  public void startPrefixMapping(String prefix, String uri) {}
153.  public void endPrefixMapping(String prefix) {}
154.  public void ignorableWhitespace(char[] ch, int start, int end) {}
155.  public void processingInstruction(String target, String data) {}
156.  public void setDocumentLocator(Locator locator) {}
157.  public void skippedEntity(String name) {}
158.
159.  /*********** getType ************/
160.
161.  int getType()
162.  {
163.     return (requestType);
164.  }
165.
166.  /*********** valueReturn ************/
167.
168.  public String valueReturn()
169.  {
170.   return st;
171.  }
```

```
172.
173.    /*********** vectorReturn ************/
174.
175.    public Vector vectorReturn()
176.    {
177.     return values;
178.    }
179.   }// End MyContentHandler...
```

- Lines 1□5: Contain import statements for packages whose classes are being used by the SParser class.

- Lines 9□13: Contain class and variable declarations.

- Line 17: Declares the method perform().

- Line 21: Creates an object of type SAXParser. SAXParser is an event-based parser wherein various methods are called depending upon the events encountered during parsing. For example, the method startDocument() is called when parsing of a document begins, startElement() is called when a new XML element/tag is encountered, and so on. The other type of parsers are tree-based, but they are beyond the scope of this book.

- Line 22: Creates an object of type MyContentHandler used to store tags and data from the passed XML.

- Line 23: Sets the content handler created in Line 22 as the content handler for the object, parser, which is of XMLReader type (See Line 12).

- Line 24: Calls the method parse(), passing the String uri as a parameter. Note this URI will refer to file "response.xml" as explained in the MainScreen class.

- Lines 28□31:Catch an Exception of type IOException resulting due to an error in reading data from the given URI.

- Lines: 32□35: Catcha SAXException that occurs if the SAXParser object cannot be created.

- Lines 40□43:Define the valueReturn() method of SParser class that calls the valueReturn() method of class MyContentHandler and returns its value.

- Lines 47□50:Define the vectorReturn() method of SParser class that calls the vectorReturn() method of MyContenthandler and returns the value defined in it.

- Lines 54□57:Define the getType() method for SParser class that returns the value from the getType() method of MyContentHandler class.

- Line 63: Declares the class MyContentHandler.

- Lines 65□69:Variable declarations/initialization.

- Line 73: Declares the startElement() method that is called when a new XML element is encountered.

- Lines 76☐79:Set the value of variable `requestType` to 1 if the string `localName` contains "AUTH".

- Lines 80☐83:Set `requestType` to 2 if `localName` contains "REGISTER".

- Lines 84☐87:Set `requestType` to 3 if `localName` contains "MSG".

- Lines 88☐91:Set `requestType` to 4 if `localName` contains "QUIT".

- Lines 92☐95:Set `requestType` to 5 if `localName` contains "FRIENDLIST".

- Lines 96☐99:Set `requestType` to 6 if `localName` contains "NOTIFYFRIENDS".

- Lines 100☐103: Set`requestType` to 7 if `localName` contains "ROSTER".

- Lines 104☐107: Set`requestType` to 8 if `localName` contains "FRIENDSTATUS".

- Lines 108☐111: Set`requestType` to 9 if `localName` contains "DELETESTATUS".

- Lines 112☐115: Set`requestType` to 10 if `localName` contains "UNREGISTER".

- Lines 116☐119: Set`requestType` to 11 if `localName` contains "ADDGATEWAY".

- Lines 121☐128: Contain a`for` loop that runs through the length of the attributes type array `atts`; if the `LocalName` value at current index is "name," it adds the current attribute value of `atts` to the vector `values`.

- Lines 133☐138: Define the method `characters()` that retrieves in the String `temp` the data between an XML value tag.

- Lines 142☐145: Define the `startDocument()` method called at the beginning of the document and initilizes the String variable `st`.

- Lines 149☐157: Methods of`SAXParser` class that are not being used by the class but need to be declared as per Java's implementation specifications.

- Lines: 161☐164: Define the `getType()` method of the class `MyContentHandler` that returns the value of `requestType` set in the method `startElement()`.

- Lines 168☐171: Define the method `valueReturn()` that returns the String `st`, defined in `startDocument()` or `characters()`.

- Lines 175☐178: Define the `vectorReturn()` method that returns the vector values set by the method `startElement()`.

Login class

The flow chart of the `Login` class is presented in Figure 5-11. Listing 5-3 contains the code for this class, followed by a detailed description of the code.

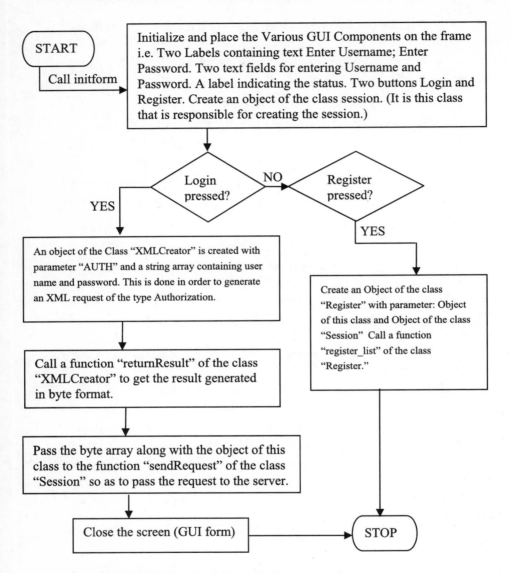

Figure 5-11: Technical flow chart for the Login class

Listing 5-3: Login.java

```
1.    import javax.swing.*;
2.    import javax.swing.event.*;
3.    import java.awt.*;
4.    import java.awt.event.*;
5.    import java.net.*;
```

```
6.    import java.io.*;
7.    import java.util.Vector;
8.
9.    /*********** Class Declaration *************/
10.
11.   public class Login extends JFrame implements ActionListener
12.   {
13.
14.   JLabel                    m_CompanyLogo;
15.   JLabel                    m_LoginName;
16.   JLabel                    m_Password;
17.   JLabel                    m_LoginStatus;
18.   JTextField                m_EnterLoginName;
19.   JPasswordField            m_EnterPassword;
20.   JButton                   m_Login;
21.   JButton                   m_Register;
22.
23.   Session                   userSession;
24.   Register                  register;
25.
26.   String                    LoginName     = new String();
27.   String                    PassWord      = new String();
28.   String                    MessageLabel  = new String();
29.
30.   /*********** Constructor *************/
31.
32.   Login(String Name, String PassWord, String MessageLabel)
33.   {
34.    this.LoginName          = Name;
35.    this.PassWord           = PassWord;
36.    this.MessageLabel       = MessageLabel;
37.    initForm();
38.   }
39.
40.   /*********** Overloaded Constructor *************/
41.
42.   Login()
43.   {
44.    MessageLabel = "Enter Name and Password";
45.    initForm();
46.   }
47.
48.   /*********** initForm *************/
49.
50.   void initForm()
51.   {
52.    setTitle("Login -- Instant Messenger");
53.    setResizable(false);
54.
```

```
55.    getContentPane().setLayout(null);
56.
57.    setSize(320,150);
58.    setLocation(250,150);
59.
60.    Insets insets = getInsets();
61.
62.    addWindowListener (new java.awt.event.WindowAdapter () {
63.    public void windowClosing (java.awt.event.WindowEvent evt) {
64.     System.exit(0);
65.    }
66.    }
67.    );
68.
69.    m_CompanyLogo = new JLabel("© Dreamtech Software India Inc.");
70.    m_CompanyLogo.setFont(new Font("sansSerif", Font.PLAIN, 11));
71.    m_CompanyLogo.setBounds(70 + insets.left, insets.top + 7, 200,
10);
72.    m_CompanyLogo.setForeground(Color.blue);
73.
74.    getContentPane().add(m_CompanyLogo);
75.
76.    m_LoginName = new JLabel("Login Name");
77.    m_LoginName.setBounds(30 + insets.left, insets.top + 40, 70, 10);
78.    m_LoginName.setFont(new Font("sansSerif", Font.PLAIN, 11));
79.
80.    getContentPane().add(m_LoginName);
81.
82.    m_EnterLoginName = new JTextField(LoginName,50);
83.    m_EnterLoginName.setBounds(105 + insets.left, insets.top + 40,
185, 20);
84.
85.    getContentPane().add(m_EnterLoginName);
86.
87.    m_Password = new JLabel("Password");
88.    m_Password.setBounds(30 + insets.left, insets.top + 65, 70, 10);
89.    m_Password.setFont(new Font("sansSerif", Font.PLAIN, 11));
90.
91.    getContentPane().add(m_Password);
92.
93.    m_EnterPassword = new JPasswordField(PassWord,50);
94.    m_EnterPassword.setBounds(105 + insets.left, insets.top + 65, 185,
20);
95.
96.    getContentPane().add(m_EnterPassword);
97.
98.    m_Login = new JButton("Login");
99.    m_Login.setBounds(105 + insets.left, insets.top + 90, 90, 20);
100.
```

```
101.    m_Login.addActionListener(this);
102.
103.    getContentPane().add(m_Login);
104.
105.    m_Register = new JButton("Register");
106.    m_Register.setBounds(200 + insets.left, insets.top + 90, 90, 20);
107.    m_Register.addActionListener(this);
108.
109.    getContentPane().add(m_Register);
110.
111.    m_LoginStatus = new JLabel(MessageLabel);
112.    m_LoginStatus.setBounds(5 + insets.left, insets.top + 110, 170,
10);
113.    m_LoginStatus.setFont(new Font("sansSerif", Font.PLAIN, 11));
114.
115.    getContentPane().add(m_LoginStatus);
116.
117.    userSession =        new Session();
118.    if (userSession.returnResult() == -1)
119.    {
120.      JOptionPane.showMessageDialog(this,"There is no Server to
          satisfy your request ","Instant
          Messenger",JOptionPane.INFORMATION_MESSAGE);
121.
122.      System.exit(0);
123.    }
124.  }
125.  /*********** actionPerformed ************/
126.
127.  public void actionPerformed(ActionEvent at)
128.  {
129.    Object source = at.getSource();
130.
131.    if(source.equals(m_Register))
132.    {
133.        register = new Register(this, userSession);
134.        register.register_list();
135.    }
136.    else if(source.equals(m_Login))
137.    {
138.      XMLCreator        createRequest;
139.      byte      [] RequestGenerated;
140.
141.      String [] val = new String[2];
142.
143.      val[0] = m_EnterLoginName.getText();
144.      val[1] = new String(m_EnterPassword.getPassword());
145.
146.      createRequest           = new XMLCreator("AUTH", val);
```

```
147.       RequestGenerated      = createRequest.returnResult();
148.       userSession.sendRequest(this, RequestGenerated, null);
149.   }
150. }
151.
152. /*********** main ************/
153.
154. public static void main(String[] args)
155. {
156.   Login login = new Login();
157.   login.show();
158. }
159. } // End Login...
```

- Lines 1□7: Contain Java import statements for the packages containing classes being used by the Login class; for example, javax.swing contains classes to build the GUI; the java.awt.event is used to recognise the window-closing event, and so on.

- Line 11: Contains the class declaration.

- Line 14□21: Declare the various elements of the login GUI.

- Line 23: Declares the Session object used to create a new session.

- Line 24: Declares an object of the Register class used only if a user chooses the Register option.

- Lines 26□28: Declare string variables that will contain the user informationand the response message to be displayed on the user's GUI.

- Lines 32□38: Contain the constructor version that takes the user's login name, password, and response message as parameters. This constructor is not called in the first instance (that is, when the application is started). It is called when incorrect login information is given or after a user registers for the first time. The constructor sets the values of user variables (Lines 34□36) andcalls the initForm() method (Line 37).

- Lines 42□46: Contain the constructor version without parameters. This versionis called in the first instance (that is, when the application is started). It sets the label MessageLabel (Line 44) and calls the initForm() method (Line 45).

- Line 50: Declares the initForm() method.

- Line 52: Sets the title of the login window.

- Line 53: Sets the Resizable property of the window to false (that is, the user cannot resize the window).

- Line 55: Passes a null to the setLayout() method to set absolute positioning for the content pane.

- Lines 57□58: Set the size (widthin pixels x height in pixels) and location (x-coordinate, y-coordinate) of the login window from the top-left corner of the screen.

- Line 60: Uses the method getInsets() to initailize an object of type Insets.

- Lines 62□66: Implement the windowlistener that recognizes a window-closing event and exits the login program if the login window is closed.

- Lines 69□72:Define the m_CompanyLogo label and set its font (Line 70), its boundaries (Line 71), and its foreground color (Line 72).

- Line 74: Adds the label m_CompanyLogo to the content pane.

- Lines 76□78:Define the m_LoginName label and set its boundaries and font.

- Line 80: Adds the m_LoginName label to the content pane.

- Lines 82□85: Define the text field where the user types her login name, set its boundaries, and add it to the content pane.

- Lines 87□91:Define the label m_Password, set its boundaries and font, and add it to the content pane.

- Lines 93□96: Define thetext field that accepts user's password, set its boundaries, and add it to the content pane.

- Lines 98□99: Define the Login button and set its boundaries.

- Line 101: Adds an action listener to the Login button.

- Line 103: Adds the Login button to the content pane.

- Lines 105□109: These lines definethe Register button, set its boundaries, add anaction listener to it, and add it to the content pane.

- Line 111: Defines the m_LoginStatus label that gives the login status of the user when the parametrised constructor of the Login class is called.

- Lines 112□115: Set the boundaries ofthe m_LoginStatus label, set its font, and add it to the content pane.

- Line 117: Creates an object of the Session class by calling its constructor.

- Lines 118□124:Check the return value from the Session object. If the return value is □ 1, indicating that the session cannot be established, the message "There is No Server To Satisfy your Request" is displayed in a dialog box, and the client program exits.

- Line 127: Declares the actionPerformed() method that recognises what button on the login window has been clicked.

- Lines 131□135: Definethe action to be taken if the action event is triggerred by the Register button; an object of the Register class is created and the register_list() method is called.

- Lines 136□148: Definethe action to be taken if the login button is pressed.

  - Line 138: Creates an object of the XMLCreator class.

  - Line 139: Declares the variable RequestGenerated of type byte that receives the generated XML request.

- Line 141: Declares the String array `val` used to store the user's login name and password.
- Lines 143□144: Set the user'slogin name as the first element of the `val` array and the password as the second element.
- Line 146: Calls the constructor of `XMLCreator` class by passing the string "AUTH" to denote that an authorization request is to be generated and passes the `val` array that contains the user data for the respective XML tags in the request.
- Line 147: Retrieves the output XML from the `XMLCreator` class into the `RequestGenerated` variable by calling the `returnResult()` method of the `XMLCreator` class.
- Line 148: Calls the `sendRequest()` method of the `Session` class through its object `userSession` to send the request to the server.
- Lines 154□158: Definethe `main()` method of the `Login` class that calls the no-parameter constructor to present the user with the login window.

Session class

The flow chart of `Session` class is presented in Figure 5-12. Listing 5-4 contains the code for this class, followed by a detailed description of the code.

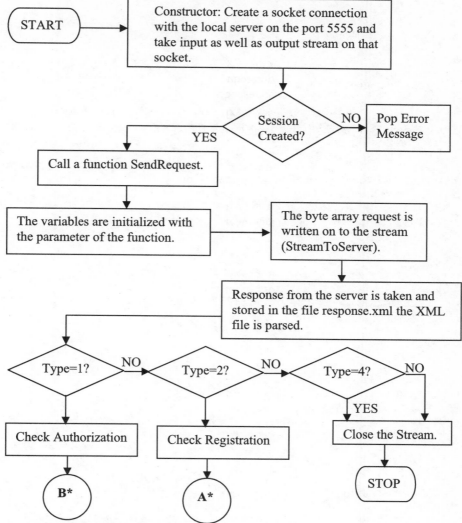

Figure 5-12: Technical flow chart for the Session class

Listing 5-4: Session.java

```
1.   import java.io.*;
2.   import java.net.*;
3.   import javax.swing.*;
4.
```

```
5.   /*********** class Declaration ************/
6.
7.   public class Session
8.   {
9.
10.  Socket                 socket;
11.  Socket                 sc;
12.  ServerSocket  serversocket;
13.
14.  BufferedInputStream  StreamFromLocalServer= null;
15.  BufferedOutputStream StreamToLocalServer          = null;
16.
17.  int            loop         = 100;
18.  byte []        buffer       = new byte[32];
19.  int            temp         = 0;
20.  String FinalString          = new String();
21.  int    sessionVal           = 0;
22.
23.  Login          screen;
24.  Register       regScreen ;
25.
26.  SParser Parser = new SParser();
27.
28.  /*********** constructor ************/
29.
30.  Session()
31.  {
32.  try
33.  {
34.
35.   socket = new Socket (SERVERIP, 5555);
36.   StreamFromLocalServer = new
      BufferedInputStream(socket.getInputStream());
37.   StreamToLocalServer = new
      BufferedOutputStream(socket.getOutputStream());
38.   sessionVal                = 1;
39.  }
40.  catch(Exception e)
41.  {
42.   System.out.println("Exception in Constructor of Session.java" +
e);
43.   sessionVal = -1;
44.  }
45.  } // End Constructor...
46.
47.  /*********** returnResult ************/
48.
49.  int returnResult()
50.  {
```

```
51.   return  sessionVal;
52.   }
53.
54.   /************ sendRequest *************/
55.
56.   void sendRequest(Login screen, byte request[], Register regScreen)
57.   {
58.
59.   this.screen        = screen;
60.   this.regScreen     = regScreen;
61.
62.    try
63.     {
64.    StreamToLocalServer.write(request, 0, request.length);
65.    StreamToLocalServer.flush();
66.
67.    if (screen == null)
68.    {
69.      System.exit(0);
70.    }
71.
72.    FinalString  = new String();
73.    loop = 100;
74.
75.    while (loop != 0)
76.    {
77.     temp        = StreamFromLocalServer.read(buffer, 0, 32);
78.     String str = new String (buffer, 0, temp);
79.     FinalString = FinalString + str;
80.     loop        = StreamFromLocalServer.available();
81.
82.    }
83.
84.    byte [] tempbytes = FinalString.getBytes();
85.    FileOutputStream TempOutFile = new
    FileOutputStream(""response.xml"");
86.    TempOutFile.write(tempbytes, 0, tempbytes.length);
87.    TempOutFile.close();
88.
89.    Parser.perform(""response.xml"");
90.
91.    if (Parser.getType() == 1)
92.    {
93.      checkAuthorization();
94.    }
95.    if (Parser.getType() == 2)
96.    {
97.      checkRegisteration();
98.    }
```

```
99.   if (Parser.getType() == 4)
100.    {
101.      StreamFromLocalServer.close();
102.      StreamToLocalServer.close();
103.    }
104.  }
105.  catch(Exception e)
106.    {
107.     System.out.println("Exception in Session.java :"+e);

108.  }
109.  }
110.
111.  /*********** checkAuthorization ************/
112.
113.  void checkAuthorization() throws Exception
114.  {
115.  String value = Parser.valueReturn();
116.  char info = value.charAt(0);
117.
118.  if(info == '0')
119.  {
120.   System.out.println("Success");
121.   String userName     = screen.m_EnterLoginName.getText();
122.   String passWord     = new
       String(screen.m_EnterPassword.getPassword());
123.
124.   MainScreen showScreen = new MainScreen(userName, passWord,
       StreamFromLocalServer, StreamToLocalServer);
125.
126.   screen.dispose();
127.  }
128.  else if(info == '1')
129.  {
130.   screen.dispose();
131.   StreamFromLocalServer.close();
132.   StreamToLocalServer.close();
133.   Login loginAgain = new Login("", "","UnRegistered User");
134.   loginAgain.show();
135.  }
136.  else if(info == '2')
137.  {
138.   screen.dispose();
139.   StreamFromLocalServer.close();
140.   StreamToLocalServer.close();
141.   Login loginAgain = new Login("", "","Invalid Password");
142.   loginAgain.show();
143.
144.  }
```

```
145.   else
146.   {
147.    screen.dispose();
148.    StreamFromLocalServer.close();
149.    StreamToLocalServer.close();
150.    Login loginAgain = new Login("", "","Critical Error Try Again.");
151.    loginAgain.show();
152.
153.   }
154.   }
155.
156.   /************ checkRegisteration *************/
157.
158.   void checkRegisteration() throws Exception
159.   {
160.   String value = Parser.valueReturn();
161.   char info = value.charAt(0);
162.
163.   if(info == '0')
164.   {
165.    // Call the Main_Screen from here...
166.   screen.dispose();
167.   regScreen.dispose();
168.
169.   String userName      = regScreen.m_LoginName.getText();
170.   String passWord      = new
       String(regScreen.m_Password.getPassword());
171.
172.   StreamFromLocalServer.close();
173.   StreamToLocalServer.close();
174.   Login loginAgain = new Login(userName, passWord,"Registration
       Successful.. Press Login to Log !");
175.   loginAgain.show();
176.
177.   }
178.   else if(info == '1')
179.   {
180.    screen.dispose();
181.    regScreen.dispose();
182.
183.    StreamFromLocalServer.close();
184.    StreamToLocalServer.close();
185.    Login loginAgain = new Login("", "","User Already Exits... Try
Again !");
186.    loginAgain.show();
187.   }
188.   else
189.   {
190.    screen.dispose();
```

```
191.    regScreen.dispose();
192.
193.    StreamFromLocalServer.close();
194.    StreamToLocalServer.close();
195.    Login loginAgain = new Login("", "","Critical Error... Please Try
Again !");
196.    loginAgain.show();
197.
198.    }
199.    }
200.    }      // End Session...
```

- Lines 1□3: Contain the Java import statements for packages whose classes are used by the Session class.

- Lines 7□21: Contain class and variabledeclarations/initialization.

- Line 23: Declares an object of the Login class.

- Line 24: Declares an object of the Register class.

- Line 26: Declares an object of the SParser class.

- Lines 30□45:Containontain the constructor of the Session class:

  - Line 35: Creates a socket on the client machine on port 5555, corresponding to a connection with the Server. As mentioned in the "Establishing connection with the local server" section, you need to replace "SERVERIP" with the IP address of the machine on which the server code is being run.

  - Line 36: Creates a buffered input stream to read from the server.

  - Line 37: Creates a buffered output stream to write to the server.

  - Line 38: Sets the value of the sessionVal to 1.

  - Lines 40□44:Contain the catch block that displays the Exception message and sets the sessionVal value to □1 to indicate that the server could not be reached.

- Lines 49□52:Define the returnResult() method that returns the value of the variable sessionVal to the calling class/method.

- Line 56: Declares the sendRequest() method that accepts a Login object, a request XML as a byte array, and a Register object.

- Lines 59□60:Initialize the Login and Register objects with the arguments given by the calling method.

- Lines 62□65: Theselines send the request to the server within a try block. The flush() method commits the output stream.

- Lines 67□70:If the Login object is null, the program exits.

- Lines 72□73: These linesinitiallize the two respective variables.

- Lines 75☐82:The Session class waits in a loop to receive the response from the server 32 bytes at a time and appends it to the String variable FinalString. The available() method (Line 80) checks if more data from the server is available.

- Line 84: Retrieves the string response from the server in a byte array.

- Line 85: Opens an output stream to the "response.xml" file.

- Lines 86☐87: Write the server's response tothe "response.xml" file and close the file.

- Line 89: Calls the SParser class'perform() method through its object, Parser, sending the "response.xml" file name as argument.

- Lines 91☐94:Check the call the getType() method of the SParser class that returns an integer denoting the type of request. The value 1 denotes an authorization request, and the checkAuthorization() method of Session class is called.

- Lines 95☐98:Call the checkRegistration() method of the Session class if the requestType value is 2.

- Lines 99☐103: Close the input and output streams to and from the server if the requestType is 4, which denotes a Quit request.

- Lines 105☐108: Contain thecatch block corresponding to the try statements of Line 62 that print the Exception description if the Session class fails to perform read/write operations.

- Lines 113☐154: Contain the codefor the checkAuthorization() method.

  - Line 115: Retrieves the parsed XML from the SParser value in the string variable value.

  - Line 116: Retrieves the first character of the string variable value in the variable info.

  - Lines 118☐127: Use anif clause to check if the value of the variable info is 0, which means a successful login. The user's name and password are retrived in their respective variables using the screen object of the Login class (Line 121☐122); the MainScreen class is invoked through its object, showScreen (Line 124); and the object of the Login class, screen, is disposed.

  - Lines 128☐135: Definethe program execution in the event of the value of variable info being 1. The previous object, screen, of the Login class is disposed (Line 130); the streams to and from the server are closed (Line 131☐132); a newLogin object, loginAgain, is created that invokes the parametrized constructor of the Login class with the message label "UnRegistered User" (Line 133); and the login GUI is displayed again (Line 134).

  - Lines 136☐142: Definethe program execution in the event of the value of variable info being 2. The previous object, screen, of the Login class is disposed (Line 138); the streams to and from the server are closed (Line 139☐140); a newLogin object, loginAgain, is created that invokes the parametrized constructor of the

`Login` class with the message label "Invalid Password" (Line 141); and the login GUI is displayed again (Line 142).

- Lines 145☐153: Definethe program execution in the event that the value of variable `info` is not equal to any of the values defined previously. The previous object, `screen`, of the `Login` class is disposed (Line 147); the streams to and from the server are closed (Line 148☐149); a new`Login` object, `loginAgain`, is created that invokes the parametrized constructor of the `Login` class with the message label "Critical Error Try Again" (Line 150); and the Login GUI is displayed again (Line 151).

- Lines 158☐199:Contain the code for the `checkRegisteration()` method.

  - Line 160: Retrieves the parsed XML from the `SParser` value in the string variable `value`.

  - Line 161: Retrieves the first character of the string variable `value` in the variable `info`.

  - Lines 163☐177: Use an`if` clause to check if the value of the variable `info` is 0, which means successful registration. The objects of `Login` and `Register` class are disposed (Line 166☐167). The user'sname and password are retrived in their respective variables (Line 169☐170); the streams toand from the server are closed (Line 172☐173); the`Login` class'parametrized constructor is called with the message label "Registration Successful. Press Login to Log !" (Line 174); and the Login GUI is displayed again (Line 175).

  - Lines 178☐187:Define the program execution in the event of the value of variable `info` being 1. The objects of the `Login` and `Register` classes are disposed (Line 180☐181); the streams to and fromthe server are closed (Line 183☐184); a new `Login` object, `loginAgain`, is created that invokes the parametrised constructor of `Login` class with the message label "User Already Exits... Try Again!" (Line 185); and the Login GUI is displayed again (Line 186).

  - Lines 188☐198: Definethe program execution in the event the value of variable `info` is neither 0 nor 1. The objects of the `Login` and `Register` classes are disposed (Line 190☐191); the streams to and fromthe server are closed (Line 193☐194); a new `Login` object, `loginAgain`, is created that invokes the parametrized constructor of the `Login` class with the message label "Critical Error... Please Try Again!" (Line 195); and the Login GUI is displayed again (Line 196).

Register class

The flow chart of the `Register` class is presented in Figure 5-13. Listing 5-5 contains the code for this class, followed by a detailed description of the code.

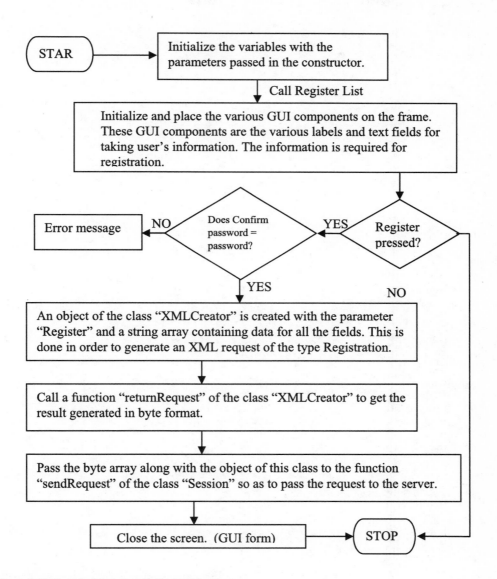

Figure 5-13: Technical flow chart for the Register class

Listing 5-5: Register.java

```
1.   import javax.swing.*;
2.   import javax.swing.event.*;
3.   import java.awt.*;
4.   import java.awt.event.*;
5.   import java.net.*;
6.   import java.io.*;
7.
8.   /*********** class Declaration ************/
9.
10.  public class  Register extends JFrame implements ActionListener
11.  {
12.
13.  JLabel                    m_Status;
14.  JLabel                    m_Heading;
15.  JLabel                    m_CompanyLogo;
16.  JLabel                    m_EnterLoginName;
17.  JTextField                m_LoginName;
18.  JLabel                    m_EnterPassword;
19.  JPasswordField            m_Password;
20.  JLabel                    m_EnterConfPassword;
21.  JPasswordField            m_ConfirmPassword;
22.  JLabel                    m_EnterAdd1;
23.  JTextField                m_Add1;
24.  JLabel                    m_EnterAdd2;
25.  JTextField                m_Add2;
26.  JLabel                    m_EnterPhone1;
27.  JTextField                m_Phone1;
28.  JLabel                    m_EnterPhone2;
29.  JTextField                m_Phone2;
30.  JLabel                    m_EnterEmail1;
31.  JTextField                m_Email1;
32.  JLabel                    m_EnterEmail2;
33.  JTextField                m_Email2;
34.  JLabel                    m_EnterCity;
35.  JTextField                m_City;
36.  JLabel                    m_EnterPin;
37.  JTextField                m_Pin;
38.  JLabel                    m_EnterProfession;
39.  JTextField                m_Profession;
40.  JButton                   m_Register;
41.  String [] requestString = new String[12];
42.
43.  Login               screen;
44.  Session             userSession;
45.
```

```
46.   /*********** constructor************/
47.
48.   Register(Login screen, Session userSession)
49.   {
50.   this.screen                = screen;
51.   this.userSession     = userSession;
52.   }
53.
54.   /*********** register_list ************/
55.
56.   public void register_list()
57.   {
58.   setTitle("Register -- InstantMessenger");
59.   getContentPane().setLayout(null);
60.   setResizable(false);
61.
62.   setSize(475,300);
63.   setVisible(true);
64.
65.   addWindowListener( new WindowAdapter()
66.    { public void WindowClosing(WindowEvent e)
67.      {
68.          dispose();
69.      }
70.    });
71.
72.   m_Heading = new JLabel("Provide your Personal Details..");
73.   m_Heading.setBounds(140,   3, 200, 14);
74.   m_Heading.setFont(new Font("sansSerif", Font.BOLD, 12));
75.   m_Heading.setForeground(Color.blue);
76.   getContentPane().add(m_Heading);
77.
78.   m_CompanyLogo = new JLabel("© DreamTech Software India Inc.");
79.   m_CompanyLogo.setBounds(250 ,   21, 200, 10);
80.   m_CompanyLogo.setFont(new Font("sansSerif", Font.PLAIN, 12));
81.   m_CompanyLogo.setForeground(Color.blue);
82.   getContentPane().add(m_CompanyLogo);
83.
84.   m_EnterLoginName = new JLabel("Login Name");
85.   m_EnterLoginName.setBounds(20  ,   50, 70, 10);
86.   m_EnterLoginName.setFont(new Font("sansSerif", Font.PLAIN, 11));
87.   getContentPane().add(m_EnterLoginName);
88.
89.   m_LoginName = new JTextField(50);
90.   m_LoginName.setBounds(110 ,   50, 200, 20);
91.   getContentPane().add(m_LoginName);
92.
93.   m_EnterPassword = new JLabel("Password");
94.   m_EnterPassword.setBounds(20  ,   75, 70, 10);
```

```
95.  m_EnterPassword.setFont(new Font("sansSerif", Font.PLAIN, 11));
96.  getContentPane().add(m_EnterPassword);
97.
98.  m_Password = new JPasswordField(30);
99.  m_Password.setBounds(110  ,   75, 110, 20);
100. getContentPane().add(m_Password);
101.
102. m_EnterConfPassword = new JLabel("Confirm Password");
103. m_EnterConfPassword.setBounds(240  ,   75, 90, 10);
104. m_EnterConfPassword.setFont(new Font("sansSerif", Font.PLAIN,
11));
105. getContentPane().add(m_EnterConfPassword);
106.
107. m_ConfirmPassword = new JPasswordField(30);
108. m_ConfirmPassword.setBounds(340  ,   75, 110, 20);
109. getContentPane().add(m_ConfirmPassword);
110.
111. m_EnterAdd1 = new JLabel("Address1");
112. m_EnterAdd1.setBounds(20  ,   100, 70, 10);
113. m_EnterAdd1.setFont(new Font("sansSerif", Font.PLAIN, 11));
114. getContentPane().add(m_EnterAdd1);
115.
116. m_Add1 = new JTextField(30);
117. m_Add1.setBounds(110  ,   100, 110, 20);
118. getContentPane().add(m_Add1);
119.
120. m_EnterAdd2 = new JLabel("Address2");
121. m_EnterAdd2.setBounds(240  ,   100, 90, 10);
122. m_EnterAdd2.setFont(new Font("sansSerif", Font.PLAIN, 11));
123. getContentPane().add(m_EnterAdd2);
124.
125. m_Add2 = new JTextField(30);
126. m_Add2.setBounds(340  ,   100, 110, 20);
127. getContentPane().add(m_Add2);
128.
129. m_EnterPhone1 = new JLabel("Phone1");
130. m_EnterPhone1.setBounds(20  ,   125, 70, 10);
131. m_EnterPhone1.setFont(new Font("sansSerif", Font.PLAIN, 11));
132. getContentPane().add(m_EnterPhone1);
133.
134. m_Phone1 = new JTextField(30);
135. m_Phone1.setBounds(110  ,   125, 110, 20);
136. getContentPane().add(m_Phone1);
137.
138. m_EnterPhone2 = new JLabel("Phone2");
139. m_EnterPhone2.setBounds(240  ,   125, 90, 10);
140. m_EnterPhone2.setFont(new Font("sansSerif", Font.PLAIN, 11));
141. getContentPane().add(m_EnterPhone2);
142.
```

```
143.    m_Phone2 = new JTextField(30);
144.    m_Phone2.setBounds(340  ,   125, 110, 20);
145.    getContentPane().add(m_Phone2);
146.
147.    m_EnterEmail1 = new JLabel("Email1");
148.    m_EnterEmail1.setBounds(20  ,    150, 70, 10);
149.    m_EnterEmail1.setFont(new Font("sansSerif", Font.PLAIN, 11));
150.    getContentPane().add(m_EnterEmail1);
151.
152.    m_Email1 = new JTextField(30);
153.    m_Email1.setBounds(110  ,    150, 110, 20);
154.    getContentPane().add(m_Email1);
155.
156.    m_EnterEmail2 = new JLabel("Email2");
157.    m_EnterEmail2.setBounds(240  ,    150, 90, 10);
158.    m_EnterEmail2.setFont(new Font("sansSerif", Font.PLAIN, 11));
159.    getContentPane().add(m_EnterEmail2);
160.
161.    m_Email2 = new JTextField(30);
162.    m_Email2.setBounds(340  ,    150, 110, 20);
163.    getContentPane().add(m_Email2);
164.
165.    m_EnterCity = new JLabel("City");
166.    m_EnterCity.setBounds(20  ,    175, 70, 10);
167.    m_EnterCity.setFont(new Font("sansSerif", Font.PLAIN, 11));
168.    getContentPane().add(m_EnterCity);
169.
170.    m_City = new JTextField(30);
171.    m_City.setBounds(110  ,    175, 110, 20);
172.    getContentPane().add(m_City);
173.
174.    m_EnterPin = new JLabel("Pin");
175.    m_EnterPin.setBounds(240  ,    175, 90, 10);
176.    m_EnterPin.setFont(new Font("sansSerif", Font.PLAIN, 11));
177.    getContentPane().add(m_EnterPin);
178.
179.    m_Pin = new JTextField(30);
180.    m_Pin.setBounds(340  ,    175, 110, 20);
181.    getContentPane().add(m_Pin);
182.
183.    m_EnterProfession = new JLabel("Profession");
184.    m_EnterProfession.setBounds(20  ,    200, 70, 10);
185.    m_EnterProfession.setFont(new Font("sansSerif", Font.PLAIN, 11));
186.    getContentPane().add(m_EnterProfession);
187.
188.    m_Profession = new JTextField(30);
189.    m_Profession.setBounds(110  ,    200, 110, 20);
190.    getContentPane().add(m_Profession);
191.
```

```
192.    m_Register = new JButton("Register");
193.    m_Register.setBounds(170  ,   235, 100, 20);
194.    m_Register.addActionListener(this);
195.    getContentPane().add(m_Register);
196.
197.    m_Status = new JLabel("");
198.    m_Status.setBounds(5  ,   255, 170, 10);
199.    m_Status.setFont(new Font("sansSerif", Font.PLAIN, 11));
200.    getContentPane().add(m_Status);
201.    }
202.
203.    /*********** actionPerformed *************/
204.
205.    public void actionPerformed(ActionEvent e)
206.    {
207.    if(e.getSource() == m_Register)
208.    {
209.
210.    XMLCreator           createRequest;
211.    byte    []           RequestGenerated;
212.    int          clear  = 0;
213.
214.    requestString[0]     = m_LoginName.getText();
215.    requestString[1]     = new String(m_Password.getPassword());
216.    requestString[2]     = new String(m_ConfirmPassword.getPassword());
217.    requestString[3]     = m_Add1.getText();
218.    requestString[4]     = m_Add2.getText();
219.    requestString[5]     = m_Phone1.getText();
220.    requestString[6]     = m_Phone2.getText();
221.    requestString[7]     = m_Email1.getText();
222.    requestString[8]     = m_Email2.getText();
223.    requestString[9]     = m_City.getText();
224.    requestString[10]    = m_Pin.getText();
225.    requestString[11]    = m_Profession.getText();
226.
227.
228.    if (requestString[1].equals(requestString[2]))
229.    {
230.     clear = 1;
231.    }
232.    else
233.    {
234.      JOptionPane.showMessageDialog(this,"Password and Confirm
Password Fields Do Not Match.. ","Instant
Messenger",JOptionPane.ERROR_MESSAGE);
235.      m_Password.setText("");
236.      m_ConfirmPassword.setText("");
237.      clear = 0;
238.    }
```

```
239.  if (clear == 1)
240.  {
241.    createRequest        = new XMLCreator("REGISTER", requestString);
242.    RequestGenerated     = createRequest.returnResult();
243.    userSession.sendRequest(screen, RequestGenerated, this);
244.  }
245.  }
246.  }
247.  }        // End Register.
```

- Lines 1□6: Contain the Java import statements for Java packages.

- Line 10: The class declaration.

- Lines 13□41:Declare various user-defined variables derived from the `javax.swing` package. Collectively, these variables form the elements of the registration GUI.

- Line 43: Declares an object of the `Login` class.

- Line 44: Declares an object of the `Session` class.

- Lines 48□52:Define the constructor for the `Register` class that sets the objects of the `Login` and `Session` classes with the arguments passed to the constructor.

- Line 56: Declares the `register_list()` method that creates the registration GUI.

- Line 58: Sets the title of the registration window.

- Line 59: Passes a `null` to the `setLayout()` method to set absolute positioning for the content pane.

- Line 60: Sets the `Resizable` property of the window to `false` (that is, the user cannot resize the window).

- Line 62: Sets the size (width in pixels x height in pixels) of the registration window.

- Lines 65□70: Implement the windowlistener that recognizes a window-closing event and disposes the registration window.

- Lines 72□76: Create a new label (Line 72), set its bounds (Line 73), set its font (Line 74), set its text color (Line 75), and add it to the content pane (Line 76).

- Lines 78□82: Create a new label (Line 78), set its bounds (Line 79), set its font (Line 80), set its text color (Line 81), and add it to the content pane (Line 82).

- Lines 84□87: Create a new label (Line 84), set its bounds (Line 85), set its font (Line 86), and add it to the content pane (Line 87).

- Lines 89□91: Create the text fieldfor login name (Line 89), set its bounds (Line 90), and add it to the content pane (Line 91).

- Lines 93□96: Create a new label (Line 93), set its bounds (Line 94), set its font (Line 95), and add it to the content pane (Line 96).

- Lines 98□100: Create the password field for password (Line 98), set its bounds (Line 99), and add it to the content pane (Line 100).

- Lines 102□105: Create a new label (Line 102), set its bounds (Line 103), set its font (Line 104), and add it to the content pane (Line 105).

- Lines 107□109: Create the passwordfield for password confirmation (Line 107), set its bounds (Line 108), and add it to the content pane (Line 109).

- Lines 111□114: Create a new label (Line 111), set its bounds (Line 112), set its font (Line 113), and add it to the content pane (Line 114).

- Lines 116□118:Create the text field for user's address (Line 116), set its bounds (Line 117), and add it to the content pane (Line 118).

- Lines 120□123: Create a new label (Line 120), set its bounds (Line 121), set its font (Line 122), and add it to the content pane (Line 123).

- Lines 125□127:Create another text field for the user's address (Line 125), set its bounds (Line 126), and add it to the content pane (Line 127).

- Lines 129□132:Create a new label (Line 129), set its bounds (Line 130), set its font (Line 131), and add it to the content pane (Line 132).

- Lines 134□136: Create a text fieldfor user's telephone number (Line 134), set its bounds (Line 135), and add it to the content pane (Line 136).

- Lines 138□141:Create a new label (Line 138), set its bounds (Line 139), set its font (Line 140), and add it to the content pane (Line 141).

- Lines 143□145:Create another text field for user's telephone number (Line 143), set its bounds (Line 144), and add it to the content pane (Line 145).

- Lines 147□150: Create a new label (Line 147), set its bounds (Line 148), set its font (Line 149), and add it to the content pane (Line 150).

- Lines 152□154:Create the text field for user's e-mail ID (Line 152), set its bounds (Line 153), and add it to the content pane (Line 154).

- Lines 156□159: Create a new label (Line 156), set its bounds (Line 157), set its font (Line 158), and add it to the content pane (Line 159).

- Lines 161□163: Create anothertext field for user's e-mail ID (Line 161), set its bounds (Line 162), and add it to the content pane (Line 163).

- Lines 165□168:Create a new label (Line 165), set its bounds (Line 166), set its font (Line 167), and add it to the content pane (Line 168).

- Lines 170□172:Create a text field for user's city (Line 170), set its bounds (Line 171), and add it to the content pane (Line 172).

- Lines 174□177: Create a new label (Line 174), set its bounds (Line 175), set its font (Line 176), and add it to the content pane (Line 177).

- Lines 179□181: Create a textfield for user's Pincode (Line 179), set its bounds (Line 180), and add it to the content pane (Line 181).

- Lines 183□186: Create a new label (Line 183), set its bounds (Line 184), set its font (Line 185), and add it to the content pane (Line 186).

- Lines 188□190: Create a text fieldfor user's profession (Line 188), set its bounds (Line 189), and add it to the content pane (Line 190).

- Lines 192□195: Create a new button(Line 192), set its bounds (Line 193), set its font (Line 194) and add it to the content pane (Line 195).

- Line 197□200: Create a label fieldfor the status (Line 197), set its bounds (Line 198), set its font (Line 199), and add it to the content pane (Line 200).

- Line 205: Declares the `actionPerformed()` method.

- Line 207: Checks if the source of the action event is the button `m_Register` (that is, if the `m_Register` button (for registration) has been clicked).

- Line 210: Declares an object of the `XMLCreator` class.

- Line 211□212: Declare user-defined variables.

- Line 214□225: Retrievethe entries made by the user in various input fields and puts them in the string array `requestString`.

- Line 228□238: Use an`if-else` clause to check if the element at index 1 of the `requestString` array is the same as the element at index 2; this checks whether the same entries have been made in password and confirm password fields. If they match, the value of the variable `clear` is set to 1; otherwise, a dialog box is displayed with the message "Password and Confirm Password Fields Do Not Match."; `clear` is set to 0.

- Line 239□244: Contain an`if` clause that checks for the value of the variable `clear`. If it is 1, the `XMLCreator` class is called with the argument "REGISTER" that informs that a registration request is to be generated and with the second argument `requestString` that contains all the user entries that need to be enclosed in their respective XML tags. The XML thus created is retrieved in the byte array `RequestGenerated`, and this request is passed to the `sendRequest()` method of the `Session` class.

MainScreen class

The flow chart of `MainScreen` class is presented in Figure 5-14. Listing 5-6 contains the code for this class, followed by a detailed description of the code.

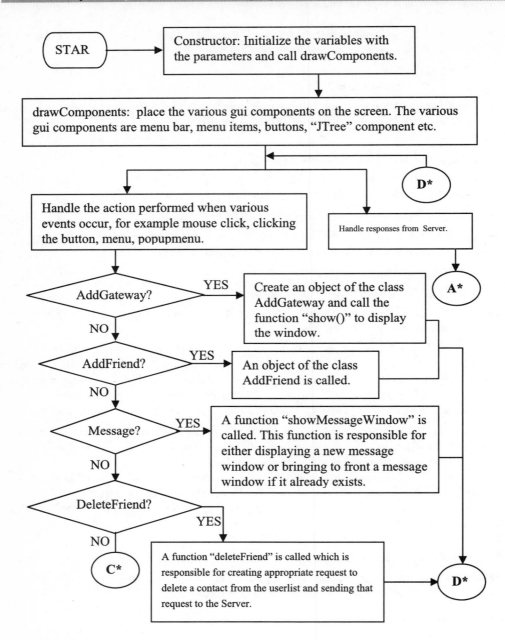

Figure 5-14(a): Technical flow chart for MainScreen class

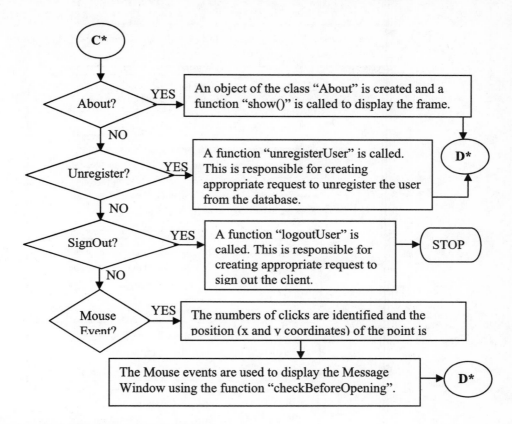

Figure 5-14(b): Technical flow chart for MainScreen class

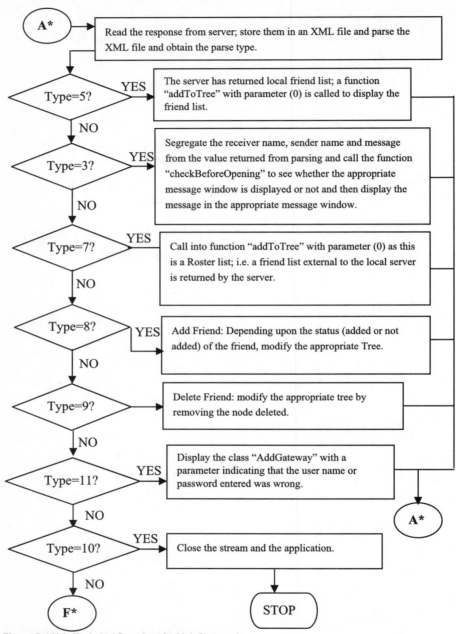

Figure 5-14(c): Technical flow chart for MainScreen class

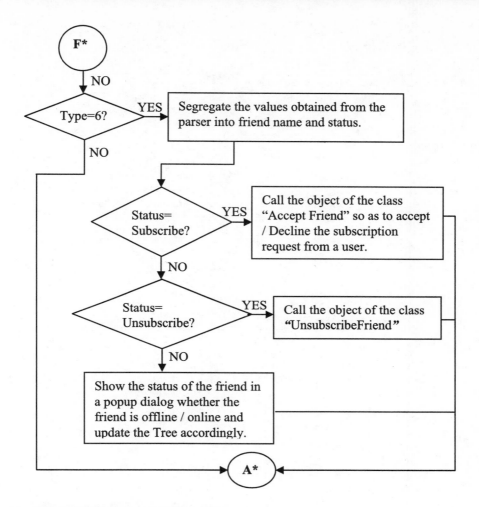

Figure 5-14(d): Technical flow chart for MainScreen class

Listing 5-6: MainScreen.java

```
1.   import java.awt.event.*;
2.   import java.awt.*;
3.   import javax.swing.*;
4.   import javax.swing.tree.*;
5.   import javax.swing.event.*;
6.   import java.net.*;
7.   import java.io.*;
8.   import java.util.*;
9.   import javax.swing.text.*;
```

```
10.
11.    /*********** Class Declaration ************/
12.
13.    public class MainScreen extends JFrame implements ActionListener ,
MouseListener, ChangeListener,Runnable
14.    {
15.    JMenuBar                        m_Menubar;
16.    JMenu                           m_Menu;
17.
18.    JMenuItem                       m_SignOutMenuItem;
19.    JMenuItem                       m_UnregisterMenuItem;
20.    JMenuItem                       m_MessageMenuItem;
21.    JMenuItem                       m_AddFriendMenuItem;
22.    JMenuItem                       m_DeleteFriendMenuItem;
23.    JMenuItem                       m_AboutMenuItem;
24.    JMenuItem                       m_AddGatewayMenuItem;
25.
26.
27.    JButton                         m_Message;
28.    JButton                         m_Delete;
29.    JButton                         m_Add;
30.    JLabel                          m_Status;
31.    JLabel                          m_StatusPosition;
32.    JLabel                          m_ConnectionStatus;
33.    JPopupMenu                      m_PopupMenu;
34.    JTabbedPane                     m_TabbedPane;
35.    JScrollPane                     m_ScrollPane1;
36.    JScrollPane                     m_ScrollPane2;
37.
38.    DefaultMutableTreeNode          m_TreeRoot1;
39.    DefaultMutableTreeNode          m_TreeSubRoot1;
40.    DefaultMutableTreeNode          m_TreeSubRoot2;
41.
42.    DefaultMutableTreeNode          m_TreeRoot2;
43.    DefaultMutableTreeNode          m_TreeChild;
44.    DefaultTreeModel                m_TreeModel1;
45.    DefaultTreeModel                m_TreeModel2;
46.    DefaultTreeCellRenderer         m_renderer;
47.    JTree                           m_friendsOnline        ;
48.    JTree                           m_friendsOffline;
49.
50.    AddFriend                       m_addFriendInList;
51.
52.    BufferedOutputStream StreamToServer;
53.    BufferedInputStream     StreamFromServer;
54.
55.    Vector FriendName          = new Vector();
56.    Vector FriendIP            = new Vector();
57.    Vector FriendStatus        = new Vector();
```

```
58.   boolean        updateTree     = false;
59.   String user                   = new String();
60.
61.   SParser Parser = new SParser();
62.   String originalString          = new String();
63.
64.   int m_posOnScreenX = 0;
65.   int m_posOnScreenY    = 0;
66.   String userName,password,status;
67.
68.   Vector ListOfMessageWindowsByName = new Vector();
69.   Vector ListOfMessageWindowsByObject = new Vector();
70.
71.   Vector JabberFriendName  = new Vector();
72.   Vector JabberFriendID   = new Vector();
73.   Vector JabberFriendStatus  = new Vector();
74.   Vector JabberFriendSubscription  = new Vector();
75.
76.   JMenuItem                          m_PopMenuItem;
77.   JMenuItem                          m_PopMenuItem1;
78.
79.   int  addToTreeRoster  = 0;
80.   String [] maintainUserTree = new String[100];
81.
82.   /*********** Constructor ***************/
83.
84.   MainScreen(String userName, String password,BufferedInputStream
StreamFromServer,BufferedOutputStream StreamToServer) throws Exception
85.   {
86.    this.userName              = userName;
87.    this.password              = password;
88.    this.StreamToServer        = StreamToServer;
89.    this.StreamFromServer      = StreamFromServer;
90.
91.    drawComponents();
92.    Thread         TreeUpdate = new Thread(this);
93.    TreeUpdate.start();
94.   }
95.
96.   /*********** drawComponents ************/
97.
98.   void drawComponents()
99.   {
100.   setTitle("Instant Messenger");
101.   setResizable(false);
102.   getContentPane().setLayout(null);
103.   setSize(258,415);
104.   setLocation(300,100);
105.   setVisible(true);
```

```
106.
107.    addWindowListener( new WindowAdapter()
108.    { public void windowClosing(WindowEvent e)
109.        {
110.                try
111.                {
112.                        logoutUser();
113.                }
114.                catch(IOException ef)
115.                {
116.                        System.out.println("Window Event"+ef);

117.                }
118.                System.exit(1);
119.        }
120.    });
121.
122.    getContentPane().setCursor(new Cursor(Cursor.DEFAULT_CURSOR));
123.
124.    m_Menubar = new JMenuBar();
125.    m_Menu = new JMenu("Login");
126.
127.    m_AddGatewayMenuItem = new JMenuItem("Add a GateWay");
128.    m_AddGatewayMenuItem.addActionListener(this);
129.    m_Menu.add(m_AddGatewayMenuItem);
130.
131.    m_UnregisterMenuItem = new JMenuItem("Unregister");
132.    m_UnregisterMenuItem.addActionListener(this);
133.    m_Menu.add(m_UnregisterMenuItem);
134.
135.    m_SignOutMenuItem = new JMenuItem("Sign Out of Messenger");
136.    m_SignOutMenuItem.addActionListener(this);
137.    m_Menu.add(m_SignOutMenuItem);
138.
139.    m_Menubar.add(m_Menu);
140.
141.    m_Menu = new JMenu("Message");
142.    m_Menubar.add(m_Menu);
143.
144.    m_MessageMenuItem = new  JMenuItem("Send A Message");
145.    m_MessageMenuItem.addActionListener(this);
146.    m_Menu.add(m_MessageMenuItem);
147.
148.    m_Menu = new  JMenu("Friends");
149.    m_Menubar.add(m_Menu);
150.
151.    m_AddFriendMenuItem = new  JMenuItem("Add Friend");
152.    m_AddFriendMenuItem.addActionListener(this);
153.    m_Menu.add(m_AddFriendMenuItem);
```

```
154.
155.    m_DeleteFriendMenuItem = new  JMenuItem("Delete Friends...");

156.    m_DeleteFriendMenuItem.addActionListener(this);
157.    m_Menu.add(m_DeleteFriendMenuItem);
158.
159.
160.    m_Menu = new  JMenu("Help");
161.    m_Menubar.add(m_Menu);
162.
163.    m_AboutMenuItem = new  JMenuItem("About");
164.    m_AboutMenuItem.addActionListener(this);
165.    m_Menu.add(m_AboutMenuItem);
166.
167.    m_Menubar.setBounds(0, 0, 200, 15);
168.
169.    this.setJMenuBar(m_Menubar);
170.
171.    m_Message = new  JButton("Message");
172.    m_Message.setBounds(0 , 20, 80, 30);
173.    m_Message.setFont(new Font("sansSerif", Font.BOLD, 10));
174.    m_Message.addActionListener(this);
175.    getContentPane().add(m_Message);
176.
177.    m_Add = new  JButton("Add Friend");
178.    m_Add.setBounds(80,20, 100, 30);
179.    m_Add.setFont(new Font("sansSerif", Font.PLAIN, 9));
180.    m_Add.addActionListener(this);
181.    getContentPane().add(m_Add);
182.
183.
184.    m_Delete = new  JButton("Delete");
185.    m_Delete.setBounds(180,20, 70, 30);
186.    m_Delete.setFont(new Font("sansSerif", Font.PLAIN, 9));
187.    m_Delete.addActionListener(this);
188.    getContentPane().add(m_Delete);
189.
190.
191.    m_TabbedPane = new  JTabbedPane();
192.    m_TabbedPane.setBounds(0 ,   67, 250, 275);
193.
194.    m_TabbedPane.setTabPlacement(JTabbedPane.BOTTOM);
195.    m_TabbedPane.addChangeListener(this);
196.    getContentPane().add(m_TabbedPane);
197.
198.    m_Status = new  JLabel("status");
199.    m_Status.setBounds(10  ,   300, 50, 15);
200.    m_Status.setFont(new Font("sansSerif", Font.PLAIN, 10));
201.    getContentPane().add(m_Status);
```

```
202.
203.    m_StatusPosition = new  JLabel();
204.    m_StatusPosition.setBounds(50  ,   300, 150, 15);
205.    m_StatusPosition.setFont(new Font("sansSerif", Font.PLAIN, 10));
206.    getContentPane().add(m_StatusPosition);
207.    m_StatusPosition.setText("I'm Available");
208.
209.    m_ConnectionStatus = new  JLabel(new ImageIcon("white-ball.gif"),
        SwingConstants.LEFT);
210.    m_ConnectionStatus.setBounds(10,350, 150, 15);
211.    getContentPane().add(m_ConnectionStatus);
212.    m_ConnectionStatus.setText("Connecting");
213.
214.    m_PopupMenu = new  JPopupMenu();
215.    m_PopMenuItem = new JMenuItem("Send An Instant Message");
216.    m_PopMenuItem1 = new JMenuItem("Delete Contact");
217.    m_PopMenuItem.addActionListener(this);
218.    m_PopMenuItem1.addActionListener(this);
219.
220.    m_PopupMenu.add(m_PopMenuItem);
221.    m_PopupMenu.add(m_PopMenuItem1);
222.
223.    addMouseListener(this);
224.    getContentPane().add(m_PopupMenu);
225.
226.    m_TreeRoot1 = new DefaultMutableTreeNode("Friends");
227.    m_renderer = new DefaultTreeCellRenderer();
228.    m_TreeModel1 = new DefaultTreeModel(m_TreeRoot1);
229.
230.    m_friendsOnline = new JTree(m_TreeModel1);
231.    m_friendsOnline.putClientProperty("JTree.lineStyle", "Angled");
232.
233.    m_TreeRoot2 = new DefaultMutableTreeNode("Friends");
234.    m_TreeModel2 = new DefaultTreeModel(m_TreeRoot2);
235.    m_friendsOffline = new JTree(m_TreeModel2);
236.
237.    m_friendsOnline.addMouseListener(this);
238.    m_friendsOffline.addMouseListener(this);
239.    m_ScrollPane1 = new JScrollPane(m_friendsOnline);
240.    m_ScrollPane2 = new JScrollPane(m_friendsOffline);
241.    m_ScrollPane1.setBounds(0  ,   67, 250, 225);
242.    m_ScrollPane2.setBounds(0  ,   67, 250, 225);
243.    m_TabbedPane.addTab("friends",m_ScrollPane1);
244.    m_TabbedPane.setSelectedIndex(0);
245.    }     // End constructor....
246.
247.    /********** Add To Tree    **********/
248.
249.    void AddToTree(int val)
```

```
250.    {
251.    getContentPane().setCursor(new Cursor(Cursor.WAIT_CURSOR));
252.
253.    try
254.    {
255.    if (val == 0)
256.    {
257.    originalString       =       "Friend List For  \" "+user+" \"";
258.    m_TreeRoot1 = new DefaultMutableTreeNode(originalString);
259.    m_TreeSubRoot1 = new DefaultMutableTreeNode("ON-LINE");
260.    m_TreeSubRoot2 = new DefaultMutableTreeNode("OFF-LINE");
261.    m_TreeRoot1.add(m_TreeSubRoot1);
262.    m_TreeRoot1.add(m_TreeSubRoot2);
263.    m_TreeModel1 = new DefaultTreeModel(m_TreeRoot1);
264.    m_renderer.setOpenIcon(new ImageIcon("red-ball.gif"));
265.    m_renderer.setClosedIcon(new ImageIcon("yellow-ball.gif"));
266.    m_renderer.setLeafIcon(new ImageIcon("blue-ball.gif"));
267.    m_renderer.setBackgroundSelectionColor(Color.green);
268.    m_friendsOnline.setCellRenderer(m_renderer);
269.
270.    for (int i=0;i<FriendName.size();i++)
271.    {
272.      m_TreeChild = new
DefaultMutableTreeNode(FriendName.elementAt(i));
273.      maintainUserTree[i]          =
(String)FriendName.elementAt(i);
274.      if (FriendStatus.elementAt(i).equals("0"))
275.      m_TreeSubRoot2.add(m_TreeChild);
276.      else
277.        m_TreeSubRoot1.add(m_TreeChild);
278.    }
279.    m_friendsOnline.setModel(m_TreeModel1);
280.
281.    m_TreeModel1.reload();
282.    updateTree = false;
283.    }
284.    else if(val == 1)
285.    {
286.    for (int i=0;i<JabberFriendID.size();i++)
287.    {
288.    String      str   = (String)JabberFriendID.elementAt(i);
289.    String      temp = (String)JabberFriendSubscription.elementAt(i);
290.    if (!(str.indexOf("registered")!= -1))
291.    {
292.    int index = str.indexOf("@");
293.    if (index!= -1)
294.    {
295.     str = str.substring(0, index);
296.    }
```

```
297.
298.    if (temp.equalsIgnoreCase("to"))
299.    {
300.    str = str+"(Requested)";
301.    }
302.    else if (temp.equalsIgnoreCase("from"))
303.    {
304.    str = str+"(Requesting)";
305.    }
306.    else if (temp.equalsIgnoreCase("none"))
307.    {
308.    str = str+"(Pending)";
309.
310.    }
311.
312.    m_TreeChild = new DefaultMutableTreeNode(str);
313.    m_TreeSubRoot2.add(m_TreeChild);
314.    m_TreeModel1.reload();
315.    }
316.
317.    }
318.    }
319.    else
320.    {
321.    for (int i=0;i<JabberFriendID.size();i++)
322.    {
323.
324.    String      str   = (String)JabberFriendID.elementAt(i);
325.    String temp = (String)JabberFriendSubscription.elementAt(i);
326.    if (str.indexOf("registered")!= -1)
327.    {
328.    continue;
329.
330.    }
331.    int index;
332.    index      = 0;
333.    index = str.indexOf("@");
334.    if (index!= -1)
335.    {
336.    str = str.substring(0, index);
337.    }
338.
339.    if (temp.equalsIgnoreCase("none"))
340.    {
341.    continue;
342.    }
343.    else if (temp.equalsIgnoreCase("to"))
344.    {
345.    str = str+"(Requested)";
```

```
346.     }
347.     else if (temp.equalsIgnoreCase("from"))
348.     {
349.     str = str+"(Requesting)";
350.     }
351.
352.     m_TreeChild = new DefaultMutableTreeNode(str);
353.
354.     Enumeration m_TempTreeChildren   =
         m_TreeSubRoot2.depthFirstEnumeration();
355.     boolean        found                          =    false;
356.     found                              =    false;
357.     index                    =    0;
358.     while (m_TempTreeChildren.hasMoreElements())
359.     {
360.     String tempStr = (m_TempTreeChildren.nextElement()).toString();
361.     if (str.indexOf(tempStr)!= -1)
362.     {
363.       found = true;
364.       break;
365.     }
366.     else
367.       index++;
368.     }
369.     if (found)
370.       continue;
371.     else
372.     {
373.       m_TempTreeChildren        =
     m_TreeSubRoot1.depthFirstEnumeration();
374.     index                    =    0;
375.     while (m_TempTreeChildren.hasMoreElements())
376.     {
377.     String tempStr = (m_TempTreeChildren.nextElement()).toString();
378.     if (tempStr.indexOf(str)!= -1)
379.       {
380.       found = true;
381.       break;
382.       }
383.     else
384.       index++;
385.     }
386.     if (found)
387.     continue;
388.       else
389.       {
390.     m_TreeSubRoot2.add(m_TreeChild);
391.     m_TreeModel1.reload();
392.       }
```

```
393.    }
394.   }
395.   }
396.   for (int i = 0;i < m_friendsOnline.getRowCount();i++ )
397.    m_friendsOnline.expandRow(i);
398.   }
399.   catch(Exception e)
400.   {
401.   System.out.println("Error in Add To Tree.."+ e);
402.   e.printStackTrace(System.out);
403.   }
404.   getContentPane().setCursor(new Cursor(Cursor.DEFAULT_CURSOR));
405.
406.   }
407.
408.   /************* ActionPerformed *************/
409.
410.   public void actionPerformed (ActionEvent ae)
411.   {
412.
413.   if (ae.getSource() == m_AddGatewayMenuItem)
414.   {
415.   System.out.println("Add Gateway...");
416.
417.    AddGateway GatewayScreen = new AddGateway(this,userName);
418.    GatewayScreen.show();
419.   }
420.   if (ae.getSource() == m_Add)
421.   {
422.    m_addFriendInList = new AddFriend(this, userName);
423.   }
424.   if (ae.getSource() == m_Message)
425.   {
426.    showMessageWindow();
427.   }
428.   if (ae.getSource() == m_PopMenuItem)
429.   {
430.    showMessageWindow();
431.   }
432.   if (ae.getSource() == m_PopMenuItem1)
433.   {
434.    deleteFriend();
435.   }
436.   if (ae.getSource() == m_Delete)
437.   {
438.    deleteFriend();
439.   }
440.   if (ae.getSource() == m_AddFriendMenuItem)
441.   {
```

```
442.   m_addFriendInList = new AddFriend(this, userName);
443.  }
444.  if (ae.getSource() == m_AboutMenuItem)
445.  {
446.     About aboutDialog = new About(this,"About -- Instant
           Messenger", true);
447.     aboutDialog.show();
448.  }
449.  if (ae.getSource() == m_MessageMenuItem)
450.  {
451.    showMessageWindow();
452.  }
453.  if (ae.getSource() == m_DeleteFriendMenuItem)
454.  {
455.    deleteFriend();
456.  }
457.  if (ae.getSource() == m_UnregisterMenuItem)
458.  {
459.   try
460.   {
461.       unregisterUser();
462.   }
463.   catch (Exception e)
464.   {
465.     System.out.println("Exception in Log Out User "+e);
466.     e.printStackTrace(System.out);
467.   }
468.  }
469.  if (ae.getSource() == m_SignOutMenuItem)
470.  {
471.   try
472.   {
473.       logoutUser();
474.   }
475.   catch (Exception e)
476.   {
477.     System.out.println("Exception in Log Out User "+e);
478.     e.printStackTrace(System.out);
479.   }
480.   System.exit(0);
481.  }
482.  }
483.  /*********** Mouse Events ************/
484.  public void mouseReleased(MouseEvent me) {}
485.  public void mouseEntered(MouseEvent me) {}
486.  public void mouseExited(MouseEvent me) {}
487.  public void mousePressed(MouseEvent me){}
488.  public void valueChanged(TreeSelectionEvent tr){}
489.  public void stateChanged(ChangeEvent ch){}
```

```
490.   /************ Mouse Clicked ********/
491.   public void mouseClicked(MouseEvent me)
492.   {
493.     int x = me.getX();
494.     int y = me.getY();
495.     boolean  eventInTree = false;
496.
497.     if (me.getClickCount() == 2)
498.     {
499.         try
500.         {
501.               JTree m_friendsOnline= (JTree)me.getSource();
502.               eventInTree    = true;
503.         }
504.         catch (Exception e)
505.         {
506.           System.out.println("Exception occured:OutSide Tree
                 Region");
507.           eventInTree = false;
508.         }
509.         if (eventInTree)
510.         {
511.             int result = 0;
512.             int clickedRow   = m_friendsOnline.getRowForLocation(x,
y);
513.             if (clickedRow != -1)
514.             {
515.                 TreePath path =
                 m_friendsOnline.getPathForRow(clickedRow);
516.                 TreeNode node =
             (TreeNode)path.getLastPathComponent();
517.
518.     if (node.getParent() == null)
519.       result = -2;
520.     else if (((node.toString()).equalsIgnoreCase("ON-LINE"))
||((node.toString()).equalsIgnoreCase("OFF-LINE")))
521.       result = -2;
522.     else if (((node.getParent()).toString()).equalsIgnoreCase("OFF-
LINE"))
523.       result = -2;
524.     else
525.       result =   CheckBeforeOpening(node.toString());
526.
527.     if (result == -1)
528.       {
529.        Message   msgWindow = new Message(user, node.toString(), this,
StreamToServer);
530.        msgWindow.show();
```

```
531.
     ListOfMessageWindowsByName.add((Object)node.toString());
532.
     ListOfMessageWindowsByObject.add((Object)msgWindow);
533.    }
534.   else if (result != -2)
535.    {
536.    Message   msg =
(Message)(ListOfMessageWindowsByObject.elementAt(result));
537.    msg.toFront();
538.    msg.show();
539.    }
540.    }
541.     }
542.    }
543.    else if((me.getModifiers() & InputEvent.BUTTON1_MASK) ==
     InputEvent.BUTTON1_MASK)
544.    {
545.      m_posOnScreenX =      me.getX();
546.      m_posOnScreenY =      me.getY();
547.    }
548.    else if ((me.getModifiers() & InputEvent.BUTTON3_MASK) ==
     InputEvent.BUTTON3_MASK)
549.    {
550.      m_posOnScreenX =      me.getX();
551.      m_posOnScreenY =      me.getY();
552.
553.      int clickedRow =
          m_friendsOnline.getRowForLocation(m_posOnScreenX,
   m_posOnScreenY);
554.         if (clickedRow != -1)
555.         {
556.   TreePath path      = m_friendsOnline.getPathForRow(clickedRow);
557.   TreeNode node   = (TreeNode)path.getLastPathComponent();
558.
559.   String     str         = node.toString();
560.    int result = -1;
561.
562.    if ((node.getParent() == null) ||(str.equalsIgnoreCase("OFF-
LINE"))||(str.equalsIgnoreCase("ON-LINE")))
563.    {
564.   result = -1;
565.   }
566.    else
567.    {
568.    result = 0;
569.   }
570.
571.    if (result == 0)
```

```
572.      {
573.      if (((node.getParent()).toString()).equalsIgnoreCase("OFF-
LINE"))
574.        m_PopMenuItem.setEnabled(false);
575.      else
576.        m_PopMenuItem.setEnabled(true);
577.
578.
      m_PopupMenu.show(m_friendsOnline,m_posOnScreenX, m_posOnScreenY);
579.      }
580.    }
581.    }
582.
583.  }
584.
585.  /******** run() *************/
586.
587.  public void run()
588.  {
589.    try
590.    {
591.     while (true)
592.     {
593.     int        loop        = 100;
594.     byte[]     buffer      = new byte[1];
595.     int        temp        = 0;
596.     String     FinalString = new String();
597.
598.     while (loop != 0)
599.     {
600.        temp            = StreamFromServer.read(buffer, 0, 1);
601.        if (temp < 0)
602.               break;
603.        String str    = new String (buffer, 0, temp);
604.        FinalString    = FinalString + str;
605.        loop           = StreamFromServer.available();
606.        if (FinalString.indexOf("</InstantMessenger>")!=
    -1)
607.               break;
608.     }
609.     FinalString = FinalString.trim();
610.
611.     byte [] tempbytes = FinalString.getBytes();
612.     if(tempbytes.length == 0)
613.        continue;
614.     FileOutputStream TempOutFile      = new
FileOutputStream("response.xml");
615.     TempOutFile.write(tempbytes, 0, tempbytes.length);
616.     TempOutFile.close();
```

```
617.
618.
619.    String ReturnVal = new String();
620.
621.    Parser.perform("\"response.xml\"");
622.    ReturnVal   = Parser.valueReturn();
623.
624.
625.    if (Parser.getType() == 5)
626.    {
627.        StringTokenizer tokens = null;
628.        tokens = new StringTokenizer(ReturnVal,"~");
629.        Vector FriendName           = new Vector();
630.        Vector FriendIP             = new Vector();
631.        Vector FriendStatus   = new Vector();
632.        String userName = new String();
633.        userName = tokens.nextToken();
634.
635.        while (tokens.hasMoreTokens())
636.        {
637.                FriendName.add(tokens.nextToken());
638.                FriendStatus.add(tokens.nextToken());
639.        }
640.
641.        this.user           = userName;
642.        this.FriendName     = FriendName;
643.        this.FriendIP           = FriendIP;
644.        this.FriendStatus       = FriendStatus;
645.    getContentPane().setCursor(new Cursor(Cursor.WAIT_CURSOR));
646.        AddToTree(0);
647.    getContentPane().setCursor(new Cursor(Cursor.DEFAULT_CURSOR));
648.
649.    m_ConnectionStatus.setIcon(new ImageIcon("pink-ball.gif"));
650.    m_ConnectionStatus.setText("Connected");
651.
652.
653.    }
654.    else if (Parser.getType() == 3)
655.    {
656.        String sender           = new String();
657.        String receiver         = new String();
658.        String userMessage      = new String();
659.        StringTokenizer tokens  = null;
660.
661.        ReturnVal               = Parser.valueReturn();
662.        System.out.println(ReturnVal);
663.
664.        tokens                  = new
StringTokenizer(ReturnVal,"~");
```

```
665.
666.        receiver                      = tokens.nextToken();
667.        sender                        = tokens.nextToken();
668.        userMessage                   = tokens.nextToken();
669.
670.        // Break Return Val into Sender Receiver and Message..
671.        int result = CheckBeforeOpening(sender);
672.        if (result == -1)
673.        {
674.         Message msgWindow = new Message(receiver, sender, this,
             StreamToServer);
675.         msgWindow.show();
676.         ListOfMessageWindowsByName.add((Object)sender);
677.         ListOfMessageWindowsByObject.add((Object)msgWindow);
678.
679.
680.         Style m_TempStyle  = (Style)
             msgWindow.m_Attributes.get("receiver");
681.         try
682.         {
683.

msgWindow.m_Document.insertString(msgWindow.m_Document.getLength(),
sender+" :\n", m_TempStyle);
684.
685.           m_TempStyle =
               (Style)msgWindow.m_Attributes.get("receiverMessage");
686.
687.

     msgWindow.m_Document.insertString(msgWindow.m_Document.getLength(),
     userMessage+"\n", m_TempStyle);
688.         }
689.         catch (Exception e)
690.         {
691.          System.out.println("Exception occured:"+e);
692.         }
693.
694.        }
695.        else
696.        {
697.          Message      msg =
             (Message)(ListOfMessageWindowsByObject.elementAt(result));
698.          msg.toFront();
699.          msg.show();
700.
701.          Stylem_TempStyle  = (Style)
              msg.m_Attributes.get("receiver");
702.          try
703.          {
```

```
704.              msg.m_Document.insertString(msg.m_Document.getLength(),
                  sender+" :\n", m_TempStyle);
705.
706.          m_TempStyle= (Style)
                  msg.m_Attributes.get("receiverMessage");
707.
708.          msg.m_Document.insertString(msg.m_Document.getLength(),
                  userMessage+"\n", m_TempStyle);
709.          }
710.          catch (Exception e)
711.          {
712.          System.out.println("Exception occured:"+e);
713.          }
714.      }
715.  }
716.  else if (Parser.getType() == 6)
717.  {
718.
719.      JDialog            m_notifyDialog;
720.      JLabel             m_label;
721.      JLabel             m_label1;
722.      JLabel             m_label2;
723.      String             m_ReturnVal = new String();
724.      String             m_FriendName = new String();
725.      String             m_status = new String();
726.      StringTokenizer    m_token = null;
727.      GraphicsConfigurationm_gc;
728.      Rectangle bounds ;
729.
730.
731.      m_ReturnVal    = Parser.valueReturn();
732.
733.      m_token = new StringTokenizer(m_ReturnVal, "~");
734.
735.      m_FriendName   =    m_token.nextToken();
736.      m_status           =        m_token.nextToken();
737.
738.
739.      if (m_status.equalsIgnoreCase("SUBSCRIBE"))
740.      {
741.       AcceptFriend acceptRequest = new AcceptFriend(this,
m_FriendName, userName);
742.              acceptRequest.show();
743.      }
744.      else if (m_status.equalsIgnoreCase("UNSUBSCRIBE"))
745.      {
746.      UnsubscribeFriend unsubscribeRequest = new
UnsubscribeFriend(this, m_FriendName, userName);
747.      unsubscribeRequest.show();
```

```
748.        }
749.        else
750.        {
751.        m_notifyDialog = new JDialog();
752.        m_notifyDialog.setTitle("Friend");
753.        m_notifyDialog.setSize(150, 100);
754.        m_notifyDialog.getContentPane().setLayout(null);
755.        m_gc  = m_notifyDialog.getGraphicsConfiguration();
756.        bounds = m_gc.getBounds();
757.        m_notifyDialog.setLocation(bounds.width -150, bounds.height-
140);
758.
759.        String tempName      = m_FriendName;
760.        int indexP = tempName.indexOf("%");
761.        if (indexP!= -1)
762.        {
763.            tempName        =       tempName.substring(0, indexP);
764.        }
765.        m_label = new JLabel(tempName);
766.        m_label.setFont(new Font("sansSerif", Font.BOLD, 11));
767.        m_label.setBounds(10, 7, 130, 15);
768.        m_label.setForeground(Color.blue);
769.        m_notifyDialog.getContentPane().add(m_label);
770.
771.        m_label1 = new JLabel(" is ");
772.        m_label1.setFont(new Font("sansSerif", Font.BOLD, 11));
773.        m_label1.setBounds(25, 25, 40, 15);
774.        m_label1.setForeground(Color.black);
775.        m_notifyDialog.getContentPane().add(m_label1);
776.
777.        m_label2 = new JLabel(m_status);
778.        m_label2.setFont(new Font("sansSerif", Font.BOLD, 11));
779.        m_label2.setBounds(10, 43, 90, 15);
780.        m_label2.setForeground(Color.blue);
781.        m_notifyDialog.getContentPane().add(m_label2);
782.        m_notifyDialog.setVisible(true);
783.
784.        if (m_status.equalsIgnoreCase("OFF-LINE"))
785.        {
786.            booleanfound = false;
787.            DefaultMutableTreeNode m_TempTreeNode = new
                DefaultMutableTreeNode(m_FriendName);
788.
789.
790.            Enumeration m_TreeChildren   =
                m_TreeSubRoot1.depthFirstEnumeration();
791.            int                  index              =   0;
792.            while (m_TreeChildren.hasMoreElements())
793.                {
```

```
794.                      String str =
                          (m_TreeChildren.nextElement()).toString();
795.                      if
(str.toLowerCase().indexOf(m_FriendName.toLowerCase())!= -1)
796.                      {
797.                          found = true;
798.                          break;
799.                      }
800.                      else
801.                          index++;
802.              }
803.              if (found)
804.              {
805.                      m_TreeSubRoot1.remove(index);
806.                      m_TreeSubRoot2.add(m_TempTreeNode);
807.                      m_TreeModel1.reload();
808.              }
809.
810.      for (int i = 0;i < m_friendsOnline.getRowCount();i++ )
811.                      m_friendsOnline.expandRow(i);
812.      }
813.      else if (m_status.equalsIgnoreCase("ON-LINE"))
814.      {
815.              boolean found = false;
816.              DefaultMutableTreeNode m_TempTreeNode = new
DefaultMutableTreeNode(m_FriendName);
817.
818.
819.              Enumeration m_TreeChildren   =
                  m_TreeSubRoot2.depthFirstEnumeration();
820.              int index = 0;
821.              while (m_TreeChildren.hasMoreElements())
822.              {
823.                      String str =
                          (m_TreeChildren.nextElement()).toString();
824.                      if
(str.toLowerCase().indexOf(m_FriendName.toLowerCase())!= -1)
825.                      {
826.                          found = true;
827.                          break;
828.                      }
829.                      else
830.                          index++;
831.              }
832.
833.              if (found)
834.              {
835.                      m_TreeSubRoot2.remove(index);
836.                      m_TreeSubRoot1.add(m_TempTreeNode);
```

```
837.                    m_TreeModel1.reload();
838.              }
839.            for (int i = 0;i < m_friendsOnline.getRowCount();i++
)
840.                    m_friendsOnline.expandRow(i);
841.        }
842.      this.toFront();
843.      try
844.      {
845.            Thread.sleep(5000);
846.      }
847.      catch(Exception ex)
848.      {
849.            System.out.println("Error in Sleep :" +ex);
850.      }
851.
852.      m_notifyDialog.setVisible(false);
853.    }
854.  }
855.  else if (Parser.getType() == 7)
856.  {
857.      StringTokenizer tokens = null;
858.      tokens = new StringTokenizer(ReturnVal,"~");
859.
860.      JabberFriendID                   = new Vector();
861.      JabberFriendSubscription         = new Vector();
862.
863.      while (tokens.hasMoreTokens())
864.      {
865.        JabberFriendID.add((Object)tokens.nextToken());
866.        JabberFriendSubscription.add((Object)tokens.nextToken());
867.      }
868.      getContentPane().setCursor(new Cursor(Cursor.WAIT_CURSOR));
869.      addToTreeRoster++;
870.      AddToTree(addToTreeRoster);
871.      getContentPane().setCursor(new
          Cursor(Cursor.DEFAULT_CURSOR));
872.  }
873.  else if (Parser.getType() == 8)
874.  {
875.      StringTokenizer tokens = null;
876.      tokens = new StringTokenizer(ReturnVal,"~");
877.      int i = 0;
878.      String val [] = new String[4];
879.
880.      while (tokens.hasMoreTokens())
881.            val[i++] = tokens.nextToken();
882.
```

```
883.        if
((val[2].equalsIgnoreCase("0"))&&(val[3].equalsIgnoreCase("1")))
884.        {
885.          DefaultMutableTreeNode m_TreeChild = new
DefaultMutableTreeNode(val[1]);
886.          m_TreeSubRoot1.add(m_TreeChild);
887.          m_TreeModel1.reload();
888.          for (int j = 0;j < m_friendsOnline.getRowCount();j++ )
889.               m_friendsOnline.expandRow(j);
890.
891.        }
892.        else if
((val[2].equalsIgnoreCase("0"))&&(val[3].equalsIgnoreCase("0")))
893.        {
894.          DefaultMutableTreeNode m_TreeChild = new
DefaultMutableTreeNode(val[1]);
895.          m_TreeSubRoot2.add(m_TreeChild);
896.          m_TreeModel1.reload();
897.          for (int j = 0;j < m_friendsOnline.getRowCount();j++ )
898.               m_friendsOnline.expandRow(j);
899.
900.        }
901.        else if (val[2].equalsIgnoreCase("2"))
902.        {
903.        JOptionPane.showMessageDialog(this,"Friend \"" + val[1] +"\"
Already exists...","Instant Messenger",JOptionPane.INFORMATION_MESSAGE);
904.        }
905.    }
906.    else if (Parser.getType() == 9)
907.    {
908.        boolean found = false;
909.
910.        StringTokenizer tokens = null;
911.        tokens = new StringTokenizer(ReturnVal,"~");
912.        int i = 0;
913.        String val [] = new String[3];
914.
915.        while (tokens.hasMoreTokens())
916.             val[i++] = tokens.nextToken();
917.
918.        if (val[2].equalsIgnoreCase("0"))
919.        {
920.
921.          Enumeration m_TempTreeChildren   =
m_TreeSubRoot2.depthFirstEnumeration();
922.          int                index              =   0;
923.          while (m_TempTreeChildren.hasMoreElements())
924.          {
```

```
925.              String str =
(m_TempTreeChildren.nextElement()).toString();
926.              if (val[1].indexOf(str)!= -1)
927.              {
928.                found = true;
929.                break;
930.              }
931.              else
932.                index++;
933.          }
934.
935.        if (found)
936.        {
937.              m_TreeSubRoot2.remove(index);
938.              m_TreeModel1.reload();
939.        }
940.        else
941.        {
942.              m_TempTreeChildren    =
                  m_TreeSubRoot1.depthFirstEnumeration();
943.              index             =    0;
944.              while (m_TempTreeChildren.hasMoreElements())
945.              {
946.                String str =
                    (m_TempTreeChildren.nextElement()).toString();
947.                if (val[1].indexOf(str)!= -1)
948.                {
949.                 found = true;
950.                 break;
951.                }
952.                else
953.                    index++;
954.          }
955.          if (found)
956.          {
957.              m_TreeSubRoot1.remove(index);
958.              m_TreeModel1.reload();
959.          }
960.        }
961.
962.        for (int j = 0;j < m_friendsOnline.getRowCount();j++ )
963.              m_friendsOnline.expandRow(j);
964.
965.
966.        JOptionPane.showMessageDialog(this,"Friend \"" + val[1] +"\"
Removed Successfully... ","Instant
Messenger",JOptionPane.INFORMATION_MESSAGE);
967.      }
968.    }
```

```
969.      else if (Parser.getType() == 11)
970.      {
971.          AddGateway AddGateway = new AddGateway(this,userName,"Wrong
User Name or Password Please Try Again!");
972.          AddGateway.show();
973.      }
974.      else if (Parser.getType() == 10)
975.      {
976.         StreamToServer.close();
977.         StreamFromServer.close();
978.         System.exit(0);
979.      }
980.      }
981.   }
982.   catch(Exception e)
983.   {
984.     System.out.println("Exception in Class ListenerForLocalServer in
the Run Method"+e);
985.     e.printStackTrace(System.out);
986.   }
987.   }// End Run
988.
989.   /*********************** CheckBeforeOpening
**************************/
990.
991.   int CheckBeforeOpening(String toUser)
992.   {
993.   for (int i = 0;i<ListOfMessageWindowsByName.size() ;i++ )
994.   {
995.       String str = new String();
996.       str    = (String)ListOfMessageWindowsByName.elementAt(i);
997.       if (str.equalsIgnoreCase(toUser))
998.       {
999.
1000.        return i;
1001.       }
1002.   }
1003.   return -1;
1004.   }
1005.
1006.   /******************** logoutUser ************/
1007.
1008.   void logoutUser() throws IOException
1009.   {
1010.      String [] values = new String[1];
1011.      values [0] = userName;
1012.
1013.      XMLCreator      createRequest;
1014.      byte     []            RequestGenerated;
```

```
1015.
1016.      createRequest   = new XMLCreator("QUIT", values);
1017.      RequestGenerated        = createRequest.returnResult();
1018.
1019.      StreamToServer.write(RequestGenerated, 0,
RequestGenerated.length);
1020.      StreamToServer.flush();
1021.
1022.  }
1023.
1024.  /************  showMessageWindow  *************/
1025.
1026.  void showMessageWindow()
1027.  {
1028.  int result = -11;
1029.  int clickedRow      =
m_friendsOnline.getRowForLocation(m_posOnScreenX, m_posOnScreenY);
1030.
1031.  if (clickedRow > 0)
1032.  {
1033.         TreePath path= m_friendsOnline.getPathForRow(clickedRow);
1034.         TreeNode node    = (TreeNode)path.getLastPathComponent();
1035.
1036.         if (((node.getParent()).toString()).equalsIgnoreCase("OFF-
LINE"))
1037.         {
1038.              result = -2;
1039.              JOptionPane.showMessageDialog(this,"Cannot Send
Message to an OFF-Line User.","Instant
Messenger",JOptionPane.INFORMATION_MESSAGE);
1040.         }
1041.         else if (((node.toString()).equalsIgnoreCase("ON-LINE"))
||((node.toString()).equalsIgnoreCase("OFF-LINE")))
1042.         {
1043.           result = -2;
1044.         }
1045.         else
1046.          result =    CheckBeforeOpening(node.toString());
1047.
1048.         if (result == -1)
1049.         {
1050.              MessagemsgWindow = new Message(user, node.toString(),
this, StreamToServer);
1051.              msgWindow.show();
1052.
 ListOfMessageWindowsByName.add((Object)node.toString());
1053.              ListOfMessageWindowsByObject.add((Object)msgWindow);
1054.         }
1055.         else if (result != -2)
```

```
1056.          {
1057.          Message      msg =
(Message)(ListOfMessageWindowsByObject.elementAt(result));
1058.          msg.toFront();
1059.          msg.show();
1060.          }
1061.   }
1062.
1063.   }
1064.
1065.   /********* deleteFriend()   ******************/
1066.
1067.   void deleteFriend()
1068.   {
1069.   int result = -11;
1070.   int clickedRow     =
m_friendsOnline.getRowForLocation(m_posOnScreenX, m_posOnScreenY);
1071.
1072.   if (clickedRow > 0)
1073.   {
1074.    TreePath path      = m_friendsOnline.getPathForRow(clickedRow);
1075.    TreeNode node      = (TreeNode)path.getLastPathComponent();
1076.
1077.    if (((node.toString()).equalsIgnoreCase("ON-LINE"))
||((node.toString()).equalsIgnoreCase("OFF-LINE")))
1078.    {
1079.      result = -2;
1080.    }
1081.    else
1082.    {
1083.      String [] values = new String[2];
1084.      values[0] = user;
1085.      values[1] = node.toString();
1086.      int indexCheck = values[1].indexOf("(");
1087.      if (indexCheck!= -1)
1088.      {
1089.        values[1] = values[1].substring(0, indexCheck);
1090.      }
1091.
1092.      XMLCreator        createRequest;
1093.      byte      []            RequestGenerated;
1094.
1095.      createRequest      = new XMLCreator("DELETEFRIEND", values);
1096.      RequestGenerated   = createRequest.returnResult();
1097.
1098.      try
1099.      {
1100.      StreamToServer.write(RequestGenerated, 0,
        RequestGenerated.length);
```

```
1101.        StreamToServer.flush();
1102.      }
1103.      catch (Exception e)
1104.      {
1105.          System.out.println("Delete Friend Name:"+e);
1106.      }
1107.
1108.    }
1109.    }
1110.    }
1111.    /********** UnregisterUser()  ************/
1112.
1113.    void unregisterUser()throws Exception
1114.    {
1115.    String [] values = new String[1];
1116.    values [0] = userName;
1117.
1118.    XMLCreator   createRequest;
1119.    byte []              RequestGenerated;
1120.
1121.    createRequest        = new XMLCreator("UNREGISTER", values);
1122.    RequestGenerated     = createRequest.returnResult();
1123.
1124.    StreamToServer.write(RequestGenerated, 0,
RequestGenerated.length);
1125.    StreamToServer.flush();
1126.    }
1127. }/// End Main Screen..
```

- Lines 1□9: Contain Java import statements for packages used by theMainScreen class.

- Lines 13□80: Contain class and variable declarations/intialization.

- Line 84: Declares the constructor of MainScreen class.

- Lines 86□89: Initialize user-defined variables using parameter values ofthe constructor.

- Line 91: Calls the drawComponents() method.

- Lines 92□93: Create a new Threadand start the thread. The start() method makes a call to the run() method of MainScreen class.

- Line 98: Declares the drawComponents() method.

- Lines 100□101: Set the title of the MainScreen GUI window and set its Resizable property to false.

- Line 102: Sets the elements of the GUI to absolute positioning by passing a null argument to the setLayout() method.

- Lines 103□104: Set the size (width x height) in pixels andlocation (x-coordinate, y-coordinate) of the Main Screen window.

- Line 105: Sets the `Visible` property of the window to true.
- Lines 107□120: Implement the Window Listener that recognizes a window-closing event. When the window is closed, the method `windowClosing()` tries to call the `logoutUser()` method. If an `Exception` occurs during the call to `logoutUser()`, the exception is printed. The program then exits.
- Line 122: Sets a cursor in the container.
- Line 124: Creates a menu bar named `m_Menubar`.
- Lines 125: Creates a new menu titled "Login."
- Lines 127□129:Create a menu item labelled "Add a Gateway," add action listener to this menu item, and add it to the "Login" menu.
- Lines 131□133:Create a menu item labelled "Unregister", add action listener to this menu item, and add the item to "Login" menu.
- Lines 135□137: Create a menuitem "Sign out of Messenger", add action listener to it, and add the item to "Login" menu.
- Line 139: Adds the "Login" menu to the menu bar.
- Lines 141□142: Create a new Menulabelled "Message" and add it to the menu bar.
- Lines 144□146: Create a menuitem labelled "Send A Message", add action listener to it, and add it to the "Message" menu.
- Lines 148□149: Create a third menu labelled "Friends" and add it to the menu bar.
- Lines 151□153: Create a menuitem labelled "Add Friend", add action listener to it, and add it to the "Friends" menu.
- Lines 155□157: Create a menuitem labelled "Delete Friends…" add action listener to it, and add it to the "Friends" menu.
- Lines 160□161: Create a fourthmenu labelled "Help" and add it to the menu bar.
- Lines 163□165: Create a menuitem labelled "About", add action listener to it, and add the item to the "Help" menu.
- Line 167: Sets the bounds of the menu bar created in Line 124 (x-coordinate, y-coordinate, width, height).
- Line 169: Sets the menu bar in the window container.
- Line 171: Creates a new button labelled "Message".
- Line 172: This line sets the bounds (x-coordinate, y-coordinate, width, height) of the "Message" button.
- Line 173: Sets the font for the label of the button (font face is sans-serif, type-face is bold, and font-size is 10 points).
- Line 174: Adds action listener to the "Message" button.

- Line 175: Adds the "Message" button to the container.
- Line 177□181: Create a button labelled"Add Friend", set its bounds, set its font, add action listener to it, and add the button to the container.
- Line 184□188: Createa button labelled "Delete", set its bounds, set its font, add action listener to it, and add the button to the container.
- Lines 191□192: Create a tab-paneand set its bounds.
- Line 194: Sets the tab(s) at the bottom of the tab-pane.
- Line 195: Adds change-listener to the tab-pane to enable it to recognize when the user clicks another tab.
- Line 196: Adds the tab-pane to the container.
- Line 198□201: Create a label "status", set its bounds, set its font, andadd the label to the container.
- Line 203□206: Create a new label namedm_StatusPosition, set its bounds, set its font, and add it to the container.
- Line 207: Sets the text of the label, m_StatusPosition to "I'm Available".
- Lines 209□211: Create a new image label using the image "white-ball.gif", set its bounds, and add it to the container.
- Line 212: Sets the text "Connecting" for the preceding label.
- Line 214: Creates a new pop-up menu.
- Lines 215□216: Create two menuitems for the pop-up menu.
- Lines 217□218: Addaction listener to the pop-up menu items.
- Lines 220□221: Addthe two menu items to the pop-up menu of Line 214.
- Line 223: Adds a mouse listener to the MainScreen window.
- Line 224: Adds the pop-up menu to the container.
- Line 226: Creates a tree node labelled "Friends."
- Line 227: Creates a tree-cell renderer.
- Line 228: Creates a tree-model for the tree node labelled "Friends".
- Line 230: Creates a new tree with the tree-model in Line 228.
- Line 231: Sets the visual attribute for the tree component that appears as a dotted line joining tree elements in their proper hierarchy (see Figure 5-2).
- Line 233□234: Create another tree node, again labelled "Friends". and createsa new tree-model for it.
- Line 235: Creates a new tree for the second tree model.
- Lines 237□238: Addmouse-listener to the two tree models.

- Lines 239☐240: Create two scroll panes, one each for the two tree models defined previously.

- Lines 241☐242: Set the bounds ofthe two scroll-panes.

- Lines 243: Adds the tab "friends" to the tab-pane created in Line 191.

- Line 244: Sets the selected tab-index of the tab-pane to 0, that is, the first tab is selected by default.

- Line 249: Declares the AddToTree() method.

- Line 251: Sets the cursor in the container to a waiting-cursor (indicating that some processing is going on).

- Line 255: Checks if the variable val contains the value 0; if it does, the if block statements (Line 257☐282)are executed.

- Line 257: Sets the value of the string variable originalString.

- Line 258: Creates a tree-node that acts as the parent/root node for the tree structure of user's friend list.

- Lines 259☐260: Create two tree-nodes that act as subnodes tothe root-node of Line 258 and show the user's "ON-LINE" and "OFF-LINE" friends.

- Lines 261☐262: Addthe two subnodes to the root note.

- Lines 263: Creates the tree model for the root tree node.

- Lines 264: Sets the image "red-ball.gif" as the open icon, that is, the icon that will be used for the parent nodes when the complete tree is displayed on the window.

- Line 265: Sets the image "yellow-ball.gif" as the closed icon, that is, the icon that will be displayed when the tree is compact, not yet being shown fully on the window.

- Line 266: Sets the image "blue-ball.gif" as the leaf icon, that is, the icon that will be used for the leaf nodes (the friend names).

- Line 267: Sets the highlight color to be green for the selected row in the tree structure.

- Line 268: Calls the setCellRenderer() to display the tree in the window as per settings in Lines 264☐267.

- Lines 270☐278: Run afor loop that loops through the elements in the Vector FriendName for each element in FriendName; the entry at corresponding index in the FriendStatus vector is checked (Line 274). If the value of the element at current index of FriendStatus is 0, the current element of FriendName is added as a child to the "OFFLINE" tree-node (Line 275); otherwise, it is added to the "ONLINE" tree-node.

- Line 279: Sets the tree model defined in line 263 for the tree m_friendsOnline.

- Line 281: Reloads the tree model, thereby updating the tree-structure of the friend list.

- Line 282: Sets the boolean updateTree to false.

- Line 284: Contains the `else` clause for the `if` of Line 255 that checks whether or not the value of variable `val` is 1.
- Lines 286□317:Run a `for` loop till the last element of the vector `JabberFriendID`.
  - Lines 288□289: Retrievethe current element of Vectors `JabbeFriendID` and `JabberFriendSubscription` into the String variables `str` and `temp`, respectively.
  - Line 290: Checks if the index of the string "registered" in variable `str` is not □1, that is, `str` contains the string "registered".
  - Line 292: Extracts the index of the character "@" in variable `str` to the variable `index`.
  - Lines 293□296: Checks that the value ofvariable `index` is not □1, that is, the character "@" exists in variable `str`, and extracts the characters from index 0 to the index of char "@" from the var `str`.
  - Lines 298□301: Ifthe variable `temp` contains the string "to", the string "(Requested)" is appended to variable `str`.
  - Lines 302□305: Ifthe variable `temp` contains the string "from", the string "(Requesting)" is appended to variable `str`.
  - Lines 306□310: Ifthe variable `temp` contains the string "none", the string "(Pending)" is appended to variable `str`.
- Line 312: Sets the variable `str` as the label for a new tree-node (child-node).
- Line 313: Adds the node of Line 312 to the "OFF-LINE" friends node.
- Line 314: Reloads the tree-model.
- Line 319: This line contains the `else` clause for the `if` of line 255 and `else if` of Line 284.
- Line 321□394: Use afor loop to loop through the elements of vector `JabberFriendID`.
  - Lines 324□325: Retrievethe current element of the Vectors `JabberFriendID` and `JabberFriendSubscription` in the variables `str` and `temp`, respectively.
  - Lines 326□330:Check if the string "registered" exists within the variable `str`, and if it does, continue with execution of the loop.
  - Lines 331□332:Declare and initialize the variable `index`.
  - Line 333: Assigns the index of character "@" to the variable `index`.
  - Lines 334□337: Check if variable`index` is not □1 and extract the substring from 0 to the value contained in variable `index` from the variable `str`.
  - Lines 339□342: Check if variable`temp` contains "none", and if it does, transfer control back to the loop condition.

- Lines 343□346: Ifvariable `temp` contains "to", the string "(Requested)" is appended to `str`.

- Lines 347□350: Ifthe variable `temp` contains "from", the string "(Requesting)" is appended to `str`.

- Line 352: Sets `str` as a child tree node.

- Line 354: Gets the enumeration from the "OFFLINE" tree node into the variable `m_TempTreeChildren`.

- Lines 355□357: Initializes variables.

- Line 358: Runs a `while` loop that checks if the Enumeration `m_TempTreeChildren` contains more elements.

- Line 360: Retrieves the next element in `m_TempTreeChildren` to the string, `tempStr`.

- Lines 361□365: If the string given by`tempStr` exists in variable `str`, the boolean `found` is set to `true`, and the program control exits the `while` loop.

- Lines 366□367: If`tempStr` does not exist within `str`, the value of variable `index` is incremented.

- Lines 369□370: Ifboolean `found` is `true`, the program control returns to the `for` loop (Line 321).

- Line 371: Specifies `else` clause corresponding to `if` clause of line 369.

- Line 373: Retrieves enumeration elements from "ONLINE" tree node.

- Line 374: Sets variable `index` to 0.

- Line 375: Contains the controlling `while` condition that checks if the last element in `m_TempTreeChildren` is reached.

- Line 377: Retrieves the next element in `m_TempTreeChildren` to `tempStr`.

- Lines 378□383: If`tempStr` contains the string given by the variable `str`, boolean `found` is set to `true`, and the `while` loop of Line 375 is exit.

- Line 383: `Else` clause of the `if` statement in line 378 that increments variable `index`.

- Lines 386□387: Ifthe boolean `found` is `true`, program control returns to the `for` loop (Line 321).

- Lines 388□393:`Else` clause that adds the child tree node to the "OFFLINE" friends' node and reloads the tree-model.

- Lines 396□398:Cause the tree nodes to expandfully displaying each child node, by default any addition to the treecontracts the nodes.

- Lines 399□403:`Catch` block for `try` of Line 253 that prints the `Exception` and prints the stack-trace to the console. The stack trace traces back the `Exception` to its point of occurrence.

- Line 404: Resets the cursor to the default cursor style.

- Line 410: Declares the `actionPerformed()` method.

- Lines 413□419: If 'Add Gateway" menu item is clicked, the constructor of `AddGateway` class is called (Line 417), and the `AddGateway` GUI window is shown on screen.

- Lines 420□423: If the "Add Friend" button is clicked, the `AddFriend` class constructor is called.

- Lines 424□427: If the "Message" button is clicked, the `showMessageWindow()` method of `MainScreen` class is called.

- Lines 428□431: If the "Send An Instant Message" menu item within the pop-up menu is chosen, `showMessageWindow()` method is called.

- Lines 432□435: If the "Delete Contact" item is selected from the pop-up menu, `deleteFriend()` method of `MainScreen` class is called.

- Lines 436□439: If the "Delete" button is pressed, `deleteFriend()` method is called.

- Lines 440□443: If the "Add Friend" item in "Friends" menu is clicked, the constructor of class `AddFriend` is called.

- Lines 444□447: If the "About" item is selected from the "Help" menu, the constructor of class `About` is called.

- Lines 449□452: If 'Send A Message" item is chosen from the "Message" menu, `showMessageWindow()` method is called.

- Lines 453□456: If the "Delete Friends" item is selected from the "Friends" menu, `deleteFriend()` method is called.

- Lines 457□468: If the "Unregister" item is chosen from the "Login" menu, the method `unregisterUser()` of `MainScreen` class is called, and the `Exception` is printed if the user cannot be unregistered.

- Lines 469□482: If the "Sign Out of Messenger" item is chosen from the "Login" menu, the method `logoutUser()` of `MainScreen` class is called.

- Lines 484□489: Declare the methods that are implemented by the `MouseListener` and `ChangeListener` interfaces but are not being used by `MainScreen` class. Since a class implementing an interface is obliged to define all methods of that interface, these methods are being defined. (The other option is to use adapter classes.)

- Line 491: Declares the `mouseclicked()` method that takes a mouse event as parameter.

- Lines 493□494: Retrieve the x and y coordinates of mouse position in variables x and y, respectively.

- Lines 495: Sets the boolean `eventInTree` to `false`.

- Lines 497: Checks if the mouse event is a double-click of the mouse.

- Lines 501: Retrieves the object of mouse event from the Tree, that is, the friend list.
- Line 502: Sets `eventInTree` to `true`.
- Lines 504□508: Contain the `catch` block that is executed if the mouse is double-clicked outside the tree-region. The error message "Exception Occurred: Outside Tree Region" is printed, and the boolean `eventInTree` is set to `false`.
- Line 509-511: If the mouse left key was pressed in the tree region then initialize the variable `result` to 0.
- Line 512: Retrieves the row in the `m_friendsOnline` tree that has been clicked.
- Line 513: Checks whether the variable `clickedRow` is equal to □1 ornot, which means a row within the tree structure is clicked.
- Line 515: Retrieves the path of the row that has been clicked. The path specifies if the row is a parent node, a parent-child node, or a parent-child-child node. Notice that "Friends for Username" is the parent node. "ONLINE" and "OFFLINE" are the parent-child nodes and the names of the friends are the parent-child-child nodes.
- Line 516: Retrieves the node that is the last in the path. For example, if a user clicks on the row "Friends for Username", then the row in itself will be the last row; if "ONLINE' is clicked, "OFFLINE" will be the last node. For example, if the user has 3 friends A, B, and C online and he/she clicks on A, then C will be the last node and so on.
- Lines 518□519:Check if the parent of the clicked row is `null` and set `result` to □2.
- Lines 520□521: Set`result` to □2 f the "ON-LINE" or "OFF-LINE" node is clicked.
- Lines 522□523: Set the value of`result` to □2 if the parent of the clicked node is "OFF-LINE", that is, an offline friend's name has been clicked.
- Lines 524□525: Call`CheckBeforeOpening()` method and assign its result value to the variable `result`, if none of the previous `if` clauses (Lines 518, 520, or 522) succeed. This means the user has clicked the name of an online friend.
- Lines 526□533: Define action to be taken if `CheckBeforeOpening()` method returns the value □1. (Remember from previous discussions that this value indicates that an Instant Message window for the friend whose name has been clicked does not exist.)
  - Line 529: Calls the class `Message`.
  - Lines 530: Opens a new Instant Message window.
  - Line 531: Adds the name of the friend as the next element of the vector `ListOfMessageWindowsByName`.
  - Line 532: Adds the window object of Line 529 to the vector `ListOfMessageWindowsByObject`.
- Lines 534□540: If`CheckBeforeOpening()` does not return the value □2, meaning an Instant Message window for the friend already exists, that window is retrieved by using

the index returned by the CheckBeforeOpening() method (this index is stored in variable result).

- Lines 537☐538: Bring the said messagewindow to the front and show it on the screen.

- Lines 543: Checks for mouse event modifiers, that is, if the mouse has been left-clicked, but only once, not double-clicked. If the user single-clicks a user name, the if condition of this line will be true. BUTTON1_MASK is a predefined variable signifying a single-click.

- Lines 544☐545: Obtain the x and y coordinates ofthe mouse when a friend's name is single-clicked.

- Lines 548: Checks if the mouse has been right-clicked. BUTTON3_MASK is another predefined variable of class InputEvent that signifies a right-click of the mouse.

- Lines 550☐551:Retrieve the x and y coordinates of the mouse when it is right-clicked.

- Lines 553: Retrieves the row in the tree that has been right-clicked.

- Lines 554: Checks that the row returned is not ☐1, meaning the row is not withinthe tree structure.

- Lines 556: Retrieves the path of the row. (See Line 515 for details.)

- Lines 557: Retrieves the node that forms the last component of the path. (See Line 516 for details.)

- Lines 559☐560: Initialize the stringvariable str and the integer result.

- Lines 562: This if clause checks to see if the parent of the node is null (meaning the parent node itself has been right☐clicked) or if the node is the "OFF-LINE" node or the "ON-LINE" node.

- Line 564: Sets the value of variable result to ☐1 f the if condition of Line 562 is satisfied.

- Line 568: Sets the variable result to 0 if the if clause of Line 562 is not satisfied.

- Line 571☐579: Define actions to be taken ifresult variable has the value 0.

  - Lines 573☐574: Ifthe parent node of the node clicked by user is "OFF-LINE", the pop-menu item "Send An Instant Message" named m_PopMenuItem is disabled.

  - Lines 575☐576: Ifthe parent node is not "OFF-LINE", i.e., it is "ON-LINE", m_PopMenuItem is enabled.

  - Line 578: Shows the pop-up menu at the position where the mouse is clicked.

- Line 587: Declares the run() method.

- Lines 589☐591: Beginan infinite while loop within a try block.

- Lines 593☐596: Contain variable declaration/initialization.

- Line 598: Begins a while loop to read the Data from the Server.

- Line 600: Reads the stream from the server one byte at a time.

- Lines 601☐602: Exit thewhile loop of Line 598 if no byte to be read is available from the server.

- Lines 603☐604: Assignthe byte read from server to variable `str` and append this to the variable `FinalString`.

- Line 605: Sets the value of `loop` variable to check if the stream from the Server is available.

- Lines 606☐607: Exit thewhile loop of Line 598 (equivalent to stop-reading from server) if the string `</InstantMessenger>` exists within the variable `FinalString`. Notice that this is the closing XML tag that indicates completion of an XML response from the server.

- Line 609: Removes trailing/leading spaces from the variable `FinalString`.

- Line 611: Retrieves the `FinalString` variable's value into a byte array, `tempbytes`.

- Lines 612☐613: Ifthe length of the response is 0, the program control goes back to Line 591 to read from the server.

- Line 614: If the length of `tempbytes` (the response from server) is not 0, an output stream is opened to write to the file "response.xml".

- Line 615: Writes the server's response in variable `tempbytes` to the "response.xml" file.

- Line 616: Closes the file output stream.

- Line 619: Creates a new string variable named `ReturnVal`.

- Line 621: Calls the `perform()` method of `SParser` class (`Parser` is the object of `SParser` class) to parse the "response.xml" file.

- Line 622: Retrieves the return value from class `SParser` into the variable `ReturnVal`.

- Line 625: Checks to see if the `SParser` returns a request type 5. The value 5 denotes a friend list.

- Line 627: Variable declaration/initialization.

- Line 628: Splits the string variable `ReturnVal` using the character "~" as a delimiter.

- Lines 629☐632: Declare the variables to hold values fromXML tags.

- Line 633: Retrieves the next value from the string tokenizer.

- Lines 635☐639: Addthe Friend Name and his/her status to respective vectors, while the `StringTokenizer` variable `tokens` contains more values.

- Lines 641☐644: Set the value of uservariables.

- Line 645: Sts the cursor to a wait-cursor.

- Line 646: Adds the friend list to the tree. The argument 0 denotes the local friend list.

- Line: 647: Sets the cursor to the default cursor.
- Line 649: Sets the image-icon "pink-ball.gif" for the label m_Connection Status.
- Line 650: Sets the text "Connected" for the label m_Connection Status.
- Line 654: Checks whether the SParser class has returned the value 3 that stands for a message request.
- Lines 656☐659: Variable declarations/initialization.
- Line 661: Puts the value returned by the SParser class with variable ReturnVal.
- Line 664: Splits the ReturnVal using "~" as delimiter.
- Lines 666☐668: Assignthe next three values in the string tokenizer tokens to the three variables: receiver, sender, and userMessage, respectively.
- Line 671: Calls the CheckBeforeOpening() method to see if Instant Message window corresponding to the friend already exists.
- Lines 672☐694: Contain actionsto be performed if CheckBeforeOpening() returns the value ☐1.
  - Line 674: Creates a new message window by calling the Message class.
  - Line 675: Displays the Instant Message window on the client screen.
  - Lines 676☐677: Addsthe friend's name and window object to their respective vectors.
  - Line 680: Calls the Style class to get the color for the sender's name.
  - Line 683: Appends the friend's name (sender) to the Instant Message window using the color of Line 680.
  - Line 685: Retrieves the color for messages received.
  - Line 687: Appends the message received using the color of Line 685.
  - Lines 689☐692:Catch block that catches an Exception if the message cannot be appended to the Instant Message window.
- Lines 695☐714: Specifythe else clause for if statement of Line 672.
  - Line 697: The Instant Message window is retrieved using the index returned by CheckBeforeOpening() method.
  - Lins 698☐699: Brings the windowto the front and shows it.
  - Line 701: Retrieves color for sender's name.
  - Line 704: Appends the sender's name to the message window.
  - Line 706: Retrieves the color for messages received.
  - Line 708: Appends the message received to the Instant Message window.
  - Line 710☐713: Catch anyException that may occur if the message cannot be appended to the window.

- Line 716: Checks if SParser returns the type as value 6, meaning a notify-friends request.

- Lines 719□728: Variable declarations.

- Line 731: Sets the variable m_ReturnVal by the values returned by the method value Return(). This method returns string containing the data within XML value tags.

- Line 733: Splits m_ReturnVal using the delimiter "~". Various tokens/values in m_token now belong to different XML value tags.

- Lines 735□736: Assignthe next two tokens to the variables m_FriendName and m_status. Notice that since each XML request/response has a fixed structure, once a request type is known, the order in which XML elements appear is also known, and the token values can be correctly assigned to variables meant to contain values from respective XML tags.

- Lines 739□743:If the string in m_status is "SUBSCRIBE", a call to the constructor of AcceptFriend class is made and the corresponding dialog box is displayed.

- Lines 744□748: Ifthe string m_status contains "UNSUBSCRIBE", the constructor of class UnsubscribeFriend is called and the corresponding dialog box is displayed.

- Lines 749□853: Ifm_status is neither of the above, it is treated as a notification of friend's status response.

  - Lines 751□753: Create a dialog box,set its title to "Friend", and set its size.

  - Line 754: Sets the elements of the dialog box to absolute positioning.]

  - Line 755: Obtain an object of class GraphicsConfiguration to get the screen coordinates .

  - Line 756: Retrieves the bounds for the dialog box.

  - Line 757: Sets the location of the dialog box.

  - Line 759: Sets the value of variable tempName with the name of the friend.

  - Line 760: Assigns to variable indexP the index of character "%" in Friend's name.

  - Lines 761□764: If"%" is contained within tempName, the substring up to the index of "%" is taken into the variable tempName.

  - Line 765□769: Create a new label whose text contains the friend's name, set its font, set its bounds, set its text color, and add it to the dialog box.

  - Lines 771□775:Create a label "is", set its font, set its bounds, set its text color, and add it to the dialog box.

  - Lines 777□781:Create a label whose text contains the status of the friend, set its font, set its bounds, set its text color, and add it to the dialog box.

  - Line 782: Sets the Visible property of the dialog box to true.

- Lines 784□812: Check ifthe friend's status is "OFF-LINE", create a tree node with the friend's name, and check if the friend name already exists within the "OFF-LINE" node. If it doesn't, that is, if the friend was previously in the "ON-LINE" list, he/she is removed from "ONLINE" and added to "OFF-LINE". A `for` loop is run through the length of the friend list to expand the tree (Lines 810-811).

- Lines: 813□841: If friend's statusis "ON-LINE", these lines create a tree-node with the friend's name and check if the name exists in "ON-LINE" friends; if not, it is removed from "OFF-LINE" list and added to the "ON-LINE" list. A `for` loop is run through the length of the friend list to expand the tree (Lines 839□840).

- Lines 843□850:Calls the `sleep()` method for 5 seconds and catches an `Exception` if it occurs. This is to ensure that the notification is visible for 5 seconds.

- Line 852: The dialog box is removed by setting its `Visible` property to false.

- Line 855: Checks if `SParser` class returns 7, meaning roster or Jabber friend list.

- Line 857□858: Split theReturnVal variable using the character "~" as delimiter.

- Lines 860□861: Create two new vectors.

- Lines 863□872: Run awhile loop as long as tokens exist in the `StringTokenizer` variable tokens.

  - Line 865□866: The next two tokens are added to the VectorsJabberFriendID and JabberFriendSubscription.

  - Line 868: The cursor is converted to a wait-cursor while the roster is added to the friend's tree structure

  - Line 869: Increments addToTreeRoster. This contains the number of times the roster is being updated. When the roster is added for the first time, this value is 1.

  - Line 870: Calls AddToTree(), passing the addToTreeRoster as an argument.

  - Line 871: The cursor is set to default cursor.

- Line 873: Checks if `SParser` has returned the value 8, which means FRIENDSTATUS response.

- Lines 875□876: Split theReturnVal and store the values in `StringTokenizer` variable tokens.

- Lines 877□878: Variable declarations/initializaton:

- Lines 880□881: Execute awhile loop till more tokens remain in variable tokens.

- Line 881: The next token value is put as the next element of val [ ] array.

- Lines 883□887: Ifthe last two elements in val [ ] array are 0 and 1, respectively, the value of the second element in val [ ] is used to create a tree node (Line 885). This node is added to the "ON-LINE" friends' node and the tree model is reloaded.

- Lines 888□889: The tree that gets contracted duringalterations is expanded by running a `for` loop that expands each row.

- Lines 892□900: Iflast two elements in `val[ ]` are both 0, the value of second element in `val[ ]` is converted to a tree-node and added to "OFF-LINE" friends node. The tree is reloaded, and each row expanded using a `for` loop.

- Lines 901□904: Ifthe third element in `val[ ]` array is 2, a message box is displayed that shows the message "FriendName Already Exists…" indicating that the friend has already been added to user's friend list.

- Line 906: Checks if `SParser` returns the value 9, which indicates a delete request.

- Lines 908□910: Variable declarations/initialization.

- Line 911: Splits the string `ReturnVal` using "~" as delimiter.

- Lines 912□913: Intialize the integeri to 0 and declare `val[ ]` as an array of 3 string elements.

- Line 915: Decalres a `while` loop that checks if the string tokenizer has more values/tokens.

- Line 916: Retrieves the token value in the `val[ ]` array as the next element.

- Lines 918□933: Ifthe third value in `val[ ]` array is 0, the enumeration from the "OFF-LINE" list is obtained. Each enumeration element is retrieved in the string `str` (Line 925), and it is checked if the value given in `str` exists in the second element of `val[ ]` array (Line 926). If `str` exists in `val[1]` value, `found` is set to `true` and the loop of Line 923 is exit; otherwise, the value of variable `index` is incremented.

- Lines 935□939: Ifthe boolean `found` is `true`, meaning the friend's name (`val[1]`) was found in the "OFF-LINE" list, the corresponding index is removed and the tree-model is reloaded.

- Lines 940□960: The sameprocess from Line 923□939is repeated, this time with enumeration elements from the "ON-LINE" friends node.

- Lines 962□963: The tree rowsare expanded one by one after the friend's index has been deleted.

- Line 966: Shows the message "Friend Friendname Removed Successfully…".

- Line 969: Checks if the value 11 is returned by `SParser`, that is, for an Add Gateway request.

- Lines 971□972: The constructor ofclass `AddGateway` is called and its GUI window is displayed.

- Lines 974□979:Close the input and output stream from and to the server and exit the program if `SParser` returns the value 10, which is for an unregister request.

- Lines 982□986: Contain the catch block corresponding to try of line 589 that catches an Exception in the run() method, traces back the Exception to its occurrence, and prints the trace to the console.
- Lines 991□1004: These lines define the CheckBeforeOpening() method.
  - Lines 993□1002: A for loop is run for the entire length of the vector ListOfMessageWindowsByName to check if any element matches the value toUser passed to the method. If the user name is found, the corresponding index is returned (Line 1000).
  - Line 1003: The value □1 is returned if the name is not found in ListOfMessageWindowsByName.
- Lines 1008□1022: Define the logoutUser() method.
  - Lines 1010□1014: Variable declaration/initialization.
  - Line 1016: Calls the XMLCreator class to form a "QUIT" request.
  - Line 1017: The return value of XMLCreator is retrieved in variable RequestGenerated.
  - Line 1019: The request is written to the server.
  - Line 1020: The request data is committed using the flush() method.
- Line 1026: This line declares the showMessageWindow() method.
- Line 1028: Initializes the variable result to □11.
- Line 1029: Obtains the row in the friend list's tree structure the user has clicked.
- Line 1031: Checks if the row number returned in Line 1029 is greater than 0.
- Lines 1033□1034: Obtain the path for the clicked row and the node that forms the last component in this path.
- Lines 1036□1040: If the parent of the last component node, retrieved in line 1034 (that is also the parent for the clicked row), is the "OFF-LINE" friend's node, the variable result is set to □2 and a message box is displayed with the message, "Cannot Send Message to an OFF□Line User".
- Lines 1041□1044: Specify the else if clause for the if statement in line 1036. If the last component node is "ON-LINE" or "OFF-LINE" friend's node, the variable result is set to □2.
- Lines 1045□1046: Specify the else clause; if neither of the conditions in Line 1036 and Line 1041 are satisfied, meaning the name of a friend has been clicked, the return value from the method CheckBeforeOpening() is assigned to the variable result.
- Lines 1048□1060: Specify what actions are to be taken depending upon the value returned by CheckBeforeOpening() method.

- Lines 1048□1054: If the value returned is □1, a new Instant Message window is opened by calling the constructor of `Message` class (Line 1050). Also the friend's name is added to the `ListOfMessageWindowsByName`, and the window object of Line 1050 is added to the vector `ListOfMessageWindowsByObject`.

- Line 1055□1060: Ifthe return value is □2, the Instant Message window, given by`msg` (Line 1057), that already exists for the friend is retrieved using the returned index, and that message window is brought to the front of the screen.

- Line 1067: Declares the method `deletefriend()`.

- Line 1069: Intializes variable `result` to □11.

- Line 1070: Obtains the row that has been clicked.

- Line 1072: Checks if index of the returned row is greater than 0.

- Lines 1074□1075: Obtain the path to the row clicked and the last component node in that path.

- Lines 1077□1080: Set result to □2f the clicked node is "ON-LINE" or "OFF-LINE" friends' node.

- 1081□1108: Specifythe `else` clause for `if` statement of Line 1077.

  - Lines 1083□1085:Declare a new string array `values[ ]` and set the user name and the friend's node as the two values at its first two indices.

  - Line 1086: Puts in variable `indexCheck` the index of the occurrence of character "(" in the node value.

  - Lines 1087□1090:Truncate the value of second element in `values[ ]` array to the substring from index 0 to the index returned in the variable `indexCheck`.

  - Lines 1092□1093: Declare an object of`XMLCreator` class and a byte array, `RequestGenerated`.

  - Lines 1095□1096:Call the `XMLCreator` class to form a Delete Friend request and retrieve the result value from `XMLCreator` to the variable `RequestGenerated`.

  - Lines 1098□1102: Write the request XML created by`XMLCreator` to the server.

  - Lines 1103□1106: Catch the`Exception` thrown by the `try` of line 1098, if the stream to the server cannot be written.

- Line 1113: Declares the `unregisterUser()` method.

- Lines 1115□1116: Declare the string`array` `values` and assign the user name to the first value in it.

- Lines 118□1119: Callthe class `XMLCreator` to form an UNREGISTER request and retrieve its return value in the variable `RequestGenerated`.

- Lines 1124□1125: Write the request to the server.

Message class

The flow chart of `Message` class is presented in Figure 5-15. Listing 5-7 contains the code for this class, followed by a detailed description of the code.

Figure 5-15: Technical flow chart for the Message class

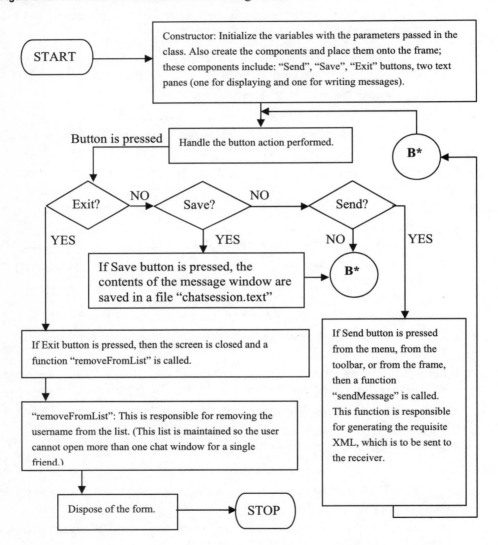

Listing 5-7: Message.java

```
1.  import javax.swing.*;
2.  import javax.swing.event.*;
3.  import java.awt.*;
4.  import java.awt.event.*;
5.  import java.net.*;
6.  import java.io.*;
7.  import java.util.*;
8.  import javax.swing.text.*;
9.
10.   /******** Class Declaration *********/
11.
12.   public class Message extends JFrame        implements
ActionListener, KeyListener
13.   {
14.
15.   DefaultStyledDocument            m_Document;
16.   Style                           m_Style;
17.   StyleContext                    m_StyleContext;
18.   Hashtable                       m_Attributes;
19.
20.   JLabel                          m_CompanyLogo;
21.
22.   JLabel                          m_Client;
23.
24.   JTextPane                       m_DisplayMessage;
25.   JScrollPane                     m_DisplayScroll;
26.
27.   JTextPane                       m_WriteMessage;
28.   JScrollPane                     m_WriteScroll;
29.
30.   JButton                         m_Send;
31.
32.   JMenuBar                        m_menuBar;
33.   JSeparator                      m_Separator;
34.
35.
36.   JMenu                           m_File;
37.   JMenuItem                       m_MenuSend;
38.   JMenuItem                       m_Save;
39.   JMenuItem                       m_MenuClose;
40.
41.   JMenu                           m_View;
42.   JMenuItem                       m_TextSize;
43.   JMenuItem                       m_BKColor;
44.
```

```
45.    JMenu                          m_Help;
46.    JMenuItem                      m_About;
47.
48.    JToolBar                       m_ToolBar;
49.    JButton                        m_ToolSend;
50.    JButton                        m_ToolClose;
51.    JButton                        m_ToolHelp;
52.
53.    Color                          m_messageSendColor;
54.    Color                          m_messageReceivedColor;
55.
56.    Color                          m_SenderColor;
57.    Color                          m_ReceiverColor;
58.
59.    boolean                        m_enterKeyPressed     = false;
60.
61.    Component                      m_Strut;
62.    Container                      m_Container;
63.
64.    String fromUser                = new String();
65.    String toUser                  = new String();
66.    MainScreen                     userScreen;
67.    BufferedOutputStream           StreamToServer;
68.    FileOutputStream               sessionFile;
69.
70.
71.
72.    /**********   Constructor **************/
73.
74.    Message(String fromUser, String toUser, MainScreen userScreen,
BufferedOutputStream StreamToServer)
75.    {
76.
77.    super("Instant Message.");
78.
79.    setSize(300, 500);
80.    setResizable(false);
81.
82.    this.fromUser       = fromUser;
83.    this.toUser         = toUser;
84.    this.userScreen     = userScreen;
85.    this.StreamToServer = StreamToServer;
86.
87.    m_Container    =      getContentPane();
88.    m_Container.setLayout(null);
89.
90.    m_messageSendColor          = new Color(0, 0, 0);
91.    m_messageReceivedColor      = new Color(0, 0, 0);
92.
```

```
93.   m_SenderColor                = new Color(0, 0, 255);
94.   m_ReceiverColor              = new Color(255, 0, 0);
95.
96.   m_menuBar                    = new JMenuBar() ;
97.
98.   m_File                       = new JMenu("File");
99.
100.  m_MenuSend                   = new JMenuItem("Send");
101.  m_MenuSend.addActionListener(this);
102.  m_MenuSend.setEnabled(false);
103.  m_File.add(m_MenuSend);
104.
105.  m_Separator        = new JSeparator() ;
106.  m_File.add(m_Separator);
107.
108.  m_Save                       = new JMenuItem("Save");
109.  m_Save.addActionListener(this);
110.  m_File.add(m_Save);
111.
112.  m_Separator        = new JSeparator() ;
113.  m_File.add(m_Separator);
114.
115.  m_MenuClose                  = new JMenuItem("Close");
116.  m_MenuClose.addActionListener(this);
117.  m_File.add(m_MenuClose);
118.
119.  m_View                       = new JMenu("View");
120.
121.  m_TextSize         = new JMenuItem("TextSize");
122.  m_TextSize.addActionListener(this);
123.  m_View.add(m_TextSize);
124.
125.  m_Separator        = new JSeparator() ;
126.  m_View.add(m_Separator);
127.
128.  m_BKColor          = new JMenuItem("Color");
129.  m_BKColor.addActionListener(this);
130.  m_View.add(m_BKColor);
131.
132.  m_Help                       = new JMenu("Help");
133.
134.  m_About                      = new JMenuItem("About");
135.  m_About.addActionListener(this);
136.  m_Help.add(m_About);
137.
138.  m_menuBar.add(m_File);
139.  m_menuBar.add(m_View);
140.  m_menuBar.add(m_Help);
141.
```

```
142.    setJMenuBar(m_menuBar);
143.
144.    m_ToolBar            = new JToolBar();
145.
146.    m_ToolBar.setFloatable(false);
147.
148.    m_ToolSend           = new JButton(new ImageIcon("SEND.jpeg"));
149.    m_ToolSend.setEnabled(false);
150.    m_ToolClose          = new JButton(new ImageIcon("EXIT.jpeg"));
151.    m_ToolHelp           = new JButton(new ImageIcon("HELP.jpeg"));
152.
153.    m_ToolSend.setToolTipText("Send Message");
154.    m_ToolClose.setToolTipText("Close Message Window..");
155.    m_ToolHelp.setToolTipText("About..");
156.
157.    m_ToolSend.addActionListener(this);
158.    m_ToolClose.addActionListener(this);
159.    m_ToolHelp.addActionListener(this);
160.
161.    m_ToolBar.add(m_ToolSend);
162.    m_ToolBar.addSeparator();
163.    m_ToolBar.add(m_ToolHelp);
164.    m_ToolBar.addSeparator();
165.    m_ToolBar.add(m_ToolClose);
166.
167.    m_ToolBar.setBounds(0, 0, 200, 50);
168.
169.    m_Container.add(m_ToolBar);
170.
171.    m_Client             = new JLabel("To:        "+toUser);
172.    m_Client.setForeground(Color.blue);
173.    m_Client.setBounds(5, 45, 130, 25);
174.    m_Container.add(m_Client);
175.
176.    m_StyleContext            = new StyleContext();
177.    m_Document                = new
DefaultStyledDocument(m_StyleContext);
178.    m_Attributes        = new Hashtable();
179.
180.    addStyle();
181.
182.    m_DisplayMessage    = new JTextPane(m_Document);
183.    m_DisplayScroll     = new JScrollPane(m_DisplayMessage);
184.    m_DisplayScroll.setBounds(3, 68, 289, 285);
185.    m_Container.add(m_DisplayScroll);
186.    m_DisplayMessage.setEditable(false);
187.
188.    m_WriteMessage            = new JTextPane();
189.    m_WriteMessage.addKeyListener(this);
```

```
190.   m_WriteScroll              = new JScrollPane(m_WriteMessage);
191.   m_WriteScroll.setBounds(3, 363, 215, 75);
192.   m_Container.add(m_WriteScroll);
193.
194.   m_Send                           = new JButton("Send");
195.   m_Send.setMnemonic('S');
196.   m_Send.setFont(new Font("sansSerif", Font.BOLD, 12));
197.   m_Send.setForeground(Color.blue);
198.   m_Send.setBounds(225, 363, 65, 75);
199.   m_Send.setEnabled(false);
200.   m_Send.addActionListener(this);
201.   m_Container.add(m_Send);
202.
203.
204.   addWindowListener (new java.awt.event.WindowAdapter () {
205.   public void windowClosing (java.awt.event.WindowEvent evt) {
206.    // Remove from the List....
207.    dispose();
208.    removeFromList();
209.   }
210.   }
211.   );
212.   }// End Constructor....
213.
214.   /********** removeFromList  ***************/
215.
216.   void removeFromList()
217.   {
218.   String str = new String();
219.   for (int i = 0;i<userScreen.ListOfMessageWindowsByName.size();i++
)
220.   {
221.   str =
(String)userScreen.ListOfMessageWindowsByName.elementAt(i);
222.   if (str.equalsIgnoreCase(toUser))
223.   {
224.    userScreen.ListOfMessageWindowsByName.removeElementAt(i);
225.    userScreen.ListOfMessageWindowsByObject.removeElementAt(i);
226.   }
227.   }
228.   }
229.
230.   /******** actionPerformed  **************/
231.
232.   public void actionPerformed(ActionEvent ae)
233.   {
234.
235.    if (ae.getSource() == m_Send)
236.    {
```

```
237.          sendMessage();
238.      }
239.      else if (ae.getSource() == m_MenuSend)
240.      {
241.          sendMessage();
242.      }
243.      else if (ae.getSource() == m_ToolSend)
244.      {
245.          sendMessage();
246.      }
247.      else if (ae.getSource() == m_MenuClose)
248.      {
249.          dispose();
250.          removeFromList();
251.      }
252.      else if (ae.getSource() == m_ToolClose)
253.      {
254.          dispose();
255.          removeFromList();
256.      }
257.      else if (ae.getSource() == m_Save)
258.      {
259.          try
260.          {
261.              sessionFile = new FileOutputStream("ChatSession.txt");
262.          }
263.          catch (Exception e)
264.          {
265.            System.out.println("Exception occured:"+e);
266.          }
267.
268.          String text    = m_DisplayMessage.getText();
269.          byte    [] textBytes = text.getBytes();
270.          try
271.          {
272.            sessionFile.write(textBytes, 0, textBytes.length);
273.          }
274.          catch (Exception e)
275.          {
276.            System.out.println("Exception occured:"+e);
277.          }
278.
279.          try
280.          {
281.            sessionFile.close();
282.          }
283.          catch (Exception e)
284.          {
285.            System.out.println("Exception occured:"+e);
```

```
286.         }
287.    }
288.    else if (ae.getSource() == m_TextSize)
289.    {
290.    }
291.    else if (ae.getSource() == m_BKColor)
292.    {
293.      ColorPreference colorPreference = new ColorPreference(this,
"Color Preferences", true);
294.      colorPreference.show();
295.      addStyle();
296.    }
297.    else if (ae.getSource() == m_About)
298.    {
299.      About aboutDialog = new About(this,"About -- Instant Message",
true);
300.      aboutDialog.show();
301.    }
302.    else if (ae.getSource() == m_ToolHelp)
303.    {
304.      About aboutDialog = new About(this,"About -- Instant Message",
true);
305.      aboutDialog.show();
306.    }
307.
308.    }// End ActionListener...
309.
310.    /********** sendMessage ***************/
311.
312.    void sendMessage()
313.    {
314.    String       str    = m_WriteMessage.getText();
315.
316.    if (str.indexOf("\n") == -1)
317.      str = str + "\n";
318.    m_WriteMessage.setText("");
319.
320.    Style m_TempStyle    = (Style) m_Attributes.get("sender");
321.    try
322.    {
323.      m_Document.insertString(m_Document.getLength(), fromUser+" :\n",
m_TempStyle);
324.
325.      m_TempStyle        = (Style) m_Attributes.get("senderMessage");
326.
327.      m_Document.insertString(m_Document.getLength(), str+"\n",
m_TempStyle);
328.    }
329.    catch (Exception e)
```

```
330.  {
331.     System.out.println("Exception occured:"+e);
332.  }
333.
334.  m_Send.setEnabled(false);
335.  m_ToolSend.setEnabled(false);
336.  m_MenuSend.setEnabled(false);
337.
338.  String [] values = new String[3];
339.
340.  values[0] = toUser;
341.  values[1] = fromUser;
342.  values[2] = str;
343.
344.  XMLCreator   createRequest;
345.  byte  []        RequestGenerated;
346.
347.  createRequest        = new XMLCreator("MSG", values);
348.  RequestGenerated     = createRequest.returnResult();
349.
350.  try
351.  {
352.     StreamToServer.write(RequestGenerated, 0,
RequestGenerated.length);
353.     StreamToServer.flush();
354.  }
355.  catch(Exception ef)
356.  {
357.     System.out.println("Exception in Message.java"+ef);
358.  }
359.  }
360.
361.  /********** Key listener ******************/
362.
363.  public void keyTyped(KeyEvent ke)
364.  {
365.  m_Send.setEnabled(true);
366.  m_ToolSend.setEnabled(true);
367.  m_MenuSend.setEnabled(true);
368.  }
369.  public void keyPressed(KeyEvent ke){}
370.  public void keyReleased(KeyEvent ke)
371.  {
372.  if (ke.getKeyCode() == KeyEvent.VK_ENTER)
373.  {
374.  sendMessage();
375.  m_WriteMessage.setText("");
376.  m_Send.setEnabled(false);
377.  m_ToolSend.setEnabled(false);
```

```
378.    m_MenuSend.setEnabled(false);
379.    }
380.    }
381.
382.    /********** addStyle   ******************/
383.    void addStyle()
384.    {
385.    m_Style                     = m_StyleContext.addStyle(null,
null);
386.    StyleConstants.setBold(m_Style, true);
387.    StyleConstants.setForeground(m_Style, m_SenderColor);
388.    m_Attributes.put("sender", m_Style);
389.
390.    m_Style                     = m_StyleContext.addStyle(null,
null);
391.    StyleConstants.setBold(m_Style, true);
392.    StyleConstants.setForeground(m_Style, m_messageSendColor);
393.    m_Attributes.put("senderMessage", m_Style);
394.
395.    m_Style                     = m_StyleContext.addStyle(null,
null);
396.    StyleConstants.setBold(m_Style, true);
397.    StyleConstants.setForeground(m_Style, m_ReceiverColor);
398.    m_Attributes.put("receiver", m_Style);
399.
400.    m_Style                     = m_StyleContext.addStyle(null,
null);
401.    StyleConstants.setBold(m_Style, true);
402.    StyleConstants.setForeground(m_Style, m_messageReceivedColor);
403.    m_Attributes.put("receiverMessage", m_Style);
404.    }
405.    } //   End Message..
```

- Lines 1□8: Contain the Java import statements.
- Lines 12□68:Contain the class and variable declarations.
- Line 74: Declares the default constructor.
- Line 77: Calls the constructor of the superclass (JFrame) to set the title of the window to "Instant Message."
- Lines 79□80: Set the size of the message window (width x height) in pixels and set the window's Resizable property to false.
- Lines 82□85:Set the class variables with values received as arguments in the constructor.
- Lines 87□88: Create the container/content paneand set it to absolute positioning by passing a null value to the setLayout() method.

- Lines 90□94: Set the default colors for the messages and user names. The messages sent and received are set to black color (Line 90□91), and the sender's (user's) nameappears in blue (Line 93); the name of the friend appears in red (Line 94).

- Line 96: Creates a menubar using the JMenubar class.

- Line 98: Creates a new menu named "File".

- Lines 100□103: Create a menuitem, "Send", add action listener to it, disable it by setting the Enabled property to false, and add this menu item to the "File" menu created in Line 98.

- Lines 105□106: Create a new separator that separates the "Send"menu item from the next item in the menu and add the separator to the menu "File". By default, this separator is a horizontal line.

- Lines 108□110: Create a secondmenu item "Save", add action listener to it, and add it to the "File" menu.

- Lines 112□113: Adda second separator after the "Save" menu item.

- Lines 115□117:Create a third menu item, "Close", add action listener to it, and add it to the "File" menu.

- Line 119: Creates the second menu, "View".

- Lines 121□123: Create a menu item,"TextSize", add action listener to it, and add the item to the "View" menu.

- Lines 125□126: Create a separator andadd it to the "View" menu.

- Lines 128□130:Create a second menu item, "Color", add the action listener to it, and add this item to the "View" menu.

- Line 132: Creates a third menu, "Help".

- Lines 134□136: Create a menuitem "About", add action listener to it, and add this item to the "Help" menu.

- Lines 138□142: Addthe three menus, "File", "View", and "About", to the menu bar and set the menu bar in the message window.

- Line 144: Creates a toolbar named m_ToolBar.

- Line 146: Sets the Floatable property of the toolbar to false, that is, it is not a floating pallette.

- Lines 148□149: Create animage button (an image that acts as a button) using the image "SEND.jpeg" and set its Enabled property to false.

- Lines 150□151: Create two moreimage buttons using the images "EXIT.jpeg" and "HELP.jpeg".

- Lines 153☐155: Set the tooltips for the three image buttons created in the previous lines, that is, when the mouse is over one of the buttons, the respective text set as the tool tip is displayed.

- Lines 157☐159:Add action listener to the three toolbar buttons created in Lines 148, 150, and 151.

- Line 161: Adds the "Send Message" button icon to the toolbar m_ToolBar.

- Line 162: Adds a separator to the toolbar.

- Line 163: Adds the "About" button icon to the toolbar.

- Line 164: Adds another separator to the toolbar.

- Line 165: Adds the "Close" button icon to the toolbar.

- Line 167: Boundsounds for the toolbar (x-coordinate, y-coordinate, width, height).

- Line 169: Adds the toolbar to the container.

- Lines 171☐174: Create a label,set its text color, set its bounds, and add it to the client.

- Lines 176☐178: Specifyvariable declarations.

- Line 180: Calls the addStyle() method.

- Line 182: Creates a text pane that displays the user's and his/her friend's messages.

- Line 183: Creates a scroll pane to which the text pane of Line 182 is added.

- Lines 184-185:Sets the bounds of the scrollbar on the visible area and adds the scrollbar on to the displayable container.

- Line 186: Sets the Editable property of the text pane to false.

- Line 188: Creates another text pane where messages (s) to be sent can be typed by the user.

- Line 189: Adds key listener to the text pane of Line 188.

- Line 190: Adds the message text pane of Line 188 to a scroll pane.

- Lines 191☐192: Set the bounds for the scroll paneand add it to the container.

- Line 194: Creates a new button labelled "Send".

- Line 195: Sets Alt+S as the keyboard shortcut equivalent to clicking the "Send" button.

- Lines 196☐198: Set the font, foregroundcolor, and bounds for the text pane.

- Line 199: Disables the "Send" button.

- Lines 200☐201: Addaction listener to "Send" button and add it to the container.

- Lines 204☐211: Implement the window listener that disposes ofthe message window when it is closed and calls the method removefromList().

- Line: 216: Declares the removeFromList() method.

- Line 218: Creates a new string.

- Lines 219□227: Run a for loop for the entire size of the vector `ListOfMessageWindowsByName` and check each element against the value of the variable `toUser` (Line 222). If a match is found, the entry at that index of the two vectors `ListOfMessageWindowsByName` and `ListOfMessageWindowsByObject` is removed.

- Line 232: Declares the `actionPerformed()` method.

- Lines 235□238: If the "Send" button is pressed, the method `sendMessage()` is called.

- Lines 239□242: If the "Send" item within the "File" menu is chosen, `sendMessage()` is called.

- Lines 243□246: If the Send image icon from the tool-bar is chosen, `sendMessage()` is called.

- Lines 247□256: If the "Close" item from the "File" menu is chosen (Line 247) or if the close image icon from the toolbar is chosen (Line 252), the message window is disposed of, and method `removeFromList()` is called.

- Lines 257□266: If the "Save" item under the "File" menu is chosen, a file output stream is opened to the file titled "ChatSession.txt"; and if the stream cannot be created, an `Exception` is caught (Line 263).

- Line 268: The text in the text-pane that displays all the chat messages is retrieved in the string `text`.

- Line 269: The text is then stored in the byte array `textBytes`.

- Lines 270□277: Try to write the bytes from `textBytes` to "ChatSession.txt" and catch an `Exception` if the write operation fails.

- Lines 279□285: Try to close the file output stream and catch an `Exception` if the close operation fails.

- Lines 291□296: If the "color" item under the "View" menu is chosen, the class `ColorPreference` is called, and then the method `addStyle()` is called to effect the change in color settings made by the user in `ColorPreference` class.

- Lines 297□306: If the menu item "About" under the "Help" menu is chosen (Line 297) or if the About image icon is pressed in the toolbar (Line 302), the `About` class constructor is called, and the corresponding dialog box is shown.

- Line 312: Declares the `sendMessage()` method.

- Line 314: Assigns the text from the message text pane (that is, the text written by the user) to the string `str`.

- Lines 316□317: Check for the line break character "\n" in the user message and, if it is not found, append this character to the variable `str`.

- Line 318: Clears the text from the `m_WriteMessage` pane.

- Line 320: Obtains the value of the attribute recognized as "sender". This retrieves the sender-color setting for the user.

- Line 323: Appends the user's name to the text pane containing all messages using the color settings of Line 320.

- Lines 325□327: Retrieves the colorset for displaying messages sent by the user and adds the user message to the display pane using this color.

- Lines 329□332: Catch an `Exception` if the message cannot be written to the display window.

- Lines 334□336: Disable the "Send" Button, disable the menu item for sending a message, and disable the tool-bar icon for sending a message.

- Lines 338□342: Create a string array, `values [ ]`, and assign the recipient's name, the sender's name, and the message as its three elements.

- Lines 344□345: Declare an object of `XMLCreator` and a byte array.

- Lines 347□348: Call the `XMLCreator` class to form a message request, and its return value(s) is stored in the `RequestGenerated` byte array.

- Lines 350□358: Write the XML request to the server and catch an `Exception` if the write operation fails.

- Line 363: Declares the `keyTyped()` method.

- Lines 365□367: Enable all the three options (button, tool icon, and menu item) to send a message.

- Line 369: This line recognizes an event when a key is pressed.

- Line 370: This line recognizes an event when a key is released.

- Line 372: Checks if the key released is the same as the `VK_ENTER` variable for the `KeyEvent` class (which signifies that the user has released the Enter key on the keyboard).

- Lines 374□378: If the clause in Line 372 is satisfied, the method `sendMessage()` is called, the text in the message text pane is set to blank, and the three send-message options are disabled.

- Line 383: Declares the `addStyle()` method.

- Line 385: Creates a `Style` object.

- Line 386: Sets the text in the `m_Style` object to bold.

- Line 387: Sets the color of text in `m_Style` object to `m_SenderColor`.

- Line 388: Specifies that `m_Style` will be recognized as the attribute "sender".

- Lines 390□393: Create another `Style` object and set its text to bold and its color to `m_messageSendColor`. This style is recognized by the "senderMessage" attribute (line 393).

- Lines 395□403: Create two morestyles with text color specified by m_ReceiverColorand m_messageReceived color. The two styles are recognized as "receiver" and "receiverMessage".

AddFriend class

The flow chart of AddFriend class is presented in Figure 5-16. Listing 5-8 contains the code for this class, followed by a detailed description of the code.

Figure 5-16: Technical flow chart for the AddFriend class

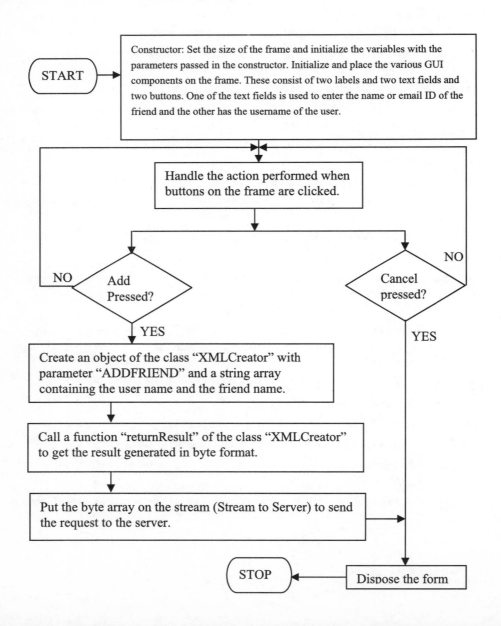

Listing 5-8: AddFriend.java

```
1.   import javax.swing.*;
2.   import javax.swing.event.*;
3.   import java.awt.*;
4.   import java.awt.event.*;
5.   import javax.swing.table.*;
6.   import java.io.*;
7.   import java.net.*;
8.   import java.util.*;
9.   import javax.swing.tree.*;
10.
11.  /*********** Class Declaration ************/
12.
13.  public class  AddFriend extends JDialog implements ActionListener
14.  {
15.
16.  JLabel                              m_EnterFriendName ;
17.  JTextField                          m_FriendName ;
18.
19.  JLabel                              m_EnterUserName ;
20.  JTextField                          m_UserName;
21.
22.  JButton                             m_AddFriend;
23.  JButton                             m_Cancel;
24.  String                              urlName;
25.
26.  String                              FriendName = new String();
27.  String                              userName = new String();
28.
29.  Container                           cont;
30.  MainScreen                          screen;
31.  BufferedOutputStream                StreamToServer;
32.
33.  /*********** Constructor ************/
34.
35.  AddFriend(MainScreen  screen, String userName )
36.  {
37.   setTitle("Add Friend --- Instant Messenger");
38.   setSize(250,150);
39.   setLocation(300,200);
40.   setVisible(true);
41.
42.   this.screen                    = screen;
43.   this.userName                  = userName;
44.   this.StreamToServer            = screen.StreamToServer;
45.
```

```
46.    cont = getContentPane();
47.    cont.setLayout(null);
48.
49.    addWindowListener( new WindowAdapter()
50.    { public void windowClosing(WindowEvent e)
51.      {
52.          dispose();
53.      }
54.    });
55.
56.    m_EnterFriendName  = new JLabel(" Friend ID ");
57.    m_EnterFriendName .setBounds(10, 5, 50, 10);
58.    cont.add(m_EnterFriendName );
59.
60.    m_FriendName  = new JTextField(30);
61.    m_FriendName .setBounds(80,5, 140, 20);
62.    cont.add(m_FriendName );
63.
64.    m_EnterUserName  = new JLabel(" User ID ");
65.    m_EnterUserName .setBounds(20,35, 50, 10);
66.    cont.add(m_EnterUserName );
67.
68.    m_UserName = new JTextField(30);
69.    m_UserName.setBounds(80,35, 140, 20);
70.    m_UserName.setText(userName);
71.    m_UserName.disable();
72.    cont.add(m_UserName);
73.
74.    m_AddFriend = new JButton("Ok");
75.    m_AddFriend.setBounds(20,60, 90, 20);
76.    m_AddFriend.addActionListener(this);
77.    cont.add(m_AddFriend);
78.
79.    m_Cancel = new JButton("Cancel");
80.    m_Cancel.setBounds(130, 60, 90, 20);
81.    m_Cancel.setFont(new Font("sansSerif", Font.PLAIN, 11));
82.    m_Cancel.addActionListener(this);
83.    cont.add(m_Cancel);
84.  }
85.
86.  public void actionPerformed(ActionEvent e)
87.  {
88.
89.   Object source = e.getSource();
90.
91.   if(source.equals(m_Cancel))
92.   {
93.    dispose();
94.   }    // end of if (source.equals(m_Cancel))
```

```
95.
96.    else if(source.equals(m_AddFriend))
97.    {
98.       XMLCreator createRequest;
99.       byte          []              RequestGenerated;
100.
101.      String[] values          = new String[2];
102.      values[0]                = userName;
103.      values[1]                = m_FriendName .getText();
104.      createRequest            = new XMLCreator("ADDFRIEND", values);
105.      RequestGenerated         = createRequest.returnResult();
106.      try
107.      {
108.          StreamToServer.write(RequestGenerated, 0,
RequestGenerated.length);
109.          StreamToServer.flush();
110.      }
111.      catch(IOException exception)
112.      {
113.          System.out.println("Exception in Add Friend " + exception);
114.      }
115.
116.      dispose();
117.    }
118.
119. }
120. }      // End Add Friend...
```

- Lines 1□9: These lines are the Java import statements that import packages whose classes are being used by the AddFriend class.

- Line 13: Contains the class declaration.

- Lines 16□29:Contain user-defined variable declarations that form the elements of the Add Friend GUI.

- Line 30: Declares a variable of the MainScreen class.

- Line 31: Declares the user-defined variable for the output stream to server.

- Line 35: Declares the contructor of AddFriend class.

- Line 37: Sets the title of the Add Friend window.

- Lines 38□40: Set the size(width x height) in pixels, set the location (x-coordinate, y-coordinate) of Add Friend window, and set its Visible property to true.

- Lines 42□44: Set the three variables screen, userName, and StreamToServer using the arguments passed to the construtor.

- Lines 46□47: Get the container/content paneand set its elements to absolute positioning.

- Lines 49□53: Implement the windowlistener that recognizes a window-closing event and dispose of the Add Friend window, that is, take the window off the screen.

- Lines 56□58: Create a new label "Friend ID", set its boundaries (x-coordinate, y-coordinate, width, height), and add it to the container.

- Lines 60□62: Create a text field, set its boundaries, and add it to the container.

- Lines 64□66: Create a label "User ID", set itsboundaries, and add it to the container.

- Lines 68□69: Create a text field and set its boundaries.

- Line 70: Sets the user's name in the text field created previously.

- Line 71: Disables the text field.

- Line 72: Adds the text field to the container.

- Lines 74□77: Create a button labelled"Ok", set its boundaries, add an action listener to it, and add this button to the container.

- Lines 79□83: Create a button labelled "Cancel",set its boundaries, set its font, add an action listener to it, and add it to the container.

- Line 86: Declares the `actionPerformed()` method.

- Line 89: Retrieves the source of the action event into the object `source`.

- Lines 91□94:Dispose the Add Friend window if the "Cancel" button is pressed.

- Lines 96□105: Definethe code execution in the event the "Ok" button is pressed:

  - Lines 98□101:Contain variable declarations.

  - Lines 102□103: Assignthe user's name and friend's name to the first and second elements of the string array `values`.

  - Line 104: Calls the `XMLCreator` class.

  - Line 105: Retrieves the XML returned by `XMLCreator` class into the variable `RequestGenerated`.

- Lines 106□110: Use the output streamto write the XML request to the server within a `try` block. The `flush()` method commits the request data.

- Lines 111□114: Contain thecatch block corresponding to the `try` of line 106.

- Line 116: Disposes the Add Friend window.

AcceptFriend class

The flow chart of `AcceptFriend` class is presented in Figure 5-17. Listing 5-9 contains the code for this class, followed by a detailed description of the code.

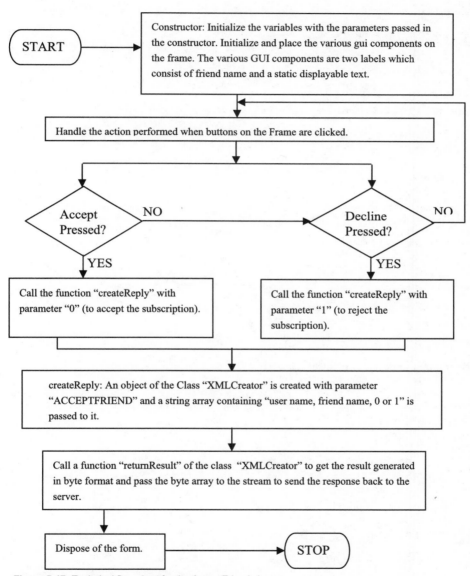

Figure 5-17: Technical flow chart for the AcceptFriend class

Listing 5-9: AcceptFriend.java

```
1.    import javax.swing.*;
2.    import javax.swing.event.*;
3.    import java.awt.*;
4.    import java.awt.event.*;
5.    import javax.swing.table.*;
6.    import java.io.*;
7.    import java.net.*;
8.    import java.util.*;
9.
10.   /*********** Accept Friend ************/
11.
12.   class  AcceptFriend extends JFrame implements ActionListener
13.   {
14.
15.   JLabel                          m_FriendName ;
16.   JLabel                          m_InfoLabel;
17.   JButton                         m_Accept;
18.   JButton                         m_Decline;
19.
20.   Container                       cont;
21.   MainScreen                      screen;
22.   BufferedOutputStream StreamToServer;
23.   String                          userName = new String();
24.
25.   String                          urlName;
26.
27.   String                          FriendName = new String();
28.
29.   /*********** Constructor ************/
30.
31.   AcceptFriend(MainScreen  screen, String FriendName, String
      userName)
32.   {
33.    setTitle("Accept Friend --- Instant Messenger");
34.    setSize(320,120);
35.    setLocation(300,200);
36.    setResizable(false);
37.    setVisible(true);
38.
39.    cont = getContentPane();
40.    cont.setLayout(null);
41.
42.    this.screen                   = screen;
43.    this.FriendName               = FriendName;
44.    this.userName                 = userName;
45.
46.    this.StreamToServer           = screen.StreamToServer;
```

```
47.
48.    addWindowListener( new WindowAdapter()
49.    { public void windowClosing(WindowEvent e)
50.    {
51.         dispose();
52.    }
53.    });
54.
55.
56.    m_FriendName   = new JLabel(FriendName);
57.    m_FriendName.setBounds(10 , 5, 300, 30);
58.    m_FriendName.setFont(new Font("sansSerif", Font.BOLD, 12));
59.    m_FriendName.setForeground(Color.blue);
60.    cont.add(m_FriendName  );
61.
62.    m_InfoLabel  = new JLabel("Wants to View Your Online Presence..
");
63.    m_InfoLabel.setBounds(10 , 25, 300, 30);
64.    m_InfoLabel.setFont(new Font("sansSerif", Font.PLAIN, 12));
65.    m_InfoLabel.setForeground(Color.black);
66.    cont.add(m_InfoLabel);
67.
68.
69.    m_Accept = new JButton("Accept");
70.    m_Accept.setBounds(50 , 60, 100, 20);
71.    m_Accept.addActionListener(this);
72.    cont.add(m_Accept);
73.
74.    m_Decline = new JButton("Decline");
75.    m_Decline.setBounds(160 , 60, 100, 20);
76.    m_Decline.addActionListener(this);
77.    cont.add(m_Decline);
78.    }
79.
80.    /*********** actionPerformed ************/
81.
82.    public void actionPerformed(ActionEvent e)
83.    {
84.
85.    Object source = e.getSource();
86.
87.    if(source.equals(m_Decline))
88.    {
89.     createReply("1");
90.     dispose();
91.    }    // end of if (source.equals(b_cancel))
92.
93.    else if(source.equals(m_Accept))
94.    {
```

```
95.     createReply("0");
96.     dispose();
97.   }
98.  }
99.
100.  /*********** createReply ************/
101.
102.  void createReply(String str)
103.  {
104.      XMLCreator               createRequest;
105.      byte        []           RequestGenerated;
106.
107.      String[] values          = new String[3];
108.      values[0]                = userName;
109.      values[1]                = FriendName;
110.      values[2]                = str;
111.
112.      createRequest            = new XMLCreator("ACCEPTFRIEND",
values);
113.      RequestGenerated         = createRequest.returnResult();
114.      try
115.      {
116.          StreamToServer.write(RequestGenerated, 0,
RequestGenerated.length);
117.          StreamToServer.flush();
118.      }
119.      catch(IOException exception)
120.      {
121.          System.out.println("Exception in Add Friend " + exception);
122.      }
123.   }
124.  }// End Accept Friend.
```

- Lines 1□8: Contain Java import statements for packages whose classes are being used by the AcceptFriend class.

- Lines 12□27: Contain class and variable declarations.

- Line 31: Declares the constructor for AcceptFriend class.

- Line 33: Sets the title of Accept Friend window.

- Lines 34□35:Set the size and location of Accept Friend window.

- Line 36: Sets the Reisizable property of Accept Friend window to false.

- Line 37: Sets the Visible property of Accept Friend window to true.

- Lines 39□40: Get the container and set its elements toabsolute positioning.

- Lines 42□44: Set the values of three variables,screen, FriendName and userName, with constructor parameters.

- Line 46: Sets the output stream to the server.
- Lines 48☐53: Implement the windowlistener that recognizes a window-closing event and take the Accept Friend window off the screen.
- Lines 56☐59: Create a label containing the name of the friend, set its boundaries, set its font, and set its text color.
- Line 60: Adds the label to the container.
- Lines 62☐65: Create a label "Wants to viewYour Online Presence", set its boundaries, set its font, and set its text color.
- Line 66: Adds the label to the container.
- Lines 69☐70: Create a button labelled"Accept" and set its bounds.
- Line 71: Adds an action listener to the Accept button.
- Line 72: Adds the Accept button to the container.
- Lines 74☐75: Create a button labelled"Decline" and set its bounds.
- Line 76: Adds an action listener to the Decline button.
- Line 77: Adds the Decline button to the container.
- Line 82: Declares the `actionPerformed()` method.
- Line 85: Obtains the source of the action event
- Lines 87☐91: Check ifthe "Decline" button is clicked, call the `createReply()` method passing 1 as the argument, and dispose the Accept Friend window.
- Lines 93☐97: Checkif the "Accept" button has been clicked, call the `createReply()` method with 0 as the argument, and dispose the Accept Friend window.
- Line 102: Declares the `createReply()` method.
- Lines 104☐107: Contain variable declarations.
- Line 108: Puts the user's name as the first element of string array named `values`.
- Line 109: Sets the friend's name as the second element of array `values`.
- Line 110: Sets the parameter value passed to `createReply()` method as the third element of `values` array.
- Line 112: Calls the `XMLCreator` class to form an "ACCEPTFRIEND" request.
- Line 113: Retrieves the XML returned by `XMLCreator` class in the variable `RequestGenerated`.
- Lines 114☐118: Write the XML request tothe server within a `try` block. The `flush()` method commits the request data.
- Lines 119☐122: Contain thecatch block corresponding to the `try` of line 114. If the method fails to write to the server, the `Exception` is printed to the console.

AddGateway class

The flow chart of AddGateway class is presented in Figure 5-18.

Figure 5-18: Technical flow chart for the AddGateway class

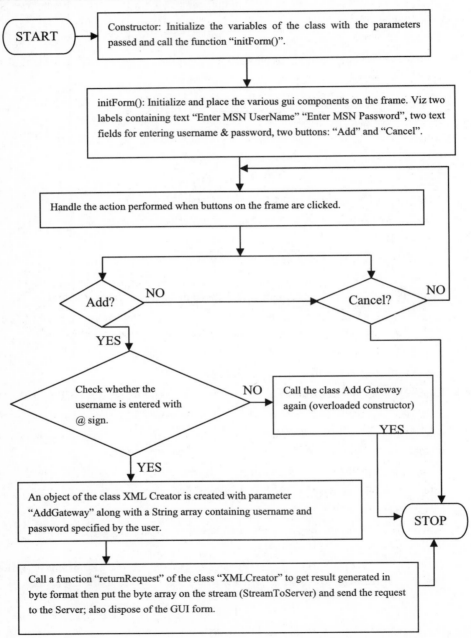

Listing 5-10 contains the code for this class. A detailed explanation follows.

Listing 5-10: AddGateway.java

```
1.   import javax.swing.*;
2.   import javax.swing.event.*;
3.   import java.awt.*;
4.   import java.awt.event.*;
5.   import java.io.*;
6.
7.   /*********** Class Declaration *************/
8.
9.   public class AddGateway extends JFrame implements ActionListener
10.  {
11.
12.  JLabel                        m_CompanyLogo;
13.  JLabel                        m_LoginName;
14.  JLabel                        m_Password;
15.  JLabel                        m_LoginStatus;
16.  JTextField                    m_EnterLoginName;
17.  JPasswordField                m_EnterPassword;
18.  JButton                       m_AddIt;
19.  JButton                       m_Cancel;
20.
21.  MainScreen                        screen;
22.  BufferedOutputStream StreamToServer;
23.  String                        userName      = new String();
24.  String                        messageLabel  = new String();
25.
26.  /*********** Constructor *************/
27.
28.  AddGateway(MainScreen  screen, String userName)
29.  {
30.
31.  this.screen              = screen;
32.  this.userName            = userName;
33.  this.StreamToServer      = screen.StreamToServer;
34.  messageLabel             = "Enter your MSN Name and Password";
35.  initForm();
36.  }
37.
38.  /*********** OverLoaded Constructor *************/
39.
40.  AddGateway(MainScreen  screen, String userName , String
MessageLabel)
41.  {
42.
43.  this.screen              = screen;
44.  this.userName            = userName;
```

```
45.   this.StreamToServer        = screen.StreamToServer;
46.   this.messageLabel          = MessageLabel;
47.   initForm();
48.   }
49.
50.   /*********** initForm ************/
51.
52.   void initForm()
53.   {
54.   setTitle("AddGateway -- Instant Messenger");
55.   setResizable(false);
56.   getContentPane().setLayout(null);
57.   setSize(330,165);
58.   setLocation(250,150);
59.
60.   addWindowListener (new java.awt.event.WindowAdapter () {
61.   public void windowClosing (java.awt.event.WindowEvent evt) {
62.    dispose();
63.   }
64.   }
65.   );
66.
67.   m_CompanyLogo = new JLabel("© Dreamtech Software India Inc.");
68.   m_CompanyLogo.setFont(new Font("sansSerif", Font.BOLD, 12));
69.   m_CompanyLogo.setBounds(40,7, 220, 10);
70.   m_CompanyLogo.setForeground(Color.blue);
71.   getContentPane().add(m_CompanyLogo);
72.
73.   m_LoginName = new JLabel("MSN Login Name");
74.   m_LoginName.setBounds(15 ,40, 100, 12);
75.   m_LoginName.setFont(new Font("sansSerif", Font.BOLD, 11));

76.   getContentPane().add(m_LoginName);
77.
78.   m_EnterLoginName = new JTextField();
79.   m_EnterLoginName.setBounds(125,40, 185, 20);
80.   getContentPane().add(m_EnterLoginName);
81.
82.   m_Password = new JLabel("MSN Password");
83.   m_Password.setBounds(15,65, 120, 12);
84.   m_Password.setFont(new Font("sansSerif", Font.BOLD, 11));
85.   getContentPane().add(m_Password);
86.
87.   m_EnterPassword = new JPasswordField();
88.   m_EnterPassword.setBounds(125,65, 185, 20);
89.   getContentPane().add(m_EnterPassword);
90.
91.   m_AddIt = new JButton("Add");
92.   m_AddIt.setBounds(85,90, 90, 20);
```

```
93.   m_AddIt.addActionListener(this);
94.   getContentPane().add(m_AddIt);
95.
96.   m_Cancel = new JButton("Cancel");
97.   m_Cancel.setBounds(200,90, 90, 20);
98.   m_Cancel.addActionListener(this);
99.   getContentPane().add(m_Cancel);
100.
101.  m_LoginStatus = new JLabel(messageLabel);
102.  m_LoginStatus.setBounds(5,120, 270, 15);
103.  m_LoginStatus.setFont(new Font("sansSerif", Font.BOLD, 12));

104.  getContentPane().add(m_LoginStatus);
105.
106.  }
107.
108.  /************ actionPerformed ************/
109.
110.  public void actionPerformed(ActionEvent at)
111.  {
112.  Object source = at.getSource();
113.  if(source.equals(m_Cancel))
114.  {
115.    dispose();
116.  }
117.  else if(source.equals(m_AddIt))
118.  {
119.      XMLCreator         createRequest;
120.      byte        []     RequestGenerated;
121.
122.      String [] val                   = new String[3];
123.
124.      val[0]                          = userName;
125.      val[1]                          = m_EnterLoginName.getText();
126.      char [] rawPassword  = m_EnterPassword.getPassword();
127.
128.      for (int i=0;i<rawPassword.length;i++ )
129.      {
130.      rawPassword[i] += 10;
131.      }
132.      val[2]                          = new String(rawPassword);
133.
134.      if (val[1].indexOf("@") == -1)
135.      {
136.      this.dispose();
137.      AddGateway AddGateway = new AddGateway(screen,userName,"Wrong
User Name Please Try Again!");
138.      AddGateway.show();
```

```
139.      }
140.     else
141.     {
142.     createRequest   = new XMLCreator("ADDGATEWAY", val);
143.     RequestGenerated = createRequest.returnResult();
144.     try
145.     {
146.        StreamToServer.write(RequestGenerated, 0,
RequestGenerated.length);
147.        StreamToServer.flush();
148.     }
149.     catch(IOException exception)
150.     {
151.        System.out.println("Exception in Add Gateway " + exception);
152.     }
153.     dispose();
154.     }
155.  }
156.  }
157.  }// End Add Gateway...
```

- Lines 1□5: Contain the Java import statements.
- Lines 9□24: Declare the classAddGateway and its user-defined variables.
- Lines 28□36:Define the constructor.
  - Lines 31□33:Set the variables screen, userName, and StreamToServer using values passed to the constructor.
  - Line 34: Creates a label.
  - Line 35: Calls the initform() method that displays the AddGateway GUI window.
- Lines 40□48: Define a second constructor that receives 3 parameters and is called after an invalid Add Gateway attempt.
  - Lines 43□46: Set user-defined variables using values passed to the constructor.
  - Line 47: Calls the initForm() method.
- Line 52: Declares the method initForm().
- Line 54: Sets the title of the window.
- Line 55: Sets the Resizable property to false.
- Line 56: Sets absolute positioning for the GUI elements.
- Lines 57□58: Set the size and location the window.
- Lines 60□65: Implement the window listener that disposesthe window when it receives a window closing event, that is, when the user closes the window.

- Lines 67□70: Create a label, set its font, set its bounds, and set its textcolor.
- Line 71: Adds the label to the container.
- Lines 73□75: Create a label, set its bounds, and set its text color.
- Line 76: Adds the label to the container.
- Lines 78□79: Create a text field and set its bounds.
- Line 80: Adds the text field to the container.
- Lines 82□85: Create a label, set its bounds, set its font, and addit to the container.
- Lines 87□89: Create a password field, set its bounds, and add it to the container.
- Lines 91□94: Create a button labelled "Add", set its bounds, add action listener to it, and add the button to the container.
- Lines 96□99: Createa button labelled "Cancel", set its bounds, add action listener to it, and add the button to the container.
- Lines 101□104: Create a labelwith its text defined by the string variable `messageLabel`, set its bounds, set its font, and add the label to the container.
- Line 110: Declares the `actionPerformed()` method.
- Line 112: Retrieves the source of the action event.
- Lines 113□116: Definethat if the Cancel button is clicked, the window is to be disposed.
- Line 117: Begins the `else if` clause that defines steps to be taken if the "Add" button is clicked.
- Lines 119□122:Contain variable declarations.
- Lines 124□125: Setthe user's name as the first element of `val[ ]` array and the user's login name for the gateway (this will be the same as the e-mail ID of the user for the gateway it is seeking to add) as the second element.
- Line 126: Retrieves the raw password in a character array.
- Lines 128□131: Loopthrough a `for` loop to add 10 to each character of the raw password. This is a very basic encryption being done to protect the password.
- Line 132: Converts the raw password into a string and sets it as the third element of the `val[ ]` array.
- Lines 134□139: These lines check for the index ofcharacter "@" in the user's gateway login name; and if this character is absent, the window is disposed, a new object of `AddGateway` is created that calls the constructor with three parameters (line 137), and a new `AddGateway` window is displayed with the label "Wrong User Name Please Try Again!".
- Line 140: Specifies the `else` clause of the `if` statement in Line 134.
- Line 142: Calls the `XMLCreator` class to form an `ADDGATEWAY` request.

- Line 143: Retrieves the request XML in the variable `RequestGenerated`.
- Lines 144☐148: Write the response tothe server; the method `flush()` commits the request data.
- Lines 149☐152:Compose the `catch` block of `try` in Line 144.
- Line 153: Disposes the `AddGateway` window.

UnsubscribeFriend class

The flow chart of `UnsubscribeFriend` class is presented in Figure 5-19. Listing 5-11 contains the code for this class, followed by a detailed description of the code.

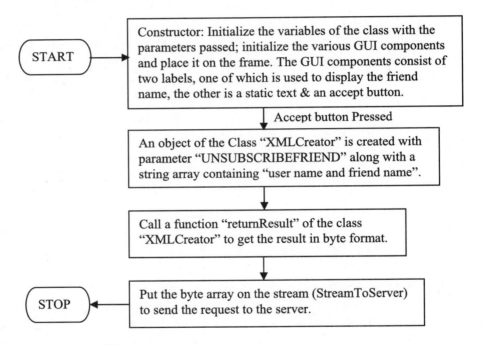

Figure 5-19: Technical flow chart for the UnsubscribeFriend class

Listing 5-11: UnsubscribeFriend.java

```
1.    import javax.swing.*;
2.    import javax.swing.event.*;
3.    import java.awt.*;
4.    import java.awt.event.*;
5.    import javax.swing.table.*;
6.    import java.io.*;
7.    import java.net.*;
8.    import java.util.*;
```

```
9.
10.   /*********** Class Declaration ************/
11.
12.   public class  UnsubscribeFriend extends JFrame implements
ActionListener
13.   {
14.
15.   JLabel                m_FriendName;
16.   JLabel                m_StaticText;
17.
18.   JButton               m_Ok;
19.
20.   String FriendName     = new String();
21.
22.   Container             cont;
23.   MainScreen            screen;
24.   BufferedOutputStream  StreamToServer;
25.   String userName       = new String();
26.
27.   /*********** Constructor ************/
28.
29.   UnsubscribeFriend(MainScreen  screen, String FriendName, String
userName)
30.   {
31.    setTitle("UnSubscribe --- Instant Messenger");
32.    setSize(320,120);
33.    setLocation(300,200);
34.    setResizable(false);
35.    setVisible(true);
36.
37.   38.   39.
40.    cont = getContentPane();
41.    cont.setLayout(null);
42.
43.    this.screen                   = screen;
44.    this.FriendName               = FriendName;
45.    this.userName                 = userName;
46.
47.    this.StreamToServer           = screen.StreamToServer;
48.
49.
50.
51.    addWindowListener( new WindowAdapter()
52.    { public void windowClosing(WindowEvent e)
53.     {
54.         dispose();
55.         createReply();
56.     }
57.    });
```

```
58.
59.
60.    m_FriendName = new JLabel(FriendName);
61.    m_FriendName.setBounds(10 , 5, 300, 30);
62.    m_FriendName.setFont(new Font("sansSerif", Font.BOLD, 12));
63.    m_FriendName.setForeground(Color.blue);
64.    cont.add(m_FriendName);
65.
66.
67.    m_StaticText = new JLabel("Has removed You from his/her Friend
List.. ");
68.    m_StaticText.setBounds(10 , 25, 300, 30);
69.    m_StaticText.setFont(new Font("sansSerif", Font.PLAIN, 12));
70.    m_StaticText.setForeground(Color.black);
71.    cont.add(m_StaticText);
72.
73.    m_Ok = new JButton("Ok");
74.    m_Ok.setBounds(90 , 60, 100, 20);
75.    m_Ok.addActionListener(this);
76.    cont.add(m_Ok);
77.    }
78.
79.    /*********** actionPerformed ************/
80.
81.    public void actionPerformed(ActionEvent ae)
82.    {
83.    if (ae.getSource() == m_Ok)
84.    {
85.      dispose();
86.      createReply();
87.    }
88.    }
89.
90.    /*********** createReply ************/
91.
92.    void createReply()
93.    {
94.    XMLCreator               createRequest;
95.    byte []                  RequestGenerated;
96.
97.    String[] values          = new String[2];
98.    values[0]                = userName;
99.    values[1]                = FriendName;
100.
101.    createRequest            = new XMLCreator("UNSUBSCRIBEFRIEND",
values);
102.    RequestGenerated         = createRequest.returnResult();
103.
104.    try
```

```
105.    {
106.    StreamToServer.write(RequestGenerated, 0,
RequestGenerated.length);
107.    StreamToServer.flush();
108.    }
109.    catch(IOException exception)
110.    {
111.    System.out.println("Exception in Add Friend " + exception);
112.    }
113.    }
114. }// End UnsubscribeFriend...
```

- Lines 1□8: Contain Java import statements.
- Lines 12□25: Declare the class and user-definedvariables.
- Line 29: Declares the constructor for UnsubscribeFriend class.
- Lines 31□33: Set the title, size, andlocation of the Unsubscribe Friend window.
- Lines 34□35:Set the Unsubscribe Friend window's Resizable property to false and Visible property to true.
- Lines 40□41: Get the container object and set its elements toabsolute positioning.
- Lines 43□45: Use the values passed to the constructor's parameters to set the values of the variables screen, FriendName, and userName.
- Line 47: Sets the output stream to the server.
- Lines 51□57: Implement the window listener that recognizes the window-closingevent. It disposes the Unsubscribe window and calls the createReply() method.
- Lines 60□64: Create a label withthe friend's name, set its bounds, set its font, set its text color, and add it to the container.
- Lines 67□71: Create a label with the text "Has removed You from his/her Friend List..", set its bounds, set its font, set its text color, and add it to the container.
- Lines: 73□74: Createa button labelled "Ok" and set its bounds.
- Line 75: Adds an action listener to the "Ok" button.
- Line 76: Adds the "Ok" button to the container.
- Lines 81□88:Define the actionPerformed() method. If the "Ok" button is clicked (Line 83), the window is disposed, and the method createReply() is called.
- Line 92: Declares the createReply() method.
- Lines 94□97:Contain variable declarations.
- Lines 98□99: The user's name is set as the first element of the string array values[ ], and the friend's name is set as its second element.
- Line 101: Calls the XMLCreator class to form an "UNSUBSCRIBEFRIEND" request.

- Line 102: Retrieves the XML request into the byte array `RequestGenerated`.
- Lines 104□108: Write the request in variable`RequestGenerated` to the server.
- Lines 109□112: Contain the`catch` block corresponding to the `try` of Line 104 that prints an `Exception` if the request cannot be written to the server.

ColorPreference class

Listing 5-12 contains the code for `ColorPreference` class, followed by a detailed description of the code.

Listing 5-12: ColorPreference.java

```java
1.   import javax.swing.*;
2.   import javax.swing.event.*;
3.   import java.awt.*;
4.   import java.awt.event.*;
5.
6.
7.   public class ColorPreference extends JDialog implements
ActionListener
8.   {
9.   Container       m_contentPane;
10.
11.  JLabel          m_OutGoingMessageColor;
12.  JButton         m_ColorOutGoing;
13.
14.  JLabel          m_senderColor;
15.  JButton         m_ColorSender;
16.
17.  JLabel          m_InComingMessageColor;
18.  JButton         m_ColorInComing;
19.
20.  JLabel          m_FriendColor;
21.  JButton         m_ColorFriend;
22.
23.  JButton         m_Ok;
24.  JButton         m_Cancel;
25.
26.  Message         frame;
27.
28.  /************* Constructor ********************/
29.
30.  ColorPreference(Message frame, String title, boolean modal)
31.  {
32.   super(frame, title, modal);
33.
34.   this.frame = frame;
35.   setSize(290, 200);
```

```
36.    setResizable(false);
37.
38.    m_contentPane = getContentPane();
39.    m_contentPane.setLayout(null);
40.
41.    m_OutGoingMessageColor = new JLabel("Message Color Settings.");
42.    m_OutGoingMessageColor.setFont(new Font("sansSerif", Font.BOLD,
12));
43.    m_OutGoingMessageColor.setForeground(Color.black);
44.    m_OutGoingMessageColor.setBounds(10, 15, 150, 25) ;
45.    m_contentPane.add(m_OutGoingMessageColor);
46.
47.    m_ColorOutGoing = new JButton();
48.    m_ColorOutGoing.setBackground(frame.m_messageSendColor);
49.    m_ColorOutGoing.setBounds(200, 15, 75, 25) ;
50.    m_ColorOutGoing.addActionListener(this);
51.    m_contentPane.add(m_ColorOutGoing);
52.
53.    m_senderColor = new JLabel("Sender Color Settings.");
54.    m_senderColor.setFont(new Font("sansSerif", Font.BOLD, 12));
55.    m_senderColor.setForeground(Color.black);
56.    m_senderColor.setBounds(10, 45, 150, 25) ;
57.    m_contentPane.add(m_senderColor);
58.
59.    m_ColorSender = new JButton();
60.    m_ColorSender.setBackground(frame.m_SenderColor);
61.    m_ColorSender.setBounds(200, 45, 75, 25) ;
62.    m_ColorSender.addActionListener(this);
63.    m_contentPane.add(m_ColorSender);
64.
65.
66.    m_InComingMessageColor = new JLabel("Incoming Message Color. ");
67.    m_InComingMessageColor.setFont(new Font("sansSerif", Font.BOLD,
12));
68.    m_InComingMessageColor.setForeground(Color.black);
69.    m_InComingMessageColor.setBounds(10, 80, 150, 25) ;
70.    m_contentPane.add(m_InComingMessageColor);
71.
72.    m_ColorInComing = new JButton();
73.    m_ColorInComing.setBackground(frame.m_messageReceivedColor);
74.    m_ColorInComing.setBounds(200, 80, 75, 25) ;
75.    m_ColorInComing.addActionListener(this);
76.    m_contentPane.add(m_ColorInComing);
77.
78.    m_FriendColor = new JLabel("Friend Color Settings.");
79.    m_FriendColor.setFont(new Font("sansSerif", Font.BOLD, 12));
80.    m_FriendColor.setForeground(Color.black);
81.    m_FriendColor.setBounds(10, 110, 150, 25) ;
82.    m_contentPane.add(m_FriendColor);
```

```
83.
84.    m_ColorFriend = new JButton();
85.    m_ColorFriend.setBackground(frame.m_ReceiverColor);
86.    m_ColorFriend.setBounds(200, 110, 75, 25) ;
87.    m_ColorFriend.addActionListener(this);
88.    m_contentPane.add(m_ColorFriend);
89.
90.
91.    m_Ok = new JButton("Ok");
92.    m_Ok.setMnemonic('O');
93.    m_Ok.setBounds(65, 140, 75, 25) ;
94.    m_Ok.addActionListener(this);
95.    m_contentPane.add(m_Ok);
96.
97.    m_Cancel = new JButton("Cancel");
98.    m_Cancel.setMnemonic('C');
99.    m_Cancel.setBounds(150, 140, 75, 25) ;
100.   m_Cancel.addActionListener(this);
101.   m_contentPane.add(m_Cancel);
102.
103.   addWindowListener (new java.awt.event.WindowAdapter () {
104.    public void windowClosing (java.awt.event.WindowEvent evt) {
105.    dispose();
106.   }
107.     }
108.     );
109.   }
110.
111.   /********************** actionPerformed ******************/
112.
113.   public void actionPerformed(ActionEvent ae)
114.   {
115.
116.   if (ae.getSource() == m_Ok)
117.   {
118.    frame.m_messageSendColor   = m_ColorOutGoing.getBackground();
119.    frame.m_SenderColor                      =
m_ColorSender.getBackground();
120.    frame.m_messageReceivedColor = m_ColorInComing.getBackground();
121.    frame.m_ReceiverColor              =
m_ColorFriend.getBackground();
122.    JOptionPane.showMessageDialog(this,"The Changes would be
applicable from next send or received message.. ","Instant
Messenger",JOptionPane.INFORMATION_MESSAGE);
123.    dispose();
124.   }
125.   else if (ae.getSource() == m_Cancel)
126.   {
127.     dispose();
```

```
128.  }
129.  else if (ae.getSource() == m_ColorOutGoing)
130.  {
131.    Color color = JColorChooser.showDialog(this, "Select a New
Color...", m_ColorOutGoing.getBackground());
132.    m_ColorOutGoing.setBackground(color);
133.  }
134.  else if (ae.getSource() == m_ColorSender)
135.  {
136.    Color color = JColorChooser.showDialog(this, "Select a New
Color...", m_ColorSender.getBackground());
137.    m_ColorSender.setBackground(color);
138.  }
139.  else if (ae.getSource() == m_ColorInComing )
140.  {
141.    Color color = JColorChooser.showDialog(this, "Select a New
Color...", m_ColorInComing.getBackground());
142.    m_ColorInComing.setBackground(color);
143.  }
144.  else if (ae.getSource() == m_ColorFriend)
145.  {
146.    Color color = JColorChooser.showDialog(this, "Select a New
Color...", m_ColorFriend.getBackground());
147.    m_ColorFriend.setBackground(color);
148.  }
149.  }
150. }
```

- Lines 1☐4: Java import statements.
- Lines 7☐24: Contain class and user-defined variable declarations.
- Line 26: Declares an object of the Message class.
- Line 30: Declares the class constructor.
- Line 32: Calls the constructor of the super class (JDialog).
- Line 34: Initialize the variable with the parameter passed in the constructor.
- Line 35: Sets the size (width x height) of the Dialog box in pixels.
- Line 36: Sets the Resizable property to false.
- Lines 38☐39: Get the contentpane and set it to absolute positioning.
- Lines 41☐45: Definea label with the text "Message Color Settings."; set its font, text color, and boundaries; and add it to the container/content pane.
- Lines 47☐51: Define a button, set its background color and boundaries, add an action listener to it, and add the button to the container/content pane.

- Lines 53□57: Definea label with the text "Sender Color Settings."; set its font, text color, and boundaries; and add it to the container/content pane.
- Lines 59□63: Define a button, set its background color and boundaries, add an action listener to it, and add the button to the container/content pane.
- Lines 66□70: Define a label with the text "Incoming Message Color."; set its font, text, color, and boundaries; and add it to the container/content pane.
- Lines 72□76: Define a button, set its background color and boundaries, add an action-listener to it, and add the button to the container/content pane.
- Lines 78□82: Definea label with the text "Friend Color Settings."; set its font, text color, and boundaries; and add it to the container/content pane.
- Lines 84□88: Define a button, set its background color and boundaries, add an actionListener to it, and add the button to the container/content pane.
- Lines 91□95: Define the "Ok" button, setits keyboard shortcut to Alt+O, set its boundaries, add an actionListener to it, and add the button to the container/content pane.
- Lines 97□101: Definethe "Cancel" button, set its keyboard shortcut to Alt+C, set its boundaries, add an actionListener to it, and add the button to the container/content pane.
- Lines 103□108: Implement the window listener that recognizes a window-closingevent and disposes the Color Preference dialog box.
- Line 113: Declares the `actionPerformed()` method.
- Line 116: Checks if the source of the action event is the "Ok" button.
- Lines 118□123: List the actionsto be taken if the "Ok" button is pressed.
  - Line 118: Sets the color-type variable `m_messageSendColor` (defined in the `Message` class) to the background of `m_ColorOutGoing` button.
  - Line 119: Sets the color-type variable `m_SenderColor` (defined in the `Message` class) to the background of `m_ColorSender` button.
  - Line 120: Sets the color-type variable `m_messageReceivedColor` (defined in the `Message` class) to the background of `m_ColorInComing` button.
  - Line 121: Sets the color-type variable `m_ReceiverColor` (defined in the `Message` class) to the background of `m_ColorFriend` button.
  - Line 122: Displays the message "The Changes would be applicable from next send or received message.. ".
  - Line 123: Closes the ColorPreference dialog box.
- Lines 125□128: Check ifthe "Cancel" button is clicked and close the Color Preference dialog box.
- Lines 129□148: These lines present a colorchooser using the `JcolorChooser` class. The `showDialog()` method takes four parameters. These parameters are explained

below for Line 131. The showDialog() methods of Lines 136, 141 and 146 are explained in a similar manner.

- The first parameter, this, refers to the current dialog box.

- The second parameter, "Select a new color..." sets the title of the color chooser to "Select a New Color...".

- The third parameter, m_ColorOutGoing.getBackground(), sets the selected color to the background of the button that has been clicked.

- The fourth parameter, m_ColorOutGoing.setBackground(color) sets the background of the clicked button to the color chosen by the user. For example, if the user clicks the m_ColorOutGoing button whose background is set to color A (see Line 48), when the color chooser appears, it has the color A preselected. Suppose the user chooses color B from the color chooser; then the background of the m_ColorOutGoing button is set to B.

About class

Listing 5-13 contains the code for About class, followed by a detailed description of the code.

Listing 5-13: About.java

```
1.   import javax.swing.*;
2.   import javax.swing.event.*;
3.   import java.awt.*;
4.   import java.awt.event.*;
5.
6.   /*********** Class Declaration ************/
7.
8.   public class About extends JDialog implements ActionListener
9.   {
10.  JButton        m_ok;
11.  JLabel         m_CopyRight;
12.  JLabel         m_CompanyLabel;
13.  Point          m_point;
14.
15.  Container      m_contentPane;
16.
17.  /*********** Constructor ************/
18.
19.  About(JFrame frame, String title, boolean modal)
20.  {
21.  super(frame, title, modal);
22.  setSize(290, 100);
23.  setResizable(false);
24.  m_point = frame.getLocationOnScreen();
25.  setLocation(m_point.x, m_point.y+m_point.y);
26.  m_contentPane = getContentPane();
```

```
27.   m_contentPane.setLayout(null);
28.
29.   m_CopyRight = new JLabel("Copyright (C) 2001-2002 ");
30.   m_CopyRight.setFont(new Font("sansSerif", Font.BOLD, 12));
31.   m_CopyRight.setForeground(Color.blue);
32.   m_CopyRight.setBounds(10, 15, 150, 25) ;
33.   m_contentPane.add(m_CopyRight);
34.
35.   m_CompanyLabel = new JLabel("M/s. DreamTech Software India Inc. ");
36.   m_CompanyLabel.setFont(new Font("sansSerif", Font.BOLD, 12));
37.   m_CompanyLabel.setForeground(Color.blue);
38.   m_CompanyLabel.setBounds(10, 35, 250, 25) ;
39.   m_contentPane.add(m_CompanyLabel);
40.
41.
42.   m_ok = new JButton("Ok");
43.   m_ok.setBounds(230, 15, 50, 25) ;
44.   m_ok.setMnemonic('O');
45.   m_ok.addActionListener(this);
46.   m_contentPane.add(m_ok);
47.
48.
49.   addWindowListener (new java.awt.event.WindowAdapter () {
50.   public void windowClosing (java.awt.event.WindowEvent evt) {
51.    dispose();
52.   }
53.   }
54.   );
55.   }
56.
57.   /*********** actionPerformed ************/
58.
59.   public void actionPerformed(ActionEvent ae)
60.   {
61.   if (ae.getSource() == m_ok)
62.   {
63.    dispose();
64.   }
65.   }
66.   } // End About...
```

- Lines 1□4: Java import statements.
- Lines 8□15: Contain class and user-defined variable declarations.
- Line 19: Declares the class constructor.
- Line 21: Calls the constructor of the super class (JDialog).
- Line 22: Sets the size (width x height) of the dialog box in pixels.

- Line 23: Sets the `Resizable` property to false.

- Line 24: Calls the `getLocationOnScreen()` method to get the x and y coordinates of the calling frame/window.

- Line 25: Sets the location of the dialog box.

- Lines 26□27: Get the contentpane and set it to absolute positioning.

- Lines 29□33: Define a label with the text "Copyright (C) 2001-2002 "; set its font, text color, and boundaries; and add it to the container/content pane.

- Lines 35□39: Define a label with the text "Ms. DreamTech Software India Inc. "; set its font, text color, and boundaries; and add it to the container/content pane.

- Lines 42□43: Create a buttonm_ok and set its boundaries.

- Line 44: Sets the mnemonic "O" for the m_ok button, that is, pressing Alt+O acts as the keyboard equivalent to pressing the m_ok button.

- Line 45: Adds actionListener to the m_ok button.

- Line 46: Adds the m_ok button to the content pane.

- Lines 49□53: Implement the windowlistener that recognizes a window-closing event and disposes the About dialog box.

- Lines 59□65: Define the`actionPerformed()` method. If the m_ok button is pressed, the About window is disposed.

Summary

In this chapter, you have seen how the client side (Java) of the Instant Messenger application has been developed. This chapter has also discussed what functions are taken care of by the client application and how various user-defined Java classes have been integrated to perform these functions. It is also amply clear from the discussions in this chapter that the client application is complementary to the server application that forms the backbone of the Instant Messenger. The user-defined Java classes that form the client application have been explained in detail, with the technical-flow diagrams providing insight into the working of each class. By the end of this chapter, you get a fair idea of the working of the complete Instant Messenger application. The only thing left, insofar as this application is concerned, is the C# client; that is covered in the next chapter.

Chapter 6

Instant Messaging Client (C#)

For the purpose of completing the C# Version of the Instant Messaging application, this chapter presents a comprehensive discussion on the C# Client module. We discuss all possible scenarios involved in developing the Client module, and we provide all relevant code listings and detailed explanations.

Client Module Tasks

Generally, the Client module is responsible for performing the following tasks:

- Establishing a connection with the server, thereby initiaiting the session with the server.
- Programming client requests so that they can be delivered to the server. Since the communication standard of the application is XML oriented, it is the responsibility of the Client module to format various client requests in XML structures that are understood and recognized by the server. Also the Client module is entitled to maintain various GUI based forms to provide easy and interactive usage of the application for users of all levels of the user.
- Analyzing and parsing server responses so that the end user is aware of them.

Connection with the server

Whenever the user runs the Client module, the start up form of the application is displayed, as shown in Figure 6-1. As soon as this form is displayed on the user's screen, the Client module's connection with the server starts developing automatically without any effort from the user.

Once the connection between the Client module and the server is established, the server assigns a unique thread to this connection. For each connection, a unique thread is assigned to maintain a distinction among the users. Thus far, only a connection, not a session, is established between the client and the server. For establishing a connection with the server, the Client module of our application needs the assistance of the sckClient class, which inherits the features and functionality of TcpClient class, as follows:

```
public class sckClient : System.Net.Sockets.TcpClient
```

Figure 6-1: Start Up Form of the Client module

The constructor of the sckClient class is implemented in the Connect() function of the frmJabberClient class. A new instance of the sckClient class is made to establish the connection with the server. The following code snippet will help you understand the connection process.

```
clientSocket=new sckClient();
try
{
  clientSocket.Connect("pratul",5555);
}
catch
{
  try
  {
    clientSocket.Connect("gaurav",5555);
  }
  catch
  {
    MessageBox.Show("Can't connect to the server","Connection Error");
    Application.Exit();
  }
}
```

In the preceding code snippet, the connection with the server, named pratul, is presented. This server listens to all incoming client requests on port 5555. The server pratul may sometimes not be available to cater the client requests. To handle such a situation, another server, gaurav, is kept on reserve. gaurav, too, listens to all client requests on port 5555.

Encode client requests

After establishing a connection between the Client module and the server, the user is free to make requests as per his/her requirements. The possible client requests are described in the following sections.

Various clients' requests are fired from the `frmJabberClient` class. This class maintains various functions to handle different kinds of requests. Whenever a request is initiated by the user, the corresponding function of the `frmJabberClient` class is executed. This function calls the `XmlFormat` class and hands over the request for appropriate treatment. The `XmlFormat` class transforms the client requests in the application's XML norm. To accomplish the XML norm, the `XmlFormat` class maintains various functions for each type of client request. For example, a user initiates the request for deleting a friend from his/her friend list; this request is faced by the `DelFriend()` function of the `frmJabberClient` class. The `DelFriend()` function makes a call to the `XmlFormat` class to pass on the delete a friend request, so that it can be transformed into a suitable XML structure. The `XmlFormat` class calls its `DeleteFriendXML()` function to transform the user request in XML format.

Once the XML structure is created, the only task remaining is to gain the XML, which delivers the request of the user to the server. To accomplish this task, the `GetXml()` function of the `XmlFormat` class is used to return the XML.

Registration request

On successful connection, a login window comes up for registering new users for the application. To register, the user clicks the Registration button. Immediately after the click, a registration window comes up on the desktop screen, as shown in Figure 6-2.

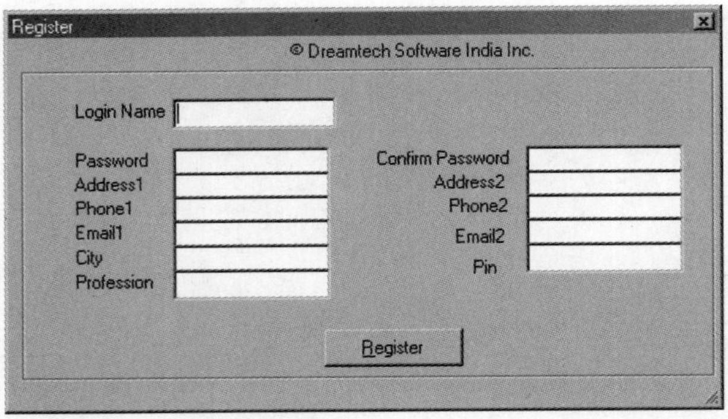

Figure 6-2: Registration window

Some fields shown in the registration window, such as Login Name, Password and Confirm Password, must be filled by the user to facilitate quick registration. After supplying all the required information, the user clicks the Register button to complete the registration process.

To process the information filled by the user for registration, the `ProcessRegisterAction()` function of `frmJabberClient` is contacted. This function takes the `frmRegister` class as a parameter. Using the `GetLoginInfo()` function of `frmRegister` class, the information entered by the user is accepted and handed over to the constructor of the `XmlFormat` class with REGISTER and the string type array (strParam) as parameters. The following code will help you understand the process of retrieving and handing over the user's registration request to the concerned authorities.

```csharp
public class frmJabberClient : System.Windows.Forms.Form
{ ...........................................
  private void ProcessRegisterAction(frmRegister frmReg)
  {
    XmlFormat xmlReg;
    strParam=new String[11];
    ...........................
    strParam=frmReg.GetLoginInfo();
    xmlReg=new XmlFormat("REGISTER",strParam);
    WriteMsg(xmlReg.GetXml());
    }
}
```

In turn, the constructor of `XmlFormat` class invokes the `RegisterXML()` function of `XmlFormat` class, which finally transform the registration request of the user in appropriate XML format and returns the XML by using the `GetXml()` function. You will understand how the `RegisterXML()` function of `XmlFormat` class finalizes the client's registration request from the following code snippet. The following code snippet displays the working of the `RegisterXML()` function.

```csharp
public XmlFormat(string strType,string []param)
{
  strXml= "<?xml version=\'1.0\' encoding=\'utf-8\'?>
      <InstantMessenger>";

  ...................................
  else if (strType.ToUpper().CompareTo("REGISTER")==0)
  {
    RegisterXML(param);
  }
  strXml+= "</InstantMessenger>";
}

private void RegisterXML(String []param)
{
  strXml+= "<Register>";
  strXml+= "<UserName>"+param[0]+"</UserName>";
  strXml+= "<Password>"+param[1]+"</Password>";
  strXml+= "<sAdd1>"+param[2]+"</sAdd1>";
  strXml+= "<sAdd2>"+param[3]+"</sAdd2>";
  strXml+= "<sPhone1>"+param[4]+"</sPhone1>";
  strXml+= "<sPhone2>"+param[5]+"</sPhone2>";
  strXml+= "<sEmail1>"+param[6]+"</sEmail1>";
  strXml+= "<sEmail2>"+param[7]+"</sEmail2>";
  strXml+= "<sPin>"+param[8]+"</sPin>";
  strXml+= "<sCity>"+param[9]+"</sCity>";
  strXml+= "<sProfession>"+param[10]+"</sProfession>";
```

```
    strXml+= "</Register>";
}
```

Login request

To log on to the application network, a user has to go through an authentication process in which he/she has to supply the login name and password. Through the login name and password supplied by the user, the server can find whether the user who wants to enter the application network has been authorized to avail of the resources and services of the network. You can access the Login window by the clicking the Login button placed on the start up form of the Client module. The Login window of our application appears as in Figure 6-3:

Figure 6-3: Login window

In the background working of the Client module, the `GetLoginInfo()` function of `frmJabberClient` is approached. The `GetLoginInfo()` takes the `frmLogin` class as a parameter. With the help of the `GetLoginInfo()` function of the `frmLogin` class, the authentication information submitted by the user is retrieved, as shown in the following code.

```
public class frmJabberClient : System.Windows.Forms.Form
{ ......................................
    private void GetLoginInfo()(frmLogin frmLog)
    {
        XmlFormat xmlLog;

        ...........................................
        strParam=new String[2];
        strParam=frmLog.GetLoginInfo();

        ...........................................
        xmlLog=new XmlFormat("AUTH",strParam);
        WriteMsg(xmlLog.GetXml());
    }
```

The client request is handed over to the `XmlFormat` class, with "AUTH" as the parameter. The `AuthXML()` function of the `XmlFormat` class finally accomplishes the task by forming the login request of the user in appropriate XML structure.

```
public XmlFormat(string strType,string []param)
{
```

```
    strXml= "<?xml version=\'1.0\' encoding=\'utf-8\'?>
<InstantMessenger>";
    if (strType.ToUpper().CompareTo("AUTH")==0)
    {
      AuthXML(param);
    }
    strXml+= "</InstantMessanger>";
}
private void AuthXML(String []param)
{
  strXml+= "<Auth>";
  strXml+= "<UserName>"+param[0]+"</UserName>";
  strXml+= "<Password>"+param[1]+"</Password>";
  strXml+= "</Auth>";
}
```

The key elements of the `<Auth>` tag are the login name of the user (`<UserName>`) and his/her password (`<Password>`). If no error is found in the information supplied by the user, he/she becomes online with the application net. In this case, a window as shown in Figure 6-4 appears on the desktop screen of the user.

Figure 6-4: Entry in application network

Request to deliver a message to a friend

The most common type of request faced by the Client module is designing the user message in suitable XML format and handing it over to the server for its delivery to the target user. The Message window in our application appears as in Figure 6-5.

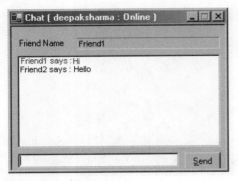

Figure 6-5: Message window

Each time a user clicks the Send button to send the message, the click event of the Send button is fired, which calls the XmlFormat class for structuring the message in application's XML standard. When the client request is of "Message" type, the parameter for the XmlFormat class becomes 'MSG' and a string type array (strParam). The following code will help you understand the Client module function in sending a message.

```csharp
public class frmSendMessage : System.Windows.Forms.Form
{
    private void cmdSend Click(object sender, System.EventArgs e)
    {
        ...........................................
        XmlFormat xmlReg=new XmlFormat("MSG",strParam);
    }
}

public XmlFormat(string strType,string []param)
{
    strXml= "<?xml version=\'1.0\' encoding=\'utf-8\'?>
<InstantMessenger>";
    ...............................................

    else if (strType.ToUpper().CompareTo("MSG")==0)
    {
        MessageXML(param);
    }
    strXml+= "</InstantMessenger>";
}

private void MessageXML(String []param)
{
    strXml+= "<MSG>";
    strXml+= "<Target>" +param[0]+ "</Target>";
    strXml+= "<Source>" +param[1]+ "</Source>";
    strXml+= "<Text>"   +param[2]+ "</Text>";
```

```
    strXml+= "</MSG>";
}
```

The <MSG> tag represents the message type request. The key attributes of the <MSG> tag are name of the user for whom the message is intended (<Target>), the name of the sender of the message (<Source>), and the content of the message (<Text>).

Request to add a friend

This request is generally made when a user is interested in including the other user in his/her list of friends. It is not mandatory that the user and the other user who is to be included as a friend must know each other. The only prerequisite is that both of them be the registered users of the application. The window that entertains the request to add a friend is shown in Figure 6-6.

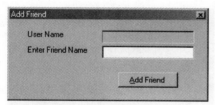

Figure 6-6: Add Friend window

To formulate the client request of including the friend, the AddFriend() function of the frmJabberClient class comes into play. This function accesses the name of the friend selected by the user for inclusion in the friend list by the GetFriendName() function of frmAddFriend class. Once the friend name is obtained, the task of forming the request is handed over to the XmlFormat class, with "ADDFRIEND" as the parameter. The following code will help you understand the mechanism involved in gaining the friend name and handing over the request to the XmlFormat class.

```csharp
public class frmJabberClient : System.Windows.Forms.Form
{
    ..............................................
    ................................... .
    private void AddFriend()
    {
        ...................................................

    strFriendName=frmAddFrnd.GetFriendName();
        ...................................................
        string []strParam=new string[2];
        strParam[0]=strLogin;
        strParam[1]=strFriendName;
        XmlFormat xmlAdd=new XmlFormat("ADDFRIEND",strParam);
```

```
        WriteMsg(xmlAdd.GetXml());
    }
}
```

The `XmlFormat` class, on receiving the request, calls the `AddFriendXML()` function. The
following code illustrates the involvement of the `XmlFormat` class and its associated
function, `AddFriendXML()`.

```
public XmlFormat(string strType,string []param)
{
    strXml= "<?xml version=\'1.0\' encoding=\'utf-8\'?>
<InstantMessenger>";
    ................
    else if (strType.ToUpper().CompareTo("ADDFRIEND")==0)
    {
        AddFriendXML(param);
    }
    strXml+= "</InstantMessenger>";
}

private void AddFriendXML(String []param)
{
    strXml+= "<AddFriend>";
    strXml+= "<UserName>"+param[0]+"</UserName>";
    strXml+= "<FriendName>"+param[1]+"</FriendName>";
    strXml+= "</AddFriend>";
}
```

You must have noticed in the preceding code snippet that the user request to add a friend is
headed by the `<AddFriend>` tag, which comprises the user name (`<UserName>`) interested
in making the friend and the name of the other user (`<FriendName>`) who is to be made a
friend.

Notification request confirming acceptance of a friend

Whenever a user adds another user to his/her list of friends, the Instant Messaging application
usually sends the notification to the other user, prompting that a certain user has requested to
include him/her in his/her list of friends. On receipt of such a request, the target user is
provided with two options: to accept or reject the friendship proposal. For conveying his/her
intention, a dialog box is also displayed with Yes and No options. In our application, such
notification requests are handled by the `frmAddConfirm` class, which has the `Accept()`
function that delivers the friendship offer to the intended user. The following code snippet will
help you understand the working of the `Accept()` function.

```
public class AddConfirm : System.Windows.Forms.Form
{
    ..........................
```

```
    private void Accept(string strCode)
    {
      string []strParam=new String[3];
      strParam[0]=frmJabberClient.strLogin;
      strParam[1]=strFriend.ToLower();
      strParam[2]=strCode;
      XmlFormat xmlAccept =new XmlFormat("ACCEPTFRIEND",strParam);
      frmJabberClient.WriteMsg(xmlAccept.GetXml());
      xmlAccept=null;
    }
}
```

The `Accept()` function invokes the constructor of the `XmlFormat` class, with
ACCEPTFRIEND as the parameter. The `XmlFormat` class converts the user's request for
adding a friend in appropriate XML format.

```
public XmlFormat(string strType,string []param)
{
    strXml= "<?xml version=\'1.0\'   encoding=\'utf-
8\'?><InstantMessenger>";
    .............................. . .
    else if (strType.ToUpper().CompareTo("ACCEPTFRIEND")==0)
    {
       AcceptFriendXML(param);
    }
}
  .......................... . .
  private void AcceptFriendXML(String []param)
  {
    strXml+= "<AcceptFriend>";
    strXml+= "<UserName>"+param[0]+"</UserName>";
    strXml+= "<FriendName>"+param[1]+"</FriendName>";
    strXml+= "<Status>"+param[2]+"</Status>";
    strXml+= "</AcceptFriend>";
  }
```

From the constructor of the `XmlFormat` class, the `AcceptFriendXML()` function is called,
which forms the XML responsible for delivering the user request. In the XML structure, the
`<Status>` element holds the reply of the opposite user: whether he/she accepts or rejects the
friendship proposal of the user.

Request to add a gateway

Whenever the user wants to communicate with his/her friends over the MSN Instant
Messenger, he/she includes the gateway for MSN in the Client module. It must be remembered
that the gateway for MSN is included for once. This gateway enables the user to obtain the list
of MSN friends and to deliver instant messages to them. A message that the user intends to
deliver to the MSN user is first faced either by the local or Jabber server. On receiving the

message, the server hands it over to the gateway, which further delivers it to the MSN server. On receiving the messages, the MSN server accesses the name of the target user and delivers the message to him/her. The only prerequisite for a user to use the gateway is possession of an account on the MSN network. The window to add the gateway appears as shown in Figure 6-7.

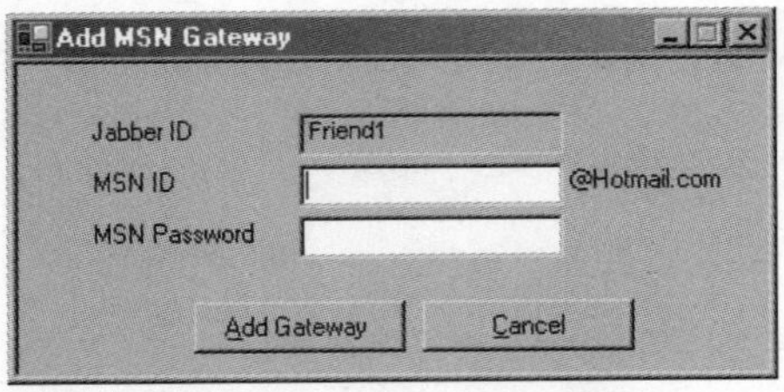

Figure 6-7: Add Gateway window

The `AddGateway` class manages the task of including the gateway for MSN. When the user clicks the Add Gateway button, the code written inside the click event of the button is executed, and the `XmlFormat` class is called with 'ADDGATEWAY' as the parameter. The following code snippet will help you understand this process.

```
public class AddGateway : System.Windows.Forms.Form
{
    ....................................

    private void cmdAddGateway_Click(object sender, System.EventArgs e)
    {
        XmlFormat xmlAddGateway=new XmlFormat("ADDGATEWAY",strParam);
        frmJabberClient.WriteMsg(xmlAddGateway.GetXml());
    }
}
```

The XmlFormat transforms the client request of including the gateway as per the following coding.

```
public XmlFormat(string strType,string []param)
{
  strXml= "<?xml version=\'1.0\' encoding=\'utf-8\'?>
<InstantMessanger>";
    ....................................
    else if (strType.ToUpper().CompareTo("ADDGATEWAY")==0)
    {
      AddGateway(param);
    }
    strXml+= "</InstantMessanger>";
}


public void AddGateway(String []param)
{
```

```
strXml+="<AddGateway>";
strXml+="<UserName>" + param[0] + "</UserName>";
strXml+="<MSNUserName>" + param[1] + "</MSNUserName>";
strXml+="<MSNPassword>" + param[2] + "</MSNPassword>";
strXml+="</AddGateway>";
}
```

The client request for including the gateway is headed by the <AddGateway> tag. While forming the XML structure, the name of the user for Jabber and MSN is required. The user's password for MSN is also required.

Request to delete a friend

The user raises this request when he/she wants to delete some friend from his/her list of friends. To delete a friend from the friend list, you can use the Delete menu or right-click the mouse button over the friend's name to use the Delete option of the pop-up menu for quick deletion. The window to delete the friend appears as shown in Figure 6-8.

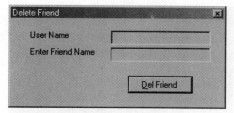

Figure 6-8: Delete Friend window

The request to delete a friend is handled by the DelFriend() function of the frmJabberClient class. On being invoked, this function hands over the request to the XmlFormat class for appropriate treatment. The DeleteFriendXML() function in the XmlFormat class formulates the appropriate XML structure required for the request. The following code snippet will help you understand the mechanism involved in creating the request to delete a friend.

```
public class frmJabberClient : System.Windows.Forms.Form
{

    ............................... .

  private void DelFriend()
  {

    ............................... .

    XmlFormat xmlDel=new XmlFormat("DELETEFRIEND",strParam);
  }
}

public XmlFormat(string strType,string []param)
{
```

```
        strXml= "<?xml version=\'1.0\' encoding=\'utf-8\'?>
<InstantMessenger>";
        ............................... .
        else if (strType.ToUpper().CompareTo("DELETEFRIEND")==0)
        {
           DeleteFriendXML(param);
        }
        strXml+= "</InstantMessenger>";
}

private void DeleteFriendXML(String []param)
{
   strXml+= "<DeleteFriend>";
   strXml+= "<UserName>"+param[0]+"</UserName>";
   strXml+= "<FriendName>"+param[1]+"</FriendName>";
   strXml+= "</DeleteFriend>";
}
```

Request to unregister a user

The user generates this request when he/she wants to unregister his/her account from the application network. Once the request for removing the account is processed by the application, the user is deprived of entry into the network, and he/she has no access to the resources and services of the application. To trigger the request for removal of the account, you need to select the Unregister option from the Login menu.

The unregistration request of the user is first faced by the UnRegister() function of frmJabberClient class. Thereafter, the Unregister() function hands over the request to the XmlFormat class, which calls its member function UnRegisterXML() to formulate the unregister request in appropriate XML structure. The following code snippet provides you with better insight into the nuances of the unregister request.

```
public class frmJabberClient : System.Windows.Forms.Form
{
   ............................... .
   private void UnRegister()
   {
       ............................... .
       XmlFormat xmlUnReg=new XmlFormat("UNREGISTER",strParam);
   }
}

public XmlFormat(string strType,string []param)
{
    strXml= "<?xml version=\'1.0\' encoding=\'utf-8\'?>
<InstantMessanger>";
    ............................... .
    else if (strType.ToUpper().CompareTo("UNREGISTER")==0)
```

```
    {
        UnRegisterXML(param);
    }
    strXml+= "</InstantMessanger>";
}

public void UnRegisterXML(String []param)
{
    strXml+="<UnRegister>";
    strXml+=param[0];
    strXml+="</UnRegister>";
}
```

The <UnRegister> tag represents the unregister request of the client. The sub element of this type of request is the login name of the user.

Logout request

The user resorts to this request when he/she is interested in quitting the application. The user can quit the application by clicking the Logout button on the main window of the application. Clicking this button brings into operation the Quit() function of frmJabberClient class. The Quit() function takes the login name of the user as a parameter. To form the client request into XML structure, the XmlFormat class is approached with the 'QUIT' parameter, as shown in the following code.

```
public class frmJabberClient : System.Windows.Forms.Form
{
    ................... . .

    private void Quit()
    {
        string []strParam=new String[1];
        strParam[0]=strLogin;
        ................... . .
        XmlFormat xmlQuit=new XmlFormat("QUIT",strParam);
        WriteMsg(xmlQuit.GetXml());
        xmlQuit=null;
        ................... . .
        netStream.Close();
        clientSocket.Close();
    }
}
```

To transform the quit request in XML structure, the XMLFormat class makes a call to its QuitXML() function. The following code snippet illustrates how the client request to quit the application is formed.

```
public XmlFormat(string strType,string []param)
{
```

```
    strXml= "<?xml version=\'1.0\'     encoding=\'utf-8\'?>
<InstantMessenger>";
    ...........................................
    else if (strType.ToUpper().CompareTo("QUIT")==0)
    {
      QuitXML(param);
    }
    strXml+= "</InstantMessenger>";
}

private void QuitXML(String []param)
{
  strXml+= "<Quit>";
  strXml+= "<UserName>"+param[0]+"</UserName>";
  strXml+= "</Quit>";
}
```

Server Responses

As we know, the Client module creates all types of client requests. Apart from creating and encoding these requests, the Client module is responsible for receiving, analyzing, and decoding the server response for the end user. To handle server-related jobs, the Client module must be endowed with certain capabilities, so as to empower it with analytical and decision-making qualifications. Only then can the responses returned by the server be easily understood by the user. Considering the nature of the tasks to be performed by the Client module, it must be vested with following capabilities:

- Reading the response returned by the server.
- Determining the nature of responses returned by the server; the Client module must have suitable provisions for parsing the server response.
- Processing the server module. While performing various actions, the Client module must consider *time* a key factor. If the Client module realizes that certain server responses are taking more time than normal processing, it must put such responses under the watch of the timer to avoid any blocking of normal proceedings.
- Maintaining GUI forms to display the server response.

In the following sections, you come to understand how the Client module addresses various server responses. First, you should understand how the Client module reads responses from the server.

How the Client module reads server responses

In our application, the ReadMsg() function of the frmJabberClient class takes the responsibility of reading the server responses. When the Client module successfully establishes its connection with the server, a thread is started, which helps the Client module iterate through the entire message or response from the server. To read the responses, the Client module stores the server response in a temporary file, which is named after the login name of the user. Once the entire response is stored and read, the next action of the Client module is to parse the server response to determine its type. For parsing the server response, a separate function named `ParseXml()` is written in the `frmJabberClient` class. The `ParseXml()` function is called from the `ReadMsg()` function itself. The main task of the `ParseXml()` function is to identify the type of response and retrieve the contents of the server response. Finally, after determining the type of response, the `processXml()` function comes into play. It takes the appropriate action on the server response and displays the response to the end user. All of this is outlined in the following code.

```csharp
public class frmJabberClient : System.Windows.Forms.Form
{
    ...........................
    ...........................
    private void ReadMsg()
    {
        ...........................
        System.IO.StreamWriter streamXml;
        if (System.IO.File.Exists(strLogin + "temp" +".xml"))
        {
            System.IO.File.Delete(strLogin + "temp" +".xml");
        }
        streamXml=System.IO.File.CreateText(strLogin + "temp" + ".xml");
        streamXml.Write(str);
        streamXml.Close();
        ...........................
        int iCode=parseXml(strLogin + "temp" +".xml");
        if (iCode!=-1) processXml(iCode);
        if (iCode==1)
    }
```

Types of server responses

As discussed previously, the `parseXml()` and `processXml()` functions of the `frmJabberClient` class handle the task of parsing and processing the server responses. While detailing each server response individually, the working of `parseXml()` and `processXml()` are discussed hand to hand. Whenever the Client module parses a response of the server, an integer value is assigned to the response to denote its type. This integer value is used for representing the type of response when processing needs to be carried out by the `processXml()` function. In the succeeding sections, server responses are lined up. While explaining them, the role of the `parseXml()` function is discussed. Thereafter, the working of the `processXml()` function is explained.

Response to login request

The Client module recognizes the server response for the login request by reading the name of the first child of the XML file. If the name of the first child turns out to be AUTH, the Client module fetches the attributes of child nodes present under the AUTH. On successful parsing of the response, the integer value 0 is denoted to login type. Next, the `processXml()` function comes into play. The following code snippet displays how the `parseXml()` function parses the server response for the authorization type of the request.

```
private int parseXml(string strFile)
{
   System.Xml.XmlDocument xmlDoc=new System.Xml.XmlDocument();
   System.Xml.XmlNode xNode;
   strXmlElements=null;
   ....................................

 try
 {
  xmlDoc.Load(strFile);
  if(xNode.FirstChild.Name.ToUpper().CompareTo("AUTH")==0)
  {
   strXmlElements=new string[1];
    If(xNode.FirstChild.ChildNodes.Item(0).Name.ToUpper().
      CompareTo("INT")==0)
     {
 strXmlElements[0]=xNode.FirstChild.ChildNodes.Item(0).InnerText.Trim();
       return 0;
     }
  }
  ....................................

}
```

If the login information entered by the user is correct, the `processXml()` function takes the appropriate action and displays 'Successful Login' on the status bar of the corresponding form. Similar to the status bar effect, the button on the toolbar is converted from login to logout. If the login name or password entered by the user is incorrect, the `Login()` function is called, which redisplays the login form for the user and replaces the misspelled information. The following code will help you understand the processing of the server response by `processXml()`.

```
private void processXml(int iXmlType)
{
 switch (iXmlType)
 {
  case 0:
  if (strXmlElements[0]=="0")
  {
    bLogin=true;
    msgQueue=new Queue();
```

```
    statusBarClient.Text="Succesfuly Login.";
    toolbarClient.Buttons[2].Text="Logout";
    ........................................
    else if (strXmlElements[0]=="1")
    {
     Login(strLogin,1);
    }
    else if (strXmlElements[0]=="2")
    {
     Login(strLogin,2);
    }
}
```

If user enters the incorrect login name, the integer value 1 is passed with the Login()
function. For the wrong password, the integer value 2 is supplied.

Response to registration request

After determining the server response to the registration request, the Client module returns the
integer value 1. After parsing and analyzing the Server module's response, the
processXml() function is called by the Client module. The following code snippet displays
how the Client module parses the server response for a registration request.

```
private int parseXml(string strFile)
{
    ........................................
    else if (xNode.FirstChild.Name.ToUpper().CompareTo("REGISTER")==0)
    {
      ........................................
      if
(xNode.FirstChild.ChildNodes.Item(0).Name.ToUpper().CompareTo("INT")==0)
      {
        strXmlElements[0]=xNode.FirstChild.ChildNodes.Item(0).InnerText;
        return 1;
      }
    }
    ........................................
}
```

When the processXml() function is called, the connection with the server ends but is soon
revived. This time, the authorization request is created with the help of the XmlFormat class.
The constructor of the XmlFormat class is used to create the login request login. If the
registration process cannot be completed successfully, perhaps due to a clash of similar login
names, the entire process of registration has to be repeated. The following code snippet will
help you understand the working of the processXml() function.

```
private void processXml(int iXmlType)
{
    ........................................
```

```
case 1:
{
 CloseConnection();
 string []strParam=new String[2];
 Connect();
 strParam[0]=strLogin;
 strParam[1]=strPassword;
 XmlFormat xmlLog=new XmlFormat("AUTH",strParam);
 WriteMsg(xmlLog.GetXml());
 else if (strXmlElements[0]=="1")
 {
   CloseConnection();
   Connect();
   Register(strLogin,1);
 }
}
}
```

If the registration process fails, the integer value 1 is passed to `Register()`. `Register()` invokes the registration process again.

Receive a friend list from the server

Whenever the user succeeds at establishing the connection with the application's server, he/she automatically receives the friend list without making any request. This friend list comprises names of the user's friends and their current statuses — online or offline. The following code snippet illustrates how the Client module parses the server response and retrieves friend list from it.

```
private int parseXml(string strFile)
{
........................
else if (xNode.FirstChild.Name.ToUpper().CompareTo("FRIENDLIST")==0)
{
 strXmlElements=new string[(xNode.FirstChild.ChildNodes.Count-1)/2+1]
........................
 strXmlElements[0]=xNode.FirstChild.ChildNodes.Item(0).InnerText;
........................
 for (int j=1;j<xNode.FirstChild.ChildNodes.Count;j+=2,k++)
 {
........................
if (xNode.FirstChild.ChildNodes.Item(j).Name.ToUpper().
      CompareTo("FRIENDNAME")==0)
strXmlElements[k]=xNode.FirstChild.ChildNodes.Item(j).InnerText;
........................
if (xNode.FirstChild.ChildNodes.Item(j+1).Name.ToUpper().
      CompareTo("STATUS")==0)
      strXmlElements[k]=xNode.FirstChild.ChildNodes.
      Item(j+1).InnerText.Trim()+strXmlElements[k];
```

```
}
 return 2;
}
```

When the friend list is parsed and the names of the friends, along with their statuses, are retrieved, and control over the application falls into the hands of the `processXml()` function. Since the length of the friend list can vary from user to user, the list takes some time to appear on the application's form. Hence, the `processXml()` function puts the processing of the friend list under the timer's consideration. An integer value is assigned to the timer, which denotes the processing of the friend list. The following code will help you understand this process.

```
private void processXml(int iXmlType)
{
   .............................................
   case 2:
   iFListCmd=0;
   fList=strXmlElements;
   break;
}
```

In the preceding code, the value of the `iFListCmd` variable determines the command for the timer. In our case, for obtaining the friend list, the command for the timer is set to `0`.

`processXml()` is only set to the command for the timer. It is the responsibility of the timer to update its list of commands, which occurs every 200 milliseconds. Each time the timer runs, its command list is checked to determine the latest command. The timer then takes the necessary steps to process the response. The following code snippet displays the action the timer executes in retrieving the friend list.

```
private void timerIM_Tick(object sender, System.EventArgs e)
{
   ..............................
   case 0:
   for (int i=1;i<fList.Length;i++)
   {
     if (fList[i].Substring(0,1)=="0")
     iImgIdx=3;
     else
     iImgIdx=2;
     AddFriendInTree(fList[i].Substring(1),iImgIdx);
   }
   treeFriendList.TopNode.Expand();
   break;
   ..............................
}
```

As you see in the preceding code snippet, the substring of array `fList` is searched. The `fList` array holds the friend list. If the value of the substring comes is 0, which means the user is offline, an appropriate image is set against the name of the friend to indicate his/her status. If the user is online, the corresponding image is set. Finally, after placing the images against the friends' names, the friend list is added in the friend tree, and the size of the friend-list tree is adjusted accordingly. The preceding code snippet shows the working of the timer.

Receive a message from a friend

The Client module, after parsing the message of the other user, transported and handed over by the server, denotes this type of response as 3. While parsing the message type response, the Client module obtains the names of the sender and receiver of the message and the content of the message. The following code snippet will help you understand the role of the parseXml() function in parsing the message.

```
private int parseXml(string strFile)
{
..........................................
else if (xNode.FirstChild.Name.ToUpper().CompareTo("MSG")==0)
{
  ..............................
if (xNode.FirstChild.ChildNodes.Item(j).Name.ToUpper().
    CompareTo("TARGET")==0)
    strXmlElements[0]=xNode.FirstChild.ChildNodes.Item(j).InnerText;
if (xNode.FirstChild.ChildNodes.Item(j).Name.ToUpper().
    CompareTo("SOURCE")==0)
    ...............................
}
return 3;
}
```

On being processed by the processXml() function, the GetMsgfrm() and MessageRecieved() functions are called.

```
private void processXml(int iXmlType)
{
.........................................
  case 3:
.........................................
frmSendMessage frmMsg=null;
frmMsg=GetMsgfrm(strXmlElements[1]);
frmMsg.MessageRecieved(strXmlElements[2]);
frmMsg.Show();
frmMsg.BringToFront();
}
```

The GetMsgfrm() function queues the messages for the user and displays the chatting window for each friend of the user. The MessageRecieved() function displays the chatting message of the friend to the user in customized colors.

Response to inclusion in a user's friend list

Whenever a user of the Instant Messaging application wishes to include you on his/her list of friends, he/she sends you a notification request, mentioning that he/she wishes to include you on his/her friends list. In return to the request, the user sends his/her response to accept or decline the request. Now consider the same scenario for our application in which the other user on his/her friend list sends a notification request. The name of a notification is SUBSCRIBE. The SUBSCRIBE notification is assigned a string value 2. The following code snippet will help you understand this process.

```
else if (xNode.FirstChild.Name.ToUpper().CompareTo("NOTIFYFRIENDS")==0)
...........................................
...........................................
else if (xNode.FirstChild.ChildNodes.Item(j).InnerText.Trim().
ToUpper().CompareTo("SUBSCRIBE")==0)
{
   strXmlElements[0]="2" + strXmlElements[0];
}
return 5;
```

As mentioned previously, all notification messages from the server are processed by the timer. Thus, when `processXml()` is called for processing the notification, it is handed over to the timer. The following code snippet illustrates how the `processXml()` function hands over the task to the timer.

```
private void processXml(int iXmlType)
{
...........................................
case 5:
iFListCmd=1;
strFriendNotify=strXmlElements[0];
break;
}
```

For processing the notification messages, the command for the timer is set as 1. When the processing reaches the timer, the `AddConfirm()` function is called, which delivers the message to the user to be included on the friend list. The message states that a particular user has requested to view your online status.

```
private void timerIM_Tick (object sender, System.EventArgs e)
{
........................... .
if (sNotify=="2")
{
   AddConfirm(strFriendNotify.Substring(1));
}
........................... .
}
```

Response to deletion from a user's friend list

When a user proceeds to delete you from his/her friend list, the Instant Messaging application sends a notification mentioning that the other user has requested this deletion. Whenever the user needs to omit a friend from the friend list, our Instant Messaging application delivers the notification to the target user. This type of notification is called UNSUBSCRIBE. To mark this notification, string type value 4 is assigned. The following code snippet is based on the preceding discussion.

```
if (xNode.FirstChild.ChildNodes.Item(j).Name.ToUpper().
    CompareTo("STATUS")==0)
{
  strSts=xNode.FirstChild.ChildNodes.Item(j).InnerText;
  elseif (xNode.FirstChild.ChildNodes.Item(j).InnerText.Trim().
    ToUpper().CompareTo("UNSUBSCRIBE")==0)
  {
    strXmlElements[0]="4" + strXmlElements[0];
  }
  return 5;
}
```

The processXml() function is called to process the server's response. For processing the server response, the processXml() function puts the response of the server under the consideration of the timer. The following code snippet displays the working of processXml().

```
private void processXml(int iXmlType)
{
  ....................................................
  case 5:
  iFList.Cmd=1;
  strFriendNotify=strXmlElements[0];
  break;
}
```

When the timer takes over the responsibility of completing the process to delete the friend from the friend list of the user. To accomplish the task, the timer calls the DelConfirm() function. The DelConfirm() function delivers the message to the target user, prompting that he/she has been deleted from the friend list of the user. Finally, the assistance of the XmlFormat class is taken up for formulating the appropriate XML structure, which holds the names of the user and his/her friend. The following code snippet illustrates the working of timer.

```
private void timerIM_Tick(object sender, System.EventArgs e)
{
  ................................
  else if (sNotify=="4")
  {
```

```
    DelConfirm(strFriendNotify.Substring(1));
  }
}
```

Response to an Add Friend request

Since being added to the friend list of a user is not a one-way process, you can also include other users in your friend list. When you have delivered your request to add a friend, the server brings back the response to your Add Friend request. The child node named FRIENDSTATUS heads the response of the server. When the parseXml() function starts parsing the server response, it obtains the friend name, his/her reply (STATUS)—whether he/she has rejected or accepted the proposal and his/her current status. Here we assume that the user has accepted the friendship proposal. Once, the response is parsed, the integer value 6 is assigned to such type of response parsing. The following code snippet illustrates the working of the parseXml() function in analyzing the server response for the Add Friend request.

```
else if (xNode.FirstChild.Name.ToUpper().CompareTo("FRIENDSTATUS")==0)
{
  if (xNode.FirstChild.ChildNodes.Item(j).Name.ToUpper().
    CompareTo("FRIENDNAME")==0)
    strXmlElements[0]=xNode.FirstChild.ChildNodes.Item(j).InnerText;
  if (xNode.FirstChild.ChildNodes.Item(j).Name.ToUpper().
    CompareTo("STATUS")==0)
    strXmlElements[0]+=xNode.FirstChild.ChildNodes.Item(j).InnerText;
  if (xNode.FirstChild.ChildNodes.Item(j).Name.ToUpper().
    CompareTo("ONLINE")==0)
    strXmlElements[0]=xNode.FirstChild.ChildNodes.Item(j).InnerText+
                                 strXmlElements[0];
  return 6;
}
```

On receiving the Server module's response for the Add friend request, the processXml() function processes the server response. The processXml() puts the processing of the Add Friend request under the consideration of the timer. The command for the timer is set to 2.

```
case 6:
iFListCmd=2;
```

The timer starts processing the response by first of all looking for the status of the user — whether he/she is online or offline. An online friend is denoted by 0, whereas 1 marks an online friend. Based on the status of the user, a suitable image is placed against the name of the friend. The AddFriendInTree() function is called with the friend name and the image as parameters, and the size of the friend-list tree is expanded accordingly. The following code snippet displays how the timer process the Add Friend request and performs a suitable action in adding the friend to the friend list of the user.

```
private void timerIM_Tick(object sender, System.EventArgs e)
{
..........................................................
 case 2:
 if (strFriendNotify.Substring(strFriendNotify.Length-1)=="0")
 {
  if (strFriendNotify.Substring(0,1)=="0")
  iImgIdx=3;
  else
  iImgIdx=2;
  AddFriendInTree(strFriendNotify.Substring(1,strFriendNotify.
                      Length-2,ImgIdx);
  treeFriendList.TopNode.Expand();
 }
}
```

Response to an unregister request

The user may wish to remove his/her account from the Instant Messaging application, thereby quitting all the facilities and services provided by the application. In our application, whenever the server responds to the unregistration request, the parseXml() function parses the response and retrieves the name of the user who makes the request. This type of client request is assigned the integer value 8. Next, the processXml() takes the suitable steps to fulfill the client request. The following code snippet illustrates the working of parseXml() function in parsing the server response.

```
else if (xNode.FirstChild.Name.ToUpper().CompareTo("UNREGISTER")==0)
{
 strXmlElements=new string[1];
 strXmlElements[0]=xNode.FirstChild.InnerText;
 return 8;
}
```

The processXml() function displays the message box to the user, prompting him/her that he/she has been unregistered from the application, followed with a call to the CloseConnection() function. The CloseConnection() function handles the job of closing down the stream and socket connection of the Client module with the server, there by providing smooth exit to the user from the application.

```
case 8:
if (strXmlElements[0]=="0")
MessageBox.Show("Unregistered");
CloseConnection();
Application.Exit();
break;
```

Response to an add gateway request

If the user wants to communicate with his/her friends who use MSN Instant Messenger, he/she needs to include the gateway for MSN Instant Messaging application. The following code snippet illustrates the working of the `parseXml()` function in the server response for the gateway request.

```
else if (xNode.FirstChild.Name.ToUpper().CompareTo("ADDGATEWAY")==0)
{
 strXmlElements=new string[1];
 strXmlElements[0]=xNode.FirstChild.InnerText;
 return 9;
}
```

The `processXml()` function comes into action when the gateway cannot be added. To display the failure, a message is displayed on the status bar of the Client module's form.

```
case 9:
if (strXmlElements[0]=="-1")
{
 statusBarClient.Text="Error : Can't Add gateway";
}
break;
```

Technical Documentation

This section covers the complete coding involved in building the Client module. For better understanding to the readers, the flow charts of various classes that are provided followed with code listing and explanation of the code listing.

Figure 6-9 illustrates the working of the `Main.cs` class.

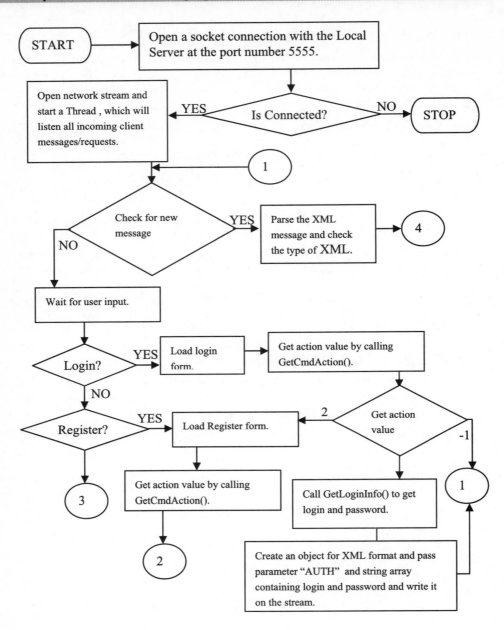

Figure 6-9(a): Flowchart of Main.cs

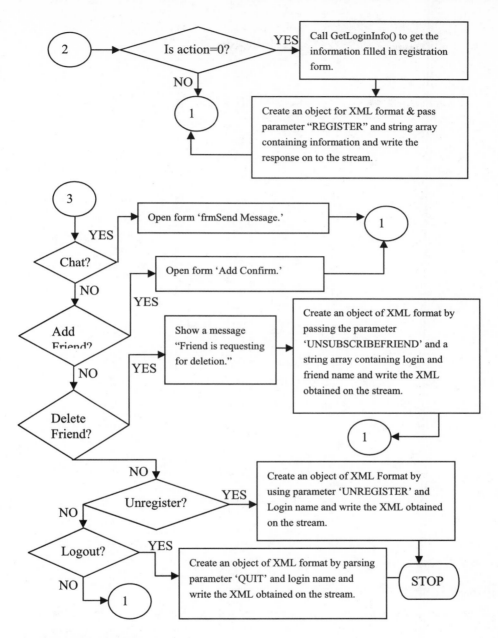

Figure 6-9(b): Flowchart of Main.cs

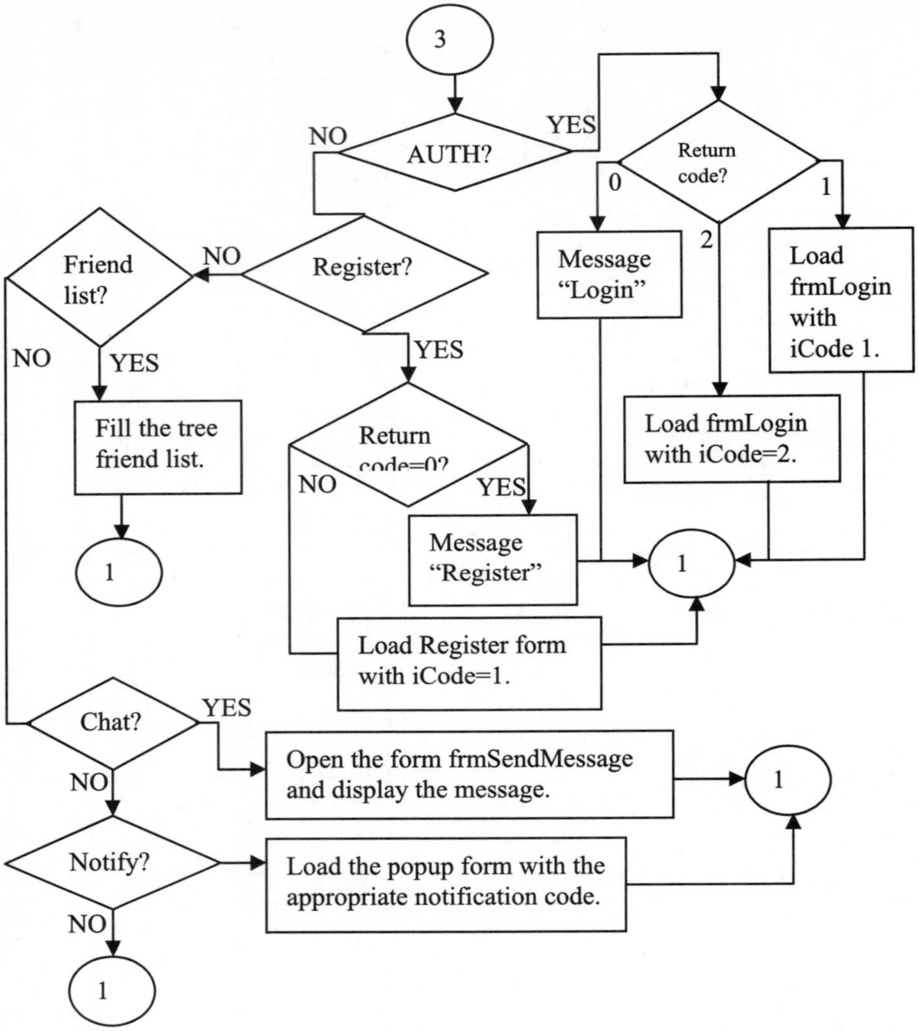

Figure 6-9(c): Flowchart of Main.cs

Listing 6-1: Main.cs

The following code listing has the Main() function that acts like the entry point for the application. The listing has various other functions like for Reading and writing the messages and analyzing the Server's response.

```csharp
 1 using System;
 2 using System.Drawing;
 3 using System.Collections;
 4 using System.ComponentModel;
 5 using System.Windows.Forms;
 6 using System.Data;
 7 using Jabber;
 8 using System.Net;
 9 using System.Net.Sockets;
10 using System.Xml;
11 using System.Threading;
12
13
14 namespace Jabber
15 {
16   /// <summary>
17   /// Summary description for Form1.
18   /// </summary>
19   public class frmJabberClient : System.Windows.Forms.Form
20   {
21     private System.Windows.Forms.ToolBar toolbarClient;
22     private System.Windows.Forms.StatusBar statusBarClient;
23     private System.Windows.Forms.ImageList imageListClient;
24     private System.Windows.Forms.ToolBarButton btnAdd;
25     private System.Windows.Forms.ToolBarButton btnSend;
26     private System.ComponentModel.IContainer components;
27
28
29     public System.Windows.Forms.TreeView treeFriendList;
30     private System.Windows.Forms.Timer timerIM;
31     private System.Windows.Forms.ContextMenu contextMenuIM;
32     private System.Windows.Forms.MenuItem menuAddFriend;
33     private System.Windows.Forms.MenuItem menuSendMsg;
34     private System.Windows.Forms.MenuItem menuDelFriend;
35     private System.Windows.Forms.MainMenu mainMenuIM;
36     private System.Windows.Forms.MenuItem menuItem1;
37     private System.Windows.Forms.MenuItem menuLogin;
38     private System.Windows.Forms.MenuItem menuSignIn;
39     private System.Windows.Forms.MenuItem menuUnRegister;
40     private System.Windows.Forms.MenuItem menuMessage;
41     private System.Windows.Forms.MenuItem menuSend;
42     private System.Windows.Forms.MenuItem menuFriends;
43     private System.Windows.Forms.MenuItem menuAdd;
44     private System.Windows.Forms.MenuItem menuDel;
45     private System.Windows.Forms.MenuItem menuHelp;
46     private System.Windows.Forms.MenuItem menuAbout;
47     private System.Windows.Forms.ToolBarButton btnAbout;
48     private System.Windows.Forms.ToolBarButton btnQuit;
49     private System.Windows.Forms.Label lblCopyrights;
```

```
50
51     //user defined variables.
52     public string strNotify;
53     public static string strLogin;
54     public bool bLogin;
55     public int iFListCmd;
56     public string strFriendNotify;
57     private sckClient clientSocket;
58     private static NetworkStream netStream=null;
59     private Thread thrd;
60     private bool bClose;
61     private bool bShown;
62     private Queue msgQueue;
63     public string []fList=null;
64     public string []strXmlElements=null;
65     private System.Windows.Forms.MenuItem mnuAddGateway;
66     private string strPassword="";
67
68
69   public frmJabberClient()
70   {
71     //
72     // Required for Windows Form Designer support
73     //
74     InitializeComponent();
75
76     //
77     // TODO: Add any constructor code after InitializeComponent
         // call
78             //
79
80 bClose=true;
81 bShown=false;
82 bLogin=false;
83 iFListCmd=-1;
84
85 }
86
87   /// <summary>
88   /// Clean up any resources being used.
89   /// </summary>
90   protected override void Dispose( bool disposing )
91   {
92     if( disposing )
93     {
94       if (components != null)
95       {
96         components.Dispose();
97       }
```

```
 98     }
 99     base.Dispose( disposing );
100   }
101
102   #region Windows Form Designer generated code
103   /// <summary>
104   /// Required method for Designer support - do not modify
105   /// the contents of this method with the code editor.
106   /// </summary>
107   private void InitializeComponent()
108   {
109     this.components = new System.ComponentModel.Container();
110     System.Resources.ResourceManager resources = new
             System.Resources.ResourceManager(typeof(frmJabberClient));
111     this.menuSendMsg = new System.Windows.Forms.MenuItem();
112     this.btnQuit = new System.Windows.Forms.ToolBarButton();
113     this.lblCopyrights = new System.Windows.Forms.Label();
114     this.menuAddFriend = new System.Windows.Forms.MenuItem();
115     this.menuFriends = new System.Windows.Forms.MenuItem();
116     this.menuAdd = new System.Windows.Forms.MenuItem();
117     this.menuDel = new System.Windows.Forms.MenuItem();
118     this.mnuAddGateway = new System.Windows.Forms.MenuItem();
119     this.menuSend = new System.Windows.Forms.MenuItem();
120     this.btnSend = new System.Windows.Forms.ToolBarButton();
121     this.menuSignIn = new System.Windows.Forms.MenuItem();
122     this.imageListClient = new
               System.Windows.Forms.ImageList(this.components);
123     this.menuHelp = new System.Windows.Forms.MenuItem();
124     this.menuAbout = new System.Windows.Forms.MenuItem();
125     this.toolbarClient = new System.Windows.Forms.ToolBar();
126     this.btnAdd = new System.Windows.Forms.ToolBarButton();
127     this.btnAbout = new System.Windows.Forms.ToolBarButton();
128     this.statusBarClient = new System.Windows.Forms.StatusBar();
129     this.menuItem1 = new System.Windows.Forms.MenuItem();
130     this.menuUnRegister = new System.Windows.Forms.MenuItem();
131     this.menuDelFriend = new System.Windows.Forms.MenuItem();
132     this.treeFriendList = new System.Windows.Forms.TreeView();
133     this.contextMenuIM = new System.Windows.Forms.ContextMenu();
134     this.menuMessage = new System.Windows.Forms.MenuItem();
135     this.menuLogin = new System.Windows.Forms.MenuItem();
136     this.timerIM = new
             System.Windows.Forms.Timer(this.components);
137     this.mainMenuIM = new System.Windows.Forms.MainMenu();
138     this.SuspendLayout();
139     //
140     // menuSendMsg
141     //
142     this.menuSendMsg.Index = 1;
143     this.menuSendMsg.Text = "&Send Message";
```

```
144    this.menuSendMsg.Click += new
               System.EventHandler(this.menuSendMsg_Click);
145    //
146    // btnQuit
147    //
148    this.btnQuit.ImageIndex = 8;
149    this.btnQuit.Text = "Login";
150    //
151    // lblCopyrights
152    //
153    this.lblCopyrights.ForeColor = System.Drawing.Color.Blue;
154    this.lblCopyrights.Location = new System.Drawing.Point(8, 48);
155    this.lblCopyrights.Name = "lblCopyrights";
156    this.lblCopyrights.Size = new System.Drawing.Size(208, 16);
157    this.lblCopyrights.TabIndex = 0;
158    this.lblCopyrights.Text = "© Dreamtech Software India Inc.";
159    this.lblCopyrights.TextAlign =
           System.Drawing.ContentAlignment.BottomCenter;
160    //
161    // menuAddFriend
162    //
163    this.menuAddFriend.Index = 0;
164    this.menuAddFriend.Text = "&Add Friend";
165    this.menuAddFriend.Click += new
           System.EventHandler(this.menuAddFriend_Click);
166    //
167    // menuFriends
168    //
169    this.menuFriends.Index = 2;
170    this.menuFriends.MenuItems.AddRange(new
           System.Windows.Forms.MenuItem[] {
171    this.menuAdd,
172    this.menuDel,
173    this.mnuAddGateway});
174    this.menuFriends.Text = "&Friends";
175    //
176    // menuAdd
177    //
178    this.menuAdd.Index = 0;
179    this.menuAdd.Text = "&Add Friend";
180    this.menuAdd.Click += new
           System.EventHandler(this.menuAdd_Click);
181    //
182    // menuDel
183    //
184    this.menuDel.Index = 1;
185    this.menuDel.Text = "&Del Friend";
186    this.menuDel.Click += new
           System.EventHandler(this.menuDel_Click);
```

```
187    //
188    // mnuAddGateway
189    //
190    this.mnuAddGateway.Index = 2;
191    this.mnuAddGateway.Text = "ADD &Gateway";
192    this.mnuAddGateway.Click += new
           System.EventHandler(this.mnuAddGateway_Click);
193    //
194    // menuSend
195    //
196    this.menuSend.Index = 0;
197    this.menuSend.Text = "&Send Message";
198    this.menuSend.Click += new
           System.EventHandler(this.menuSend_Click);
199    //
200    // btnSend
201    //
202    this.btnSend.ImageIndex = 1;
203    this.btnSend.Text = "Chat";
204    //
205    // menuSignIn
206    //
207    this.menuSignIn.Index = 0;
208    this.menuSignIn.Text = "&Sign in";
209    this.menuSignIn.Click += new
           System.EventHandler(this.menuSignIn_Click);
210    //
211    // imageListClient
212    //
213    this.imageListClient.ColorDepth =
           System.Windows.Forms.ColorDepth.Depth8Bit;
214    this.imageListClient.ImageSize = new System.Drawing.Size(16,
                                                  16);
215    this.imageListClient.ImageStream =
           ((System.Windows.Forms.ImageListStreamer)(resources.
           GetObject("imageListClient.ImageStream")));
216    this.imageListClient.TransparentColor =
           System.Drawing.Color.Transparent;
217    //
218    // menuHelp
219    //
220    this.menuHelp.Index = 3;
221    this.menuHelp.MenuItems.AddRange(new
           System.Windows.Forms.MenuItem[] {
222    this.menuAbout});
223    this.menuHelp.Text = "&Help";
224    //
225    // menuAbout
226    //
```

```
227    this.menuAbout.Index = 0;
228    this.menuAbout.Text = "&About";
229    this.menuAbout.Click += new
           System.EventHandler(this.menuAbout_Click);
230    //
231    // toolbarClient
232    //
233    this.toolbarClient.AutoSize = false;
234    this.toolbarClient.Buttons.AddRange(new
           System.Windows.Forms.ToolBarButton[] {
235    this.btnAdd,
236    this.btnSend,
237    this.btnQuit,
238    this.btnAbout});
239    this.toolbarClient.ButtonSize = new System.Drawing.Size(50, 40);
240    this.toolbarClient.DropDownArrows = true;
241    this.toolbarClient.ImageList = this.imageListClient;
242    this.toolbarClient.Name = "toolbarClient";
243    this.toolbarClient.ShowToolTips = true;
244    this.toolbarClient.Size = new System.Drawing.Size(208, 48);
245    this.toolbarClient.TabIndex = 0;
246    this.toolbarClient.Wrappable = false;
247    this.toolbarClient.ButtonClick += new
           System.Windows.Forms.ToolBarButtonClickEventHandler
           (this.toolbarClient_ButtonClick);
248    //
249    // btnAdd
250    //
251    this.btnAdd.ImageIndex = 0;
252    this.btnAdd.Text = "Add";
253    //
254    // btnAbout
255    //
256    this.btnAbout.ImageIndex = 4;
257    this.btnAbout.Text = "About";
258    //
259    // statusBarClient
260    //
261    this.statusBarClient.Location = new System.Drawing.Point(0, 156);
262    this.statusBarClient.Name = "statusBarClient";
263    this.statusBarClient.Size = new System.Drawing.Size(208, 16);
264    this.statusBarClient.TabIndex = 1;
265    //
266    // menuItem1
267    //
268    this.menuItem1.Index = -1;
269    this.menuItem1.Text = "";
270    //
271    // menuUnRegister
```

```
272    //
273    this.menuUnRegister.Index = 1;
274    this.menuUnRegister.Text = "&Un-Register";
275    this.menuUnRegister.Click += new
          System.EventHandler(this.menuUnRegister_Click);
276    //
277    // menuDelFriend
278    //
279    this.menuDelFriend.Index = 2;
280    this.menuDelFriend.Text = "&Delete Friend";
281    this.menuDelFriend.Click += new
          System.EventHandler(this.menuDelFriend_Click);
282    //
283    // treeFriendList
284    //
285    this.treeFriendList.ContextMenu = this.contextMenuIM;
286    this.treeFriendList.ImageList = this.imageListClient;
287    this.treeFriendList.Location = new System.Drawing.Point(8, 72);
288    this.treeFriendList.Name = "treeFriendList";
289    this.treeFriendList.Nodes.AddRange(new
          System.Windows.Forms.TreeNode[] {
290    new System.Windows.Forms.TreeNode("Friends", 5, 5)});
291    this.treeFriendList.Size = new System.Drawing.Size(192, 192);
292    this.treeFriendList.TabIndex = 2;
293    this.treeFriendList.DoubleClick += new
          System.EventHandler(this.treeFriendList_DoubleClick);
294    //
295    // contextMenuIM
296    //
297    this.contextMenuIM.MenuItems.AddRange(new
          System.Windows.Forms.MenuItem[] {
298    this.menuAddFriend,
299    this.menuSendMsg,
300    this.menuDelFriend});
301    //
302    // menuMessage
303    //
304    this.menuMessage.Index = 1;
305    this.menuMessage.MenuItems.AddRange(new
          System.Windows.Forms.MenuItem[] {
306    this.menuSend});
307    this.menuMessage.Text = "&Message";
308    //
309    // menuLogin
310    //
311    this.menuLogin.Index = 0;
312    this.menuLogin.MenuItems.AddRange(new
          System.Windows.Forms.MenuItem[] {
313    this.menuSignIn,
```

```
314   this.menuUnRegister});
315   this.menuLogin.Text = "&Login";
316   //
317   // timerIM
318   //
319   this.timerIM.Enabled = true;
320   this.timerIM.Interval = 200;
321   this.timerIM.Tick += new
          System.EventHandler(this.timerIM_Tick);
322   //
323   // mainMenuIM
324   //
325   this.mainMenuIM.MenuItems.AddRange(new
          System.Windows.Forms.MenuItem[] {
326   this.menuLogin,
327   this.menuMessage,
328   this.menuFriends,
329   this.menuHelp});
330   //
331   // frmJabberClient
332   //
333   this.AutoScaleBaseSize = new System.Drawing.Size(5, 13);
334   this.ClientSize = new System.Drawing.Size(208, 172);
335   this.Controls.AddRange(new System.Windows.Forms.Control[] {
336   this.lblCopyrights,
337   this.treeFriendList,
338   this.statusBarClient,
339   this.toolbarClient});
340   this.MaximizeBox = false;
341   this.Menu = this.mainMenuIM;
342   this.Name = "frmJabberClient";
343   this.Text = "Jabber Client";
344   this.Resize += new
                  System.EventHandler(this.frmJabberClient_Resize);
345   this.Closing += new  System.ComponentModel.CancelEventHandler
      (this.frmJabberClient_Closing);
346   this.Activated += new
          System.EventHandler(this.frmJabberClient_Activated);
347   this.ResumeLayout(false);
348
349   }
350   #endregion
351
352   /// <summary>
353   /// The main entry point for the application.
354   /// </summary>
355   [STAThread]
356   static void Main()
357   {
```

```
358    Application.Run(new frmJabberClient());
359  }
360
361  private void toolbarClient_ButtonClick(object sender,
362        System.Windows.Forms.ToolBarButtonClickEventArgs e)
362  {
363  if (e.Button.Text.CompareTo("Chat")==0)
364  {
365    SendMessage();
366    return;
367  }
368
369  if (e.Button.Text.CompareTo("About")==0)
370  {
371      About();
372  return;
373  }
374
375  if (e.Button.Text.CompareTo("Add")==0)
376  {
377    AddFriend();
378    return;
379  }
380
381
382  if (e.Button.Text.CompareTo("Login")==0)
383  {
384    Login("",0);
385    return;
386  }
387  if (e.Button.Text.CompareTo("Logout")==0)
388  {
389    Quit();
390  }
391  }
392
393  private void Quit()
394  {
395    string []strParam=new String[1];
396    strParam[0]=strLogin;
397
398  if (bLogin)
399  {
400    XmlFormat xmlQuit=new XmlFormat("QUIT",strParam);
401    WriteMsg(xmlQuit.GetXml());
402    xmlQuit=null;
403  }
404    bClose=true;
405
```

```
406
407   if (clientSocket==null) return;
408   if (clientSocket.IsConnected())
409   {
410     netStream.Close();
411     clientSocket.Close();
412   }
413   netStream=null;
414   clientSocket=null;
415   bClose=true;
416
417   Application.Exit();
418   return;
419   }
420
421
422   private void frmJabberClient_Activated(object sender,
                        System.EventArgs e)
423   {
424     if (!bShown)
425     {
426       Connect();
427       bShown=true;
428       Login("",0);
429     }
430   }
431
432   private void frmJabberClient_Resize(object sender,
                        System.EventArgs e)
433   {
434     if (this.Height<304) this.Height=304;
435     if (this.Width<208) this.Width=208;
436     treeFriendList.Width=this.Width-treeFriendList.Left-8;
437     treeFriendList.Height=statusBarClient.Top-
                        toolbarClient.Height-lblCopyrights.Height-16;
438     treeFriendList.Top=toolbarClient.Height
                                        +lblCopyrights.Height+8;
439     lblCopyrights.Width=treeFriendList.Width;
440     treeFriendList.Left=4;
441   }
442
443   private void ProcessLoginAction(frmLogin frmLog)
444   {
445     string []strParam=null;
446     int action=frmLog.GetCmdAction();
447     XmlFormat xmlLog;
448
449     switch (action)
450     {
```

```
451        case 0:
452          strParam=new String[2];
453
454          strParam=frmLog.GetLoginInfo();
455          strLogin=strParam[0];
456
457          xmlLog=new XmlFormat("AUTH",strParam);
458          WriteMsg(xmlLog.GetXml());
459          xmlLog=null;
460          break;
461          case 1:
462            Register("",0);
463            break;
464          case -1: //skip
465          break;
466          }
467  }
468
469  private void ProcessRegisterAction(frmRegister frmReg)
470  {
471      string []strParam=null;
472      XmlFormat xmlReg;
473
474      int act=frmReg.GetCmdAction();
475
476      switch (act)
477      {
478          case 0:
479          strParam=new String[11];
480          strParam=frmReg.GetLoginInfo();
481
482          this.Text=strParam[0];
483          strLogin=strParam[0];
484          strPassword=strParam[1];
485
486          xmlReg=new XmlFormat("REGISTER",strParam);
487          WriteMsg(xmlReg.GetXml());
488          xmlReg=null;
489          break;
490          default:
491          break;
492          }
493  }
494
495  private void Connect()
496  {
497      clientSocket=new sckClient();
498      try
499      {
```

```
500         clientSocket.Connect("pratul",5555);
501     }
502    catch
503    {
504       try
505       {
506         clientSocket.Connect("gaurav",5555);
507       }
508       catch
509       {
510
511  MessageBox.Show("Can't connect to the server","Connection
Error");
512         Application.Exit();
513         return;
514       }
515    }
516
517       //while (!sck.IsConnected()); //wait
518       netStream=clientSocket.GetStream();
519
520
521       thrd=new Thread(new ThreadStart(ReadMsg));
522       thrd.Start();
523       bClose=false;
524  }
525
526  private void ReadMsg()
527  {
528    byte bData;
529    string str="",strEndTag="</InstantMessanger>";
530    char []ch=strEndTag.ToCharArray();
531    bool bMatch=false;
532    int i=0,len=strEndTag.Length;
533   bool bCharFound=false;
534
535    while (true)
536    {
537    Application.DoEvents();
538    if (bClose) return;
539
540    try
541    {
542
543       bCharFound=false;
544       while (netStream.DataAvailable)
545       {
546         if (bClose) return;
547         Application.DoEvents();
```

```
548          char chByte;
549
550          bData=(byte)netStream.ReadByte();
551
552          chByte=(char)bData;
553          if (!bCharFound)
554          {
555      if (chByte==' ' || chByte=='\r' || chByte=='\n' || chByte=='\t')
556          {
557             continue;
558          }
559          else
560          {
561             bCharFound=true;
562          }
563      }
564
565      if ((chByte==ch[i]))
566      {
567         i++;
568      }
569      else
570      {
571         i=0;
572      }
573
574      str+=((char)bData).ToString();
575
576      if (i==len)
577      {
578         bMatch=true;
579         break;
580      }
581  }
582
583      if (bMatch)
584      {
585         bMatch=false;
586         System.IO.StreamWriter streamXml;
587         if (System.IO.File.Exists(strLogin + "temp" +".xml"))
588         {
589            System.IO.File.Delete(strLogin + "temp" +".xml");
590         }
591         streamXml=System.IO.File.CreateText
             (strLogin + "temp" + ".xml");
592         streamXml.Write(str);
593         streamXml.Close();
594         str="";
595         i=0;
```

```
596
597      int iCode=parseXml(strLogin + "temp" +".xml");
598      if (iCode!=-1) processXml(iCode);
599      if (iCode==1)
600      {
601        bClose=true;
602        return;
603      }
604    }
605  }
606    catch(Exception ex)
607    {
608
609      MessageBox.Show(ex.ToString(),"Session closed on error");
610      bClose=true;
611      return;
612    }
613  }
614 }
615
616  public static int WriteMsg(string strMsg)
617  {
618    if (netStream==null)
619    return 1;
620    if (!netStream.CanWrite)
621    return 1;
622
623    int len=strMsg.Length;
624    char []chData=new Char[len];
625    byte []bData=new byte[len];
626
627    chData=strMsg.ToCharArray();
628    for (int i=0;i<len;i++)
629    {
630      bData[i]=(byte)chData[i];
631    }
632    try
633    {
634      netStream.Write(bData,0,len);
635    }
636    catch
637    {
638      bData=null;
639      chData=null;
640      return 1;
641    }
642    bData=null;
643    chData=null;
644    return 0;
```

```
645   }
646
647   private void frmJabberClient_Closing(object sender,
                System.ComponentModel.CancelEventArgs e)
648   {
649     if (bClose==true)
650     {
651       return;
652     }
653     Quit();
654   }
655
656   private int parseXml(string strFile)
657   {
658     System.Xml.XmlDocument xmlDoc=new System.Xml.XmlDocument();
659     System.Xml.XmlNode xNode;
660
661     strXmlElements=null;
662
663     try
664     {
665       xmlDoc.Load(strFile);
666       if (xmlDoc.ChildNodes.Count<2)
667       {
668         return(-1);
669       }
670       xNode=xmlDoc.ChildNodes.Item(1);
671   if (xNode.Name.Trim().ToUpper().CompareTo("INSTANTMESSANGER")!=0)
672     {
673       return(-1);
674     }
675
676     if (xNode.FirstChild.Name.ToUpper().CompareTo("AUTH")==0)
677     {
678       strXmlElements=new string[1];
679       if (xNode.FirstChild.ChildNodes.Item(0).Name.
                ToUpper().CompareTo("INT")==0)
680       {
681         strXmlElements[0]=
                xNode.FirstChild.ChildNodes.Item(0).InnerText.Trim();
682         return 0;
683       }
684       else
685       {
686         return -1;
687       }
688     }
689   else if (xNode.FirstChild.Name.ToUpper().CompareTo("REGISTER")==0)
690     {
```

```
691        strXmlElements=new string[1];
692      if xNode.FirstChild.ChildNodes.Item(0).
             Name.ToUpper().CompareTo("INT")==0)
693        {
694  strXmlElements[0]=xNode.FirstChild.ChildNodes.Item(0).InnerText;
695        return 1;
696        }
697        else
698        {
699          return -1;
700        }
701      }
702     else if (xNode.FirstChild.Name.ToUpper().CompareTo
                ("FRIENDLIST")==0)
703      {
704        strXmlElements=new
           string[(xNode.FirstChild.ChildNodes.Count-1)/2+1];
705        if (xNode.FirstChild.ChildNodes.Count<1)
706        {
707          return(-1);
708        }
709        else
710        {
711     strXmlElements[0]=xNode.FirstChild.ChildNodes.Item(0).InnerText;
712        }
713
714     int k=1;
715     for (int j=1;j<xNode.FirstChild.ChildNodes.Count;j+=2,k++)
716     {
717         if (xNode.FirstChild.ChildNodes.Item(j).Name.ToUpper().
             CompareTo("FRIENDNAME")==0)
718     strXmlElements[k]=xNode.FirstChild.ChildNodes.Item(j).InnerText;
719         else
720         return -1;
721     if (xNode.FirstChild.ChildNodes.Item(j+1).Name.ToUpper().
           CompareTo("STATUS")==0)
722     strXmlElements[k]=xNode.FirstChild.ChildNodes.
           Item(j+1).InnerText.Trim() +strXmlElements[k];
723     else
724       return -1;
725     }
726       return 2;
727     }
728     else if (xNode.FirstChild.Name.ToUpper().CompareTo("MSG")==0)
729     {
730       strXmlElements=new string[3];
731       for (int j=0;j<xNode.FirstChild.ChildNodes.Count;j++)
732       {
733         if (xNode.FirstChild.ChildNodes.Item(j).Name.
```

```
734            ToUpper().CompareTo("TARGET")==0)
     strXmlElements[0]=xNode.FirstChild.ChildNodes.Item(j).InnerText;
735          if (xNode.FirstChild.ChildNodes.Item(j).
               Name.ToUpper().CompareTo("SOURCE")==0)
736    strXmlElements[1]=xNode.FirstChild.ChildNodes.Item(j).InnerText;
737           if (xNode.FirstChild.ChildNodes.Item(j).Name.
                ToUpper().CompareTo("TEXT")==0)
738    strXmlElements[2]=xNode.FirstChild.ChildNodes.Item(j).InnerText;
739        }
740      if (strXmlElements[0]=="" || strXmlElements[1]=="" ||
           strXmlElements[2]=="") //invalid xml
741      {
742         return -1;
743      }
744      else
745         return 3;
746      }
747      else if (xNode.FirstChild.Name.ToUpper().CompareTo("ROSTER")==0)
748      {
749        int k=0;
750     strXmlElements=new String[(xNode.FirstChild.ChildNodes.Count)/2];
751
752        for (int j=0;j<xNode.FirstChild.ChildNodes.Count;j+=2,k++)
753        {
754          if (xNode.FirstChild.ChildNodes.Item(j).Name.ToUpper().
                 CompareTo("FRIENDID")==0)
755    strXmlElements[k]=xNode.FirstChild.ChildNodes.Item(j).InnerText;
756          else
757          return -1;
758          if (xNode.FirstChild.ChildNodes.Item(j+1).Name.ToUpper().
                 CompareTo("SUBSCRIPTION")==0)
759          {
760            if (xNode.FirstChild.ChildNodes.Item(j+1).
                   InnerText.ToUpper().CompareTo("NONE")==0)
761            {
762                strXmlElements[k]+="0";
763            }
764        else if (xNode.FirstChild.ChildNodes.Item(j+1).InnerText.
                ToUpper().CompareTo("FROM")==0)
765        strXmlElements[k]+="1";
766        else if (xNode.FirstChild.ChildNodes.Item(j+1).InnerText.
                ToUpper().CompareTo("TO")==0)
767        strXmlElements[k]+="2";
768        else if (xNode.FirstChild.ChildNodes.Item(j+1).InnerText.
                ToUpper().CompareTo("BOTH")==0)
769        strXmlElements[k]+="3";
770          }
771          else
772           return -1;
```

```
773     }
774   return 4;
775   }
776     else if (xNode.FirstChild.Name.ToUpper().CompareTo
        ("NOTIFYFRIENDS")==0)
777     {
778       strXmlElements=new String[1];
779
780       string strSts="";
781       for (int j=0;j<xNode.FirstChild.ChildNodes.Count;j++)
782       {
783 if (xNode.FirstChild.ChildNodes.Item(j).Name.ToUpper().
        CompareTo("USERNAME")==0)
784 {
785 strXmlElements[0]=xNode.FirstChild.ChildNodes.Item(j).InnerText;
786 }
787 if (xNode.FirstChild.ChildNodes.Item(j).Name.ToUpper().
        CompareTo("STATUS")==0)
788 {
789   strSts=xNode.FirstChild.ChildNodes.Item(j).InnerText;
790 if (xNode.FirstChild.ChildNodes.Item(j).InnerText.Trim().
        ToUpper().CompareTo("ON-LINE")==0)
791 {
792   strXmlElements[0]="1" + strXmlElements[0];
793 }
794 else if (xNode.FirstChild.ChildNodes.Item(j).InnerText.
        Trim().ToUpper().CompareTo("SUBSCRIBE")==0)
795 {
796   strXmlElements[0]="2" + strXmlElements[0];
797 }
798 else if (xNode.FirstChild.ChildNodes.Item(j).InnerText.
        Trim().ToUpper().CompareTo("SUBSCRIBED")==0)
799 {
800   strXmlElements[0]="3" + strXmlElements[0];
801 }
802 else if (xNode.FirstChild.ChildNodes.Item(j).InnerText.
        Trim().ToUpper().CompareTo("UNSUBSCRIBE")==0)
803 {
804   strXmlElements[0]="4" + strXmlElements[0];
805 }
806 else if (xNode.FirstChild.ChildNodes.Item(j).InnerText.
        Trim().ToUpper().CompareTo("UNSUBSCRIBED")==0)
807 {
808   strXmlElements[0]="5" + strXmlElements[0];
809 }
810 else
811 {
812   strXmlElements[0]="0" + strXmlElements[0];
813 }
```

```
814
815         }
816     }
817     return 5;
818  }
819  else if (xNode.FirstChild.Name.ToUpper().
        CompareTo("FRIENDSTATUS")==0)
820  {
821     strXmlElements=new string[1];
822
823  for (intj=0;j<xNode.FirstChild.ChildNodes.Count;j++)
824  {
825     if (xNode.FirstChild.ChildNodes.Item(j).Name.ToUpper().
        CompareTo("FRIENDNAME")==0)
826  strXmlElements[0]=xNode.FirstChild.ChildNodes.Item(j).InnerText;
827     if (xNode.FirstChild.ChildNodes.Item(j).Name.ToUpper().
        CompareTo("STATUS")==0)
828  strXmlElements[0]+=xNode.FirstChild.ChildNodes.Item(j).InnerText;
829     if (xNode.FirstChild.ChildNodes.Item(j).Name.ToUpper().
        CompareTo("ONLINE")==0)
830  strXmlElements[0]=xNode.FirstChild.ChildNodes.Item(j).InnerText +
                              strXmlElements[0];
831  }
832  return 6;
833  }
834  else if (xNode.FirstChild.Name.ToUpper().CompareTo
        ("DELETESTATUS")==0)
835  {
836     strXmlElements=new string[1];
837
838     for (int j=0;j<xNode.FirstChild.ChildNodes.Count;j++)
839     {
840      if (xNode.FirstChild.ChildNodes.Item(j).Name.ToUpper().
        CompareTo("FRIENDNAME")==0)
841  strXmlElements[0]=xNode.FirstChild.ChildNodes.Item(j).InnerText;
842  if (xNode.FirstChild.ChildNodes.Item(j).Name.ToUpper().
        CompareTo("STATUS")==0)
843  strXmlElements[0]+=xNode.FirstChild.ChildNodes.Item(j).InnerText;
844  }
845  return 7;
846  }
847  else if (xNode.FirstChild.Name.ToUpper().CompareTo
        ("UNREGISTER")==0)
848  {
849     strXmlElements=new string[1];
850
851     strXmlElements[0]=xNode.FirstChild.InnerText;
852      return 8;
```

```
853      }
854      else if (xNode.FirstChild.Name.ToUpper().CompareTo
           ("ADDGATEWAY")==0)
855      {
856        strXmlElements=new string[1];
857
858        strXmlElements[0]=xNode.FirstChild.InnerText;
859        return 9;
860      }
861    }
862    catch
863    {
864      return(-1);
865    }
866     return -1;
867    }
868
869    private void processXml(int iXmlType)
870    {
871      switch (iXmlType)
872      {
873        case 0:
874        if (strXmlElements[0]=="0")
875        {
876          bLogin=true;
877
878          msgQueue=new Queue();
879
880          statusBarClient.Text="Succesfuly Login.";
881          toolbarClient.Buttons[2].Text="Logout";
882          menuSignIn.Text="&Sign out";
883          toolbarClient.Buttons[2].ImageIndex=9;
884          this.Text=strLogin + " (online)";
885        }
886    else if (strXmlElements[0]=="1")
887    {
888      Login(strLogin,1);
889    }
890    else if (strXmlElements[0]=="2")
891    {
892      Login(strLogin,2);
893    }
894    else if (strXmlElements[0]=="-1")
895    {
896      MessageBox.Show("Closing
           Application","Critical Error");
897      Application.Exit();
898    }
899    break;
```

```
900   case 1:
901     if (strXmlElements[0].Trim()=="0")
902     {
903       bLogin=true;
904       bClose=true;
905
906       CloseConnection();
907
908       string []strParam=new String[2];
909
910       Connect();
911       strParam[0]=strLogin;
912       strParam[1]=strPassword;
913
914
915       XmlFormat xmlLog=new XmlFormat("AUTH",strParam);
916       WriteMsg(xmlLog.GetXml());
917       xmlLog=null;
918       statusBarClient.Text="Login....";
919     }
920     else if (strXmlElements[0]=="1")
921     {
922       CloseConnection();
923       Connect();
924       Register(strLogin,1);
925     }
926     else
927     {
928       MessageBox.Show("Closing
          Application","Critical Error");
929       Application.Exit();
930     }
931     break;
932      case 2:
933     if (!bLogin) return;
934     iFListCmd=0; //set command for timer_event
935     fList=strXmlElements;
936     break;
937     case 3:
938       if (!bLogin) return;
939       frmSendMessage frmMsg=null;
940       frmMsg=GetMsgfrm(strXmlElements[1]);
941       frmMsg.MessageRecieved(strXmlElements[2]);
942       frmMsg.Show();
943       frmMsg.BringToFront();
944       Application.DoEvents();
945       break;
946     case 4:
947       iFListCmd=6;
```

```
948        fList=strXmlElements;
949        break;
950    case 5:
951        iFListCmd=1;
952        strFriendNotify=strXmlElements[0];
953        break;
954    case 6:
955        iFListCmd=2;
956        strFriendNotify=strXmlElements[0];
957        break;
958    case 7:
959        iFListCmd=3;
960        strFriendNotify=strXmlElements[0];
961        break;
962    case 8:
963        if (strXmlElements[0]=="0")
964        MessageBox.Show("Unregistered");
965        CloseConnection();
966        Application.Exit();
967        break;
968        case 9:
969        if (strXmlElements[0]=="-1")
970        {
971           statusBarClient.Text="Error : Can't Add gateway";
972        }
973        break;
974    }
975 }
976
977 private void CloseConnection()
978 {
979   try
980   {
981     bClose=true;
982     bLogin=false;
983     iFListCmd=-1;
984
985     thrd=null;
986
987     if (netStream!=null && netStream.CanRead)
988     netStream.Close();
989     netStream=null;
990
991     if (clientSocket!=null && clientSocket.IsConnected())
992     clientSocket.Close();
993     clientSocket=null;
994   }
995   catch
996   {
```

```
 997        //skip...
 998      }
 999  }
1000
1001  private frmSendMessage GetMsgfrm(string strFriend)
1002  {
1003     object []objMsgFrm=null;
1004     frmSendMessage frmMsg=null;
1005
1006     objMsgFrm=msgQueue.ToArray();
1007     for(int f=0;f<objMsgFrm.Length;f++)
1008     {
1009        frmMsg=(frmSendMessage)objMsgFrm[f];
1010        if (frmMsg.friendname.Trim().ToUpper().
                 CompareTo(strFriend.ToUpper())==0)
1011        {
1012           return((frmSendMessage)objMsgFrm[f]);
1013        }
1014     }
1015
1016     objMsgFrm=null;
1017     frmMsg=null;
1018
1019     frmMsg=new frmSendMessage(strFriend);
1020     msgQueue.Enqueue((object)frmMsg);
1021     return frmMsg;
1022  }
1023
1024  private void treeFriendList_DoubleClick(object sender,
                              System.EventArgs e)
1025  {
1026     SendMessage();
1027  }
1028
1029  private void timerIM_Tick(object sender, System.EventArgs e)
1030  {
1031     int iCmd=iFListCmd,iLen=0;
1032     string sImg="",sNotify="";
1033     frmSendMessage frmChat=null;
1034
1035  try
1036  {
1037     if (iFListCmd!=-1)
1038     {
1039        iFListCmd=-1;
1040
1041        TreeNode node =new TreeNode();
1042        int iImgIdx=0;
1043        node=this.treeFriendList.TopNode;
```

```
1044
1045        switch(iCmd)
1046        {
1047          case 0:
1048          for (int i=1;i<fList.Length;i++)
1049          {
1050          if (fList[i].Substring(0,1)=="0")
1051              iImgIdx=3;
1052          else
1053              iImgIdx=2;
1054              AddFriendInTree(fList[i].Substring(1),iImgIdx);
1055        }
1056        treeFriendList.TopNode.Expand();
1057        break;
1058        case 1: //notification
1059          int img=3;
1060
1061          sNotify=strFriendNotify.Substring(0,1);
1062          if (sNotify=="1")
1063          {
1064            img=2;
1065          }
1066          else if (sNotify=="0")
1067          {
1068            img=3;
1069            frmChat=GetMsgfrm(strFriendNotify.Substring(1));
1070            frmChat.CloseChat();
1071          }
1072          else if (sNotify=="5")
1073          {
1074            frmChat=GetMsgfrm(strFriendNotify.Substring(1));
1075            frmChat.CloseChat();
1076          }
1077          else img=-1;
1078
1079        if (img!=-1) //replace icon
1080        {
1081          DelFriendFromTree(strFriendNotify.Substring(1));
1082          AddFriendInTree(strFriendNotify.Substring(1),img);
1083        }
1084        //popup form : this will notify friend's status.
1085        frmPopup frmPop=new frmPopup(strFriendNotify.Substring(1),
                      sNotify);
1086        frmPop.Top=Screen.PrimaryScreen.WorkingArea.Bottom;
1087        frmPop.Left=Screen.PrimaryScreen.WorkingArea.Width-
                frmPop.Width;
1088        frmPop.Height=40;
1089        frmPop.TopMost=true;
1090        frmPop.Show();
```

```
1091
1092        if (sNotify=="2")
1093        {
1094          AddConfirm(strFriendNotify.Substring(1));
1095        }
1096        else if (sNotify=="4")
1097        {
1098          DelConfirm(strFriendNotify.Substring(1));
1099        }
1100        break;
1101      case 2: //add local friend
1102      if (strFriendNotify.Substring(strFriendNotify.Length-
1)=="0")
1103        {
1104          if (strFriendNotify.Substring(0,1)=="0")
1105           iImgIdx=3;
1106          else
1107           iImgIdx=2;
1108
1109          AddFriendInTree(strFriendNotify.Substring(1,
                  strFriendNotify.Length-2),iImgIdx);
1110          treeFriendList.TopNode.Expand();
1111        }
1112      else
1113      MessageBox.Show("Can't Add " + strFriendNotify.Substring(1,
              strFriendNotify.Length-2) + " as friend");
1114      break;
1115      case 3: //del local friend
1116      if (strFriendNotify.Substring(strFriendNotify.Length-1)=="0")
1117        {
1118          string strFrnd=
      strFriendNotify.Substring(0,strFriendNotify.Length-1).ToUpper();
1119        DelFriendFromTree(strFrnd);
1120        frmChat=GetMsgfrm(strFrnd);
1121        frmChat.CloseChat();
1122        }
1123      else
1124        MessageBox.Show("Can't Delete " +
strFriendNotify.Substring
                (1,strFriendNotify.Length-1) + " as friend");
1125      break;
1126      case 6: //roster
1127        for (int i=0;i<fList.Length;i++)
1128        {
1129           iLen=fList[i].Length;
1130           sImg=fList[i].Substring(iLen-1,1);
1131           if (sImg!="0")
1132           AddFriendInTree(ExtractFriendName(fList[i].Substring
              (0,iLen-1)),3);
```

```
1133    else
1134    DelFriendFromTree(ExtractFriendName(fList[i].
            Substring(0,iLen-1)));
1135
1136            }
1137      treeFriendList.TopNode.Expand();
1138      break;
1139          }
1140        }
1141    }
1142    catch
1143    {
1144
1145    }
1146  }
1147
1148    private void AddFriendInTree(string strFriend,int iImgIdx)
1149    {
1150      foreach( TreeNode trNode in this.treeFriendList.TopNode.Nodes)
1151      {
1152        if (trNode.Text.ToUpper()==strFriend.ToUpper())
1153        {
1154          return;
1155        }
1156      }
1157
1158      TreeNode child=new TreeNode(strFriend,iImgIdx,iImgIdx);
1159      treeFriendList.TopNode.Nodes.Add(child);
1160      child=null;
1161    }
1162
1163    private void DelFriendFromTree(string strFriend)
1164    {
1165      TreeNode node =new TreeNode();
1166      node=this.treeFriendList.TopNode;
1167
1168      foreach( TreeNode trNode in node.Nodes)
1169      {
1170        if (trNode.Text.ToUpper()==strFriend.ToUpper())
1171        {
1172          treeFriendList.TopNode.Nodes.Remove(trNode);
1173          return;
1174        }
1175      }
1176    }
1177
1178    private void AddConfirm(string strFriend)
1179    {
1180
```

```
1181      Jabber.AddConfirm frmAddConfirm=new AddConfirm(strFriend);
1182      frmAddConfirm.Show();
1183    }
1184
1185    private void DelConfirm(string strFriend)
1186    {
1187      MessageBox.Show(strFriend.ToUpper() + " is requesting for
              deletion","Request for deletion");
1188      string []strParam=new String[2];
1189      strParam[0]=strLogin;
1190      strParam[1]=strFriend;
1191      XmlFormat xmlAccept =new
              XmlFormat("UNSUBSCRIBEFRIEND",strParam);
1192      WriteMsg(xmlAccept.GetXml());
1193      xmlAccept=null;
1194    }
1195
1196    private string ExtractFriendName(string strName)
1197    {
1198      int index=strName.IndexOf("@");
1199
1200      if (index!=-1)
1201      return strName.Substring(0,index);
1202      return strName;
1203    }
1204
1205 private void menuAddFriend_Click(object sender, System.EventArgs
e)
1206 {
1207    AddFriend();
1208 }
1209
1210  private void menuSendMsg_Click(object sender, System.EventArgs e)
1211  {
1212    SendMessage();
1213  }
1214
1215 private void menuDelFriend_Click(object sender, System.EventArgs
e)
1216  {
1217    DelFriend();
1218  }
1219
1220  private void menuAbout_Click(object sender, System.EventArgs e)
1221  {
1222    About();
1223  }
1224
1225   private void Login(string strLog,int iCmd)
```

```
1226  {
1227     frmLogin frmLog=new frmLogin(strLog,iCmd);
1228     frmLog.ShowDialog();
1229     ProceessLoginAction(frmLog);
1230     frmLog=null;
1231  }
1232  private void Register(string strReg,int iCmd)
1233  {
1234     frmRegister frmReg=new frmRegister(strReg,iCmd);
1235     frmReg.ShowDialog();
1236     ProcessRegisterAction(frmReg);
1237     frmReg=null;
1238  }
1239  private void About()
1240  {
1241     frmAbout frmAb=new frmAbout();
1242     frmAb.ShowDialog();
1243     frmAb=null;
1244  }
1245  private void AddFriend()
1246  {
1247     if (!bLogin) return;
1248
1249     string strFriendName="";
1250     frmAddFriend frmAddFrnd=new frmAddFriend(strLogin,0,"");
1251     frmAddFrnd.ShowDialog();
1252     strFriendName=frmAddFrnd.GetFriendName();
1253     frmAddFrnd=null;
1254     if (strFriendName!="")
1255     {
1256       string []strParam=new string[2];
1257       strParam[0]=strLogin;
1258       strParam[1]=strFriendName;
1259       XmlFormat xmlAdd=new XmlFormat("ADDFRIEND",strParam);
1260
1261       WriteMsg(xmlAdd.GetXml());
1262       xmlAdd=null;
1263       strParam=null;
1264     }
1265  }
1266
1267  private void SendMessage()
1268  {
1269     if (!bLogin) return;
1270
1271     string strFriendName=treeFriendList.SelectedNode.Text;
1272     if (strFriendName.Trim()=="") return;
1273     if (strFriendName.CompareTo("Friends")==0) return;
1274     if (treeFriendList.SelectedNode.ImageIndex!=2)
```

```
1275    return;
1276
1277    frmSendMessage frmMsg=null;
1278    frmMsg=GetMsgfrm(strFriendName);
1279
1280    frmMsg.Show();
1281
1282  }
1283
1284  private void DelFriend()
1285  {
1286    if (!bLogin) return;
1287
1288    if (treeFriendList.SelectedNode.Text.Trim()=="") return;
1289    if (treeFriendList.SelectedNode.Text.Trim().
                    CompareTo("Friends")==0) return;
1290
1291    frmAddFriend frmDel=new
    frmAddFriend(strLogin,1,treeFriendList.SelectedNode.Text.Trim());
1292    frmDel.ShowDialog();
1293
1294    string []strParam=new string[2];
1295    strParam[0]=strLogin;
1296    strParam[1]=ExtractFriendName(frmDel.GetFriendName());
1297
1298    if (strParam[1].Trim()=="") return;
1299
1300    XmlFormat xmlDel=new XmlFormat("DELETEFRIEND",strParam);
1301    WriteMsg(xmlDel.GetXml());
1302    frmDel=null;
1303    strParam=null;
1304 }
1305
1306  private void menuAdd_Click(object sender, System.EventArgs e)
1307  {
1308    AddFriend();
1309  }
1310
1311  private void menuSend_Click(object sender, System.EventArgs e)
1312  {
1313    SendMessage();
1314  }
1315
1316  private void menuDel_Click(object sender, System.EventArgs e)
1317  {
1318    DelFriend();
1319  }
1320
1321  private void menuSignIn_Click(object sender, System.EventArgs e)
```

```
1322  {
1323     if (menuSignIn.Text=="&Sign in")
1324     Login("",0);
1325     else
1326     Quit();
1327  }
1328
1329  private void menuUnRegister_Click(object sender, System.EventArgs
e)
1330  {
1331     UnRegister();
1332  }
1333
1334  private void UnRegister()
1335  {
1336     if (!bLogin) return;
1337     string []strParam=new string[1];
1338     strParam[0]=strLogin;
1339
1340     XmlFormat xmlUnReg=new XmlFormat("UNREGISTER",strParam);
1341     WriteMsg(xmlUnReg.GetXml());
1342     xmlUnReg=null;
1343  }
1344
1345  private void mnuAddGateway_Click(object sender, System.EventArgs
e)
1346  {
1347     AddGateway frmAddGateway=new AddGateway();
1348     frmAddGateway.Show();
1349     frmAddGateway=null;
1350  }
1351  }
1352  }
```

Code Description- Main.cs

- Lines 1-11: The namespaces required for building the application are included.

- Line 14: The namespace Jabber is implemented. This namespace serves as the common place for various classes and functions that are acting like the building blocks for the application.

- Line 19: Declaresthe publicly accessible class frmJabberClient is deployed. This class is inherited from the C# defined class System.Windows.Forms.Form. The System.Windows.Forms.Form is used for designing the windows based forms.

- Lines 21-49: Designer variables required to build the form are declared.

- Lines 52-66: Declares user-defined variables.

- Lines 69-85: The default constructor of class `frmJabberClient` is implemented. Inside the constructor, the boolean variables are assigned appropriate values, and the integer type variable `iFListCmd` is set to □1.

- Lines 90-100: Implements the protected `Dispose()` function. This function is responsible for releasing and cleaning up all resources held by the application once they are no longer used by the application.

- Lines 107-349: Implements the mandatory function `Initialize Component()`. This function generates the appropriate code required for designing the application form. The users are asked not to alter the code, as such an attempt can affect the the application.

- Lines 356-359: Deploys the `Main()` function is implemented. This function serves as the entry point for the Client module of the application.

- Lines 361-391: The implementation of the private function `toolbarClient`. This function handles the task of determining the name of the button that receive the click event by the user. Once this function determines the button, it makes a call to the appropriate function, which handles further operations.

- Lines 393-419: The `Quit()` function is implemented. This function comes into action whenever the user initiates a request to quit the application.

  - Lines 395-396: A string type array `strParam` is declared here. In next step variable, `strLogin` is assigned to this array. The `strLogin` variable holds the login name of the client.

  - Lines 398-404: The boolean variable `blogin` is passed with a `TRUE` value to determine whether the user who is willing to quit is logged in or not. If the user is logged in, an object `xmlQuit` of the `XmlFormat` class is built with `QUIT` as the parameter; the login name of the user is passed, and the variable `bClose` is set to `TRUE`.

  - Lines 407-419: Ensures that after successful processing of the client request to quit the application, the connection with the Server module might left opened. To determine the status of the connection with the Server module, the `IsConnected()` function of clientSocket is called by the Client module. If it is found that connection with the server module is still alive even after processing of the client's quit request, the Close() method of netStream and clientSocket are called to close down the connection between the Client and Server module.

- Lines 422-430: Manages the task of laying down the connection with the server and displaying the login form.

- Lines 432-441 The `Resize` property of `frmJabberClient` is implemented. Whenever the window is resized, this code adjusts the size of the friend list tree in fixed proportion to the size of the window.

- Lines 443-467: Implements the `GetLoginInfo()` function is responsible for processing the login request of the user. For deciding the route taken by the user, the

GetCmdAction() function of frmLog is used, which helps in determining the button clicked by the user during the login process.

- Line 447: An object xmlLog of the XmlFormat class is declared. The xmlLog helps in formulating the client request in XML standard.

- Lines 449-460: Checks the value of action variable. If the value of the variable action turns out to be 0, which means the user has clicked the Login button, the login information of the user □ login name and password — are retreived using the GetLoginInfo() function of the frmLogin class. Once the request arrives at the XmlFormat class, it forms the authentication request for the client.

- Lines 461-463: Checks the value of action variable.If the value of action variable turns out to be 1, the user request is for registration.

- Lines 469-493: Whenever the client request is of registration type, the ProcessRegisterAction() function comes into action. For beginning the process, this function takes the object of frmRegister as a parameter.

  - Lines 471-474: The objects strParam and xmlReg of String Array and XmlFormat class are created, respectively, and the command button action raised by the user is trapped in the integer-type variable act.

  - Lines 478-489: Checks the value of variable act. If the value of the act variable emerges as 0, these lines will execute. In these lines, the login information (login name and password) entered by the user during the registration process is stored in strParam with REGISTRATION as the parameter, and message is written for handing over the client request to higher authorities (server) for validation. If there is any other request apart from registration, the process will simply break up.

- Lines 495-524: Establishes the Client module connection with the local server.

  - Lines 497-507: The object clientSocket is created to establish connection with the server at port 5555. The server named pratul is tried for establishing connection. If the connection with the first server cannot be achieved, the second server, gaurav, is tried for connectivity.

  - Lines 508-515: If the connection with either of the servers cannot be established, these lines comes into existence.

  - Lines 517-523: When connection with any of the servers is launched, after waiting for a while, the stream is obtained by the netStream object for delivering requests and receiving responses to and from the server. Once the stream is obtained, a new Thread is created and started to read messages from the server.

- Lines 526-614: Implements the ReadMsg() function, which handles the task of reading the message for the Client module.

- Lines 529: Declares two string type variables, `str` and `strEndTag`. The `strEndTag` variable is initialized with the end tag of every XML Message `</InstantMessenger>` to mark the end of the total message length, which is converted into character type and stored in `ch` array of char type.

- Lines 535-550: Checks whether any data is still left for reading. If such data is found, it is read from the stream in byte type format and stored in the variable `bData`.

- Line 552: Converts the byte type data stored in the `bData` variable into character type and stores the characterized data in variable `chByte`.

- Lines 553-563: While reading the message, some empty space may be encountered by the `ReadMsg()` function. To ignore all these empty values, this code snippet comes into play. When empty value or blank character is found, the value of the variable `bCharFound` is set to TRUE.

- Lines 565-572: Responsible for comparing the end tag of the message read with the end tag (`</InstantMessenger>`) of standard XML of our application to ensure the validity of the XML structure. In case any mismatch is found, the entire process of comparing the tags is repeated. The recurence of the comparison process takes place by setting the value of the variable `i` to 0.

- Line 574: Converts the message into string type and stores the data in variable `str`.

- Lines 576-580: If the end tag of the message turns out to be equal to the standard end tag of the application's XML structure, the value of the variable `bMatch` is set to TRUE, and control comes out of the loop.

- Lines 583-595: Once the message is read and legalized, it is stored in a temporary file. For storing the message, an instance `streamXml` of the `StreamWriter` class is created, which writes the message on a temporary file. The name of such a temporary file is laid upon the login name of the user. If such a file exists, the file is deleted, and a new file is created again, and data is written to it. After writing the data, `streamXml` is closed, and the variables `str` and `i` are set free to cater to the next message.

- Lines 597-604: After writing the message to the file, its parsing and processing needs to be carried out. To accomplish these tasks, this code is utilized. It calls the `parseXml()` function, which determines the type of XML and fetches its contents. In next step, this code calls the `processXml()` function, which takes appropriate action on the type of XML determined by the `parseXml()` function.

- Lines 606-612: Exeutes when some the ReadMsg() function faces some error in reading the message coming from the Server module. Consequently an error message is displayed to the user notifying him/her about the failure while reading the message followed with closure of the process as well as session.

- Lines 616-645: Implements the WriteMsg() function, which is used in the application for writing the message by the user. The WriteMsg() function heavily depends upon the availability of the network stream.

  - Lines 618-621: Determines the availability of the network stream. If the network stream is unavailable or if data cannot be written over the stream, these lines get executed, and the process halts. To indicate the problem, integer value 1 is returned.

  - Lines 623-627: Determines the length of the message and stored in the integer type variable len. Also two arrays chData and bData of type character and byte respectively are declared.

  - Lines 628-635: Using the For Loop structure, each character of the message is converted into byte type. Once the entire message becomes byte formatted, it gets stored in byte type array bData and written on the stream by using the Write() function of netStream.

  - Lines 636-641: If data cannot be written on the stream, this code snippet comes into action. bData and chData are set to NULL, and integer value 1 is returned to notify the failure.

  - Lines 642-644: When message is put on the stream successfully, bData and chData are set to NULL. It is mandatory to free these variables so that whenever any new message needs to be delivered, the junk values of previous message do not get attached with new message.

- Lines 647-654: Closes the client form. Whenever such as request is raised by the client, the bClose variable is set to TRUE to initiate the process, and the Quit() function is called.

- Lines 656-867: The parseXml() function of the frmJabberClient class is implemented. This function takes the string- ype parameter strFile to hold the name of the file that is about to be parsed by the function.

  - Lines 658-659: The objects xmlDoc and xNode of the system-defined classes XmlDocument and XmlNode are created, respectively. The file that needs to be parsed will be loaded in the xmlDoc by using the Load() function.

  - Lines 663-669: The response trapped by the strFile variable is loaded in the xmlDoc object. Before determining and parsing the response, the Client module checks the validity of the XML document by looking for the number of child nodes in the document. If the number of child nodes is more than 2, the error code □1 is returned, and the parsing stops immediately.

  - Lines 670-674: The number of child nodes might be okay but they might not be of the type supported by the application, especially the Client module. These lines take care of such exceptions. If the child node is other than INSTANTMESSANGER, the parsing of the document will not take place due to an invalid XML structure. Once the structure of the XML is checked, the next target is to determine the type of response returned by the server and to parse it to retreive the contents. To do this, all possible responses of the server are lined up. Based upon the nature of the responses, the corresponding code block is executed.

- Lines 676-688: Executed when the type of response returned by the server is of AUTH type against the authorization request made by the user. The text of the first item of the child node is retrieved and stored in strXmlElements. Finally, to mark the successful parsing of the AUTH type, a response integer value 0 is returned; otherwise □1 is returned.

- Lines 689-701: If the response to be parsed is of REGISTER type, this code comes into action. Like the authorization response, the first Item of the child node from the first child of the XML document node is retrieved. On successful parsing of the response, integer value 1 is returned; otherwise □1.

- Lines 702-727: Comes into play when the Client module faces the response from the server for the friend list type of request. This code retrieves the FriendList for the user and contains the names of his/her friends along with their statuses — online or offline. On successful retrieval of the friends' names and their statuses, integer value 2 is returned. Any exception such as an inappropriate number of child nodes or missing elements in the child nodes the parseXml() function returns an integer value □1to the Client module to notify the error in the structure of the XML.

- Lines 728-746: If the server response is for the message request, this code comes into existence. The server response for such client requests is represented by the name of the first child □ 'MSG'. The MSG first childcomprises three child nodes— 'TARGET', 'SOURCE', and 'TEXT'. This code obtains the contents of these child nodes; on successful retrieval of the contents, integer value 3 is returned. If any of the child nodes are empty or holding no value, an error occurs. Integer value □1 is returned.

- Lines 747-774: Parses the server response if it is meant for roster type of request. Out of the roster list, the names of the friends are retrieved. The subscription or relation between the user and the friends is determined. Each subscription is represented by the value ranging between 0-3.

- Lines 776-818: Comes are utilized when the notifications returned from the server need to be parsed. This type of server response is identified by the first child, namely, NOTIFYFRIENDS, of the XML file. For parsing the notification, the name of the user for whom the notification is intended is fetched out. In the second step, the status of the notification is determined. The status element determines the type of notification.

- Lines 790-797: If the status is of ON-LINE type to mark the availability of the opposite user or if the status element holds the SUBSCRIBE value, which symbolizes that the user has received the request to become the friend of the other user, these lines come into action.

- Lines 798-801: If the client has included some other user in his/her list of friends, the friend sends him/her his/her confirmation to become a friend of the client. In such a case, the nature of the notification is of SUBSCRIBED type. As a result, this code snippet gets executed.

- Lines 802-805: In contrast to including or getting included in the friend list of the other users, it might be possible that some friend of the user deletes him/her from his/her list of friends. In such a situation, the notification faced by the user would be of UNSUBSCRIBE type. And to execute such a client request, this code takes the responsibility.

- Lines 806-809: Whenever the user receives the request for deletion from the friend list from his/her friend, he/she responds by sending the confirmation message to mark the confirmed delete. Such notification is known as UNSUBSCRIBED. And to cater to such request, this code snippet is utilized.

- Line 817: On successful processing of various types of notification, the integer value 5 is returned.

- Lines 819-833: The server could also return the response of FRIENDSTATUS type. Such a response is returned by the server when one user accepts the friendship request of the other user. Whenever such a situation of accepting the friendship proposal comes into existence, the server fetches the name of the user to whom the request of friendship is made, checks the STATUS element to make sure that the desired name has successfully been added as a friend, and detects the availability of the friend — whether he/she is offline or online. Once the response is parsed successfully without encountering any errors, an integer value of 6 is returned.

- Lines 834-845: If some user wants to delete a friend from his/her friend list and wants to inform the friend about the move, the server delivers the DELETESTATUS to the target user. While parsing the DELETESTATUS response of the server, the Client module retrieves the name of the friend who has initiated the process. Once the the friend is deleted successfully and the process is completed without facing any errors, an integer value of 7 is returned to wind up the process.

- Lines 847-853: Executed when the server responds to UNREGISTER type of request. The contents of the response are retreived, and on successful completion of the process, the integer value 8 is returned.

- Lines 854-859: Comes into play when the server replies to the client request for adding the gateway to the application for the MSN Messaging Service.Once the process is completed smoothly, integer value 9 is returned.

- Lines 869-975: Implements the processXml() function, which is responsible for taking appropriate action on the server responses parsed by the parseXML() function. Based on the return value of parsed responses, the processXml() function decides the course of action. Once the type of response is decided for processing, the value of variable `strXmlElements` is looked upon to decide the action to be taken for parsing the response.

- Lines 873-885: Checks the server's response for authorization type of request. Once the login information entered by the user is validated by the server without finding any errors, the text 'Successful Login' appears on the status bar of the Client module, and the caption of the button placed on the toolbar changes from 'Login' to 'Logout'. Along with these changes, the menu option 'Sign In' tuns into 'Sign out'.

- Lines 886-893: Ensures that if the login name or password entered by the user is incorrect, the login form is redisplayed and the user is prompted to replace the misspelled information.

- Lines 894-898: Comes into existence when the user is unable to log on to the network due to technical or other problems like busy a server or the unavailibility of the server.

- Lines 900-931: Takes care of the actions that are to be taken to process the response returned for the registration request. As the processing of the registration request begins, the connection with the server is closed and reestablished by sending the authorization request in XML format using the `XmlFormat` class with `AUTH` as parameter. Now the status bar displays the text 'Login' to let the user know that he/she will soon get logged on to the network.

- Lines 932-936: Retreives the friend list from of the server response. Since this process can take some time, it is assigned to the timer event, which will be discussed later in the documentation.

- Lines 937-945: Manages the task of resolving the chat message returned by the server. To process the chat-message response, the name of the message sender and the content of the message are accessed using the `GetMsgFrm()` and `MessageRecieved()` functions, respectively, and the chat form is displayed.

- Lines 946-953: Caters to the task of processing the roster and notify responses returned by the server. Since both processes are time consuming and may block the working of the application, the responsibility of processing these events is handed over to the timer.

- Lines 954-961: Takes the responsibility of sending the notification to the local friend about his/her inclusion in and deletion from the friend list of some other user. Since these requests can take some time in getting the response from the target user, the services of the timer are once again used for processing these requests.

- Lines 962-967: Required when the unregister type of response needs to handled. On execution of this code, a message box is displayed to the user, notifying that he/she has been unregistered from the application; thereafter, the user's connectivity with the server is snapped and he/she exits the application.

- Lines 968-973: Comes into existence when the gateway for the MSN Network could not be added successfully by the user. To let the user know about the faliure, a text is displayed on the status bar, mentioning that due to some error the gateway could not be included in the application.

- Lines 977-999: Implements the `CloseConnection()` function, which snaps the connection with the server whenever the user unregisters himself/herself from the application or wishes to quit the application. To begin shutting down the connection, this function checks whether the thread, socket connection, and network stream between the Client module and the server are active or not. If it finds that these resources are still active, it closes and sets them to `Null` to wipe out all junk and undetected data.

- Lines 1001-1022: Deploys the `frmSendMessage()`. The `frmSendMessage()` function displays the message of each friend in a separate form.

  - Lines 1006-1014: Searches the name of the friend who has sent the message. On being found, this code snippet returns a form containing the message of the friend.

  - Lines 1019-1021: If the friend name is not available in the message queue, a new instance of the Send Message form is displayed and added to `msgQueue`. Finally, the form is retuned by this code to display the message that has been sent by the friend.

- Lines 1024-1027: Invokes the `SendMessage()` function when the user double clicks the left mouse button over the friend name in the friend list to deliver the message.

- Lines 1029-1146: Implements the `timerIM_Tick()` function, in which various responses set on the timer command are processed.

  - Lines 1035-1039: Sets the `iFListCmd` free to handle more timer commands for upcoming processes that need to be put under the consideration of timer.

  - Lines 1047-1057: Determines the total length of the friend list out of the `fLIst` array of the string type. Once the length is obtained, the substring of `fList` is gained to determine the status of the user, whether he/she is offline (0) or online (1), and the image in the friend list corresponding to the friend name is adjusted accordingly. The `AddFriendInTree()` function is called to include friend(s) in the friend list. The size of the top node of the friend tree is also expanded accordingly.

  - Lines 1058-1059: Starts the processing of various types of notifications. At the start-up of the processing, the offline image is displayed.

  - Lines 1061-1071: Fetches the status of the user by searching the substring of the `strNotifyFriend` variable and storing it in the `sNotify` variable. If `sNotify = 1` (means status of notification is ONLINE), the online image is displayed. In contrast, if `sNotify = 0` (means status of notification is OFFLINE), the offline image is displayed, and the Chatting dialog box is closed.

  - Lines 1072-1076: If the notification is of UNSUBSCRIBED type (`sNotify = 5`), the Chatting window, through any means remaining open, is closed by this code snippet.

  - Lines 1077-1083: Reponsible for deleting the friend from the friend list.

- Lines 1085-1090: Displays a pop-up menu at the bottom of the screen to display the status of the friend whenever he/she becomes online or offline.

- Lines 1092-1095: Processes the SUBSCRIBE notification (sNotify=2). To begin the process, the constructor of the AddConfirm class is called.

- Lines 1096-1099: Handles the task of processing the UNSUBSCRIBE Notification. It makes a call to the DelConfirm() function to take care of the rest of the proceeings to delete the friend.

- Lines 1148-1161: Implements AddFriendInTree() function, which handles the task of adding friends to the friend-list tree. For including the friend in the friend list, a new TreeNode is added to the friend-list tree.

- Lines 1163-1176: Holds the working of DelFriendFromTree() function, which is responsible for allowing the user to delete a friend from his/her list of friends.

- Lines 1178-1183: Implements the AddConfirm() function, which displays the dialog box to add a friend.

- Lines 1185-1194: Deploys the DelConfirm() function, which enables the user to send a notification message to the friend whenever he/she wishes to delete some friend from his/her friend list. After delivering the notification message, the login name of the user and his/her friend's name is retrieved, and the constructor of the XmlFormat class is called with the UNSUBSCRIBEFRIEND parameter. The message is written using WriteMsg() function to wind up the process.

- Lines 1196-1203: Puts into service the ExtractFriendName() function, which takes the friend name as a string-type parameter. The ExtractFriendName() function extracts only the name of the friend from his/her full login name.

- Lines 1205-1208: Executed when the user clicks the mouse on the AddFriend menu option. As a resul,t AddFriend() is called to take over the rest of the proceedings.

- Lines 1210-1213: Whenever the user clicks the Send Message menu option to deliver the message to the intended friend or user, this code comes into action. SendMessage() is called to deliver the message.

- Lines 1215-1218: Starts when the user clicks the Delete Friend menu option to delete some friend from his/her friend list. To make sure the process commences smoothly, the assistance of DelFriend() is taken up.

- Lines 1220-1223: Comes into action whenever the user clicks the About menu option to view the details of the application such as the application version, the vendor's name and so on. Immediately after this menu option is clicked, the About() function is called. The about function displays information such as application version and the name of the software vender.

- Lines 1225-1231: Implements the Login() function, which takes the login name and integer type variables as parameters. Whenever this code is executed, the Login dialog box is displayed. To process the login information, the `ProceessLoginAction()` function is used.

- Lines 1232-1238: Implements the `Register()` fucntion, which takes the login name opted by the user and an integer type variable. On execution, this code displays the registration form; to process the information entered by the user for registration, the `ProcessRegisterAction()` function is called.

- Lines 1239-1244: Responsible for displaying the About dialog box.

- Lines 1245-1265: The execution path of the `AddFriend()` function, which allows the user to add a friend to his/her list of friends. The variable `strfriendName` is deliberately left empty so that the user can add a friend specifically by supplying the friend name.

  - Lines 1249-1252: The constructor of the `frmAddFriend` class is called, and parameters of the login name and an integer value 0 indicate that the user is adding the friend. An empty parameter is passed, which later will go to store the name of the friend selected by the user for inclusion in his/her friend list. Finally, the name of the friend selected by the user is accessed by putting `GetFriendName()` into practice.

  - Lines 1254-1265: Checks whether the variable `strFriendName` is empty or not. Variable strfriendName holds the name of the friend which is selected by the user for inclusion in the friend list. If the variable `strFriendName` is not empty, the constructor of the `XmlFormat` class is called to form the request for adding a friend in the predefiend XML norm for the application. While creating the request, ADDFRIEND and `strParam` are passed as parameters in the constructor of the `XmlFormat` class. The parameter `strParam` conatins the login name of the user and the name of the friend.

- Lines 1267-1282: Implements the `SendMessage()` function, which handles the task of imposing certain validations before the desired message can be delivered to the target user. The `Send Message()` function ensures that the friend name is not empty and that the name selected by the user is not the parent node 'Friends' of the friend-list tree.

  - Line 1274: Makes sure that the friend selected by the user for delivering the message is online. This is determined by checking the image placed before the friend names. If the image is different from the login image, the process stops.

- Lines 1284-1304: Deploys the `DelFriend()` function, which enables the user to delete his/her friend(s) from the friend list.

  - Lines 1288-1289: Ensure that the friend name selected by the user is not empty; if already selected, the name must not be 'Friends'— the name of the node in the friend-list tree.

  - Lines 1291-1292: Calls the constructor of the `frmAddFriend` class, which takes the following parameters: login name of the user, integer value 1 (to indicate that deletion of the friend is occuring), and the name of the friend selected from the friend-list tree. After having all required parameters, the dialog box todelete the friend is shown by using the `ShowDialog()` function of `frmAddFriend` class.

- Lines 1294-1304: The login name of the user and the friend name are put in the array of string type. If the name of the friend is empty, the process is halted immediately; otherwise, the constructor of the `XmlFormat` class is called with the `DELETEFRIEND` parameter to manufacture the suitable XML to commence the process.

- Lines 1306-1309: Comes into action when the user clicks the Add Friend menu option to include a friend in his/her list of friends. To complete the process initiated by the user, the `AddFriend()` function is called, which takes care of rest of the proceedings.

- Lines 1311-1314: The Send Message menu option, on being clicked by the user, invokes the `SendMessage()` function to complete the client request to deliver the message to the target user.

- Lines 1316-1319: Executed when the user clicks the Delete Friend menu option to delete a friend from his/her list of friends. The user's click invokes the `DelFriend()` function to complete the process.

- Lines 1321-1327: Used when the user clicks the SignIn menu opion to log on to the application network. After the user's click, the `Login()` function is called. If the user is already logged in, the `Quit` option is placed on the menu.

- Lines 1329-1332: Executed when the user clicks the Unregister menu option to remove his/her account from the application database. The request is fulfilled by calling the `UnRegister()` function.

- Lines 1334-1343: Implements the `UnRegister()` function, which allows the user to remove or delete his/her account from the application. To remove the user's account, his/her login name is required. Once the login name is obtained, the constructor of the `XmlFormat` class is called with UNREGISTER and the login name of the user as parameters.

- Lines 1345-1350: Comes into action when the user clicks the Add Gateway menu option. As a result of the click, this code displays the dialog box to include the gateway for MSN Network.

Figure 6-10 illustrates the working of frmLogin.cs class. The frmLogin class enables the user to log on the application.

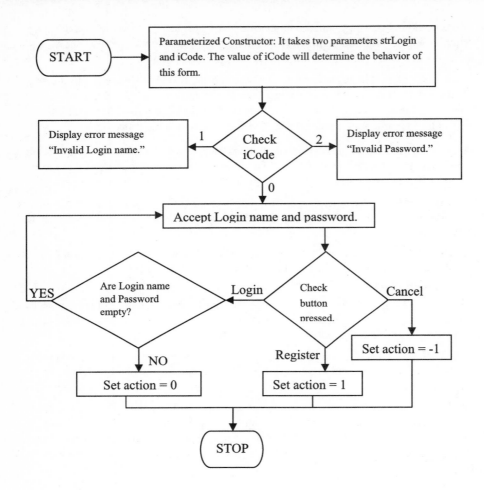

Figure 6-10: Flowchart of frmLogin.cs

Listing 6-2: frmLogin.cs

The following code listing provides the code for designing the login form and allowing the user to use this form to logon the application.

```
1 using System;
2 using System.Drawing;
3 using System.Collections;
4 using System.ComponentModel;
5 using System.Windows.Forms;
```

```
 6 using System.Net;
 7 using System.Net.Sockets;
 8 using System.Xml;
 9
10 namespace Jabber
11 {
12   /// <summary>
13   /// Summary description for Login.
14   /// </summary>
15   public class frmLogin : System.Windows.Forms.Form
16   {
17     private System.Windows.Forms.Label lblCopyrights;
18     private System.Windows.Forms.StatusBar IMstatusBar;
19     private System.Windows.Forms.GroupBox grpBxLogin;
20     private System.Windows.Forms.Button cmdRegister;
21     private System.Windows.Forms.Button cmdLogin;
22     private System.Windows.Forms.TextBox txtPassword;
23     private System.Windows.Forms.TextBox txtLoginName;
24     private System.Windows.Forms.Label lblPassword;
25     private System.Windows.Forms.Label lblName;
26   /// <summary>
27   /// Required designer variable.
28   /// </summary>
29   private System.ComponentModel.Container components = null;
30
31   private int action; //0 : login, 1 : register, -1 : cancel
32   private int iCode;
33   private bool bMsgShow;
34
35   public frmLogin(string strLogin,int iCode)
36   {
37     //
38     // Required for Windows Form Designer support
39     //
40     InitializeComponent();
41
42     //
43     // TODO: Add any constructor code after
44     InitializeComponent call
44     //
45
46     action=-1;
47     txtLoginName.Text=strLogin;
48     this.iCode=iCode;
49     bMsgShow=false;
50   }
51
52   /// <summary>
53   /// Clean up any resources being used.
```

```
54 /// </summary>
55 protected override void Dispose( bool disposing )
56 {
57   if( disposing )
58   {
59     if(components != null)
60     {
61       components.Dispose();
62     }
63   }
64   base.Dispose( disposing );
65 }
66
67 #region Windows Form Designer generated code
68 /// <summary>
69 /// Required method for Designer support - do not modify
70 /// the contents of this method with the code editor.
71 /// </summary>
72 private void InitializeComponent()
73 {
74   this.txtPassword = new System.Windows.Forms.TextBox();
75   this.lblCopyrights = new System.Windows.Forms.Label();
76   this.cmdLogin = new System.Windows.Forms.Button();
77   this.grpBxLogin = new System.Windows.Forms.GroupBox();
78   this.cmdRegister = new System.Windows.Forms.Button();
79   this.txtLoginName = new System.Windows.Forms.TextBox();
80   this.lblPassword = new System.Windows.Forms.Label();
81   this.lblName = new System.Windows.Forms.Label();
82   this.IMstatusBar = new
        System.Windows.Forms.StatusBar();
83   this.grpBxLogin.SuspendLayout();
84   this.SuspendLayout();
85   //
86   // txtPassword
87   //
88   this.txtPassword.Location = new System.Drawing.Point(112, 48);
89   this.txtPassword.MaxLength = 20;
90   this.txtPassword.Name = "txtPassword";
91   this.txtPassword.PasswordChar = '*';
92   this.txtPassword.Size = new System.Drawing.Size(112, 20);
93   this.txtPassword.TabIndex = 2;
94   this.txtPassword.Text = "";
95   this.txtPassword.KeyPress += new
        System.Windows.Forms.KeyPressEventHandler
        (this.txtPassword_KeyPress);
96   //
97   // lblCopyrights
98   //
99     this.lblCopyrights.ForeColor = System.Drawing.Color.Blue;
```

```
100     this.lblCopyrights.Location = new System.Drawing.Point(8, 0);
101     this.lblCopyrights.Name = "lblCopyrights";
102     this.lblCopyrights.Size = new System.Drawing.Size(240, 16);
103     this.lblCopyrights.TabIndex = 0;
104     this.lblCopyrights.Text = "© Dreamtech Software India Inc.";
105     this.lblCopyrights.TextAlign =
            System.Drawing.ContentAlignment.BottomCenter;
106     //
107     // cmdLogin
108     //
109     this.cmdLogin.Location = new System.Drawing.Point(56, 80);
110     this.cmdLogin.Name = "cmdLogin";
111     this.cmdLogin.Size = new System.Drawing.Size(72, 25);
112     this.cmdLogin.TabIndex = 4;
113     this.cmdLogin.Text = "&Login";
114     this.cmdLogin.Click += new
            System.EventHandler(this.cmdLogin_Click);
115     //
116     // grpBxLogin
117     //
118     this.grpBxLogin.Controls.AddRange(new
            System.Windows.Forms.Control[] {
119     this.cmdRegister,
120     this.cmdLogin,
121     this.txtPassword,
122     this.txtLoginName,
123     this.lblPassword,
124     this.lblName});
125     this.grpBxLogin.Location = new System.Drawing.Point(8, 16);
126     this.grpBxLogin.Name = "grpBxLogin";
127     this.grpBxLogin.Size = new System.Drawing.Size(248, 112);
128     this.grpBxLogin.TabIndex = 0;
129     this.grpBxLogin.TabStop = false;
130     //
131     // cmdRegister
132     //
133     this.cmdRegister.Location = new System.Drawing.Point(136, 80);
134     this.cmdRegister.Name = "cmdRegister";
135     this.cmdRegister.Size = new System.Drawing.Size(72, 24);
136     this.cmdRegister.TabIndex = 5;
137     this.cmdRegister.Text = "&Register";
138     this.cmdRegister.Click += new
            System.EventHandler(this.cmdRegister_Click);
139     //
140     // txtLoginName
141     //
142     this.txtLoginName.Location = new System.Drawing.Point(112, 24);
143     this.txtLoginName.MaxLength = 20;
144     this.txtLoginName.Name = "txtLoginName";
```

```
145     this.txtLoginName.Size = new System.Drawing.Size(112, 20);
146     this.txtLoginName.TabIndex = 1;
147     this.txtLoginName.Text = "";
148     this.txtLoginName.KeyPress += new
            System.Windows.Forms.KeyPressEventHandler
             (this.txtLoginName_KeyPress);
149     //
150     // lblPassword
151     //
152     this.lblPassword.Location = new System.Drawing.Point(32, 48);
153     this.lblPassword.Name = "lblPassword";
154     this.lblPassword.Size = new System.Drawing.Size(80, 16);
155     this.lblPassword.TabIndex = 1;
156     this.lblPassword.Text = "Password";
157     //
158     // lblName
159     //
160     this.lblName.Location = new System.Drawing.Point(32, 24);
161     this.lblName.Name = "lblName";
162     this.lblName.Size = new System.Drawing.Size(80, 16);
163     this.lblName.TabIndex = 0;
164     this.lblName.Text = "Login Name";
165     //
166     // IMstatusBar
167     //
168     this.IMstatusBar.Location = new System.Drawing.Point(0, 140);
169     this.IMstatusBar.Name = "IMstatusBar";
170     this.IMstatusBar.Size = new System.Drawing.Size(262, 24);
171     this.IMstatusBar.TabIndex = 2;
172     //
173     // frmLogin
174     //
175     this.AutoScaleBaseSize = new System.Drawing.Size(5, 13);
176     this.ClientSize = new System.Drawing.Size(262, 164);
177     this.Controls.AddRange(new System.Windows.Forms.Control[] {
178     this.lblCopyrights,
179     this.IMstatusBar,
180     this.grpBxLogin});
181     this.FormBorderStyle =
            System.Windows.Forms.FormBorderStyle.FixedToolWindow;
182     this.Name = "frmLogin";
183     this.StartPosition =
            System.Windows.Forms.FormStartPosition.CenterParent;
184     this.Text = "Login";
185     this.Load += new System.EventHandler(this.Login_Load);
186     this.Activated += new
            System.EventHandler(this.frmLogin_Activated);
187     this.grpBxLogin.ResumeLayout(false);
188     this.ResumeLayout(false);
```

```
189
190   }
191   #endregion
192
193   private void Login_Load(object sender, System.EventArgs e)
194   {
195
196   }
197
198   private void cmdLogin_Click(object sender, System.EventArgs e)
199   {
200      if (txtLoginName.Text.Trim()=="")
201      {
202        MessageBox.Show("Login can't be empty");
203        txtLoginName.Focus();
204        return;
205      }
206
207      if (txtPassword.Text.Trim()=="")
208      {
209        MessageBox.Show("Password can't be empty");
210        txtPassword.Focus();
211        return;
212      }
213      action=0;
214      this.Close();
215   }
216   public string[] GetLoginInfo()
217   {
218      string []strReturn=new string[2];
219      strReturn[0]=txtLoginName.Text.Trim();
220      strReturn[1]=txtPassword.Text.Trim();
221
222      return  strReturn;
223   }
224
225   private void cmdRegister_Click(object sender, System.EventArgs e)
226   {
227      action=1;
228      this.Close();
229   }
230
231   public int GetCmdAction()
232   {
233      int act=action;
234      action=-1; //clear last action
235      return act;
236   }
237
```

```
238 private void frmLogin_Activated(object sender, System.EventArgs e)
239 {
240    if (bMsgShow) return;
241    bMsgShow=true;
242
243    if (iCode==1)
244    {
245      MessageBox.Show("Invlaid Login Name","Error");
246      txtLoginName.Focus();
247            }
248            else if (iCode==2)
249            {
250                    MessageBox.Show("Invlaid Password","Error");
251                    txtPassword.Focus();
252            }
253    }
254
255    private void txtLoginName_KeyPress(object sender,
               System.Windows.Forms.KeyPressEventArgs e)
256    {
257            if (((int)e.KeyChar)==13)
258                    cmdLogin_Click(sender,e);
259    }
260
261    private void txtPassword_KeyPress(object sender,
               System.Windows.Forms.KeyPressEventArgs e)
262    {
263            if (((int)e.KeyChar)==13)
264                    cmdLogin_Click(sender,e);
265    }
266 }
267 }
```

- Lines 1-8: Includes namespaces that are required for building the class, which provide a login facility and validations for the user.

- Lines 15: The publicly accessible class frmLogin is declared, which is inherited from the System.Windows.Forms.Form class.

- Lines 17-25: Declaring required design variables that will be required during the designing course of the login form.

- Lines 31-33: User-defined variables are declared. The Integer type variable action can have three values □ 0 for Login, 1 for Register, and □1 for canceling the process. On the other hand, the iCode variable is responsible for deciding the behaviour of the form. If the value of iCode = 1, it means invalid login name; iCode =2 means invalid password and iCode= 0 means successful login.

- Lines 35-50: In these lines, the default constructor of the login class is implemented with two parameters — strLogin and iCode. Inside the constructor, it is made sure that if the user clicks the Cancel button, the login name of the user remains present on the corresponding textbox of the form and the rest of the process is stopped.

- Lines 55-65: In these lines, the `Dispose()` function is implemented, which performs the clean up task by freeing up all resources held by the application once they are no longer required.

- Lines 72-191: Hold the implementation of the `Initialize Component()` function, which provides appropriate designing effects to the designer variables. Since code between mentioned lines is autogenerated, the users must not to alter it, as any such attempt could affect the normal working of the application.

- Lines 198-215: Perform appropriate validation whenever the user clicks the Login button to step into the application.

  - Lines 200-205: If the user clicks the Login button, leaving the login name field empty, these lines get executed.

  - Lines 207-212: If the user clicks the Login button without entering the password, these lines get executed.

  - Lines 213-214: If the user clicks the Login button without leaving the login and password field blank, he/she is allowed entry to the application network, and immediately the login form is closed.

- Lines 216-223: The `GetLoginInfo()` function implemented in these lines is responsible for collecting the login information (login name and password) submitted by the user during the log on process.

  - Lines 218-222: To collect the login information, the string-type array `strReturn` is created with the length of two indexes. In the first index, the login name is stored. In the second index, the password of the user is stored. This function returns the same string, which holds the login information of the user.

- Lines 225-229: Handles the click event raised by the user on the Register button. On successful registration, the action variable is set to 1, and the login form is closed.

- Lines 231-236: Implements the `GetCmdAction()` function, which keeps track of the last button pressed during the logon process. The default button is Cancel (-1), which is also used to clear the last action.

- Lines 238-253: Responsible for returning the appropriate feedback to the user if some error occurs during the logon process. To determine the possible error, the value of the `iCode` variable is used. If `iCode` carries value 1, the message "Invalid Login name" is displayed; if `iCode =2`, the message "Invalid Password" is shown.

- Lines 255-265: Permit the Enter key to work for the Login button. If the cursor location is either on the login name or the passowrd textbox, and you press the Enter button from the keyboard, immediately the Login button gets activated.

Figure 6-11 illustrates the working of the `frmRegister.cs` class. The `frmRegister` class is used in the application to register the new users.

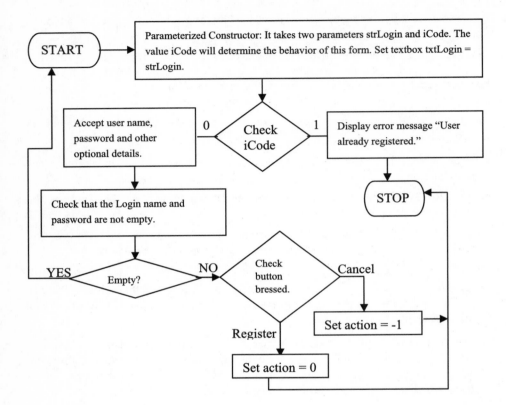

Figure 6-11: Flow chart of frmRegister.cs

Listing 6-3: frmRegister.cs

The following code listing provides the code for designing the registration form. Also entire code to handle the registration process is provided in the code listing.

```
1 using System;
2 using System.Drawing;
3 using System.Collections;
4 using System.ComponentModel;
5 using System.Windows.Forms;
6 using System.Net;
7 using System.Net.Sockets;
```

```
 8 using Jabber;
 9 using System.Xml;
10
11 namespace Jabber
12 {
13  /// <summary>
14  /// Summary description for Register.
15  /// </summary>
16  public class frmRegister : System.Windows.Forms.Form
17  {
18    private System.Windows.Forms.GroupBox grpBxRegister;
19    private System.Windows.Forms.Button cmdRegister;
20    private System.Windows.Forms.TextBox txtProfession;
21    private System.Windows.Forms.TextBox txtPin;
22    private System.Windows.Forms.TextBox txtCity;
23    private System.Windows.Forms.TextBox txtEmail2;
24    private System.Windows.Forms.TextBox txtEmail1;
25    private System.Windows.Forms.TextBox txtPhone2;
26    private System.Windows.Forms.TextBox txtPhone1;
27    private System.Windows.Forms.TextBox txtAddress2;
28    private System.Windows.Forms.TextBox txtAddress1;
29    private System.Windows.Forms.TextBox txtConfirmPass;
30    private System.Windows.Forms.TextBox txtPass;
31    private System.Windows.Forms.TextBox txtLogin;
32    private System.Windows.Forms.Label label12;
33    private System.Windows.Forms.Label label11;
34    private System.Windows.Forms.Label label10;
35    private System.Windows.Forms.Label label9;
36    private System.Windows.Forms.Label label8;
37    private System.Windows.Forms.Label label7;
38    private System.Windows.Forms.Label label6;
39    private System.Windows.Forms.Label label5;
40    private System.Windows.Forms.Label label4;
41    private System.Windows.Forms.Label label3;
42    private System.Windows.Forms.Label label2;
43    private System.Windows.Forms.Label label1;
44    private System.Windows.Forms.Label lblCopyrights;
45    private System.Windows.Forms.StatusBar IMstatusBar;
46    /// <summary>
47    /// Required designer variable.
48    /// </summary>
49    private System.ComponentModel.Container components = null;
50
51    private int action;
52    private int iCode;
53    private bool bMsgShow;
54
55
56  public frmRegister(string strLogin,int iCode)
```

```
57 {
58   //
59   // Required for Windows Form Designer support
60   //
61   InitializeComponent();
62
63   //
64   // TODO: Add any constructor code after InitializeComponent
        // call
65   //
66
67   action=-1;
68   txtLogin.Text=strLogin;
69   this.iCode=iCode;
70   bMsgShow=false;
71 }
72
73 /// <summary>
74 /// Clean up any resources being used.
75 /// </summary>
76 protected override void Dispose( bool disposing )
77 {
78   if( disposing )
79   {
80     if(components != null)
81     {
82       components.Dispose();
83     }
84   }
85   base.Dispose( disposing );
86 }
87
88   #region Windows Form Designer generated code
89   /// <summary>
90   /// Required method for Designer support - do not modify
91   /// the contents of this method with the code editor.
92   /// </summary>
93   private void InitializeComponent()
94   {
95     this.label8 = new System.Windows.Forms.Label();
96     this.label9 = new System.Windows.Forms.Label();
97     this.label4 = new System.Windows.Forms.Label();
98     this.label5 = new System.Windows.Forms.Label();
99     this.label6 = new System.Windows.Forms.Label();
100    this.label7 = new System.Windows.Forms.Label();
101    this.label1 = new System.Windows.Forms.Label();
102    this.txtPhone2 = new System.Windows.Forms.TextBox();
103    this.label3 = new System.Windows.Forms.Label();
104    this.txtPhone1 = new System.Windows.Forms.TextBox();
```

```
105       this.txtAddress1 = new System.Windows.Forms.TextBox();
106       this.cmdRegister = new System.Windows.Forms.Button();
107       this.label10 = new System.Windows.Forms.Label();
108       this.txtEmail2 = new System.Windows.Forms.TextBox();
109       this.txtConfirmPass = new System.Windows.Forms.TextBox();
110       this.txtEmail1 = new System.Windows.Forms.TextBox();
111       this.txtPass = new System.Windows.Forms.TextBox();
112       this.txtCity = new System.Windows.Forms.TextBox();
113       this.IMstatusBar = new System.Windows.Forms.StatusBar();
114       this.label2 = new System.Windows.Forms.Label();
115       this.txtPin = new System.Windows.Forms.TextBox();
116       this.txtAddress2 = new System.Windows.Forms.TextBox();
117       this.label11 = new System.Windows.Forms.Label();
118       this.lblCopyrights = new System.Windows.Forms.Label();
119       this.txtLogin = new System.Windows.Forms.TextBox();
120       this.label12 = new System.Windows.Forms.Label();
121       this.txtProfession = new System.Windows.Forms.TextBox();
122       this.grpBxRegister = new System.Windows.Forms.GroupBox();
123       this.grpBxRegister.SuspendLayout();
124       this.SuspendLayout();
125       //
126       // label8
127       //
128       this.label8.Location = new System.Drawing.Point(32, 104);
129       this.label8.Name = "label8";
130       this.label8.Size = new System.Drawing.Size(104, 16);
131       this.label8.TabIndex = 7;
132       this.label8.Text = "Email1";
133       this.label8.TextAlign =
              System.Drawing.ContentAlignment.MiddleLeft;
134       //
135       // label9
136       //
137       this.label9.Location = new System.Drawing.Point(224, 104);
138       this.label9.Name = "label9";
139       this.label9.Size = new System.Drawing.Size(88, 24);
140       this.label9.TabIndex = 8;
141       this.label9.Text = "Email2";
142       this.label9.TextAlign =
              System.Drawing.ContentAlignment.MiddleRight;
143       //
144       // label4
145       //
146       this.label4.Location = new System.Drawing.Point(32, 72);
147       this.label4.Name = "label4";
148       this.label4.Size = new System.Drawing.Size(96, 16);
149       this.label4.TabIndex = 3;
150       this.label4.Text = "Address1";
```

```
151    this.label4.TextAlign =
           System.Drawing.ContentAlignment.MiddleLeft;
152    //
153    // label5
154    //
155    this.label5.Location = new System.Drawing.Point(224, 72);
156    this.label5.Name = "label5";
157    this.label5.Size = new System.Drawing.Size(88, 16);
158    this.label5.TabIndex = 4;
159    this.label5.Text = "Address2";
160    this.label5.TextAlign =
           System.Drawing.ContentAlignment.MiddleRight;
161    //
162    // label6
163    //
164    this.label6.Location = new System.Drawing.Point(32, 88);
165    this.label6.Name = "label6";
166    this.label6.Size = new System.Drawing.Size(112, 16);
167    this.label6.TabIndex = 5;
168    this.label6.Text = "Phone1";
169    this.label6.TextAlign =
           System.Drawing.ContentAlignment.MiddleLeft;
170    //
171    // label7
172    //
173    this.label7.Location = new System.Drawing.Point(224, 88);
174    this.label7.Name = "label7";
175    this.label7.Size = new System.Drawing.Size(88, 16);
176    this.label7.TabIndex = 6;
177    this.label7.Text = "Phone2";
178    this.label7.TextAlign =
           System.Drawing.ContentAlignment.MiddleRight;
179    //
180    // label1
181    //
182    this.label1.Location = new System.Drawing.Point(32, 24);
183    this.label1.Name = "label1";
184    this.label1.Size = new System.Drawing.Size(72, 16);
185    this.label1.TabIndex = 0;
186    this.label1.Text = "Login Name";
187    this.label1.TextAlign =
           System.Drawing.ContentAlignment.MiddleLeft;
188    //
189    // txtPhone2
190    //
191    this.txtPhone2.Location = new System.Drawing.Point(320, 88);
192    this.txtPhone2.MaxLength = 20;
193    this.txtPhone2.Name = "txtPhone2";
194    this.txtPhone2.TabIndex = 7;
```

```
195  this.txtPhone2.Text = "";
196  //
197  // label3
198  //
199  this.label3.Location = new System.Drawing.Point(208, 56);
200  this.label3.Name = "label3";
201  this.label3.Size = new System.Drawing.Size(112, 16);
202  this.label3.TabIndex = 2;
203  this.label3.Text = "Confirm Password";
204  this.label3.TextAlign =
         System.Drawing.ContentAlignment.MiddleRight;
205  //
206  // txtPhone1
207  //
208  this.txtPhone1.Location = new System.Drawing.Point(96, 88);
209  this.txtPhone1.MaxLength = 20;
210  this.txtPhone1.Name = "txtPhone1";
211  this.txtPhone1.TabIndex = 6;
212  this.txtPhone1.Text = "";
213  //
214  // txtAddress1
215  //
216  this.txtAddress1.Location = new System.Drawing.Point(96, 72);
217  this.txtAddress1.MaxLength = 100;
218  this.txtAddress1.Name = "txtAddress1";
219  this.txtAddress1.TabIndex = 4;
220  this.txtAddress1.Text = "";
221  //
222  // cmdRegister
223  //
224  this.cmdRegister.Location = new System.Drawing.Point(192, 176);
225  this.cmdRegister.Name = "cmdRegister";
226  this.cmdRegister.Size = new System.Drawing.Size(88, 24);
227  this.cmdRegister.TabIndex = 13;
228  this.cmdRegister.Text = "&Register";
229  this.cmdRegister.Click += new
         System.EventHandler(this.cmdRegister_Click);
230  //
231  // label10
232  //
233  this.label10.Location = new System.Drawing.Point(32, 120);
234  this.label10.Name = "label10";
235  this.label10.Size = new System.Drawing.Size(88, 16);
236  this.label10.TabIndex = 9;
237  this.label10.Text = "City";
238  this.label10.TextAlign =
         System.Drawing.ContentAlignment.MiddleLeft;
239  //
240  // txtEmail2
```

```
241  //
242  this.txtEmail2.Location = new System.Drawing.Point(320, 104);
243  this.txtEmail2.MaxLength = 50;
244  this.txtEmail2.Name = "txtEmail2";
245  this.txtEmail2.TabIndex = 9;
246  this.txtEmail2.Text = "";
247  //
248  // txtConfirmPass
249  //
250  this.txtConfirmPass.Location = new System.Drawing.Point(320, 56);
251  this.txtConfirmPass.MaxLength = 20;
252  this.txtConfirmPass.Name = "txtConfirmPass";
253  this.txtConfirmPass.PasswordChar = '*';
254  this.txtConfirmPass.TabIndex = 3;
255  this.txtConfirmPass.Text = "";
256  //
257  // txtEmail1
258  //
259  this.txtEmail1.Location = new System.Drawing.Point(96, 104);
260  this.txtEmail1.MaxLength = 50;
261  this.txtEmail1.Name = "txtEmail1";
262  this.txtEmail1.TabIndex = 8;
263  this.txtEmail1.Text = "";
264  //
265  // txtPass
266  //
267  this.txtPass.Location = new System.Drawing.Point(96, 56);
268  this.txtPass.MaxLength = 20;
269  this.txtPass.Name = "txtPass";
270  this.txtPass.PasswordChar = '*';
271  this.txtPass.TabIndex = 2;
272  this.txtPass.Text = "";
273  //
274  // txtCity
275  //
276  this.txtCity.Location = new System.Drawing.Point(96, 120);
277  this.txtCity.MaxLength = 20;
278  this.txtCity.Name = "txtCity";
279  this.txtCity.TabIndex = 10;
280  this.txtCity.Text = "";
281  //
282  // IMstatusBar
283  //
284  this.IMstatusBar.Location = new System.Drawing.Point(0, 231);
285  this.IMstatusBar.Name = "IMstatusBar";
286  this.IMstatusBar.Size = new System.Drawing.Size(452, 16);
287  this.IMstatusBar.TabIndex = 2;
288  //
289  // label2
```

```
290  //
291  this.label2.Location = new System.Drawing.Point(32, 56);
292  this.label2.Name = "label2";
293  this.label2.Size = new System.Drawing.Size(112, 16);
294  this.label2.TabIndex = 1;
295  this.label2.Text = "Password";
296  this.label2.TextAlign =
           System.Drawing.ContentAlignment.MiddleLeft;
297  //
298  // txtPin
299  //
300  this.txtPin.Location = new System.Drawing.Point(320, 120);
301  this.txtPin.MaxLength = 20;
302  this.txtPin.Name = "txtPin";
303  this.txtPin.TabIndex = 11;
304  this.txtPin.Text = "";
305  //
306  // txtAddress2
307  //
308  this.txtAddress2.Location = new System.Drawing.Point(320, 72);
309  this.txtAddress2.MaxLength = 100;
310  this.txtAddress2.Name = "txtAddress2";
311  this.txtAddress2.TabIndex = 5;
312  this.txtAddress2.Text = "";
313  //
314  // label11
315  //
316  this.label11.Location = new System.Drawing.Point(208, 128);
317  this.label11.Name = "label11";
318  this.label11.Size = new System.Drawing.Size(96, 16);
319  this.label11.TabIndex = 10;
320  this.label11.Text = "Pin";
321  this.label11.TextAlign =
                   System.Drawing.ContentAlignment.MiddleRight;
322  //
323  // lblCopyrights
324  //
325  this.lblCopyrights.ForeColor = System.Drawing.Color.Blue;
326  this.lblCopyrights.Name = "lblCopyrights";
327  this.lblCopyrights.Size = new System.Drawing.Size(520, 16);
328  this.lblCopyrights.TabIndex = 0;
329  this.lblCopyrights.Text = "© Dreamtech Software India Inc.";
330  this.lblCopyrights.TextAlign =
           System.Drawing.ContentAlignment.BottomCenter;
331  //
332  // txtLogin
333  //
334  this.txtLogin.Location = new System.Drawing.Point(96, 24);
335  this.txtLogin.MaxLength = 20;
```

```
336  this.txtLogin.Name = "txtLogin";
337  this.txtLogin.Size = new System.Drawing.Size(104, 20);
338  this.txtLogin.TabIndex = 1;
339  this.txtLogin.Text = "";
340  //
341  // label12
342  //
343  this.label12.Location = new System.Drawing.Point(32, 136);
344  this.label12.Name = "label12";
345  this.label12.Size = new System.Drawing.Size(80, 16);
346  this.label12.TabIndex = 11;
347  this.label12.Text = "Profession";
348  this.label12.TextAlign =
         System.Drawing.ContentAlignment.MiddleLeft;
349  //
350  // txtProfession
351  //
352  this.txtProfession.Location = new System.Drawing.Point(96, 136);
353  this.txtProfession.MaxLength = 20;
354  this.txtProfession.Name = "txtProfession";
355  this.txtProfession.TabIndex = 12;
356  this.txtProfession.Text = "";
357  //
358  // grpBxRegister
359  //
360  this.grpBxRegister.Controls.AddRange(new
         System.Windows.Forms.Control[] {
361  this.cmdRegister,
362  this.txtProfession,
363  this.txtPin,
364  this.txtCity,
365  this.txtEmail2,
366  this.txtEmail1,
367  this.txtPhone2,
368  this.txtPhone1,
369  this.txtAddress2,
370  this.txtAddress1,
371  this.txtConfirmPass,
372  this.txtPass,
373  this.txtLogin,
374  this.label12,
375  this.label11,
376  this.label10,
377  this.label9,
378  this.label8,
379  this.label7,
380  this.label6,
381  this.label5,
382  this.label4,
```

```
383   this.label3,
384   this.label2,
385   this.label1});
386   this.grpBxRegister.Location = new
          System.Drawing.Point(8, 16);
387   this.grpBxRegister.Name = "grpBxRegister";
388   this.grpBxRegister.Size = new System.Drawing.Size(440, 208);
389   this.grpBxRegister.TabIndex = 0;
390   this.grpBxRegister.TabStop = false;
391   //
392   // frmRegister
393   //
394   this.AutoScaleBaseSize = new System.Drawing.Size(5, 13);
395   this.ClientSize = new System.Drawing.Size(452, 247);
396   this.Controls.AddRange(new System.Windows.Forms.Control[] {
397   this.grpBxRegister,
398   this.lblCopyrights,
399   this.IMstatusBar});
400   this.FormBorderStyle =
          System.Windows.Forms.FormBorderStyle.FixedToolWindow;
401   this.Name = "frmRegister";
402   this.StartPosition =
          System.Windows.Forms.FormStartPosition.CenterParent;
403   this.Text = "Register";
404   this.Activated += new
          System.EventHandler(this.frmRegister_Activated);
405   this.grpBxRegister.ResumeLayout(false);
406   this.ResumeLayout(false);
407
408   }
409   #endregion
410
411   private void cmdRegister_Click(object sender, System.EventArgs e)
412   {
413     if (txtLogin.Text.Trim()=="")
414     {
415       MessageBox.Show("Login can't be empty");
416       txtLogin.Focus();
417       return;
418   }
419   if (txtPass.Text.Trim()=="")
420   {
421     MessageBox.Show("Password can't be empty");
422     txtPass.Focus();
423     return;
424   }
425   if (txtConfirmPass.Text.Trim()=="")
426   {
427     MessageBox.Show("Confirm Password can't be empty");
```

```
428    txtConfirmPass.Focus();
429    return;
430  }
431  if (txtPass.Text.CompareTo(txtConfirmPass.Text)!=0)
432  {
433    MessageBox.Show("Password mismatch");
434    txtPass.Focus();
435    return;
436  }
437
438    action=0;
439    this.Close();
440  }
441  public string[] GetLoginInfo()
442  {
443    string []strReturn=new string[11];
444
445    strReturn[0]=txtLogin.Text.Trim();
446    strReturn[1]=txtPass.Text.Trim();
447    strReturn[2]=txtAddress1.Text.Trim();
448    strReturn[3]=txtAddress2.Text.Trim();
449    strReturn[4]=txtPhone1.Text.Trim();
450    strReturn[5]=txtPhone2.Text.Trim();
451    strReturn[6]=txtEmail1.Text.Trim();
452    strReturn[7]=txtEmail2.Text.Trim();
453    strReturn[8]=txtPin.Text.Trim();
454    strReturn[9]=txtCity.Text.Trim();
455    strReturn[10]=txtProfession.Text.Trim();
456
457    return strReturn;
458  }
459  public int GetCmdAction()
460  {
461    int act=action;
462    action=-1; //clear last action
463    return act;
464  }
465
466  private void frmRegister_Activated(object sender,
           System.EventArgs e)
467  {
468    if (bMsgShow) return;
469    bMsgShow=true;
470
471  if (iCode==1)
472    {
473  MessageBox.Show("User already exist.Try another user name id",
                    "Error");
474      txtLogin.Focus();
```

```
475        }
476    }
477    }
478 }
```

- Lines 1-9: Include namespaces required for building this section of the Client module.

- Line 16: Implements the publicly accessible class frmRegister, which is inherited from System.Windows.Forms.Form class.

- Lines 18-45: Declaring required designer variables that will be used in designing the register form.

- Lines 51-53: Declare some user-defined variables.

- Lines 56-71: The default constructor of thefrmRegister class is implemented. The constructor takes two parameters — strLogin and iCode. The value of iCode determines the behavior of the register form, whereas strLogin carries the login name opted by the user during registration process.

- Lines 76-86: The Dispose() function is implemented, which manages the task of releasing all resources once they are no longer required by the application.

- Lines 88-408: Hold the code of the Initialize Component() function, which is must for designing the form using designer variables. The coding of the Initialize Component() function is autogenerated, and the user must not alter the code to prevent the appearance of any fault in the application.

- Lines 411-440: Comes into action when the user clicks the Register button. It checks the information submitted by the user and ensures that no validations such as empty password and login name are ignored while registering the user.

  - 413-424: If the user clicks the Registration button without entering the login name or password, these lines get executed.

  - 425-430: If the user clicks the Registration button, leaving the confirmation password field empty, these lines get executed.

  - 431-436: The password and confirmation password might vary. In such a scenario, these lines get executed.

  - 438-439: When the user does not skip information, the value of action variable is set to 0, which indicates that the user information has been successfully received.

- Lines 441-458: The GetLoginInfo() function is implemented, which is responsible for getting the information submitted by the user during the registration process. For handling the user information, a string-type array strReturn with an index length of 11 is used, which is capable of holding mandatory user information such as the login name and password, as well as optional registration information such as the user's address and e-mail address.

- Lines 459-464: Implements the GetCmdAction() function. This function is used to determine the last command button pressed during the registration process.

- Lines 466-476: Responsible for activating the registration form again. The registration form is activated again for the same user when the login name opted by the user is already taken by some other user.

Listing 6-4: sckClient.cs

The following code listing provides the code to establish the socket connection.

```
1 using System;
2 using System.Net;
3 using System.Net.Sockets;
4
5 namespace Jabber
6 {
7  /// <summary>
8  /// Summary description for sckClient.
9  /// </summary>
10  public class sckClient : System.Net.Sockets.TcpClient
11  {
12    public sckClient()
13    {
14      //
15      // TODO: Add constructor logic here
16      //
17    }
18
19  // this function will return the connection status
20  // of socket by using protected prpoperty Active.
21  public bool IsConnected()
22  {
23    return base.Active;
24  }
25  }
26 }
```

- Lines 1-3: The namespaces required for incorporating the networking feature in the application are included.

- Line 10: Implements a publicly accessible class, sckClient, which is inherited from the System.Net.Sockets.TcpClient class.

- Lines 12-17: Implement the default constructor of the sckClient class.

- Lines 21-24: Implement the publicly accessible function IsConnected(), which returns a boolean type value. This function returns the connection status of the socket by using the protected Active property.

Listing 6-5: XmlFormat.cs

The following code listing provides the code of XML norms, which is deployed in our application. The following code listing has various functions that handle the task of creating XML for specific task.

```
1 using System;
2
3 namespace Jabber
4 {
5 /// <summary>
6 /// Summary description for XmlFormat.
7 /// </summary>
8 public class XmlFormat
9 {
10   private string strXml;
11   public XmlFormat()
12     {
13     //
14     // TODO: Add constructor logic here
15     //
16     }
17
18 //overloaded constructor
19 public XmlFormat(string strType,string []param)
20 {
21    strXml= "<?xml version=\'1.0\' encoding=\'utf-
       8\'?><InstantMessanger>";
22
23    if (strType.ToUpper().CompareTo("AUTH")==0)
24    {
25    AuthXML(param);
26    }
27    else if (strType.ToUpper().CompareTo("REGISTER")==0)
28    {
29      RegisterXML(param);
30    }
31    else if (strType.ToUpper().CompareTo("MSG")==0)
32    {
33       MessageXML(param);
34    }
35    else if (strType.ToUpper().CompareTo("ADDFRIEND")==0)
36    {
37      AddFriendXML(param);
38    }
39    else if (strType.ToUpper().CompareTo("DELETEFRIEND")==0)
40    {
41      DeleteFriendXML(param);
42    }
```

```
43    else if (strType.ToUpper().CompareTo("ACCEPTFRIEND")==0)
44    {
45      AcceptFriendXML(param);
46    }
47    else if (strType.ToUpper().CompareTo("UNSUBSCRIBEFRIEND")==0)
48    {
49      UnsubscribeFriendXML(param);
50    }
51    else if (strType.ToUpper().CompareTo("ADDGATEWAY")==0)
52    {
53      AddGateway(param);
54    }
55    else if (strType.ToUpper().CompareTo("UNREGISTER")==0)
56    {
57      UnRegisterXML(param);
58    }
59    else if (strType.ToUpper().CompareTo("QUIT")==0)
60    {
61      QuitXML(param);
62    }
63    strXml+= "</InstantMessanger>";
64
65  }
66  private void AuthXML(String []param)
67  {
68    strXml+= "<Auth>";
69    strXml+= "<UserName>"+param[0]+"</UserName>";
70    strXml+= "<Password>"+param[1]+"</Password>";
71    strXml+= "</Auth>";
72  }
73
74  private void RegisterXML(String []param)
75  {
76    strXml+= "<Register>";
77    strXml+= "<UserName>"+param[0]+"</UserName>";
78    strXml+= "<Password>"+param[1]+"</Password>";
79    strXml+= "<sAdd1>"+param[2]+"</sAdd1>";
80    strXml+= "<sAdd2>"+param[3]+"</sAdd2>";
81    strXml+= "<sPhone1>"+param[4]+"</sPhone1>";
82    strXml+= "<sPhone2>"+param[5]+"</sPhone2>";
83    strXml+= "<sEmail1>"+param[6]+"</sEmail1>";
84    strXml+= "<sEmail2>"+param[7]+"</sEmail2>";
85    strXml+= "<sPin>"+param[8]+"</sPin>";
86    strXml+= "<sCity>"+param[9]+"</sCity>";
87    strXml+= "<sProfession>"+param[10]+"</sProfession>";
88    strXml+= "</Register>";
89  }
90
91  private void QuitXML(String []param)
```

```
 92  {
 93    strXml+= "<Quit>";
 94    strXml+= "<UserName>"+param[0]+"</UserName>";
 95    strXml+= "</Quit>";
 96  }
 97
 98  private void MessageXML(String []param)
 99  {
100    strXml+= "<MSG>";
101    strXml+= "<Target>" + param[0] + "</Target>";
102    strXml+= "<Source>" + param[1] + "</Source>";
103    strXml+= "<Text>" + param[2] + "</Text>";
104    strXml+= "</MSG>";
105  }
106
107  private void AddFriendXML(String []param)
108  {
109    strXml+= "<AddFriend>";
110    strXml+= "<UserName>"+param[0]+"</UserName>";
111    strXml+= "<FriendName>"+param[1]+"</FriendName>";
112    strXml+= "</AddFriend>";
113  }
114  private void DeleteFriendXML(String []param)
115  {
116    strXml+= "<DeleteFriend>";
117    strXml+= "<UserName>"+param[0]+"</UserName>";
118    strXml+= "<FriendName>"+param[1]+"</FriendName>";
119    strXml+= "</DeleteFriend>";
120  }
121  private void AcceptFriendXML(String []param)
122  {
123    strXml+= "<AcceptFriend>";
124    strXml+= "<UserName>"+param[0]+"</UserName>";
125    strXml+= "<FriendName>"+param[1]+"</FriendName>";
126    strXml+= "<Status>"+param[2]+"</Status>";
127    strXml+= "</AcceptFriend>";
128  }
129  private void UnsubscribeFriendXML(String []param)
130  {
131    strXml+= "<UnsubscribeFriend>";
132    strXml+= "<UserName>"+param[0]+"</UserName>";
133    strXml+= "<FriendName>"+param[1]+"</FriendName>";
134    strXml+= "</UnsubscribeFriend>";
135  }
136
137  public void UnRegisterXML(String []param)
138  {
139    strXml+="<UnRegister>";
140    strXml+=param[0];
```

```
141    strXml+="</UnRegister>";
142  }
143
144  public void AddGateway(String []param)
145  {
146    strXml+="<AddGateway>";
147    strXml+="<UserName>" + param[0] + "</UserName>";
148    strXml+="<MSNUserName>" + param[1] + "</MSNUserName>";
149    strXml+="<MSNPassword>" + param[2] + "</MSNPassword>";
150    strXml+="</AddGateway>";
151  }
152
153  public string GetXml()
154  {
155    return strXml;
156  }
157 }
158 }
```

- Line 1: For including the necessary namespace `System`.

- Line 8: Declares the publicly accessible class `XMLFormat`. This class is responsible for creating different types of client requests in XML format such as deleting or adding a friend, authentication request, logout, and so on.

- Line 10: A string-type variable, `strXml`, is declared. This variable carries the main tag for the client request to mark the beginning and end of requests — `<InstantMessenger>` and `</InstantMessenger>`.

- Lines 19-65: Implement the overloaded constructor of the class `XmlFormat`. This constructor takes two string-type parameters □`strType` and array `param`. The variable `strType` holds the type of client request, whereas the array `param` retains the content and information required for creating the request.

- Lines 23-62: The type of request is determined, and corresponding function(s) are called to form the request in appropriate XML format.

In the following code explanation, various functions responsible for manufacturing appropriate XML formats for client requests are discussed. The functions take the string array type parameter, which holds the information in accordance with the nature of the request. Whenever the request is formed, a set of tags (start and end) is added under the main tag (`<InstantMessanger>` and `</Instant Messanger>`) to mark the mode of request.

- Lines 66-72: The private function `AuthXML()` is implemented. This function is responsible for formulating the authentication request for the client by appending the user's login name and password inside the `<Auth>` and `</Auth>` tags.

- Lines 74-89: Implement private the function `RegisterXML()`. This function is responsible for creating the format for the registration request. Inside the `<Register>` and `</Register>` tags, the registration information is added and is stored in `param`.

- Lines 91-96: Undertakes the implementation of the `QuitXML()` function, which caters to the task of forming the quit request of the client. The `<Quit>` tag represents the quit request, and the login name of the user dominates such a request.

- Lines 98-105: Implements the `MessageXML()` function, which manages the task of writing the message in appropriate XML format. The `<MSG>` tag marks such as request. Under the `<MSG>` tag, the names of the sender and target the user are mentioned, along with the message content.

- Lines 107-113: The `AddFriendXML()` function is in charge of making the appropriate XML format whenever a user initiates to add another user as his/her friend. The `<AddFriend>` tag represents such as request. Whenever this request is formed, the names of the users, the one including another user and the one being included as friend, are passed.

- Lines 114-120: The `DeleteFriendXML()` function is responsible for forming the client request whenever he/she is deleting the other user from his/her friend list. Like the `AddFriendXML()` function, this function takes user names, the one deleting and the one being deleted, as parameters.

- Lines 121-128: Implements the `AcceptFriendXML()` function, which formulates the XML for accepting the friendship proposal forwarded by the user. Usually, the friend to whom the user has proposed for friend ship is responsible for generating this XML.

- Lines 129-135: Comes into action when the user deletes some friend(s) from his/her friend list. While forming the required XML, the `UnsubscribeFriendXML()` function takes names of the user and his/her friend as required parameters. The `<UnsubscribeFriend>` tag represents such requests.

- Lines 137-142: The `UnRegisterXML()` function undertakes the responsibility of making the unregister XML request for the client whenever he/she wishes to remove his/her account from the application database. The `<UnRegister>` tag denotes this client request, and it takes the login name of the user as a guideline.

- Lines 144-151: Allows the user to add the MSN gateway. To add the gateway, the code implements the `AddGateway()` function, which forms the suitable XML request for the client to accomplish the task. In the request, the login name of the user of the application and the authentication information of MSN (MSN login name and password) are supplied.

- Lines 153-156: Implements the `GetXml()` function, which returns the string-type variable `strXml`. This variable contains the format of XML request(s).

Figure 6-12 illustrates the working AddGateway class. The AddGateway class handles the task of including the gateway for MSN Instant Messenger.

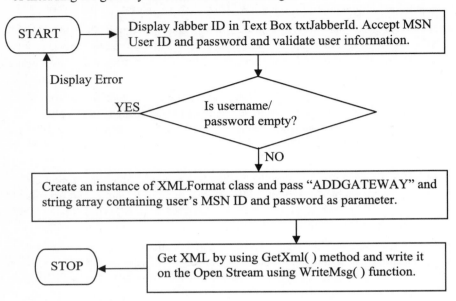

Figure 6-12: Flow Chart of Add Gateway

Listing 6-6: AddGateway.cs

The following code listing provides the code to include the gateway for the MSN Instant Messenger in the application so that user could communicate with MSN's users.

```
1 using System;
2 using System.Drawing;
3 using System.Collections;
4 using System.ComponentModel;
5 using System.Windows.Forms;
6
7 namespace Jabber
8 {
9  /// <summary>
10  /// Summary description for AddGateway.
11  /// </summary>
12  public class AddGateway : System.Windows.Forms.Form
13  {
14    private System.Windows.Forms.Label label1;
15    private System.Windows.Forms.TextBox txtJabberId;
16    private System.Windows.Forms.Label label2;
17    private System.Windows.Forms.TextBox txtMsnId;
```

```
18      private System.Windows.Forms.Label label3;
19      private System.Windows.Forms.TextBox txtMsnPassword;
20      private System.Windows.Forms.Button cmdAddGateway;
21      private System.Windows.Forms.Button cmdCancel;
22      private System.Windows.Forms.Label label4;
23      /// <summary>
24      /// Required designer variable.
25      /// </summary>
26      private System.ComponentModel.Container components = null;
27
28      public AddGateway()
29        {
30          //
31          // Required for Windows Form Designer support
32          //
33          InitializeComponent();
34
35          //
36          // TODO: Add any constructor code after InitializeComponent
                // call
37          //
38
39          txtJabberId.Text=frmJabberClient.strLogin;
40        }
41
42  /// <summary>
43  /// Clean up any resources being used.
44  /// </summary>
45  protected override void Dispose( bool disposing )
46  {
47    if( disposing )
48    {
49      if(components != null)
50        {
51          components.Dispose();
52        }
53    }
54    base.Dispose( disposing );
55  }
56
57  #region Windows Form Designer generated code
58  /// <summary>
59  /// Required method for Designer support - do not modify
60  /// the contents of this method with the code editor.
61  /// </summary>
62  private void InitializeComponent()
63  {
64    this.txtJabberId = new System.Windows.Forms.TextBox();
65    this.cmdAddGateway = new System.Windows.Forms.Button();
```

```
66    this.cmdCancel = new System.Windows.Forms.Button();
67    this.label3 = new System.Windows.Forms.Label();
68    this.label4 = new System.Windows.Forms.Label();
69    this.txtMsnPassword = new System.Windows.Forms.TextBox();
70    this.label1 = new System.Windows.Forms.Label();
71    this.label2 = new System.Windows.Forms.Label();
72    this.txtMsnId = new System.Windows.Forms.TextBox();
73    this.SuspendLayout();
74    //
75    // txtJabberId
76    //
77    this.txtJabberId.Enabled = false;
78    this.txtJabberId.Location = new System.Drawing.Point(128, 24);
79    this.txtJabberId.MaxLength = 20;
80    this.txtJabberId.Name = "txtJabberId";
81    this.txtJabberId.Size = new System.Drawing.Size(120, 20);
82    this.txtJabberId.TabIndex = 1;
83    this.txtJabberId.Text = "";
84    //
85    // cmdAddGateway
86    //
87   this.cmdAddGateway.Location = new System.Drawing.Point(80, 112);
88    this.cmdAddGateway.Name = "cmdAddGateway";
89    this.cmdAddGateway.Size = new System.Drawing.Size(96, 24);
90    this.cmdAddGateway.TabIndex = 6;
91    this.cmdAddGateway.Text = "&Add Gateway";
92    this.cmdAddGateway.Click += new
          System.EventHandler(this.cmdAddGateway_Click);
93    //
94    // cmdCancel
95    //
96    this.cmdCancel.Location = new System.Drawing.Point(184, 112);
97    this.cmdCancel.Name = "cmdCancel";
98    this.cmdCancel.Size = new System.Drawing.Size(96, 24);
99    this.cmdCancel.TabIndex = 7;
100   this.cmdCancel.Text = "&Cancel";
101   this.cmdCancel.Click += new
          System.EventHandler(this.cmdCancel_Click);
102   //
103   // label3
104   //
105   this.label3.Location = new System.Drawing.Point(32, 72);
106   this.label3.Name = "label3";
107   this.label3.Size = new System.Drawing.Size(88, 16);
108   this.label3.TabIndex = 4;
109   this.label3.Text = "MSN Password";
110   this.label3.TextAlign =
          System.Drawing.ContentAlignment.MiddleLeft;
111   //
```

```
112     // label4
113     //
114     this.label4.Location = new System.Drawing.Point(248, 48);
115     this.label4.Name = "label4";
116     this.label4.Size = new System.Drawing.Size(80, 16);
117     this.label4.TabIndex = 8;
118     this.label4.Text = "@Hotmail.com";
119     this.label4.TextAlign =
            System.Drawing.ContentAlignment.MiddleLeft;
120     //
121     // txtMsnPassword
122     //
123  this.txtMsnPassword.Location = new System.Drawing.Point(128, 72);

124     this.txtMsnPassword.MaxLength = 50;
125     this.txtMsnPassword.Name = "txtMsnPassword";
126     this.txtMsnPassword.PasswordChar = '*';
127     this.txtMsnPassword.Size = new System.Drawing.Size(120, 20);
128     this.txtMsnPassword.TabIndex = 5;
129     this.txtMsnPassword.Text = "";
130     //
131     // label1
132     //
133     this.label1.Location = new System.Drawing.Point(32, 24);
134     this.label1.Name = "label1";
135     this.label1.Size = new System.Drawing.Size(88, 16);
136     this.label1.TabIndex = 0;
137     this.label1.Text = "Jabber ID";
138     this.label1.TextAlign =
            System.Drawing.ContentAlignment.MiddleLeft;
139     //
140     // label2
141     //
142     this.label2.Location = new System.Drawing.Point(32, 48);
143     this.label2.Name = "label2";
144     this.label2.Size = new System.Drawing.Size(80, 16);
145     this.label2.TabIndex = 2;
146     this.label2.Text = "MSN ID";
147     this.label2.TextAlign =
            System.Drawing.ContentAlignment.MiddleLeft;
148     //
149     // txtMsnId
150     //
151     this.txtMsnId.Location = new System.Drawing.Point(128, 48);
152     this.txtMsnId.MaxLength = 50;
153     this.txtMsnId.Name = "txtMsnId";
154     this.txtMsnId.Size = new System.Drawing.Size(120, 20);
155     this.txtMsnId.TabIndex = 3;
156     this.txtMsnId.Text = "";
```

```
157    //
158    // AddGateway
159    //
160    this.AutoScaleBaseSize = new System.Drawing.Size(5, 13);
161    this.ClientSize = new System.Drawing.Size(340, 145);
162    this.Controls.AddRange(new System.Windows.Forms.Control[] {
163    this.label4,
164    this.cmdCancel,
165    this.cmdAddGateway,
166    this.txtMsnPassword,
167    this.label3,
168    this.txtMsnId,
169    this.label2,
170    this.txtJabberId,
171    this.label1});
172    this.FormBorderStyle =
           System.Windows.Forms.FormBorderStyle.Fixed3D;
173    this.MaximizeBox = false;
174    this.Name = "AddGateway";
175    this.StartPosition =
           System.Windows.Forms.FormStartPosition.CenterParent;
176    this.Text = "Add MSN Gateway";
177    this.ResumeLayout(false);
178
179    }
180    #endregion
181
182    private void cmdCancel_Click(object sender, System.EventArgs e)
183    {
184       this.Close();
185    }
186
187    private void cmdAddGateway_Click(object sender, System.EventArgs
e)
188    {
189       if (txtMsnId.Text.Trim()=="")
190       {
191         MessageBox.Show("MSN ID can't be empty");
192         txtMsnId.Focus();
193         return;
194       }
195       if (txtMsnId.Text.IndexOf("@")!=-1 ||
                        txtMsnId.Text.IndexOf(".")!=-1)
196       {
197         MessageBox.Show("Invalid id.");
198         txtMsnId.Focus();
199         return;
200       }
201       if (txtMsnPassword.Text.Trim()=="")
```

```
202      {
203        MessageBox.Show("MSN Password can't be empty");
204        txtMsnPassword.Focus();
205        return;
206      }
207
208
209        string []strParam=new String[3];
210        char []chPassword=null;
211
212        strParam[0]=frmJabberClient.strLogin;
213        strParam[1]=txtMsnId.Text.Trim() + "@hotmail.com";
214        chPassword=txtMsnPassword.Text.Trim().ToCharArray();
215        for (int i=0;i<chPassword.Length;i++)
216        {
217          chPassword[i]=(char)(((byte)chPassword[i])+10);
218          strParam[2]+=chPassword[i].ToString();
219        }
220
221        XmlFormat xmlAddGateway=new
XmlFormat("ADDGATEWAY",strParam);
222        frmJabberClient.WriteMsg(xmlAddGateway.GetXml());
223        xmlAddGateway=null;
224
225        this.Close();
226      }
227   }
228 }
```

- Lines 1-5: Include necessary namespaces required to build the classes and various other functions needed by the application.

- Line 12: Declares a public class `AddGateway`, inherited from `System.Windows.Forms.Form class`.

- Lines 14-22: Declares various designer variables required for designing the form.

- Lines 28-40: Implements the default constructor of the class `AddGateway`.

- Lines 45-55: Implements the `Dispose()` function, which sets free all resources once they are no longer required by the application.

- Lines 62-179: Implements the autogenerated coding of the `InitializeComponent()` function, a must for form-designer variables.

- Lines 182-185: Comes into action whenever the user clicks the Cancel button. The user's click leads to immediate closure of the form.

- Lines 187-226: Works when the user clicks on the `Add Gateway` button placed on the form. It ensures that certain validations are adhered to.

- Lines 189-194: Makes sure that the MSN ID is not left null. If the ID is null, an error message is displayed to the user, and the cursor is set on the text box.

- Lines 195-200: Ensures another validation. The user might type special characters such as '@' or dot (.) while entering the MSN ID. In response to such characters in the MSN ID, an error message appears, which informs the user about the cause of the error. When entering the login name for the MSN Network, only name is required.

- Lines 201-206: Makes sure that the password for logging on to the MSN Messenger can't be left blank.

- Lines 209-210: The arrays strParam and chPassword of string and character type are declared. The strParam is assigned the job of retaining the login names of the user for the local application and MSN Instant Messenging Service. The chPassword will be used for storing the password for the MSN Messenging Service.

- Lines 212-214: Adds the login name and the MSN login name of the user in strParam. The MSN password of the user is converted into CharArray type and stored in chPassword.

- Lines 215-219: Calculates the total length of the password. Each character of the password is converted into byte, and 10 is added in the ASCII value of each character to make it encrypted. Once all characters of the password are encrypted, they are again stored in character-type array and converted into string. The encrypted password is stored in strParam.

- Line 221: A new instance of xmlAddGateway of XmlFormat is created, and the ADDGATEWAY parameter is passed along with strParam, which holds the user's login information.

- Line 222: The WriteMsg() function is called to write the message. For squaring up the task, the GetXml() function is used.

Figure 6-13 illustrates the working of the frmAddConfirm.cs class.

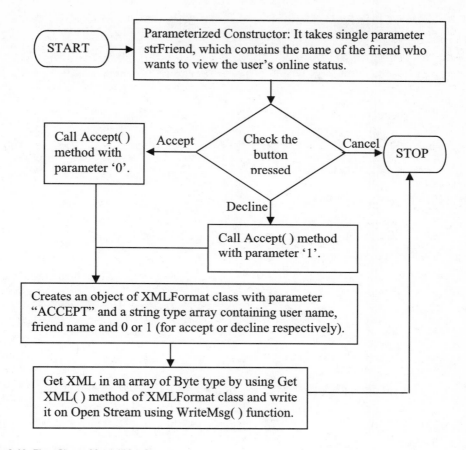

Figure 6-13: Flow Chart of frmAddConfirm.cs

Listing 6-7: AddConfirm.cs

The following code listing provides the code to add a friend in the friend list and ensures that friend gets included successfully.

```
1 using System;
2 using System.Drawing;
3 using System.Collections;
4 using System.ComponentModel;
5 using System.Windows.Forms;
6
7 namespace Jabber
8 {
9  /// <summary>
10  /// Summary description for AddConfirm.
```

```
11   /// </summary>
12   public class AddConfirm : System.Windows.Forms.Form
13   {
14     private System.Windows.Forms.Label lblMessage;
15     private System.Windows.Forms.Button cmdAccept;
16     private System.Windows.Forms.Button cmdDecline;
17
18     private string strFriend;
19     /// <summary>
20     /// Required designer variable.
21     /// </summary>
22     private System.ComponentModel.Container components = null;
23
24   public AddConfirm(string strFriend)
25   {
26     //
27     // Required for Windows Form Designer support
28     //
29     InitializeComponent();
30
31     //
32     // TODO: Add any constructor code after InitializeComponent
33     //       call
34     //
35     this.strFriend=strFriend;
36
37     lblMessage.Text=strFriend.ToUpper() + " has requested you to
                                view your online status";
38   }
39
40   /// <summary>
41   /// Clean up any resources being used.
42   /// </summary>
43   protected override void Dispose( bool disposing )
44   {
45     if( disposing )
46     {
47       if(components != null)
48       {
49         components.Dispose();
50       }
51     }
52     base.Dispose( disposing );
53   }
54
55   #region Windows Form Designer generated code
56   /// <summary>
57   /// Required method for Designer support - do not modify
```

```
 58   /// the contents of this method with the code editor.
 59   /// </summary>
 60   private void InitializeComponent()
 61   {
 62     this.cmdDecline = new System.Windows.Forms.Button();
 63     this.cmdAccept = new System.Windows.Forms.Button();
 64     this.lblMessage = new System.Windows.Forms.Label();
 65     this.SuspendLayout();
 66     //
 67     // cmdDecline
 68     //
 69     this.cmdDecline.Location = new System.Drawing.Point(160, 72);
 70     this.cmdDecline.Name = "cmdDecline";
 71     this.cmdDecline.Size = new System.Drawing.Size(72, 24);
 72     this.cmdDecline.TabIndex = 2;
 73     this.cmdDecline.Text = "&Decline";
 74     this.cmdDecline.Click += new
         System.EventHandler(this.cmdDecline_Click);
 75     //
 76     // cmdAccept
 77     //
 78     this.cmdAccept.Location = new System.Drawing.Point(80, 72);
 79     this.cmdAccept.Name = "cmdAccept";
 80     this.cmdAccept.Size = new System.Drawing.Size(72, 24);
 81     this.cmdAccept.TabIndex = 1;
 82     this.cmdAccept.Text = "&Accept";
 83     this.cmdAccept.Click += new
         System.EventHandler(this.cmdAccept_Click);
 84     //
 85     // lblMessage
 86     //
 87     this.lblMessage.BorderStyle =
         System.Windows.Forms.BorderStyle.Fixed3D;
 88     this.lblMessage.Location = new System.Drawing.Point(8, 16);
 89     this.lblMessage.Name = "lblMessage";
 90     this.lblMessage.Size = new System.Drawing.Size(288, 40);
 91     this.lblMessage.TabIndex = 0;
 92     this.lblMessage.TextAlign =
         System.Drawing.ContentAlignment.MiddleCenter;
 93     //
 94     // AddConfirm
 95     //
 96     this.AutoScaleBaseSize = new System.Drawing.Size(5, 13);
 97     this.ClientSize = new System.Drawing.Size(306, 103);
 98     this.Controls.AddRange(new System.Windows.Forms.Control[] {
 99     this.cmdDecline,
100     this.cmdAccept,
101     this.lblMessage});
```

```
102    this.FormBorderStyle =
            System.Windows.Forms.FormBorderStyle.Fixed3D;
103    this.MaximizeBox = false;
104    this.Name = "AddConfirm";
105    this.StartPosition =
            System.Windows.Forms.FormStartPosition.CenterParent;
106    this.Text = "Add Confirmation";
107    this.Closing += new
            System.ComponentModel.CancelEventHandler
                (this.AddConfirm_Closing);
108    this.ResumeLayout(false);
109
110  }
111  #endregion
112
113  private void cmdAccept_Click(object sender, System.EventArgs e)
114  {
115    Accept("0");
116    this.Close();
117  }
118
119  private void cmdDecline_Click(object sender, System.EventArgs e)
120  {
121    Accept("1");
122    this.Close();
123  }
124
125  private void Accept(string strCode)
126  {
127    this.Hide();
128    string []strParam=new String[3];
129    strParam[0]=frmJabberClient.strLogin;
130    strParam[1]=strFriend.ToLower();
131    strParam[2]=strCode;
132    XmlFormat xmlAccept =new XmlFormat("ACCEPTFRIEND",strParam);
133    frmJabberClient.WriteMsg(xmlAccept.GetXml());
134    xmlAccept=null;
135  }
136
137  private void AddConfirm_Closing(object sender,
                System.ComponentModel.CancelEventArgs e)
138  {
139    e.Cancel=true;
140  }
141  }
142 }
```

- Lines 1-5: Include necessary namespaces required for building the application.

- Line 12: Implements the publicly accessible class `AddConfirm`, which is inherited from `System.Windows.Forms.Form`.

- Lines 14-16: Declares designer variables required for designing various controls for the form.

- Line 18: A string type variable, `strFriend`, is declared. This variable retains the name of the user interested in viewing the online status of the friend.

- Lines 24-38: Implements the default constructor of the `AddConfirm` class.

  - 37: The text of the label `lblMessage` notifies the user that the other user wishes to view his/her online status.

- Lines 60-110: Implementation of the `InitializeComponent()` function, mandatory for designer variables. Since this code is autogenerated, the users must not alter it to prevent hampering the normal working of the application.

- Lines 113-117: Works when the user clicks the Accept button to allow the visited user view his/her online status. After accepting the request of the user, the form closes down.

- Lines 119-123: It might be possible that the user is not interested in sharing his/her online status with visitors. To reject their requests, he/she can click the Decline button. As in the case of request acceptance, after rejecting the request of the visitor, the form closes down.

- Lines 125-135: Implements the `Accept()` function. It takes a string-type variable as a parameter. This variable keeps the status of the user □ whether he/she is online or offline.

  - Lines 128-131: A string-type array, `param`, is declared to store the name of the user whose status is about to be viewed, his/her status, and the name of the user viewing the status.

  - Lines 132-133: A new instance, `xmlAccept`, of the class `XmlFormat` is created with ACCEPTFRIEND as a parameter; the `GetXml()` function of `xmlAccept` is called by the `WriteMsg()` function to write the appropriate message.

- Lines 137-140: Closes the form when the user clicks the Cancel button.

Figure 6-14 illustrates the working of `frmAddFriend.cs` class. The Client module uses this class to let user add friend in the friend list. It must be remembered that `frmAddConfirm.cs` class only checks whether the friend is included in the friend list of the user or not.

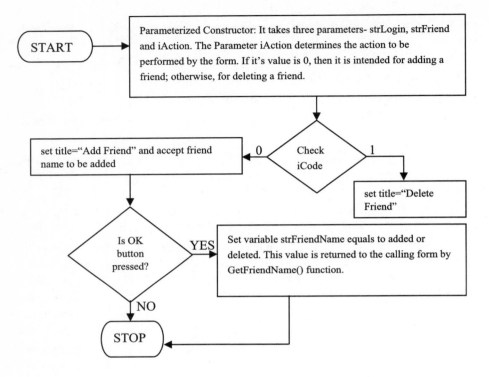

Figure 6-14: Flow Chart of frmAdd.cs

Listing 6-8: frmAddFreind.cs

The following code listing provides the code to include the friend in the friend list of the user.

```
1 using System;
2 using System.Drawing;
3 using System.Collections;
4 using System.ComponentModel;
5 using System.Windows.Forms;
6
7 namespace Jabber
8 {
9  /// <summary>
10  /// Summary description for frmAddFriend.
11  /// </summary>
12  public class frmAddFriend : System.Windows.Forms.Form
13  {
```

```
14      private System.Windows.Forms.Label label1;
15      private System.Windows.Forms.TextBox txtFriendName;
16      private System.Windows.Forms.Label label2;
17      private System.Windows.Forms.TextBox txtUserName;
18      /// <summary>
19      /// Required designer variable.
20      /// </summary>
21      private System.ComponentModel.Container components = null;
22      private System.Windows.Forms.Button cmdAddFriend;
23      private string strFriendName;
24
25  public frmAddFriend(string strLogin,int iAction,string strFriend)
26   {
27      //
28      // Required for Windows Form Designer support
29      //
30      InitializeComponent();
31
32      //
33      // TODO: Add any constructor code after InitializeComponent
        // call
34      //
35      txtUserName.Text=strLogin;
36      strFriendName="";
37
38      if (iAction==0)
39      {
40          this.Text="Add Friend";
41          cmdAddFriend.Text="&Add Friend";
42      }
43      else
44      {
45      this.Text="Delete Friend";
46      cmdAddFriend.Text="&Del Friend";
47      txtFriendName.Text=strFriend;
48      txtFriendName.Enabled=false;
49      }
50   }
51
52  /// <summary>
53  /// Clean up any resources being used.
54  /// </summary>
55  protected override void Dispose( bool disposing )
56   {
57      if( disposing )
58      {
59          if(components != null)
60          {
61              components.Dispose();
```

```
62      }
63    }
64    base.Dispose( disposing );
65  }
66
67  #region Windows Form Designer generated code
68  /// <summary>
69  /// Required method for Designer support - do not modify
70  /// the contents of this method with the code editor.
71  /// </summary>
72  private void InitializeComponent()
73  {
74    this.txtFriendName = new System.Windows.Forms.TextBox();
75    this.label1 = new System.Windows.Forms.Label();
76    this.label2 = new System.Windows.Forms.Label();
77    this.cmdAddFriend = new System.Windows.Forms.Button();
78    this.txtUserName = new System.Windows.Forms.TextBox();
79    this.SuspendLayout();
80    //
81    // txtFriendName
82    //
83   this.txtFriendName.Location = new System.Drawing.Point(136, 40);
84    this.txtFriendName.MaxLength = 20;
85    this.txtFriendName.Name = "txtFriendName";
86    this.txtFriendName.Size = new System.Drawing.Size(136, 20);
87    this.txtFriendName.TabIndex = 1;
88    this.txtFriendName.Text = "";
89    //
90    // label1
91    //
92    this.label1.Location = new System.Drawing.Point(24, 40);
93            this.label1.Name = "label1";
94    this.label1.Size = new System.Drawing.Size(104, 16);
95    this.label1.TabIndex = 0;
96    this.label1.Text = "Enter Friend Name";
97    //
98    // label2
99    //
100   this.label2.Location = new System.Drawing.Point(24, 16);
101   this.label2.Name = "label2";
102   this.label2.Size = new System.Drawing.Size(104, 16);
103   this.label2.TabIndex = 3;
104   this.label2.Text = "User Name";
105   //
106   // cmdAddFriend
107   //
108   this.cmdAddFriend.Location = new System.Drawing.Point(160, 80);
109   this.cmdAddFriend.Name = "cmdAddFriend";
110   this.cmdAddFriend.Size = new System.Drawing.Size(88, 24);
```

```
111     this.cmdAddFriend.TabIndex = 2;
112     this.cmdAddFriend.Text = "&Add Friend";
113     this.cmdAddFriend.Click += new
           System.EventHandler(this.cmdAddFriend_Click);
114     //
115     // txtUserName
116     //
117     this.txtUserName.Enabled = false;
118     this.txtUserName.Location = new System.Drawing.Point(136, 16);
119     this.txtUserName.MaxLength = 20;
120     this.txtUserName.Name = "txtUserName";
121     this.txtUserName.Size = new System.Drawing.Size(136, 20);
122     this.txtUserName.TabIndex = 4;
123     this.txtUserName.Text = "";
124     //
125     // frmAddFriend
126     //
127     this.AutoScaleBaseSize = new System.Drawing.Size(5, 13);
128     this.ClientSize = new System.Drawing.Size(292, 127);
129     this.Controls.AddRange(new System.Windows.Forms.Control[] {
130     this.txtUserName,
131     this.label2,
132     this.cmdAddFriend,
133     this.txtFriendName,
134     this.label1});
135     this.FormBorderStyle =
           System.Windows.Forms.FormBorderStyle.FixedToolWindow;
136     this.Name = "frmAddFriend";
137     this.StartPosition =
           System.Windows.Forms.FormStartPosition.CenterParent;
138     this.Text = "Add Friend";
139     this.ResumeLayout(false);
140
141   }
142   #endregion
143
144   public string GetFriendName()
145   {
146     return strFriendName;
147   }
148
149 private void cmdAddFriend_Click(object sender, System.EventArgs e)
150 {
151     strFriendName=txtFriendName.Text.Trim();
152     if (txtFriendName.Text.Trim()=="")
153     {
154       MessageBox.Show("Friend name can't be empty","Error");
155       txtFriendName.Focus();
156     }
```

```
157     else
158     {
159       this.Close();
160     }
161   }
162 }
163 }
```

- Lines 1-5: Include necessary namespaces required for building the application.

- Line 12: Sets up the class `frmAddFriend` with public accessibility.

- Lines 14-23: Declares necessary designer variables that will be taken up in designing the form.

- Lines 25-50: Groups the implementation of the default constructor of `frmAddFriend` class. The constructor takes three parameters. The first parameter (`strLogin`) holds the login name of the user; the second parameter decides the action that the form will take. If `action = 0`, it indicates that the user is interested in adding the friend, otherwise deleting the friend from his/her friend list. The third parameter takes the name of the friend. Based upon the value of the action variable, the caption of the command button changes.

- Lines 55-65: Implements the `Dispose()` function, which performs the clean up task by freeing up all resources once they are no longer required by the application.

- Lines 72-141: Puts the `InitializeComponent()` function into service, which is required by designer variables. This code is autogenerated, and the users must not alter or modify it to prevent any setback to the working of the application.

- Lines 144-147: Deploys the `GetFriendName()` function. This function returns the name of the friend, which is about to be added by the user in his/her friend list.

- Lines 149-161: Comes into action whenever the user clicks on the Add Friend button to include the other user in his/her friend list. If the user leaves the friend name NULL and initiates the process, an error message is shown, informing the user that validation has been overruled and focus is set on the empty field. If no validation is challenged by the user, the process is completed, smoothly followed by the closure of the form.

Figure 6-15 illustrates the working of `frmSendMessage.cs` class. The Client module uses this class to deliver messages among the users.

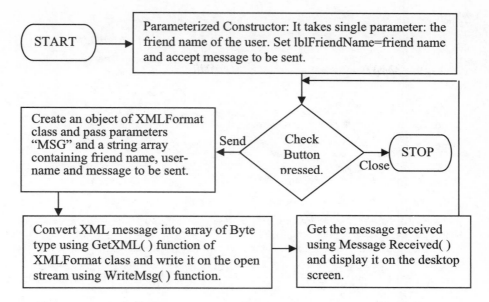

Figure 6-15: Flow Chart of frmSendMessage.cs

Listing 6-9: frmSendMessage.cs

The following code listing provides the code to design the window for delivering the message and also technique involved in exchanging the messages among users.

```
1 using System;
2 using System.Drawing;
3 using System.Collections;
4 using System.ComponentModel;
5 using System.Windows.Forms;
6 using System.Net;
7 using System.Net.Sockets;
8
9 namespace Jabber
10 {
11   /// <summary>
12   /// Summary description for SendMessage.
13   /// </summary>
14   public class frmSendMessage : System.Windows.Forms.Form
15   {
16     private System.Windows.Forms.Label label1;
17     private System.Windows.Forms.TextBox txtMessageSend;
18     /// <summary>
19     /// Required designer variable.
20     /// </summary>
21     private System.ComponentModel.Container components = null;
```

```
22    private System.Windows.Forms.Label lblFriendName;
23    private string username;
24    private System.Windows.Forms.Button cmdSend;
25    private System.Windows.Forms.RichTextBox txtMessages;
26    public string friendname;
27
28
29  public frmSendMessage(string friendname)
30  {
31    //
32    // Required for Windows Form Designer support
33    //
34    InitializeComponent();
35
36    //
37    // TODO: Add any constructor code after InitializeComponent
      // call
38    //
39
40    this.username=frmJabberClient.strLogin;
41    this.friendname=friendname;
42    lblFriendName.Text=friendname;
43    this.Text="Chat ( " + frmJabberClient.strLogin + " : Online)";
44
45  }
46
47  public void MessageRecieved(string msg)
48  {
49    int iLen=0,iTotal=0;
50    string str=friendname + " says: ";
51    iLen=str.Length;
52    iTotal=txtMessages.Text.Length;
53
54    txtMessages.AppendText(str);
55    txtMessages.SelectionStart=iTotal;
56    txtMessages.SelectionLength=iLen;
57
58    txtMessages.SelectionColor=System.Drawing.Color.Red;
59
60    txtMessages.AppendText(msg + "\r\n");
61    this.Focus();
62    txtMessageSend.Focus();
63  }
64
65  /// <summary>
66  /// Clean up any resources being used.
67  /// </summary>
68  protected override void Dispose( bool disposing )
69  {
```

```
70      if( disposing )
71      {
72         if(components != null)
73         {
74            components.Dispose();
75         }
76      }
77      base.Dispose( disposing );
78   }
79
80   #region Windows Form Designer generated code
81   /// <summary>
82   /// Required method for Designer support - do not modify
83   /// the contents of this method with the code editor.
84   /// </summary>
85   private void InitializeComponent()
86   {
87      this.cmdSend = new System.Windows.Forms.Button();
88      this.label1 = new System.Windows.Forms.Label();
89      this.lblFriendName = new System.Windows.Forms.Label();
90      this.txtMessages = new System.Windows.Forms.RichTextBox();
91      this.txtMessageSend = new System.Windows.Forms.TextBox();
92      this.SuspendLayout();
93      //
94      // cmdSend
95      //
96      this.cmdSend.Location = new System.Drawing.Point(232, 176);
97      this.cmdSend.Name = "cmdSend";
98      this.cmdSend.Size = new System.Drawing.Size(48, 24);
99      this.cmdSend.TabIndex = 2;
100     this.cmdSend.Text = "&Send";
101     this.cmdSend.Click += new
            System.EventHandler(this.cmdSend_Click);
102     //
103     // label1
104     //
105     this.label1.Location = new System.Drawing.Point(8, 16);
106     this.label1.Name = "label1";
107     this.label1.Size = new System.Drawing.Size(80, 16);
108     this.label1.TabIndex = 0;
109     this.label1.Text = "Friend Name";
110     //
111     // lblFriendName
112     //
113     this.lblFriendName.BorderStyle =
            System.Windows.Forms.BorderStyle.Fixed3D;
114     this.lblFriendName.Location = new System.Drawing.Point(88, 16);
115     this.lblFriendName.Name = "lblFriendName";
116     this.lblFriendName.Size = new System.Drawing.Size(192, 16);
```

```
117    this.lblFriendName.TabIndex = 4;
118    this.lblFriendName.TextAlign =
           System.Drawing.ContentAlignment.MiddleLeft;
119    //
120    // txtMessages
121    //
122    this.txtMessages.Location = new System.Drawing.Point(8, 40);
123    this.txtMessages.Name = "txtMessages";
124    this.txtMessages.ReadOnly = true;
125    this.txtMessages.ScrollBars =
           System.Windows.Forms.RichTextBoxScrollBars.Vertical;
126    this.txtMessages.Size = new System.Drawing.Size(272, 128);
127    this.txtMessages.TabIndex = 5;
128    this.txtMessages.Text = "";
129    //
130    // txtMessageSend
131    //
132 this.txtMessageSend.Location = new System.Drawing.Point(8, 176);
133    this.txtMessageSend.MaxLength = 255;
134    this.txtMessageSend.Name = "txtMessageSend";
135    this.txtMessageSend.Size = new System.Drawing.Size(216, 20);
136    this.txtMessageSend.TabIndex = 1;
137    this.txtMessageSend.Text = "";
138    this.txtMessageSend.KeyPress += new
           System.Windows.Forms.KeyPressEventHandler
               (this.txtMessageSend_KeyPress);
139    //
140    // frmSendMessage
141    //
142    this.AutoScaleBaseSize = new System.Drawing.Size(5, 13);
143    this.ClientSize = new System.Drawing.Size(286, 198);
144    this.Controls.AddRange(new System.Windows.Forms.Control[] {
145    this.txtMessages,
146    this.cmdSend,
147    this.txtMessageSend,
148    this.lblFriendName,
149    this.label1});
150    this.FormBorderStyle =
           System.Windows.Forms.FormBorderStyle.Fixed3D;
151    this.MaximizeBox = false;
152    this.Name = "frmSendMessage";
153    this.StartPosition =
           System.Windows.Forms.FormStartPosition.CenterParent;
154    this.Text = "SendMessage";
155    this.TopMost = true;
156    this.Closing += new
           System.ComponentModel.CancelEventHandler
               (this.frmSendMessage_Closing);
```

```
157    this.Activated += new
          System.EventHandler(this.frmSendMessage_Activated);
158    this.ResumeLayout(false);
159
160  }
161  #endregion
162
163  private void cmdSend_Click(object sender, System.EventArgs e)
164  {
165    if (txtMessageSend.Text.Trim()=="") return;
166
167    int iLen=0,iTotal=0;
168    string str=username + " says : ";
169    string []strParam=new string[3];
170
171    iLen=str.Length;
172    iTotal=txtMessages.Text.Length;
173
174    txtMessages.AppendText(str);
175    txtMessages.SelectionStart=iTotal;
176    txtMessages.SelectionLength=iLen;
177
178    txtMessages.SelectionColor=System.Drawing.Color.Blue;
179
180    strParam[0]=friendname;
181    strParam[1]=username;
182    strParam[2]=txtMessageSend.Text;
183
184    txtMessages.AppendText(txtMessageSend.Text + "\r\n");
185    txtMessageSend.Text="";
186    txtMessageSend.Focus();
187
188    XmlFormat xmlReg=new XmlFormat("MSG",strParam);
189    if (frmJabberClient.WriteMsg(xmlReg.GetXml())!=0)
190    {
191      xmlReg=null;
192      MessageBox.Show("Can't Send Message.","Error");
193      this.Close();
194    }
195    xmlReg=null;
196  }
197
198  private void frmSendMessage_Activated(object sender,
                              System.EventArgs e)
199  {
200      txtMessageSend.Focus();
201  }
202
```

```
203   private void frmSendMessage_Closing(object sender,
                         System.ComponentModel.CancelEventArgs e)
204   {
205     e.Cancel=true;
206     Close();
207   }
208
209   private void txtMessageSend_KeyPress(object sender,
                         System.Windows.Forms.KeyPressEventArgs e)
210   {
211     if (e.KeyChar==(char)13)
212     {
213       cmdSend_Click(sender,e);
214     }
215   }
216   private void Close()
217   {
218     this.Hide();
219     txtMessages.Text="";
220     txtMessageSend.Text="";
221   }
222   public void CloseChat()
223   {
224     Close();
225     MessageBox.Show(friendname + " has gone offline","Closing
                chat window");
226   }
227   }
228 }
```

- Lines 1-7: Inlcude namespaces required for building the application.

- Line 14: Declares the publicly accessible class `frmSendMessage`, inherited from `System.Windows.Forms.Form` class.

- Lines 16-26: Declares a designer variable, which will be required in designing the form. Also, one user-defined variable, `friendname`, is declared.

- Lines 29-45: Implements the default constructor of the `frmSendMessage` class. This constructor takes the string-type parameter `friendname`, which holds the name of the friend.

- Lines 47-63: Implements the `MessageRecieved()` function, which takes the string type parameter. The parameter usually holds the contents of the message.

  - Lines 51-52: The length of the current message and the total length of all messages are retreived and stored in the `iLen` and `iTotal` variables.

  - Lines 54-58: The messages are appended in the textbox `txtMessages`, which serves as the container for all messages. The color of the messages received is set to red.

- Line 60: Each message in the `txtMessages` text box begins with a new row.

- Lines 85-160: Implements the `Initialize Component()`. The code of this function is autogenerated, and users must not alter it.

- Lines 163-194: Executed when the user clicks the Send button of the message form to deliver the message to the other user.

  - Lines 171-172: The length of the messages is obtained. The length of the current message is stored in the `iLen` variable, whereas the aggregate length of all messages is held by the `iTotal` variable.

  - Lines 174-176: The messages sent by the user are appended in the `txtMessages` box, which serves as the container for all messages sent by the user.

  - Line 178: The color of the message sent by the user is set to blue.

  - Lines 180-182: The names of the user and his/her friend and the content of the message are stored in string-type array `strParam`.

  - Lines 188-194: Calls the constructor of the `XmlFormat` class, with the parameter MSG to denote the type of XML to be formed and the `strParam`. If the XML cannot be written, an error message is displayed, and the message box is closed, followed by cleaning up the `xmlReg`.

- Lines 198-201: Used to set the focus on the send message textbox whenever the Send Message form is activated.

- Lines 203-207: Comes into action when the user wishes to close the Send Message form.

- Lines 209-214: Works for the Enter key. Whenever the user, after typing the message, hits the Enter key, the Send button is clicked, and the message is delivered.

- Lines 216-221: In this code snippet, the `Close()` function is implemented, which comes into action whenever the user closes the Send Message form. On being invoked, the `Close()` function hides the form and clears the message textbox and the list of messages.

- Lines 222-226: Deploys the `CloseChat()` function. This function is responsible for closing the chat window whenever the user logs out. It also delivers the log-out message to his/her friend.

Figure 6-16 illustrates the working of `frmPopup.cs` class. The Client module uses this class to display a pop up menu to notify the user about notifications and messages of his/her friends.

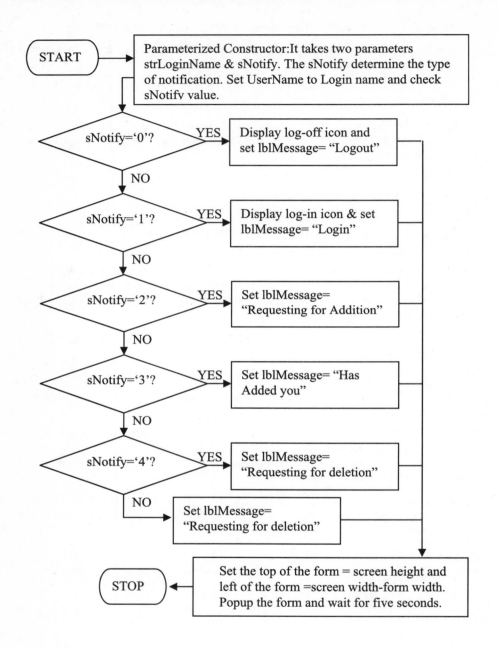

Figure 6-16: Flow Chart of frmPopup class

Listing 6-10: frmPopup.cs

The following code listing provides the code to design and implement a pop menu in the application.

```
 1 using System;
 2 using System.Drawing;
 3 using System.Collections;
 4 using System.ComponentModel;
 5 using System.Windows.Forms;
 6 using System.Threading;
 7
 8 namespace Jabber
 9 {
10   /// <summary>
11   /// Summary description for frmPopup.
12   /// </summary>
13   public class frmPopup : System.Windows.Forms.Form
14   {
15     /// <summary>
16     /// Required designer variable.
17     /// </summary>
18     private System.ComponentModel.Container components = null;
19     private System.Windows.Forms.Panel panel1;
20     private System.Windows.Forms.PictureBox pictureOnLine;
21     private System.Windows.Forms.Label lblMessage;
22     private System.Windows.Forms.Label lblUserName;
23     private System.Windows.Forms.PictureBox pictureOffLine;
24     private bool bActivate;
25     private string strFriend="";
26
27   public frmPopup(String strLoginName,string sNotify)
28   {
29     //
30     // Required for Windows Form Designer support
31     //
32     InitializeComponent();
33
34     //
35     // TODO: Add any constructor code after InitializeComponent
36     //       call
37
38     lblUserName.Text=strLoginName;
39
40     pictureOffLine.Visible=false;
41     pictureOnLine.Visible=false;
```

```
42
43    switch (sNotify.ToCharArray()[0])
44    {
45      case '0':
46        pictureOffLine.Visible=true;
47        lblMessage.Text="Log-out";
48      break;
49      case '1':
50        pictureOnLine.Visible=true;
51        lblMessage.Text="Log-in";
52      break;
53      case '2':
54        lblMessage.Text="requesting for addition";
55      break;
56      case '3':
57        lblMessage.Text="has added you in his list";
58      break;
59      case '4':
60        lblMessage.Text="requesting for deletion";
61      break;
62      case '5':
63        lblMessage.Text="has deleted you from the friend list";
64      break;
65    }
66    bActivate=false;
67  }
68  /// <summary>
69  /// Clean up any resources being used.
70  /// </summary>
71  protected override void Dispose( bool disposing )
72  {
73    if( disposing )
74    {
75      if(components != null)
76      {
77        components.Dispose();
78      }
79    }
80    base.Dispose( disposing );
81  }
82
83  #region Windows Form Designer generated code
84  /// <summary>
85  /// Required method for Designer support - do not modify
86  /// the contents of this method with the code editor.
87  /// </summary>
88  private void InitializeComponent()
89  {
```

```
90     System.Resources.ResourceManager resources = new
          System.Resources.ResourceManager(typeof(frmPopup));
91     this.lblUserName = new System.Windows.Forms.Label();
92     this.panel1 = new System.Windows.Forms.Panel();
93     this.pictureOnLine = new System.Windows.Forms.PictureBox();
94     this.lblMessage = new System.Windows.Forms.Label();
95     this.pictureOffLine = new System.Windows.Forms.PictureBox();
96     this.panel1.SuspendLayout();
97     this.SuspendLayout();
98     //
99     // lblUserName
100    //
101    this.lblUserName.Font = new System.Drawing.Font("Microsoft
          Sans Serif", 9.75F, System.Drawing.FontStyle.Regular,
          System.Drawing.GraphicsUnit.Point, ((System.Byte)(0)));
102    this.lblUserName.Location = new System.Drawing.Point(32, 8);
103    this.lblUserName.Name = "lblUserName";
104    this.lblUserName.Size = new System.Drawing.Size(120, 16);
105    this.lblUserName.TabIndex = 2;
106    this.lblUserName.TextAlign =
          System.Drawing.ContentAlignment.MiddleCenter;
107    //
108    // panel1
109    //
110    this.panel1.BorderStyle =
          System.Windows.Forms.BorderStyle.Fixed3D;
111    this.panel1.Controls.AddRange(new
          System.Windows.Forms.Control[] {
112    this.pictureOnLine,
113    this.lblMessage,
114    this.lblUserName,
115    this.pictureOffLine});
116    this.panel1.Name = "panel1";
117    this.panel1.Size = new System.Drawing.Size(168, 48);
118    this.panel1.TabIndex = 4;
119    //
120    // pictureOnLine
121    //
122    this.pictureOnLine.Image =
          ((System.Drawing.Bitmap)(resources.GetObject
              ("pictureOnLine.Image")));
123    this.pictureOnLine.Location = new System.Drawing.Point(8, 0);
124    this.pictureOnLine.Name = "pictureOnLine";
125    this.pictureOnLine.Size = new System.Drawing.Size(24, 16);
126    this.pictureOnLine.TabIndex = 1;
127    this.pictureOnLine.TabStop = false;
128    //
129    // lblMessage
130    //
```

```
131    this.lblMessage.Font = new System.Drawing.Font("Microsoft
            Sans Serif", 9F, System.Drawing.FontStyle.Regular,
            System.Drawing.GraphicsUnit.Point, ((System.Byte)(0)));
132    this.lblMessage.Location = new System.Drawing.Point(8, 24);
133    this.lblMessage.Name = "lblMessage";
134    this.lblMessage.Size = new System.Drawing.Size(160, 16);
135    this.lblMessage.TabIndex = 3;
136    this.lblMessage.TextAlign =
        System.Drawing.ContentAlignment.MiddleCenter;
137    //
138    // pictureOffLine
139    //
140    this.pictureOffLine.Image = (System.Drawing.Bitmap)
        (resources.GetObject("pictureOffLine.Image")));
141    this.pictureOffLine.Location = new System.Drawing.Point(8, 0);
142    this.pictureOffLine.Name = "pictureOffLine";
143    this.pictureOffLine.Size = new System.Drawing.Size(24, 24);
144    this.pictureOffLine.TabIndex = 0;
145    this.pictureOffLine.TabStop = false;
146    //
147    // frmPopup
148    //
149    this.AutoScaleBaseSize = new System.Drawing.Size(5, 13);
150    this.ClientSize = new System.Drawing.Size(176, 56);
151    this.Controls.AddRange(new System.Windows.Forms.Control[] {
152    this.panel1});
153    this.FormBorderStyle =
        System.Windows.Forms.FormBorderStyle.None;
154    this.Location = new System.Drawing.Point(0, -100);
155    this.Name = "frmPopup";
156    this.ShowInTaskbar = false;
157    this.Text = "frmPopup";
158    this.Activated += new
        System.EventHandler(this.frmPopup_Activated);
159    this.panel1.ResumeLayout(false);
160    this.ResumeLayout(false);
161
162    }
163    #endregion
164
165
166    private void popupMsg()
167    {
168      int height=0;
169      this.Top=Screen.PrimaryScreen.WorkingArea.Bottom;
170      this.Left=Screen.PrimaryScreen.WorkingArea.Width-this.Width;
171      height=50;
172
173      bActivate=true;
```

```
174    for (int i=0;i<height;i++)
175    {
176        this.Top=Screen.PrimaryScreen.WorkingArea.Height-i;
177        this.Height=i;
178        Thread.Sleep(20);
179    }
180
181    Thread.Sleep(5000);
182
183    for (int i=0;i<height;i++)
184    {
185      this.Top=Screen.PrimaryScreen.WorkingArea.Height+i-height;
186      this.Height-=1;
187      Thread.Sleep(20);
188    }
189    this.Close();
190  }
191
192 private void frmPopup_Activated(object sender, System.EventArgs e)
193  {
194      if (bActivate==false)
195      {
196          this.Top=Screen.PrimaryScreen.WorkingArea.Bottom;
197
198          Thread thrMsg=new Thread(new ThreadStart(popupMsg));
199          thrMsg.Start();
200      }
201    }
202  }
203 }
```

- Lines 1-6: Include various namespaces required while building the application.

- Line 13: Declares the publicly accessible class frmPopup, which is inherited from System.Windows.Forms.Form class.

- Lines 18-23: Declares various designer variables required while creating the GUI for the frmPopup class.

- Lines 24-25: Declares user-defined variables bActive and strFriend of Bool and String type, respectively.

- Lines 27-65: Implements the deault constructor of the frmPopup class. The constructor of frmPopup class takes the two string type variables — strLoginName and sNotify. strLoginName holds the login name of the user, whereas sNotify carries the type of notification to symbolize the status or activity of the user.

  - Lines 38-41: The label on the form is populated with the users's login name, whereas the pictures that indicate the online and offline staus of the user are kept invisible.

- Line 43: The possible notification value is converted into Char type and stored in `sNotify` variable.

- Lines 45-52: Comes into existence when the status of the user becomes either offline (0) or online (1). Based on the user status, the `lblMessage` is populated with 'Logout' and 'Login' message, respectively, and the picture that symbolizes the offline or online status is made visible accordingly.

- Lines 53-55: Executed when the user requests to add the other user in his/her friend list. As a result, the `lblMessage` is filled with message prompting the firiend of the user is requesting for adition in the friend list.

- Lines 56-58: Delivers the notification when some other user has added the currently logged in user in the friend list after obtaining the consesus of the currently logged in user.

- Lines 59-61: Responsible for delivering the notification for deletion to the target user whenever the user decides to delete him/her from his/her friend list.

- Lines 62-64: Delivers the notification when another user deletes the currently logged in user from his/her friend list.

- Lines 88-162: Implements the default `InitializeComponent()` function. The code of this function is autogenerated, and the users must not alter it.

- Lines 166-190: Deploys the `popupMsg()` function. This function holds the responsibility of showing a popup menu at the right-bottom of the desktop screen to notify the user about status requests and the demands of other users.

  - Lines 168-171: Sets the coordinates and height of the popup menu.

  - Lines 173-179: Lifts the popup menu at nominal speed. The speed for uplifting the popup menu is set by the means of thread. The sleep value of thread is assigned as 2 milliseconds.

  - Line 181: Keeps the popup menu visible on the desktop screen for 5 seconds.

  - Lines 183-189: After remaining visible for 5 seconds on the screen, this code starts pulling down the popup menu gradually at speed hiding 50 pixels in 2 milliseconds. The hiding begins with the total height of the popup menu and ends when the menu is pulled down.

- Lines 192-199: Displays a popup menu at the right-bottom of the screen. For displaying the popup menu, a thread is started.

Listing 6-11: About.cs

The following code listing provides the code for designing the About dialog for the application.

```
1 using System;
2 using System.Drawing;
```

```
 3 using System.Collections;
 4 using System.ComponentModel;
 5 using System.Windows.Forms;
 6
 7 namespace Jabber
 8 {
 9   /// <summary>
10   /// Summary description for About.
11   /// </summary>
12   public class frmAbout : System.Windows.Forms.Form
13   {
14     private System.Windows.Forms.Label lblCopyrights;
15     private System.Windows.Forms.Label labelJabber;
16     /// <summary>
17     /// Required designer variable.
18     /// </summary>
19     private System.ComponentModel.Container components = null;
20
21   public frmAbout()
22   {
23     //
24     // Required for Windows Form Designer support
25     //
26     InitializeComponent();
27
28     //
29     // TODO: Add any constructor code after InitializeComponent
30     // call
31   }
32
33   /// <summary>
34   /// Clean up any resources being used.
35   /// </summary>
36   protected override void Dispose( bool disposing )
37   {
38     if( disposing )
39     {
40       if(components != null)
41       {
42         components.Dispose();
43       }
44     }
45     base.Dispose( disposing );
46   }
47
48   #region Windows Form Designer generated code
49   /// <summary>
50   /// Required method for Designer support - do not modify
```

```
51  /// the contents of this method with the code editor.
52  /// </summary>
53  private void InitializeComponent()
54  {
55    this.lblCopyrights = new System.Windows.Forms.Label();
56    this.labelJabber = new System.Windows.Forms.Label();
57    this.SuspendLayout();
58    //
59    // lblCopyrights
60    //
61    this.lblCopyrights.ForeColor = System.Drawing.Color.Blue;
62    this.lblCopyrights.Location = new System.Drawing.Point(16, 16);
63    this.lblCopyrights.Name = "lblCopyrights";
64    this.lblCopyrights.Size = new System.Drawing.Size(208, 16);
65    this.lblCopyrights.TabIndex = 0;
66    this.lblCopyrights.Text = "© Dreamtech Software India Inc.";
67    this.lblCopyrights.TextAlign =
        System.Drawing.ContentAlignment.BottomCenter;
68    //
69    // labelJabber
70    //
71    this.labelJabber.ForeColor = System.Drawing.Color.Blue;
72    this.labelJabber.Location = new System.Drawing.Point(16, 40);
73    this.labelJabber.Name = "labelJabber";
74    this.labelJabber.Size = new System.Drawing.Size(208, 16);
75    this.labelJabber.TabIndex = 0;
76    this.labelJabber.Text = "Jabber Instant Messanger Client";
77    this.labelJabber.TextAlign =
        System.Drawing.ContentAlignment.BottomCenter;
78    //
79    // frmAbout
80    //
81    this.AutoScaleBaseSize = new System.Drawing.Size(5, 13);
82    this.ClientSize = new System.Drawing.Size(242, 74);
83    this.Controls.AddRange(new System.Windows.Forms.Control[] {
84    this.labelJabber,
85    this.lblCopyrights});
86    this.FormBorderStyle =
        System.Windows.Forms.FormBorderStyle.FixedToolWindow;
87    this.Name = "frmAbout";
88    this.StartPosition =
        System.Windows.Forms.FormStartPosition.CenterParent;
89    this.Text = "About";
90    this.ResumeLayout(false);
91
92  }
93  #endregion
94  }
95 }
```

- Lines 1-5: Include namespaces required to build the application.

- Line 12: Implements the `frmAbout` class, inherited from `System.Windows.Forms.Form`

- Lines 21-31: Implements the default constructor of the `frmAbout` class.

- Lines 36-46: Implements the `Dispose()` function, which performs the clean-up task by releasing all the resources used up in the application.

- Lines 53-93: Deploys the InitializeComponent() function, which initializes various designer variables that are required for the application.

Summary

The chapter provides all the documentation and code required to build the Client module for an Instant Messaging application. Because it is the origin of all requests, the Client module's manner of making various requests and the GUI support the Client module extends for making requests have been explained. Details regarding the working of the Client module in making various types of requests have been backed up by an account of how the Client module analyzes server responses.

Chapter 7

Enhancing Instant Messaging

The implementation of the Instant Messaging application using Java and C# is covered in previous chapters. Implicit in the previous discussions is the fact that the Instant Messaging application is built for computer-to-computer communication. However, market considerations demand that applications built to work on personal computers (PCs) should be able to communicate with other consumer devices such as set-top boxes, handheld devices, and so on. This chapter provides insight into how Java 2 Micro Edition (J2ME) can be used to port the Instant Messaging application to handheld devices. The scope of enhancing this application, along with relevant design considerations, is outlined in this chapter. Also included are the design techniques, with complete code and technical documentation, to run the Instant Messaging Client on handheld devices.

Introduction to J2ME

The first question that comes to mind is why J2ME? Why not simply use the application designed in Java 2 Standard Edition (J2SE) or Java 2 Enterprise Edition (J2EE) for handheld devices? The answer lies in the basic design of these handheld devices. These devices are conceptually designed to be handy and compact; hence, they are small, lightweight, and portable. They have limited computing power, limited memory, a small display area, and limited input power (being battery operated). Besides, most of these handheld devices work on proprietary software, with little or no compatibility with other brands or other devices. Hence, what is required is a platform on which a memory-efficient, device-independent or platform-independent application can be built. An application designed in J2SE, for example, cannot run in a limited memory space of 16K□512K, which happensto be the typical range of memory for handheld devices. The solution lies in J2ME, the third platform (after J2EE and J2SE) offered by Sun Microsystems.

J2ME is Java's platform for embedded and small consumer electronic devices. The J2ME technology has been developed specifically to work within constrained resources (for instance, within a limited memory range of 128K□512K. It should, however, be notedthat J2ME is not restricted to lower-end devices only. It can also be used on higher-end devices, such as set-top boxes, with as much computing power as a PC. Since J2ME is upwardly scalable to work with J2SE and J2EE, it enables these small consumer devices to be networked with servers or PCs.

The J2ME platform consists of a J2ME Virtual Machine and a set of APIs that are suitable for consumer and embedded devices. The J2ME technology can be divided into two primary components — configurations and profiles. These components can be understood if you think of J2ME in terms of a layered technology, with one layer working upon the other. The base layer is formed by a configuration, upon which operates the second layer, formed by a profile. Figure 7-1 illustrates this concept. A configuration is composed of the low-level APIs and the J2ME Virtual Machine; both of these provide an interface with a device's operating system. A profile built on top of a configuration is composed of APIs that provide functionality to build the user interface and develop the classes required to build an application.

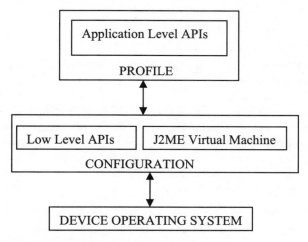

Figure 7-1: The concept of configurations and profiles

Think of a configuration as an abstract entity that provides basic J2ME functionality to a device, whereas a profile is what utilizes this configuration to allow the actual implementation of that functionality. For example, a configuration may support J2ME input/output functions on a family of devices, but the implementation of the input/output streams and their associated methods, properties, and so on depends upon the profile being used. Configurations and profiles are complementary to each other; both are required to develop and run a J2ME application.

The development of J2ME configurations, profiles, and so on has been a Community Process Program. In this program, Sun Microsystems and various companies manufacturing and marketing consumer devices have come together to develop a platform that provides industry-oriented solutions. It should also be noted that, like other Community Development Programs, J2ME is being continually upgraded to enhance and optimize J2ME-based services.

J2ME Virtual Machine

As mentioned earlier, J2ME is used for devices with limited memory. This means that the Java 2 Virtual Machine (JVM) meant for PCs and servers cannot be used with low-end electronic devices such as mobile phones, two-way pagers, hand-held devices, screen phones, smart phones, and so on. In addition, J2ME targets high-end electronic devices such as set-top boxes, car navigation systems, and handheld PCs that have much better resources. However, they still don't accommodate the large size of the conventional JVM. Therefore, to support the J2ME technology, two smaller Virtual Machines have been developed. These are, the K Virtual Machine (KVM), which has a smaller footprint than CVM and is used with low-end devices, and the C Virtual Machine (CVM), which has a footprint larger than KVM and is used with high-end devices.

K Virtual Machine (KVM)

The K Virtual Machine (KVM) has been developed keeping in mind the constraints of small mobile devices being manufactured in the industry. The KVM is a highly optimized version of the conventional JVM, with a size as small as 50K. Since KVM was specifically designed for very small environments that are proprietary, it has also been made highly customizable to enable manufacturers to adapt it to suit their particular device. The design considerations for KVM ensure that it is capable of running on low-power processors. The KVM can run on any system that has a 16-bit/32-bit processor and 160-512K of total memory. Nevertheless, the size reduction has occurred at the expense of a vast number of packages that are not supported by the KVM. As of now, the KVM has no support for certain features such as determinism, long and float data types, and so on.

The K Virtual Machine can theoretically run several profiles, but it cannot run perfectly all the profiles and APIs that aren't specifically designed for it, just as it cannot be used to run the Connected Device Configuration (CDC). It is meant for Connected Limited Device Configuration (CLDC). Presently, KVM supports only one profile — Mobile Information Device Profile (MIDP). This means that applications written for the more capable C Virtual Machine (CVM) or for the conventional JVM most probably cannot run on the KVM without some changes. However, the converse is not true — applications written for KVM can easily run on the CVM or the normal JVM. CVM, CDC, CLDC, and MIDP are discussed in forthcoming sections.

C Virtual Machine (CVM)

The C Virtual Machine was developed to provide additional functions not available in KVM that high-end electronic devices are capable of supporting. Its capabilities come very close to those of the conventional Java Virtual Machine (JVM). You may wonder why CVM was necessary at all if it is almost as powerful as the normal JVM. The most logical reason, perhaps, is that the devices for which CVM has been developed are meant to do specific work. They are not supposed to carry out extensive computing as desktop PCs do. Hence, what is required for these high-end devices such as set-top boxes, hand-held PCs, and so on is a smaller footprint of the conventional JVM without much loss in terms of functionality. Therefore, the CVM has been designed as a full-featured virtual machine that supports many features that are missing in KVM. Only a small portion of the functionality has been sacrificed to optimize it. Being introduced only recently, CVM has not been used extensively till now, but Sun Microsystems claims that CVM has the following advantages over the K Virtual Machine:

- If CVM is used with a real-time operating system, it knows how to work with it using the real-time capabilities.

- Memory use in CVM is more efficient. This is achieved by making it more exact, reducing the garbage collection pause times, totally separating the virtual machine from the memory system and so on.

- If you use CVM, you can directly map Java threads to native threads and run Java classes from read-only memory.

- Synchronization can be done with a small number of machine instructions, which increases the speed of synchronization.

- Besides being used with dynamically loaded classes, CVM can be used with the so-called ROMable classes. As a result, the virtual machine takes less time to start; fragmentation is reduced, and data sharing increases. This also means you can execute byte codes from ROM.

- Native threads are supported by CVM, and internal synchronization and exact garbage collection work with these.

- The footprint of CVM is only a little more than half that of JDK and about one-sixth less than that of Personal Java.

- All the VM specifications and libraries of JDK 1.3 are supported, including weak references, serialization, RMI, and so on.

- It is easier to add functionality to interfaces in CVM.

The CVM is used with the Connected Device Configuration (CDC) that uses the Foundation Profile.

J2ME configurations

J2ME configurations have been classified into two categories — Connected, Limited Device Configuration (CLDC) for low-end devices with 128K□512K memoryand Connected Device Configuration (CDC) for 512K+ devices. Thus, the choice of configuration depends upon the device specifications. These configurations are nested so that if an application runs on a low-end configuration, it will also be able to run on a high-end configuration. While developing an application, keep in mind that only one configuration can be used at a time.

Connected, Limited Device Configuration (CLDC)

CLDC is meant for small devices such as mobile phones, with constrained resources. CLDC is ideally suited for devices with a 16/32-bit microprocessor and can work on an available memory as low as 160K. It uses the small K Virtual Machine (KVM), discussed earlier in the chapter, and a limited set of libraries. Together, the KVM and the libraries can be stored in just 128K of memory space. Limited functionality is the price paid for using the memory-efficient CLDC. For example, the most commonly used J2SE packages, such as `java.lang.awt`, `java.lang.beans`, and others, have been dropped. In fact, CLDC contains only the following four packages:

- `java.io`: A stripped-down version of the J2SE `java.io` package. It contains the classes required for data input and output using streams.

- `java.lang`: A stripped-down version of the J2SE `java.lang` package. It contains the classes that are basic to the Java language, such as the wrapper classes for data types.

- `java.util`: A stripped-down version of the J2SE `java.util` package. It contains classes such as `Calender`, `Date`, `Vector`, and `Random`.

- `javax.microedition.io`: A newly introduced CLDC-specific class that defines the Generic Connection Framework. It contains the classes for handling all types of connections by using the same framework.

The emphasis in CLDC is providing just the basic functionality to conserve memory. Although certain basic features of J2SE are altogether missing in CLDC, certain implementations have been altered to make them simpler. The following list discusses these features of CLDC:

- Data types `long` and `float` are not supported. All the methods of J2SE inherited classes that use these data types have been removed.

- The number of runtime errors has been reduced significantly for the classes included in CLDC. In fact, only the following three errors (`java.lang.Error`, `java.lang.OutOfMemoryError`, and `java.lang.VirtualMachineError`) are available. Other errors are handled in an implementation-specific manner.

- To make garbage collection simple, support for finalization is not provided. There is no `finalize` method in the `java.lang.Object` class.

- Java Native Interface (JNI), which provides a means to access the local hardware, is not supported in CLDC. The purpose is to eliminate platform-dependence so that the applications can be ported to any platform containing the virtual machine.

- You can use threads but not thread groups or daemon threads.

- In the standard edition, you can mark objects for possible garbage collection. This cannot be done with CLDC. In other words, there is no support for weak references.

- Verification of classes to check whether the code is well formed is done off-device — that is, on the desktop system on which the applications are developed — by a tool called *preverifier*. You must do preverification explicitly after you compile your code.

- A different security model is used in CLDC that is somewhat similar to the one used in browsers for downloaded applets. The reason is that the model used in the standard edition is too heavy for small devices, and the security needs of the connected devices are similar to those of the browsers.

In our Instant Messaging application, we have used CLDC with Mobile Information Device Profile (MIDP) to provide the complete J2ME runtime environment.

Connected Device Configuration (CDC)

CDC is used on high-end electronic devices with better resources than handheld devices. These high-end devices run typically on 32-bit microprocessors and have 2MB of memory available for storing the virtual machine and libraries. CDC contains the C Virtual Machine (CVM), discussed earlier in the chapter. CVM is a full-featured virtual machine, providing the functionality of the Java 2 Virtual machine, but it has a smaller footprint. In addition to the CVM that provides the Java 2 Virtual Machine feature set, CDC contains a much higher number of APIs than CLDC and provides full Java-language support. CDC provides better networking support and a more flexible security mechanism. The packages contained in CDC are as follows:

- `java.io`
- `java.lang`
- `java.lang.ref`
- `java.lang.reflect`
- `java.math`
- `java.net`
- `java.security`
- `java.security.cert`
- `java.text`
- `java.text.resources`
- `java.util`
- `java.util.jar`
- `java.util.zip`
- `javax.microedition.io`

Some of the important features of this configuration are as follows:

- Full Java-language and virtual-machine support are provided, according to the Java Language Specification and the Java Virtual Machine Specification.

- The interfaces between parts of the runtime environment, such as the garbage collector, interpreter, and so on, are clearly defined; it is easy to add new features to the virtual machine.

- Cleanup and shutdown of the virtual machine is efficient, freeing up all memory and stopping threads without any leaks.

- Java threads can be mapped directly to native threads, and Java classes can be run from read-only memory.

- Native threads are supported by CVM, and internal synchronization and exact garbage collection work with these.

- All the VM specifications and libraries of JDK 1.3 are supported, including weak references, serialization, RMI, and so on.

CDC uses the Foundation Profile that provides functionality common to all target devices.

J2ME Profiles

As mentioned earlier, a configuration just provides a base that is capable of supporting J2ME applications. The profiles are what bring in the functionality. For example, without a profile, a developer cannot create a graphical user interface (GUI). A profile may add other kinds of functionality, such as better networking support, database management, distributed computing, and so on. Like configurations, profiles may be device-category specific. Some profiles may be useful for small devices, but others may be suitable for less-constrained devices. For example, MIDP or PDA Profile is used for mobile phones and PDA-like devices, respectively, on top of CLDC. On the other hand, Personal Profile is used for devices such as set-top boxes, on top of CDC.

Mobile Information Device Profile (MIDP)

CLDC can be used for writing applications for small devices. However, it gives you limited functionality; for example, there is no way to provide a graphical user interface. Therefore, it is necessary that a profile be used to build an effective application. The only profile so far available for small devices is the Mobile Information Device Profile (MIDP). The MIDP specification, being part of the Java Community Process, has been developed by a group of device manufacturers, software vendors, and other interested parties. The most common mobile information devices are cell phones, so this profile is considered the profile for cell phones. Now that the Palm port has become available, it can be used for Palm devices also.

MIDP sticks to the CLDC approach of minimizing resource usage but provides ways to add a good user interface within the given constraints. It introduces a new application model in which every application is called a MIDlet. A MIDlet behaves somewhat like an applet. It can have three states: active, paused, and destroyed. The application-manager software manages the lifecycle of the application. There is also a method to make data persistent.

The classes that MIDP contains, in addition to those provided by the CLDC, are as follows:

- `javax.microedition.midlet`: Defines the application model used in MIDP. It has a single class, `MIDlet`, with methods for enabling the application-managing software to create, pause, and destroy the application and perform some other tasks.

- `javax.microedition.lcdui`: Responsible for providing the user interface. It includes classes such as those for creating user-interface elements (buttons, text fields, choice groups, gauges, images, and so on) and for handling events (listeners). This is basically a game-oriented user interface package but can be used for other UI purposes.

- `javax.microedition.rms`: Provides the capability to make data persistent. For this purpose, the main class included is `RecordStore`. In addition, there are interfaces for comparison, enumeration, filtering, and listening.

> **NOTE:** MIDP has been used in our Instant Messaging application.

Foundation Profile

This profile is just an extension of CDC. CDC APIs do not provide the complete functionality available in Java Standard Edition. Therefore, to obtain functionality comparable to that of Java Standard Edition, one has to use the APIs of the Foundation Profile on top of CDC. The Foundation Profile acts as an extension of CDC to achieve Java 2 Standard Edition functionality. Profiles are normally supposed to add GUI functionality to configurations, but the Foundation Profile does not do this. There is no GUI package in this profile. Another peculiarity about this profile is that it is mandatory. You must use it along with CDC to prepare the ground for adding another profile. CDC, if combined with the Foundation Profile, adds up to complete the basic Java API set as available in the standard edition. The only exception is the user interface — that is, there is no `java.awt` package.

The classes this profile contains, in addition to those provided by the CDC, are as follows:

- `java.security.acl`
- `java.security.interfaces`
- `java.security.spec`

Figure 7-2 depicts the J2ME environment, summarizing what this chapter has discussed about it thus far.

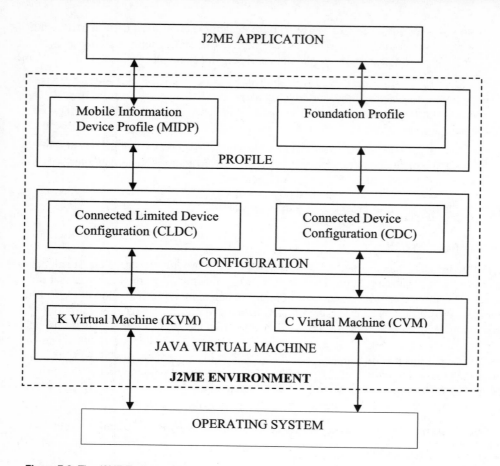

Figure 7-2: The J2ME Environment

Readers who are inclined to know more about J2ME may refer to the book *Wireless Programming with J2ME: Cracking the Code*, by Dreamtech Software Team (Hungry Minds, 2002) or *Java 2 Micro Edition* by Eric Giguere (John Wiley and Sons, Inc., 2000).

Design Techniques

The J2ME client developed for handheld devices is quite similar to the one developed in J2SE; however, there are certain classes/methods that are specific to J2ME. For example, the main class, `MIDP_Messenger`, that provides the user interface extends the `MIDlet` class that is not found in J2SE or J2EE. This section discusses the implementations that are crucial to developing the Instant Messaging Client in J2ME.

Introduction to MIDlets

A MIDlet is a small application that is programmed to conform to the Mobile Information Device Profile (MIDP). MIDlets are akin to applets. Just as applets run in a Web browser, MIDlets require the J2ME runtime environment. The two packages `javax.microedition.midlet` and `javax.microedition.lcdui` are central to the development of MIDlets. While `javax.microedition.midlet` provides the MIDlet framework to the user class that extends the MIDlet class, the `javax.microedition.lcdui` package provides GUI components. The specification for the MIDlet class governs the structure of a MIDlet. For example, a MIDlet must have the `startApp()`, `pauseApp()`, and `destroyApp()` methods. Listing 7-1 demonstrates a MIDlet.

Listing 7-1 MIDlet example

```
import javax.microedition.midlet.*;
import javax.microedition.io.*;
import javax.microedition.lcdui.*;
import java.util.*;

public class HelloJ2ME extends MIDlet implements CommandListener
{
 private Display       m_Display;
 private Command       m_Ok;
 private Command       m_Cancel;
 private Form          m_Form;


 public HelloJ2ME()
 {
   m_Display = Display.getDisplay(this);
   m_Ok      = new Command("OK",Command.SCREEN,3);
   m_Cancel  = new Command("CANCEL",Command.SCREEN,2);
 }

 public void startApp()
 {
  m_Form = new Form("Hello J2ME");
  m_Form.append("Hello From J2ME...");
  m_Form.addCommand(m_Ok);
  m_Form.addCommand(m_Cancel);
  m_Form.setCommandListener(this);
  m_Display.setCurrent(m_Form);
 }

 public void pauseApp()
 {}
```

```
public void destroyApp(boolean unconditional)
{
  notifyDestroyed();
}

public void commandAction(Command m_command, Displayable m_displayable)
{
  if (m_command == m_Ok)
  {
   Alert m_alert = new Alert("Message", "User Pressed OK Button !",
   null, AlertType.INFO);
   m_alert.setTimeout(5000);
   m_Display.setCurrent(m_alert,m_displayable);
  }
  else if (m_command == m_Cancel)
  {
   System.out.println("User Pressed Cancel Button...");
   destroyApp(true);
  }
 }
}
```

Before discussing the working of the MIDlet, I want to show how it can be run using the J2ME Wireless Tool Kit. Version 1.0.3 of J2ME is available on the CD accompanying this book. Double click on the `j2me_wireless_toolkit_1_0_3_win.exe` file on the CD to run the setup that will itself guide you on how to install J2ME Wireless Toolkit on your computer. However, to be able to run the J2ME code you also need to have JDK installed on your computer (JDK is also available on the CD). After installing the J2ME Wireless Tool Kit take the following steps:

1. Run the Ktoolbar from the Start menu or from the J2MEWTK directory. For example, if the J2MEWTK directory is `c:\J2MEWTK`, use the command prompt to reach its bin directory:

   ```
   c:\J2MEWTK>cd bin    <Enter>
   c:\J2MEWTK\bin>ktoolbar
   ```

2. A screen as shown in Figure 7-3 pops up.

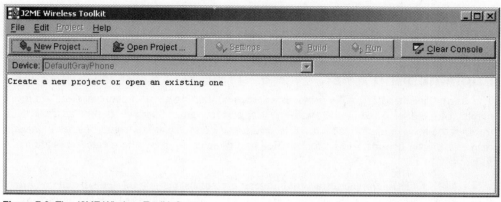

Figure 7-3: The J2ME Wireless Toolkit Screen

3. On this screen, click the New Project button.

   a. Enter a name for the project (for example, "HelloProgram").

   b. For the MIDlet class name, enter "HelloJ2ME".

4. Go to the directory `c:\J2MEWTK\apps\HelloProgram\src`, and place the source-code file `"HelloJ2ME.java"` in it.

5. Go to the pop up screen again, and press the Build button.

6. After the build operation is completed, press Run; the result of the `HelloJ2ME` class appears as in Figure 7-4.

Figure 7-4: Output from the HelloJ2ME class

If the user presses the "OK" button, the message "User Pressed OK Button !" is displayed for five seconds. If, however, the user presses the "CANCEL" button, the MIDlet is destroyed. Notice in the code for the MIDlet that a MIDlet implements a `CommandListener` instead of the `ActionListener` implemented in the J2SE classes. It defines the `commandAction()` method that takes an object of the type `Command` to recognize a user action.

Thus, J2ME uses certain interfaces, classes, and methods that are not in J2SE. However, once you are familiar with the new interfaces, classes, and methods, you realize that the concepts and procedures remain the same as in J2SE.

Implementing a list

The `List` class in MIDP APIs provides a screen containing a list of choices. A list on the display of the device can interact with the user and recognize user events such as traversing through the list. As mentioned earlier, `commandAction` is used to trigger the application's response to user actions. Lists are classified into three categories. These categories are as follows:

- IMPLICIT: Encompasses a simple, menu type of list (unrelated items listed one after the other). In such a list, the element of the list that has the focus is selected before any command listener is called.

- EXCLUSIVE: The select operation changes the selected element in the list, but the application is not notified until a command action occurs. This is akin to a radio-button list where selecting an option automatically deselects the option previously selected.

- MULTIPLE: Akin to checkbox elements where a select operation toggles the state of the element in focus. Here, too, the application is not notified until a command action occurs.

Listing 7-2 is an example depicting the `List` class. Take note in this example that the `MenuCheck` class depicts how a menu works on a handheld device. For the sake of simplicity, no actual action is performed by the class; instead, text messages are displayed to indicate the list item that has been selected by the user.

Listing 7-2: The MenuCheck class

```
import javax.microedition.midlet.*;
import javax.microedition.io.*;
import javax.microedition.lcdui.*;

public class MenuCheck extends MIDlet implements CommandListener
{
 private Display display = null;
 Command ok = null;
 Command quit = null;
 List menu = null;
 Form ui_form = null;
 StringItem si = null;
 public MenuCheck()
 {
  display = Display.getDisplay(this);
  quit = new Command("Quit",Command.SCREEN,2);
 }
 public void startApp()
```

```
{
 menu = new List("Various Options..",List.IMPLICIT);
 menu.append("TextField",null);
 menu.append("Ticker",null);
 menu.append("Alert",null);
 menu.setCommandListener(this);
 display.setCurrent(menu);
 ui_form = new Form("User's Choice...");
 si = new StringItem("User Entered ..", "");
 ui_form.append(si);
 ui_form.addCommand(quit);
 ui_form.setCommandListener(this);
}
public void pauseApp()
{
 menu = null;
}
public void destroyApp(boolean unconditional)
{
 menu = null;
 notifyDestroyed();
}
public void commandAction(Command c, Displayable d)
{
 if ( c == quit )
 {
  destroyApp(true);
 }
 else
 {
 List down = (List)display.getCurrent();
      switch(down.getSelectedIndex()) {
      case 0: si.setText("Text Field...");break;
      case 1: si.setText("Ticker...");break;
      case 2: si.setText("Alert...");break;
 }
 display.setCurrent(ui_form);
 }
}
}  // End MenuCheck......
```

The getDisplay() method of the Display class is used to get the display area for the
MIDlet. The startApp() method is then defined that creates a menu-list with three elements
in it and adds a command listener to the list. Figure 7-5 shows how the MIDlet appears on the
handheld screen.

Figure 7-5: The GUI for the class MenuCheck

A look at the `commandAction()` method shows that a `StringItem` variable (akin to a label in J2SE) is updated when the selected element of the list is changed. If, however, the user chooses to quit, the `destroyApp()` method is called, and the MIDlet is taken off the screen.

Implementing a socket

Sockets are implemented in J2ME using the `StreamConnection` interface. (Recall that the `Socket` class was used in J2SE to create sockets.) In addition, the input and output functions are performed using the `DataInputStream` and `DataOutputStream` classes, respectively. These classes allow Java primitive types to be read/written in a device-independent/portable manner. The `read()` and `write()` methods that read data from the input stream or write data to the output stream in the form of bytes remain practically the same.

Listing 7-3 shows how read/write operations are performed in J2ME. This example consists of two programs. The first program is a MIDlet that runs on the hand-held device at the user-end. The second is a standard Java program that runs on the server and implements a server-socket to listen to communication from the client. (Server-sockets are discussed in Chapter 3.) The MIDlet opens a connection to a specific port on the server. It then uses this connection to send messages to the server and to read responses from the server.

Listing 7-3: Read/write operations in J2ME

```
import javax.microedition.midlet.*;
import javax.microedition.io.*;
import javax.microedition.lcdui.*;
import java.util.*;
import java.io.*;


public class SocketCheck extends MIDlet implements CommandListener
{
  private Display        m_Display;
  private Command        m_Ok;
  private Command        m_Cancel;
  private Form           m_Form;
  private TextField      m_TextField;
```

```
private TextField        m_ReplyField;
InputStream              m_inputStream;
OutputStream             m_outputStream;
DataOutputStream         m_dataOutputStream;
DataInputStream          m_dataInputStream;
StreamConnection         socketC;
public SocketCheck()
{
  m_Display   = Display.getDisplay(this);
  m_Ok        = new Command("OK",Command.SCREEN,3);
  m_Cancel    = new Command("CANCEL",Command.SCREEN,2);
}
public void startApp()
{
 m_Form = new Form("Socket Check");
 m_TextField = new TextField("Enter Text Here ","",40,0);
 m_ReplyField = new TextField("Reply From Server ","",70,0);
 m_Form.append(m_TextField);
 m_Form.append(m_ReplyField);
 m_Form.addCommand(m_Ok);
 m_Form.addCommand(m_Cancel);
 m_Form.setCommandListener(this);
 m_Display.setCurrent(m_Form);
 try
 {

  socketC= (StreamConnection)
          Connector.open("socket://ServerIPAddress:5555");
  if (socketC != null)
    System.out.println("Connection Successfully established ");

  m_outputStream = socketC.openOutputStream();
  m_dataOutputStream = new DataOutputStream(m_outputStream);
  m_inputStream = socketC.openInputStream();
  m_dataInputStream = new DataInputStream(m_inputStream);
 }
 catch(IOException ae)
 {
   System.out.println("Couldn't open socket. Either server is not
   started (start it from ../serverforsocket/ using the command java
   server ), or port is already in use.... "  );
   destroyApp(true);
 }
}
public void pauseApp(){}
public void destroyApp(boolean unconditional)
{
  notifyDestroyed();
}
```

```
public void commandAction(Command m_command, Displayable m_displayable)
{
  if (m_command == m_Ok)
  {
    try
    {
    String str =  m_TextField.getString();
    m_outputStream.write((str+"\n").getBytes());
    StringBuffer sb = new StringBuffer();
    int b;
    while ((b=m_inputStream.read()) != 13)
    {
      sb.append((char)b);
    }
    String reply = sb.toString();
    m_ReplyField.setString(reply);
  }
  catch(IOException e)
  {
   System.out.println("IOException" + e);
  }
  }
  else if (m_command == m_Cancel)
  {
   System.out.println("User Pressed Cancel Button...");
   destroyApp(true);
  }
 }
}
```

Note that the Connector class is being typecast into a StreamConnection; its open() method is being used to open a connection to the server. The Connector class encompasses all the methods to create connection objects for all kinds of connections (that is, a connection to a server port, a connection to a file, a connection to an http address, and so on). Though the open() method in this example takes a single parameter, it may take up to three parameters:

```
open(String name, int modevalue, Boolean timeoutflag)
```

The first parameter, name, has the general form:

```
(scheme):[(target)]:[(params)]
```

scheme denotes the protocol name or the type of connection such as socket, http, and so on. target denotes the network address to which connection is to be made and could contain a URL to a server port, URL to a file or database, and so on. params allows the connecting class to send any values to the target URL, if required (akin to query-string values). Note that target and params are both optional and may not be present. This would be the case when a connectionless datagram is being sent.

The second parameter, `modevalue`, denotes whether the connection is being used for READ, WRITE, or READ-WRITE functions. If this parameter is absent, the connection is opened with READ_WRITE as default mode.

The third parameter, `timeoutflag`, is a boolean value that indicates whether the code is equipped to handle timeout exceptions.

When the MIDlet is run, it displays two text boxes: one to accept text typed by the user and the other to display messages received from the server. Figure 7-6 shows the `SocketCheck` GUI on the display of the handheld device.

Figure 7-6: The GUI For SocketClass class

When the user keys a message and presses the OK button, the MIDlet writes this message to the output stream as bytes. It then uses the input stream to read from the connection and displays this message in its respective textbox.

The server program works as an echo-server; it reads the message from the client MIDlet and outputs the same message to be read by the MIDlet. The code for the server program follows: Note that this server program is in Java Standard Edition and therefore would require Java Runtime Environment for execution.

```
import java.io.*;
import java.net.*;
public class server
 {
 public static void main(String args[])
 {
  try
  {
  ServerSocket server_soc = new ServerSocket (5555);
  Socket sc;
  sc = server_soc.accept();
  BufferedReader br = new BufferedReader (new
                    InputStreamReader(sc.getInputStream()));
  PrintWriter pw = new PrintWriter (new BufferedWriter(new
               OutputStreamWriter(sc.getOutputStream())),true);
  while (true)
  {
```

```
    String str = br.readLine();
    System.out.println("strstsr" +str);
    pw.println(str);
    }
    }
  catch(Exception ae)
  {
  }
 }
}
```

Hence, the text displayed in the second text box that appears below the text "Reply From Server" (see Figure 7-6) is the same as the message entered by the user.

Handling XML

In the J2ME client, the XML is parsed using the KXML parser. This is a SAX-based parser that parses an XML based on tags, attributes, and so on available in the XM (that is, it performs tag-by-tag parsing). (The other type of parser is DOM-based; it treats the complete XML as a single tree-entity and parses it on the whole.) In addition, as is expected, the KXML parser is very small, approximately 9K. The KXML parser can be obtained from www.kxml.org upon downloading place the org package obtained in the folder tmpclasses of your package. This would place the XML parser package in the classpath.

The parsing process in J2ME differs from that in J2SE. Here, the predefined variables such as START_TAG, END_TAG and TEXT are used to identify starting and ending tags as well as the data within the tags. Listing 7-4 displays an XML parser that clarifies the concepts of how XML is being parsed in the J2ME client application.

The XMLHandling class begins with displaying the single XML tag <Mode>Data in the Tag</Mode> on the device's screen, along with an "OK" and "CANCEL" button. If the user clicks on the "OK" button, result from the parsed XML is displayed on the screen (see Figure 7-7). If the user clicks the "CANCEL" button, the MIDlet is destroyed. Listing 7-4 contains the code for the XMLHandling class.

Listing 7-4: The XMLHandling class

```
import javax.microedition.midlet.*;
import javax.microedition.io.*;
import javax.microedition.lcdui.*;
import java.io.InputStream;
import java.util.*;
import java.io.*;
/**
 *  Packages used by the XML parser...
 *
 */
import org.kxml.*;
```

```
import org.kxml.io.*;
import org.kxml.parser.*;
public class XMLHandling extends MIDlet implements CommandListener
{
AbstractXmlParser                m_parser;
ParseEvent                       m_ParseEvent;
private Display                   m_Display;
private Command                  m_Ok;
private Command                  m_Cancel;
private Form                     m_Form;
private Form                     m_FormResult;
String                           m_XMLString = new String();
ByteArrayInputStream             m_stream;
String                           m_resultString = new String();
public XMLHandling()
{
  m_Display        = Display.getDisplay(this);
  m_Ok             = new Command("OK",Command.SCREEN,3);
  m_Cancel         = new Command("CANCEL",Command.SCREEN,2);
}
public void startApp()
{
 m_Form = new Form("XML Handling.");
 m_Form.append("Press \"OK\" to parse the XML. \n");
 m_XMLString        = "<Mode>\nData in the Tag\n</Mode>";
 m_Form.append(m_XMLString);
 m_Form.addCommand(m_Ok);
 m_Form.addCommand(m_Cancel);
 m_Form.setCommandListener(this);
 m_Display.setCurrent(m_Form);
 m_FormResult = new Form("XML Result.");
 m_FormResult.addCommand(m_Cancel);
 m_FormResult.setCommandListener(this);
}
public void pauseApp(){}
public void destroyApp(boolean unconditional)
{
 notifyDestroyed();
}

public void commandAction(Command m_command, Displayable m_displayable)
{
if (m_command == m_Ok)
 {
 try
  {
   byte[] m_byteArray = m_XMLString.getBytes();
   m_stream = new ByteArrayInputStream(m_byteArray);
   m_parser = new XMLParser(new InputStreamReader(m_stream));
```

```
 }
 catch(IOException ex)
 {
  System.out.println("IOException occured");
 }
 parseData();
 m_FormResult.append(m_resultString);
 m_Display.setCurrent(m_FormResult);
  }
  else if (m_command == m_Cancel)
  {
    System.out.println("User Pressed Cancel Button...");
    destroyApp(true);
  }
}
void parseData()
 {
  do
  {
   try
   {
 m_ParseEvent = m_parser.read ();
/** Start Tag is encountered.. and Appended to a string.*/
 if(m_ParseEvent.getType()==Xml.START_TAG)
 {
  StartTag stag = (StartTag)m_ParseEvent;
  String name = stag.getName();
  m_resultString = m_resultString + "Start Tag :"+name + "\n";
 }
/** text between tags is encountered and appended to the String. */
 if(m_ParseEvent.getType()== Xml.TEXT)
 {
  TextEvent tevent = (TextEvent)m_ParseEvent;
  String name = tevent.getText();
  name = name.trim();
  m_resultString = m_resultString +"Data :  "+name + "\n";
 }
/**  End Tag is encountered.. and Appended to a string. */
 if(m_ParseEvent.getType()== Xml.END_TAG)
 {
  EndTag end_tag = (EndTag)m_ParseEvent;
  String name = end_tag.getName();
  m_resultString = m_resultString + "End Tag : "+name + "\n";
 }
}
catch(IOException ex)
{
 System.out.println("Exception occured");
}
```

```
}
while (!(m_ParseEvent instanceof EndDocument));
System.out.println("**** END OF DOCUMENT ****"); // End of document
  }
}
```

The `AbstractXmlParser` class is used to parse the XML. When an XML tag or data within tags is encountered, an event of type `ParseEvent` is generated. The names of the tags and the data are assigned to respective variables and displayed on the screen. The results from the parsed XML are displayed as shown in Figure 7-7.

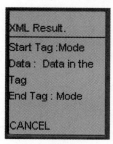

Figure 7-7: Parsed output from the XMLHandling class

Programming Client Requests

Two J2ME classes work together to recognize user events and to send user requests to the server: `MIDP_Messenger` and `XMLCreatorCell`. The MIDlet `MIDP_Messenger` provides the user interface necessary for the working of the Instant Messaging application, and the XMLCreatorCell class works in the background, generating XML requests as and when it is called by the `MIDP_Messenger` class.

1. The `MIDP_Messenger` GUI is based on the `List` class. Recall that the client application starts with a login or a registration request from the user. Following the same concept, the constructor of the `MIDP_Messenger` class creates a list with two elements, "Login" and "Registration", at the onset. The constructor also adds a command listener to the list and provides an "OK" and an "EXIT" button.

```
public MIDP_Messenger()
{
try
  {
m_display = Display.getDisplay(this);
m_midpmainlist = new List("Starting Screen", List.IMPLICIT,
                                  m_midpoptions, null);
m_midpokcommand = new Command("OK", Command.OK, 0);
m_midpexitcommand = new Command("EXIT", Command.EXIT, 0);
m_midpmainlist.addCommand(m_midpokcommand);
m_midpmainlist.addCommand(m_midpexitcommand);
```

```
m_midpmainlist.setCommandListener(this);
m_parser = new DataParser();
m_addchatlistfriend = new List("List of Friends", List.IMPLICIT);
 }
```

2. Four parameter values have been passed while creating a `List` object. The first value containing the string "Starting Screen" is the name of the list. The second value, `List.IMPLICIT`, denotes the type of list. The third value, `m_midpoptions`, is a string array containing values for the list elements (here these elements are "Login" and "Registration"). The fourth value that is a null parameter here accepts an image array for any image icons that the application developer may want to use in the list. The first display on the screen of the handheld is as shown in Figure 7-8.

Figure 7-8: The starting screen of the J2ME Instant Messaging client

3. When the user presses the "OK" button, the Login or the Registration GUI appears, depending upon the list item in focus when the button is pressed. The index of the selected item is obtained to determine the list element that the user has focused upon before pressing "OK".

```
public void commandAction(Command a, Displayable d)
{
 if (a == m_midpokcommand )
{
String m_select_options =

m_midpmainlist.getString(m_midpmainlist.getSelectedIndex());
if (m_select_options.equals("Login"))
        {
        m_loginform = new Form("Login Screen");
.........
else if(m_select_options.equals("Registration"))
        {
        m_registrationform = new Form("Registration");
----
```

4. The GUI for registration appears on the device dispay as shown in Figure 7-9. The GUI for login is similar except that it contains only two input boxes one for the user's name and the other for the user's password.

Figure 7-9: The Registration GUI

> **NOTE:** Notice the *down* arrow between the "Back" and the "OK" buttons. This arrow indicates that more elements exist in the GUI (that are not visible due to space constraints). Pressing this arrow scrolls down the display to the hidden elements.

5. After the user enters the login/registration information and presses the "OK" button, the information entered by the user is retrieved in the string array `value`. These values are then passed to the `XMLCreatorCell` class to create a login or registration XML request.

```
if (a == m_registrationokcommand)
{
        String[] value = {
m_registrationnamefield.getString(),m_registrationpasswordfield.getStr
ing(),m_registrationconfirmpasswordfield.getString(),"","","","",m_reg
istrationemailfield.getString(),"","","","" };
        m_xmlcreator = new XMLCreatorCell("REGISTER", value);

if (a == m_loginokcommand)
{

        String[] value = { m_loginnamefield.getString() ,
                                m_loginpasswordfield.getString()};
        m_sender_name = m_loginnamefield.getString();
        m_xmlcreator = new XMLCreatorCell("AUTH", value);
```

6. The `XMLCreatorCell` class calls the appropriate methods, depending upon the request type to generate the XML request.

```
if (type.equals("AUTH"))
    {
        CreateAuthXML(params);
    }
```

```
else if (type.equals("REGISTER"))
{
        CreateRegisterXML(params);
}
```

7. The `MIDP_Messenger` class uses the `returnResult()` method of `XMLCreatorCell` to obtain the XML request in a byte array. This XML request is subsequently written to the output stream.

```
byte[] m_loginstream  = m_xmlcreator.returnResult();
try
{
        m_dataoutputstream.write(m_loginstream, 0,
m_loginstream.length);
        m_dataoutputstream.flush();
}
```

8. Upon successful login, the user's friend list is displayed on the handheld device's display, as shown in Figure 7-10.

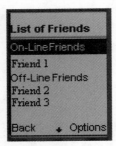

Figure 7-10: The friend list

The list of friends shows the names of the friends along with their respective status. The friend list is also derived from the `List` class and is of `IMPLICIT` type. The Options button in the right hand corner (see Figure 7-10) provides options such as deleting a friend, chatting with a friend, and so on. The index of the selected friend is obtained to associate the chosen option with that particular friend. For example, if the focus is on Friend 1 and the chat option is chosen, the program takes care that the message keyed in is subsequently sent to Friend 1.

The Instant Messaging options available to the user, such as sending a message, adding a friend, and so on, are also displayed as a list derived from the `List` class, as shown in Figure 7-11.

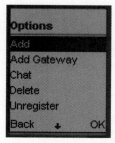

Figure 7-11: The Instant Messaging Options list

The user can now choose any option from the list, and the display will show the corresponding GUI. For the Add Gateway option, a form seeking the user's MSN or Hotmail username and password appears on the display. The user is supposed to enter his/her username and password to be able to add a gateway. As is mentioned in Chapter 5, the user needs to have an MSN or Hotmail account to add a gateway.

When a user wants to chat with a friend, a message window like the one shown in Figure 7-12 appears. The user can type his/her message in the text box and press "OK" to send it.

Figure 7-12: The GUI to send a message

When a user receives a message from a friend, the message is shown on the display with the caption, "Message From Jane" where *Jane* is the name of the friend from whom the message is received.

When a user chooses to add a friend, a form with the caption "Add Friend" appears on the display. The form contains an input field for the friend's name and a "Back" and "OK" button. After the user enters the friend's name and presses "OK", an add-friend request is generated using the XMLCreatorCell class and is sent to the server by the MIDP_Messenger class.

When another user adds you as a friend, a form like the one in Figure 7-13 appears that provides the option of accepting or declining ("Discard" button) to accept the other user as a friend. The name of the user who wishes to add you as a friend also appears on the screen.

Figure 7-13: Notification when another user adds you as friend

When another user removes you from his/her friend list, a notification GUI similar to Figure 7-13 is displayed, except that it provides a single `Accept` option, the `Discard` option is not available.

The remaining requests for unregistration, deleting a friend, quitting, and so on do not require a GUI; instead, the requested operation is performed by the application, and the results of the operation are obvious to the user. For example, if a delete-friend request is made, the friend list will be updated to show deletion of the friend's name.

Each of the requests is handled by the `MIDP_Messenger` class that in turn calls the `XMLCreatorCell` class to generate the appropriate XML. Note that the XML format of various requests remains the same as in the J2SE client. This XML is then written to the server by the `MIDP_Messenger` class. The `MIDP_Messenger` class, in conjunction with the `XMLCreatorCell` class, handles all requests made by the user and communicates these requests to the server.

Handling Responses

This topic is covered in two parts. In the first part, the possible ways of communication from the server to the client are discussed; in the second part, how the J2ME client handles the server responses is explained.

The Push-Pull technology

The server-to-client communication is based on two technologies, the *Push* technology or the *Pull* technology. In the Push technology, the server *pushes* the data to the client. This means that whenever the server has some data for the client, it initiates communication with the client on its own and sends the data. Thus, in the Push technology, the server plays an active role. Examples of Push technology are broadcasts and Netmeetings. In these cases, the server sends the data to all the clients connected to its network. All media broadcasts fall under the Push category.

In Pull technology, however, the server plays a passive role. The client checks if any data meant for it is available on the server. When such data is available, the client *pulls* this data from the server. Take note that for the J2ME application Push technology is not available, i.e., no methods, classes, etc., are available that are used by the server to push data to the J2ME client. One possible reason is that it is not feasible for these devices to remain connected to a network all the time, which happens to be a primary requirement for the Push technology. Other reasons are bandwidth and memory constraints. Further, even though the Push technology can be implemented in J2SE for PCs, it is not advisable to use it because of the following disadvantages:

- The load on the server increases, since a program running on the server is responsible for initiating communication with clients and sending their respective data.

- Since different clients may be connected via different types of connections such as dial-up, leased line, and so on, the server has to synchronize data transmission with the available client-bandwidth. In the absence of synchronization, data for low-bandwidth clients may get queued up at the server.

- The server has to be designed so that it is capable of pushing data to a maximum anticipated number of clients at all times. Since the number of clients actually logged into the service is likely to be fewer than this maximum, costly server resources are wasted.

These concerns give Pull technology an advantage over Push technology for the Instant Messaging application. As mentioned in the previous section, the `ListenerForCell` class that works on the client side is responsible for pulling the client data whenever it is available on the server. The server does not try to initiate data-transfer; instead, it holds the data until the client reads it. Note that the J2SE application discussed in Chapter 3 and Chapter 5 is based on Pull technology, too.

How the J2ME client handles server responses

The responses received from the server are handled by the remaining two classes in the J2ME client. These classes are `ListenerForCell` and `DataParser`.

1. An object of the `ListenerForCell` class is instantiated when the user chooses the option to log in to or register with the messenger service. This object of the `ListenerForCell` class runs an infinite loop to read the server's response to the authorization/registration request. Subsequently, the `ListenerForCell` class handles the information/response sent by the server.

```
public void run()
{
        m_firsttimenotifyfriends = new Vector();
 try
 {
  while (true)
  {
m_parser = new DataParser();
int           m_loop         = 100;
```

```
byte[] m_buffer        = new byte[1];
int            m_temp        = 0;
String m_FinalString = new String();
m_listoffriends                = new Vector();
while (m_loop != 0)
{
        m_temp        = m_datainputstream.read(m_buffer, 0, 1);
        String m_str = new String (m_buffer, 0, m_temp);
        m_FinalString = m_FinalString + m_str;
        if (m_FinalString.indexOf("</InstantMessenger>") != -1)
        {
         m_loop = 0;
        }
```

2. One byte at a time is read from the server and each time, the presence of the last XML tag, `</InstantMessenger>`, is checked within the received XML. If the tag is present, it means that the XML being read is now complete. This results in the value of the `while` loop variable, the `m_loop` being set to 0. If, however, the last tag is not encountered in the received XML, the program goes back to the `while` loop that reads data from the server.

> **NOTE:** The previous code snippet contains two `while` loops. The first `while` loop (immediately after the `try` statement) is the infinite loop that is run to listen to communication from the server. Do not confuse it with the second `while` loop that serves to actually read XML data from the server. The second loop is exited every time a complete XML is received from the server (to enable further processing of this XML). However, the first loop runs until the user exits the application.
>
> Since, the second `while` loop is nested within the first, it also means that even after exiting the second loop, the program execution will return to it repeatedly to read subsequent XML responses from the server.

3. After a complete XML has been received from the server, the `DataParser` class is called to parse the received XML.

```
m_parser.sourceurl(m_FinalString);
m_parser.firsttag();
String m_first = m_parser.firststring();
```

4. The `sourceurl()` method of the `DataParser` class creates an object of the class `AbstractXmlParser` and sets it to parse the XML received as a parameter value.

```
public void sourceurl(String xmldata)
{
try
{
        byte[] m_b = xmldata.getBytes();
        m_stream = new ByteArrayInputStream(m_b);
```

```
        m_parser = new XmlParser(new InputStreamReader(m_stream));
}
catch(IOException ex)
{
        System.out.println("IOException occured");
}
}
```

5. The `firsttag()` method of `DataParser` class sets the request type for the incoming XML data by identifying the first XML tag.

```
public void firsttag()
{
do
{
        try
        {
         m_event = m_parser.read();
                if (m_event.getType() == Xml.START_TAG)
                {
                if (m_event.getName().equals("auth"))
                {
                  m_firstvaluestring = m_event.getName();
                  return;
                }
                else if(m_event.getName().equals("FriendList"))
                {
                  m_firstvaluestring = m_event.getName();
                  return;
                }
```

6. The `firststring()` method of `DataParser` returns the string that contains the request type. Depending on the request type, the `ListenerForCell` class calls the appropriate method of the `DataParser` class. For example, for an authorization/login request type, the `authcall()` method is called.

```
if (m_first.trim().equals("auth"))
{
        m_parser.authcall();
        m_auth = m_parser.auth();
}
```

7. The method `authcall()` separates the XML value from the XML value tag (Recall that this value indicates whether or not the login is successful).

```
public void authcall()
{
do
{
        try
        {
                m_event = m_parser.read();
                if (m_event.getType() == Xml.START_TAG)
                {
                }
                else if(m_event.getType() == Xml.TEXT)
                {
                   TextEvent m_tx = (TextEvent)m_event;
                   m_authstring = m_tx.getText();
                }
                else if(m_event.getType() == Xml.END_TAG)
                {
                }
        }
        catch (IOException e)
        {
                System.out.println(e);
        }
}
while (!(m_event instanceof EndDocument));
}
```

8. The method auth() returns the string containing the value within the XML value tags.

9. The program control then goes back to the while loop to wait for the next server communication that happens to be the user's friend list. The method listoffriends() in the DataParser class generates the friend list as a string. The method returnthefriendslist() returns this string to the ListenerForCell class to be subsequently shown on the device's display.

10. The ListenerForCell class goes back to the loop that reads from the server. Subsequent communication from the server is generated when the user makes a request. Once again, the ListenerForCell class reads these responses, parses them, and processes them. Thus, the ListenerForCell class keeps waiting for the server's communication as long as the user remains logged into the messenger service. When the user chooses the option to quit or unregister, the object of ListenerForCell class is destroyed. This, however, is done by the MIDP_Messenger class in its destroyApp() method.

Thus, we have seen that the J2ME client application for the Instant Messaging application is composed of four classes: MIDP_Messenger, XMLCreatorCell, ListenerForCell, and

`DataParser`. While the first two classes contain user interfaces and methods to handle user requests, the last two handle server responses.

This sums up the discussions in this chapter. Listings of complete working codes, technical flow charts, and line-by-line explanation of code for the four classes used in the J2ME Instant Messaging client are available on the CD accompanying this book. Please refer to the CD documentation to locate the exact folder where you can find the technical documentation for the J2ME classes.

Summary

This chapter explains how the Instant Messaging client can be extended to handheld electronic devices such as mobile phones, hand-held PCs, and so on by using J2ME. Because of the resource constraints of these devices, the client has been built on a limited number of classes and methods offered by J2ME (the `List` and `Form` classes being most notable). A noteworthy point is that though the J2ME client provides all the basic services provided by the J2SE client, the number of user-defined classes used in J2ME is just four, as opposed to the 13 classes used in the J2SE client (refer to Chapter 5 for these classes).

Appendix A

What's on the CD-ROM

This appendix provides you with information regarding the contents of the CD that accompanies this book. For the latest and the greatest information, please refer to the ReadMe file located at the root of the CD. Here is what you will find:

- Hardware/software requirements
- Using the CD with Windows
- What's on the CD
- Troubleshooting

Hardware/Software Requirements

This section lets you know the different software and hardware requirements that your system needs to meet to be able to host the applications on the CD.

Hardware requirements

Make sure your computer meets the minimum system requirements listed in this section. If your computer doesn't meet most of these requirements, you may encounter problems when using the contents of the CD.

For Windows 9*x*, Windows 2000, Windows NT4 (with SP 4 or later), Windows Me, or Windows XP:

- PC with a Pentium processor running at 120 Mhz or faster
- If you are running the Java version of the Instant Messaging application, a Minimum of 32 MB of total RAM should be installed on your computer; for best performance, we recommend at least 64 MB.
- To run the C# version of the Instant Messaging application, you need to have a minimum of 128 MB of the total RAM installed on your computer; for best performance, we recommend 256 MB or more.
- Ethernet network interface card (NIC) or a modem with a speed of at least 28,800 bps
- A CD-ROM drive

Software requirements

This section lists the software you need to have on your computer to be able to run the two versions of the Instant Messaging application on the CD.

The Java version

Following is the software the user must have on his or her system to run the Java version of this software:

- JDK (Java Development Kit) — This is the Software Development Kit for developing standard Java applications. The Java version of our application has been developed using this kit. You can download it from: `http://java.sun.com/j2se/1.3/`. It is available on the CD as well.

- XForte for Java release 3.0 — The Forte for Java release 3.0 software is an integrated development environment used for developing Java applications. Use this to develop the Java version of our application. It is an IDE provided by Sun Microsystems. You can download it from: `http://www.sun.com/forte/ffj/`. It is available on the CD as well.

- Xerces XML parser for Java — The XML parser is required for parsing the XML data. The Java version of the application internally uses this XML parser. This XML parser is available at: `http://xml.apache.org/dist/xerces-j/`. It is available on the CD as well.

- Tomcat 3.0 — Tomcat is the servlet container used in the official reference implementation for the Java Servlet and JavaServer Pages technologies. You can get this at: `http://jakarta.apache.org/tomcat/`. It is available on the CD as well.

The C# Version

Following is the software the user needs to have on his or her system to run the C# version of this software.

- Microsoft XML Parser 3.0 or above — The XML parser class is needed for parsing the XML data. The C# version of the application internally uses this XML parser. This XML parser may be procured at: `http://msdn.microsoft.com/library/default.asp?url=/nhp/default.asp?contentid=28000438`.

- Microsoft Visual Studio .NET — The C# version of our application has been developed using this kit.

- SQL Server 2000 — The Instant Messaging application uses this RDBMS (Relational Data Base Management System) to manage the user database. Additional information regarding this SQL Server 2000 is available at: `http://www.microsoft.com/sql/default.asp`.

- Acrobat Reader 5.0 — Software for viewing Adobe PDF files. You need this software to read the eBook version of this book. You can download this software from: `http://www.adobe.com/products/acrobat/readermain.html`. It is available on the CD as well.

Using the CD with Windows

To install the items from the CD to your hard drive, follow these steps:

1. Insert the CD in the computer's CD-ROM drive of your computer.

2. A window will appear with the following options: Install, Explore, eBook, Links, and Exit.

   - **Install:** Gives you the option to install the supplied software and/or the author-created samples on the CD-ROM.

   - **Explore:** Allows you to view the contents of the CD-ROM in its directory structure.

   - **eBook:** Allows you to view an electronic version of the book.

   - **Links:** Opens a hyperlinked page of Web sites.

   - **Exit:** Closes the autorun window.

If you do not have autorun enabled or if the autorun window does not appear, perform the following steps to access the CD.

1. Click Start → Run.

2. In the dialog box that appears, type *d*:\setup.exe, where *d* is the letter denoting your CD-ROM drive. This brings up the autorun window described previously.

3. Choose the Install, Explore, eBook, Links, or Exit option from the menu. (See Step 2 in the preceding list for a description of these options.)

CD Contents

The following sections provide a summary of the software and other materials you will find on the CD.

Author-created materials

All author-created materials of the book, including code listings and samples, are on the CD in the folder named "Instant Messaging Source Code."

The source code is further categorized into three subfolders, namely, Java (Standard Edition), C# (which consists of the two versions in which this application has been built), and Java (Micro Edition), which is the enhancement of our Instant Messaging application. A brief description of the various files/subfolders in each folder is provided here as an aid to handling the CD-ROM effectively.

Java (Standard Edition) Folder

In this folder, you will find three more subfolders, namely, Client, Server, and WebServices, in which you will find their respective source codes.

Client Folder

- **org:** Handles all operations necessary for XML parsing.

- **Login.java:** Becomes operative when the client/user starts the Instant Messaing application. It enables the user to login to the Instant Messaging server or to register to the Instant Messaging server in case the user is using the application for the first time.

- **MainScreen.java:** This class, as the name suggests, is the most important of the client applications and does a whole lot of work. For example, it displays the friend list to the user, lets the user send messages to any other user, and lets the user add or delete friends.

- **Register.java:** Responisible for registering the user in the local domain as well as to the Jabber server.

- **Session.java:** Helps in creating a session of the client with the server.

- **SParser.java:** Responsible for parsing the XML requests and responses.

- **Message.java:** Responsible for showing a GUI that the user can use to send/receive messages to other users.

- **AddFriend.java:** Responsible for adding a friend to the users' friend list.

- **AcceptFriend.java:** Responsible for accepting a request from any other user.

- **AddGateway.java:** Responsible for adding the friend list of any other messaging service (MSN and so on) to the current friend list.

- **UnsubscribeFriend.java:** Responsible for removing a friend from the friend list.

- **XMLCreator.java:** Responsible for generating requests in XML format.

- **ColorPreference.java:** Responsible for changing the visual attributes of the message screen.

- **About.java:** Responsible for displaying a dialog indicating who has created this application.

- There are some other resources that have no use in programming but are included to improve the visual attribute of the application. They are certain .gif files and certain icons. Their names are as follows:

  - `yellow-ball.gif`
  - `white-ball.gif`
  - `red-ball.gif`
  - `pink-ball.gif`
  - `blue-ball.gif`

- green-ball.gif
- EXIT.ICO
- help.ico
- SEND.ICO

Server Folder

- **org:** Handles all operations necessary for XML parsing.
- **StartUpScreen.java:** Comes into action when the client/user starts the Instant Messaing application server. It enables the user to start a server that hosts all the clients.
- **Server.java:** The most important class of the server application; it handles requests of various clients, maintains the databases with the help of Web services, and so on.
- **ListenerForJabber.java:** Responsible for sending and receiving requests from the Jabber server.
- **XMLParser.java:** Responsible for parsing the XML requests and responses.
- **CreateXML.java:** Responsible for generating requests in XML format.

WebServices Folder

- **AddFriend.jsp:** Responsible for adding a friend to the users' friend list by updating the database accordingly.
- **DeleteContact.jsp:** Responsible for removing a friend from the users' friend list by updating the database accordingly.
- **FriendList.jsp:** Responsible for generating the friend list of a particular user from the database.
- **Login.jsp:** Responsible for updating the user status in the database.
- **Logout.jsp:** Responsible for updating user status in the database.
- **Register.jsp:** Responsible for adding a new user to the database.
- **Unregister.jsp:** Responsible for removing a user from the database.
- **NotifyFriends.java:** Responsible for notifying the friends of a particular user about his/her status(Online / offline).

How to run the application

To run the Java version of the application, copy all the folders under the folder Java (Standard Edition) to a folder on the hard disk. Copy all the .jsps and servlets from the Web services to the Tomcat (WebService Container) WEB-INF directory. To run the server, go to the command prompt switch to the server directory and type the following command: **java StartUpScreen.java**. To run the client, go to the command prompt switch to the client directory and type **java Client.java**. The process has been made easier for the users by providing the installation option in the setup application for the CD that copies the required files to the location specified by the user.

C# folder

This part describes the contents present for the C# version of the Instant Messaging application on this CD-ROM. In this folder, you will find two more subfolders, namely, Jabber and JIM, in which you will find their respective source codes and a file named `InstMsgServ.asmx`, the Web service file that handles the Web service for the C# application. The functions used up in this Web service are as follows:

- **AddFriend:** Responsible for adding a friend to the users' friend list and updating the database accordingly.

- **DeleteContact:** Responsible for removing a friend from the users' friend list and updating the database accordingly.

- **FriendList:** Responsible for generating the friend list of a particular user in the database.

- **Login:** Responsible for updating user login status in the database.

- **Logout:** Responsible updating the database record of the user, by indicating that user has logged out of the instant messaging system.

- **Register:** Responsible for adding a user to the database.

- **Unregister:** Responsible for removing a user from the database.

- **NotifyFriends:** Responsible for notifying the friends of a particular user about his or her status (online/offline).

Jabber folder

- **icons:** Contains various icons used in the application.

- **Main.cs:** Assumes action when the user starts the client.

- **sckClient.cs:** Responsible for establishing connectivity with the server.

- **Register.cs:** Handles the registration process.

- **Login.cs:** Comes into play when the user logs on to the server. It sends the user information to the local server.

- **SendMessage.cs:** Responsible for showing a GUI that the user can use to send/receive messages to other users.

- **XmlFormat.cs:** Responsible for generating requests in XML format.

- **frmPopup.cs:** Responsible for various popup features used in the application (for example, displaying that a certain friend of the user is online/offline).

- **frmAddFriend.cs:** Responsible for adding a friend to the user's friend list.

- **AddGateway.cs:** Responsible for adding the friend list of any other messaging service (for instance, MSN) to the current friend list.
- **AddConfirm.cs:** Responsible for accepting a request from any other user.
- **About.cs:** Responsible for displaying a dialog indicating who has created this application.

JIM Folder

- **Main.cs:** Comes into action when the user starts the client.
- **SckListener.cs:** Responsible for establishing connectivity with the client.
- **SocketThread.cs:** A multiutility class that has a lot of functions (connecting to Jabber server, parsing the XML responses and requests received by the server, and so on).
- **XmlFormat.cs:** Responsible for generating responses in XML format.
- **JabberXml.cs:** Responsible for generating requests for the Jabber server in XML format supported by the Jabber.

How to run the application

To build the C# version of this application, copy all the contents of the C# folder to a folder on your hard disk, and compile the project files or solution files of the client, the server, and the InstMsgServ.asmx using Microsoft Visual Studio .NET Beta 2. Following this, double click the exe files of each, that is, the Jabber.exe and JIM.exe, which have been generated by the Microsoft Visual Studio .NET environment. The process has been made easier for users by providing the installation option in the setup application for the CD, which copies the required files on the location specified by the user.

Java (Micro Edition) Folder

- **org:** Handles all operations necessary for XML parsing.
- **MIDP_Messenger.java:** The most important class of the Micro-Edition Application. It displays the friend list to the user, lets the user send messages to other users, and lets the user add/delete friends, and so on.
- **DataParser.java:** Responsible for parsing the XML requests and responses.
- **ListenerForCell.java:** Responsible for sending and receiving requests from the server.
- **XMLCreatorCell.java:** Responsible for generating requests in XML format.

How to run the application

To build the Micro Edition version of this application, copy all the contents of the Java(Micro Edition) folder to a folder on your hard disk, and compile the project files or solution files using J2MEWTK (J2ME Wireless Toolkit) after adding the org folder at an appropriate place. Now just run the project from J2MEWTK. The process has been made easier for users by providing the installation option in the setup application for the CD, which copies the required files on the location specified by the user.

Applications

The following applications are on the CD:

Tomcat Server Folder

- **Tomcat Server 3.0:** With the tomcat environment, development of Java Servlets and JSP is possible without having to install a full-fledged Web server as entailed by ASP, CGI, Perl, and so on. In the Tomcat environment, all classes are available, as suited to the server-side Java programming environment.

Java Developers Kit Folder

- **Forte for Java release 3.0:** An integrated development environment used for devloping Java applications. It is an IDE provided by Sun Microsystems.
- **Java 2 SDK:** A software-development kit for Java Standard Edition; required for developing Java applications.
- **Java 2 Platform Micro Edition, Wireless Toolkit 1.0.x (J2ME):** A software-development kit for Java Micro-Edition; required for developing Java applications for handheld devices.

Acrobat Reader Folder

- **Acrobat Reader 5.0:** This software enables you to view the Adobe PDF files over a liberal range of hardware and operating systems. You can avail the Acrobat reader 5.0 for adding digital signature to files even while remaining connected to your Web browser or for converting your office documents to Adobe PDF files for the Acrobat Reader for Palm OS.

Xerces Folder

- **Xerces Java Parser 1.4.4 Release :** Enables you to parse the XML files.

kXML

- **kXML:** XML parser for Palm and other handheld devices. This is used with the application built in Java Micro Edition.

Shareware programs are fully functional trial versions of copyrighted programs. If you like particular programs, you may register with their authors for a nominal fee and receive licenses, enhanced versions, and technical support. *Freeware programs* are copyrighted games, applications, and utilities free for personal use. Unlike shareware, these programs do not require a fee or provide technical support. *GNU software* is governed by its own license, which is included inside the folder of the GNU product. See the GNU license for more details.

Trial, demo, or evaluation versions are usually limited either by time or functionality (such as being unable to save projects). Some trial versions are very sensitive to system date changes. If you alter your computer's date, the programs will "time out" and will no longer be functional.

eBook version of Instant Messaging Systems: Cracking the Code

The complete text of this book is on the CD in Adobe's Portable Document Format (PDF). You can read and search through the file with the Adobe Acrobat Reader (also included on the CD).

Troubleshooting

If you have difficulty installing or using any of the materials on the companion CD, try the following solutions:

- **Turn off any anti-virus software that you may have running:** Installers sometimes mimic virus activity and can make your computer incorrectly believe that it is being infected by a virus. (Be sure to turn the anti-virus software back on later.)

- **Close all running programs:** The more programs you're running, the less memory is available to other programs. Installers also typically update files and programs; if you keep other programs running, installation may not work properly.

- **Reference the ReadMe:** Please refer to the ReadMe file located at the root of the CD-ROM for the latest product information at the time of publication.

- **Make sure you are online:** The applications (the Instant Messaging applications) on this CD are developed assuming that the the user has access to an Internet/Intranet connection. These applications will not work if the user is not connected to the Internet or Intranet. The user must ensure that he or she is connected to the Internet or Intranet for these applications to run smothly.

If you still have trouble with the CD, please call the Wiley Customer Care phone number: (800) 762-2974. Outside the United States, call 1 (317) 572-3994. You can also contact Wiley Customer Service by e-mail at techsupdum@hungryminds.com. Wiley will provide technical support only for installation and other general quality control items; for technical support on the applications themselves, consult the program's vendor or author.

Appendix B

Instant Messaging Software Resources

The following table gives a list of URLs, which provide information on the Instant Messaging systems and software.

URL	Explanation
http://www.howstuffworks.com/instantmessaging.htm	Introduction to Instant Messaging.
http://www.jabber.org	Jabber Instant Messaging Application.
http://docs.jabber.org/jpg	Jabber's Programmers Guide (JPG).
http://java.sun.com	JDK 1.3.
http://java.sun.com	J2MEWTK 1.3.
http://www.kxml.org	KXML xml parser for J2ME.
http://xml.apache.org/	Xerces XML Parser for Java 2 Standard Edition.
http://jakarta.apache.org/tomcat/	Tomcat (Web Server Container).
http://java.sun.com	Forte for Java Community Edition.
http://msdn.microsoft.com/vstudio/	Visual Studio .NET.
http://www.microsoft.com/sql/default.asp	SQL Server 2000.
http://www.microsoft.com	IIS Internet Information Server.
http://messenger.yahoo.com	Yahoo Instant Messenger.
http://messenger.msn.com	MSN Instant Messenger.
http://www.icq.com	ICQ Instant Messenger.
http://www.aol.com/index.adp	AOL Instant Messenger.

X□Y□Z

Terms and conditions of the license & export for Java™ 2 SDK, Standard Edition 1.4.0
Sun Microsystems, Inc.
Binary Code License Agreement

READ THE TERMS OF THIS AGREEMENT AND ANY PROVIDED SUPPLEMENTAL LICENSE TERMS (COLLECTIVELY "AGREEMENT") CAREFULLY BEFORE OPENING THE SOFTWARE MEDIA PACKAGE. BY OPENING THE SOFTWARE MEDIA PACKAGE, YOU AGREE TO THE TERMS OF THIS AGREEMENT. IF YOU ARE ACCESSING THE SOFTWARE ELECTRONICALLY, INDICATE YOUR ACCEPTANCE OF THESE TERMS BY SELECTING THE "ACCEPT" BUTTON AT THE END OF THIS AGREEMENT. IF YOU DO NOT AGREE TO ALL THESE TERMS, PROMPTLY RETURN THE UNUSED SOFTWARE TO YOUR PLACE OF PURCHASE FOR A REFUND OR, IF THE SOFTWARE IS ACCESSED ELECTRONICALLY, SELECT THE "DECLINE" BUTTON AT THE END OF THIS AGREEMENT.

1. LICENSE TO USE. Sun grants you a non-exclusive and non-transferable license for the internal use only of the accompanying software and documentation and any error corrections provided by Sun (collectively "Software"), by the number of users and the class of computer hardware for which the corresponding fee has been paid.

2. RESTRICTIONS. Software is confidential and copyrighted. Title to Software and all associated intellectual property rights is retained by Sun and/or its licensors. Except as specifically authorized in any Supplemental License Terms, you may not make copies of Software, other than a single copy of Software for archival purposes. Unless enforcement is prohibited by applicable law, you may not modify, decompile, or reverse engineer Software. You acknowledge that Software is not designed, licensed or intended for use in the design, construction, operation or maintenance of any nuclear facility. Sun disclaims any express or implied warranty of fitness for such uses. No right, title or interest in or to any trademark, service mark, logo or trade name of Sun or its licensors is granted under this Agreement.

3. LIMITED WARRANTY. Sun warrants to you that for a period of ninety (90) days from the date of purchase, as evidenced by a copy of the receipt, the media on which Software is furnished (if any) will be free of defects in materials and workmanship under normal use. Except for the foregoing, Software is provided "AS IS". Your exclusive remedy and Sun's entire liability under this limited warranty will be at Sun's option to replace Software media or refund the fee paid for Software.

4. DISCLAIMER OF WARRANTY. UNLESS SPECIFIED IN THIS AGREEMENT, ALL EXPRESS OR IMPLIED CONDITIONS, REPRESENTATIONS AND WARRANTIES, INCLUDING ANY IMPLIED WARRANTY OF MERCHANTABILITY, FITNESS FOR A PARTICULAR PURPOSE OR NON-INFRINGEMENT ARE DISCLAIMED, EXCEPT TO THE EXTENT THAT THESE DISCLAIMERS ARE HELD TO BE LEGALLY INVALID.

5. LIMITATION OF LIABILITY. TO THE EXTENT NOT PROHIBITED BY LAW, IN NO EVENT WILL SUN OR ITS LICENSORS BE LIABLE FOR ANY LOST REVENUE, PROFIT OR DATA, OR FOR SPECIAL, INDIRECT, CONSEQUENTIAL, INCIDENTAL OR PUNITIVE DAMAGES, HOWEVER CAUSED REGARDLESS OF THE THEORY OF LIABILITY, ARISING OUT OF OR RELATED TO THE USE OF OR INABILITY TO USE SOFTWARE, EVEN IF SUN HAS BEEN ADVISED OF THE POSSIBILITY OF SUCH DAMAGES. In no event will Sun's liability to you, whether in contract, tort (including negligence), or otherwise, exceed the amount paid by you for Software under this Agreement. The foregoing limitations will apply even if the above stated warranty fails of its essential purpose.

6. Termination. This Agreement is effective until terminated. You may terminate this Agreement at any time by destroying all copies of Software. This Agreement will terminate immediately without notice from Sun if you fail to comply with any provision of this Agreement. Upon Termination, you must destroy all copies of Software.

7. Export Regulations. All Software and technical data delivered under this Agreement are subject to US export control laws and may be subject to export or import regulations in other countries. You agree to comply strictly with all such laws and regulations and acknowledge that you have the responsibility to obtain such licenses to export, re-export, or import as may be required after delivery to you.

8. U.S. Government Restricted Rights. If Software is being acquired by or on behalf of the U.S. Government or by a U.S. Government prime contractor or subcontractor (at any tier), then the Government's rights in Software and accompanying documentation will be only as set forth in this Agreement; this is in accordance with 48 CFR 227.7201 through 227.7202-4 (for Department of Defense (DOD) acquisitions) and with 48 CFR 2.101 and 12.212 (for non-DOD acquisitions).

9. Governing Law. Any action related to this Agreement will be governed by California law and controlling U.S. federal law. No choice of law rules of any jurisdiction will apply.

10. Severability. If any provision of this Agreement is held to be unenforceable, this Agreement will remain in effect with the provision omitted, unless omission would frustrate the intent of the parties, in which case this Agreement will immediately terminate.

11. Integration. This Agreement is the entire agreement between you and Sun relating to its subject matter. It supersedes all prior or contemporaneous oral or written communications, proposals, representations and warranties and prevails over any conflicting or additional terms of any quote, order, acknowledgment, or other communication between the parties relating to its subject matter during the term of this Agreement. No modification of this Agreement will be binding, unless in writing and signed by an authorized representative of each party.

JAVA™ 2 SOFTWARE DEVELOPMENT KIT (J2SDK), STANDARD EDITION, VERSION 1.4.X SUPPLEMENTAL LICENSE TERMS

These supplemental license terms ("Supplemental Terms") add to or modify the terms of the Binary Code License Agreement (collectively, the "Agreement"). Capitalized terms not defined in these Supplemental Terms shall have the same meanings ascribed to them in the Agreement. These Supplemental Terms shall supersede any inconsistent or conflicting terms in the Agreement, or in any license contained within the Software.

1. Software Internal Use and Development License Grant. Subject to the terms and conditions of this Agreement, including, but not limited to Section 4 (Java Technology Restrictions) of these Supplemental Terms, Sun grants you a non-exclusive, non-transferable, limited license to reproduce internally and use internally the binary form of the Software complete and unmodified for the sole purpose of designing, developing and testing your Java applets and applications intended to run on the Java platform ("Programs").

2. License to Distribute Software. Subject to the terms and conditions of this Agreement, including, but not limited to Section 4 (Java Technology Restrictions) of these Supplemental Terms, Sun grants you a non-exclusive, non-transferable, limited license to reproduce and distribute the Software, provided that (i) you distribute the Software complete and unmodified (unless otherwise specified in the applicable README file) and only bundled as part of, and for the sole purpose of running, your Programs, (ii) the Programs add significant and primary functionality to the Software, (iii) you do not distribute additional software intended to replace any component(s) of the Software (unless otherwise specified in the applicable README file), (iv) you do not remove or alter any proprietary legends or notices contained in the Software, (v) you only distribute the Software subject to a license agreement that protects Sun's interests consistent with the terms contained in this Agreement, and (vi) you agree to defend and indemnify Sun and its licensors from and against any damages, costs, liabilities, settlement amounts and/or expenses (including attorneys' fees) incurred in connection with any claim, lawsuit or action by any third party that arises or results from the use or distribution of any and all Programs and/or Software. (vi) include the following statement as part of product documentation (whether hard copy or electronic), as a part of a copyright page or proprietary rights notice page, in an "About" box or in any other form reasonably designed to make the statement visible to users of the Software: "This product includes code licensed from RSA Security, Inc.", and (vii) include the statement, "Some portions licensed from IBM are available at http://oss.software.ibm.com/icu4j/".

3. License to Distribute Redistributables. Subject to the terms and conditions of this Agreement, including but not limited to Section 4 (Java Technology Restrictions) of these Supplemental Terms, Sun grants you a non-exclusive, non-transferable, limited license to reproduce and distribute those files specifically identified as redistributable in the Software "README" file ("Redistributables") provided that: (i) you distribute the Redistributables complete and unmodified (unless otherwise specified in the applicable README file), and only bundled as part of Programs, (ii) you do not distribute

additional software intended to supersede any component(s) of the Redistributables (unless otherwise specified in the applicable README file), (iii) you do not remove or alter any proprietary legends or notices contained in or on the Redistributables, (iv) you only distribute the Redistributables pursuant to a license agreement that protects Sun's interests consistent with the terms contained in the Agreement, (v) you agree to defend and indemnify Sun and its licensors from and against any damages, costs, liabilities, settlement amounts and/or expenses (including attorneys' fees) incurred in connection with any claim, lawsuit or action by any third party that arises or results from the use or distribution of any and all Programs and/or Software, (vi) include the following statement as part of product documentation (whether hard copy or electronic), as a part of a copyright page or proprietary rights notice page, in an "About" box or in any other form reasonably designed to make the statement visible to users of the Software: "This product includes code licensed from RSA Security, Inc.", and (vii) include the statement, "Some portions licensed from IBM are available at http://oss.software.ibm.com/icu4j/".

4. **Java Technology Restrictions.** You may not modify the Java Platform Interface ("JPI", identified as classes contained within the "java" package or any subpackages of the "java" package), by creating additional classes within the JPI or otherwise causing the addition to or modification of the classes in the JPI. In the event that you create an additional class and associated API(s) which (i) extends the functionality of the Java platform, and (ii) is exposed to third party software developers for the purpose of developing additional software which invokes such additional API, you must promptly publish broadly an accurate specification for such API for free use by all developers. You may not create, or authorize your licensees to create, additional classes, interfaces, or subpackages that are in any way identified as "java", "javax", "sun" or similar convention as specified by Sun in any naming convention designation.

5. **Notice of Automatic Software Updates from Sun.** You acknowledge that the Software may automatically download, install, and execute applets, applications, software extensions, and updated versions of the Software from Sun ("Software Updates"), which may require you to accept updated terms and conditions for installation. If additional terms and conditions are not presented on installation, the Software Updates will be considered part of the Software and subject to the terms and conditions of the Agreement.

6. **Notice of Automatic Downloads.** You acknowledge that, by your use of the Software and/or by requesting services that require use of the Software, the Software may automatically download, install, and execute software applications from sources other than Sun ("Other Software"). Sun makes no representations of a relationship of any kind to licensors of Other Software. TO THE EXTENT NOT PROHIBITED BY LAW, IN NO EVENT WILL SUN OR ITS LICENSORS BE LIABLE FOR ANY LOST REVENUE, PROFIT OR DATA, OR FOR SPECIAL, INDIRECT, CONSEQUENTIAL, INCIDENTAL OR PUNITIVE DAMAGES, HOWEVER CAUSED REGARDLESS OF THE THEORY OF LIABILITY, ARISING OUT OF OR RELATED TO THE USE OF OR INABILITY TO USE OTHER SOFTWARE, EVEN IF SUN HAS BEEN ADVISED OF THE POSSIBILITY OF SUCH DAMAGES.

7. **Trademarks and Logos.** You acknowledge and agree as between you and Sun that Sun owns the SUN, SOLARIS, JAVA, JINI, FORTE, and iPLANET trademarks and all SUN, SOLARIS, JAVA, JINI, FORTE, and iPLANET-related trademarks, service marks, logos

and other brand designations ("Sun Marks"), and you agree to comply with the Sun Trademark and Logo Usage Requirements currently located at http://www.sun.com/policies/trademarks. Any use you make of the Sun Marks inures to Sun's benefit.

8. Source Code. Software may contain source code that is provided solely for reference purposes pursuant to the terms of this Agreement. Source code may not be redistributed unless expressly provided for in this Agreement.

9. Termination for Infringement. Either party may terminate this Agreement immediately should any Software become, or in either party's opinion be likely to become, the subject of a claim of infringement of any intellectual property right.

For inquiries please contact: Sun Microsystems, Inc. 901 San Antonio Road, Palo Alto, California 94303

(LFI#109998/Form ID#011801)

Terms and conditions of the license & export for Java(TM) 2 Micro Edition Wireless Toolkit 1.0.3 Sun Microsystems, Inc.
Binary Code License Agreement

READ THE TERMS OF THIS AGREEMENT AND ANY PROVIDED SUPPLEMENTAL LICENSE TERMS (COLLECTIVELY "AGREEMENT") CAREFULLY BEFORE OPENING THE SOFTWARE MEDIA PACKAGE. BY OPENING THE SOFTWARE MEDIA PACKAGE, YOU AGREE TO THE TERMS OF THIS AGREEMENT. IF YOU ARE ACCESSING THE SOFTWARE ELECTRONICALLY, INDICATE YOUR ACCEPTANCE OF THESE TERMS BY SELECTING THE "ACCEPT" BUTTON AT THE END OF THIS AGREEMENT. IF YOU DO NOT AGREE TO ALL THESE TERMS, PROMPTLY RETURN THE UNUSED SOFTWARE TO YOUR PLACE OF PURCHASE FOR A REFUND OR, IF THE SOFTWARE IS ACCESSED ELECTRONICALLY, SELECT THE "DECLINE" BUTTON AT THE END OF THIS AGREEMENT.

1. LICENSE TO USE. Sun grants you a non-exclusive and non-transferable license for the internal use only of the accompanying software and documentation and any error corrections provided by Sun (collectively "Software"), by the number of users and the class of computer hardware for which the corresponding fee has been paid.

2. RESTRICTIONS. Software is confidential and copyrighted. Title to Software and all associated intellectual property rights is retained by Sun and/or its licensors. Except as specifically authorized in any Supplemental License Terms, you may not make copies of Software, other than a single copy of Software for archival purposes. Unless enforcement is prohibited by applicable law, you may not modify, decompile, or reverse engineer Software. You acknowledge that Software is not designed, licensed or intended for use in the design, construction, operation or maintenance of any nuclear facility. Sun disclaims any express or implied warranty of fitness for such uses. No right, title or

interest in or to any trademark, service mark, logo or trade name of Sun or its licensors is granted under this Agreement.

3. LIMITED WARRANTY. Sun warrants to you that for a period of ninety (90) days from the date of purchase, as evidenced by a copy of the receipt, the media on which Software is furnished (if any) will be free of defects in materials and workmanship under normal use. Except for the foregoing, Software is provided "AS IS". Your exclusive remedy and Sun's entire liability under this limited warranty will be at Sun's option to replace Software media or refund the fee paid for Software.

4. DISCLAIMER OF WARRANTY. UNLESS SPECIFIED IN THIS AGREEMENT, ALL EXPRESS OR IMPLIED CONDITIONS, REPRESENTATIONS AND WARRANTIES, INCLUDING ANY IMPLIED WARRANTY OF MERCHANTABILITY, FITNESS FOR A PARTICULAR PURPOSE OR NON-INFRINGEMENT ARE DISCLAIMED, EXCEPT TO THE EXTENT THAT THESE DISCLAIMERS ARE HELD TO BE LEGALLY INVALID.

5. LIMITATION OF LIABILITY. TO THE EXTENT NOT PROHIBITED BY LAW, IN NO EVENT WILL SUN OR ITS LICENSORS BE LIABLE FOR ANY LOST REVENUE, PROFIT OR DATA, OR FOR SPECIAL, INDIRECT, CONSEQUENTIAL, INCIDENTAL OR PUNITIVE DAMAGES, HOWEVER CAUSED REGARDLESS OF THE THEORY OF LIABILITY, ARISING OUT OF OR RELATED TO THE USE OF OR INABILITY TO USE SOFTWARE, EVEN IF SUN HAS BEEN ADVISED OF THE POSSIBILITY OF SUCH DAMAGES. In no event will Sun's liability to you, whether in contract, tort (including negligence), or otherwise, exceed the amount paid by you for Software under this Agreement. The foregoing limitations will apply even if the above stated warranty fails of its essential purpose.

6. Termination. This Agreement is effective until terminated. You may terminate this Agreement at any time by destroying all copies of Software. This Agreement will terminate immediately without notice from Sun if you fail to comply with any provision of this Agreement. Upon Termination, you must destroy all copies of Software.

7. Export Regulations. All Software and technical data delivered under this Agreement are subject to US export control laws and may be subject to export or import regulations in other countries. You agree to comply strictly with all such laws and regulations and acknowledge that you have the responsibility to obtain such licenses to export, re-export, or import as may be required after delivery to you.

8. U.S. Government Restricted Rights. If Software is being acquired by or on behalf of the U.S. Government or by a U.S. Government prime contractor or subcontractor (at any tier), then the Government's rights in Software and accompanying documentation will be only as set forth in this Agreement; this is in accordance with 48 CFR 227.7201 through 227.7202-4 (for Department of Defense (DOD) acquisitions) and with 48 CFR 2.101 and 12.212 (for non-DOD acquisitions).

9. Governing Law. Any action related to this Agreement will be governed by California law and controlling U.S. federal law. No choice of law rules of any jurisdiction will apply.

10. Severability. If any provision of this Agreement is held to be unenforceable, this Agreement will remain in effect with the provision omitted, unless omission would

frustrate the intent of the parties, in which case this Agreement will immediately terminate.

11. Integration. This Agreement is the entire agreement between you and Sun relating to its subject matter. It supersedes all prior or contemporaneous oral or written communications, proposals, representations and warranties and prevails over any conflicting or additional terms of any quote, order, acknowledgment, or other communication between the parties relating to its subject matter during the term of this Agreement. No modification of this Agreement will be binding, unless in writing and signed by an authorized representative of each party.

JAVA™ DEVELOPMENT TOOLS
J2ME™ WIRELESS TOOLKIT (J2ME WTK),
VERSION 1.0.x
SUPPLEMENTAL LICENSE TERMS

These supplemental license terms ("Supplemental Terms") add to or modify the terms of the Binary Code License Agreement (collectively, the "Agreement"). Capitalized terms not defined in these Supplemental Terms shall have the same meanings ascribed to them in the Agreement. These Supplemental Terms shall supersede any inconsistent or conflicting terms in the Agreement, or in any license contained within the Software.

1. Software Internal Use and Development License Grant. Subject to the terms and conditions of this Agreement, including, but not limited to Section 2 (Java(TM) Technology Restrictions) of these Supplemental Terms, Sun grants you a non-exclusive, non-transferable, limited license to reproduce internally and use internally the binary form of the Software complete and unmodified for the sole purpose of designing, developing and testing your Java applets and applications intended to run on the Java platform ("Programs") provided that any executable output generated by a compiler that is contained in the Software must (a) only be compiled from source code that conforms to the corresponding version of the OEM Java Language Specification; (b) be in the class file format defined by the corresponding version of the OEM Java Virtual Machine Specification; and (c) execute properly on a reference runtime, as specified by Sun, associated with such version of the Java platform.

2. Java Technology Restrictions. You may not modify the Java Platform Interface ("JPI", identified as classes contained within the "java" package or any subpackages of the "java" package), by creating additional classes within the JPI or otherwise causing the addition to or modification of the classes in the JPI. In the event that you create an additional class and associated API(s) which (i) extends the functionality of the Java platform, and (ii) is exposed to third party software developers for the purpose of developing additional software which invokes such additional API, you must promptly publish broadly an accurate specification for such API for free use by all developers. You may not create, or authorize your licensees to create, additional classes, interfaces, or subpackages that are in any way identified as "java", "javax", "sun" or similar convention as specified by Sun in any naming convention designation.

3. Java Runtime Availability. Refer to the appropriate version of the Java Runtime Environment binary code license (currently located at http://www.java.sun.com/jdk/index.html) for the availability of runtime code which may be distributed with Java applets and applications.

4. Trademarks and Logos. You acknowledge and agree as between you and Sun that Sun owns the SUN, SOLARIS, JAVA, JINI, FORTE, and iPLANET trademarks and all SUN, SOLARIS, JAVA, JINI, FORTE, and iPLANET-related trademarks, service marks, logos and other brand designations ("Sun Marks"), and you agree to comply with the Sun Trademark and Logo Usage Requirements currently located at http://www.sun.com/policies/trademarks. Any use you make of the Sun Marks inures to Sun's benefit.

5. Source Code. Software may contain source code that is provided solely for reference purposes pursuant to the terms of this Agreement. Source code may not be redistributed unless expressly provided for in this Agreement.

6. Termination for Infringement. Either party may terminate this Agreement immediately should any Software become, or in either party's opinion be likely to become, the subject of a claim of infringement of any intellectual property right.

For inquiries please contact: Sun Microsystems, Inc. 901 San Antonio Road, Palo Alto, California 94303

(LFI#101620/Form ID#011801)

Forte for Java, release 3.0, Enterprise Edition Try and Buy, Multi-Language

To obtain Forte for Java, release 3.0, Enterprise Edition Try and Buy, Multi-Language, you must agree to the software license below.

Sun Microsystems Inc. Try and Buy Binary Software License Agreement

SUN IS WILLING TO LICENSE THE ACCOMPANYING BINARY SOFTWARE IN MACHINE- READABLE FORM, TOGETHER WITH ACCOMPANYING DOCUMENTATION (COLLECTIVELY "SOFTWARE") TO YOU ONLY UPON THE CONDITION THAT YOU ACCEPT ALL OF THE TERMS AND CONDITION CONTAINED IN THIS TRY AND BUY LICENSE AGREEMENT. READ THE TERMS AND CONDITIONS OF THIS AGREEMENT CAREFULLY BEFORE OPENING THE SOFTWARE MEDIA PACKAGE. BY OPENING THE SOFTWARE MEDIA PACKAGE, YOU AGREE TO THE TERMS OF THIS AGREEMENT. IF YOU ARE ACCESSING THE SOFTWARE ELECTRONICALLY, INDICATE YOUR ACCEPTANCE OF THESE TERMS BY SELECTING THE "ACCEPT" BUTTON AT THE END OF THIS AGREEMENT. IF YOU DO NOT AGREE TO ALL THESE TERMS, PROMPTLY RETURN THE UNUSED SOFTWARE TO YOUR PLACE OF PURCHASE FOR A

REFUND OR, IF THE SOFTWARE IS ACCESSED ELECTRONICALLY, SELECT THE "DECLINE" BUTTON AT THE END OF THIS AGREEMENT.

LICENSE TO EVALUATE (TRY) THE SOFTWARE: If you have not paid the applicable license fees for the Software, the Binary Code License Agreement ("BCL") and the Evaluation Terms ("Evaluation Terms") below shall apply. The BCL and the Evaluation Terms shall collectively be referred to as the Evaluation Agreement ("Evaluation Agreement").

LICENSE TO USE (BUY) THE SOFTWARE: If you have paid the applicable license fees for the Software, the BCL and the Supplemental Terms ("Supplemental Terms") provided following the BCL shall apply. The BCL and the Supplemental Terms shall collectively be referred to as the Agreement ("Agreement").

EVALUATION TERMS

If you have not paid the applicable license fees for the Software, the terms of the Evaluation Agreement shall apply. These Evaluation Terms add to or modify the terms of the BCL. Capitalized terms not defined in these Evaluation Terms shall inconsistent or conflicting terms in the BCL below, or in any license contained within the Software.

1. LICENSE TO EVALUATE. Sun grants to you, a non-exclusive, non-transferable, royalty-free and limited license to use the Software internally for the purposes of evaluation only for sixty (60) days after the date you install the Software on your system ("Evaluation Period"). No license is granted to you for any other purpose. You may not sell, rent, loan or otherwise encumber or transfer the Software in whole or in part, to any third party. Licensee shall have no right to use the Software for productive or commercial use.

2. TIMEBOMB. Software may contain a timebomb mechanism. You agree to hold Sun harmless from any claims based on your use of Software for any purposes other than those of internal evaluation.

3. TERMINATION AND/OR EXPIRATION. Upon expiration of the Evaluation Period, unless terminated earlier by Sun, you agree to immediately cease use of and destroy Software.

4. NO SUPPORT. Sun is under no obligation to support Software or to provide upgrades or error corrections ("Software Updates") to the Software. If Sun, at its sole option, supplies Software Updates to you, the Software Updates will be considered part of Software, and subject to the terms

5. NO SUPPLEMENTAL TERMS. The Supplemental Terms following the BCL do not apply to the Evaluation Agreement.

Sun Microsystems, Inc. Binary Code License Agreement

READ THE TERMS OF THIS AGREEMENT AND ANY PROVIDED SUPPLEMENTAL LICENSE TERMS (COLLECTIVELY "AGREEMENT") CAREFULLY BEFORE OPENING THE SOFTWARE MEDIA PACKAGE. BY OPENING THE SOFTWARE MEDIA PACKAGE, YOU AGREE TO THE TERMS OF THIS AGREEMENT. IF YOU

ARE ACCESSING THE SOFTWARE ELECTRONICALLY, INDICATE YOUR ACCEPTANCE OF THESE TERMS BY SELECTING THE "ACCEPT" BUTTON AT THE END OF THIS AGREEMENT. IF YOU DO NOT AGREE TO ALL THESE TERMS, PROMPTLY RETURN THE UNUSED SOFTWARE TO YOUR PLACE OF PURCHASE FOR A REFUND OR, IF THE SOFTWARE IS ACCESSED ELECTRONICALLY, SELECT THE "DECLINE" BUTTON AT THE END OF THIS AGREEMENT.

1. LICENSE TO USE. Sun grants you a non-exclusive and non-transferable license for the internal use only of the accompanying software and documentation and any error corrections provided by Sun (collectively "Software"), by the number of users and the class of computer hardware for which the corresponding fee has been paid.

2. RESTRICTIONS. Software is confidential and copyrighted. Title to Software and all associated intellectual property rights is retained by Sun and/or its licensors. Except as specifically authorized in any Supplemental License Terms, you may not make copies of Software, other than a single copy of Software for archival purposes. Unless enforcement is prohibited by applicable law, you may not modify, decompile, or reverse engineer Software. You acknowledge that Software is not designed, licensed or intended for use in the design, construction, operation or maintenance of any nuclear facility. Sun disclaims any express or implied warranty of fitness for such uses. No right, title or interest in or to any trademark, service mark, logo or trade name of Sun or its licensors is granted under this Agreement.

3. LIMITED WARRANTY. Sun warrants to you that for a period of ninety (90) days from the date of purchase, as evidenced by a copy of the receipt, the media on which Software is furnished (if any) will be free of defects in materials and workmanship under normal use. Except for the foregoing, Software is provided "AS IS". Your exclusive remedy and Sun's entire liability under this limited warranty will be at Sun's option to replace Software media or refund the fee paid for Software.

4. DISCLAIMER OF WARRANTY. UNLESS SPECIFIED IN THIS AGREEMENT, ALL EXPRESS OR IMPLIED CONDITIONS, REPRESENTATIONS AND WARRANTIES, INCLUDING ANY IMPLIED WARRANTY OF MERCHANTABILITY, FITNESS FOR A PARTICULAR PURPOSE OR NON-INFRINGEMENT ARE DISCLAIMED, EXCEPT TO THE EXTENT THAT THESE DISCLAIMERS ARE HELD TO BE LEGALLY INVALID.

5. .LIMITATION OF LIABILITY. TO THE EXTENT NOT PROHIBITED BY LAW, IN NO EVENT WILL SUN OR ITS LICENSORS BE LIABLE FOR ANY LOST REVENUE, PROFIT OR DATA, OR FOR SPECIAL, INDIRECT, CONSEQUENTIAL, INCIDENTAL OR PUNITIVE DAMAGES, HOWEVER CAUSED REGARDLESS OF THE THEORY OF LIABILITY, ARISING OUT OF OR RELATED TO THE USE OF OR INABILITY TO USE SOFTWARE, EVEN IF SUN HAS BEEN ADVISED OF THE POSSIBILITY OF SUCH DAMAGES. In no event will Sun's liability to you, whether in contract, tort (including negligence), or otherwise, exceed the amount paid by you for Software under this Agreement. The foregoing limitations will apply even if the above stated warranty fails of its essential purpose.

6. Termination. This Agreement is effective until terminated. You may terminate this Agreement at any time by destroying all copies of Software. This Agreement will

terminate immediately without notice from Sun if you fail to comply with any provision of this Agreement. Upon Termination, you must destroy all copies of Software.

7. Export Regulations. All Software and technical data delivered under this Agreement are subject to US export control laws and may be subject to export or import regulations in other countries. You agree to comply strictly with all such laws and regulations and acknowledge that you have the responsibility to obtain such licenses to export, re-export, or import as may be required after

8. U.S. Government Restricted Rights. If Software is being acquired by or on behalf of the U.S. Government or by a U.S. Government prime contractor or subcontractor (at any tier), then the Government's rights in Software and accompanying documentation will be only as set forth in this Agreement; this is in accordance with 48 CFR 227.7201 through 227.7202-4 (for Department of Defense (DOD) acquisitions) and with 48 CFR 2.101 and 12.212 (for non-DOD acquisitions).

9. Governing Law. Any action related to this Agreement will be governed by California law and controlling U.S. federal law. No choice of law rules of any jurisdiction will apply.

10. Severability. If any provision of this Agreement is held to be unenforceable, this Agreement will remain in effect with the provision omitted, unless omission would frustrate the intent of the parties, in which case this Agreement will immediately terminate.

11. Integration. This Agreement is the entire agreement between you and Sun relating to its subject matter. It supersedes all prior or contemporaneous oral or written communications, proposals, representations and warranties and prevails over any conflicting or additional terms of any quote, order, acknowledgment, or other communication between the parties relating to its subject matter during the term of this Agreement. No modification of this Agreement will be binding, unless in writing and signed by an authorized representative of each party.

FORTE™ FOR JAVA™, RELEASE 3.0, ENTERPRISE EDITION SUPPLEMENTAL LICENSE TERMS

These supplemental license terms ("Supplemental Terms") add to or modify the terms of the Binary Code License Agreement (collectively, the "Agreement"). Capitalized terms not defined in these Supplemental Terms shall have the same meanings ascribed to them in the Agreement. These Supplemental Terms shall supersede any inconsistent or conflicting terms in the Agreement, or in any license contained within the Software.

1. Software Internal Use and Development License Grant. Subject to the terms and conditions of this Agreement, including, but not limited to Section 3 (Java(TM) Technology Restrictions) of these Supplemental Terms, Sun grants you a non-exclusive, non-transferable, limited license to use internally the binary form of the Software complete and unmodified for the sole purpose of designing, developing and testing your Java applets and applications intended to run on the Java platform.

2. License to Distribute Redistributables. Subject to the terms and conditions of this Agreement, including but not limited to Section 3 (Java Technology Restrictions) of these Supplemental Terms, Sun grants you a non-exclusive, non-transferable, limited license to reproduce and distribute the binary form of those files specifically identified as redistributable in the Software "RELEASE NOTES" file ("Redistributables") provided that: (i) you distribute the Redistributables complete and unmodified (unless otherwise specified in the applicable RELEASE NOTES file), and only bundled as part of Programs, (ii) you do not distribute additional software intended to supersede any component(s) of the Redistributables, (iii) you do not remove or alter any proprietary legends or notices contained in or on the Redistributables, (iv) for a particular version of the Java platform, any executable output generated by a compiler that is contained in the Software must (a) only be compiled from source code that conforms to the corresponding version of the OEM Java Language Specification; (b) be in the class file format defined by the corresponding version of the OEM Java Virtual Machine Specification; and (c) execute properly on a reference runtime, as specified by Sun, associated with such version of the Java platform, (v) you only distribute the Redistributables pursuant to a license agreement that protects Sun's interests consistent with the terms contained in the Agreement, and (v) you agree to defend and indemnify Sun and its licensors from and against any damages, costs, liabilities, settlement amounts and/or expenses (including attorneys' fees) incurred in connection with any claim, lawsuit or action by any third party that arises or results from the use or distribution of any and all Programs and/or Software.

3. Java Technology Restrictions. You may not modify the Java Platform Interface ("JPI", identified as classes contained within the "java" package or any subpackages of the "java" package), by creating additional classes within the JPI or otherwise causing the addition to or modification of the classes in the JPI. In the event that you create an additional class and associated API(s) which (i) extends the functionality of the Java platform, and (ii) is exposed to third party software developers for the purpose of developing additional software which invokes such additional API, you must promptly publish broadly an accurate specification for such API for free use by all developers. You may not create, or authorize your licensees to create, additional classes, interfaces, or subpackages that are in any way identified as "java", "javax", "sun" or similar convention as specified by Sun in any

4. Java Runtime Availability. Refer to the appropriate version of the Java Runtime Environment binary code license (currently located at http://www.java.sun.com/jdk/index.html) for the availability of runtime code which may be distributed with Java applets and applications.

5. 5. Trademarks and Logos. You acknowledge and agree as between you and Sun that Sun owns the SUN, SOLARIS, JAVA, JINI, FORTE, and iPLANET trademarks and all SUN, SOLARIS, JAVA, JINI, FORTE, and iPLANET-related trademarks, service marks, logos and other brand designations ("Sun Marks"), and you agree to comply with the Sun Trademark and Logo Usage Requirements currently located at http://www.sun.com/policies/trademarks. Any use you make of the Sun Marks inures to Sun's benefit.

6. Source Code. Software may contain source code that is provided solely for reference purposes pursuant to the terms of this Agreement. Source code may not be redistributed unless expressly provided for in this Agreement.

7. Termination for Infringement. Either party may terminate this Agreement immediately should any Software become, or in either party's opinion be likely to become, the subject of a claim of infringement of any intellectual property right.

For inquiries please contact: Sun Microsystems, Inc. 901 San Antonio Road, Palo Alto, California 94303

(LFI#91206/Form ID#011801)

Forte for Java, release 3.0, Community Edition, English

To obtain Forte for Java, release 3.0, Community Edition, English, you must agree to the software license below.

Sun Microsystems, Inc. Binary Code License Agreement

READ THE TERMS OF THIS AGREEMENT AND ANY PROVIDED SUPPLEMENTAL LICENSE TERMS (COLLECTIVELY "AGREEMENT") CAREFULLY BEFORE OPENING THE SOFTWARE MEDIA PACKAGE. BY OPENING THE SOFTWARE MEDIA PACKAGE, YOU AGREE TO THE TERMS OF THIS AGREEMENT. IF YOU ARE ACCESSING THE SOFTWARE ELECTRONICALLY, INDICATE YOUR ACCEPTANCE OF THESE TERMS BY SELECTING THE "ACCEPT" BUTTON AT THE END OF THIS AGREEMENT. IF YOU DO NOT AGREE TO ALL THESE TERMS, PROMPTLY RETURN THE UNUSED SOFTWARE TO YOUR PLACE OF PURCHASE FOR A REFUND OR, IF THE SOFTWARE IS ACCESSED ELECTRONICALLY, SELECT THE "DECLINE" BUTTON AT THE END OF THIS AGREEMENT.

1. LICENSE TO USE. Sun grants you a non-exclusive and non-transferable license for the internal use only of the accompanying software and documentation and any error corrections provided by Sun (collectively "Software"), by the number of users and the class of computer hardware for which the corresponding fee has been paid.

2. RESTRICTIONS. Software is confidential and copyrighted. Title to Software and all associated intellectual property rights is retained by Sun and/or its licensors. Except as specifically authorized in any Supplemental License Terms, you may not make copies of Software, other than a single copy of Software for archival purposes. Unless enforcement is prohibited by applicable law, you may not modify, decompile, or reverse engineer Software. You acknowledge that Software is not designed, licensed or intended for use in the design, construction, operation or maintenance of any nuclear facility. Sun disclaims any express or implied warranty of fitness for such uses. No right, title or interest in or to any trademark, service mark, logo or trade name of Sun or its licensors is granted under this Agreement.

3. LIMITED WARRANTY. Sun warrants to you that for a period of ninety (90) days from the date of purchase, as evidenced by a copy of the receipt, the media on which Software is furnished (if any) will be free of defects in materials and workmanship under normal use. Except for the foregoing, Software is provided "AS IS". Your exclusive remedy and Sun's entire liability under this limited warranty will be at Sun's option to replace Software media or refund the fee paid for Software.

4. DISCLAIMER OF WARRANTY. UNLESS SPECIFIED IN THIS AGREEMENT, ALL EXPRESS OR IMPLIED CONDITIONS, REPRESENTATIONS AND WARRANTIES, INCLUDING ANY IMPLIED WARRANTY OF MERCHANTABILITY, FITNESS FOR A PARTICULAR PURPOSE OR NON-INFRINGEMENT ARE DISCLAIMED, EXCEPT TO THE EXTENT THAT THESE DISCLAIMERS ARE HELD TO BE LEGALLY INVALID.

5. 5. LIMITATION OF LIABILITY. TO THE EXTENT NOT PROHIBITED BY LAW, IN NO EVENT WILL SUN OR ITS LICENSORS BE LIABLE FOR ANY LOST REVENUE, PROFIT OR DATA, OR FOR SPECIAL, INDIRECT, CONSEQUENTIAL, INCIDENTAL OR PUNITIVE DAMAGES, HOWEVER CAUSED REGARDLESS OF THE THEORY OF LIABILITY, ARISING OUT OF OR RELATED TO THE USE OF OR INABILITY TO USE SOFTWARE, EVEN IF SUN HAS BEEN ADVISED OF THE POSSIBILITY OF SUCH DAMAGES. In no event will Sun's liability to you, whether in contract, tort (including negligence), or otherwise, exceed the amount paid by you for Software under this Agreement. The foregoing limitations will apply even if the above stated warranty fails of its essential purpose.

6. Termination. This Agreement is effective until terminated. You may terminate this Agreement at any time by destroying all copies of Software. This Agreement will terminate immediately without notice from Sun if you fail to comply with any provision of this Agreement. Upon Termination, you must destroy all copies of Software.

7. Export Regulations. All Software and technical data delivered under this Agreement are subject to US export control laws and may be subject to export or import regulations in other countries. You agree to comply strictly with all such laws and regulations and acknowledge that you have the responsibility to obtain such licenses to export, re-export, or import as may be required after delivery to you.

8. U.S. Government Restricted Rights. If Software is being acquired by or on behalf of the U.S. Government or by a U.S. Government prime contractor or subcontractor (at any tier), then the Government's rights in Software and accompanying documentation will be only as set forth in this Agreement; this is in accordance with 48 CFR 227.7201 through 227.7202-4 (for Department of Defense (DOD) acquisitions) and with 48 CFR 2.101 and 12.212 (for non-DOD acquisitions).

9. Governing Law. Any action related to this Agreement will be governed by California law and controlling U.S. federal law. No choice of law rules of any jurisdiction will apply.

10. Severability. If any provision of this Agreement is held to be unenforceable, this Agreement will remain in effect with the provision omitted, unless omission would frustrate the intent of the parties, in which case this Agreement will immediately terminate.

11. Integration. This Agreement is the entire agreement between you and Sun relating to its subject matter. It supersedes all prior or contemporaneous oral or written communications, proposals, representations and warranties and prevails over any conflicting or additional terms of any quote, order, acknowledgment, or other communication between the parties relating to its subject matter during the term of this Agreement. No modification of this Agreement will be binding, unless in writing and signed by an authorized representative of each party.

FORTE™ FOR JAVA™, RELEASE 3.0, COMMUNITY EDITION SUPPLEMENTAL LICENSE TERMS

These supplemental license terms ("Supplemental Terms") add to or modify the terms of the Binary Code License Agreement (collectively, the "Agreement"). Capitalized terms not defined in these Supplemental Terms shall have the same meanings ascribed to them in the Agreement. These Supplement contained within the Software.

1. 1. Software Internal Use and Development License Grant. Subject to the terms and conditions of this Agreement, including, but not limited to Section 4 (Java(TM) Technology Restrictions) of these Supplemental Terms, Sun grants you a non-exclusive, non-transferable, limited license to reproduce internally and use internally the binary form of the Software complete and unmodified for

2. License to Distribute Software. Subject to the terms and conditions of this Agreement, including, but not limited to Section 4 (Java (TM) Technology Restrictions) of these Supplemental Terms, Sun grants you a non-exclusive, non-transferable, limited license to reproduce and distribute the Software in binary code form only, provided that (i) you distribute the Software complete and unmodified and only bundled as part of, and for the sole purpose of running, your Programs, (ii) the Programs add significant and primary functionality to the Software, (iii) you do not distribute additional software intended to replace any component(s) of the Software, (iv) for a particular version of the Java platform, any executable output generated by a compiler that is contained in the Software must (a) only be compiled from source code that conforms to the corresponding version of the OEM Java Language Specification; (b) be in the class file format defined by the corresponding version of the OEM Java Virtual Machine Specification; and (c) execute properly on a reference runtime, as specified by Sun, associated with such version of the Java platform, (v) you do not remove or alter any proprietary legends or notices contained in the Software, (v) you only distribute the Software subject to a license agreement that protects Sun's interests consistent with the terms contained in this Agreement, and (vi) you agree to defend and indemnify Sun and its licensors from and against any damages, costs, liabilities, settlement amounts and/or expenses (including attorneys' fees) incurred in connection with any claim, lawsuit or action by any third party that arises or

3. License to Distribute Redistributables. Subject to the terms and conditions of this Agreement, including but not limited to Section 4 (Java Technology Restrictions) of these Supplemental Terms, Sun grants you a non-exclusive, non-transferable, limited

license to reproduce and distribute the binary form of those files specifically identified as redistributable in the Software "RELEASE NOTES" file ("Redistributables") provided that: (i) you distribute the Redistributables complete and unmodified (unless otherwise specified in the applicable RELEASE NOTES file), and only bundled as part of Programs, (ii) you do not distribute additional software intended to supersede any component(s) of the Redistributables, (iii) you do not remove or alter any proprietary legends or notices contained in or on the Redistributables, (iv) for a particular version of the Java platform, any executable output generated by a compiler that is contained in the Software must (a) only be compiled from source code that conforms to the corresponding version of the OEM Java Language Specification; (b) be in the class file format defined by the corresponding version of the OEM Java Virtual Machine Specification; and (c) execute properly on a reference runtime, as specified by Sun, associated with such version of the Java platform, (v) you only distribute the Redistributables pursuant to a license agreement that protects Sun's interests consistent with the terms contained in the Agreement, and (v) you agree to defend and indemnify Sun and its licensors from and against any damages, costs, liabilities, settlement amounts and/or expenses (including attorneys' fees) incurred in connection with any claim, lawsuit or action by any third party that arises or results from the use or distribution of any and all Programs and/or Software.

4. **Java Technology Restrictions.** You may not modify the Java Platform Interface ("JPI", identified as classes contained within the "java" package or any subpackages of the "java" package), by creating additional classes within the JPI or otherwise causing the addition to or modification of the classes in the JPI. In the event that you create an additional class and associated API(s) which (i) extends the functionality of the Java platform, and (ii) is exposed to third party software developers for the purpose of developing additional software which invokes such additional API, you must promptly publish broadly an accurate specification for such API for free use by all developers. You may not create, or authorize your licensees to create, additional classes, interfaces, or subpackages that are in any way identified as "java", "javax", "sun" or similar convention as specified by Sun in any naming convention designation.

5. **Java Runtime Availability.** Refer to the appropriate version of the Java Runtime Environment binary code license (currently located at http://www.java.sun.com/jdk/index.html) for the availability of runtime code which may be distributed with Java applets and applications.

6. **Trademarks and Logos.** You acknowledge and agree as between you and Sun that Sun owns the SUN, SOLARIS, JAVA, JINI, FORTE, and iPLANET trademarks and all SUN, SOLARIS, JAVA, JINI, FORTE, and iPLANET-related trademarks, service marks, logos and other brand designations ("Sun Marks"), and you agree to comply with the Sun Trademark and Logo Usage Requirements currently located at http://www.sun.com/policies/trademarks. Any use you make of the Sun Marks inures to Sun's benefit.

7. **Source Code.** Software may contain source code that is provided solely for reference purposes pursuant to the terms of this Agreement. Source code may not be redistributed unless expressly provided for in this Agreement.

8. Termination for Infringement. Either party may terminate this Agreement immediately should any Software become, or in either party's opinion be likely to become, the subject of a claim of infringement of any intellectual property right.

For inquiries please contact: Sun Microsystems, Inc. 901 San Antonio Road, Palo Alto, California 94303

(LFI#91205/Form ID#011801)

Wiley Publishing, Inc.
End-User License Agreement

READ THIS. You should carefully read these terms and conditions before opening the software packet(s) included with this book "Book". This is a license agreement "Agreement" between you and Wiley Publishing, Inc."WPI". By opening the accompanying software packet(s), you acknowledge that you have read and accept the following terms and conditions. If you do not agree and do not want to be bound by such terms and conditions, promptly return the Book and the unopened software packet(s) to the place you obtained them for a full refund.

1. **License Grant.** WPI grants to you (either an individual or entity) a nonexclusive license to use one copy of the enclosed software program(s) (collectively, the "Software" solely for your own personal or non-commercial purposes on a single computer (whether a standard computer or a workstation component of a multi-user network). The Software is in use on a computer when it is loaded into temporary memory (RAM) or installed into permanent memory (hard disk, CD-ROM, or other storage device). WPI reserves all rights not expressly granted herein.

2. **Ownership.** WPI is the owner of all right, title, and interest, including copyright, in and to the compilation of the Software recorded on the disk(s) or CD-ROM "Software Media". Copyright to the individual programs recorded on the Software Media is owned by the author or other authorized copyright ownerof each program. Ownership of the Software and all proprietary rights relatingthereto remain with WPI and its licensers.

3. **Restrictions On Use and Transfer.** (a) You may only (i) make one copy of the Software for backup or archival purposes, or (ii) transfer the Software to a single hard disk, provided that you keep the original for backup or archival purposes. You may not (i) rent or lease the Software, (ii) copy or reproduce the Software through a LAN or other network system or through any computer subscriber system or bulletin- board system, or (iii) modify, adapt, or create derivative works based on the Software. (b) You may not reverse engineer, decompile, or disassemble the Software. You may transfer the Software and user documentation on a permanent basis, provided that the transferee agrees to accept the terms and conditions of this Agreement and you retain no copies. If the Software is an update or has been updated, any transfer must include the most recent update and all prior versions.

4. **Restrictions on Use of Individual Programs.** You must follow the individual requirements and restrictions detailed for each individual program in the About the CD-ROM appendix of this Book. These limitations are also contained in the individual license agreements recorded on the Software Media. These limitations may include a requirement that after using the program for a specified period of time, the user must pay a registration fee or discontinue use. By opening the Software packet(s), you will be agreeing to abide by the licenses and restrictions for these individual programs that are detailed in the About the CD-ROM appendix and on the Software Media. None of the material on this Software Media or listed in this Book may ever be redistributed, in original or modified form, for commercialpurposes.

5. **Limited Warranty.** (a) WPI warrants that the Software and Software Media are free from defects in materials and workmanship under normal use for a period of sixty (60) days from the date of purchase of this Book. If WPI receives notification within the warranty period of defects in materials or workmanship, WPI will replace the defective Software Media. (b) WPI AND THE AUTHOR OF THE BOOK DISCLAIM ALL OTHER WARRANTIES, EXPRESS OR IMPLIED, INCLUDING WITHOUT LIMITATION IMPLIED WARRANTIES OF MERCHANTABILITY AND FITNESS FOR A PARTICULAR PURPOSE, WITH RESPECT TO THE SOFTWARE, THE PROGRAMS, THE SOURCE CODE CONTAINED THEREIN, AND/OR THE TECHNIQUES DESCRIBED IN THIS BOOK. WPI DOES NOT WARRANT THAT THE FUNCTIONS CONTAINED IN THE SOFTWARE WILL MEET YOUR REQUIREMENTS OR THAT THE OPERATION OF THE SOFTWARE WILL BE ERROR FREE. (c) This limited warranty gives you specific legal rights, andyou may have other rights that vary from jurisdiction to jurisdiction.

6. **Remedies.** (a) WPI's entire liability and your exclusive remedy for defects in materials and workmanship shall be limited to replacement of the Software Media, which may be returned to WPI with a copy of your receipt at the following address: Software Media Fulfillment Department, Attn.: *Instant Messaging Systems: Cracking the Code*, Wiley Publishing, Inc., 10475 Crosspoint Blvd., Indianapolis, IN 46256, or call 1-800-762-2974. Please allow four to six weeks for delivery. This Limited Warranty is void if failure of the Software Media has resulted from accident, abuse, or misapplication. Any replacement Software Media will be warranted for the remainder of the original warranty period or thirty (30) days, whichever is longer. (b) In no event shall WPI or the author be liable for any damages whatsoever (including without limitation damages for loss of business profits, business interruption, loss of business information, or any other pecuniary loss) arising from the use of or inability to use the Book or the Software, even if WPI has been advised of the possibility of such damages. (c) Because some jurisdictions do not allow the exclusion or limitation of liability for consequential or incidental damages, the above limitation or exclusion may not apply to you.

7. **U.S. Government Restricted Rights.** Use, duplication, or disclosure of the Software for or on behalf of the United States of America, its agencies and/or instrumentalities "U.S. Government" is subject to restrictions as stated in paragraph (c)(1)(ii) of the Rights in Technical Data and Computer Software clause of DFARS 252.227-7013, or subparagraphs (c) (1) and (2) of the Commercial Computer Software - Restricted Rights clause at FAR 52.227-19, and in similar clauses in the NASA FAR supplement, as applicable.

8. **General.** This Agreement constitutes the entire understanding of the parties and revokes and supersedes all prior agreements, oral or written, between them and may not be modified or amended except in a writing signed by both parties hereto that specifically refers to this Agreement. This Agreement shall take precedence over any other documents that may be in conflict herewith. If any one or more provisions contained in this Agreement are held by any court or tribunal to be invalid, illegal, or otherwise unenforceable, each and every other provision shall remain in full force and effect.

Important CD-ROM Information

Use of the Forte for Java, release 3.0, Community Edition, Java 2 Micro Edition Wireless Toolkit 1.0.3, and Java 2 Software Development Kit Standard Edition version 1.4 for Windows software is subject to the Sun Microsystems, Inc. Binary Code License agreement on page 685 of the accompanying book. Read this agreement carefully. By opening this package, you are agreeing to be bound by the terms and conditions of this agreement.